P9-CBT-324

Nazis on the Run

Nazis on the Run

How Hitler's Henchmen Fled Justice

GERALD STEINACHER

OXFORD
UNIVERSITY PRESS

OXFORD
UNIVERSITY PRESS

Great Clarendon Street, Oxford OX2 6DP

Oxford University Press is a department of the University of Oxford.
It furthers the University's objective of excellence in research, scholarship,
and education by publishing worldwide in

Oxford New York

Auckland Cape Town Dar es Salaam Hong Kong Karachi
Kuala Lumpur Madrid Melbourne Mexico City Nairobi
New Delhi Shanghai Taipei Toronto

With offices in

Argentina Austria Brazil Chile Czech Republic France Greece
Guatemala Hungary Italy Japan Poland Portugal Singapore
South Korea Switzerland Thailand Turkey Ukraine Vietnam

Oxford is a registered trade mark of Oxford University Press
in the UK and in certain other countries

Published in the United States
by Oxford University Press Inc., New York

British Library Cataloguing in Publication Data

Data available

Library of Congress Cataloging in Publication Data

Data available

Typeset by SPI Publisher Services, Pondicherry, India
Printed in Great Britain
on acid-free paper by
Clays Ltd, St Ives plc

ISBN 978-0-19-957686-9

1 3 5 7 9 10 8 6 4 2

This book was made possible in part through a Center for Advanced Holocaust Studies Fellowship
at the United States Holocaust Memorial Museum in Washington, DC. The statements made and
views expressed, however, are solely the responsibility of the author.

Jacket photo: International Committee of the Red Cross travel document for Adolf Eichmann
alias Riccardo Klement; Fundación Memoria del Holocausto, Buenos Aires.

Preface and Acknowledgements

This book originated as a professorial thesis (*Habilitation*) delivered to the Leopold Franzens University in Innsbruck in 2007. It has been shortened and rewritten for publication. Lengthy periods of archive research in Europe and the United States were required for the investigation of this subject over the past five years.

Without the support of various institutions and certain individuals this work would not have been possible. First I should like to thank the United States Holocaust Memorial Museum, where I was allowed to work on my thesis in the context of a Research Fellowship. I was able to consult the archives of the Holocaust Museum in detail and received invaluable feedback from a number of people including Peter Black, Jürgen Matthäus, Lisa Yavnai, Bruce Tapper, Suzanne Brown-Fleming, Jan Lambertz, and Richard Breitman.

I also received important suggestions and support from the staff of the archives I consulted in Europe and the United States. In particular, I should like to thank Marija Fueg of the Archive of the International Red Cross in Geneva, John E. Taylor in College Park, Maryland, Harald Toniatti of the State Archive in Bozen, and Elisabeth Klamper of the Documentation Centre of Austrian Resistance in Vienna. Matteo Sanfilippo was a great source of help to me when dealing with the problems involved in the Roman archives. I should like to thank Johann Hörist, the Rector of Santa Maria dell'Anima, the German and Austrian national church in Rome, for his help and support in my study of the Anima's archive.

Over the years, conversations with colleagues and friends have been motivating and encouraging in various ways. Many ideas, suggestions, questions, and connections arose out of these encounters. At this point I should like to express particular thanks to Hans Heiss, Leopold Steurer, Stas Nikolova, Andrea Di Michele, Horst Schreiber, Renate Telser, and Christof Mauch. They have supported my research even during difficult phases, and without the advice and encouragement of Hans Heiss and Leopold Steurer this book would never have existed. They have also corrected a number of chapters in terms of language, form, and content, and invested a great deal of time in doing so. I should especially thank my mentor Rolf Steininger, Innsbruck, who has always sympathetically accompanied my professional and academic progress. As head of the Institute at Innsbruck University, Rolf Steininger has always closely interwoven regional with international contemporary history: a perspective that continues to inform my work today. During my period of study in the United States, Günter Bischof in New Orleans opened up a new (and wide) world of contemporary historical research that gave my scholarly work a new direction. I wish to thank Linda and Eric Christenson for their repeated hospitality over the past few years in the United States. Carlo Gentile and Kurt Schrimm have allowed me an insight into the trials of Nazi war criminals in Italy and Germany during the 1990s. Shraga Elam provided a great deal of background information on Operation Bernhard. Uki Goñi and Luis Moraes in Buenos Aires made a considerable contribution to my better understanding of Argentinian politics and contemporary history. The historians Wolfgang Benz, Klaus Larres, Reiner Pommerin, and Anton Pelinka contributed valuable suggestions to the reworking of my post-doctoral thesis.

Eva Trafojer, Norbert Sparer, Christian Url, Tanja Schluchter, and Thomas Pardatscher sacrificed many hours to the formal revision of individual chapters of this work, which made the final revision considerably easier for me. Lou Bessette in Montreal, Quebec, helped to translate the introduction to this edition; Harald Dunajtschik drew up the index of proper names and contributed many additional suggestions for improvement. Thanks to Shaun Whiteside for his excellent English translation and Jennifer Shimek for the accurate final copy editing of the book.

I owe a debt of thanks to the de Rachewiltz family for their hospitality at Brunnenburg Castle near Meran: a true refuge for thinkers. It was there and at the Center for European Studies at Harvard University that the final version of the English edition was produced. I would also like to extend my thanks to my friends and like-minded colleagues Georg Mischi, Pietro Fogale, and Philipp Trafoier, who patiently endured lengthy discussions of this book's subject matter and individual research problems.

My family and friends have shown a great deal of understanding for my work and have kept me from losing touch with life outside academia. To them, and particularly to my brother Werner, this book is dedicated.

G.S.

Washington D.C., Harvard/Boston, and Brunnenburg near Meran
2010

People can face the truth.

Ingeborg Bachmann

Some people hoped a 'line' would be drawn under the National Socialist past. Some were thinking less of the dead victims than of the living perpetrators.

German Federal President Horst Köhler, winter 2008

Contents

List of Illustrations   xi
List of Abbreviations   xiii
Introduction   xv

1. The Nazi Escape Route through Italy   1
   1. Italy as a Country of Refuge   3
   2. Refugees, Prisoners of War, and War Criminals   8
   3. Illegal Immigrants   15
   4. Smuggling Goods and People   23
   5. South Tyrol, the Nazi Bolt-Hole   32
   6. Fake Papers   43

2. The Co-Responsibility of the International Red Cross   55
   1. Red Cross Travel Documents   56
   2. How the ICRC Issued Travel Documents in Italy   61
   3. The Routine Nature of False Documentation   69
   4. The Red Cross Calls a Halt   77
   5. The Red Cross on the Escape Route   84
   6. Escaping with Ethnic German Identity   90

3. The Vatican Network   101
   1. The Vatican Relief Commission   102
   2. The National Subcommittees   110
   3. The Network of Bishop Alois Hudal   118
   4. The Monsignor and the Croatian Fascists   128
   5. The Role of the Church in South Tyrol   139
   6. Denazification through Baptism   148

4. The Intelligence Service Ratline   159
   1. Operation Bernhard   161
   2. The Special Case of Italy   169
   3. 'Recycled' War Criminals   177
   4. The Origins of the Italian Ratline   183
   5. The Ratline Players   195
   6. Escape along the Ratline   199

5. Destination Argentina   211
   1. Argentinian Immigration Policy   212
   2. The Recruitment of Specialists   218
   3. Argentinian Diplomats and Agents in Italy   226
   4. Perón's Escape Agents in Italy   232
   5. Austrian Pioneers in the Escape Network   241
   6. The Escape of the Concentration Camp Commandants   248
   7. A New Start in Argentina   258

Conclusion   271

Notes   290
Bibliography   342
Index of Names   365
General Index   372

List of Illustrations

1. Map of the escape routes through the Alps to South Tyrol and from there to the port of Genoa. (Institut für Zeitgeschichte, Innsbruck)

2. Gerhard Bast, an Austrian Gestapo officer. (Martin Pollack)

3. Gabor Kemény with young Hungarian soldiers. (US National Archives, College Park)

4. The wife and daughter of Heinrich Himmler, Reichsführer of the SS, near Bozen. (US National Archives, College Park)

5. Jean Luchaire at the time of his arrest in Meran; next to him stands his daughter Corinne, a well-known actress at the time. (US National Archives, College Park)

6. Adolf Eichmann's travel document from the International Committee of the Red Cross (ICRC) under the alias of Riccardo Klement. (ICRC archives, Geneva)

7. Josef Mengele's travel document from the ICRC under the alias of Helmut Gregor. (ICRC archives, Geneva)

8. Franz Stangl's travel document from the ICRC. (ICRC archives, Geneva)

9. Bishop Alois Hudal. (Gerald Steinacher)

10. Archbishop Spellman agrees to financially support the Austrian Refugee Committee in Rome. (Catholic University of America)

11. The former SS-Sturmbannführer Erich Priebke's travel document from the ICRC under the alias of Otto Pape. (ICRC archives, Geneva)

12. Ante Pavelić, the leader of fascist Croatia, and his war minister in the German propaganda journal *Signal*, 1941.

13. The seriously ill Gerda Bormann in the hospital in Meran. (Anna Sigmund)

14. Allied officers in front of Hotel Greif in the Bolzano town centre a few days after the capitulation of the Germans in Italy in May 1945. (US National Archives, College Park)

15. German Special Police, South Tyrol, May 1945. (US National Archives, College Park)

16. Karl Wolff, the Höchste SS- and Polizeiführer for Italy, in a prisoner-of-war camp in Bolzano in May 1945. (US National Archives, College Park)

17. The former chief of the Gestapo in Lyons, Klaus Barbie's travel document from the ICRC under the alias of Klaus Altmann. (ICRC archives, Geneva)

18. Frederik R. Benson, right, next to the just captured Gerhard Lausegger. (Michael Gehler)

19. The family of the Austrian engineer Walter Haasler in front of the Pyramids. (Privately owned)

20. Adolf Eichmann in Jerusalem. (United States Holocaust Memorial Museum)

List of Abbreviations

ACC	Allied Control Commission
ACS	Archivio Centrale dello Stato
AGIUS	Assistenza Giuridica agli Stranieri
AMG	Allied Military Government
CAPRI	Compañía Argentina para Proyectos y Realizaciones Industriales—Fuldner y Cía
CEANA	Comisión para el Esclarecimiento de las Actividades del Nacionalsocialismo en la Argentina
CIA	Central Intelligence Agency
CIC	Counter Intelligence Corps
DAV	Deutsche Antinazistische Vereinigung
DAIE	Delegación Argentina de Inmigración en Europa
DPs	Displaced Persons
FBI	Federal Bureau of Investigation
Gestapo	Geheime Staatspolizei
ICRC	International Committee of the Red Cross
IRO	International Refugee Organization
NARA	US National Archives and Record Administration
NCWC	National Catholic Welfare Conference
NSDAP	Nationalsozialistische Deutsche Arbeiterpartei, German National Socialist (Nazi) Party
ODESSA	Organisation der ehemaligen SS-Angehörigen
OSS	Office of Strategic Services
PCA	Pontificia Commissione Assistenza (Profughi)
SD	Sicherheitsdienst, German Security Service
SS	Schutzstaffel, Nazi 'Protection Squadron' led by Heinrich Himmler
UNRRA	United Nations Relief and Rehabilitation Administration
USHMM	United States Holocaust Memorial Museum
US	United States
USSR	Union of Soviet Socialist Republics

Introduction

In 1967 Simon Wiesenthal, known as the 'Nazi hunter', wrote in his book *The Murderers among Us*:

> Late in 1947 I began to trace the escape routes of important missing Nazis who were now on the wanted lists of several nations. I knew that towards the end of the war all prominent SS leaders and Gestapo members had received from the RSHA [Reichssicherheitshauptamt, Reich Main Security Office] false personal documents bearing new names. But I was less interested in names than in routes. It was essential to find out where they had gone and by what means, and who had helped them and paid for it all.[1]

Wiesenthal was referring at this time to a large gap in the research into the background of the flight of SS members and war criminals overseas—a gap that he himself did not close, and which has not yet been filled even decades later. This book reconstructs the flight and the escape routes of the Nazi perpetrators after 1945.

The history of the twentieth century is defined to a particularly high degree by National Socialism and the Second World War with its mass crimes and genocides. As a result, the study of National Socialism has gained a great deal of ground over the last few decades. The number of books, essays, internet texts, films, and TV documentaries on the subject is vast. Research into Nazi perpetrators has now become centrally important. The socialization, motives, and actions of the planners, executives, and agents of the genocide occupy centre stage, as for example in the recent much-discussed novel by Jonathan Littell, *The Kindly Ones*.[2]

But the flight of war criminals and SS members is generally overlooked. It is only in the past few years that this subject has increasingly attracted attention, but after the end of the war numerous Nazi war criminals and National Socialists evaded punishment by escaping overseas. The circumstances which allowed them to do so and routes they followed, as well as the issue of who helped the war criminals, was not the subject of close investigation.[3]

For decades, imaginative ideas of supposedly powerful secret organizations such as ODESSA (Organisation der ehemaligen SS-Angehörigen, Organisation of former SS members) were a strikingly unrealistic model. The ODESSA myth, based on claims by Simon Wiesenthal, became the incarnation of the conspiracy myth of the secret survival of the National Socialist elite. Foremost among the proponents of such ideas is Frederick Forsyth's 1972 novel *The Odessa File*, the story of a tightly knit band of former SS men who formed the secret 'Odessa organization'. Both the novel and the film based on it became wildly popular across the globe. This vividly drawn conspiratorial group—which was rumoured to have vast financial resources at its disposal and was jealously guarded its members, inserting them into positions of great influence in the post-war world—was over time accepted as fact. ODESSA became known as the biggest fugitive organization of all time, a powerful SS brotherhood operating on a global scale behind a nearly impenetrable veil of secrecy. Tight discipline and an autocratic structure ensured that its members were poised to revive Nazism, strike again, and impose a brutal dystopia on the world. But this picture of Nazi fugitives and their escape routes strayed rather far from the objective truth.

The shadowy ODESSA had actually garnered serious attention in 1946 and 1947 from the likes of the US Counter Intelligence Corps (CIC). Despite dogged research, however, CIC agents were never able to uncover any concrete facts about the founding, structure, or precise activities of the fabled group. They even began to suspect that some small and insignificant circles of former SS men, taking pleasure in the rumours, had adopted the name 'ODESSA' to create an air of mystery around their fraternity. Most of the information about ODESSA that made its way to the CIC was extraordinarily vague and its origins not quite credible, propped up as it was more by hearsay than by fact. Yet the Americans at least initially opted to believe that the Nazi underground would enjoy a long life after the war, and they eagerly seized upon every small incident or sign that supported this fear.

This Cold War climate of distrust gave rise to quite a formidable tale, said to have unfolded at a hotel named Maison Rouge, which still exists in Strasburg today. Bestsellers and the popular press continue to invoke the fascinating story of a secret conference held there on 10 August 1944, in which economic leaders of the Third Reich together with the

SS plotted out a course for the afterlife of Nazism. It was believed by many, including such authorities as Simon Wiesenthal, that the participants planned to transfer several billion Goldmarks safely abroad for 'underwriting the greatest fugitive organization in world history'. Wiesenthal confidently announced that participants at the conference had included coal baron Emil Kirdorf and steel magnates Fritz Thyssen and Gustav Krupp, all implicated in the use of forced labour from concentration camps. To this day, not a single piece of evidence has turned up to support this incredible story of a high-level meeting to plan the emergence of the Fourth Reich. In fact, Kirdorf had already died in 1938, Krupp had relinquished his position in 1943, and Thyssen was imprisoned in the Sachsenhausen concentration camp at the time.[4]

In his lifetime, Simon Wiesenthal chose to invoke ODESSA time and again, clearly intrigued by a plausible symbol that resonated with the difficulties of post-war reckoning. The legendary Strasburg meeting and its supposed role in laying the ground for the ODESSA figured in his 1967 book, *The Murderers among Us*. He claimed to have learned about the organization in 1950 from 'Hans', a German former intelligence operative with insider knowledge: refuges for Nazis on the run had been established in a series of way stations such as monasteries at twenty-five-mile intervals; the final stage involved sailing from the port of Genoa to the Argentina of General Perón.

The Vienna Nazi hunter ultimately used the image of this organization to explain all actual and alleged escapes, both by prominent criminals and the 'foot soldiers' in the Nazi machinery of genocide and destruction. ODESSA conveniently stood in for the complicated and shady phenomenon of a Nazi exodus. Inexhaustible in his pursuit of perpetrators and justice, Wiesenthal had found a serviceable symbol to keep alive public anxiety and outrage about conniving former SS men and the impunity of their actions.

Individual escape stories such as that of Adolf Eichmann have by now been spectacularly retold, but at the same time little research has yet been carried out into the subject of Nazi flight, as for a long time contemporary historians showed very little interest in the subject. Holger Meding, a Latin America specialist at Cologne University, gives three reasons for the lack of interest of researchers into the subject that prevailed for so long: the archives that remained inaccessible until a few years ago, the flippant treatment of the escape stories (or even their invention) by journalists, and the sensationalist approach towards invented or true individual cases such as those of Joseph Mengele, Adolf Eichmann, and Martin Bormann, which has deterred academic historians.[5]

Changing conditions have encouraged new inquiry into the subject of escape aid for fleeing National Socialists, SS men, and collaborators. New political conditions resulting in, among other things, the opening of archives and the freedom to re-examine the past, have contributed significantly to the improved state of academic research and growing public interest. With the end of the Cold War, the political will to address this subject has also grown; the shield that had protected those SS officers and war criminals who were still alive and in hiding no longer exists. After the fall of the Berlin Wall in 1989 and the end of the Cold War, many international archives were opened, legal authorities resumed investigations, and some governments set up commissions of historians to examine Nazi flight in the post-war years.

Historians such as Heinz Schneppen have in recent years shown that an all-powerful, mythical organization like ODESSA never existed. This research also makes abundantly clear that simple monocausal models do not adequately account for the complicated relationships that facilitated Nazi flight. Former Nazis and SS men had indisputably forged bonds and support networks that secured their escape from Germany. These loose associations gradually became more concrete in 1946 and thereafter, and often consisted of small groups of men who had fought together. The network maintained by former members of the Waffen-SS, for instance, shows how ties forged on the battlefield and in combat units later served to jump-start and support post-war careers. These men often helped one another not only to escape from Europe, but also to put down roots in their new countries of residence.

Most of the research herein is devoted to Italy, since that country was to become an all-important highway for war criminals (*Reichsautobahn für Kriegsverbrecher*) on their way to overseas destinations. Of course, this happened over time and as conditions allowed. The Allied military occupation of Italy was only lifted in December of 1945 and deterred fugitives from leaving from there earlier. But the research in this book shows that the escape route through Italy began functioning in 1946 and that the majority of Nazis fleeing from Europe passed through Italian harbours on their journey abroad. Significant in helping the fugitives was the German-speaking population of the Alto Adige (South Tyrol), a border region subjected to intense Italianization under Benito Mussolini. Often banned from using the German language and from referring to Tyrolean culture, the population kept alive strong bonds with German ethno-nationalism, even in the face of Hitler's rejection to defend its cause against Mussolini. By the end of 1945 South Tyrol was also the first German-language region on the escape route to be freed from Allied military government controls.

The book highlights how this set of conditions facilitated the emergence of an escape hatch (*Nazi-Schlupfloch*) in the conveniently located region of South Tyrol. Former Nazis and SS officers fleeing from Germany or Eastern Europe to Italy crossed the Austrian territory that lay in between. They could be taken over the Brenner Pass on traditional smuggling routes, which entailed far fewer risks than travelling through heavily policed northern gateways such as the ports of Rotterdam and Hamburg. Some smugglers made no distinction: in addition to German immigrants whose destination was South America, their clientele often included Jews who were illegally fleeing Europe to settle in Palestine. In a macabre fashion, the paths of fugitive Nazi criminals along the escape routes over the Alps often crossed with those of their victims. South Tyrol became a natural hub for members of SS and business circles to reunite and forge connections between Germany, Italy, Spain, and Argentina that would secure their escape. Fugitives were often made so welcome in this border region that some chose to stay for months and even years, working on local farms or living on borrowed money to raise funds for emigration visas and steamship fares. Networks of assistance in South Tyrol were evidently well organized and able to provide war criminals and SS officers on the run with essential items, among them new identity papers under false names.

Beyond this, the book takes a hard look at the International Committee of the Red Cross (ICRC). This organization derived its influence and power above all from its moral standing as a neutral humanitarian intermediary. The question of whether this position was tenable in a world of realpolitik cropped up repeatedly in this research. It is well known that the ICRC failed to speak out against the Holocaust, despite having clear information on what was unfolding for the Jews of Europe. The organization apparently made a tactical decision not to protest, for fear that this would endanger its ability to carry on aid work in

German-occupied Europe. Moral authority thus gave way to practical considerations. But how did the Committee actually react when Nazis and war criminals began using Red Cross services to elude Allied justice? A central element deals with deciphering ICRC discussions in Geneva over this dilemma. Historian Jean-Claude Favez and others have already shown the organization's role during World War II, particularly its failure to denounce the systematic murder of the Jews up to 1945. Yet the story of the ICRC in the immediate post-war years remains largely unwritten, and this book is the first serious attempt to close this gap.

The ICRC, albeit never a willing partner, evidently extended a significant helping hand to the fugitives. Hiding among the Displaced Persons (DPs) were such well-known criminals as Adolf Eichmann, Josef Mengele, and Franz Stangl, who used transit papers from the ICRC to flee abroad. In this way tainted biographies were transformed into spotless identities. Although the ICRC has acknowledged that it served as an accessory in these cases and has publicly apologized, its action went well beyond helping a few people. This book provides proof that travel papers issued by the Committee made it possible for thousands of Nazis, war criminals, and collaborators from all over Europe to slip through the hands of justice and to find refuge in North and South America, Spain, and the Near East. By the middle of 1951, the Red Cross had issued at least 120,000 travel documents in what must be regarded as an extremely problematic operation. The organization's vetting procedure for issuing identity papers may have been quite lax, indeed very insufficient, but its operations functioned surprisingly well, given the huge numbers of refugees making claims on its personnel.

Nazis on the Run details the ICRC's entanglement in the rescue operation that was exploited by fugitives and shows what the leaders of the organization actually knew. It establishes beyond doubt that Paul Ruegger, then president of the ICRC, was aware that Red Cross travel documents were not always going into the right hands, but that he nevertheless chose not to intervene. Again, a question about the lack of proper action on the part of the ICRC must be asked: why did the Committee not act quickly and effectively when the massive scale of the travel documents scandal became known? Once more, practical considerations came into play. The ICRC apparently saw the cases related to the scandal as just a few 'bad apples' in the huge throng of

DPs and did not want this matter to jeopardize its whole refugee assistance programme. Whenever the question came up, Red Cross officials were quick to insist that the Allies and the Vatican were ultimately responsible for weeding out suspect cases. This book identifies a chain of deferred responsibility.

Nazis on the Run also examines the extent to which the background and political beliefs of certain ICRC leaders played a role in this process of dodging responsibility and failing to verify adequately applicants' details before issuing new identity papers. It is obvious that President Carl Jacob Burckhardt had a history of pro-German sympathies and was at least latently anti-Semitic. Did this have a concrete effect on the involvement of the International Red Cross in assistance provided to the Nazi ratline? The question will remain on the table until further research on the biographies and decisions of the ICRC leadership is carried out. This book makes it clear, however, that strongly anticommunist convictions and concerns influenced the ICRC decision makers. One could say that the organization never acted along strictly neutral lines and, from time to time, allowed itself to be marshalled as a weapon in the early Cold War. This is supported by a careful scrutiny of the Red Cross representatives in Italy immediately after the war and of decisions made at headquarters in Geneva about aid for DPs.

The book documents the close cooperation between the ICRC and Vatican relief agencies for refugees in Italy. The attitude of the Vatican and Pope Pius XII during the Nazi years has been the subject of ongoing historical debate, particularly the Pontiff's silence on the Holocaust as it unfolded. As in the case of the ICRC, the Vatican's conflict between moral standards and realpolitik becomes obvious in hindsight. Many leaders of the Catholic Church—sometimes knowingly, at other times unwittingly—were also involved in large-scale Nazi smuggling. A key motive for the clergy was the need to fight against 'godless communism'. Correspondence between bishops in the United States and the Vatican reveals that the fear of a communist takeover in Italy was then paramount and founded partly on the fact that Italy had the strongest communist party in post-war Western Europe. Of special interest in this political context is the role of the Vatican Pontifical Assistance Commission for Refugees, an important charitable organization under the supervision of Under-Secretary of State Giovanni Montini (later

Paul VI). The commission (sponsored by the American Catholic Church) was central to the overall strategy against communism at the outset of the Cold War, as State Department officials documented at the time. Evidence suggests that some figures in the Vatican used the organization as a tool in the fight against the common enemy, the rise of Soviet influence in Europe. A key player in this process was Alois Hudal, Rector of the College of Santa Maria dell'Anima in Rome (and a convinced Nationalist and admirer of Adolf Hitler). A bishop since 1933 and Assistant to the Papal Throne, Hudal enjoyed close personal ties to Pope Pius XII for many years. Although his influence waned at the Vatican and within the church hierarchy from 1943 onwards, he was still able to obtain special papal blessings for the Nazi aid pro-gramme. Hudal in later years became a scapegoat for the Vatican, but his practices while in office were by no means the exception: the Vatican refugee committees for Croats, Slovenes, Ukrainians, and Hungarians acted in similar fashion, aiding former fascists and Nazi collaborators to escape those countries.

The Catholic Church proved to be highly adaptable and flexible in the complex political situation that was emerging. Consider the Church's history during fascist rule: in 1929, the Holy See and Italy had signed the Lateran Treaty, ending years of antagonism between the Church and the Italian State. In the very first article of this conciliation treaty, Italy recognized the Catholic Apostolic Roman religion as the only state religion. The importance of the Treaty in the evolution of events across the spectrum in Europe, before, during, and after the war, can-not be overstated. Journalist John Cornwell suggests that the Italian Concordat (Lateran Treaty) foreshadowed the 1933 Reich Concordat, a deal reached after much protracted wrangling between Hitler and Cardinal Secretary of State Eugenio Pacelli (later Pius XII).

The Italian Concordat worked as an alliance of sorts between the Church and the fascist regime and allowed both to agree on most issues, at least until 1938 when the Mussolini regime introduced race laws directed against the Jews and Slavs in Italy and the black African popu-lations in the Italian colonies. Indeed, relations between fascists and the clergy in Italy remained largely unproblematic up to 1943. Even after the Nazis took control of northern Italy in September 1943, there was no evidence of general anti-Catholic policies. In some cases, SS officials and church representatives in northern Italy forged ties in their common fear of a communist takeover in the region. The same cannot be said of the situation that prevailed in Austria and Germany, where the Catholic Church repeatedly found itself in conflict with the Nazi regime, especially regarding Nazi race ideology. The regime sometimes openly attacked bishops, persecuted priests and sent them to concentration camps, and shut down monasteries.

After the war, changing circumstances along with the ever-increasing fear of communist expansion weighed heavily in the way the Church now understood its role in the world. With the liberation of Rome by Allied troops in 1944, the Catholic Church 'discovered' democracy. Pius XII declared that the Church would view democracy—if purified by Christian influence—as a form of government on par with monarchy. Prior to this, the Church had traditionally aligned with the monarchy and authoritarian regimes, finding them more acceptable than the alternatives. It now saw itself as a stabilizing force in post-war Italy as one of the few indisputable authorities in the vacuum left by fascism, National Socialism, and civil war. Certainly, the Church continued to wield great influence over society and would not readily relinquish this position. Fascist ideologies of 'master races' (*Herrenrassen*), the cult of war, and extreme nationalism had led Europe into catastrophe, and Christian churches wanted to turn the tide by regaining their supremacy in society and politics. Religious anti-Judaism (as distinguished from anti-Semitic racism) may have played a role in helping Nazis to escape. But other factors appear to have been more compelling, among them a desire to help Catholics irrespective of their political background and, above all, a determination to lead the opposition to communism in the chaotic and unpredictable situation in post-war Europe.

It was very much part of the Church's policy at the time to welcome the return of 'renegade' Catholics and to embrace converted Protestants. This book presents unprecedented evidence that some priests on occasion went so far as to offer 're-baptism' to non-Catholic (mostly Protestant) Germans who sought the clergy's assistance in their flight from likely retribution. The return to the Church of some lapsed members—men who had been temporarily 'waylaid by the seductions of Nazism'—was also greeted with enthusiasm. Certain members of the Catholic Church saw this as an opportunity to re-Christianize Europe after years of the pagan Nazi rule. Denazification through baptism clearly operated on the margins of church doctrine, but exceptional times bred exceptional measures; the fact it was practised suggests that those in the Church who helped fugitives may have needed strong symbols to assuage their ambivalence over an extremely complex situation. Many questions remain, but the Vatican Archives are still only accessible for the years up to 1939. Thus the book's research relies heavily on scholarly literature, witness testimonies, and archives from the German National Church of the Anima in Rome, the Catholic Church of America, and regional churches. I also had the opportunity to conduct a revealing interview with Monsignor Joseph Prader, a close confidant of Bishop Hudal, on these and related activities.

One cannot ignore the role of the Western Allies, particularly the involvement of the US intelligence services in assisting refugees with a Nazi past and in recycling SS agents at the beginning of the Cold War. The Allies were also gearing up to put a stop to the 'clear and present danger' of communist expansion. Cold War concerns now trumped post-war reckoning with Nazi crimes. At the same time, US intelligence operations were undergoing radical internal changes, one of them being the disbanding of the Office of Strategic Services (OSS, the precursor to the Central Intelligence Agency, CIA) in 1945. This left the Counter Intelligence Corps (CIC) seriously understaffed and unprepared for newly emerging challenges; in dire need of new sources of information, its operations often seemed amateurish and slightly desperate.

In this context, underground networks born of the collaboration between the ICRC and the Catholic Church to help Nazis escape became useful to the Allies themselves. As early as 1947, the CIC itself was using a 'ratline', as it was called in intelligence jargon. It smuggled former SS men recruited to advise US intelligence agencies out of Soviet-occupied areas of Austria and eastern Europe into Italy and on to South America. From the CIC's perspective, SS men and German counterintelligence agents had special expertise on the Soviet Union and Eastern Europe that could serve its post-war purposes. Scholars such as Richard Breitman, Norman Goda, Timothy Naftali, Robert Wolfe, and Kerstin von Lingen have documented this configuration in great detail over the past years. In the end, the unsavoury new agents recruited by the CIC produced very little valuable information on the Soviet Union and its satellite states and allies. This book expands on these histories by delving further into the concerns and conditions prevailing in Italy at the time and by closely examining the secret contacts already fostered between the SS in Italy and the OSS under Allen Dulles up to the end of 1945. Until now, historical research had focused particularly on the role of Dulles and his intricate network of contacts. These were crucial in defining the methods of Allied intelligence gathering, but also in identifying likely participants for the Italian ratline. One network, for instance, surfaced from Operation Bernhard, a large-scale counterfeiting operation recently brought to world audiences through the Oscar-winning Austrian movie *The Counterfeiters* (*Die Fälscher*). After 1945 some SS agents connected with Operation Bernhard went on to organize escape routes and facilities across Italy and became a part of the CIC ratline. But for the investigation of the precise connections between Operation Bernhard and the ratline further research is required. In describing the various links, I am able to bring a better understanding of the central position that Italy occupied in the chain of events.

This study does not focus strictly on Argentina as a destination for Nazis on the run. Despite popular assumptions, this South American country was only one of several that held considerable attraction for war criminals, Nazis, and fascists in flight. Some researchers attribute Argentina's open-door policy mainly to a sympathetic attitude towards Nazi ideology, but this book provides a more balanced picture. Argentina's interest in hosting the fugitives had its basis in the same motives found in other countries (most prominently, the United States, Great Britain, the Soviet Union, and France). All of them put out the welcome mat for Germans and Austrians deemed useful, regardless of their political background or wartime activities; this spoke of a desire to pursue national interests with the help of a vast pool of unemployed Nazi migrants, men with special skills—who incidentally had something to hide. The works of Uki Goñi, Holger Meding, Heinz Schneppen, Carlota Jackisch, and other scholars have shown that the Argentine government also made particular efforts to recruit German specialists with a military background or technical expertise. This study draws from such literature as well as from new Italian and American archival sources. The practical steps taken in the recruitment process by Argentinian officials is particularly striking. Both legal and illegal recruiting was carried out by Argentinians of German extraction and, in Italy, by SS officers lying low.

Once in Argentina, fugitive Nazis had indeed found a safe haven, for extradition from that country was highly unlikely. How many war criminals and Nazis fled overseas? It is still difficult to pin down precise figures, for much depends on definitions of perpetrators of crimes under National Socialism (who is a perpetrator?) and selection by nationality (it was by no means only Germans and Austrians who fled). Fundamentally, one must distinguish between (1) high-ranking Nazis and SS officers, (2) war criminals and Holocaust perpetrators, and (3) fascists and collaborators from across Europe. It is sometimes difficult to make clear distinctions. According to Argentinian sources, some 180 prominent or seriously implicated Nazi officials and SS officers entered the country from Europe through the Buenos Aires harbour on the Río de la Plata River. Historian Holger Meding, for his part, puts arrival figures at between 300 and 800 high-level Nazis, including some fifty known war criminals and mass murderers. They were joined by thousands of collaborators and fascists from Italy, Hungary, Slovenia, Belgium, Croatia, and other countries. Among them were such prominent figures as Ante Pavelić, the former head of state of Croatia.

As mentioned already, Argentina was hardly the only desirable destination for fugitives. Spain or countries in the Near East or in North and South America—including the United States and Canada—appear to have been sought-after places to relocate. For example, in 1946, some 9,000 Ukrainians from the Waffen-SS Division Galizien found their way via Italy to Great Britain and from there to Canadian shores, passing themselves off as agricultural settlers eager to work on Canada's vast tracts of farmland. Their numbers may have included former concentration camp personnel. A clear statistical picture concerning those who fled abroad will only emerge once records have been thoroughly examined for all major countries that accepted new immigrants, and not just Argentina.

For this book, I visited numerous international archives over a five-year period and assessed their contents. They include the relevant national archives in Italy, Austria, Germany, the United States, Great Britain, and Switzerland as well as regional, church, and corporate archives. I consulted intensively the Archive of the International Red Cross Committee in Geneva; this was also the first time that the internal correspondence of the Red Cross during those years was examined. Entirely fresh insights into escape aid also came from the archives of the National Catholic Welfare Conference in Washington, DC. In addition, I closely evaluated the rich deposits of the US National

Archives. Along with the documents of the International Red Cross, they form the backbone of this richly sourced book. The Central State Archive and the Istituto Santa Maria dell'Anima in Rome, state archives elsewhere in Italy, and parish offices and city archives supplied important missing pieces for the understanding of the post-war situation in Italy.

Nazis on the Run is the first book to bring together and analyse all the structures used by Nazis in their flight. It gives a more complete picture of the organizations involved and of the links between them. First it depicts the role of Italy and, in particular, the South Tyrol in the transit of Nazis fleeing Europe. In the chapters that follow, the structures of the escape route are examined: the role of the International Committee of the Red Cross, the role of players inside the Vatican, and the actions of the intelligence agencies in the post-war years. The last chapter is devoted to Argentina, to which many of the perpetrators escaped. It is my hope that this fresh, transnational, and interdisciplinary outlook will provide a new understanding of how so many Nazis managed to escape justice after 1945.

1

The Nazi Escape Route
through Italy

In January 1949, the US Consulate in Bremen reported to the US State Department:

> I have the honor to report that I have had conversations with several well-informed persons who had occasion to investigate the underground route followed by Germans, particularly former Schutzstaffel (SS) members and their relatives and other politically suspicious persons, which leads via the Tirol and Italy to the Argentine. From what I have been able to learn, there is no longer any question but that a well-established and well-marked route exists.[1]

In this matter, the American diplomats were entirely correct. Their leading informer about Nazi escape routes to South America was a major figure—Dr Paul Schmidt, the former chief of the Press Department at the German Foreign Office. Schmidt described the escape routes in the greatest detail since he himself had attempted to escape via Bavaria, Salzburg, and the Tyrol to Genoa, Italy, in order to flee by ship to Argentina. But he did not leave and informed the US authorities instead. Others, mostly Nazis and SS men involved in the Holocaust or war crimes, managed to escape justice by fleeing to overseas territories.

The majority of the fleeing SS members and Nazis took the route overseas via Italy. There were other escape routes such as the 'Swiss hub',[2] or Spain, a destination to which thousands of Nazi perpetrators were able to escape between 1943 and 1946,[3] but from 1946 onwards, the exodus through Italy became extremely popular. For all those who wanted to leave the ruins of Europe and emigrate overseas, the shortest routes from Central and Eastern Europe led to port cities, chiefly Genoa and Trieste. Because the four occupying powers controlled Germany and Austria and Tito's communists ruled Yugoslavia, the route through Italy was shorter and presented fewer bureaucratic hurdles. For that reason, the country quickly became a hub for streams of refugees; war criminals also managed to escape quite easily through Italy. At the end of the war, hundreds of thousands of refugees and deportees from Central and Eastern Europe were on the move. To this day, their fate has largely been ignored; memory of them seems to have been erased in their countries of origin and in the ones through which they passed. In Austria alone, an estimated 1.5 million foreigners travelled through its restored sovereign territory in the spring of 1945.[4] This stampede of people made checks of personal documents and precise inspections impossible; the Italian authorities also had little interest in keeping their uninvited guests in the country and so had little interest in finding fault with their papers. As a result, SS men and war criminals disappeared into the crowd of refugees. The danger of being discovered shrank from month to month. The Allied Military Government in Italy was dissolved early on 31 December 1945. After that, the checks of personal papers became even more casual. Once the Allies and Italy signed the 1947 peace treaty, the Allied checks stopped completely. The Italian authorities were stretched thin and the security situation was desperate, so war criminals had little fear of discovery by them.

To understand what was happening at the time on the road between Brenner, Rome, and Genoa, the chaos of the post-war years must be understood: millions of refugees were in transit, either trying to find their homes and families or to start a new life. Those fleeing were not only wanted Nazis and war criminals, but also people expelled from the Eastern German territories, Nazi collaborators and anticommunists from European countries occupied by the Red Army, deserters, prisoners of war, forced labourers, displaced people, soldiers, and, finally, the survivors of the extermination and concentration camps. Various Jewish underground organizations also took advantage of the chaos in order to smuggle Holocaust survivors illegally through the British sea blockade to Palestine. In this case, too, the most advantageous route led to Italy, from which the emigrants' risky journey could continue on organized ship transports.

Genoa and Rome in particular were the contact points for many refugees as they set off for a supposedly 'new and better life' overseas. Tracking the large number of Germans and Austrians who emigrated to South America establishes that Italy posed few bureaucratic obstacles to their emigration. The possibility of escaping via Italy without major difficulties soon became public knowledge.

The chief obstacles to emigration existed in Central Europe; the inner-German borders with their controls, and the Alps, which acted as a geographical barrier to Italy that had to be overcome. But for centuries an established smuggling route traversed this 'green line'. Having reached Italy, the would-be emigrants had to rely on their own resources: they had entered the country illegally, with little money, and usually with sketchy documentation, without residence permits, and with no knowledge of the language. They were aware of the danger of being arrested by the carabinieri, and—to avoid that fate—they turned for help to institutions they believed they could trust: the Red Cross, the Catholic Church, and international refugee organizations. These organizations did help them—without checking who ultimately benefited from their aid. Everything quickly settled into a routine. In this way, thousands of SS members reached Italy.

1. Italy as a Country of Refuge

Understanding the flight of Nazi war criminals requires looking more closely at the situation in Italy. SS members and Nazi war criminals generally disappeared into the crowd of refugees. They lived in the same camps and accommodations and made the same subsequent journey overseas. The refugees were initially divided into categories by the Allied authorities. Even in the beginning, the Supreme Headquarters, Allied Expeditionary Force (SHAEF) distinguished between the terms 'refugees', for civilians who were temporarily homeless within their own national boundaries, and Displaced Persons (DPs). Displaced Persons were defined as a group of civilians who were outside their national boundaries by reason of war. The Allies defined two large groups of DPs thus:

United Nations Displaced Persons, citizens of the Allied nations, as well as those who could be given equal status with them, such as citizens of neutral states.

Enemy or Ex-Enemy Displaced Persons, or citizens of enemy states such as Germany and Austria as well as ex-enemy states such as Italy.[5]

According to the estimates of the US military authorities, at the end of the war in 1945 there were around 6.5 million Displaced Persons in Germany alone. Most of these were former forced labourers, but there were also countless Germans among them who were stranded far from their hometowns. In June 1945 in Bozen, Allied Headquarters held its first major conference on the current state of prisoners of war and Displaced Persons. The participants were very optimistic, believing they would be able to find a solution to the matter. But generally they had to acknowledge that thousands of refugees could not return to their homelands, and hundreds of thousands were de facto stateless. In June 1945, this explicitly meant Serbian nationalists, people from eastern Poland, and Ukrainians. They were to be housed in camps in Italy complete with their own churches and schools. For the foreseeable future, these people would have no choice but to lead life in Italian refugee camps because 'it was apparent that there was nowhere else for them to go'.[6]

The Allied military authorities bore primary responsibility for the DP camps; since 1943 they had been supported in this by the forty-four nation United Nations Relief and Rehabilitation Administration (UNRRA). UNRRA and above all its successor, the International Refugee Organization (IRO), were responsible for the mass of refugees. Members of former enemy states (Ex-Enemy Displaced Persons) did not fall under the auspices of UNRRA and the IRO. This group included all German nationals, but also 'ethnic Germans' (Volksdeutsche), which was the term for German speakers and members of the German cultural circle who were not German, Austrian, or Swiss citizens. The ethnic Germans lived mostly in Eastern and Southern Europe (Romania, Yugoslavia, Poland, and the Soviet Union). In Italy, South Tyroleans, too, were deemed to be ethnic Germans. In 1945/6, a regular westward migration of these peoples occurred.[7] As well as the ethnic Germans, Reich Germans were expelled from Silesia or eastern Prussia. Finally, the expulsion of the Sudeten Germans from Czechoslovakia began; most of them found a new home in Austria.[8]

Non-German refugees from the Soviet Union, Poland, Czechoslovakia, Hungary, and Yugoslavia, on the other hand, were to be 'brought home'. In the second half of 1945, UNRRA began major operations to repatriate millions of Displaced Persons. By the beginning of 1946, three-quarters of the original DPs in Europe had been returned to their own countries. But hundreds of thousands of refugees in Western Europe who had no intention of returning to their—now communist—homelands still existed. Original agreements reached by UNRRA with the Soviet Union decreed that all former Soviet citizens were to be handed over to Moscow—regardless of the will of the people in question. But in 1946, a million refugees from Central and Eastern Europe were still in Austria, Italy, and Germany. In June 1947, 650,000 refugees still lived in the camps in the three UNRRA-supported countries.

For years, the majority of refugees led a wretched life in the refugee camps. In the first post-war years, the Italian peninsula was scattered with three kinds of camps: first were the prisoner-of-war camps in which the soldiers of the Axis forces (above all from the German Reich, Austria, and Croatia) were interned, then the actual refugee camps, and finally the prison camps. The inmates of the latter were German refugees and former Axis soldiers who had committed crimes such as theft, black-marketeering, prostitution, and so forth, or whom the authorities found suspicious. Conditions in these camps varied greatly. Some were former Nazi transit camps or fascist confinement camps, such as the ones at Fossoli, Bozen (Bolzano), and Alatri; others were built after 1945 specifically for refugees, while still others were set up provisionally in villas, barracks, or even cinemas. In 1947, the Italian Foreign Ministry estimated that the Allies were in charge of some 80,000 people inside camps and 500,000 outside them. It seems these figures were revised slightly upwards so that Allied support for the large number of refugees could be requested with even greater urgency. At the time, Anglo-American authorities in Italy actually worked on the basis of 60,000 camp inmates and around 200,000 people in need of help who were housed outside of camps.[9]

After the war, the Allied authorities in Italy gradually withdrew from refugee care. On 31 December 1945, the Allied Military Government (AMG) was dissolved. With the 1947 Peace Treaty, Italy assumed responsibility for the refugees that they saw as the 'human flotsam and jetsam of war'. The Italian government wanted to deal with them as little as possible and had no desire to pay for their upkeep. The Allies did not want to find themselves once again burdened with hundreds of thousands of refugees, and they were keen to pass the task on to an international organization.

After UNRRA was dissolved in June 1947, the desperate situation of a million refugees escalated because their repatriation was no longer possible. The establishment of an additional organization for refugees received particular support from the United States; on 1 July 1947, the IRO finally went into operation.[10] The IRO defined refugees as people who were outside the country of their citizenship or their permanent place of residence, while Displaced Persons were people who had been deported from their homes by the Axis powers or a power allied to them during the Second World War, or who were forced to leave their homes due to a work contract. Excluded from the care of the IRO, once again, were people of German descent in the ethnic sense (German citizens or members of German minorities in other countries).[11]

Even at the time of the IRO's foundation, the tensions between East and West were clearly apparent. Because the Soviets regarded those people left in the camps as 'traitors and war criminals, nothing else', a refugee problem no longer existed as far as they were concerned. The Soviets accused the West of encouraging the formation of anticommunist movements and groups in the camps. The Western representatives reassured the Soviet diplomats by promising to support the repatriation of the Eastern refugees within the context of the IRO.[12] In the first two post-war years, 93 per cent of Soviet citizens were repatriated—many against their will. Among the Poles, the return quota was only 66 per cent, and only 42 per cent of the fleeing Slovenes, Croatians, and Serbs returned to Yugoslavia.[13]

In 1948 the newly founded IRO assumed control of almost all refugee housing and camps in Italy, while the Italian Interior Ministry administrated only a few camps, most of whose internees were foreigners considered suspicious on political or criminal grounds; these included the camps of Fossoli, Fraschette, Farfa Sabina (for women), Alberobello, Lipari, and Ustica.[14] According to the terms of the treaty between the IRO and the Italian government, refugees were either to be sent back to their countries of origin or made to emigrate overseas. But many refugees had already been in Italy for years and had settled there, found work, and started families. These refugees had no desire to be uprooted again because they already saw a better future for themselves and their families in Italy than elsewhere. But the Italian government nevertheless tried to get rid of the refugees as completely as possible. In some cases, this was not difficult; after several gruelling years in refugee camps, thousands were ready to leave Italy. But at the same time, new transports of refugees were still arriving in Italy. Even after the opening of German and Dutch ports, Italy remained the most important transit country. The IRO evacuated refugees from Germany and Austria to Italy in order to make it easier for them to continue on their way. In theory, the refugees were to travel by train via the Brenner Pass and to board a ship in Genoa, if possible without any great delay. But in reality the refugees were often displaced several times, so that months and years passed. Thus between 1946 and 1956 large numbers of people in Italy were looking for work and housing or the chance of going abroad and 'wandering' through the country.

Unlike UNRRA, the IRO worked independently of the military and even had its own fleet of refugee ships. It established treaties with various church and international aid organizations such as the International Red Cross. The US Joint Distribution Committee, for example, had paid for Jewish deportees. The US Catholic Church financed the outward passage of Catholics from Central and Eastern Europe, while the Evangelical church associations provided financial support for their members. The logistics, however, were generally handled by the IRO, which ran emigration offices worldwide, particularly in South America, Canada, North Africa, and Europe.[15] The IRO Headquarters in Geneva was responsible for around 1.5 million refugees. The largest groups were formed of 300,000 Poles, 150,000 people from the Baltic, 107,000 Ukrainians, and 30,000 Yugoslavians. In addition, over 500,000 refugees lived outside the camps. The constant influx of new refugees from the East, including above all Jews and people fleeing the communist regimes in Eastern European countries, made the IRO's work more difficult. Initially, the IRO's administrative policies and procedures regarding these Eastern refugees were not complete and well organized, but over time, the IRO considerably extended its jurisdiction and its mandate. However, ambiguities and capriciousness remained the order of the day. At the same time, political refugees and 'dissidents' also fell under the auspices of the IRO, which considered that the best solution still lay in the repatriation of these people to their countries of origin. Actual force was soon abandoned, but IRO planners continued to apply psychological pressure and advise the refugees to return to their original homelands.[16]

It soon became clear, however, that the IRO had no chance of sending all the refugees back to Eastern Europe; only a small proportion returned to their homes in what had become Soviet-controlled Eastern

Europe. Thus the refugees either were integrated into Western Europe or emigrated to South or North America or Australia or New Zealand. Still, the problem of what to do with the refugees had no clear resolution in the foreseeable future; from 1949 onwards, the IRO ceased to pay any attention to the new refugees constantly flowing in from Eastern Europe. Instead, the IRO's work focused on resettling and reintegrating the people displaced by the Second World War. As a result, in 1949 the United Nations began to set up the United Nations High Commission for Refugees (UNHCR); as a permanent international organization, it would from that point forward dedicate itself to the worldwide care of refugees.[17]

The IRO was determined to fulfil all the expectations of the Italian government, and so encouraged the overseas passage of refugees. The refugee organization established treaties with several countries, particularly in South America, that were interested in receiving workers from Europe. These first attempts were relatively unsuccessful, not least because the South Americans were unwilling to recruit refugees from Eastern Europe. Religious and racist prejudices against the supposedly inferior Slavs played a considerable part in this.[18] South American states also refused entry permits to Jewish refugees because anti-Semitism was widespread. In 1947, for example, the Brazilian Foreign Minister announced to the IRO that he would violently resist the issuing of visas to Jewish refugees because Jews would cause trouble in Brazil, settle only in the cities, keep to themselves, and dominate the property market. Moreover, they were also actively involved in the black market. Brazil would continue to take in refugees, but no Jews, for the reasons given, the Minister said by way of conclusion.[19] Attitudes such as this deepened the difficulty of the IRO's work. From its outset, the IRO had been conceived of as a short-term organization, and it essentially ceased activity on 30 June 1950.[20] From that point onwards, the states in question and the new UNHCR were responsible for refugees.

2. Refugees, Prisoners of War, and War Criminals

As well as the refugees, large numbers of German prisoners of war found themselves in Italy. Since the end of the war, thousands of SS and Wehrmacht members had been interned in places such as the biggest prisoner-of-war camp at Rimini-Bellaria. About 150,000 troops, including officers, had handed in their weapons in northern Italy in April and early May of 1945. The German capitulation and the SS leadership's negotiation with US officials in Italy created a favourable climate for the prisoners of war. As early as the summer of 1945, the German soldiers enjoyed certain freedoms—participating in many sporting and cultural initiatives such as soccer teams, language courses, film showings, singing groups—and even a specially improvised college. 'German Headquarters Rimini-Bellaria' was largely self- administrated, and the Allies granted it a large amount of autonomy.[21] With the mass release of Wehrmacht members in the autumn of 1945, the number of internees dropped to 25,000.[22] Guard duty became increasingly lax, so much so that regular unsupervised walks in the surrounding countryside became possible. Escape from the prisoner-of-war camps thus became fairly easy.

The British tried to weed out the war criminals from the mass of German prisoners of war and set up their own 'document centre' in order to do so. But before their arrest, many SS members had acquired false papers—mostly Wehrmacht service books—which presented them as ordinary soldiers; German assistants in the document centre also torpedoed the investigation of war criminals.[23] Among the high-ranking inmates in Rimini were, for example, Otto Baum, who had commanded the 16th Tank Grenadier Division Reichsführer SS, which was involved in several massacres of civilians in Italy. Another 'illustrious person' who enjoyed a fine life in Rimini was SS-Brigadeführer and Generalmajor Desiderius Hampel, who had commanded, among others, the 13th Waffen Mountain Division of the SS, the notorious 'Handschar'. In 1943, the Handschar was formed of Bosnian Moslem volunteers to fight Tito's partisans. Also in the Rimini camp were Generals Heinrich von Vietinghoff, Traugott Herr, and Joachim Lemelsen.

Despite the increasingly lax security measures, repeated breakouts from prisoner-of-war camps did occur. In May 1947 the Roman Ministry of the Interior informed all provinces by letter that the Italian police were now engaging in raids against the many fleeing German prisoners of war 'who were wandering all over Italy'. The arrested former Wehrmacht members were delivered to the Farfa camp.[24] Also in May 1947 the security authorities in the Bozen province reported the arrest of forty German prisoners of war who had escaped to South Tyrol from the camps of northern Italy. In March 1947, the Roman chief of police provided the British with a group of sixty officials in the city to support an intensified raid against German escapees and Croatian fascists. The police investigated 150 immigrants and arrested twenty of them, but were unable to enter the Vatican's Croatian Institute at the College of San Girolamo in Rome, where many war criminals and collaborators had supposedly found refuge.[25]

Beginning in the summer of 1947, the Allied Command Mediterranean in Italy showed less and less interest in prisoners of war. The large camp in Rimini Miramare was dissolved. Germans who had been apprehended by the Italian authorities and who had escaped from Allied camps were to be interned in the Compalto camp near Mestre, but the British 'no longer had the slightest interest' in non-German prisoners-of-war.[26] The US ambassador in Rome also made it clear in 1947 that from now on the Italian government was responsible not only for prisoners of war, but also for war criminals in its own country. Henceforth the Italians were to arrest the following groups of people: former members of the German forces, excluding those who could demonstrate that they had been recruited under duress; those who had committed war crimes or crimes against the Allies; and those who had voluntarily supported the enemy (collaborators). Then the US ambassador granted the Italians one more half-hearted wish: 'I am directed to state that my Government hopes that your Government will be governed by the same policy which the United States Government has pursued in this matter, and that my Government will support through me your Government in this respect.'[27] Finally, in October 1947 Allied Supreme Command gave its final word on the matter of Nazi war criminals and prisoners of war. In a short, emotionless communication, it established that Italy would henceforth have to concern itself only with escaped prisoners of war, regardless of whether they were of German or of any other nationality. Allied Supreme Command no longer had any interest whatsoever in these people.[28] Since 1947, the Italian police had not been so diligent either, and the search for war criminals lapsed immediately.

From the very beginning, the often difficult process of distinguishing between prisoners of war, refugees, and war criminals became a major problem for the authorities. Definitions were disputed, and the relevant governmental and refugee organizations were completely overwhelmed. In addition, the mounting conflict between the Soviet Union and the

Western Allies made the search for war criminals more difficult. The Soviets had quite different definitions and ideas regarding Eastern European refugees than the other Allied powers. Moscow often regarded refugees and prisoners of war from Eastern Europe as war criminals. Severe penalties awaited them behind the Iron Curtain. The IRO also had severe difficulties dealing with these Eastern European refugees.

Initially, however, the Allies did agree upon the appropriate fate of perpetrators and collaborators. As noted earlier, war criminals and ordinary German soldiers, as acknowledged refugees, were explicitly excluded from the IRO's protection; likewise, people who had violated the nation's law through treason or collaboration were outside the scope of the IRO's work. These people were instead to be brought before an international or national court.[29] The 'Declaration on the Responsibility of Hitler's Followers for Atrocities Committed' signed at the Moscow Conference on 1 November 1943 specified the extradition of war criminals to the states in which they had allegedly committed their crimes. The most notable characteristic of the Moscow Declaration was the distinction it made between perpetrators on a smaller scale, who were to be dealt with by national courts, and the 'major war criminals'. The most prominent perpetrators were the joint concern of the Allies, and these individuals were put on trial in Nuremberg after the end of the war.[30] Italy, too, had agreed to extradite war criminals in its peace treaty with the Allies. All suspicious people were held not by the IRO, but in Allied camps, later in Italian government camps, for interrogation. In the spring of 1945, collaborators with the Nazis were extradited to their homelands—Cossacks to the Soviet Union, for example, or Croatian Ustaša Fascists to Tito's Yugoslavia. For the people in question, that meant either internment or execution. It was only from 1947 onwards that the Western Allies more or less stopped extraditing people from this group.

The Soviet Union repeatedly accused the Western Allies of encouraging Soviet Displaced Persons not to return. Moreover it argued that the British, Americans, and French were using the DPs militarily and politically, or exploiting their labour. The Soviets were determined that the refugees should be returned to Eastern Europe. The US Embassy in Moscow was able to give important domestic reasons for the Soviets' position: their chief concern was the control of anticommunists. The Soviets were well aware of how the presence of thousands of people from Eastern Europe could be used for propaganda purposes. Among the refugees were people who were able to give eye-witness accounts of conditions and crimes in Stalin's Soviet Union. Other DPs made up an ideal pool from which the West could recruit Latvian, Lithuanian, and Ukrainian nationalists and anticommunists. For the Americans, the existence of these groups fed US hopes of the Soviet Union's dissolution. At the same time, the groups could play a considerable part in supporting resistance movements against the Soviet Union. During a new war, analysts thought, these exiles could, perhaps, form the core of a government. An internal report further assumed that such groups would collaborate with foreign intelligence services. The subsequent assessment by the US diplomats was that no arguments would work against the constant attacks and accusations of the Soviets. Hence they felt an unambiguous opposition to the forced repatriation of the Eastern Europeans. The US's clearly formulated position stated that they were making concrete efforts 'to rehabilitate and resettle these unfortunates so that they may live as free men'.[31]

Soviet accusations that collaborators were given preferential treatment were not entirely without foundation;[32] relief organizations often acted as a protective intermediary on behalf of the DPs from Soviet states. Even the Cossacks, traditionally seen as fanatical anticommunists, could expect assistance from the West. Thus, for example, the Cossack National Movement in Germany thanked the IRO in August 1948 for its support of the celebration of the 'thousandth anniversary of the Cossack people and the 30th anniversary of the declaration of independence' at the Cossack Conference in Munich. Delegates from all over the world had taken part in the festivities, 'with the exception of the Soviet Union and her satellite states'. On this occasion, the Cossacks asked the IRO to give a clear indication of their nationality and not put them in the categories of 'Russians' or 'stateless people'. Once the Cossacks had ridden against the Red Army in the uniform of the Wehrmacht; now they asked for school books and feared nothing more than the possibility of being handed over to Joseph Stalin.[33]

Not only was the IRO an advocate, Catholic dignitaries in Rome repeatedly intervened on behalf of Catholic collaborators and prisoners of war in the camps of Italy. Croatian clerics called upon the Vatican not only for better conditions in the camps, but also for passports and opportunities for internees to emigrate to South America.[34] Father

Krunoslav Draganović, the secretary of the Croatian Institute at the College of San Girolamo degli Illrici in Rome, told the Italian Prime Minister Alcide De Gasperi about the situation of the Croatians in the refugee camps. Draganović condemned the conditions affecting Yugoslavs and Croatians in the Fossoli camp and was particularly enraged by the visit of a delegation from Josip Broz Tito's Yugoslavia to Fossoli: he feared that Croatians and Yugoslavians could be forcibly returned to their homeland, which was now under communist rule. According to Draganović, this was irresponsible because among one hundred interned Croatians there were only two war criminals. The rest were innocent men who should be freed immediately.[35] The Vatican also shared this attitude. In September 1947 Pope Pius XII and Under-Secretary of State for Ordinary Affairs Giovanni Montini put pressure on the IRO for the right of residence for Yugoslavian refugees, including Croatian fascists.[36]

From the point of view of the host country, Italy, the refugees would not be a burden, would not create any problems, and would soon leave. In order to emigrate, the refugees needed internationally recognized travel documents in which the visas of the immigration states could be recorded. To this end, in October 1946 in London, twenty-one countries signed the 'London Agreement' about travel permits—the IRO's so-called 'London travel document'. According to this agreement, a refugee had to fulfil certain conditions to receive travel documents from the IRO, which was responsible for the permits (which meant that Germans were excluded in principle): the applicant had to be stateless either de facto or legally and should have a legal residence permit in an IRO member country. The preparation took a great deal of time. Many South American states refused to acknowledge the documents, or else created other difficulties. Even the Swiss authorities (despite the fact that the IRO's headquarters was in Geneva) questioned the validity of the papers.[37]

The IRO set up a few offices to deal with the correct issuance of travel documents. Because IRO officials were aware that war criminals, Nazi perpetrators, and collaborators were hiding among the refugees, they stepped up controls: foreign-language documents were translated, research was carried out to assess the identities of the applicants, and any gaps that existed in one's personal story were questioned. National and local authorities were also brought in to double-check personal details. The IRO was not given the task of investigating or recording war criminals, but in Italy it often worked with the Allied occupying authorities and the Italian government who did so. The refugee applications for IRO documents had to be made by the authorities in the refugee camp or in the IRO office in Rome. From 1950 onwards, improved IRO travel documents were issued and distributed at police headquarters.[38] In 1946, the Allied authorities in Italy examined 20,000 Ukrainians and Yugoslavians so that they could identify and arrest any possible war criminals. At the same time, the Allies and the IRO exerted pressure on the refugees 'so that as many dissidents as possible returned to their homelands'.[39] In January 1947, a special British screening team was assigned to the Ukrainians and Yugoslavians. This commission, headed by Fitzroy Maclean, the former leader of the British military mission in Italy, carried out the investigations. So the ambit of the IRO was not the best place for collaborators to go into hiding. Due to their use of fake papers and their desire to travel abroad, former SS men and war criminals found the organization held little appeal, as well.[40]

Given the large number of refugees and displaced persons, it was difficult in the end for the authorities to carry out precise checks on internees. Escape from the camps, the black market, prostitution, and espionage blossomed in this *demi-monde*. A considerable number of the internees also had a dark past; the superficial checks in the camps caused little alarm, which was why the authorities showed little interest in them. Because of this attitude and in spite of the checks, war criminals and Nazi collaborators were able to escape with the help of the IRO. This fact did not remain a secret. For example, in June 1947 the Venezuelan daily newspaper *Ultimas noticias*, under the headline 'Entran Fascistas', replied to accusations in the French press that French fascists were being sheltered in Venezuela. In Europe, the article said, the view was generally held that Nazis, Falangists from Spain, and fascists from Italy were disappearing in Venezuela in their thousands, not the French fascists.[41] In a memorandum of June 1947, representatives of the IRO responded to the charges of smuggling Nazis to Venezuela. The IRO delegate in Caracas replied in great detail to the charges in a report to the US embassy and the IRO in London, confirming that war criminals were, indeed, escaping to South America. The IRO, he said, was indirectly involved in the escape of the Nazis. If possible, the problem was not to be broadcast to the world at large. If it had to be dealt with at all, then it had to happen discreetly and at the highest possible level, meaning the US government and the government of Venezuela.[42] But the IRO was by no means the only international organization from which a refugee could obtain travel papers. There were alternatives: offices and authorities that hardly ever performed checks and at which the acquisition of documents was unimaginably easy and the risk of being discovered was practically nonexistent. These included the International Red Cross, which had some gaps to close in its treatment of refugees. Initially the IRO was supposed to take care of Displaced Persons, while the Red Cross was to look after prisoners of war. Because the IRO did not generally take care of German refugees, the International Committee of the Red Cross ended up doing so. Consequently, from the very start, responsibilities were unclear—in practice there were constant overlaps. Beginning in 1944, the Red Cross began to issue travel papers to give even refugees unrecognized by the IRO the opportunity to emigrate. As mentioned above, the IRO refused to accept 'ethnic Germans' or political dissidents as refugees. Millions of ethnic Germans thus led a wretched life in camps along with others who were not included in the IRO's definition of recognized refugees.

3. Illegal Immigrants

Large number of refugees in Italy had entered the country illegally by navigating Germany's internal borders, with their checks and restrictions, and the Alps. To do so, one could resort to an institution established centuries before: smuggling. The border between Austria and Italy had been strictly guarded since 1918, but was still porous. It was a tried and tested system: experienced mountain guides knew the right paths and people; often they had acquaintances among the customs men and border guards. This time, the contraband was people.

The US State Department official in Rome, Vincent La Vista, reported on smuggling problems at the Brenner border:

> Small groups [...] continue to find their way into Italy illegally, though no large-scale organization seems to be directing this movement. Nevertheless, individuals who legally make their way to Austria for a great variety of reasons with the premeditated aim of reaching Italy cross the Italo-Austrian border with considerable baggage and with relative ease.

It would seem there exist organized bands at said border who aid any would-be illegal emigrants provided a sufficient sum is paid. One of these groups operates at Brenner-See, and another at another point behind the Brenner Pass. The second group has a standard rate of 500 Schillings per person. Not all cross the border in this manner though, for some manage to cross on their own initiative.[43]

In the economically difficult post-war years, many locals made very good livelihoods out of smuggling. Everything that could be sold or exchanged at a profit was smuggled: saccharine, insulin, cocaine, coffee, tobacco, livestock, foreign currency, and gold. People were also smuggled across the 'green border'. Post-war Italy was teeming with refugees and escapees trying to get across the mountains illegally. The unlawful escape routes over the green border were very professionally organized, and the transit of humans developed into a lucrative business. In September 1945, the carabinieri exposed just such an escape network in the Italian border town of Bozen. They arrested Alfred Pasche from Vienna, who was working as a driver for the German Red Cross, in which capacity he repeatedly carried mail in his car between Bozen and Innsbruck. That allowed the smugglers to escape the mail censorship that prevailed at the time. His 'post office' was a coffeehouse, and a regular, illegal postal traffic operated undetected for months. But Pasche wasn't just smuggling mail; he was smuggling people, too.[44]

The smugglers at the Brenner had fixed rates after the war. When Jews were involved, they usually waited until they had six people, who were then carried across for 4,000 Schillings altogether. Notorious Nazis had to pay the most: 1,000 Schillings a head. Because there were hardly any telephones, the refugees were announced with passwords by couriers or other confidants.[45] The undercover agents gave a concise account of the situation: 'In spite of all attempted controls, this method of entering Italy is so simple that it is merely a matter of walking across the border and, if apprehended, being turned back to try again the next day. The process is repeated until success is achieved.'[46] The Italian border controls were generally helpless in the face of the flow of refugees. The security officials first arrested the illegal emigrants and examined them for weapons and smuggled goods. Then as a rule they were deported again or transferred to a refugee camp.[47]

In August 1947 alone, 3,139 illegal refugees were captured by the Italian security authorities at the state border, and sent back to Austria.[48] The number who managed to cross the border to Italy was probably much higher. The flow of illegal refugees was also hugely dependent upon the season. In winter and early spring, crossing the high mountains was nearly impossible; this could be done only during the few months between June and September. In 1947, Italian security authorities registered a total of 8,315 illegal emigrants detained along the Brenner border; this represented the peak of the wave of refugees. In 1948 there were 6,908 arrests, in 1949 only 840.[49] In 1947, in the Brenner–Innsbruck–German border area alone, the Austrian authorities arrested several hundred illegal emigrants. These procedures are recorded in the files of the Austrian authorities as 'unauthorized border-crossing', 'escorting', and 'deportation'. The arrests were particularly frequent on the northern border, on the German side. The refugees first had to cross the border illegally into Austria from Germany, and then cross the border—illegally again—via a narrow strip, a 50 km corridor, to Italy.[50] At this stage of the travellers' journey, the Austrians plainly kept their eyes firmly shut, since they were glad that they would soon be rid of the refugees, for Austria was already full of refugees, and the food supply situation was desperate.

Innsbruck soon proved to be the first informal transit and collection point. From Innsbruck there were several routes to Italy. From the Tyrolean alpine spa of Nauders, travellers could reach Italy by the Reschenpass and along the Adige (Etsch) via Meran (Merano) to Bozen (Bolzano). The alternative was the path leading from Innsbruck via the Brenner to Sterzing (Vipiteno) and along the Eisack (Isarco) to Bozen. Along with the Brenner and Reschen line, the path via the Zillertal and Ahrntal to Bozen was also often used. Of course, these border crossings often took place at night and in bad weather because border patrols were less likely then.

Once they reached Italy, refugees had little to fear if they behaved calmly and found suitable housing. Illegal entry was generally risked only by individuals or small groups who had relations or acquaintances in Italy and could expect to find a place to stay. For families with children, the dangers were very great. Crossings through the high mountains were sometimes associated with terrible physical strain. The fact that the journey could also be life-threatening is borne out by the many newspaper reports of refugees dying as the result of accidents or exhaustion. Once the refugees arrived in Italy, the greatest danger lay in the possibility of being arrested by the American or Italian authorities, who generally deported illegal immigrants back over the border. Normally this was done without going through the courts, but there were exceptions to this procedure. Thus, for example, some refugees were given sentences of up to six months' imprisonment, followed by deportation.[51] The US delegation in Vienna described the procedures and the escape routes:

> This person may secure the aid of several groups presently operating in Austria to assist him in crossing the border into Italy illegally, i.e. Polish Underground operating in Innsbruck, Austria, Hungarian Underground operating in the vicinity of Klagenfurt, Steiermark [*sic*], Jewish groups operating in area of Innsbruck, Austria. These groups can either supply the person in question with false identity documents or escort him over the Brenner Pass on foot in and about the area of Geis [Gries], Tyrol, Austria. Once in Italy there is little difficulty in travel and subject may reach Rome in one or two days either by motor or rail transport.[52]

The bands of people-traffickers and forgers generally did good business with refugees, regardless of where they came from and who they were. Arrangements such as safe houses or fake passports were useful to all. The people helping them escape made no distinctions. Alongside German emigrants who had set their sights on South America as a destination, their clientele also included a large number of Jews who were—also illegally—en route for Palestine. Cynically, the transalpine escape routes of the wanted Nazi criminals often crossed those of their victims as they tried to emigrate to Palestine. Simon Wiesenthal writes on the subject:

> I know a small inn near Merano, in the Italian Tyrol, and another place near the Reschenpass between Austria and Italy, where Nazi and Jewish travellers sometimes spent the night unaware of each other's presence. The Jews were hidden on the upper floor and told not to move; and the Nazis, on the ground floor, were warned to stay inside.[53]

Between 1945 and 1947 the northern Italian border town of Meran became a stopover for Jewish emigrants to Israel. Refugees were accommodated there for a few days before being transported onwards, mostly to Bozen or Milan. The then-leader of the Jewish community in Meran remembers that an average of between 250 and 400 Jewish refugees arrived daily in Meran from February 1946 until the spring of 1947.[54] In the years 1945 until 1948, in often adventurous ways, more than 200,000 Jews escaped, mostly from Poland and Romania, through Austria and Italy to Palestine.[55] The Jewish refugee organization Ha'Bricha ('Escape') had been set up in eastern Poland and Lithuania as early as 1944/5. Bricha set up escape networks from Eastern Europe to Italy, thus helping to bring the refugees closer to their goal.[56] In early summer 1945, for example, Bricha in Innsbruck and its branch in Meran repeatedly succeeded, without difficulty, in presenting Jewish refugees as returning Italians, prisoners of war, and forced labourers, and sending them to Italy with forged papers and Italian uniforms.[57] Italian refugee transports were rarely checked.[58] In summer and autumn, transports of returning Italians entered the country almost daily. The organizers of the Jewish exodus used this circumstance and smuggled their own 'returning Italians' through the Tyrol. They were helped in this by the initial lack of interest on the part of the Allies and by the extremely careless surveillance at the Italian border.[59]

For those illegally crossing the border, the Alto Adige was the first stop in Italy. German-speaking refugees in particular generally had a friendly reception. The way over the mountains was not always easy to negotiate for those unfamiliar with the area, so the help of discreet villagers was invaluable. The former German Wehrmacht soldier Karl Fiedler entrusted himself to the refugee smugglers: 'I was surprised to find German-speaking settlements so far south. The people spoke a rather different dialect, but as a German you could make yourself understood. I managed to get something to eat, and isolated farmers also offered me a place to stay and food.'[60]

Wehrmacht soldier Rudi Wagner from Erfurt escaped from Austria to the Alto Adige in May 1945. In September 1945, a US military court sentenced him to jail in Bozen and transferred him to the Rimini prisoner-of-war camp six months later:

> It was unbearable there. Still, I did get to see Venice on a voluntary work deployment. As soon as no one was looking, out we went, this time escaping over barrack walls and barbed wire and back to the mountain valleys on either side of the Brenner. Where else? Anything was better than going back to Russian-occupied Erfurt in those days.[61]

In the end, Wagner stayed in the Tyrol.

Another German soldier, Karl Schedereit, found his way across the Brenner to Alto Adige. At the end of the war Schedereit, born in 1925 and a soldier with the Waffen-SS, assumed a new identity as Wehrmacht Lieutenant 'Robert Karrasch'. After being interned at the end of the war, he escaped from a prisoner-of-war camp to the Alto Adige, hoping to head from there to Genoa and finally to Argentina, leaving behind the ruins of Europe and his hometown, now in Poland, to make a new start across the sea. He escaped via the Reschenpass to Meran, and from there to Rome. In Rome he was supplied with a new passport. But in the end he didn't emigrate, instead staying in the Alto Adige.[62] As an unpopular 'Reich German' in Austria, 'Karrasch' was constantly exposed to the threat of denunciation. Having reached the South Tyrol (Alto Adige), he depicted the situation quite differently: as a German, Karrasch no longer feared denunciation by the ethnic Germans of the Alto Adige, most of whom were sympathetic to him.[63] His crossing into Italy at the Reschenpass is typical of this. 'Karrasch' describes this central moment in his autobiography thus:

> In the border town of Reschen Karrasch walked past the carabinieri barracks, from which light and a hubbub of voices spilled out, and back out into the night towards the distant lights of the village of Graun. The inn was full of men in dark clothes, crowding around the wooden bar. They wore hats and drank red wine, smoked cigarettes and pipes. Karrasch attempted an engaging smile. 'My standard German will betray me,' he thought. The friendly, grizzled farmer came over to him with a full glass of red wine in his hand. 'You'll have come over the border? Don't worry, son, there are no Walschen [Italians] here, just Germans! Prost!'[64]

One man who made it to Argentina from Italy was Reinhard Kops. Kops was born in Hamburg-Altona in 1914 and joined the Nazi Party in 1940.[65] The anti-Semite Kops had been an intelligence agent during the war and had worked as an expert on 'freemasons' in the Balkans and Hungary. As a member of the German espionage network, Kops was automatically arrested and interned by the British.[66] After his escape across the mountains to the Alto Adige, Kops was helped on his way, no questions asked:

> I immediately notice that these people here need no further explanation. Anyone coming from up there in those days is a refugee, and they

have to be helped. No one asks any unnecessary questions; everyone provides concise factual information, and then they add: 'On the other side of the road, about 100 metres away, is the carabinieri station. You've got to get past it quickly.'[67]

Kops soon reached Meran, where he had a safe 'starting address', 'dressed as a South Tyrolean', and enjoyed a hearty dinner. Later, he reached his actual goal, his safe house at 'Aunt Anna's'. This Meran inn, run by the ominous-sounding 'Aunt Anna', was an often-used stop for SS members, fleeing Nazi perpetrators, and war criminals on their escape. Thus, for example, Kops tells of the SS doctor Emil Gelny from Austria, who was later supposedly able to flee to Syria. Gelny was the doctor chiefly responsible for the euthanasia murders in the mental institutions of Gugging and Mauer-Öhling in Austria. So Kops, alias Hans Maler, could feel quite safe there. After several months in Aunt Anna's care, the Nazi Kops set off again, this time for Genoa, acquired the remaining papers—including a visa for Argentina—and travelled to Buenos Aires.[68] After fleeing across the border to the Alto Adige, one SS man was able to say euphorically: 'After the war, Italy was the dreamland for members of criminal organizations! That's how times change.'[69]

In the 1950s, the Viennese Karl Babor, a concentration camp doctor in Groß-Rosen and Dachau notorious for his experiments on humans, escaped, presumably also via Italy, to Ethiopia. He practised in Addis Ababa as a doctor for the European colony and the Ethiopian elite. He seems to have died in unusual circumstances in 1964: the remains of the former SS-Hauptsturmführer were found in a crocodile-infested swamp. His grave is in the foreigners' cemetery in Addis Ababa.[70]

Some of the most notorious mass murderers and war criminals also chose to escape via Italy. The name Adolf Eichmann represents murder on a scale of millions, the personification of the 'desk-bound perpetrator'. It was Eichmann who handled the 'technical' side of the planned 'extermination of European Jewry'. At the end of the war, he left his wife and three children behind in the Austrian town of Aussee; he himself went into hiding.[71] Sixteen years later, Eichmann gave an account of his fear and bewilderment:

May 1945. My beloved Reich lay in ruins. Defeated. As I stood on the shore of a little Austrian lake, I became aware that I, SS-Obersturmbannführer Adolf Eichmann, was now nothing but a hunted deer, no better off than the deer in the forest that I saw before me. [...] [My family] could stay here in the safety of the cottage on the Aussee in Ischl, my uncle's chalet. I, though, had no option but to flee.[72]

Eichmann lived in Germany under false names and with false papers until 1950. At last Eichmann had saved enough to flee to South America.[73] His escape route, like that of thousands before him, was predetermined. In SS circles, the escape route via the Alto Adige to Genoa was already widespread knowledge. In May 1950 Eichmann made contact with escape agents from the Alto Adige who smuggled him into Italy. 'Dressed in mountain gear, with a Tyrolean hat with a tuft of chamois hair [*Gamsbart*]', as he revealed years later, Eichmann first managed to escape over the border to Austria.[74] In Kufstein—and elsewhere—escape agents had supplied him with shelters and contacts. The refugee smugglers in Austria and the Alto Adige were involved because of the profits to be made from aiding escapees, but sometimes they also acted out of ideological motives or pity. In most cases, they knew very little about the true identity of the refugees. All that was clear was that they were fleeing SS men or Nazi functionaries who had to—or wanted to—get out of Europe. The 'escape aid' system and the escape route had proved successful in hundreds of cases. 'The "U-boat route" worked like clockwork,' Eichmann observed.[75] Without any great difficulty, Eichmann travelled by taxi to Innsbruck, an important transit point on the Brenner line. He had planned to go into hiding in Innsbruck with an SS comrade, but received a rude welcome: 'Get out of my house'.[76] It seems that the SS man knew about Eichmann and his role as a mass murderer. Just as Eichmann's SS superiors had done at the end of the war, the Innsbruck former SS man wanted to get rid of him as quickly as possible. Eichmann had to travel on to the next safe house. This time, he tried a relative of his uncle's in Innsbruck, where he found a considerably warmer reception: 'Good old Frau Huber gave me a schnapps, then dispatched me to another inn near the Brenner.'[77] In the little border town of Gries, just before the Brenner, he found another place to hide. Here Eichmann found himself caught up in a raid by the French occupying police. 'A number of trucks pulled into the village, and immediately it swarmed with French soldiers who were about to carry out a raid. But my hostess, who belonged to the "organization", was on the ball. "Quick—into the attic," she said.'[78]

Once again, Eichmann was lucky and avoided discovery. The land-lord organized Eichmann's crossing over the Brenner frontier. This process was all routine; thousands of war criminals and former SS men had been sent to Italy in this way. The smugglers brought Eichmann from the inn on the Brenner over the mountains to the Italian side, where the vicar of Vipiteno (Sterzing) was already waiting for him. Eichmann wrote in his diaries about the helpful cleric:

> For years [the priest] had helped all kinds of refugees. Once it had been Jews, now it was—Eichmann! I was most grateful to receive my suitcase from this excellent, cycling priest about a kilometre and a half behind the Italian border, and allowed myself the now traditional swig of alcohol to celebrate my success. This time it was a red, South Tyrolean wine! The priest directed me to a taxi-driver, who first took me to his flat. Here I left my Tyrolean costume and put on less conspicuous street clothes.[79]

This was how Adolf Eichmann described his escape via the Brenner to Italy and the help given to him by a South Tyrolean priest in illegally crossing the border: the obscene and ruthless juxtaposition of 'Jews—Eichmann' that he made in his notes during his trial in Israel in 1961 needs no further comment. Eichmann's South Tyrolean 'taxi-driver' first lodged the mass murderer in his house in Vipiteno for a few days. Eichmann then moved to the Franciscan monastery in the South Tyrol's provincial capital of Bozen, where he stayed for a considerable time.[80]

4. Smuggling Goods and People

Aiding escapees became a profitable sideline in the Alpine border region. A refugee boom occurred between autumn 1945 and summer 1946, and in 1949 the tide slowly subsided.[81] Most of the people to be ferried across were strangers to the smugglers, and the names they gave were seldom correct. A middleman brought the illegal frontier-crossers to a mountain guide who had been let in on what was happening. The guide led them along a tried and tested route to South Tyrol, where they were usually welcomed by another intermediary. It was a very safe journey: the residents of the Northern and Southern Tyrol knew one another, family connections and bonds of friendship were common, and for generations smuggling had been a reliable source of income.

The customs officers on either side of the border knew each other as well, and the same German dialect was spoken on both sides of the Brenner.[82] According to a report by the US State Department, even the South Tyrolean Alpinist and actor Luis Trenker was asked to act as a guide by former comrades: 'hardly a day passed but he was appealed to for assistance on the way by two or three persons leaving Germany for Italy by the underground route'.[83] In his 1979 autobiography *Alles gut gegangen*, Trenker quite openly discusses the help he gave to a Bulgarian diplomat who was urgently sought by the US Counter Intelligence Corps (CIC):

> 'You must help them, they are good people—they must get away from here—bring them to Italy via the Brenner, as quickly as possible!' I wanted to do what my good friend urged, so I smuggled a man, woman and two children as well as their twenty pieces of luggage amongst all sorts of dangers into the Grödnertal, where I got them identification papers and residence permits. A CIC officer in Salzburg had been pursuing him, a military court had condemned him to two years' imprisonment because he was supposed to have hidden his wife's valuable jewellery.[84]

Monsignor Karl Bayer, the head of Caritas in Rome, said of the escape aid agents in the South Tyrol: 'All those fellows had told each other which little villages on the Brenner or nearby were the best for crossing, which peasants were old Nazis or just friendly, or to be had for money. But there were enough guides anyway—old hands at smuggling, who took them across for nothing.'[85]

Josef Mengele, the doctor in the Auschwitz-Birkenau extermination camp, also used local people-smugglers on his way to Italy. Mengele fled Auschwitz in January 1945 to escape the advancing Red Army. He was already a wanted man, as a warrant from the time reveals: 'Mengele, Joseph, Dr., SS-Hauptsturmführer and camp doctor, Auschwitz Concentration Camp, June 1940 until January 1945, mass murder and other crimes.'[86] In spite of his high rank as a wanted Nazi criminal, Mengele was helped by a concatenation of factors, including the difficulty of filtering out war criminals from millions of German prisoners of war. At the same time, in spring 1945, he managed to disguise himself as a private in a Wehrmacht unit. After his release from prisoner-of-war camp, Mengele worked under the name 'Fritz Hollmann' as a farmhand in Mangolding in Bavaria.[87]

In the autumn of 1948, Mengele resolved to leave Germany and start a life elsewhere. His marriage to his first wife Irene had by that time collapsed irretrievably, and they parted. Because Mengele seemed to find it more difficult to say goodbye to the couple's son Rolf, he never entirely severed contact with his family living in the small German town of Günzburg. But his family had a considerable interest in ridding themselves of the problem of a wanted Nazi war criminal. No one wanted to jeopardize the re-launch of the family business. Mengele & Sons' wheelbarrows and combine harvesters sold well in the post-war years, so the family was in a position to finance the expensive flight of Josef Mengele, the family's black sheep. Together with his family, Mengele was looking for a way out and finally decided to emigrate to German-friendly Argentina. On Good Friday 1949, he set off from Innsbruck for the Brenner Pass. Mengele's smugglers were the Tyrolean landlord Jakob Strickner and the South Tyrolean Adolf Steiner from Meran.[88]

On Easter Sunday 1949, the Tyrolean smugglers brought Mengele from Vinaders am Brenner over the mountains to the Italian side of the Brenner Pass, where he spent the night at the Kerschbaumer Inn, a grey building whose shingles were weighted down with stones. This inn still stands in Brennerbad. His helpers had advised him, in the event of a control by a border patrol, to say that he came from Tramin near Bozen and that he had taken the route over the green border because he had lost his passport. The next day, Mengele reached Vipiteno and took a room in the Goldenes Kreuz Inn in the town centre, staying there for four weeks.[89] Mengele had sufficient funds to afford staying in a hotel rather than—like Eichmann—in a South Tyrolean monastery as a penniless guest.[90]

Many years later, the media and politicians were still fascinated by the man who assisted Mengele's escape. Jakob Strickner, who was mayor of the little border village of Gries am Brenner for twenty-four years after 1945, repeatedly boasted of helping concentration camp doctor Josef Mengele escape to Italy.[91] The landlord liked to tell his guests of his 'heroic deed'. For years hardly anyone paid him any attention. But times changed. In 1985, in the run-up to a council election, the scandal broke.[92] In that year, the German magazine _Bunte_ reported extensively on Mengele's escape route[93] and named Strickner as a possible helper—the consequences were violent controversies in the border village and a defamation trial.[94]

The local press spoke about the 'Mengele trauma in Gries'.[95] At first, Strickner denied any involvement in Mengele's flight.[96] In an initial statement he said, 'I never knew Mengele, and didn't know that I was being photographed in connection with the report on his escape. The only thing I told the reporters while hoeing the potatoes was where the green border routes to Italy are in our area.'[97] But the affair really got going after Simon Wiesenthal uncovered Strickner's Nazi past.[98] Strickner had been a member of the SS, and when that story broke, people suspected the truth of his role in Mengele's escape story. But Strickner played down his SS membership in a statement: 'I was only part of the general SS in 1938, and joined the Wehrmacht in 1941. I can prove that I helped many people, including Jews.'[99] In Strickner's curriculum vitae of 1938, which he wrote for the SS Racial Office, things sounded very different: 'I joined the NSDAP early in 1933, and the SA at the end of 1933. In January 1934 I joined the SS and was commissioned to set up the SS in Wipptal and Stubaital. I have led this area since 1934.'[100] Strickner also took part, as Ortsgruppenleiter of Steinach am Brenner, in the failed July Putsch of the National Socialists in Austria in 1934 and spent several months in prison in 1935 and 1936 for 'political reasons'.[101] After the Anschluss, the forced annexation of Austria in 1938, he enriched himself with Jewish property and 'Aryanized' an Innsbruck shop.[102] In April 1941, he had been conscripted into the Wehrmacht, and in late December 1944 discharged to Tyrol.[103] In 1945, Strickner was arrested and interned by the Allies, but in 1947 was released from prisoner-of-war camp, facing ruin. Smuggling presented itself as a possible source of making a living:

> In 1947 I came home from prison—all I had was my camp uniform. Everything I owned had been confiscated because I was in the SS. What were we supposed to live on? Almost everyone in the area was smuggling. Grease, wool, replacement parts, animals and, indeed, people crossed the border illegally.[104]

According to Wiesenthal, because of the strategic position of his inn in Vinaders am Brenner, after 1945 Strickner became an important human smuggler along the Brenner line. His inn lay a few kilometres away from the Brenner Pass. Just in front of the building, a path runs across an alpine pasture through the woods to the Italian side, to the little town of Brennerbad. This route across the green border is relatively short and easy to walk; smugglers, shepherds and cowherds used it—but so did refugees. Strickner's inn was ideally situated as the last stopover on the way to Italy. Inns in the border region were particularly popular stopping points, and it was from them that many smuggling trips began. A former South Tyrolean Wehrmacht soldier vividly describes his journey home across the mountains in 1945:

> We reached the sacristy in Vinaders in the evening, and were given soup and a heated room for the night. After a breakfast of coffee with milk I paid the kind sacristan with a packet of tobacco; we said our grateful goodbyes and asked about the path over the pass. Two more South Tyroleans joined us. On the morning of 24 December 1945 four of us risked the crossing, through waist-high snow, and slowed by several snowstorms, over the Joch, and at 12 o'clock after walking for almost six hours, drenched and frozen, we arrived at the home of the old farmer above Giggelberg near Gossensass.[105]

On the way to his home near Bozen, the badly dressed and penniless returnee received repeated help from landlords along the Brenner road: 'I will never forget those landlords, and may God reward them for all the good things they did for us!'[106] There were also prominent Nazi criminals, including Franz Stangl, the Commandant of Treblinka, sitting in the Gaststuben waiting for smugglers or intermediaries. As a rule everything went smoothly—as in the case of Armin Dadieu, the right-hand man of the Styrian Gauleiter.[107] According to the Austrian State Police, Dadieu lived unrecognized in Graz until 1948, and in March of the same year escaped from Nauders in the Tyrol to Meran.[108] Dadieu received energetic help from his compatriot Bishop Alois Hudal, who also gave him contacts with smugglers at the Reschenpass.[109] By contrast, the flight of concentration camp commandant Josef Schwammberger remains largely shrouded in darkness. Here, as in most cases, only individual fragments, snapshots, and clues remain. Only once, under questioning in May 1990, did former SS-Oberscharführer Schwammberger talk about his escape to Argentina:

> I then stayed in the Oradour camp until I released myself in February 1948. I owed that entirely to my gift for organisation. [...] On my escape I took with me two other people, one SS man and another man from Hungary. [...] The driver brought us to Matrei; from there we travelled on foot until just before the Brenner. A landlady whom my parents knew

referred me to a smuggler who could get me across the border. First of all
I spent three weeks in Brixen [in the South Tyrol], staying with my godfather's daughter. [...] A religious organisation, it might have been the
Evangelical Aid Community, gave me the price of a ticket to Argentina.
The entry permit came directly from Argentina; it was organised by a
woman who had looked after German soldiers in the South Tyrol during
the War. [...] I used this opportunity to embark on a French Liberty
vessel in Genoa. That was how I got to Buenos Aires, in 1948.[110]

A network of acquaintances became the basis of a loosely organized
escape service throughout the country. Ordinary Wehrmacht soldiers,
SS men, and war criminals could count on their comrades on either
side of the Brenner. One excellent example of this is the group of former
comrades centred around the South Tyrolean SS-Hauptsturmführer
Karl Nicolussi-Leck. After receiving tips about well-organized Nazi
people-smuggling operations, the Public Prosecutor's Office in Innsbruck launched an investigation in 1949. The authorities quickly uncovered a well-functioning escape network which included a confidant of
Nicolussi-Leck: Karl Folie.

Born in Eppan in South Tyrol in 1908, Folie lived in Matrei am
Brenner, where he survived by smuggling after the war. In 1949, he was
arrested by Austrian police after an unambiguous tip-off. He immediately admitted to having brought German and Austrian citizens illegally over the Brenner border. For individuals, he generally asked 500
Schillings; groups got a discount. On the other side of the Italian border, Folie delivered the refugees to Walter Spitaler from the South Tyrol.
In the case of Folie and Spitaler, the Public Prosecutor's Office began
an investigation 'on the grounds of suspicion of neo-Nazi activity'. The
Austrian authorities assumed that Spitaler 'was, along with Karl Folie,
helping National Socialists escape abroad via an unauthorised border-
crossing'.[111] One of their intermediaries was Willi Dressler, a former
SS-Untersturmführer, who had escaped from Salzburg's Glasenbach
camp to the Tyrol during a riot. Witnesses also spoke of the political
background to people-smuggling. Folie's wife confirmed that the people
smuggled were not apolitical 'poor devils': 'From the conversations that
they had I could tell that many of the German citizens were war criminals, or at least inculpated Nazis.'[112]

To the Austrian investigators, the escape of the Nazis across the
Brenner seemed to be controlled and financed by a 'secret organization'.

People-smuggling from Germany via Austria to Italy was well organized: at the border near Kufstein, customs officer Georg Schwentner brought the Germans to Innsbruck, Austria, then South Tyrolean Karl Troy brought them to Folie in Matrei am Brenner. On the Italian side, Spitaler took charge of the refugees and brought them to Bozen, where former SS officers were waiting for them. In 1949, a repentant refugee reported 'in strict confidence' to the Austrian authorities that:

> He had been brought over the border at the Brenner by a man named Spittaler [*sic*] who lived in Bozen and was taken to that city. He had only worked for about 3 months for pay on a farm near Bozen. There he received from Rome, without any additional actions on his part and without fingerprints, a completed Red Cross passport with an entry visa. He had also received a boat ticket to Buenos Aires. He had then used his own resources to travel to Genoa, where he had—the crossing was paid for—embarked on the steamer 'Santa Cruz' for Buenos Aires, where he had arrived on 3 November last year [1948].[113]

Walter Spitaler (code name 'Goldgasser') travelled constantly back and forth between Bozen–Brenner–Innsbruck and Bozen–Reschen. Along with Nicolussi-Leck, he was one of the main escape organizers. This was also confirmed by Folie: 'The Reich German individuals told me in most cases that they wanted to emigrate to Argentina. As I recall, Spittaler [*sic*] already had in his possession the so-called "Red Cross passports" which he then issued when the people in question were in the South Tyrol.'[114] Spitaler's confidant Nicolussi-Leck travelled constantly back and forth between Innsbruck, Bozen, and Rome and brought instructions to his brother-in-law Troy in Innsbruck. In 1955 the investigations into the people-smuggling group died down, and in 1959 the search for Spitaler was abandoned. It was only later that the Ministry of the Interior in Vienna would connect this 'secret organization' around Spitaler, Nicolussi-Leck, and Troy with ODESSA. It was through Wiesenthal, in 1969, that ODESSA became a reality, at least for the Ministry of Justice in Vienna, when it gave the old file about the Tyrolean smugglers a new cover page with the title 'ODESSA Organization'.

Nicolussi-Leck was without a doubt one of the most important organizers of escape aid for Nazis in Italy. He played a central role in the immediate post-war years, first as a people-smuggler, then as the first contact for escapees. One prominent client of Nicolussi-Leck and Spitaler was flying ace Hans-Ulrich Rudel. The much-decorated pilot decided to emigrate to Argentina after the end of the war. In his memoirs, the fighter pilot gave a detailed description of how he and his closest colleagues escaped to Italy. In the chapter 'Many Ways Lead to Rome', Rudel describes how, in 1948, with his Group Commander Herbert Bauer, his aerial gunner Ernst Niermann, technical officer Katschner, and fellow squadron-member Zeltmann he escaped across the Alps. The group's smugglers were Spitaler and Nicolussi-Leck. Rudel had the contact address of his Bozen SS comrade Nicolussi-Leck in his trouser pocket.[115] For eight days, Rudel and his travelling companions were put up in Bozen by Nicolussi-Leck and fed by him.

> After a glorious train journey, in late afternoon we arrive in Bozen where we have another contact address to which Niermann is supposed to come, too. [...] Bauer and I stay in Bozen for a few days, high above the city. It's my first time here, and I'm drinking in my fill of this wonderful country. After the ordeals of the past few days, the peace and the care we're shown are touching and do an extraordinary amount of good. I spend a lot of time in the open, in the garden with a view of the Rosengarten range. In the meantime, the question is resolved as to whether we are to travel to Genoa or whether there is a chance of flying from Rome. And then the hour of farewell is struck, both from Bozen and, sadly, from Bauer, for he goes to Genoa, and I to Rome, where I am to travel by plane to South America.[116]

Rudel's family were somehow to join him. At the Brenner, they were entrusted to Nicolussi-Leck and the South Tyrolean escape assistant Spitaler. Spitaler knew the Brenner area very well and brought Rudel's wife and children safely to Bozen. 'We were helped in every imaginable way,' Colonel Rudel later wrote.[117] One of the best-known and most photographed pilots in Germany was also travelling on this underground line: Adolf Galland. His cigar, goatee, and cocker spaniel were his trademarks. In the Second World War, he soon became one of the best fighter pilots on the Western Front. In November 1942, he had been promoted to Major General and was thus, at the age of 30, the youngest general in the German Wehrmacht. In May 1945, Galland ended up in a British prisoner-of-war camp from which he was released in 1947. In 1948 he, too, moved to South America.[118]

But escape across the mountains did not always go so smoothly. In April 1947, Gerhard Bast, the former head of the Gestapo of Linz in Upper Austria, was murdered by a refugee smuggler at the Austrian–Italian border on the Brenner. The Americans were already looking for the SS-Sturmbannführer, and in 1946 they were hot on his trail, as a report by the military secret service proves. The SS-Sturmbannführer with a 'scar on the right side of his face', born in 1911 in the German linguistic enclave of Gottschee in present-day Slovenia, was suspected of hiding at the home of a farmer between Hörsching and Wels.[119] However, in the autumn of 1946 Bast escaped into the Pustertal in the South Tyrol, where he found work and lodging as a farm labourer. The Bast example is an excellent case study of how former SS members found shelter in the South Tyrol after 1945 and then set off for South America. His son Martin Pollack wrote of his escape:

> I assume that he went to the South Tyrol, because he imagined (prob-ably rightly) that he was relatively safe there and because it was, so to speak, on the way overseas to where he wanted to flee. [...] He also knew most of the areas very well from earlier tours, which must have given him an advantage. He probably knew lots of people as well, moun-tain comrades, Hüttenwirte, etc, who could help him. Ex-Nazis, too, of course. They were everywhere.[120]

Bast lived a very withdrawn life—he hardly went into the village, didn't go to the inn, and didn't talk about himself. He had presented himself as a German army private by the name of Franz Geyer, although the locals took him for an officer, not least because of 'his dashing atti-tude' and his general level of culture. He had duelling scars on his face, which marked him as a member of a student fraternity and as an aca-demic. But Bast didn't win the hospitality of the South Tyrolean farm-ers entirely for nothing. 'There must also have been payment to these farmers,' said Bast's son. After Bast's death, South Tyrolean informants close to the farming family offered his widow gold coins in the form of gold dollars. The farmers asked the widow if she wanted to buy her late husband's coins back as mementos. It seems that Bast must have paid the farmers a great deal of money.[121]

In March 1947, Bast left the Pustertal. Before he escaped to South America, he wanted to see his wife in Innsbruck one last time. It wasn't difficult to find a guard who would smuggle him over the border in return for payment. Bast hired twenty-five year-old Rudolf G., a labourer from Brennerbad, as his mountain guide. They had almost reached the Brenner Pass when G. suddenly drew a pistol and shot the former Gestapo leader from Linz.[122] Perhaps they had argued about the price of his services, perhaps the smuggler hoped for rich pickings, but at any rate he dragged the dead man to a nearby bunker and robbed him. But the pickings were slim: 3,000 lire, 20 Schillings, a watch, and a gold ring.[123] On the body in the bunker the carabinieri found an ethnic German ID, made out in the name of Franz Geyer, a worker from Krško, Gurkfeld in Slovenia. After only a few weeks, the smuggler was arrested and sentenced to twenty years' imprisonment.[124] In his memoirs, Bast's son describes a conversation with the murderer's brother:

> Back then, he said, there had been lots of people in the area, private soldiers and others, who wanted to get over the border, some to get in, the others to get out. His family had at the time been living above Brennerbad; there had often been ten or twelve people at their house sitting in the front room waiting to be guided, he said, and he did it, too, even though he was almost a child at the time.[125]

Smuggling was a necessary part of life in the Brenner region. Making a living was so difficult that even the children had to contribute to the family upkeep. A German soldier remembers:

> At the Griesbergerhof in the neighbouring village he was one of sixteen children [...] and was ten years old when the Brenner border was closed. It was barely fifty metres from his parents' house. There was no child benefit in those days. Small wonder: work in the fields by day, smuggling by night so that his mother could buy flour to bake bread. For the people of Griesberg the border was a blessing.[126]

5. South Tyrol, the Nazi Bolt-Hole

After 1945, the border region of South Tyrol played a major role as a Nazi bolt-hole. The route taken by the escapees to South America led first across the Brenner to Italy, then usually from the port of Genoa to Argentina. The escape routes were well known: in the case of Josef Schwammberger, the Commandant of Przemysl labour camp, the Federal Police Headquarters in Innsbruck revealed that the wanted man might have 'escaped like a large percentage of former SS men via Bozen and Genoa to South America (Argentina)'.[127] The Brenner line and, thus, the local and social conditions assumed a particular importance. Many SS members and war criminals found what was effectively an ideal situation in South Tyrol: the region was a kind of 'no man's land'—territorially and constitutionally. The border region was also inhabited by a majority German-speaking population whose legal status was to remain unclear for years to come. These favourable circumstances turned South Tyrol into 'Nazi Bolt-Hole Number One'. There is not a single comparable region in Europe. War criminals could often remain in hiding in South Tyrol for several years, procure the money to travel overseas, and acquire new identification papers.

Understanding the unique region of South Tyrol requires a closer look at the history of this border area. After the First World War, the majority German-speaking Southern Tyrol was broken off from the collapsed Austro-Hungarian monarchy and annexed by Italy in 1920. During Benito Mussolini's fascist era from 1922 onwards, the German-speaking population in South Tyrol was repeatedly exposed to discrimination and oppression. The use of the German language in schools and in public was partially forbidden, and German surnames were Italianized. High levels of Italian immigration began. The South Tyroleans had suffered a great reversal: until 1918 they had been part of the powerful and dominant German-speaking people in the Austro-Hungarian Monarchy, yet almost overnight they became a powerless minority in the Italian state. During the years of Italian fascism, many of them withdrew to a private, non-public 'homeland', where they hid themselves away.[128]

After Adolf Hitler assumed power in 1933, the hopes of many South Tyroleans turned to the idea of national liberation by Nazi Germany.[129] They supported National Socialism because it was German and rejected Mussolini's fascism because it was Italian. Claus Gatterer, a South Tyrolean journalist and author, summed up his compatriots' attitude when he wrote:

> Mussolini's Fascism was more human, more corrupt and, precisely in its human imponderables more easily predictable—but it spoke Italian; it was 'alien'. Nazism was probably more brutal, more inhuman—but it did speak German. For many people 'it belonged to us', it was 'ours' because it spoke our language.[130]

But from the outset Hitler made the South Tyrol question subordinate to the alliance he was seeking to forge with Italy. In 1939, Mussolini and Hitler agreed to remove the 'South Tyrol problem' from the world once and for all; the Axis alliance between the two dictators would no longer be burdened by it. The South Tyroleans had to take a vote, the so-called 'Option', to decide whether to keep their Italian citizenship and stay in the province of Bozen, or to assume German citizenship and emigrate to the German Reich. Staying would have involved complete Italianization. Great Britain watched these developments with great concern; Winston Churchill wrote on 27 July 1939 in the *Daily Mirror*:

> The more the agreement between the German and Italian Dictators about the future of the Tyrol becomes known, the more we realise how tense and grave is the state of Europe. It looks as if Herr Hitler has consented to the transfer of the entire German-speaking population of the Province of Bozen either to Greater Germany or elsewhere in Italy—in order that the homelands on which they have dwelt for a thousand years, the valleys and mountains of that beautiful upland, may be populated with Italians. That he should be willing to do this is a proof, which should be plain to the simplest mind, how seriously he regards the situation, and how determined he is to move forward upon the path of Continental domination. This was the price—the only price that would serve to bind Mussolini to his chariot wheels.

Some 85 per cent of those required to choose the 'Option' signed the orange form to assume German citizenship and the emigration to the 'Third Reich' it implied. In most cases, the decision was not a declaration of sympathy with National Socialism, but a rejection of the oppressive policy of Italian fascism. The position of those who opted to stay in Italy, known as *Dableiber*, or 'those who decided to stay', was also made more difficult by the fact that they saw themselves faced with an uncertain future because Mussolini refused to give them any guarantees that they would be allowed to remain in South Tyrol.[131] However, emigration was stalled by the war and finally came to a complete standstill in 1943. Still, some 75,000 of the 250,000 or so German and Ladino-speaking South Tyroleans actually emigrated.

The end of the war in 1945 did not mean a 'zero hour' for South Tyrol—many questions remained unresolved. First, South Tyrol's territorial future remained unclear; would it become Austrian, or remain a part of Italy? Second, the citizenship of the South Tyroleans was also murky. Those who opted for Germany, more than 80 per cent of the population, were at first seen as stateless ethnic Germans, a state of affairs that was later crucially significant for Nazi fugitives from all over Europe. The transition from the chaos of the end of the war to a certain degree of normality would take years. As early as December 1945, the Allies withdrew from the north Italian border provinces, including South Tyrol. This made South Tyrol one of the very few German-speaking areas formerly under Nazi rule that would no longer be under the direct control of a military government.

In the last weeks of the war, senior military officers and prominent Nazis also fled into the South Tyrolean mountains. In April 1945, their families came from bombed Obersalzberg bei Berchtesgaden to South Tyrol; included among them was Reich Leader Martin Bormann's family. They did not need to fear betrayal from the Germanophile population, which had been oppressed for years by fascist Italy.[132] The arrest of Heinrich Himmler's wife and daughter by US units in a mountain hut twenty kilometres outside Bozen in May 1945 was the result of Allied investigations.[133]

In April 1945, hundreds of 'collaborationist' Frenchmen with horses and carts, on foot, or in filthy luxury cars flooded the little town of Meran. It was a 'bleak procession of despair'.[134] They were coming from the German town of Sigmaringen, the last seat of the Vichy French 'government in exile'. In South Tyrol, they hoped for assistance in the forms of money, fake papers, cars, fuel, and safe hiding-places. Rumours about Hitler's alpine fortress in Tyrol had circulated during the final months of the war, but the impregnable alpine fortress existed only in Nazi propaganda and in the fears of Allied planning units. Apart from the French, senior collaborators from Hungary, Croatia, Slovakia, and Ukraine fled to the Alps. Some prominent collaborators hoped not for the alpine fortress, but for escape to nearby Switzerland. As well as some minor officials, they included France's most prominent collaborators: Prime Minister Pierre Laval, Propaganda Minister in the 'government delegation' in Sigmaringen Jean Luchaire, party heads Marcel Déat and Marcel Bucard, General André Besson-Rapp, Education Minister Abel Bonnard, Justice Minister Maurice Gabolde, and militia commander and Police Minister Joseph Darnand. The most prominent

Vichy Frenchmen in Italy were quickly tracked down and arrested by the Americans. But during the first days of May 1945 Prime Minister Laval was able to escape by plane from Bozen to Barcelona.[135]

The Reichsbank appointee and Aryanizer of Jewish property, Maximilian Bernhuber, also hid in South Tyrol, on a farm. Bernhuber was arrested by the carabinieri in Pustertal in August 1945. The Italians accused him of a series of crimes: the theft of important artworks from Italy and France, the confiscation of the gold reserve of the Italian state bank, the withdrawal of eighty million lire in gold to buy weapons for the army of the Repubblica di Salò, the extortion of twelve billion lire as costs for the occupation of Italy, the control of the production of lire in northern Italy and its surrender to the Wehrmacht leadership. The list could go on. Thus Bernhuber had every reason to get away from the Allies and the Italian authorities.[136] As early as the autumn of 1943, Bernhuber brought Italy's gold reserves to South Tyrol and stashed them in the old Franzensfeste fortress. US special units were considerably surprised when they entered the 'vault'.[137]

The fascist leader Mario Carità, feverishly sought by the Partisans, hid on the Seiser Alm near Bozen until the end of the war. His notorious police unit in Florence and Padua—generally known simply as 'Banda Carità'—fought against partisans and spied on resistance circles. Carità's troop also included some South Tyrolean SS members. At the end of the war, the booty-laden criminal finally found lodging with a South Tyrolean family and had to hand over part of his 'fortune' to local people-smugglers. When an attempt was made by US soldiers to arrest him in May 1945, a gunfight ensued in which Carità was killed.[138]

In May 1947, SS-Sturmbannführer Alois Schintlholzer was arrested in South Tyrol. An Innsbruck native and a well-known boxer, Schintlholzer had joined the Nazi party (NSDAP) as early as 1932 and soon belonged to the hard core of Nazis in Tyrol. Because of his brutality, he quickly advanced through the ranks of the SS. Schintlholzer led a murder squad in the 1938 November Pogrom in Innsbruck and was involved in various reprisals against partisans and civilians in Italy. In a retaliatory action by the Waffen-SS, the town of Caviola was burned down, and forty people were murdered.[139] But when the end of the Third Reich was in sight, Schintlholzer prepared for the post-war period. In January 1945, he asked his SS superiors for permission to move his children to South Tyrol. He himself went into hiding in Meran in April 1945. When US agents investigated him, he escaped just in time to a remote South Tyrol valley, where he was able to lie low for a while.[140] He was eventually arrested by American units and interned in the Rimini prisoner-of-war camp. Like many prisoners, he was able to escape from there in 1946, and he moved back to South Tyrol. The authorities in Austria knew where he was staying, but South Tyrol was in Italy, and the Austrian police and courts 'had' to throw up their hands:

> After further investigations in South Tyrol, in early October 1945 it was learned that Schintlholzer had not committed suicide. He is supposed initially to have been interned in a prisoner-of-war camp, and after his inexplicable recent release, to have worked as a physical education teacher somewhere in South Tyrol. Schintlholzer's children are supposed to be living in Obermais near Meran. Further data and positive details have been impossible to establish so far.[141]

On 28 May 1947, Schintlholzer was surprised by the carabinieri while asleep in the Hotel Sulden in Prad, not far from Meran, and placed under arrest again.[142] There was a loaded pistol under his pillow and a machine-gun leaning against his bedside table. But for the daredevil Schintlholzer, this arrest did not last long either. He escaped from Italian custody—and went to Germany. In 1957, Austrian authorities issued an arrest warrant against Schintlholzer for suspicion of the murders of engineer Richard Graubart and Dr Wilhelm Bauer in the course of the Innsbruck pogrom of 9/10 November 1938. In April 1961, he handed himself over to the court in Innsbruck and spent eleven months on remand. The accusations were finally dropped, and in March 1962 Schintlholzer was a free man again.[143] The Italian authorities had twice sentenced him in absentia to life imprisonment. At this time, Schintlholzer was living in Innsbruck—only a few kilometres away from the Italian border—where he died in old age.

Still another example of a fleeing German who made his way to South Tyrol was Erich Priebke; the former SS-Sturmbannführer who first went into hiding there. From 1943 he was an officer of the Gestapo in Rome, and in March 1944 he was one of those responsible for the shooting of 335 hostages in the Ardeatine Caves near Rome. So, like his closest colleague, Karl Hass, he had to hide in South Tyrol.

Erich Priebke was born in Berlin on 29 July 1913. At the age of four-
teen he had to start earning his own livelihood and began working in
the hotel trade. On the recommendation of an acquaintance, in 1936
he went to Berlin as an Italian interpreter for the Gestapo. He quickly
made a career for himself and became head of the 'Foreign Police'
office, which coordinated press work and contact with foreign countries. In 1938, Priebke married Alice Stöll from Berlin. He also attended
the SS-Führerschule, graduating very successfully as a 'Criminal
Commissar'.[144] In February 1941, he was sent to Rome where he met
police attaché Herbert Kappler and became his closest colleague. 'That
means', Priebke wrote in a memorandum written for his trial, 'at that
time I was Number Two.'[145] Priebke quickly worked his way up through
the SS, and in September 1943 he was finally promoted to Hauptsturmführer. In July 1943, the Allies landed in Sicily and marched slowly
northwards. The defeat of the Axis powers was looming on the horizon,
but Priebke and his family had already been living in Sterzing since
1943. Sixty years later, Priebke remembered the move to Sterzing in
South Tyrol:

> When the Duce was toppled on 25 July 1943, all the families of the peo-
> ple attached to the [German] embassy [in Rome] had to return to Ger-
> many. My wife drove to Berlin with the children first, but couldn't find
> anywhere to live in the half-ruined city, so she was granted permission
> to live in Sterzing, where friends of our already had an apartment
> ready. The wagon with our possessions was sent there.[146]

When the German front in northern Italy collapsed, Priebke made
his way to Bozen, where he waited for new marching orders. Through
Gestapo Command in Bozen, his superiors informed him about the
end of the war in Italy, which was the reason why they were issuing the
officers passes and fake papers. Now Priebke had a choice: he could
wait for the Americans to arrive in Bozen, or he could withdraw into
the mountains of South Tyrol.[147] First he managed to get to Sterzing
without any difficulty and spend the first days of May 1945 there with
his family. Finally, US troops arrested Priebke on 13 May 1945 in Bozen
along with the other German officers connected to Waffen-SS General
Karl Wolff. From there his journey took him to the large prisoner-of-
war camp in Afragola near Naples and, finally, to the one in Rimini. In
July 1947, the British handed Priebke's former boss Herbert Kappler

over to Italian authorities. Kappler was found guilty of the hostage shootings in Rome and sentenced to life imprisonment. But Priebke was determined to avoid the kind of trial which Kappler had endured.

In December 1946, Priebke escaped from the Rimini camp. By this point, the Italian military prosecutor was already looking for him because of his involvement in the massacre at the Ardeatine Caves.[148] Priebke described his escape from Rimini: 'On 31 December 1946 we took advantage of the New Year celebrations. The English drank and partied, and the Poles were drunk. Five of us were able to get away: three NCOs, an officer and me. We hid in the bishop's seat, and that was where our actual flight began.'[149] According to Priebke, he and his fellow escapees received help for their onward journey from churchmen in Rome.[150] They travelled by train to Bologna, where the group separated. Priebke took a direct train to Sterzing and again went into hiding with his family in Bahnhofstrasse where his wife Alice and their two sons had been living since 1943. At first, he still lived in fear of prosecution, 'but no one looked for me there', Priebke recalled during his trial fifty years later.[151] The Priebkes' apartment in Sterzing may well have been found for them by Rudolf Stötter. The SS-Oberscharführer in Sterzing, who from 1943 was a member of the Gestapo Command in Bozen, owned a hotel in Bahnhofstrasse.[152] He was interrogated by the Allies several times about Priebke and other SS members for good reason: he did actually hide SS comrades from Bozen Gestapo Headquarters in his hotel and pointed them towards escape routes and bolt-holes in the mountains.[153] The Americans saw Stötter, probably rightly, as an important escape assistant to senior SS men in Italy, including Rudolf Thyrolf, the head of the Gestapo and Sicherheitsdienst (SD) in Bozen.[154]

Under the conditions existing in South Tyrol, it was really not difficult for many high-ranking SS members to disappear into the mountains and lie low for years. Some Nazi perpetrators and Party members did not escape to South America, but remained in South Tyrol. One example is Dr Waldemar Epp, born in Danzig in 1912. He devoted himself to the Nazi movement early on and joined the NSDAP in May 1936, at which time he was a Jungbannführer in the Hitler Youth.[155] After the annexation of Danzig to the German Reich in November 1939, he moved to Berlin, where he worked in the Foreign Office. In July 1941 he was assigned to the Press and Propaganda Office of the

Foreign Office.[156] Several official trips through occupied Europe—but also to Switzerland—followed. The diplomat then repeatedly worked from October 1944 until April 1945 in the German consulate in Milan before joining Rudolf Rahn, the German Ambassador to Italy, at headquarters on Lake Garda and later in Meran. Finally, on the day of the German surrender in Italy, 2 May 1945, Epp tried to leave South Tyrol for Switzerland, but the Swiss border guards turned him back. On 10 May 1945, Epp returned to Meran, where he left his wife and child with a South Tyrolean host family. In Meran he asked the German Evangelical pastor Julius Giese for support and a safe hiding place. In the end, on 15 May 1945, Epp was arrested by American officers along with the German embassy staff connected to the Reich Plenipotentiary in Italy, Rudolf Rahn, and the former Foreign Office head of personnel, Hans Schröder. Still, for Nazi diplomats, Meran represented a safe last refuge.[157]

Also fleeing to Meran was Dietrich von Jagow, the former German ambassador in Hungary. Jagow had been a Nazi since the early days, as his relatively low Party number, 110,538, demonstrates.[158] He ended up in northern Italy in April 1945 along with a group of German diplomats from Hungary. They had fled to South Tyrol in the wake of the Hungarian Foreign Minister in the fascist Szálasi Cabinet, Gábor Baron von Kemény.[159] Towards the end of the war, von Jagow committed suicide in a Meran hotel room.[160]

His fellow diplomat, Epp, on the other hand, was arrested as a prisoner of war and interrogated several times. After the intervention of the President of the International Committee of the Red Cross, Carl Jacob Burckhardt, Epp was transferred along with other South Tyroleans to the Bozen refugee camp, from which they were released in the autumn. Epp had cleverly presented himself as a South Tyrolean so that he could return to his wife and children. In this he succeeded. His boss, Schröder, on the other hand, had to stay interned in Terni as a Reich German Nazi diplomat. According to eye-witness reports, Hans Schröder's family was put up in the South Tyrolean village of Taufers, not far from the Swiss border.[161] The former diplomat Epp was arrested again by the carabinieri on 25 April 1946 in Toblach and sent to the camp for foreign refugees in Fossoli di Carpi near Modena, 'to await the decision of the allied commission concerning his remigration', as a memo from the camp's directors to Bozen police headquarters puts it.[162] In December

1946, Epp asked the Fossoli camp administration for a brief Christmas leave. He planned to spend the Christmas holidays with his fiancée in Toblach. He also reported on the bad state of his teeth, which he wanted to have treated by a South Tyrolean dentist.[163] That was, perhaps, how Epp finally managed to get away.[164]

Epp's attempt to escape to Switzerland and his stubborn attempts to stay in South Tyrol may also have had something to do with money. Most fugitive Holocaust perpetrators came from modest backgrounds and had hardly any funds to escape. They were dependent on the help of acquaintances, relatives, and religious charities. Only a few high-ranking Nazi bosses had stashed money abroad for their escape. A few war criminals and Holocaust perpetrators used neutral states—principally Switzerland—as safe havens for their finances. Their trust in Switzerland was not unfounded, for Switzerland was reluctant to cooperate with the Allies where the issue of 'German assets' in the country was concerned. After a brief phase of being frozen, after 1950 the Swiss bank accounts of perpetrators were mostly freed again. When the Cold War began, no one was interested in the complex process of examining assets in Swiss bank accounts. Thus after 1950 prominent perpetrators were able to access their Swiss accounts again, much to the benefit of Meran, which is not far from the Swiss border.[165]

German war criminals large and small sought refuge in Meran. Anton Malloth, a former SS man and warden in the 'Little Fortress of Theresienstadt', had also been living undisturbed in Meran for decades. 'Handsome Toni' was seen as one of the cruellest wardens in the Gestapo prison.[166] Josef Mengele's wife and son also settled in Meran in 1962. Mengele entrusted his family to former South Tyrolean people-smugglers.

After the arrest of Adolf Eichmann by the Israeli secret service in 1960, Mengele was in constant flight. His second wife, Martha Mengele, did not want to live a life underground and opted for separation.[167] In 1962 Martha Mengele moved to Parkstrasse in Meran and did not leave for Munich until 1986. The municipal registry of Meran reads: 'Housewife, married, to Josef Mengele in Uruguay in 1958.'[168] Their son Karl Heinz also lived for a time as a businessman in Meran. In 1969, Josef's brother Alois Mengele founded a branch of the Günzburg family farm machinery company and drove in person to South Tyrol for that purpose. The notary Giovanni Nicolodi in Meran noted on 30 April 1969:

'There was a visit from Herr Alois Mengele, born on 30.1.1914 in Günzburg and resident there, industrial businessman, representative of the company Karl Mengele and Sons engineering works and foundry in Günzburg.'[169]

Mengele's business partner, Franz Steiner, born 11 July 1920 in Gratsch bei Meran, worked as a businessman. Before the war, Steiner worked as a farmer in Marling bei Meran. In 1939 he opted for German citizenship and emigrated to Innsbruck in 1940, working in the tax office there.[170] His younger brother, Adolf Steiner, was born in Gratsch in 1921 and worked as a carpenter in Marling bei Meran. In the summer of 1939, he emigrated to Wörgl in Austria and appears to have stayed there until the end of the war.[171] After the war, the Steiner brothers returned to Meran and founded the South Tyrolean branch of the Mengele Company with the help of Mengele headquarters in Günzburg. Adolf Steiner had known Josef Mengele since his escape through South Tyrol in 1949. At the time, Mengele had been able to count on the Steiners' people-smuggling activities and on their comrades in South Tyrol. Now the South Tyrolean businessmen had the chance to work with the successful firm in Günzburg.[172] The foundation of the Italian firm 'Mengele & Steiner Ltd.' in Meran probably served to provide financial security for Martha Mengele and her son Karl Heinz from her first marriage.[173] But the 'Mengele & Steiner Ltd.' companies were not only concentrated in South Tyrol. 'Another activity of the company' is given as 'Collegio Germanico Ungarico—S. Maria di Galeria in Rome'. This would lead one to suspect that Mengele wanted to return the favour to friends and people-smugglers in Rome, as well. For centuries, the Collegio has been a home for German-speaking pilgrims to Rome.[174]

Even before 1945, Meran was a popular hideaway for prominent Nazis, and it became a final refuge by the end of the war. The special role played by the Italian border town of Meran after 1945 as an 'Eldorado of collaborators' was an open secret in the post-war years.[175] The newspapers at the time wrote: 'Meran is well-known as a kind of Eldorado to fish large and small.'[176]

Our newspaper has written ad nauseam about how in the post-war era South Tyrol has become the Eldorado of the Nazi fascists, who have always found generous and cordial hospitality and welcome here. Now the situation has calmed down a little, but the number of war criminals and collaborators with the fascists and Germans who have made themselves very comfortable in Bozen is still very high,

wrote the *Alto Adige* daily newspaper in May 1947.[177] However, the nationalist journal forgot to mention that the province of Bozen did not offer a refuge only to inculpated Germans, but also to numerous Italian ex-fascists, many of whom worked on the paper's staff.

6. Fake Papers

Getting hold of fake IDs was not a problem in Italy after the war. Many rings of forgers offered their services in return for good money. In addition, large numbers of real and fake delegates of international organizations and states also existed. Hundreds of fleeing SS members and Wehrmacht soldiers made use of this possibility of posing as aid and relief organization staff. For example, in his report, US investigator Vincent La Vista gives a detailed description of the activities of Dr Willi Nix in Rome. In 1944, Nix and other German exiles had set up the Central Office for Germans in Italy (ZDI), a pseudo-consulate for Germans living in Rome. At first, the Americans let this office continue working undisturbed. They even tolerated its self-designed 'Italien-Ausweis' as an identification card, precisely on the basis of the fact that the office had emerged from the German Anti-Nazi Association (Deutsche Antinazistische Vereinigung, DAV). The Office of Strategic Services (OSS) supported the German committee run by Nix, 'who might talk a lot and promises, but has very little concrete to offer', as a report of July 1944 records. Nonetheless, the Office of Strategic Services (OSS) authorized a generous finance package for the German committee.[178] Nix was not only working for the Americans; churchmen in Rome also considered him to be an important partner where aid was concerned.

Karl Heinemann, Bishop Hudal's deputy at the College of Santa Maria dell-Anima, the German Church in Rome, worked closely with Nix. Heinemann was able to turn to Nix and his committee when it came to the legalization of refugees. In a seven-line letter, stamped 'Catholic Pastoral Care for Foreigners, Rome', Heinemann recommended as an example to the head of the ZDI a Fräulein Schulze and her mother, 'in the expectation that you will be able to resolve their affair, as they deserve all manner of help'.[179] No explanation is given. The complete name of the woman in question can be found in the telephone book of Himmler's Sicherheitsdienst. The man to whom the letter was sent, Dr Nix, was a man with a fascinating past. By his own account, he had been a concentration camp inmate in Sachsenhausen and was stripped of his citizenship; in 1938 he had come via Austria to Italy—and now signed his letters to Hudal with the resounding name 'Dr Willi Nix von Lilien-Waldau'. In the years after the war, the DAV acted, according to Nix, as a shelter for 'refugees of every race and religion' in Rome who needed new ID cards. Even the Allies brought truckloads of refugees to the DAV. After the publication of the La Vista report in 1984, Dr Nix, now retired in Rome, was confronted with the past. The doctor disputed all the accusations, saying that he and his resistance committee would never have helped a single Nazi refugee.[180] As well as La Vista, US special agent Leo J. Pagmotta accused Nix of helping SS escapees from Rimini by providing them with passports so that they could continue on their journey.[181] After the discovery of Nix's activities, the Italian authorities ordered his arrest. But only minutes before the police arrived, Nix fled to the Vatican, where he found a safe refuge.[182] La Vista already suspected that Nix would act under the protection of the Vatican. Nix's flight, and the fact that he stayed in the papal state for months, were La Vista's factual confirmation of this.

While Reich Germans turned to Dr Nix for the preparation of ID cards, the 'Austrian offices' were responsible for the Austrians. The committee in Rome was founded after the retreat of the Wehrmacht in the summer of 1944. It was then run by the Austrian bishop Alois Hudal and the former Austrian ambassador to the Holy See and former Justice Minister Egon Berger-Waldenegg.[183] Issuing Austrian ID papers was soon the committee's main task. Hudal wrote about it in his memoirs: 'I signed off a thousand, but generously include a number of Reich Germans, to protect them from concentration camps and prison during those difficult months.'[184] According to their director, these offices were 'absolutely not political in character' and, as temporary Austrian consulates, were supposed to issue passports and protect Austrian interests in Italy.[185]

The Meran office saw itself as a branch of the Austrian office in Rome, and, as in Rome, issued countless passports. Austrians Fritz Rienzner and Louis Barcata, who presented themselves as 'consuls of Austria', ran the office. Before the end of the war, Rienzner had worked at the military hospital in Meran.[186] Until 1944, Barcata was an Italian correspondent for the Nazi newspaper *Das Reich* in Rome. Reich German and other refugees were generously 'included in the help of the Austrian committee'. It was of almost no importance whether a person could confirm his or her identity or not. Rienzner's identity cards had a very official-looking layout. On the first page of the passport were the words 'Republic of Austria. Austrian Office Meran'. Many of the IDs were already stamped and signed by Rienzner though they were blank! Anyone at all could enter names and personal data as he or she wished; as a result, it can hardly come as a surprise that abuse was routine. Rienzner tried to establish himself as a delegate of the Red Cross in Meran and managed to do so for a while. The Meran office thus became the first stopping point for anyone who needed fake papers—particularly those who could demonstrate Austrian origins. In April 1946, Rienzner was driven into a corner when the Italian authorities demanded that he leave the country once and for all and close this office.[187]

As a result of their investigation of Rienzner, the Italian authorities also investigated Barcata, who had worked with him in Meran, and whose past in the service of Goebbels' propaganda department was well known. Following the example of Dr Nix in Rome, he tried to reach an agreement with the American occupying powers in Italy. Barcata worked several times as an agent of the American Counter-Intelligence Corps, which gave him adequate protection for his 'escape aid' operations until 1946.

Agent Barcata later set up a propaganda newspaper in Meran and had close contacts with Argentina. With his journalist friend Rudolf Kircher, he soon found other sources of money that promised more continuity. In Meran, they founded the weekly newspaper *Der Standpunkt*, for which right-wing journalists such as Franz Hieronymus Riedl, Erich Kernmayer, Gunther Langes, and Karl Springenschmied were soon writing, generally pseudonymously. At the same time, the fees paid by *Der Standpunkt* also attracted academics formerly deployed by the SS. Prominent among them was Fritz Valjavec. Since his university days, Valjavec had been *völkisch* and nationalist by orientation, and he joined the NSDAP in 1933. He was one of the leading researchers at the Südost-Institut in Munich which was concerned with the search for 'German blood', approving the murder of others as a means of 'Germanization'. The professor established himself not only as a political adviser to senior SS men in questions relating to south-eastern Europe, but also took part after the summer of 1941 in the deployment of special command units, in the course of which hundreds of Jews and 'Communist functionaries' were murdered. After 1945, Valjavec was able to continue his scientific activity without interruption.[188] Valjavec confirmed to *Der Standpunkt*: 'Most articles are excellent and show a very high level of insight; the loss of such high-quality articles here in the rest of Germany has been painful for us to bear.'[189] The Nazi-oriented Bishop Hudal also repeatedly offered to write an article for *Der Standpunkt* in Meran, 'a newspaper that operates on a very high intellectual level'.[190]

In 1947, former Goebbels' journalists and local newspapermen in Buenos Aires set up the monthly magazine *Der Weg*, which soon became the Nazi mouthpiece in Argentina. Still an edifying journal for Argentine Germans when it was founded in 1947, over the years that followed *Der Weg* developed into a journal—and according to Holger Meding this is unparalleled in the period after the Second World War—that often represented divergent far-right and conservative ideas and subjects. Over the course of only a few years, it turned into a 'radical philosophical instruction sheet'.[191] Soon there was close collaboration between the right-wing rag *Der Standpunkt* in Meran and *Der Weg* in Buenos Aires. Some inculpated Nazi journalists wrote for both newspapers, for their philosophy and background were similar. Thus there were many personal connections between the staffs of the two papers. *Der Weg* and Dürer Verlag, its sister publishing company, finally undertook the distribution of *Der Standpunkt* in South America, while in Meran the Europavertrieb distribution company took over *Der Weg*.[192] In every respect, Meran was the perfect place for washed-up Nazis, human traffickers, and forgers: the town, not far from the Swiss border, had not been bombed; it was handily on the escape route to Genoa, and foreigners did not stand out in the town, notable for its military hospitals. Moreover, from 1946 onwards Allied controls went into abeyance.

The criminal activity in South Tyrol was diverse. Italian local administrative offices—particularly in the South Tyrol—issued SS members identity cards with false names. Numerous forgery rings produced Italian lire and a great variety of fake documents and papers of many different kinds.[193] They printed foreign currencies as well. In 1947, the authorities in Italy confiscated thousands of forged British pound notes.[194] The forged diaries of Hitler's lover Eva Braun were also fabricated in the South Tyrol at this time, and film-maker Luis Trenker acted as salesman of this 'world sensation'. The forgery was soon exposed, but Trenker emerged from the subsequent scandal almost unscathed.[195] People were not choosy about the source of their money. Some undocumented people drew ever closer to criminal groups as they earned their livelihood through prostitution,[196] drug-dealing, and currency- and people-smuggling, as well as the production of forged money: 'Many of these people have little to lose and care little for themselves and their reputation,' the newspapers reported at the time.[197]

In the South Tyrol, forgers who were not connected with the printing of counterfeit money were often discovered. Raiding police regularly found 'administrative stamps and blank forms for identity cards'.[198] It was particularly easy to get hold of new papers, including new identities, in South Tyrol. The region was, in any case, the first stopping point in Italy for refugees and former German soldiers, among others. In addition to the forgers, large numbers of aid organizations dealt with escaped prisoners of war, finding them safe lodgings and fake papers. That was something else that the local press didn't miss:

> For these people the acquisition of documents is not usually a problem, because at the end of the war these identity cards were cheerfully issued in large numbers by the Nazi mayors. These Nazi-era mayors stayed in their jobs for several months after the end of the war. Among the communities that were particularly generous in the issuing of documents we might mention Vahrn, Brixen, Algund, and Graun, but these identity cards with their declaration of 'Italian citizenship' were issued more or less in all communities.[199]

Numerous examples illustrate how forged or otherwise falsified documents obtained in the South Tyrol aided those escaping justice at the war's end. In May 1947, the South Tyrolean George Bertagnolli from Meran was arrested on suspicion of war crimes in Belluno. After the war, he went into hiding in South Tyrol with a faked South Tyrolean identity card, issued in the name Georg Greitemberg, and he found work as a driver with a Meran company. Between 1942 and 1945, Bertagnolli had helped in the forced recruitment of Italian labourers and is supposed to have commanded SS units in their combat against partisans. The press, too, asked itself the question of 'how he might have got hold of his residence permit, his position with Cadsky, the clearance certificate from the mayor and other fake documents'.[200]

Similarly, concentration camp commandant Josef Schwammberger's South Tyrolean origins facilitated his flight from justice after his year of service in the Reich. Schwammberger was born in Brixen on 14 February 1912. A short time later, he moved to Innsbruck with his parents and four siblings. In 1933 he went to Germany and worked his way up through the SS. After the Anschluss of Austria in March 1938, he joined up with the Waffen-SS in Krakow. Being 'unfit for combat' because of a stomach and intestinal complaint, he worked under the Commander of the Security Police in Krakow. Here he is supposed to have shot a 'fleeing' Jewish prisoner, his first murder. On 1 September 1942, he was made commandant of the Rozwadow forced labour camp in occupied Poland. It was now that his career as a career murderer within the SS apparatus began. He began killing 'out of a lust for murder', or else gave orders to others to do so: Ukrainian concentration camp guards killed 200 sick Jews on his orders when the Rozwadow camp was cleared in December 1942. But Schwammberger's career as a camp director continued. From February 1943 until February 1944, he was made commandant of Ghetto A in Przemysl. Unlike in Ghetto B, in Ghetto A Jews who were capable of work were better fed, since they had the task of repairing Wehrmacht equipment. This was a part of the ghetto that had been separated from the rest with barbed wire and declared to be a labour camp. By 1944 Schwammberger was supposed to have killed 250 people there with his own hands and to have ordered the murder of 700 more. Several thousand people were finally transported to the extermination camps on his orders.

Schwammberger went into hiding in Tyrol in April 1945 with false papers identifying him as 'Josef Hackel'. In the summer of that year, he was arrested in his Innsbruck bolt-hole. While he was awaiting trial, he and two other prisoners managed to escape. Their flight from an Austrian POW camp on the night of 2 January 1948 was clearly well planned. The head of the Federal Police in Innsbruck and the allied authorities immediately informed all border crossings and made it clear 'that all three are to be pursued as notorious war criminals'.[201] The authorities assumed that Schwammberger would escape to Innsbruck, where his sister lived, or to South Tyrol. Thus the border control at Brenner was on special alert with an 'express request'. After his escape, Schwammberger travelled to Matrei am Brenner and from there crossed the green border to Italy. He probably used the tried-and-tested routes for his escape. Schwammberger's first destination was Brixen, his birthplace. He met up with his wife and stayed in hiding for several weeks before continuing on his journey.[202] While in South Tyrol, he received an identity card from his hometown of Brixen, identifying him as a South Tyrol optee and, thus, 'stateless'. This ID served as a basis for his Argentinian immigration papers and for the authorities in Buenos Aires. He told the Argentinian authorities in Genoa that he was born in Bozen and spoke only Italian. He gave his profession as 'mechanic'. As a stateless South Tyrolean, Schwammberger had a right to a Red Cross passport which would facilitate his escape to South America. Having been born in South Tyrol, Schwammberger had no need to invent a South Tyrolean identity.[203] Germans and Austrians often used this opportunity to acquire a new identity—including very well-known and prominent Nazi war criminals.

On his escape through South Tyrol, Adolf Eichmann also used false papers; thus the bureaucrat par excellence of mass murder became a South Tyrolean. Eichmann received an ID issued on 2 June 1948 by the municipality of Tramin near Bozen. Thus he became Richard (Riccardo) Klement, born in 1913 in Bozen, son of one Anna Klement.[204] Eichmann's new identity was invented at random, but was extremely cleverly chosen; selecting Bozen as a birthplace was smart because Eichmann knew the South Tyrol well from the time when he had dealt with matters involving ethnic Germans. His dialect was definitely not from South Tyrol, but people didn't care. The locals obviously didn't ask him unpleasant questions about his real background or have him investigated.[205]

Auschwitz doctor Josef Mengele also became, with the help of South Tyrolean people-smugglers, a South Tyrolean: Helmut Gregor. According to his papers, Gregor was born on 6 August 1911 in Tramin and worked as a mechanic.[206] 'Salvation came from Tramin—Josef Mengele escaped thanks to an Italian ID card—he escaped with the false name Gregor from the South Tyrol'[207] as Italian newspapers put it in the summer of 2003. The personification of medical mass murder assumed an Italian identity for his new life.[208] For Mengele, his South Tyrolean people-smugglers got hold of a regular ID from a South Tyrolean municipality, like the ones issued during the German occupation between 1943 and the end of the war. Thus Mengele, too, acquired a new identity. The concentration camp doctor even submitted a residence permit from the municipality of Tramin which stated that he had been a resident in Italy since 1944. Mengele gave his address as 'Tramin, via Montello 22'. His ultimate destination, of course, was Argentina.[209] Mengele seems not to have assumed the identity of another person, such as a fallen soldier, but invented the name at random: in the register of baptisms of the parish of Tramin, no birth of any 'Helmut Gregor' is recorded for August 1911.[210]

In May 1948, Goebbels' aide Erich Müller also received an identity card issued by the municipality of Tramin, his with the name of Francesco Noelke, born on 7 December 1906 in Bozen. With this ID, he was able to apply for a Red Cross travel document. His original citizenship in the application is given as Sud-Tirolo, his current citizenship 'German because of the Option'. So Müller was presenting himself as a South Tyrolean with unresolved nationality.[211] There was never, of course, any Franz (Francesco) Nölke from Bozen. Again, the South Tyrolean people-smugglers—as in the case of Mengele, Eichmann, and many others—simply invented an identity. In February 1952, Müller applied for his name to be corrected. With the evidence of several witnesses, an Argentinian court ruled that Erich Friedrich Otto Karl Müller, born on 30 August 1902 in Münster, Westphalia, and Francesco Noelke, born on 7 December 1906 in Bozen, were one and the same person.[212]

Another refugee with invented South Tyrolean personal details is a certain 'Theodor Kremhart', who applied for a Red Cross passport in Genoa on 31 October 1949. Kremhart claimed to have been born in Tramin in South Tyrol on 2 May 1906. On 30 November 1946, a Frau Lona Kremhart wrote from Lübeck to police headquarters in Bozen inquiring into the whereabouts of her husband. According to this woman, her husband Theodor Kremhart, born on 18 September 1905 in Posen (Poznan), was a soldier in Italy. According to information from police stations in Innsbruck, Kremhart had gone to Bozen in 1946 'to fetch his belongings'. But he never came back—and remained missing. Research by the Red Cross and the Allied authorities had proved, according to Frau Kremhart, fruitless. Now the desperate woman, herself a refugee with three children, turned to the Italian authorities for support. After brief inquiries, the police in Bozen located him: Theo Kremhart had been living in Italy for a year and had an Italian identity card. Since 1946, Kremhart had actually been staying at the Gasthaus Zwölfmalgreien in Bozen.[213] Was 'Lona Kremhart' the wife of a war criminal? Had her husband told her about his new identity and his preparations to escape to South Tyrol? Would new documents, a passport and visa for Argentina, have to be organized? But as there had probably been no word from the fleeing 'Kremhart' for a long time, his wife feared the worst: something must have happened to her husband, or else he had escaped to South America without her and their three children. Perhaps his wife had only been superficially informed about her husband's new name. A sentence from the woman's letter to the police suggests as much: 'It could be that my husband's name has been changed by being written down incorrectly, for example from Kremhart to Kreinhart.'[214] Many clues suggest that a Nazi perpetrator abused the name of the man from Posen to make his escape—doing so was a fairly common practice.

Tantalizing facts hint at 'Kremhart's' identity. 'Kremhart' told the Red Cross his original citizenship was 'Italian', his current nationality 'German because of the Option'. He gave his profession as an 'expert in farm products'. Although supposedly from the South Tyrol, he gave his religious affinity as 'Protestant' which, for one originating from the small municipality of Tramin south of Bozen, was highly unusual, for very few Protestants lived in the region. As evidence of his details, he submitted an ID card issued by the municipality of Tramin in May 1948. This detail is striking and, possibly, incriminating because it suggests this man perhaps fled with Mengele and Eichmann. In April 1948 Mengele received an identity card from Tramin, as did Eichmann in June 1948 and 'Kremhart' in May 1948. One thing is clear at any rate: Theodor Kremhart, born in Tramin in 1906, never existed. The baptismal documents for those years record no one of that name.[215] But the mystery doesn't end there. According to the German Missing Peoples' Bureau in Berlin, one Theodor Kremhart, born 18 September 1905 in Poznan, really did exist. Kremhart survived the war as a soldier in a parachute unit and died in Germany in 1996.[216] But the true identity of the fleeing 'Kremhart' (supposedly born in Tramin in 1906) must (as in so many cases) remain an open question.

At any rate, Eichmann, Mengele, and Müller received ID cards from local Tramin administration offices, thus becoming citizens of South Tyrol. Why Tramin? From 1933 that municipality south of Bozen was well known as a stronghold of the *Völkische Kampfring Südtirol*, a Nazi-oriented group. The provisional mayor of the town had easily managed to set aside blank forms for identity cards during Nazi rule in South Tyrol between 1943 and 1945. The South Tyrol mayors installed by the Nazi regime remained in office until the summer of 1945 and had plenty of time to make arrangements. Additionally, in South Tyrol large numbers of forgery rings produced fake documents and currency. Blank forms were stolen and stamps copied.[217] The South Tyrolean historian Christoph von Hartungen assumes that a Nazi-inclined official at the Tramin register office issued and signed the identity cards for Mengele and friends.[218] Furthermore, no thorough denazification or defascistization of South Tyrolean municipal offices after 1945 occurred. Among the Italians, partisans of Mussolini remained in office just as much as did partisans of Hitler amongst German-speakers.

Further information about the particular role played by Tramin might have been provided by the applications made for ID cards there. According to the municipality, the archive preserves all the completed application forms for identity cards from 1927 onwards, but there are gaps. The year 1948 is missing completely:

> I can inform you that over the past 20 years I have been asked repeatedly whether an identity card was issued to the individuals you are seeking by the municipality of Tramin in the year 1948. Throughout this time the officials in the register office there have repeatedly examined the records of the issued ID cards stored in the municipal archive, but on every occasion, including yours, have had to establish that the records for 1948 are incomplete or impossible to find.[219]

During Eichmann's trial in Jerusalem in 1961, some hints of Eichmann's escape and his fake South Tyrolean identity were revealed, not least by the journalist and philosopher Hannah Arendt.[220] In his memoirs, Eichmann himself gives an account of his new identity and describes meeting his contacts in Meran:

> From there we travelled to Meran. This was—according to my new c.v.—my birthplace, and it was here that I received my *'libro desembargo'*, the landing permit for Argentina. I was given it from someone who to

my great surprise didn't want a single lira. Until then I had had to pay dearly for the services of the 'U-Boot agents'. With my entry permit in my pocket, made out in the name of Riccardo Klement, I reached Genoa.[221]

So Eichmann probably received his new ID papers for nothing, on the spot!

In Meran, Hitler's fleeing troops repeatedly received fake papers. For example, in South Tyrol, SS Standartenführer Eugen Dollmann, Hitler's intermediary and interpreter with Mussolini, received his new identity. With South Tyrolean papers Dollmann became Eugen Amonn, born in Bozen, South Tyrol. Dollmann, originally from Regensburg, had joined the NSDAP in 1934, and from 1935 ran the press department of the Party's office in Rome, where he also worked as a translator. In 1937 he joined the SS, was promoted to SS-Obersturmführer, and went on working closely with SS General Karl Wolff on Himmler's staff. As an intermediary officer with Mussolini's government and the Vatican, Dollmann became an important bearer of secret information.[222] Similarly, the case of attack pilot Hans-Ulrich Rudel can also be taken as a prime example of switched identities. South Tyrolean smugglers supplied Rudel with new ID papers and took great care of the prominent flyer.[223] Rudel was even able to choose his new name:

> I shyly ask whether I can go on using my real name. No, of course I can't. Half joking, I suggest calling myself something like Hans Meier or Paul or Saul. I couldn't care less; the main thing is that they assemble some papers so that I can get to South America. [...] The very next morning they bring me a piece of paper with the resounding name Emilio Meier! Yes, I'd have said I didn't care; they could happily call me Meier or anything they wanted. Now my name is Emil Meier, and I travel on with that name to Argentina.[224]

While Rudel fled to South America with his new identity, 'Herr Meier',[225] Rudolf Hermann, born in Plauen in 1907, also used documents from South Tyrol to travel abroad. Since September 1946, Hermann had been interned in the POW camp in Fossoli di Carpi and wanted to emigrate to South America. As evidence of his identity, Hermann submitted a British discharge paper from the Kings Own Royal Regiment Bolzano (Bozen) and a confirmation from a South Tyrolean municipality issued in December 1945.[226] He was travelling with his

Viennese comrade Hermann Hufnagl who had, as a foreign refugee, been interned along with Hermann in the Fossoli di Carpi camp near Modena. Hufnagl presented himself as a construction engineer and wanted to emigrate to Paraguay. During his journey to Italy across the Tyrolean mountains, he had acquired an ID card from the municipality of Mayrhofen in the Zillertal.[227]

In 1945, Bozen carabinieri officer Renato Galgano was able to report a rare success to his superiors: while searching a house in Bozen, he and his men had been able to arrest Josef Didinger, a former officer of the Gestapo (Geheime Staatspolizei) in Verona. Didinger, from Koblenz, clearly felt safe: he was 'equipped with false identification cards from the municipality of Mühlbach in the South Tyrol, dated 2 June 1944'. The ID was made out in the false name 'Josef Erich Müller', born in Verona, resident in Mühlbach. His South Tyrolean lover was also arrested.[228] At the same time, SS member Herbert Beuer was arrested in Meran.

Beuer had run a division of the Security Service in Milan under Walter Rauff. His chief task was the supervision of the war production and factory workers. At the end of the war on 1 May 1945, he was arrested by the Americans and interned in the Rimini POW camp. In September 1945, he was able to get out from there, probably to keep his SS past from being discovered. Then, like hundreds of other escapees from Rimini, he went into hiding in South Tyrol. First, Beuer lived with 'acquaintances in Meran'. Comrades in Meran and helpful groups found fake ID documents and a job for him. Before he could continue his journey, however, Beuer was arrested by the carabinieri.[229] 'Kremhart' from 'Tramin', on the other hand, probably managed to escape overseas from his Nazi bolt-hole. His true identity remains a mystery to this day.

2

The Co-Responsibility of the International Red Cross

In January 1947 the American delegation in Vienna passed a 'summary of information' to the Secretary of State in Washington. This referred explicitly to the flight of 'wanted war criminals' using International Red Cross travel papers:

> It is possible for any person desiring an identity document to secure an International Red Cross Identity Document through the assistance of persons operating under the protection of the Vatican. These documents can be secured without any identification on part of the securer or any investigation on part of International Red Cross. These documents may be obtained under an alias or with false nationality. Information stated in effect that reports had been received where known or wanted war criminals had reached Italy illegally and applied and received these documents under assumed names and have to date successfully evaded apprehension.[1]

For wanted SS members and collaborators, the International Committee of the Red Cross (ICRC) became a major source for the travel documents required for overseas travel. The issuing of travel papers was not traditionally one of the tasks and responsibilities of the ICRC. It was only the emergency situation of the war years and the years thereafter that forced it to take on this new task. The International Refugee Organization, by declaring that it was not responsible for the millions of 'ethnic German' refugees and anti-communists, consigned those refugees to their fate of scraping out a living in camps along with many political refugees from Eastern Europe. The majority of refugees were de facto stateless and had no valid papers. Some displaced people were integrated into German society; others emigrated. For emigration, they needed the valid travel documents that the International Red Cross issued from 1944/5. The Red Cross travel documents originally served as 'one-time travel papers' because the ICRC was and remains unable to issue passports in the narrower legal sense, since it is not a government agency.[2] But these travel papers were soon recognized by many states as substitute 'passports'. Destination countries were also supposed to check the identities of holders of these travel permits, but did not do so. Former SS members mixed among the refugees and usually presented themselves as 'stateless' ethnic Germans; thus they received the much-sought-after travel documents. By 1951 the Red Cross, mostly in Rome or Genoa, had issued at least 120,000 such *titres de voyage*. The ICRC had little previous experience as a passport authority and was not prepared for the huge numbers of applicants. As a result, it was soon completely overtaxed. Although it tried to rid itself of this unwelcome task, the ICRC went on issuing travel documents for years (it still does). The whole issuing process was ramshackle in the extreme and led in many cases to inaccurate or blatantly false identification papers. With the knowledge of the heads of the ICRC in Geneva, Max Huber and Paul Ruegger, many Nazis, fascists, collaborators, and war criminals from all over Europe managed to escape overseas.

1. Red Cross Travel Documents

The ICRC was primarily concerned with prisoners of war from the Second World War. In order to continue its humanitarian work, the ICRC did not believe it could back either side—not even to assist the victims of the concentration camps. Strict neutrality became the overriding principle of the ICRC leadership, and it was constantly invoked. After the end of the war, the Red Cross in Geneva defended itself with the argument of 'non-responsibility' against the accusations of having done little to combat the Holocaust. Only prisoners of war—and not civilian prisoners—were protected by the Geneva Convention. Consequently, the ICRC had had no legal responsibility for the protection of concentration camp inmates. No provision had been made for the well-being of civilian internees in the Geneva Conventions of 1864 and 1929.[3] A plan to this end had been negotiated in Tokyo in 1934, but its ratification was delayed by the war.[4] When the Second World War broke out, the ICRC proposed to the belligerent powers that they adopt the Tokyo draft convention in order to protect civilians. The governments concerned were, however, often unwilling to make such a humanitarian commitment.

With the League of Nations unable to function because of the war, the ICRC was by far the largest non-governmental humanitarian organization active during the Second World War. The leadership of the ICRC had known what was happening in the extermination camps since 1942/3.[5] Like the Allies and the Catholic Church, the ICRC had a worldwide network of sources and informants.[6] Yet who, the journalist Heiner Lichtenstein asks, in this context, was more in need of help under the Nazis than concentration camp inmates?[7] Care was devoted to prisoners of war, to the wounded, to victims of bombing raids. Other organizations besides the ICRC also tried to help, yet millions of prisoners of war were excluded from international aid and left to starve to death, not least because the ICRC had no mandate to help them. One case in point is Soviet POWs. The Soviet Union did not ratify the Geneva Convention of 1929, and its soldiers were, therefore, outside the scope of help the ICRC could provide.[8] Only a few months before the end of the war did the ICRC make contact with the SS leadership. In November 1944, mass murder in Auschwitz had been suspended. The Reichsführer SS, Heinrich Himmler, sought to make contact with the Western Allies via Sweden.[9] Against this background, in the spring of 1945 several meetings between high-ranking SS officers and representatives of the ICRC took place. Like Himmler, his subordinates wanted to negotiate an exchange, but mostly they wanted to get their own heads off the chopping block. Using the Jews as hostages and collaborating with the ICRC was supposed to help with that.

The likelihood that the ICRC could have done more to save human lives is revealed by the case of Raoul Wallenberg. Wallenberg, a diplomat in the Swedish embassy in Budapest, began his own rescue programme in 1944. He set up houses for Jews who supposedly planned to travel abroad for a short period to stay with relatives. Even more important were the Swedish passports, or '*Schutzpässe*', that Wallenberg issued to these Hungarian Jews. Simple though these papers were, they were also quite effective. The 'protection passes' distributed by Wallenberg and his assistants were simply unauthorized papers with no official power. But the SS often recognized them as official and released those in possession of them to the protection of the Swedish embassy. Over time, the ICRC also began to take part in the rescue action for the

Hungarian Jews by issuing protection passes and other papers.[10] Thus the idea for the ICRC identification documents began in Hungary in 1944/5. It was here that it first became apparent how much power a piece of paper could have, a power resulting from the ICRC's high reputation and powerful contacts worldwide. At the end of the war, the ICRC delegates engaged in their next major challenge, to which its members devoted themselves with more success: assisting hundreds of thousands of prisoners of war and wounded soldiers who were stranded in Western Europe in 1945.

Alongside the Allied forces, the ICRC bore the brunt of the chaotic post-war months.[11] The Red Cross faced the situation of having to care for a large number of refugees who did not want—or were unable—to return to their homelands. Ethnic cleansings became mass phenomena. In memos to the ICRC, displaced people seeking help clearly set out their motives: 'Because I am a German and cannot return to my former homeland of Pomerania, now occupied by the Poles, and don't wish to, as I don't want to have anything to do with Communism. Because my parents have very probably been deported or killed by the Russians, I would like to work in Switzerland.'[12]

The most pressing problem for everyone wishing to travel was, apart from crossing the border, the matter of replacing missing identification papers. At the end of the war, hundreds of thousands of people had no personal identity documents. Even had it been possible to pass through all controls unnoticed, obtaining the visa of a South American state required having a recognized identification paper justifying that travel was required. But travel documents of this kind could only be acquired from the occupying forces in Germany or Austria after political investigation and bureaucratic hurdles, a process that those wishing to travel sought to avoid.

Some alternatives presented themselves: supposed or real ethnic Germans could try to blend in among the refugees from their country of birth. If they managed to do so, they received a Red Cross travel paper. The ICRC issued these documents. People without a passport and with unresolved nationality had a right to a refugee identification document. Most of these travel papers were issued in Italy. From 1946 onwards these papers were recognized by many states as surrogate documents. For stateless ethnic Germans with the means to finance their journey, enough money to pay for board and lodgings upon arrival, and appropriate jobs and contacts, South American states were willing to issue visas. With these visas, the refugees could travel abroad, mostly to Brazil, Argentina, Paraguay, Bolivia, and Canada.[13] Among these countries, Argentina was the prime destination. On 29 September 1945 the delegation of the ICRC in Rome wrote to Geneva headquarters:

> Every day hundreds of men, women and children come to our delega-
> tion without valid passports and ask for ICRC documents to be able to
> leave Italy. Among these people there are particularly many stateless
> Russians and a large number of Yugoslavs (Slovenes, Croats, Serbs) who
> had to flee their country and cannot now go back. These refugees were
> never interned or deported. Practically all these people wish to travel to
> South America. Among the petitioners and particularly among the
> Yugoslavs there are often family connections and contacts in South
> America. [...] One condition for the issuing of the documents is that
> the applicants come personally to the delegation. The ICRC then exam-
> ines the documents presented (identity cards, residence permits, papers
> issued by the Italian authorities). The data of the applicant are to be
> registered in a form, we keep a copy and put them in alphabetical order,
> a copy is made available to them [ICRC headquarters].[14]

With this letter, the ICRC in Rome established its own (improvised) procedure for all paperless individuals without being able to see the consequences, especially the many instances of false certification, that would result.

At the end of 1944, the International Red Cross in Rome, on its own initiative, had begun to introduce letters of recommendation, called '*let-tres de protection*' which proved very useful for these refugees, particularly for the Yugoslavs. Although the ICRC's travel documents served origi-nally as single-use passes allowing refugees to return to their homes or to travel to a new place to settle, the ICRC in many cases extended the life of these documents. Thus travel documents from the late 1940s were still in use in the 1960s and recognized as passports. The paper was to be

> issued to all people who have been forced by the war in one way or another
> to leave their regular place of residence, on the condition that they are
> without a valid passport, that they cannot acquire a new one, that the
> country they are traveling from is the country of their residence, and that
> the country to which they wish to travel will grant them entry.[15]

The first, less detailed ICRC travel papers (*titres de voyage*) were called '10.100'. To receive a 10.100 document, all one needed were two witnesses to confirm one's data. This made for a rapid turnover, but led to falsification on a large scale. In February 1945 the identification paper commonly known as the 'Red Cross passport' was first issued by the Geneva headquarters of the ICRC. The first version of this ID remained very simple. Positive experiences with the letters of recommendation prompted the ICRC to introduce its own document which could also be recognized by diplomatic and consular agencies. Over time the presentation of the documents became increasingly sophisticated and professional. Beginning in 1947 the ICRC introduced the more detailed 'form 10.101', for which written documents rather than witness statements were required to demonstrate proof of identity.

The International Refugee Organization, initiated by the Allies, took a much stricter approach than the ICRC. The IRO issued papers only to recognized refugees. Thus 'ethnic Germans' had hardly any chance of securing an IRO document. In the eyes of the victorious powers, they belonged in the category of perpetrators—not victims—of the Second World War. The ICRC kept to a much more generous practice: any pretext, any status was accepted by the Red Cross. Although guidelines existed, the process was largely random. One indisputable precondition for Red Cross papers was the statelessness of the applicants——at least theoretically. But data such as nationality or country of origin were often missing from the applications. IRO papers, on the other hand, could be issued only after the IRO's definition of 'Displaced Person' had been satisfied. Refugees with unresolved status and without documents therefore turned to the ICRC delegations in Italy for help. The ICRC in Geneva clarified the function of ICRC papers in a memo to all delegations:

> Within the context of the 'Intergovernmental Committee' certain governments, which signed an agreement in London in October 1946, issue travel papers under certain circumstances. But unlike these passports, the ICRC travel papers are available for all refugees regardless of race, nationality, faith or political conviction.[16]

In 1949 in a memo to the ICRC correspondents, Madame E. de Ribaupierre in Geneva, director of the Division for Prisoners of War and Civilian Internees, summed up the difficult situation of refugees in Italy:

> The refugee camps in Italy fall within two different categories: those under the administration of the International Refugee Organisation (IRO) and those under Italian control. In the former are all people who

can claim the support of the IRO and thus enjoy its protection, in general the nationals of the Allied countries, the Jews and the victims of the Nazi regime regardless of their nationality. The Italian camps of Farfa Sabina, Fraschette di Alatri and Alberobello Lipari, on the other hand, hold all refugees that the authorities, for reasons of security, see themselves obliged to intern because their identification papers were not in order or because they had reached Italy illegally. As these people enjoy no support or protection from the government of their country of origin, or indeed from the institution set up specially to this end, the ICRC has energetically concerned itself with their fate. [...] The International Red Cross Committee seeks to ease their departure for a host country, helpfully dealing with their situation by issuing them with a travel document to which the necessary visas can be applied.[17]

2. How the ICRC Issued Travel Documents in Italy

Early on, Hans Wolf de Salis, the head of the ICRC in Rome, asked headquarters in Geneva to deal henceforth with the recognition of new travel documents. In particular, the potential host countries—the United States, Canada, and the South American states—were to be informed and asked for support. In January 1947, de Salis clarified the issue of the distribution of ICRC travel documents in Italy. Above all, the tasks of the ICRC delegations there—in Verona, Genoa, Milan, Naples—were to be defined. De Salis established that the help of all ICRC delegations in Italy was necessary and desirable for the distribution of travel documents, but the central file-card system was to be run by de Salis's office in Rome, located at 28 Via Gregoriana. Rome alone was to issue the documents, although applications could be made to the individual offices, to which Rome would send the issued 'passports'. In this way, de Salis was to assume control of the issue of travel documents and the central filing system (*'il nostro schedario per tutta l'Italia'*). It was now chiefly up to him and his ICRC office in Rome to determine what form the practice and control of the issuing of travel documents would take.[18]

The practice in Rome tended towards the ramshackle and the superficial. The sheer numbers of travel documents that the ICRC's Rome office produced serve as abundant examples of this. In the second half of 1948, the liaison office of the ICRC in Rome issued 6,320 travel papers. Geneva headquarters also sent hundreds of ICRC travel documents to the IRO in Italy, the refugee aid organization of the Italian

Red Cross, the American Jewish Joint Distribution Committee, and the Croatian Brotherhood in Rome.[19] From March 1945 until late October 1948, the delegation in Rome issued around 50,000 travel documents. Every two to three weeks, new blank travel paper forms had to be sent from Geneva to Rome. On 13 December 1946 alone, 7,375 forms were sent from Geneva to Rome in order to supply two weeks' demand.[20] In May 1947 in Rome, de Salis turned to Paul Kuhne of the ICRC in Geneva and requested another monthly supply of 6,000 forms for the Roman delegation: 'Thousands of refugees of various nationalities received our travel document and were also able to receive Argentinian visas by showing our "passport". These were 2,500 Poles who were turned away by the Italians, and whom the British were unable to take in. There were also several thousand Slovenes and Croatians.'[21] De Salis stressed the significance of his delegation and the necessity of the ICRC travel documents, which repeatedly ran out in a very short time because of the mass influx of refugees. The refugees often made their applications from camps, and the travel documents were then sent there. Distribution was undertaken by the camp administration in question.[22]

In addition to the Rome office, the ICRC in Genoa was particularly active and autonomous in the issuing of travel documents. In August 1948, the ICRC delegate at 12 Via Caffaro in Genoa, Dr Leo Biaggi de Blasys, investigated the recognition of Red Cross travel documents. He wrote to a large number of consulates and embassies in Italy and requested a response. The results were extremely positive. Almost all the Latin American countries recognized the ICRC's travel papers. Particularly encouraging was the answer from the Consul General of the Republic of Argentina in Genoa, Elias Juan Agusti: 'This Consulate always accepts your travel documents; our visas are always affixed to your travel documents, and these ICRC identity cards are accepted by us as travel papers and by the Directorship General for Refugees as entry documents.'[23] After such successes, de Blasys could happily report to the ICRC in Geneva: 'Our identity cards are recognised in principle as travel documents by Argentina, Bolivia, Chile, Cuba, Paraguay, Peru, Spain, Egypt, France, Mexico, Switzerland, Uruguay and El Salvador.'[24]

In October 1949 the ICRC delegation in Buenos Aires tried to resolve recurring issues related to the acknowledgement of Red Cross travel documents in South America. The recognition of the document as a kind of passport differed from state to state, de Blasys argued. Thought would have to be given to the duration of its validity; the ICRC in Buenos Aires took the view that the documents should generally be valid for a year— with the arrival of the refugees in Argentina, the Red Cross often found itself faced with the problem of providing necessary extensions.[25] Many of the immigrants to South America saw Argentina only as their first stop, generally planning to move on to other states. But to do that required valid papers, which is why pressure was often exerted on the ICRC in Argentina to extend the life of the documents. The consulates of several South American countries also argued in favour of this solution.[26] South American states urged for the longest possible validity of ICRC 'passports'. A further complication for the ICRC was the attitude of the South American countries toward the IRO. In spite of the IRO's responsibility for the refugees and their documents, its authority in this matter was often undercut. Some South American states recognized the ICRC documents, but not the IRO identification papers. The IRO was thus repeatedly forced to ask the Red Cross for 'passports' for refugees. The IRO Department of Repatriation and Resettlement in Rome, for example, wrote on 29 September 1948 to the ICRC in Rome:

> For the start of our work we need a minimum of 3,000 ICRC blank IDs. [...] For your orientation we hereby inform you that until a special agreement is reached between the IRO and the Argentine government, displaced persons wishing to travel abroad must be in possession of a Red Cross travel paper, because the Argentine authorities only accept this document for immigration to Argentina.[27]

Problems concerning the recognition of IRO travel papers were not confined to South America. The IRO office in Rome in December 1951 asked the local delegation of the Red Cross for travel papers to be issued to ethnic Germans for the purpose of emigration to Spain. Once again, where the IRO was unable to help, the Red Cross was able to step in.[28] This state of affairs was rather topsy-turvy if one bears in mind that the IRO was not responsible for 'ethnic German refugees'. Officially only the IRO was a recognized refugee organization. Now representatives of the IRO had to direct people to the ICRC so that they could receive Red Cross travel documents. The ICRC identification cards tended to be recognized much more, at least by South American countries, than the IRO documents. The IRO was unable to ignore the importance of the ICRC for ethnic Germans and other 'non-acknowedged' refugees. On the request of the refugee aid department of the Italian Red Cross in Rome, in 1948 the headquarters in Geneva announced which delegations were authorized to issue travel documents. In theory, all ICRC delegations were permitted to issue such documents, but in practice only a few did so. According to the ICRC in Geneva, the most important of these offices were the delegations in Rome, Genoa, Paris, Vienna, Salzburg, and Innsbruck.[29] Geneva headquarters often issued travel papers as well.

The Italian government had a great interest in encouraging the emigration of refugees as quickly as possible, even though that haste would result in false and inaccurate documents. The mass of homeless people was putting a serious burden on the Italian economy and the food supply. Thus in March 1946 the Italian Ministry of the Interior proposed the recognition of Red Cross travel papers despite the fact that the Italian authorities were aware of problems with the ICRC papers, which offered 'no kind of guarantee about the identity of the applicant', as the Italian Ministry of the Interior clearly stressed. In suspicious cases, the security authorities were thus directed to undertake their own investigations.[30]

Proof of the identity of the applicants presented a problem from the start. On this issue the Pontificia Commissione Assistenza (Profughi) (PCA) took action. The papal aid office in Rome briefly issued identity cards to 'displaced and stateless persons', but these were not passports in the consular sense. The introduction of ICRC travel documents was greeted with enthusiasm by the Vatican because it made emigration and a new start possible for the refugees. Unlike the church documents, the ICRC travel documents were recognized by many states. The Vatican's national aid commissions were very effective in issuing letters of recommendation to the Red Cross. By doing so, they not only confirmed the identity of the applicant, but also the supposed statelessness of an individual. With these simple letters bearing the insignia of the Vatican, the refugee turned to the Red Cross and applied for a travel document. The Red Cross thus to a large extent delegated the establishment of identity to the Vatican aid commissions.

The Croatian aid commission for refugees in Rome was particularly active in both escape aid and in the acquisition of Red Cross travel papers and visas for South America. Its deputy director, Monsignor Krunoslav Draganović, did not help only Croats; after reaching an agreement with other Vatican national aid centres, he also assisted citizens of other countries. The ICRC in Rome treated Draganović and his aid committee almost as an autonomous Red Cross delegation. The Red Cross delivered the travel documents to Draganović, who in turn distributed the documents to 'his Croats'. The ICRC Central Office in Rome produced handwritten lists with the names of applicants as well as the numbers of travel documents issued in Italy. The date of issue and the Italian delegation responsible were also noted. What is striking about this is the fact that one repeatedly comes across the entry 'Croats'. Otherwise, one sees only the name of the ICRC delegation on the lists. This is a clear indication of Draganović's special role.

The ICRC delegated responsibility to these Catholic aid commissions and thus, finally, to the Vatican. But its trust in the commissions' work was ill-advised. The PCA had barely any opportunity and often no interest in examining the details of refugees. The Director of Caritas International, Monsignor Karl Bayer, who was working in Rome at the Vatican mission at the time, said of the examination of the authenticity of papers:

> Well, yes, of course we asked questions. But at the same time we didn't have an earthly chance of checking the answers. In Rome, at that time, every kind of paper and information could be bought. If a man wanted to tell us he was born in Viareggio—no matter if he was really born in Berlin and couldn't speak a word of Italian—he only had to go down into the street and he'd find dozens of Italians willing to swear on a stack of Bibles that they knew he was born in Viareggio—for a hundred lire.[31]

So the PCA issued letters of recommendation to the ICRC. Names and other details such as nationality were immediately entered by the staff of the Vatican mission on the request of the petitioner. In most cases, the refugee visited an ICRC delegation the same day—mostly in Rome or Genoa. Only this time he could 'identify' himself with an official letter from the Vatican. But in spite of these shortcomings and the obvious drawbacks, the ICRC relied on the letters of recommendation from the PCA. In a conversation in 1984, Gertrude Dupuis, the former ICRC delegate in Rome, described why the Vatican letters were almost blindly trusted: 'Of course the world and his wife recommended people to us, but we somehow relied on the papal aid commission (PCA), it was a good address.'[32] If there were suspicions of false certification, the two organizations passed the buck. When that happened, the ICRC referred the matter to the PCA, and it, in turn, referred it to the Red Cross. In each case, the other office was supposed to be responsible for checking the accuracy of an applicant's data.

Why the Red Cross travel papers were so desirable to war criminals and Nazis would be clear to anyone who has held such a document in his or her hand. It bears the following inscription: 'This document was issued at the request of the holder, who has declared that he has neither an ordinary nor a provisional passport, and is unable to acquire one.' The document testifies: 'The undersigned delegate of the International Red Cross Committee declares that he has issued this text to allow the holder to justify his presence at his present place of residence and to facilitate his immediate or later return to his country of origin or his emigration. He confirms that he has received from him the data below.' Real or false names could be given as the individual saw fit. In fact, since the photographs were affixed only with glue and often without a stamp, they could easily be switched. The practice of using witnesses to prove identity was very easy and, thus, attractive. In the POW camps, fellow internees confirmed one another's personal details in the application forms. Ideally, a group of three men was enough: comrades from the SS or the Wehrmacht each had the two guarantors required for an ICRC travel document. After confirming each other's details, they all had this 'open sesame' document.

The whole shoddy procedure of confirming identity and issuing travel papers is well illustrated by the example of Hermann Duxneuner from Innsbruck. From May 1938, Duxneuner undertook the task of coordinating the 'de-Judaization' of Tyrol. He himself worked repeatedly as a provisional administrator and enriched himself accordingly.[33] Duxneuner also provided the lists of Jews for the assaults and murders of the particularly bloody 1938 November pogrom in Innsbruck.[34] Duxneuner worked closely with SS-Oberführer Hanns Feil, who issued the order on the basis of instructions from the Tyrolean Gauleiter Franz Hofer, to murder 'quietly' the leading male Jews in Innsbruck.[35]

As early as December 1946, Duxneuner made an application for an ICRC travel document to travel to 'Holland or Brazil'. Duxneuner described himself as a 'former Austrian' and gave his profession as

engineer. While making his application to the ICRC in Rome, Duxneuner stayed at Fossoli di Carpi refugee camp near Modena. After the
end of the war, he had hidden for several months in South Tyrol and
gave his place of residence as Bozen. He presented the Red Cross
authorities with a German passport issued by the German Consulate in
Bozen on 2 May 1945. On that date the Wehrmacht capitulated in
Italy, and Duxneuner was able to acquire new documents at the last
minute. After that, he went into hiding with South Tyrolean SS comrades. Duxneuner seems to have had very good contacts, and by
December 1946 he had received an ICRC travel document. But Duxneuner was not yet able to leave the country, for he was interned as an
'undesirable alien' in an Italian refugee camp. It was not until the summer that he was freed on the intervention of Austrian diplomats. The
Austrian political representative in Rome, Dr Buresch, repeatedly
argued for the right of residence for Austrian citizens in Italy, from
which even those inculpated of crimes benefited.[36]

For individuals who wanted to immigrate or re-migrate to Austria,
the country's diplomatic representatives issued a simple 'collective passport'. This was nothing but a simple list on letterhead of the Austrian
political representation in Rome that Buresch signed. Even alleged war
criminals were easily able to use this opportunity to leave the country
in order to be released from prisoner-of-war camps in Italy. They did
not have much to fear in terms of the examination of their personal
details and their past. The last sentence in the collective passports specifically states: 'No police investigation of the individuals named above
could be undertaken by this office.'[37] Many wanted men were able to
slip through the cracks thanks to this lack of investigation. One of them
was Hermann Duxneuner.

Duxneuner was included in the collective passport of 10 June 1947
and planned to use it to travel via Tarvis to Austria—his ticket to freedom.[38] But to do so, he had to seek an extension of and supplement to
his ICRC travel document issued in December 1946. In January 1948
the PCA asked the ICRC for a supplement to his passport. In addition
to Brazil and Holland, the list of receiving countries was to be supple-
mented with 'Switzerland, Sweden, Norway, and Belgium', which was
a very unusual procedure. But his request was granted without any
difficulty—and Duxneuner was able to move to Argentina with his SS
comrades.[39]

Kurt Baum, one of Duxneuner's fellow refugees, is another good example of SS men seeking refuge in South Tyrol. Baum had over two years to wait in South Tyrol before he left for South America, and the time passed very pleasantly. Originally from Danzig, he was arrested by US troops in Bozen in May 1945, but released again in July 1945. After his release, he lived in a castle owned by Count Cesare Strassoldo in the South Tyrolean village of Gais. The carabinieri saw the count as a 'well-known opponent of the Italians' (*nota figura di antitalianità*). Baum was engaged to the count's daughter and hoped to receive Italian citizenship through this marriage.[40] He was not initially successful in this. In August 1946, he was sent to the camp at Fossoli as an undesirable alien.

Baum presented himself as 'stateless' and told the camp administrators in Fossoli that he wanted to remain in Italy and not to return to his home town of Danzig.[41] When he was arrested, he had a residence permit from the South Tyrolean village of Gais and several letters of recommendation from church offices. He informed the carabinieri of Bruneck that he had been a Wehrmacht Unteroffizier. But 'there are widespread rumours in the village that he was a member of an SS unit', the investigating carabinieri officers reported.[42] Their suspicions were quite correct. Baum had served until 1941 in the Leibstandarte SS 'Adolf Hitler', and was an SS-Rottenführer in the Waffen-SS on the Eastern Front. In 1942 he was promoted to SS-Unterscharführer.[43] Nothing is known about war crimes relating to Baum, but he probably had his reasons for keeping his SS past quiet. Because Baum decided very early to escape overseas, on 20 December 1946 he applied for an ICRC travel document from the Red Cross delegation in in Verona. Baum presented himself as a stateless bank official wishing to emigrate to Argentina. At the time, he was in Fossoli di Carpi refugee camp near Modena, where he was a friend of Duxneuner. As proof of his identity, Baum presented his identity card from Gais. He also mentioned two witnesses, whose names appear handwritten on his application. One of these was Ludwig Jakobi, born on 14 April 1915 in Radkersburg in Styria, who presented an ICRC travel document by way of identification. Baum's second witness was his SS comrade Hermann Duxneuner from Innsbruck, who identified himself with a German passport from the Consulate in Bozen.[44] Clearly, friendships and contacts were formed in the prisoner-of-war camps; people helped one another and confirmed each other's identities. Consequently, there were no limits to potential abuse. All in all, then, questionable evidence and a procedure that was vulnerable to manipulation characterized the issuing of identity cards and travel documents. Reinhard Kops, who also escaped with a false name and an ICRC travel document, writes of the checks at the time:

> In order to get the Red Cross travel document, you had to present a few documents like a birth certificate, baptism certificate, etc. Or else you had at least to supply the testimony of two witnesses to say who you were. So there was a great need for mutual assistance. The sources were scattered all over Europe. No one went away empty-handed. Hell, where was thy victory?[45]

3. The Routine Nature of False Documentation

La Vista observes of the ICRC travel documents:

> It is to be noted that although these International Red Cross passports are recognized as perfectly valid identity documents, they in fact identify nothing. The name appearing on the passport is invariably fictitious and often is one of several aliases used by the person whose picture it bears, who in turn might have in his possession numerous other passports and identity documents bearing identically the same picture which he uses at different times, under varying circumstances, for his personal benefit. It is also noted that the picture is affixed to the passport with ordinary paste. No seal is impressed through the picture or anywhere else on the passport, making the practice, which is in common usage in Italy, of transferring or changing pictures, a very simple one. This is likewise true with the thumb print which is affixed. The thumb print is never clearly made nor legible. It is made from ordinary ink pad and never 'rolled' but rather only pressed, thus making a classification count impossible.[46]

There was no way of examining and checking the ICRC travel documents because the applications were sent immediately to Red Cross headquarters in Geneva. Once archived there, they remained under lock and key. La Vista notes with some resignation:

> Unfortunately, the International Red Cross makes it a practice to send all its records to their headquarters in Geneva, as soon as practical after each case is closed here, thus making it impossible for the investigation

to continue along those lines here. It is the opinion of this writer, however, that an examination of the records in Geneva of all passports
issued by the International Red Cross would reveal startling and unbelievable facts.[47]

The ICRC archives in Geneva were not opened until fifty years after
the La Vista report. Their contents prove La Vista to be right: the documents reveal the ICRC's involvement in the escape of SS men and
Nazi war criminals. The subsequent recommendations in the La Vista
report are unambiguous:

> This agent recommends that the investigation of the various cases men-
> tioned here be continued, and that all control points be informed of
> these events. The undersigned official further recommends that the Red
> Cross passport service be entirely suspended, and that a unified proce-
> dure against illegal emigration organisations be considered. It is also
> advised that Allied Supreme Command reach an agreement with the
> Italian authorities about the treatment of dangerous refugees.[48]

La Vista's report caused great excitement in Washington. A secret meeting was immediately called in the State Department, although no concrete decisions were reached. Otherwise, hardly any investigations were
carried out. The US ambassador in Berne was merely instructed to
discuss the procedures of his Italian office in the issuing of travel papers
with the International Red Cross Committee in Geneva.

On 11 July 1947 the State Department in Washington contacted US
Ambassador Leland Harrison in Berne about the abuse of ICRC documents; the United States government had learned that the Red Cross
had issued passports or other identification papers to 'alleged refugees'.
The Red Cross was thus acting 'as a protecting Power or to engage in
political functions'. The Red Cross documents, it was argued, were easily forged, and the applicant's identity was not subject to serious investigation. As a result such travel documents often fell into the wrong hands:
'There appears indeed to be a lively trade in the sale and alteration of
such documents after they have been issued' by the Red Cross. The
US government showed great concern and urgently requested help,
asking the International Red Cross to pursue any illegal activities by
their staff in Italy or to punish fake Red Cross delegates. The La Vista
report was presented alongside the letter from Washington as an
important basis for accusations against the ICRC. State Department

officials expressed themselves very cautiously and, of course, diplomat-
ically. It was not the International Red Cross as a whole that was under
suspicion and facing accusations, but individual 'black sheep' who were
responsible for abetting the escape of war criminals. Washington nevertheless expected fast decisions from the ICRC under its honorary
president, Max Huber: 'The United States Government cannot avoid
pointing out that a situation such as you have been directed to bring to
the attention of the responsible officials of the International Red Cross
may arouse suspicion and distrust in various quarters and it advances
this reason, as well as its knowledge that the International Red Cross
Committee wishes to keep its reputation unsullied, as grounds for
immediate and drastic action.'[49] The American representative at the
Vatican, Graham Parsons, also had an informal discussion with Monsignor Walter Carroll, a member of staff in the Secretariat of State in
the Vatican. Parsons reported on this from the Vatican to the State
Department in Washington:

> Monsignor Carroll has promised to bring this matter to the attention of
> the top Catholic authorities interested in aiding displaced persons and,
> in due course, to give me something in reply to the 'oral Message'. I have
> asked him if possible to see that consideration of this matter extends
> down to the type of agencies mentioned in La Vista's report, although
> such agencies, he said, are not connected with the Vatican. I will report
> by despatch with copies to Berne and Rome when I receive a reaction to
> our representations of today.[50]

On 22 July 1947 the ICRC in Geneva justified itself to the US authorities and defined the function of the 'travel document'. The ICRC document, officials claimed, was not valid as an identification paper; it said
nothing definitive about the holder's nationality, which it did not even
mention. The documents were supposed to enable refugees who had
been identified as 'not eligible' to emigrate. The ICRC informed the
US authorities that 25,000 travel documents had already been issued.
The ICRC left open the suspension of this service as a possibility.[51]

It was not only the US government that was concerned about the
Red Cross's methods. In March 1947, the board of the ICRC in Geneva
had spoken out about irregularities in travel documents. A letter to the
Italian ambassador Egidio Reale in Berne made reference to an event
reported in the Italian newspapers: a group of 40 refugees—under the

protection of the papal refugee aid office—had been arrested.[52] The 'suspicious' persons all carried manipulated ICRC 'passports'. The ICRC repeatedly made it clear to the Italian ambassador that it had a purely humanitarian task to perform and that it was operating in strict neutrality. The ICRC delegation in Rome was playing a very important and useful role because with the documents it issued the victims of the war would be able to return to their homes or leave beleaguered Europe. The Italian Ministry of the Interior and the Italian ambassador in Berne were once again informed of the criteria and guidelines to be used in the issuing of ICRC documents.[53]

Madame Gertrude Dupuis, for many years an ICRC delegate in Rome, confirmed the possibility of false certifications. Those wishing to emigrate had to apply in person to the Red Cross office in Rome and sign the document, but there was no chance for further investigation.[54] According to Dupuis, the ICRC in Rome continued to issue 500 *laisser-passers* a day.[55] The small staff was completely overwhelmed, and fact checking fell by the wayside. Dupuis reported on a police subpoena, in which the former 'deputy delegate' was confronted with the accusation of forgery: 'I saw some of them lying on the desk as I entered the room [...], and I could see from several feet away that they were forged. Not only were they filled out differently from how we do it for ordinary identification papers, but my signature was obviously forged.'[56]

Although forgery was a problem, the ICRC representatives did not always correctly follow the guidelines for the issuing of the papers, either. Both the heads of the ICRC in Geneva and the various delegates were aware that the papers were not being issued with the necessary care. The ICRC delegates generally relied on the information from the applicant, which made forgeries easier. At the same time, the letters of recommendation from the PCA were blindly followed, as were the letters from the refugee section of the Italian Red Cross (Assistenza Giuridica agli Stranieri, or AGIUS).[57] In various memos, ICRC headquarters referred to abuses and advised the delegates in Rome in particular to be cautious. Individual delegates watched the development with a critical eye and spontaneously informed headquarters about abuses in the issuing of papers. According to one ICRC staff member, the Swiss consulate in Italy was very lax in its issuing of documents. Thus holders of ICRC identification papers that could not confirm the identity of the bearer with any certainty could not be given a visa without further examination. The branch of the Swiss police that dealt with foreigners, on the other hand, was very cautious in its treatment of ICRC identification papers because the authorities were aware of the practice of giving false information: 'The ICRC formally gives out these cards without any guarantees, and generally relies only on the petitioner's information.' In 1948 the Swiss authorities noted with surprise:

> We are interested to learn that the ICRC is still issuing identification papers to undocumented foreigners in Italy and also, to a lesser extent, in Austria. In Italy, this happens on the express wish of the Italian authorities. Italy may have subscribed to the agreement of 15 October 1946 in London, but is technically not yet in a position to issue [IRO] papers. According to Herr Kühne's explanations, the refugees can actually travel overseas from Italy with ICRC papers.[58]

The reaction of European countries to the ICRC travel documents varied. Swiss border officials repeatedly rejected ICRC travel papers. This was the case, for example, with a woman who had escaped from eastern Germany, was staying in Meran, and wanted to travel, with a Red Cross travel document, to neighbouring Switzerland to take a position as a nanny.[59] In 1948, the French embassy in Rome and the French representatives in Germany and Austria also refused to issue visas to people with ICRC travel documents. The document was not designed for several journeys in Europe, it was argued, but only as a single-use travel document to return to Germany—or to emigrate. In the eyes of the French authorities, the ICRC document was not a regular passport.

In response to the criticism, the ICRC made various attempts to address the shortcomings in its procedures and proposed ways to restore the accuracy of and faith in the documents. In May 1947, the ICRC's prisoner-of-war division in Geneva raised the question of checking the facts on travel documents once more. Consideration was given to the idea of keeping the files of applications for ICRC travel papers in Rome, rather than sending the documents in question to Geneva straight away, which would serve to make checks easier. In addition, the ICRC encouraged the recognition of the travel documents in the Soviet Zone of Germany.[60] Attempts to improve checking an applicant's information when issuing the documents occurred, too; in August 1945, the ICRC introduced control agencies for the first time. Lists were drawn up of the issued documents, and the issuing of forms in Geneva was central-ized. The completed and signed application forms were retained in the ICRC archive, where they remain today. The travel documents them-selves were handed out to the refugees. Still, the problems persisted.

In March 1948 the ICRC delegation in Rome reported again on forged travel documents. The Swiss consul in Trieste had previously informed the ICRC in Rome about a band of forgers in Gorizia and conveyed the appropriate newspaper reports. The Gorizia forgers, led by a South American, acquired or forged ICRC travel documents. The papers were sold to Yugoslavian refugees, primarily in the area around Trieste. The ICRC in Rome asked the Italian Red Cross in Venice and Gorizia for additional information and help in rectifying the conditions that made the forgers' activities possible.[61]

In January 1949 Geneva headquarters indicated in a file memo to Frau Denise Werner in Rome its concern regarding the numbering of her office's travel documents. The numbers in the applications were often repeated, creating problems with orderly documentation and fil-ing. A check of the documentation in the card index in Geneva was thus often impossible (and impedes research even today).[62] 'I should like as soon as possible a complete examination of all the travel documents that you have sent to us in Rome since autumn 1945,' a plainly agitated Denise Werner wrote to Geneva headquarters on 15 December 1948. Only in this way could the delegation in Rome prepare precise lists and overviews, 'to test whether ICRC travel documents are also authentic' and not, for example, forged or manipulated.[63]

One example of the multiple issuing of ICRC travel documents is that of Marko Ćalušić. In Rome in November 1947, this Croatian, sup-posedly born in Potocani in 1912, applied for an ICRC travel docu-ment. He presented himself as a Catholic cleric. The photograph on his application shows a man in a monk's habit. He was able to identify himself with an identity card issued by the Papal Chancellery of the Vatican in August 1946. All the information on form no. 68,676 was stamped and confirmed by the Croatian mission in Rome. Ćalušić wanted to emigrate to Argentina, Brazil, or Chile. The travel docu-ment was issued to the 'monk' on 19 November 1947 in Via Tomacelli by Draganović. But the Croatian cleric had already made an applica-tion for an ICRC travel document with the number 26,420, two years previously. In it, he had used the same passport photograph. The hastily procured witness for the simple 10.100 form identified himself as Felice Pater Antonino Romagnoli, with an identity card from the municipality of Florence, issued in July 1944. The travel document, bearing the number 26,420, was issued for Ćalušić, but never collected. In the archive of the ICRC in Geneva are two applications from Ćalušić bearing the number 26,420.[64]

On 21 December 1948 Denise Werner once again addressed the ICRC in Geneva about the double numbering of ICRC travel documents. Her intervention was prompted by the fraudulent and abusive issuing of Red Cross papers by an IRO functionary who was arrested in November 1948. This case raised a considerable amount of dust in the media. Frau Werner thus suggested that the central office take a number of measures to prevent forgeries. The issuing of travel documents in Geneva headquarters was to be checked more precisely than before, and staff were obliged to check 'the issued or delivered forms piece by piece and without exception'. But that would take 'three times as many people and three times as much time as before,' Werner stressed. The file index in Geneva was also to be run with greater care; only through doing so would strict controls be possible. In particular, greater accuracy was needed in the numbering of travel documents, and double and multiple allocations were absolutely to be avoided. Finally, Frau Werner pointed out in a handwritten note that sales of blank ICRC forms had often occurred. One former staff member sold these 'passports' on the Roman black market, where they could be acquired for between 15,000 and 20,000 lire. The blank forms thus needed to be guarded more closely, and in uncertain situations such as the loss of cards, further research was required, she stressed.[65]

The ICRC found itself reacting to criticism more often than not. The Red Cross delegate in Rome, Madame Dupuis, later defended herself against accusations of forgery with reference to the provisional character of the papers:

> They were never meant to be passports; they were intended to provide a means of identification which at the same time would allow the holder to proceed from Italy to his next and, hopefully, permanent place of residence. You see, what was important—no, essential—at the time, was to move the thousands of refugees, to break the bottle-neck Rome had become. Italy had enormous administrative and, of course, economic difficulties of her own at the time, and it was essential to keep this

floating population moving. The identity paper usually had a validity of six months. But we know there were people who used them for much longer, particularly in South America where they were accepted as quasi-passports for years; some people are still using them now [1972].'66

The criticisms of the ICRC's internal procedures which facilitated fraud were well-founded. For example, in September 1947 a certain Heinrich Bottcher applied for an ICRC *laisser-passer* in Rome. Bottcher was supposedly born in Magdeburg and presented himself as a Sudeten German in order to acquire the desired status of 'stateless'. Magdeburg is not, in fact, in Sudetenland, but the ICRC was plainly not greatly concerned with the correctness of information. Until he emigrated to South America, Bottcher lived in the South Tyrolean mountains; from May until July 1945 he had, as a former soldier, been in an American prisoner-of-war camp in Bozen. His destination was Venezuela.67 Another typical example is that of Hungarian Radu Florian. On 23 September 1949 Florian went to the ICRC in Rome and asked for an extension of his Red Cross travel paper. After a brief examination, a staff member established that the paper had been manipulated and falsified at various points. The signature of the ICRC director in Rome, de Salis, was forged, as was the stamp. The faked identification paper was, of course, retained, and headquarters in Geneva informed.68 Whether the result of the ICRC's lack of diligence or forgery, inaccurate or false travel documents remained an issue of concern.

Thus problems persisted for the ICRC. Application forms often disappeared in the offices of the ICRC delegations in Italy. Internal inquiries produced a large number of 'missing numbers' for Red Cross headquarters in Rome.69 On several occasions, the deputy ICRC delegate in Rome, Denise Werner, informed headquarters in Geneva of 'forgeries and the sale of Red Cross travel papers in Italy'. On 4 February 1949 she gave a detailed account of this in a confidential report: in several dozen documents, the stamps, signatures of the ICRC delegate de Salis, and Argentinian visas had been forged; numbers had been invented, and photographs swapped. Apart from this, more than seventy-five applications for ICRC travel papers had disappeared. The forged papers were then presented to the IRO in Rome, and were confirmed as authentic. Italian security officials also contacted Frau Werner and confronted her with inconsistencies for which the IRO office in Rome was also investigated. The criminal court in Rome held a hearing about forgeries in January 1949. Several Hungarian refugees had innocently acquired such forgeries and informed the authorities.[70] Despite the evidence attesting to these problems, the delegates, in particular de Salis, the head of the delegation in Italy, were indignant about the suspicion with which they were treated by headquarters in Geneva.

4. The Red Cross Calls a Halt

After numerous accusations of forgery and after Swiss, Italian, and American authorities had issued inquiries, the ICRC headquarters in Geneva was forced into action. The President of the ICRC, Paul Ruegger, was now concerned with damage control. Ruegger was born in Lucerne in 1897, but grew up with the princely family of Windischgrätz in Slovenia, which was then part of the Habsburg Empire. After holding several diplomatic posts, he served as Swiss ambassador in Rome until 1942. During this time, the conservative Catholic Ruegger established close contacts with the Vatican. Between March 1943 and May 1944 Ruegger worked as a special ICRC delegate. After that, he was appointed Swiss ambassador in London. In 1948, he assumed the presidency of the ICRC.[71] When he did so, the issuance of ICRC travel documents and, thus, the escape of Nazis reached a climax.[72]

Ruegger was very pro-Italian; he admired Mussolini and the king, yet he would have to put aside any personal predispositions to act in the best interests of the ICRC. His ambitions and political attitude were symptomatic of many within the ICRC. It put him in line with his close confidant and predecessor as ICRC president, Carl Jacob Burckhardt.[73] By 1947, escape aid for Nazis was common knowledge and could no longer be ignored. At a crucial meeting on 24 May 1949, Ruegger put the accumulated problems on the table. The Red Cross representative in Geneva and Rome, the Italian Consul General in Geneva, the President of the IRO, William Hallam Tuck, and a representative of the American Jewish Joint Distribution Committee discussed the situation. Representatives of Argentina and other South American states were invited, but not present. In the discussion, Ruegger and his colleagues stressed the temporary and provisional function of the travel documents. It was only because of the chaotic refugee situation in Italy that the ICRC had been forced to assume these tasks. The ICRC was completely neutral, he argued, and helped individuals regardless of their nationality, race, religion, or political opinion.

The ICRC also assumed no responsibility for the identity of the refugees and was prepared, in principle, to stop issuing any further documents. Ruegger stressed that the Italian government was to assume this task and supply the refugees inside its borders with travel documents. But for the time being, this reform could not be implemented. Hence the Italian Red Cross and its refugee aid service in Rome (AGIUS) would step in as a brief interim solution. IRO President Tuck made it clear that the Argentinian government would accept only ICRC travel papers or national passports. The issuance of IRO travel papers or Italian travel papers to refugees was still in its building phase. Given the enormous refugee problem in Italy, the ICRC papers were still 'temporarily' issued, although in March 1949 the ICRC delegation in Rome had closed, but continued to be run as a 'liaison office'. In particular, it would help those people who were not recognized as refugees by either the Italian government or the IRO.

Ruegger declared in the course of this meeting, which lasted several hours, that the ICRC was for its part prepared to help the Italian authorities with their taking over the issuance of travel papers for refugees not entitled to IRO papers, either with advice or with the direct involvement of professional staff from the Rome office. Ruegger emphasized that this was only a suggestion on his part because the Italian government would have to assume the corresponding tasks. But AGIUS and the Italian Red Cross could play an important role in the interim. Ruegger insisted on the need to persuade the governments of host countries to acknowledge official travel documents such as those of the IRO and which in future special cases would include travel documents issued by Italian authorities. He also explained that it was a principle of the ICRC to restrict itself where possible to traditional areas of responsibility. Ruegger went on to say that the chief task of the delegations was to concern itself with prisoners of war, and this was also the reason why a large number of the most important delegations, including Washington and London, had closed. The ones that were still being run had devoted themselves to rescue actions for Jews or, according to Ruegger, played the role of neutral intermediaries in civil wars, as in Spain. He emphasized the great generosity of the Italian government to refugees of all nationalities who had sought refuge on its soil. But he repeated several times that it was also in the Italian government's interest to create a special travel permit for 'non-recognized' refugees. Finally, Ruegger proposed suspending the issue of ICRC travel documents as soon as possible.[74]

As his handling of the travel documents inadequacies and other crises illustrate, Ruegger was not one to take decisive action. In July 1950, Ercole Costa, an Italian member of staff of the ICRC in Rome, informed President Ruegger of his suspicions regarding financial abuse by the ICRC delegation in Rome. Dr Costa worked there under Hans de Salis and Denise Werner as an accountant. He referred to irregularities at the Rome office—particularly concerning income from the issuing of the 10.100 *titres de voyage*. For each form, the ICRC charged 50 lire; along with other income, this soon produced a *Fondo riservato*, a special fund from which people helped themselves. Soon its administration had fallen into chaos, Costa stressed, and in the end Frau Werner took it over. When Costa inquired into the use and regulation of the special fund, Frau Werner reacted furiously and supposedly withheld the information from him. According to Costa, other areas such as food stores and medical supplies were excluded from normal accounting procedure. He went on to observe that his positive image of the Swiss had been somewhat shaken during his period of employment with the ICRC in Rome between 1946 and 1949.[75] Ruegger replied to Costa shortly afterwards in a very brief letter. He thanked Costa for speaking openly about 'certain problems'. It was important for Ruegger to be informed about what was going on in the delegations. Ruegger went on to thank him for his appreciation and did not once refer to Costa's accusations.[76]

While the ICRC struggled with internal and external criticism, the Italian government began to flex its muscles regarding travel documents for refugees. As early as April 1948, the Italian Ministry of the Interior had introduced a travel document for foreign refugees. The basis for this was the London Agreement of 15 October 1946 within the context of the IRO. However, this document was only issued for refugees who were recognized by the IRO. According to the Ministry of the Interior, a solution for 'unrecognized' refugees would be found later. They could apply for an IRO identity card in the camps or at an IRO office and use that to apply for a visa from a host country and leave Italy. The document could thus be used only for outward travel, stressed the Italian authorities. German citizens in Italy, according to the

Ministry of the Interior, were not to be regarded as stateless, 'even if they currently have no possibility of receiving a regular German passport'. The Red Cross was instructed to cease issuing ICRC travel papers to this group.[77]

The introduction of ICRC travel documents for refugees was grounded in good intentions and, perhaps, in the success of Wallenberg's '*Schutzpässe*' for Jews, but the ICRC could not continue in this capacity forever. At the end of the war, the conscience of the ICRC leadership, stung by the ICRC's failure to assist concentration camp inmates, was probably the reason for it becoming involved in the issuance of travel documents to victims of the war. But in the end, widespread abuse forced the ICRC to suspend its work as an issuing authority of travel documents.

When news of the ICRC's plan to close its office in Rome circulated, organizations engaged in assisting refugees in Italy argued for the office to remain open because the ICRC travel documents had proved reliable and were still needed. As early as September 1947 Ferdinando Baldelli, president of the PCA in Rome, wrote to Ruegger in Geneva. Baldelli argued against the dissolution of the ICRC delegation in Rome and emphasized the effective collaboration between the Vatican and ICRC delegate de Salis.[78] In a letter to the Geneva headquarters of the ICRC in September 1948, the IRO in Rome also referred to the importance of the ICRC delegation in Rome and asked for the continued financing of this office, stressing the importance of the ICRC travel papers for the solution of the refugee problem in Italy:

> The International Refugee Organisation appreciates the value of International Red Cross passports more and more each day, and after the suggestion to close the delegation in Rome these papers will no longer be available to refugees in Italy. We view this development with great concern and regret. Thousands of Red Cross passports have been issued by the Roman delegation, and an even greater number of refugees are waiting impatiently for these passports. For these refugees, these travel documents mean the hope of a new start in a different country.[79]

The planned closure of the ICRC delegation in Rome provoked protests not only by other aid organisations, but also by refugee associations in Rome:[80] 'Since this news has spread in refugee circles, we have been receiving interventions, written and personal, from various parts of Italy and notably from the Free Territory of Trieste, which indicate the extraordinarily serious consequences of these measures for refugees.'[81] The Catholic aid commission for Croats in Rome reacted with particular vehemence. In his statement of June 1950, Father Draganović clarified his position to Ruegger:

> The International Red Cross travel document is the best document for emigrants, acknowledged by almost all states, but particularly those that accept emigrants who are not supported by the International Refugee Organisation (IRO). Apart from this, these documents were received very quickly, in contrast to the documents of other organisations. You will be aware that the IRO discriminates amongst refugees by dividing them into 'recognised' and 'not recognised', and refuses any help to the latter.[82]

Draganović stressed that it was 'easy to understand that Slovenian and Croatian refugees in particular are affected by this measure because their territories abut Italy and Italy is thus the obvious escape route'.[83] Draganović finally thanked the Red Cross for the great support it had given to Croatian refugees in Italy, giving a figure of 20,000 Croats who had been granted a new life by the Red Cross travel documents.[84]

Despite the ICRC's determination to close its office, Draganović continued to call upon the ICRC to assist refugees in his care. On 2 August 1950 Draganović asked the Geneva headquarters of the ICRC to issue travel papers for a group of Croatian refugees who wanted to emigrate to Bolivia.[85] Right until the very last minute, the priest was still trying to get hold of the coveted documents. E. de Ribaupierre, the head of the ICRC division for prisoners of war and civilian internees in Geneva, directed him towards the autonomous section of the Italian Red Cross in Rome, at 34 Via Salandra, and its aid office, AGIUS. The Italian Red Cross was to prepare the necessary documents and reach an agreement with Draganović, after which the required ICRC papers could be issued to him.[86] On 22 September 1950 Draganović once again approached Mme de Ribaupierre in Geneva for ICRC travel documents. On the advice of Geneva headquarters, Draganović visited the head of AGIUS in Rome and emphasized the enormous importance of the continued issuance of Red Cross travel documents in Rome. Draganović pulled out all the stops and wrote: 'The ICRC travel documents remain the most humane and favourable source of help for persecuted people without the most basic human rights.'[87] Draganović stubbornly refused to give up advocating for the ICRC to resume its former activity of issuing travel documents out of an office in Rome.

In the end, Draganović's efforts met with only moderate success. In May 1951 Mme de Ribaupierre told the Croatian brotherhood in Rome her views on travel documents: the closure of the ICRC's liaison office in Rome required that the issuing of travel papers be centralized. The AGIUS in Rome would prepare the documentation. Travel papers would then be issued in Geneva. In urgent cases, Draganović could turn to headquarters in Geneva and hand in the applications there. But fundamentally the issuing and extension of documents would have to be controlled via AGIUS. Headquarters in Geneva would have to be relieved of the task.[88] Draganović referred once again to the recognition of the IRO documents. According to the Croatian priest, IRO identity cards were not recognized by the Bolivian government, while ICRC travel documents were. The AGIUS in Rome had been commissioned, he said, by Geneva headquarters to issue the appropriate passports for the Croats. Draganović repeatedly made it clear that the closure of the ICRC delegation in Rome had given rise to extremely severe difficulties for refugees, a fact borne out by his direct experiences. In August 1950, he wrote to the ICRC in Geneva and informed them that 'the Minister of Justice and Migration of the Republic of Bolivia empowered Bolivia's representative in Rome to issue Bolivian entry visas to Croats recommended to the Minister by the Croatian relief committee in Rome'.[89] So the Croatian refugees were able to receive a Red Cross travel paper only with the greatest difficulty. Without a passport, Bolivian visa commitments were utterly useless. Then he asked Mme de Ribaupierre of the ICRC in Geneva to give the AGIUS aid service in Rome appropriate instructions to issue ICRC identification papers.[90] On 4 September 1950, de Ribaupierre replied to 'Monsieur l'Abbé', welcomed his interventions, and referred to the provision of Bolivian visas for Croats. For the further issuing of travel documents, Draganović was to address AGIUS in the Via Salandra in Rome. The desired passports would then be signed by Geneva headquarters and sent to AGIUS in Rome.[91] De Ribaupierre's discussions with the brotherhood in May 1951 only reiterated her previous instructions to Draganović.

The Red Cross in Genoa was, perhaps, also displeased by the new policy in Geneva. Its strategy over the next few months was one of hesitation and stalling. The ICRC in Genoa would continue to issue passports for as long as possible. The ICRC delegate in Genoa, Dr Leo Biaggi de Blasys, initially ignored the new, rather unclear instructions from the central office and played for time. On 6 July 1950 he wrote to Mme de Ribaupierre:

> In the meantime, we will continue to issue the ICRC's 10.100 travel documents to all individuals who can identify themselves and who will depart within a few days. Hence a delay in the issuing of travel documents will prevent the emigration of these people. In the meantime I should like you to inform us as soon as a definitive decision has been reached [...][92]

Eventually, the stall tactics and efforts to circumvent the ICRC's new policy were fruitless. When the ICRC delegations in Rome stopped issuing travel papers on a large scale, the flow of Nazi refugees dried up. Finally, the ICRC's liaison office in Rome closed its doors in June 1950. From January 1950 onwards, refugees had to resort to Italian refugee cards (London Agreement) or IRO documents, and the Italian Consulate General in Geneva had agreed with the ICRC that from June 1950 'non-recognized' refugees could receive a kind of confirmation to emigrate to the country of their choice. Additionally, in spite of the large number of refugees still resident in Italy, at the beginning of 1950 very few ICRC travel documents were issued. The ICRC document was thus only to be issued in exceptional cases, particularly to refugees who were not recognized as such by the Italian government. One further major concern was the problem of refugees from Trieste, which had not as yet been resolved.[93] After the protests against the closure of the ICRC liaison office in Rome, an interim solution was found. On 28 August 1950 Mme de Ribaupierre took a stand on the question of travel papers with regard to ICRC President Ruegger. The issuing of ICRC papers in Italy was now regulated by and was to be carried out via the refugee section of the Italian Red Cross (AGIUS). Over the years that followed, the director of AGIUS, Giorgio Abkhasi, did much more than that. The large number of signed applications shows that AGIUS continued with the task as the ICRC had done before.[94] As a result, the papers survived for decades and are still being issued today by the ICRC and used in various crisis zones worldwide.

5. The Red Cross on the Escape Route

The first transition and collection point for refugees on the way to the Italian ports soon turned out to be Innsbruck, where the Red Cross was based. The Red Cross gave former Wehrmacht soldiers 'their first welcome home at the Innsbruck central station'.[95] The transports of Italian forced labourers from Germany also passed through Innsbruck. They were run by the Italian Red Cross. During those years, Innsbruck became a hub between Germany and northern Italy. This transfer point saw hundreds of thousands of 'people of all nations passing through on their way home' according to notes of the Red Cross in Innsbruck.[96]

Italians returning home generally came in large groups first to Innsbruck, where they were put in the former Reichenau labour camp and were brought by truck or train to Bozen. Here they took a break from their journey to be supplied with clothes and food. Beginning in July 1945 the Brenner rail route was officially opened for homecoming transports. The trains of Italians returning home generally travelled, after a relatively short stop in Bozen, from Innsbruck to Verona. Along this route, some 3,000 people came to Italy every day; these numbers increased to around 5,000 after an agreement was reached between the Allied headquarters in Germany and Italy. An efficient system was thus created for the returning Italians, which is why people of other nationalities often chose to blend in with them.

Alongside the delegation in Genoa and Rome, the 'ICRC Delegation for Tyrol and Vorarlberg, Innsbruck' played a particularly important role in the movement of refugees. Because of its geographical location—on the shortest route between Germany and Italy—the ICRC in Innsbruck effectively offered itself up as a contact point. Just a few kilometres before the Brenner border, anyone could equip him- or herself with an ICRC travel document. Around 1948 and 1949, numerous travel documents were issued to ethnic German refugees by the ICRC in Innsbruck and sent to the towns where the individuals were living. Most of the refugees were living temporarily in the Austrian states of Salzburg, Upper Austria, or Styria. Applications from all of these regions of Austria and also from Bavaria were sent to the ICRC in Innsbruck, the gateway to Italy and, thus, to the international ports. Immediately after the war, Innsbruck had become a very important stopping-off place for refugees. At first an ICRC liaison office was set up, which, under the direction of M. Kiechl, had become a delegation in its own right. Innsbruck was in the French zone of occupation. The French consulate in Innsbruck thus often dealt with passing 'ethnic Germans' and other refugees in the occupied zone. In addition, the Swiss Consular Agency in Innsbruck and the Italian liaison office both issued transit visas to refugees. In August 1950 the head of the ICRC Delegation in Paris, William H. Michel, wrote to the Foreign Ministry in Paris and argued for a solution to this problem of multiple agencies issuing various kinds of documents.[97]

The IRO in Austria also had a branch in Innsbruck for the French zone of occupation which collaborated with the ICRC. The ICRC's chief task in Innsbruck was to issue travel documents to refugees on their way to Italy. One typical example is the ethnic German Josef Mohr from Slovenia. In January 1949, the ICRC delegation at 2 Sonnenstrasse in Innsbruck issued Mohr with an identification document. The ethnic German Mohr family had no chance of acquiring an IRO travel paper, so the IRO office in Graz turned to the ICRC in Innsbruck to 'request most courteously that the family named above, which is in possession of an Argentinian entry visa and the paid boat tickets, be issued [...] the Red Cross passports, which are recognised by the Argentinian Consul General'.[98]

Municipal and district authorities in Austria or Italy confirmed the refugees' details and their lack of any criminal record, generally without investigation and without any further information about the individuals, as the district directorate of Schärding in Upper Austria in June 1949 states:

> It is hereby certified that there are no objections concerning the emigration from Austria of the ethnic Germans from Yugoslavia Grün Peter, born on 26. 5. 1911, his wife Elisabetha, born on 12. 2. 1914, their daughter Katharina, born on 25. 8. 1934 and their daughter Eva, born on 2. 4. 1937. This certificate is valid only to be presented to the Comité International de la Croix Route in Innsbruck, towards the acquisition of a Red Cross travel document.[99]

In the case of the Innsbruck ICRC, it is striking that local church offices did not take on any duties. In Genoa and Rome, the Pontificia

Commissione Assistenza confirmed the identities of the applicants. At the ICRC delegation in Innsbruck, church offices did not issue denazification certificates, confirmations of identity, or the like. The ICRC in Innsbruck was also rather unusual in another respect: its travel documents were issued in blue, mostly for emigration to Peru—this was quite unique in the history of the Red Cross. All other ICRC travel documents were light brown in colour.[100]

For Hungary in particular, the Red Cross in Innsbruck became a major stopping-off point. There were good reasons for this. In the wake of the retreating Wehrmacht, a large number of devotees of the Fascist Hungarian Arrow Cross regime fled to western Austria and were stranded there in April 1945.[101] This was followed in 1948/9 by a second wave of Hungarian nationals fleeing the communist regime in their country. These refugees were initially housed in Austrian camps along with thousands of ethnic Germans, Yugoslavs, Ukrainians, and others. According to eyewitnesses, there were still 'lots of Nazis from Hungary among them'—above all members of the Arrow Cross. Many of them lived for years in the windy barracks of the Innsbruck camps of Höttinger Au and Reichenau. In this apparently hopeless situation, many people tried to emigrate abroad. At first, the Red Cross issued the relevant documents; then the IRO office in Innsbruck took on the task. The emigrants had to report to commissions of the countries in question, where they had to overcome many bureaucratic hurdles. They also had to be in good health and below a set age limit. Members of certain professions were also given preferential treatment. The selection of people by these commissions was something of a lottery—'like a real trade in people', eyewitnesses remembered. Particularly popular destinations were South American states, but also Canada and Australia. Many refugees remained in Tyrol forever, including a large number of Hungarians who found a new home there. In the 1950s, they were given Austrian citizenship and could move into simple blocks of flats for refugees and emigrants.[102]

Among the Hungarian Arrow Cross members who came to Tyrol with the Wehrmacht were also some individuals who perhaps used the ICRC to disguise themselves. In the summer of 1945, Dr Wilhelm Bako presented himself as the 'head of the Hungarian Red Cross in Innsbruck', where he was seemingly working on behalf of the Hungarian government. As early as October 1945 he used this new opportunity to make an application of his own to ICRC headquarters. Bako was determined to emigrate to Argentina and probably managed to do so. As his 'identity witness', he chose Captain Perrier of the French Red Cross in Innsbruck. With the low application number 7,106, Bako was also one of the first refugees with a Red Cross travel document for Argentina.[103] Bako was setting off for South America at a time when many Hungarian refugees would have desperately needed the help of the Hungarian Red Cross in Innsbruck. Bako was acting as representative of the Hungarian Red Cross in Innsbruck only for a short time. A whole group of Hungarians who had been stranded in Innsbruck at the end of the war travelled along with Bako. One of them was Dr Detre Barczy, the supposed General Secretary of the Hungarian Red Cross in Tyrol. The only evidence for his identity was the confirmation from the French Captain Perrier. Barczy also set off for Argentina with his boss.[104]

Not all the fleeing Hungarians found the refuge they sought. László Bárdossy, the anti-Semitic Foreign Minister of the Miklós Horthy regime and Prime Minister from 1941, fled to Austria in March 1945 in the face of the advancing Soviets and managed to reach Innsbruck with his wife. He was arrested by the Americans in May 1945 and handed over to the Hungarians. According to eyewitnesses, his wife lived in a small room in an Innsbruck villa, which she shared with a female Hungarian doctor who had escaped in 1944. After the end of the war, the wife of the former Prime Minister cooked for French colonial troops from Morocco, so that she at least had leftovers to eat. She also survived by selling jewellery and clothes. Mrs Bárdossy wrote several petitions to the Hungarian authorities, pleading for her husband's life. All she managed to achieve was that her husband was not hanged as a criminal but 'honourably' shot. Apart from Bárdossy, a whole series of other Arrow Cross members came to western Austria and, unlike him, fled successfully to America via Italy.[105]

One fascinating case is that of General Andras Zako, who appeared in Innsbruck in 1947 and took over the leadership of the Hungarian fascists. Zako founded the Association of Hungarian Comrades-at-Arms, which largely consisted of former officers of the Arrow Cross regime. This association was supported by the French occupying authorities in western Austria; many of their members were later used as Federal Bureau of Investigation (FBI) informants. The group around

Zako organized the emigration of the fascists to South America and the United States, where some of the Arrow Cross veterans, including war criminals, worked for the US security authorities.[106] One close colleague of Zako, Ferenc Vajta, was partly responsible for mass executions and, thus, was a wanted war criminal. Vajta had studied at the Sorbonne in Paris before the war and was a member of a Masonic lodge (Grand Orient) which was particularly active in Central and Eastern Europe. Even then, he was working for Hungarian intelligence services and, following Goebbels's guidelines, wrote adulatory articles about the Third Reich in pro-Nazi newspapers. Between 1941 and 1944, Vajta was sent on special missions by the Hungarian government, particularly to Berlin and Istanbul. In 1944, he was promoted to Hungarian Consul General in Vienna. In this office, he tried to smuggle as many refugees as possible to the West, most of them aristocrats and large landowners, along with their furniture, even saving industrial machinery and almost whole factories from the clutches of the Soviets. In the summer of 1945, he was arrested by the US Counter-Intelligence Corps and interned in Dachau. Only a few months later, he managed to escape.

Vajta fled to Innsbruck, where the French military authorities in western Austria recruited him as a spy, and he was involved in setting up the Catholic relief organization Intermarium. In April 1947 Vajta was arrested in Rome by the Italian authorities, but released after only a few days even though he was on the list of wanted war criminals and should have been handed over to the Hungarians. Subsequently, he also sought the support of the US authorities for Intermarium, and in July 1947 he was recruited by CIC agents. As a diplomat, he probably had excellent contacts with the Vatican, Great Britain, France, and Spain. His extradition was prevented several times; the Vatican offered him protection, and the Italian Prime Minister Alcide De Gasperi took personal responsibility for the Hungarian's safety. Vajta then worked for a while with CIC agents who finally moved him to Spain. In 1950, Vajta emigrated with a Red Cross travel document to Colombia, where he taught economics as professor at Bogotà University.[107]

Many German and Austrian Nazi functionaries escaped as 'Hungarian refugees or ethnic Germans' via Innsbruck to Italy, and from there to South America. The fact that the coveted International Committee of the Red Cross (ICRC) travel papers could be issued directly in Innsbruck immediately prompted people to make use of this bolt-hole.

From Innsbruck, the route led across the Brenner, with Bozen as the first stop. It is hardly surprising that the Red Cross in Bozen should also have played an important part in the travels of refugees and stateless persons. Although an especially large number of fleeing Hungarians passed through the city, plenty of contacts and safe houses existed. On the subject of the Hungarian refugees, Vincent La Vista writes:

> In Bolzano a 24 year old Hungarian night-clerk in the hotel opposite the railroad station permits Hungarians to rent a room without registering their documents, but presumably at a price. In Milan it is very easy for Hungarians to acquire a Milan Questura Carta d'identità; the exact procedure involved is unknown. In Rome it is suspected that certain elements within the 'Pontifical Assistance for Hungarians in Town', Via Parione No. 33, assist illegal emigrants to get documents under false identities. The head of the organization, Padre Josef Gallov, a Catholic priest, and Monsignor Luttor, Ferenc, are believed to be involved in these illegalities. It should be noted that Hungarians have gotten documents under false identities from the International Red Cross.[108]

Individual Red Cross delegations acted to aid escapees. Hungarian fascists were working on their network, which had important bases in Innsbruck, Bozen, and Rome. In Rome, the fascists from Hungary could also count on the support of the Red Cross. In April 1945, large numbers of Hungarian refugees in Rome founded a delegation of the Hungarian Red Cross and held discussions with Baron Apor, the Vatican ambassador of Hungary. The office of the Hungarians was set up in the rooms of the former Hungarian embassy to the Vatican. It provided shelter for many Hungarians in Rome and Italy. According to the US authorities, 'several suspects and Hungarian Nazis have been uncovered' around the Red Cross in Rome.[109] The work of the Hungarian Red Cross was given special protection by the Vatican. For example, Marten Kelemen, a former theatre director in Arad in Transylvania, came to Rome in October 1945 and organized a help group under the protection of the Pontificia Commissione di Assistenza.[110]

Italy was swarming with fake Red Cross delegates because presenting oneself as a delegate provided a measure of safety and autonomy. In particular, the fake delegates could carry out important operations in unsettled times under the protection of the Red Cross, operations such as transporting valuables to Switzerland, issuing denazification certificates to leading SS functionaries, covering up black market activities, and providing alibis for individuals suspected of a crime. One particularly shameless case is that of the former SS agent Jaac van Harten, who presented himself as the ICRC delegate for upper Italy in April 1945. Under this cover, van Harten went avidly to work within only a few weeks. He wanted to whitewash not only himself, but also his colleagues and superiors in 'Operation Bernhard', the large-scale operation by the SS to fake British banknotes for black market purposes. On 21 May 1945 the American military governor for the Province of Bozen requested that the International Red Cross in Geneva finally send an official delegate to South Tyrol: 'I am of the opinion that most of the I.R.C. delegates here now are fakers. Van Harden [*sic*] in Merano is certainly one and there are probably many more. In fact—the I.R.C. should send an official here to vet the so called I.R.C. workers.'[111]

The Catholic Monsignor Piola presented himself as the ICRC delegate in Bozen, where he looked after the provisional refugee camps. The head of the Red Cross in Meran, van Harten, he claimed, had entrusted him with the position. Finally an official ICRC delegation came to Bozen from Switzerland. The small deputation consisting of five doctors and a number of nurses and paramedics was astonished to find ICRC delegates already there—delegates of whose existence they were unaware! The Americans uncovered van Harten's activities and warned the ICRC about him because he soon became a persona non grata for the Americans. After van Harten had empowered Monsignor Piola to act as his deputy on the refugee committee of the US military authorities (AMG), they had to act quickly. Monsignor Walter Carroll of the Papal State Secretariat came to Bozen for the purpose of putting things in order. Carroll forced Piola to step down from his position on the refugee committee as the representative of the Pontificia Commissione di Assistenza.[112] On 17 May 1945 van Harten was arrested by US Intelligence in Meran. Previously, the Americans had discovered van Harten's many SS stashes, embellished with ICRC insignias and filled with rare and expensive booty.

6. Escaping with Ethnic German Identity

The International Red Cross issued a large number of travel papers to ethnic Germans so that they could start a new life abroad. War criminals and Nazis exploited this situation to leave Europe. They presented themselves as ethnic Germans and—generally without investigation—received ICRC travel documents. In many cases, the document bore a false name.

The largest group involved in this passport profiteering was, according to La Vista, a group of German Nazis who had come to Italy solely to get hold of fake identity papers and visas. They immediately left Italy via Genoa and Barcelona for South America. La Vista had seen through the system. One prominent example of a war criminal who was able to escape to South America via Italy as an 'ethnic German' was Klaus Barbie. The former head of the Gestapo in Lyons, born on 25 October 1913 in Bad Godesberg, became the mechanic Klaus Altmann, born on 25 October 1915 in Kronstadt in Transylvania. Barbie changed the year of his birth, but in spite of his new identity, he wanted to keep his birthday. On 16 March 1951 Barbie applied for a Red Cross travel document from the ICRC in Genoa. He gave his destination as 'South America, Bolivia'. As proof of identity, Altmann was able to present a provisional travel document from the Allied High Commission for Occupied Germany, issued in Munich on 21 February 1951. The details on the ICRC application were—not surprisingly—confirmed by the Croatian mission for Catholics in Rome. Here Father Krunoslav Draganović had helped Barbie with his signature.[113] Frau 'Regina Altmann' and two children, Uta Maria and Klaus Jörg, also received travel papers from the Red Cross in Genoa.[114]

In the case of Gerhard Bast, the former head of the Gestapo in Linz, the Vatican mission in Rome under Monsignor Francesco Echarri confirmed Bast's new identity: 'We request that the honourable committee supply a travel document from the International Red Cross for Herr Geyer Franz, stateless, who wants to emigrate to South America, Paraguay. Cordially yours.'[115] Equipped with this recommendation, two days later on 5 March 1947 Bast applied for a Red Cross travel document. His name was now Franz Geyer, born on 23 January 1911 in Krško, Slovenia, a stateless businessman. Bast alias Geyer filled in the application in German. Thus, for example, he gave his province of birth as 'Laibach', which the staff of the Red Cross changed to 'Ljubljana'. Bast gave his address as 'Valdaora di sotto 5 (Bolzano)'.[116] He clearly felt safe with his South Tyrolean escape assistants, likely with good reason. Several forged identification papers provided him with a perfect disguise: a birth certificate, issued in 1939 by the priest of Krško, a provisional identity card from the Bezirkshauptmannschaft in Liezen, dated 29 January 1946, and a residence permit from the Questura in Bozen, dated 22 February 1947—all documents, of course, made out in the name of one Franz Geyer from Krško bei Laibach. As a Gestapo officer, Bast had good contacts and might have acquired these documents near the end of the war.[117] A search for the identification papers for 'Franz Geyer' in the collected applications in the files of Bezirkshauptmannschaft Liezen was fruitless. Clearly, the papers for Geyer had been forged and were not issued by the authorities.[118] In March 1947, the former SS-Sturmbannführer thus already had a Red Cross travel paper with faked details. The road to South America was clear and open.

Former Gestapo officer Erich Priebke also applied for an ICRC travel document by claiming to be a displaced ethnic German from the Baltic. Priebke thus became stateless, which entitled him to a Red Cross travel document. During the weeks of preparation for his flight, Priebke stayed in Bozen. On Priebke's application for an International Red Cross travel document in 1948 his current address was given as: 'Bozen, Via Leonardo da Vinci 24'.[119] At the time, this address was occupied by facilities of the old Bozen hospital. Helpful Bozen priests had thus provided Priebke with comfortable accommodation while he waited. According to Priebke, help and papers for South America came from a priest in Bozen: 'I was helped by a Franciscan priest in Bozen and the Vatican, in the person of the Austrian bishop Alois Hudal.'[120] This included a safe hiding place in a church institution, the acquisition of a fake identity card, and contacts with like-minded priests in Rome and Genoa. The Franciscan priest Franz Pobitzer from Bozen also helped Priebke to get the new documents: 'Father Pobitzer assured us he would see to it that we received the passport from the Roman headquarters of the ICRC.'[121] In his memoirs, Priebke also describes how the churchmen found him a new identity:

> In the meantime we were on hot coals, waiting anxiously for the entry permit for Argentina. When it had finally arrived, we discovered that according to this document our name was not Priebke, but Pape, and that we were born in Riga. [...] We were rather confused about this. We asked Father Pobitzer for advice. He recommended that we leave things as they were. Quite apart from the fact that we didn't want to waste any more time and didn't know if another change of name was

possible, in the priest's view the new situation also had some positive aspects. He said I shouldn't forget that as far as the British were concerned I was still a prisoner of war on the run.[122]

On 26 July 1948, under the false name Otto Pape from Latvia, Priebke applied for a Red Cross travel document for emigration to Argentina. As proof of his identity as a stateless ethnic German, he presented a letter of recommendation from the Vatican mission in Rome and an identification card from the Austrian municipality of Krimml. Under the heading 'religious affiliation' he was now correctly able to put 'Catholic'. Perhaps he felt that was more than justified because the Catholic Church in Italy had done a great deal for him. Finally, he was able to acquire a Red Cross travel paper from the ICRC without any difficulty.[123]

Berthold Heilig, the Nazi Kreisleiter in Braunschweig, was also able to count on the help of the Red Cross when escaping. In 1948 he fled from imprisonment via Bavaria to South Tyrol. In November 1949 in Rome, Heilig applied for a Red Cross travel document in the name of 'Hans Richwitz'. Richwitz claimed to come from Posen, which made him a displaced East German; this was how he explained his supposed 'statelessness'. He gave his destination as Argentina and Paraguay, for which Father Draganović had already acquired him a visa. By way of identification, Richwitz presented a passport issued by the Finnish Foreign Ministry in Helsinki in 1940. In 1939 he had, he claimed, fought as a volunteer against the Soviets in Finland, and that was how he had received the document. Richwitz's details were sanctioned by the mission for German-speaking Catholics in Rome and signed by Monsignor Heinemann. The refugee section of the Italian Red Cross in Rome also confirmed Richwitz's details, and its director signed the application.[124] At the end of December Berthold Heilig boarded the steamer *Buenos Aires* in Genoa and arrived in Argentina on 17 January 1951.[125]

Similarly, in August 1947 Hubert Karl Freisleben, born on 20 September 1913 in Amstetten, made an application for an ICRC travel document in Austria. He presented himself as a Sudeten German and, therefore, stateless. Freisleben wanted to emigrate to the Dominican Republic or South America with his wife Gertrude and their two children. He confirmed his identity with a 'Viennese driving licence with photograph' dated 5 August 1944. The Vatican mission in Rome confirmed his desire to emigrate to South America or Santo Domingo, Dominican Republic.[126] Dr Freisleben had SS number 304,163. After the Anschluss of Austria, the doctor was 'Bereichsführer Südost der Reichsstudentenführung', based in Vienna, and in February 1938 he had joined the SS. The SS-Hauptsturmführer was by no means an opportunist, but he had joined the Sturmabteilung (SA) as early as 1931. He probably had compelling reasons for emigrating to South America because his Sudeten German origins were completely invented.[127]

The revelation of false identities, as in the prominent cases mentioned above, remains the exception. As a rule, the investigation of fake identities occurred only after lengthy war crime trials—as in the case of Barbie or Eichmann—or by chance, as in the case of Gerhard Bast who was murdered by a people-smuggler while escaping. The true identity of many refugees, however, will never be known. False details can be pinpointed in many cases, but the reality of the refugee's identity remains in the dark. Not only were many war criminals and *Wehrmacht* soldiers able to leave Europe, but they were also unlikely to be exposed then or now.

Philipp Heimberger, born in 1915, supposedly from Sibiu in Romania, is perhaps one such case. As a supposed ethnic German, Heimberger counted as stateless. He gave his profession as technical director, his religious affiliation as Protestant. The refugee Heimberger based himself in Italy, from where he organized his own emigration and the travel papers that he needed for that purpose. Heimberger lived in the South Tyrolean town of Meran. As confirmation of his identity, he presented a residence permit from the Questura in Bozen from 1947 and a Bozen postal order. His application was prepared by the Italian Red Cross and sent to Rome. Only four days later, Heimberger was able to collect his travel document from the Red Cross in Bozen. His wife Susanne and his sister-in-law Theresia went with him to the new world.[128] Was Heimberger a refugee acquiring a new identity as an ethnic German in order to travel to 'South America, South Africa or Egypt', as he told the ICRC in November 1948? Heimberger was accompanied on his travels by Wilhelm Ernst, supposedly born 1910 in Sibiu (Hermannstadt) in Transylvania. As a supposed ethnic German from Romania, Ernst was also easily able to get hold of an ICRC travel document in Rome.

In 1947, the refugee lived in the South Tyrolean village of Welschnofen, staying at the ritzy hotel 'Stella-Stern', where he candidly applied to the ICRC. Ernst even had a resident's permit for Italy, issued in February 1947 by the office of the chief of police in Bozen. On 31 March 1947, his details were confirmed by the Italian Red Cross there. The ICRC in Rome did not examine the data any further, and the Roman delegation relied upon Echarri of the Pontificia Commissione di Assistenza in Rome, which accepted the refugee's details without objection.[129] So far, so good. But these data were not subjected to even a superficial check: the details given by Heimberger and Ernst are maybe incorrect; their supposed ethnic German origin in Transylvania may be simply invented, as one can assume by examining baptismal registers in Romania. Philipp Heimberger does not appear in the baptismal registers of Hermannstadt. Neither are there any documents about his German military service. For people by the name of Ernst from Hermannstadt, however, there are two entries in the baptismal registries: Wilhelm Ernst, born in 1897, and his son of the same name, born in 1924, who died the following year.[130]

Unclear cases such as those of Ernst or Heimberger appear in their thousands in the Red Cross archives; in November 1947 Walter Schindler, born in 1921, supposedly in Bozen, applied for an ICRC *laisser-passer* in Rome. He wanted to emigrate to Switzerland with his family. Schindler gave his former nationality as Czech, thus presenting himself as a stateless Sudeten German. At the time, Schindler was living in a pension in Meran. As proof of his details, he showed Czech documents including a confirmation from the embassy in Rome. The application was accepted without objection by the Italian Red Cross in Bozen and Rome. The PCA in Rome confirmed Schindler's details in a letter of recommendation in January 1948.[131] But no Schindler is to be found in the baptismal registers of Bozen.

For South Tyrolean Nazis and other perpetrators, escape was relatively simple because the South Tyroleans were seen as stateless ethnic Germans and thus had a right to Red Cross travel documents. In many cases, they also used their real names. The state affiliation of South Tyrol was settled in favour of Italy in 1946, but the nationality of the South Tyroleans remained unresolved until 1948. In other words, most South Tyroleans were 'displaced persons'—homeless foreigners without rights. It was not until 1948 that the South Tyroleans were able to reacquire their Italian nationality. Consequently, as a German-speaking minority they were spared the fate of expulsion. The status of the South

Tyroleans as stateless ethnic Germans was a major reason for South Tyrol becoming a much desired Nazi bolt-hole.

The commandant of Przemysl camp is one notable example of a Nazi who escaped to South America as a South Tyrolean ethnic German. He was actually born in South Tyrol and was able to use the fact to his advantage. On 13 November 1948 in Rome, SS-Oberscharführer Josef Schwammberger made an application for the coveted Red Cross travel document. He hardly had to invent any of his personal details. As a South Tyrolean ethnic German from Brixen, he officially had no citizenship. He gave his profession as 'specialized mechanic', and his faith, inevitably, as Catholic. As proof of his identity, Schwammberger presented a German passport from 1938. His immigration to Argentina was already assured, and the Vatican mission confirmed his details and desire to emigrate to Argentina. The same day, he was issued the coveted Red Cross travel document in Rome.[132]

Something that was easy for South Tyrolean members of the SS would soon be possible for Nazi perpetrators from across the 'Third Reich': their escape route over the Brenner to Italy led inevitably through South Tyrol. Reich German and Austrian comrades could pass themselves off as displaced ethnic Germans. So what would have been more obvious than to describe oneself de facto as a South Tyrolean, thus making use of this option? All one needed was an identity card from a South Tyrolean municipality. Many war criminals assumed an ethnic German South Tyrolean identity because it enabled them to explain their statelessness. It was just because of this statelessness that they were eligible for an ICRC travel document.

Eventually, South Tyrolean SS comrades and escape assistants happened upon the obvious idea of the 'South Tyrolean identity cards' issued by the municipal offices. Initially, several groups and institutions worked in a very dilettante and independent manner, later becoming more and more professional and cooperative. They knew where to find safe houses where they could hide for a while and where to find civilian clothes. In South Tyrol, the loose but effective escape aid organized by the former SS men concerned itself with Reich German comrades. SS members and Wehrmacht officers were smuggled over the green border and lodged in safe houses in South Tyrol. New papers were also organized for the comrades because faked municipal identification documents were easy to secure.[133] With a letter testifying to a new name and a new place of origin, Nazi refugees were able to request a Red Cross travel document in Genoa or Rome, clearing the way to South America.

Even today, Adolf Eichmann remains the best-known case of an escaping Nazi criminal under the protection of the Red Cross. On 1 June 1950 the bureaucrat of mass murder applied for Red Cross travel documents. As proof of his personal details, Eichmann presented a South Tyrolean identification document. His new identity as Richard Klement, born in Bozen in 1913, was completely invented.[134] Eichmann thus became a stateless ethnic German from South Tyrol who had a right to a Red Cross travel document with which he could travel to South America. On Eichmann's application for a Red Cross travel document it states explicitly: 'original nationality: South Tyrol, currently: stateless'.[135] By way of confirmation, Eichmann's application was signed by a Franciscan priest. This was Father Edward Dömöter of the PCA in Rome.[136] Dömöter repeatedly worked closely with Hudal to continue assisting 'German personalities who deserve help'.[137] Eichmann, the former SS-Obersturmbannführer, finally embarked for South America in Genoa on 14 June 1950. On 14 July 1950, he reached Buenos Aires. Upon his arrival, Eichmann alias Klement gave his profession as 'technician'.[138] Two years later, Eichmann managed to bring his family, his wife Veronica, née Liebl, and his three sons—Klaus, Horst, and Dieter—over from Altaussee.[139]

The Auschwitz 'Angel of Death', Josef Mengele, was also able to escape to Argentina with the help of the Red Cross. On 16 May 1949 his flight brought him to Genoa, where Mengele wanted to secure a Red Cross travel document. Like Eichmann, Mengele based his application for a travel paper on an invented South Tyrolean origin. As a supposed ethnic German from Italy with unresolved nationality, Mengele could not receive a travel document for the crossing to South America either from the Germans or the Italians. On the application form, his former nationality appears as 'Italian', now 'German because of the option'. He used his Tramin identity card as the basis and proof of his story of statelessness. Mengele finally received the prized Red Cross travel document and travelled with it from Genoa to Argentina.[140]

Similarly, in May 1948 Goebbels' colleague Ernst Müller received an identity card from the municipality of Tramin in the name of Francesco Noelke, born in Bozen on 7 December 1906. With this identity card, he was able to apply for a Red Cross travel document in Genoa in November 1950. In the application, his original nationality is given as 'Sud Tirolo', his current one as 'German because of the option'. So Müller, too, described himself as a South Tyrolean with unresolved nationality.[141]

Often the travel groups consisted of a community of old comrades that stuck together even when escaping. These connections can generally be reconstructed—thanks to the applications—from ICRC travel documents. There are plenty of examples of fellowships of this kind. One of these is the escape of the famous fighter pilot Hans-Ulrich Rudel and his crew. In 1948, Rudel and his men travelled over the the Brenner into South Tyrol. There they found lodgings with South Tyrolean SS comrades and got hold of application forms for ICRC travel documents. In June 1948, the fighter pilot Ernst August Niermann, born in Diepholz in 1914, applied for an ICRC travel document from the delegation in Genoa. He claimed now to be an 'ex-German' and stateless. By profession, he said, he was a technician and Lutheran by religion. Niermann had been in Bozen since 1946. He gave his profession as engineer and his religion as Protestant. His destination was South America. As proof of his details, Niermann showed a German driving licence from September 1945. His emigration to Argentina was arranged by the Argentinian consul in Genoa. Niermann's application was signed and confirmed by Draganović.[142]

In June 1948 Niermann and his comrade Werner Baumbach applied for the coveted travel documents. Baumbach gave his profession as engineer and his religion as Protestant. His destination was South America. As a supporting document, Baumbach presented an identity card issued by the municipality of Salzburg in June 1947. His emigration was, like Niermann's, organized by the Argentinian commission in Genoa. In this case, too, the Croatian Father Draganović signed and confirmed the application made to the ICRC in Genoa.[143] Werner Baumbach was one of the most successful fighter pilots of the Second World War.[144] In Argentina, Baumbach was at the forefront in the training of Argentinian fighter pilots. In 1953, he crashed during a test flight over the Río de la Plata Estuary.

Herbert Bauer went, like Baumbach, to Argentina. In April 1948 Bauer applied for an ICRC travel document under his real name, giving his profession as 'pilot'. However, the Austrian presented himself as an ethnic German from Czechoslovakia, in order, as a supposed Sudeten German, to achieve the much-desired condition of 'statelessness'. His gave his destination as Argentina, his address in Rome 'Via della Pace 20', or Bishop Hudal's Anima College. So the Bozen people-smugglers passed Rudel and his colleagues on to Hudal in Rome.[145] Niermann and Bauer were comrades of flying ace Hans-Ulrich Rudel. They had spent the whole of the war together as a unit; now they were emigrating to South America with their boss.

These examples represent only a small selection of the Nazis, war criminals, and collaborators from the whole of Europe who used this practice to qualify for and receive the coveted ICRC travel documents as 'stateless' ethnic Germans. But to date, no evidence suggests that the ICRC deliberately supported an escape route for Hitler's soldiers, former Nazis, SS men, and war criminals. According to historians such as Christiane Uhlig, it seems much more likely that individual delegates did not interpret their task according to the proper guidelines, and that for a great variety of reasons, whether out of sympathy for individuals, because of their political attitudes, or simply from overwork, they more or less actively helped Nazis to escape by issuing ICRC travel papers. Because the wanted men generally used false names, it will never be possible to determine the true extent of incorrectly issued ICRC documents.[146]

The leadership of the International Red Cross in Italy had, however, been informed about it. Geneva Headquarters was also aware that the papers were helping Nazis and war criminals to escape. The attitude of ICRC President Paul Ruegger shows that the ICRC tried everything, admittedly late in the day, to step down from its task as a 'passport issuing authority'. But the desperation of thousands of refugees and the inability and unwillingness of the international community to help the displaced ethnic Germans caused the ICRC to continue with what it was doing.

Thus the ICRC bears a certain amount of moral responsiblity. Open abuse was only possible because of the manner in which the travel papers were issued, which was very amateurish, full of mistakes and glitches, and performed almost without checks of any kind. That was how Nazi war criminals and SS men were helped to escape. That the documentation could have been handled differently is shown by the example of the IRO, whose travel papers for refugees were issued only after the applicant's identity had been checked. This screening process was designed not least to filter out potential frauds or wanted war criminals. Its procedures made the IRO correspondingly unattractive amongst German and Austrian Nazi refugees.

As a humanitarian organization, the ICRC must engage in behaviour in keeping with its mission, or suffer the resulting criticism when it fails to do so. The journalist Heiner Lichtenstein sums up the ICRC's actions in the war era and thereafter:

> During the war, the International Committee of the Red Cross not only failed to speak out against the Holocaust, in Hungary it actually proved that ways to prevent the murders could be found. Soon after the war, it then set very keenly to work, not only to the benefit of the survivors of the Shoah, but also to the benefit of the murderers. While those responsible for the Holocaust were being sought everywhere in Europe, the Red Cross and Vatican staff were helping murderers to escape, and for this the ICRC is guilty of gross negligence at the very least.[147]

For its actions and inactions, the ICRC in the war and postwar era bears the burden of responsibility, along with other aid organizations, for assisting the escape of Nazis, despite its valuable service to many legitimate refugees.

3

The Vatican Network

On 15 May 1947 Vincent La Vista, a senior official with the US Embassy in Rome, wrote in strict confidence to the State Department in Washington:

> The Vatican of course is the largest single organization involved in the illegal movement of emigrants [...] The justification of the Vatican for its participation in this illegal traffic is simply the propagation of the Faith. It is the Vatican's desire to assist any person, regardless of nationality or political beliefs, as long as that person can prove himself to be a Catholic. This of course from the practical point of view is a dangerous practice. The Vatican further justifies its participation by its desire to infiltrate, not only European countries but Latin-American countries as well, with people of all political beliefs as long as they are anti-Communist and pro-Catholic Church.[1]

La Vista accompanied his secret report with a list of Catholic organizations that were engaging in illegal escape aid or were at least suspected of it. If La Vista represents the Vatican as a gigantic escape aid organization, he is plainly exaggerating because the Vatican was never officially any such thing. But his description does throw light on the fact that a series of church institutions and dignitaries were involved in aiding fascists and war criminals. After the publication of the La Vista report in the *New York Times* in 1984, the Vatican vehemently denied the involvement of the Holy See in escape aid.[2] Confronted with the revelations from Washington, the Vatican referred in 1984 to an 'impartial historical investigation' into the Vatican and its policies in the Second World War, commissioned by Paul VI and conducted by the Jesuit priests Pierre Blet, Robert A. Graham, Burkhart Schneider, and Angelo Martini between 1965 and 1981.[3] In the eleven-volume work, the authors stress that the Vatican never sheltered suspected Nazis, as La Vista expressly claimed. In 1984, Blet, a Frenchman living in Rome, criticized the US

official's observations as 'childish and absurd'. For the American priest
Father Graham, the claims that the Vatican had systematically helped
former Nazis to escape were 'nothing but a propaganda manoeuvre
against the Vatican'. Even critical church historians in Rome disputed
the idea that the Holy See deliberately encouraged the flight of war
criminals to South America. But they refused to rule out the notion that
towards the end of the war and after it war criminals found refuge in
Roman monasteries alongside many ordinary refugees. The Paris lawyer Serge Klarsfeld and his German wife Beate, who tracked down the
former SS Standartenführer Walter Rauff in Chile, conceded that 'the
Pope definitely didn't give an order, "we've got to help German
criminals"—but he probably had a place in his heart for the enemies of
the Communists.'[4] Since the publication of the La Vista report, church
leadership has had to respond to the accusation of helping war criminals
to escape: critical eyes were soon turned on the Vatican's relief commission (PCA) which repeatedly—deliberately or otherwise—helped war
criminals to escape. The mission was set up to ease the misery of refugees in Europe, but at the same time, it was an agency whose actions
were directed against the Communist Soviet Union.

1. The Vatican Relief Commission

The Vatican relief commission for refugees played a central part in the
escape of Nazis and war criminals. Millions of refugees eked out a
wretched existence in camps in Germany, Austria, and Italy, and their
future was uncertain. Because of this humanitarian emergency, the
Vatican decided to help the Catholic refugees. In April 1944 Pope Pius
XII transferred responsibility for the care of prisoners of war and
refugees to the PCA, which was run by Ferdinando Baldelli. Baldelli's
superior was Monsignor Giovanni Battista Montini, who, as Under-
Secretary of State, was in charge of current affairs in the Vatican,
including the PCA.[5] The PCA, based at 3 Borgo Santo Spirito, aside
from its Presidency and Secretariat, was divided into an administrative
sphere and a practical organizational office. Every diocese had a branch
of the Roman central office, and these branch offices, in turn, had staff
in the parishes.[6] As early as 1922, Baldelli had founded a Roman Committee for migrants which, in 1930, became the Opera Nazionale
Assistenza Religiosa Morale Operai, and in the context of which Baldelli often

worked with the future Pope Pius XII. Baldelli thus had experience in the field of refugee aid. Yet at the end of the war, he and his immediate superior, Montini, faced an almost impossible task: to assist masses of refugees while the means and agencies of the Catholic Church were still entirely uncoordinated. At first much was improvised, and clear policies and procedures, as well as the infrastructure necessary for carrying them out, were only properly put in place around 1946.[7] Montini's biographer describes the modest beginnings of the PCA thus:

> The information centre for prisoners-of-war and refugees at first had only two or three rooms, so it soon had to move to an entire storey of the Palazzo San Carlo. When it then moved to St Peter's Museum beside the Bernini Colonnades, outside the Vatican, it found itself directly involved in foreign affairs. Apart from the statistical department, Montini was in charge of all of the documentation, and assembled the now much-sought-after collected volume 'The Church and the War'.[8]

The papal coat of arms on the letterhead and the Vatican's unqualified support gave the Pontificia Commissione di Assistenza immediate authority, and at the time there were very few respected authorities in Italy. The PCA was neutral and ostensibly purely humanitarian in its mission. But since its foundation, the PCA's care of refugees had been deployed as a tool against communism and for the reinforcement of the Vatican's influence in Europe and overseas. In many respects, the Catholic Church after 1945 considered former Nazis and collaborators from Eastern Europe as 'anticommunists' first and foremost, and helped them—particularly if they were Catholic—to make a new start.

Pope Pius XII supported this aid organization wholeheartedly, and it became something like the Pope's pet project. His housekeeper, Sister Pascalina Lehnert, remembered: 'How enthusiastic Pius XII was when Monsignor Baldelli asked him to be allowed to call the "Pontificia Commissione di Assistenza" into existence. How interested the Holy Father was! It was ideal because the modest beginning corresponded with his inclination to do good in secret.'[9]

Despite his great interest in this project, Pius XII left the work of the PCA almost entirely up to Baldelli and particularly to Montini, who acted as the true head of the PCA. Montini also called the PCA into existence: 'The papal aid committee for refugees was set up at his instigation; it brought the Pope's Christian charity to every country that wasn't closed to it.'[10] At the end of the war, the Pope wanted to 'ease the misery of his beloved German people', and committed himself deeply to the PCA. 'But of course, you know, even if he liked Germans, it didn't necessarily mean that he was pro-Nazi. He had, I believe, spent a very happy time in Germany—this is where the reasons may lie, far more than in any sinister political motivations,' said the rector of the German National Church in Rome.[11] The Pope's housekeeper confirms this: 'Pius XII, who had lived and worked in Germany for almost thirteen years, knew the German people. For that reason, he suffered with them a great deal under the Hitler regime when they were exposed to subjugation and exploitation and, above all, to religious misery.'[12] These exculpatory statements must be critically challenged, since these two were close confidants of the Pope. Pius XII was certainly not 'Hitler's Pope'.[13] He did, however, try to exist between the two dictatorships of Stalin and Hitler and to preserve the interests of the Church. In order to do that, he was prepared to make compromises, particularly since 'godless' communism was unambiguously seen as the main enemy.[14] It was also difficult for the Vatican to support the Allies openly because the Soviet Union was on their side.[15]

At the end of the Second World War, the Catholic Church had only one enemy: the communist Soviet Union;[16] the Church had not regarded National Socialism the same way. In his book *Hitler's Priests*, the US historian Kevin Spicer shows that around 150 Catholic priests were members of the German National Socialist Party (NSDAP). They saw no conflict between their membership in the NSDAP and the teachings of the Catholic Church. The ideological principles that led them to turn to National Socialism included radical German nationalism, anticommunism, and anti-Semitism. After Hitler's seizure of power, National Socialist priests acted as open propagandists for the Nazi party.[17] Men such as Richard Kleine, a cleric and teacher of religion from Duderstadt, or Johann Pircher, a parish priest from the South Tyrol, built up a conspiratorial network of National Socialist priests. 'Nazi Pircher' tirelessly fought for reconciliation between the Church and the NSDAP in Vienna, and in 1938 Kleine and Pircher formed the 'Group of National Socialist Priests'—by no means the only organization for Nazi clerics. Alban Schachleiter, the exiled abbot of the Emmaus monastery near Prague, had his national pride deeply wounded by the proclamation of the independence of Czechoslovakia in 1918. He felt more and more

like the only prelate in the Catholic Church who was in a friendly relationship with Hitler. But there were other friends of Hitler in priestly
robes. They all believed, like Bishop Hudal, in a possible rapproche-
ment between National Socialism and Christianity. Philipp Häuser was
another convinced Nazi and confidant of Hitler's, and also a priest.
Invited as a guest of honour to the Nuremberg rally in 1939, he received
a silver medal from Hitler in person.[18] After the war, this history was
quickly hushed up. The Catholic Church was even seen as one of
the strongest social bastions against complete *Gleichschaltung* under the
National Socialist regime. It was only in the 1960s—prompted by
the public debate around Rolf Hochhuth's stage play *Der Stellvertreter*
(*The Deputy*, 1963)—that a more intense and critical analysis of the role
of the Christian churches during the Nazi period began.

After Hochhuth's play, Eugenio Pacelli, at first a Cardinal Secretary
of State and from 1939 Pope Pius XII, was the focus of criticism because
of his silence about the Holocaust. Brief phases of reassurance about the
role of the Pope were followed by waves of critical literature, which
stirred up feelings once more and thus counteracted the process of
exoneration that had been underway for some years. The focus of recent
analyses by John Cornwell via Michael Phayer, Susan Zuccotti, Daniel
J. Goldhagen, and Giovanni Miccoli,[19] as well as works by authors
Matteo Napolitano and Andrea Tornielli,[20] is once again the Pope's
'silence' about the murder of the Jews in Europe—even though the
genocide reached the Eternal City itself in 1943. The papal archives
could provide information about Vatican diplomacy between 1933 and
1945; however, the Vatican remains the only European state that with-
holds free access to its archives from contemporary historians. The
archives for the office of Pius XI, up to 1939, have only recently been
opened. Documents on the pontificate of Pius XII from 1939 remain
classified.[21] The archives of these years are crucial if many questions
about the Holocaust and the Second World War are to be answered
and if the many uncertainties concerning Nazi refugee assistance by
the Vatican are to be removed.

A key figure at the head of the PCA was, without a doubt, Giovanni
Battista Montini. Montini made his career within the Curia; from 1937
he worked very closely with Pacelli and remained one of the closest colleagues and confidants of Pius XII. Montini was able to count on
American support for his PCA; the United States paid millions of

dollars into the Vatican Bank to support anticommunist groups and
parties in the 1948 Italian elections.[22] In 1954 Montini was promoted to
Archbishop of Milan, an influential position and his springboard to the
papal throne in 1963. As Pope Paul VI, he remained in close contact
with the American clergy.[23] Thus, for example, he donated his papal
tiara, a present from his former Archdiocese of Milan, to the Basilica of
the National Shrine of the Immaculate Conception in Washington,
DC. Paul VI not only lacked a desire for Christian–Jewish reconciliation, but in 1945 when he was Under-Secretary of State he even seemed
to have expressed doubts about the extent of the genocide.[24] He also
defended his predecessor and mentor Pius XII in an article against the
accusations in Hochhuth's *Der Stellvertreter*.[25] In his most recent investigation, the Argentinian journalist Uki Goñi reaches the conclusion that
various cardinals, including Montini, used their influence to prepare
the way for escape assistance. Their intransigent anticommunist attitude provided the moral justification for the support of war criminals
and Nazi collaborators. The Catholic Church in Italy and the Vatican
waged their 'lonely Cold War' against communism, rescuing Catholic
refugees from Eastern Europe and Stalin's claws. At the same time, collaborators and SS men were generously helped to escape. The work of
the Vatican mission in particular should be evaluated against this background. The PCA saw itself as a kind of mercy programme of the Pope
for National Socialists and fascists, which intentionally or unintention-
ally also helped Holocaust perpetrators.[26] Former National Socialists
appeared as 'decent anticommunists', who were welcomed back into the
Church.[27] Escape assistance seemed part of a strategy in the battle
against the Soviet Union and its influence in the world.

An organization like the PCA needed appropriate funding. In Italy
alone, after the end of the war, the Vatican maintained an extensive
system of twenty-two PCA offices in the regions and 299 sections in the
dioceses that extended even into individual major parishes. One important question was whether the money for the support of refugees—
including National Socialists—came from a special fund or was centrally administrated. The historian and Jesuit Burkhart Schneider
speculates about this: ' "It is in fact because of the bank that the Vatican
got into the financial side of refugee aid. You mustn't forget that the
Vatican bank was the only source of foreign currency—so the refugee
funds almost *had* to go through it." '[28] 'In those days we had no idea

where the money for these people came from,' said the deputy delegate of the International Committee of the Red Cross in Rome. '"Certainly we never doubted that the money came from the Vatican who, after all, had quite legitimately been providing help for refugees for years." '[29] Several times in his report, La Vista emphasized the active role of the relief commission in the Vatican in helping refugees and reached the conclusion:

> Needless to say, all of the Agencies operating in conjunction with or under the protection of the Vatican are financed by Vatican funds. No attempt was made to ascertain the amount of these funds, their origin, or their method of distribution, but it is the observation of this writer that substantial sums are being spent generously in the promotion of this work.[30]

The papal relief commission received a large part of its necessary funds from the Catholic Church in the United States. The National Catholic Welfare Conference (NCWC) in Washington, DC, the leadership committee of the US Bishops, played a central role in this. Some American Catholics had made huge contributions to the papal aid organizations since their foundation and encouraged their work, as was emphasized in a brochure published by the PCA in 1947:

> The PCA is now the central aid organisation in Italy. This position was achieved by a methodical effort on the part of all participants, through the daily interest of the Pope and the help of Catholics all over the world. The support of the North American Catholics in the context of the War Relief Service of the National Welfare Conference was particularly generous.[31]

But the National Catholic Welfare Conference also worked independently of the Vatican mission. In 1943 the NCWC created its own aid organization for European war refugees, chiefly funding Catholic aid organizations in Italy. The American Bishops also funded their own local relief committees, arranged food deliveries for the starving population in Europe, and cared for the large number of refugees and exiles, above all the many Catholic clerics who had fled communism in Central and Eastern Europe.[32] In September 1944, under the patronage of the Italian government, a group was set up to coordinate aid deliveries from the United States, in which the Vatican and the Italian Red Cross were also involved. Food deliveries from the United States—funded by the NCWC—were thus to be effectively distributed to people in need.

The NCWC's aid was by no means neutral and apolitical, but was shaped by strong anticommunist tendencies. A communist seizure of power in Italy—the heartland of Catholicism—was an abhorrent thought for many people.

The Archbishop of New York, Cardinal Francis Spellman, had the greatest influence within the NCWC and thus determined the flow of money from the United States.[33] Spellman played a considerable part in ensuring that the US government, the Catholic Church in the United States, and the Vatican stood shoulder to shoulder in the struggle against communism.[34] The Cardinal was a close confidant of Pacelli; they had worked together in the Papal Secretariat of State. As a military bishop, Spellman also visited Rome on several occasions, kept close contacts with the Italian clergy, and travelled on special missions for the Pope and President Roosevelt. Spellman was even offered the directorship of the Vatican Secretariat of State, an offer that he turned down.[35] His position of power was based on his financial skills, and for many he was 'by far the greatest business head the Church has ever had in America'.[36] In the 1930s and 1940s he overhauled the shattered finances of the US Catholic Church and turned his Archdiocese of New York into a flourishing enterprise. Spellman was personally obliged to Pius XII for the promotion of his career, and he was able to show his gratitude with financial contributions to the Vatican after 1945.

The NCWC had an Italian committee at 6 Via Lucullo in Rome. Its director, Monsignor Andrew P. Landi, distributed the money—without a detour via the Vatican—directly to the national subcommittees of the PCA.[37] Monsignor Landi came from Brooklyn, where he was also involved in pastoral care. He had visited the Vatican several times in the 1930s, and in 1944 he was sent to Italy—because of his knowledge of Italian—to run the biggest church aid project in history.[38] In the Vatican, Monsignor Landi received backing for his financial transactions from his compatriot, Bishop Walter Carroll. He was responsible for emigration matters in the State Secretariat of the Vatican and was able to use diplomatic channels to persuade South American governments to take in refugees.[39]

At any rate, the attitude of the NCWC was anything but neutral and fully represented the anticommunist line of the PCA in Italy. The US State Department saw the Church's contacts behind the Iron Curtain as an important source of information and coordinated some anticommunist projects with the NCWC. The Church initially smuggled paper and printing materials and, later, clothes and money to the Eastern European underground. In 1948 the State Department and the Central Intelligence Agency (CIA) worked hand in hand with the Vatican and the NCWC to prevent the Italian communists from winning the parliamentary elections.[40] The NCWC coordinated a letter-writing campaign among Italian Americans who were to exhort their families in Italy to vote for the Christian Democrats (the postal service recorded a doubling in the number of letters to Italy during this period).[41] Because of his attitude, the papal delegate in the United States was particularly able to count on Spellman's agreement and support when he wrote to the NCWC in 1948: 'Atheistic Communism will make a police state of Italy if it gains the victory. Atheistic Communism will consider the subjugation of Italy as its greatest achievement. It aims at the destruction of Catholicity in Italy in order to limit and to nullify the world influence of the Catholic Church.'[42]

Following a meeting between IRO delegates and the Pope, in 1947 Domenico Tardini from the Vatican Secretariat of State warned the US intelligence agencies that 'the Italian government might not be strong enough on its own' to resist the pressure of the communists; Italy threatened to 'become a second Greece'. This outcome was to be prevented with all available means.[43] In Germany, Aloisius Muench, papal visitor and commissioner for refugee questions, was at the forefront of the struggle against communism. As a German American, the conservative, anti-Semitically inclined bishop tried to mediate between the Vatican and the United States.[44] Along with Carroll of the PCA in Rome and Landi of the NCWC, he took a stand for refugees from Eastern Europe. Muench and Montini from the Vatican Secretariat of State were friends, so the American bishop supported the PCA whenever he could. A general amnesty for war criminals was always one of his chief concerns. To the American High Commissioner in Germany, John McCloy, he condemned the dismissive attitude of Jewish organizations towards these amnesties, because 'such an attitude will keep alive a spirit of vindictiveness that is not good for peace and prosperity. It will reawaken racial resentments that in the interest of these very organizations should be weakened and done to death as quickly as possible.'[45] According to Muench, the Jews themselves were responsible for anti-Semitism. This attitude was quite typical of the American bishop.

The PCA set up its own emigration offices and sent several delegations to South America. They investigated the possibility of a resettlement of displaced persons from Europe and made the appropriate arrangements with the authorities. After a discussion with US Foreign Minister James Byrnes, the PCA established that, after the closure of the refugee camps in Italy, the emigration of the refugees previously accommodated in them was necessary. The Latin American countries provided the best conditions for this, Byrnes argued, and the Catholic Church, because of its position, could help with emigration. Admittedly, the International Refugee Organization had sent a committee of its own to South America, but had been comparatively unsuccessful. In response, the Catholic Church in Italy offered to help, and very soon the first 500 displaced persons were able to emigrate to Latin America. The Vatican even set up its own immigration offices in the individual countries.[46]

The Vatican emigration office also had a delegation of its own in Geneva, which at the time was the base of several international refugee organizations. The Pope's delegate to Geneva informed the Vatican and the NCWC about decisions and internal matters of the Red Cross and the IRO. The American monsignor Edward J. Killion referred several times to the supposed 'Communist and Jewish influence in the IRO'. He was convinced that the US government completely underestimated the danger of communism and that the Jews were stirring trouble with accusations that there were many Nazi collaborators among the refugees. 'You can see the utter injustice of this, when a refugee is required to show documentary evidence of non-collaboration.' The Catholic Church should have put pressure on US government circles to bring the IRO into line.[47] The letters from the Geneva delegate to his superiors in the Vatican reveal, alongside anti-Semitism, fanatical anticommunism that saw the influence of Moscow everywhere.[48]

2. The National Subcommittees

Originally, the Pope had entrusted the PCA with the duty of caring for refugees and prisoners of war. But after 1944 the practical tasks for doing so were distributed to national subcommittees in which anticommunism and nationalism were the determining guidelines.[49] These aid organizations in Rome divided the work according to the nationality of the refugees. Initially, their chief purpose was to collect information about people missing in the war, inform their relatives, and care for refugees and prisoners of war in the camps. They also issued a large number of denazification certificates and letters of acknowledgement and helped the refugees to emigrate.

The Vatican relief commission set up around twenty such subcommittees in Rome to deal with the wave of refugees from Central and Eastern Europe. At its founding in early 1944, the PCA had not yet provided for the national committees. They probably came about as the papal aid organization developed through a process in which improvisation played a large part.[50] One of these organizations was the Austrian Relief Committee, run by Bishop Alois Hudal. In the context of the PCA, Monsignor Karl Heinemann was responsible for the Germans. The Croatian committee was run by Rector Juraj Magjerec and Monsignor Krunoslav Draganović in the Roman Istituto di San Girolamo.[51] In addition, the Hungarian subcommittee led by Fathers Josef Gallov and Eduard Dömöter was particularly active. Polish, Lithuanian, Ukrainian, Russian, and Slovenian subcommittees also took care of their nationals. The PCA largely supported Catholics, while Protestant Christians were generally referred to Protestant or ecumenical aid organizations. Particularly important here was Monsignor Heinemann, the head of the Ecumenical Aid Organization in Rome. But often Heinemann didn't have to work too hard. In many cases, the Catholic national subcommittees also helped German Protestants.[52] Catholic bishops—such as Hudal—did not have a positive attitude towards German Protestantism, except when it came to German culture and the importance of the nation.[53]

The care of Catholic refugees and prisoners of war was the central task of the PCA. In the years after the war, the Italian camps held large numbers of Ustaša (Croatian fascist) soldiers and Ukrainian, German, and Austrian SS men who were mostly Catholic. In several memoirs, Vatican delegations refer to the poor conditions in the camps, where people 'were starving and freezing'.[54] In reports to the PCA, for example, Fossoli refugee camp was described as an actual concentration camp. According to these reports, the wardens—many of them former partisans—bullied the Yugoslavs and insisted that they be handed back to Tito's state. But the governor of Modena, who was responsible for the camp, did not agree to its dissolution because the 900 internees, many

of them former SS men from Germany and South Tyrol, did not want
to be transferred to the remote and equally wretched camp of Lipari, to
which 320 people had already been moved. At the same time, local
authorities were urging the closure of Fossoli because it made the local
population feel unsettled and threatened by 'hostile foreigners'.[55] Given
native Italians' concerns about the camps and the government's proposed measures to address them, internees needed someone to advocate
for them.

Intervention on behalf of the prisoners of war and refugees in Italian
camps was a key task of the PCA. Hudal, the chair of the Austrian
committee, described the poor conditions for the prisoners of war in a
detailed report to the Italian interior minister Mario Scelba. In the
camps of Farfa and Fraschette, sick refugees were not given adequate
medical care, and children were left to their own devices. No meaning-
ful activities occupied the people in the camps, and the large numbers
of ethnic Germans from territories in Eastern Europe had no representation or prospects. Among the prisoners of war from the Soviet zones
of Austria and Germany, fear of the communists was particularly great.
Furthermore, many displaced people had no chance of getting hold of
regular papers, and thus saw themselves forced to cross the borders to
Italy illegally. To these desperate people, Italy seemed like the only
country in Europe 'where the ideals of humanism and Christian fraternity still apply', according to Bishop Hudal.[56]

The national subcommittees not only advocated for camp internees
by lobbying for better accommodations and by supplying letters of recommendation, but they were also prepared to confirm in writing the
names and dates of birth with which their visitors had introduced themselves. For some refugees, this was a life-saving opportunity. With their
papers approved or issued by the Vatican, the foreigners then applied for
travel documents from the International Committee of the Red Cross,
most of which were issued without question. The Church's procedure for
assisting refugees with the acquisition of travel papers was very simple:
the papal aid committees confirmed the refugee's identity and procured
the visa, and the Red Cross supplied the travel documents.[57]

People wishing to travel overseas applied to the Red Cross for travel
documents, but they often received the coveted Red Cross documents if
they could show a letter of recommendation from the PCA.[58] Francesco
Echarri, the secretary at the PCA foreign section, signed most of the

letters of recommendation to the International Red Cross in Rome or Genoa. Letters of recommendation were issued without further investigation, and the PCA relied on the statements of the applicants. The PCA letters of recommendation consisted of a pre-printed form on which only the names, nationality, and country of destination were to be entered by Echarri by hand. The case of Josef Schwammberger, concentration camp commandant in Przemysl, is typical of thousands of others: 'This honoured committee is asked to be so kind as to issue an International Red Cross travel document for Signor Schwammberger Josef, former Austrian citizen to emigrate to Argentina. With cordial thanks, Echarri.'[59]

The former leader of one Vatican refugee operation, Father Anton Weber, claimed not to have known the true identity of many people whom his organization had helped to escape. 'Even if the war criminals had come with their real names, we would not have known at the time that they were war criminals.'[60] But in the national relief committees in Italy, some clerics had very accurate knowledge of the background of the applicants whom they helped.

Bishop Alois Hudal in Rome was a key figure in the church network in Italy, who sympathized with Nazis and war criminals. Like many other clerics, Hudal claimed to know nothing about the catastrophe that had befallen Europe and still saw the National Socialists as Europe's saviour from Bolshevism. Hudal saw himself as obliged to devote his 'entire charity work primarily to the so-called "war criminals", who are being persecuted by the Communists and "Christian" Democrats'. These persecuted people were, according to Hudal, 'in many respects personally entirely innocent, and had only been the executive organs of orders'. He had 'snatched a considerable number with fake documents from their tormentors, through flight to friendlier countries'.[61] Hudal's most thoroughly documented instance of escape assistance probably concerns the former commandant of Treblinka extermination camp, Franz Stangl:

I had no idea how one went about finding a bishop at the Vatican. I arrived in Rome and walked across a bridge over the Tiber and suddenly found myself face to face with a former comrade: there, in the middle of Rome where there were millions of people. […] 'Are you on your way to see Hulda [Hudal]?' I said yes, but that I didn't know where

to find him. [...] So I did—it couldn't have taken me more than half an
hour to get there. The Bishop came into the room where I was waiting
and he held out both his hands and said, 'You must be Franz Stangl. I
was expecting you.'[62]

Bishop Hudal welcomed Stangl to Rome with open arms. He found
him accommodations, money, and work. At first Stangl lived with
Hudal at 20 Via della Pace, then the Bishop seemingly found him a job
in the library of the Collegium Germanicum, where Stangl was able to
work until he could continue on his journey.[63] After a few weeks Stangl
had a Red Cross travel document, a ticket, a visa, and a job in a textile
factory in Styria.[64] Stangl later fled to Brazil where he found a job as a
mechanic at the Volkswagen factory in São Paulo.

The Croatian subcommittee of the PCA was particularly active in
issuing denazification certificates and falsified passports. Its chairman,
Krunoslav Draganović, procured Red Cross travel documents with
false names, thus enabling many Croatian fascists and German SS men
to flee. Draganović had a free hand where applications for travel documents and visas were concerned. Often people of other nationalities
were presented as Yugoslavs and entered on visa lists. If Draganović
received permission for visas for 300 Croatians, he had to verify the
applicants as Croatian so that they could be eligible for these papers.
One typical example of flexible attributions of nationality amongst the
relief committees is the case of the South Tyrolean Maximilian Blaas.
On his application for a Red Cross travel document in 1948, Bla[a]s,
born in 1921 in the South Tyrolean village of Partschins, mutated into
someone with 'original nationality: Yugoslavian, currently stateless'.
The 'Yugoslav Welfare Society in Rome' confirmed the Tyrolean's supposed Yugoslavian nationality. How the South Tyrolean became an
'orthodox Christian' with just a stroke of the pen is really astonishing;
as confirmation of his identity, Blaas presented his Catholic (!) baptismal certificate from Partschins near Merano. Apparently, no one was
troubled by this. Previously the Italian Red Cross in Rome had issued
him with a letter of recommendation that made no mention of any
Yugoslavian citizenship.[65] In July 1947, Blaas had made his first application to the ICRC in Rome, on this occasion with a letter of recommendation from the PCA in Rome. In this application, the entry under
the heading of 'religion' is still 'Catholic'.[66] Blaas received his Red Cross

travel document without any questions and emigrated with his whole family to South America in 1948, probably for economic reasons.[67]

Alongside the Croatians and the Austrians, the Hungarian aid committee in Rome was particularly active in the emigration of individuals with criminal or fascist pasts. The Hungarian subcommittee of the papal aid organization and the Hungarian branch of Caritas applied for thousands of visas from South American states, an especially large number of them from Peru. These activities extended far into the 1950s, when Draganović had long ceased to be active in this field. Slovenian clerics and exiled politicians feared above all that anticommunists would be extradited to Yugoslavia. In their eyes, no one was safe: 'Extradition means nothing but certain death.' Slovenian Catholic aid organizations repeatedly asked the American bishops for immediate financial help for Slovenian refugees in Italy.[68] The Slovenian committee at 8 Via dei Colli in Rome also helped former members of the Slovenian Home Guard, the Domobranci—who had formerly fought for the Germans against the partisans—and Catholic clerics. Simple but effective means to protect against deportation were identity papers and denazification certificates issued by Vatican offices.

One striking example of the Slovenian aid committee's work is that of Drago Sedmak, who was only 16 year old at the end of the war. As his Slovenian Home Guard identity card dated 1 May 1945 and his passport photograph reveal, Sedmak was seemingly still a member of the Domobranci in the last months of the war in 1945. Retreating from Tito's troops, he fled to Austria like thousands of other anticommunists. From there, he travelled through Italy and was interned in the camp for Yugoslavs in Eboli near Salerno. With the help of the Slovenian relief committee, in the spring of 1947 Sedmak applied for an ICRC travel document in Rome, and it was issued to him. There was clearly no doubt about his destination: 'Argentina'.[69]

Similarly, the Polish section of the papal relief committee at Via Stefano Rotondo in Rome became a lifeline for Polish anticommunists in exile. The Polish subcommittee asked the ICRC in Rome for a travel document for Jan Baduniec and his wife Rosaria to emigrate to Argentina and at the same time confirmed the couple's details. The Pole Baduniec, a member of the pro-Western Anders Army in Italy, applied for a Red Cross travel document in Rome. Baduniec gave his address as Polish military camp number 6 in Macerata. As proof of his identity, he presented his marriage certificate, which had been issued by a Polish field chaplain in Italy.[70]

The uncontrolled growth of aid committees under the protection of the Church led, unsurprisingly, to many instances of abuse. Under the tutelage of the Vatican, war criminals could feel just as safe as conmen and 'the human flotsam of war'. In the summer of 1944, after the retreat of the German Wehrmacht from Rome, a large number of national church relief committees sprang up. A few key examples illustrate the scope of the abuse. One in particular that benefited war criminals and collaborators appeared after the liberation of Rome by the US army: some Georgian priests, including Nazi collaborators, procured buildings in the city and asked the Holy See for permission to open a Georgian seminary. The Holy Father granted permission and gave the new institution his blessing. Months later, when a number of seminarians turned out to be SS officers with girlfriends, US units searched the seminary, where they found a state-of-the-art radio station in the cellars. The Georgian 'rector of the seminary' carried the phone number of Herbert Kappler, the German chief of police in Rome, in his wallet. SS officer Kappler had been involved in the arrest and deportation of the Roman Jews.[71] Vatican Under-Secretary of State Montini, responsible for the Vatican relief commission, was informed about cases of this kind. As a rule, Montini and the church leadership quickly hushed up such scandals. Nothing changed fundamentally; no big clean-up occurred for years. But abuse was hardly an exception.

Zoltàn Kótay, a Hungarian priest who presented himself as 'the delegate of a Vatican mission for Hungary in Germany and Austria' is a study in abuse of the papal aid committees for personal gain. With the papal coat of arms on his car, the priest did a great deal of shopping on credit. In keeping with his status, the 'papal delegate' resided in Schloss Guttenberg near Mühldorf am Inn. When his creditors insisted that he pay his debts, life slowly became difficult for the pastor, and he emigrated to America. The Hungarian aid committee, the papal representative in Germany, and even the Vatican were now confronted with the awkward problem of the debts Kótay had left behind.[72] Bishop Muench and Under-Secretary of State Montini took personal charge of the matter of alleged Vatican delegates of 'Hungarian committees in Germany'.[73] In such cases, Montini tried to calm the waves and compensate the creditors. The Vatican reacted with astonishment and contrition to the discovery of such figures in priestly robes, but the church leadership did little to oppose escape aid for collaborators and SS men.[74]

It was not until 1950 that the Vatican first began to close down the PCA subcommittees. The Holy See ceased to tolerate the controversial activities of some church dignitaries, in part due to the many scandals that had come to the attention of the Italian press. Monsignor Carroll of the Vatican was already concerned about the unclear distribution of responsibilities and the wild growth of the many organizations devoted to refugee relief. He wrote on 10 March 1947 to his superior, Monsignor Montini: 'The fact that a papal committee plays a significant part in the transportation of refugees to South America, without adequate organizational preparation for it, could expose the Holy See to rather severe criticism on the part of the authorities, who cannot differentiate between the Vatican and the committees and institutions that bear its name.'[75] Montini's behaviour suggests he was not concerned with censure of the PCA's activities, however.

As chair of the Vatican mission, Montini exerted a controlling function over the PCA. Hudal, Draganović, and the other directors reported to him on the activity of the national committees. It is thus very unlikely that Montini knew nothing about refugee relief and the escape aid for Nazis and fascists. Montini's biographer Peter Hebblethwaite devotes only a short six-line paragraph to the PCA and Montini's work. In it his role is marginalized and responsibility is transferred to Baldelli, the director of the PCA: 'Baldelli ran his own show and had his doubts about Montini.'[76] But Baldelli could not have acted against the will of his superiors. In 1959, because of his achievements in refugee relief, he was appointed titular bishop of Aperlae; a street in Rome bears his name. His promotion, coupled with his being a scapegoat, suggests connivance at the highest level, as does a US government report. After the collapse of Yugoslavia, the US State Department had begun to investigate the whereabouts of Ustaša loot. As they did so, they also uncovered the involvement of the Croatian mission of the PCA. US special delegate Stuart Eizenstat concluded his report: 'In addition to the evidence of covert Ustaša activity inside the Vatican/College of San Girolamo, there is the question of the attitude of the papal administration, which although not involved with the Ustašas, could not have been entirely unaware of what was going on.'[77]

3. The Network of Bishop Alois Hudal

Simon Wiesenthal made these concise and telling remarks about escape assistance:

> the most important escape route, the so-called 'monastery route' between Austria and Italy, came into being. Roman Catholic priests, especially Franciscans, helped [...] channel [...] fugitives from one monastery to the next, until they were received by the Caritas organisation in Rome. Best known was a monastery [...] in Rome, a monastery under the control of the Franciscans, which became a veritable transit camp for Nazi criminals. The man who organized this hideout was no less than a bishop and came from Graz: [...] Alois Hudal.[78]

The cleric's history reveals a steady ascendency in his career. Hudal, born in 1885 in Graz, Austria, attended the Fürstbischöfliche Gymnasium in his home town, graduated in theology, and was ordained as a priest. Hudal welcomed the First World War with nationalistic enthusiasm; he volunteered to serve as a field curate.[79] In 1923 Hudal was appointed rector of the Collegio Teutonico di Santa Maria dell'Anima, the German church in Rome. In this role, he was the most senior cleric among foreign Germans and Austrians in Italy and assumed extensive responsibilities.[80] The 'Anima' is tucked away down a labyrinth of alleyways at 20 Via della Pace, near the Piazza Navona.[81] Historically, the priests' college and the German-speakers' church in Rome served as a bridge between Catholics in the south (Italy) and the north (Austria, Germany); Rector Hudal continued this tradition, but because of the circumstances of the time and his dominant personality, it assumed a very different significance. In 1933 the Vatican Secretary of State, Cardinal Eugenio Pacelli, later Pope Pius XII, appointed him bishop, and shortly afterwards granted him the honorary title of 'Papal Throne Assistant'. Hudal had reached the summit of his career.[82]

Hudal, like many dignitaries of the time, was fascinated by the rise of National Socialism. After the 'seizure of power' (*Machtergreifung*) by Hitler, whose 'servant and herald abroad' he planned to be, Hudal wanted to side entirely with the German cause. According to Hudal, the Church was a natural ally of Hitler's Germany; it truly embodied the real 'principle of leadership (*Führerprinzip*)'.[83] Hudal rejected Hitler's total claim to power and the Nazis' attacks on the Church in

Germany;[84] as a priest, he demanded the role of intellectual leadership for the papacy in Europe.[85] But his role was to separate the 'good from the bad' in National Socialism, as he told the Pope. The Church's mission was to make National Socialism Christian and deploy it against communism. His goal was to represent the intellectual foundations of the Nazi movement in a book. 'That's the first mistake,' Pope Pius XI disagreed, 'there is no intellect in this movement. There is only materialism on a massive scale.'[86] Hudal ignored this criticism and remained closely connected with National Socialism even during the first few years of the dictatorship.

While Pius XI and most voices in the Catholic Church rejected the *völkisch* elements and criticized National Socialism on the grounds of *Weltanschauung*,[87] the rector of the Anima would not abandon his idea of a link between the Nazi Party and Christianity and went on dreaming of a 'Christian National Socialism'. In 1937 Hudal's book *The Foundations of National Socialism* (*Die Grundlagen des Nationalsozialismus*) was published; he sent Hitler a copy with the dedication: 'To the Siegfried of German greatness.'[88] He always saw himself as a bridge-builder between the National Socialists and the Catholic Church, as he frequently stressed:[89] 'This book is conceived as an attempt to smooth a path to the understanding of National Socialism from the Christian point of view.'[90] Hudal's book received a mixed reception, but in the end both church representatives and National Socialist offices rejected it. Hudal's attempt to 'prepare a *modus vivendi* between NS [National Socialism] and the two Christian confessions in the Reich'[91] was destined to be a failure.

Hudal's picture of the world was defined by German nationalism, anticommunism, and anti-Semitism. He was a convinced anti-Semite. 'He hated the Jews', said one former confidant.[92] It was quite possible for a bishop to be a fervent Jew-hater and at the same time condemn the racial theory of the National Socialists. After the appearance of racial anti-Semitism around 1900, a biological foundation for anti-Semitism was generally rejected by Catholics. A moderate, 'social' anti-Semitism and religious anti-Judaism, however, was part of the standard repertoire of many Catholics, in order to check the supposedly damaging influence of the Jews on religion, morals, and the economy. However, the attitude could not be based on racial lines, because 'the fight against the Jews as a race [was] anti-Christian'.[93] Hudal repeatedly made use of the anti-Semitic resentment that was then current, by, for example,

attacking the 'predominance' of the Jews in academic posts.[94] He had
no objection to laws that protected 'one's own property' in an emergency 'against a deluge of foreign element';[95] therefore, he approved of
the 'Nuremberg Racial Laws'. As rector of the Anima, Hudal was also
a contact for the German and Austrian community in Rome. The
Anima also contained Catholics of Jewish descent towards whom Hudal
behaved with complete propriety. While it would be easy to judge Hudal
as singularly biased, one must remember that Hudal's religious anti-
Judaism was shared by large sections of the clergy at the time.[96]

The collapse of the 'Third Reich' did not fundamentally alter Hudal's
attitude. But initially he knew how to adapt without undergoing any
internal transformation or distancing himself from the Nazi system.[97] If
until 1944 he still described himself as 'the German bishop in Rome',
an office that didn't even exist in the Catholic Church, on the day of the
liberation of Rome by the Allies he became the representative of
annexed Austria. In the summer of 1944, the 'German bishop in Rome'
promptly mutated into the 'Austrian bishop in Rome'. After the Wehrmacht's retreat from Rome, Hudal founded the Austrian Liberation
Committee with 'Rome Austrians', the chief task of which would soon
be to issue Austrian identity papers. Hudal turned a blind eye to national
origin and also issued confirmations for Germans. After a few months,
however, the Austrian cards were no longer in great demand. Hudal
had learned that some people had chosen to give back the cards he had
issued and to describe themselves as 'stateless' instead. There was a
good reason for this: statelessness was the precondition for the receipt of
a Red Cross travel document, and Hudal would soon be instrumental
in issuing these.[98] After the end of his activities on his own Austrian
committee and the PCA committee that came after it, he took charge
of other assistance measures.

On the model of the Croatians, Hungarians, and Slovenians, Hudal
set up the 'Assistenza Austriaca' as an Austrian committee of the PCA.
This gave the bishop far more leeway than had the Austrian Liberation
Committee which he had set up himself. Now Hudal was able to act
with the authority of the Vatican and rely on its financial support, as
well as that of the American Catholic bishops. Sometimes the NCWC
even paid money directly to the national missions, including Hudal's.
In September 1944, the New York Archbishop Francis Spellman met
Hudal's confidant Baron Berger-Waldenegg, who asked him for support

for the Austrian mission in Rome. Spellman then asked the American bishops for 'financial aid to Austrians in Rome'. The American Catholic Bishops' Conference finally authorized a sum of '200 dollars a month' for the support of the committee. In November 1944 this emergency relief was passed on to the American Monsignor and PCA representative Walter Carroll, who accepted a cheque for 400 dollars (for the running costs for September and October 1944) on Hudal's behalf.[99] But, on this occasion, the Archbishop of Chicago, Samuel Alphonsus Cardinal Stritch, stressed expressly that a definitive regulation should be introduced for the support of the Austrians in Italy at the next US Bishops' conference.[100]

Hudal's financial support came from secular as well as religious sources. In 1944–6 the US military administration and the US military intelligence service, the OSS, also helped to finance the Austrian committee in Rome. In July 1944 the US secret service contacted Berger-Waldenegg and provided financial subsidies to the Austrians. The Austrian committee thus began collaborating with the OSS agents in the sphere of espionage, while the Americans avoided giving them any official political recognition. The monthly support of 1,500 dollars for Berger-Waldenegg was a huge sum at the time.[101] As early as 1947, however, the Americans were very concerned about Bishop Hudal's activities. His frequent exchanges of letters with well-known right-wing extremists fell into the hands of the Allied mail censors, but after a brief hearing, the Allies let Hudal and his associates do as they pleased.[102]

Hudal and his relief committee became a contact point for many desperate homeless people, among them Nazi war criminals. The Assistenza Austriaca was based at the Anima church at 20 Via della Pace in Rome. Four to five Nazi refugees were always hiding with Hudal at the Anima. Their rooms were handily close to a secret passage leading to a tower and then to the church crypt. According to Hudal's confidant Joseph Prader, it was an 'ideal hiding place'. Most of the Anima employees didn't know the precise background of the hidden individuals, but the identities of senior fascists, carabinieri officers, or SS men were hard to hide.[103] Events at the Anima were an open secret in Rome. The Vatican had, at first, tolerated them in silence. On 4 April 1949 Giovanni Montini, on behalf of the Vatican's Secretary of State, wrote to Hudal: 'Most Reverend Excellency, I have the pleasant duty of passing on to your most reverend Excellency the sum of 30,000 lire, which please find enclosed, as an extraordinary support that the Holy Father is generously minded to give to the Austrians.'[104] He went on to inform Hudal that 'the Pope blesses Hudal's work'. The blessing was for his refugee relief, which indirectly included the Nazi refugees.

Refugee relief focused on the acquisition of travel documents, for it was the most important precondition for flight. Even when people managed to get hold of an assurance of a visa and raise the money for the journey, without a travel document these preparations were entirely useless. But Hudal and the relief committees were easily able to help with the travel documents. Even Hudal's contact in Buenos Aires repeatedly asked him for travel papers:

> For your protégé, Oblt. [Oberleutnant] Schmidtke, I have presented the documents to the government in order to acquire entry papers. When we will receive the entry permit, I am, however, unable to say. It could take 8 days, but it's equally possible it could take 3 months. As soon as I have the paper, I will send it to you; that seems to me to be the safest thing! I hear from Austria that there are huge numbers of ethnic Germans, mostly in Vienna, some of whom already have entry papers to come here, but have no travel documents, which means that they are unable to leave the country. If your Reverend Excellency could intervene as an intermediary, I would be most grateful. The rumour is circulating here that since 1 January [1949] this year no Red Cross documents are being issued in Italy.[105]

Bishop Hudal supplied numerous Nazi refugees with these coveted Red Cross papers. According to Gertrude Dupuis, the ICRC delegate in Rome, 'it was relatively easy for [Hudal] to achieve this. You mustn't forget, he was a bishop [...], and how could we deny the word of a priest?'[106] With the help of a national church relief committee and the receipt of a Red Cross travel document and food cards, the refugee could apply for a residence permit from the Italian authorities. 'Now the refugee can wait safely in Italy until he receives an entry permit from the consulates of Central or South American states.'[107] Yet Hudal was not content to assist those in his care with receiving travel documents and then watch them wait for entry visas.

To move this entry permit process along, a tireless Bishop Hudal addressed the Argentinian head of state Juan Domingo Perón directly, as a letter of 31 August 1948 confirms. In it he asked for 5,000 visas for German and Austrian 'soldiers'. These were not refugees, Hudal explained, but 'anti-Bolshevik fighters' whose 'sacrifices during the war had saved Europe from Soviet domination'. In short, he was asking for visas for German and Austrian National Socialists and Waffen-SS men.[108] Hudal kept a close eye on the careers of his protégés in Argentina and kept close contact with them and the Argentinian government.[109] Fighter pilot Rudel noted gratefully about Bishop Hudal: 'Through him, Rome became a refuge and a salvation for many victims of persecution after the "liberation". And some of my own comrades found their way to freedom via Rome, because Rome is full of people of good will.'[110] The CIA reported about Hudal in 1953:

> Many Wehrmacht and SS veterans went from a center in Munich through Innsbruck, Bern and Rome, to Beirut and Damascus. Some of those going to Spain and South America also passed through Rome. A transit and recruiting center existed there under the protection of German Bishop Alois Hudal, who was known as the 'Brown Bishop' because of his marked sympathy for the Nazi movement. Monsignor Hudal was reported as fully informed about the objectives of the 'international Waffen-SS' and as helping SS people abroad. Bruderschaft [Nazi brotherhood] leader [and former SS-Obersturmbannführer] Alfred Franke-Griegsch [Gricksch], travelling disguised as a monk, visited Hudal (and also met with British Fascist Sir Oswald Mosley) in Rome in 1950.[111]

Hudal was not apologetic about his activities and pursued them with great diligence.

Given the openness with which Hudal conducted his escape aid, it is not surprising that others had knowledge of the extent of his assistance. Joseph Prader, then a church secretary in Rome who was constantly in the Anima, now openly admits that after 1945 he and Hudal had also helped well-known National Socialists: 'Yes, we did that; afterwards the clerics were needed again, and we helped. We issued denazification certificates and letters of recommendation by the dozen.'[112]

Not only was Hudal active in escape aid, he also intervened several times in war crimes trials. On 10 September 1946 he issued a denazification certificate for General Kurt Mältzer, the former Stadtkommandant of Rome, on the grounds that Mältzer had always treated his prisoners well.[113] The General was jointly responsible for the shooting of 335 Italian hostages in March 1944. This was a reprisal for the killing of thirty-three German soldiers in Via Rasella in Rome. In 1951 similarly, Hudal asked US President Harry S. Truman for support for former German Foreign

Minister Konstantin von Neurath.[114] Hudal also often defended former members of the Waffen-SS, and in 1946 he wrote to the British Commander of Terni prisoner-of-war camp: 'In the last years of the war, membership of the so-called Waffen-SS no longer meant anything special.'[115] Hudal also campaigned in the name of Germany and, thus, semi-officially for the German prisoners of war and interned war criminals in Italy. Until 1951 he administrated a fund of his own for this. With the foundation of West Germany (FRG) and the opening of a German General Consulate in Rome, however, Hudal had to call this off. In a cordial letter in June 1951, Eberhard Rotberg of the Federal Justice Ministry thanked him for the bishop's support for his compatriots.[116] Then Hudal turned directly to German Federal Chancellor Konrad Adenauer, asking for commitment and support for the interned war criminals.[117] Hudal's advocacy knew no bounds.

For his work on their behalf, former Nazis thanked the bishop and held him in high regard. A dedication 'To his Excellency, the Most Reverend Bishop Dr Alois Hudal in Honour and Gratitude', found on the back of a postcard, attests to this. One Johannes P. Greil had written it at the advent of the New Year in 1949. Greil chose a motif from the Holy Year 1950: a radial cross rising from the cupola of St Peter's, cutting through barbed wire. The drawing picked up a favourite idea of Hudal's: the 'Holy Year' was to serve as an opportunity to save perpetrators from persecution and imprisonment through a general amnesty. Three years later, on 4 March 1953, Greil sent another few lines: 'Esteemed Excellency! General Remer, the well-known man of 20 July 1944, is staying temporarily in Rome, and asks you whether you would find a visit from him agreeable. PS: The gentlemen are travelling incognito!' In right-wing circles, Otto Ernst Remer is 'the well-known man of the twentieth of July'. The young major, commander of the Berlin Guard Battalion, had been ordered to arrest Joseph Goebbels after the planned Stauffenberg putsch. But Goebbels persuaded him to phone Hitler, who promoted Remer to colonel on the spot and ordered the arrest of the conspirators. Remer, who was still following Hitler obediently in July 1944, was a major general at the end of the war. On 4 December 1954, after he had been in hiding in Italy, Greil announced some good news: 'Reverend Excellency! I spent most of this year in northern Italy. Every now and again I visited Germany, risking my neck each time. But at least these excursions were not a waste of time.

At last I have all the papers required to make the leap to South America.'[118] Greil planned to leave Rome and embark a few days later from Genoa on the *Corrientes* for Buenos Aires. He cheerfully wrote:

> I shall allow myself, rocking on the waves of the Atlantic, to empty a little bottle on this New Year's night to your Rev. Excellency. But I am also moved, Rev. Excellency, to say a thousand words of thanks for all your kindness and help, which you have so generously given me over the past six years. Where would I be today, if I had not, in times of serious need, been able to creep beneath your Rev. Excellency's protective wings.[119]

No petitioner for help had to conceal his Nazi past from Hudal. On 26 March 1948 Walther Ottowitz from Graz applied for a Red Cross travel document in Rome, giving his original nationality as 'Austrian', currently 'stateless'. But as an Austrian, he was obliged to provide evidence for his supposed statelessness to the Red Cross. Here his compatriot, Bishop Hudal, was very helpful. In a solemn declaration, Ottowitz stated that he had been a member of the Austrian Legion. He had joined the NSDAP and the SA as early as 1932, and in 1934, after the failed Nazi putsch in Austria, had fled to Bavaria. As an illegal Nazi activist, he was expatriated by the Austrian government in 1936; after the end of the war, his nationality was not restored. Ottowitz's declaration was confirmed by Hudal with the official 'Anima' seal. Hudal went on to confirm, in Ottowitz's favour, 'that for political reasons he is ineligible, as a former member of the illegal Legion, for either an Austrian or a German passport, and should thus be seen as a person without nationality'. The Vatican relief commission in Rome accordingly classified Ottowitz as 'ex-Austrian, stateless'. At last the former Nazi could emigrate to Argentina.[120] Unlike the details of Ottowitz's case, those relating to Josef Schwammberger's escape to South America are still unclear. Even decades later, Schwammberger remained silent about having gone into hiding abroad. When being questioned by chief prosecutor Kurt Schrimm he said only, 'The Pope paid for my journey to South America.'[121] He may have been referring to the help he received from Bishop Hudal and the papal relief organization for refugees.

While the Vatican had endured Hudal's assistance to Nazi fugitives and war criminals, once that assistance became public, it was forced to act. The case of SS Sturmbannführer Otto Gustav Wächter, who was responsible for war crimes in Cracow and eastern Galicia, brought the issue to a head. Wächter was staying—thanks to Hudal—in Rome. Wächter, from Vienna, was one of the leading Nazis in Austria, and he had been involved in the failed Nazi putsch of 1934. From January 1942 he occupied the office of governor of the District of Galicia, and at the end of the war he went into hiding in Rome, where in 1949 he died in his monastery hiding place.[122] After Wächter's death, Italian newspapers reported for the first time on the assistance that Hudal gave the former governor of Galicia as he tried to make his escape.[123] In response, Hudal repeatedly and defiantly justified his support for Wächter:

> Along with Italian priests, I took on Lieutenant General Wächter, who was seriously ill, and if I found myself in a similar situation again, I would do exactly the same thing, but with greater devotion, love, and courage, because in these sad times of ours, filled with injustices that cry out to heaven, I see the priest's great and holy vocation as being a helping angel of love, reconciliation and mercy, prepared to put his own life on the line.[124]

Hudal's behaviour in the Wächter case and the press reactions to it were not without consequences. He was summoned by Monsignor Montini in the papal Secretariat of State, who is said to have expressed his disapproval with the words, 'A Nazi bishop must not defend himself!'[125] But Hudal was unbending: 'I told Monsignor Montini: "If what I did in the Wächter case does not represent Christianity, and heroic Christianity at that, I have been wrong in choosing this religion." '[126] This open defiance of his superior contributed to the end of Hudal's refugee mission.

On 3 February 1950 Monsignor Baldelli laconically informed Bishop Hudal of the Austrian committee that it had been decided for financial reasons to dissolve some committees, including the Austrian one—as there were no longer any 'true and actual refugees'.[127] Hudal thus no longer had the Church's blessing for his refugee assistance. But even after this clear signal from the Vatican, he failed to read the signs of the times.

Pope Pius XII skilfully and publicly distanced himself from the Nazi-tainted Hudal in order to avoid any awkward situations. But he did nothing about Hudal's commitment to former National Socialists: 'If Monsignor Hudal wishes to help needy Germans in Rome and Italy, he should do so, but in his own name and his own expense; the Anima certainly has considerable funds at its disposal,' he replied to an application from Hudal as early as November 1944.[128] Bishop Jakob Weinbacher, Hudal's successor at the Anima and an acknowledged opponent of the Nazis, refers to the once-close relationship between Hudal and the Pope:

> Bishop Hudal was very close to Pope Pius XII—there is no doubt of that; they were friends. I talked a lot with him and this certainly emerged very clearly. But he never spoke about the things he did after the war. He was...well, perhaps 'secretive' is too strong a word, but certainly he was very discreet about it; he didn't like to talk about it at all. One knew his political position, of course, so one was careful.[129]

But in Rome everyone knew that Hudal was supplying refugees with visas, travel documents, and denazification certificates. Weinbacher went on, 'I think he also helped other people, but there is no doubt that among those he eventually assisted were a great many of the Nazi higher-ups.'[130] With the liberation of Rome by the Allies in 1944, Hudal slowly lost more and more influence with the Pope as the church leadership 'discovered' Western democracy. The pro-Nazi attitude of the 'German bishop' in Rome was probably the essential reason for complaints to the Pope from the Austrian bishops.[131] Pius XII knew about the accusations against Hudal and likely would not have dropped his former protégé if he had not become a liability for the Church.

All the other national committees of the PCA worked in a similar way; Bishop Hudal was, with his attitude and the assistance he gave to SS men and war criminals, by no means an exception. Unlike others, however, he repeatedly boasted publicly, even in the mass media, about his actions, which damaged the standing of the Church. Hudal thus became an irritant in the context of the Vatican mission. Cardinal Michael Faulhaber, Archbishop of Munich and temporary vice-rector of the Anima, even referred to his episcopal colleague as 'court theologian of the NSDAP',[132] even though he himself had for a long time maintained bridges between fascism and the Church. After 1945, however, he changed his position and distanced himself from Hudal.[133] The Wächter case was the final straw. The Italian press reported at length on Hudal's refugee assistance: the events could no longer be hushed up. Pope Pius XII, Under-Secretary of State Montini, and the Austrian bishops no longer saw keeping their compromised colleague in the national Church in Rome as sustainable.[134] In April 1951 the Austrian bishops requested that Bishop Hudal step down.[135] After his demission in 1952—he supposedly left the building by the back door—he retired to his little villa in Grottaferrata near Rome.[136] After being stripped of his post as rector of the Anima, he grew visibly bitter, but remained loyal to his original idea: an association of Christianity and National Socialism.[137] Bishop Hudal died in Rome on 13 May 1963. The Catholic historian Ludwig Volk rightly described Hudal's memoirs, in which he once again set out his whole vision of the world, as the document of a stubborn rejection of reality and a frightening level of obstinacy.[138]

4. The Monsignor and the Croatian Fascists

Bishop Hudal was by no means an isolated example of a Catholic priest helping Nazis flee justice. Another prominent example was the above-mentioned Croatian Father Krunoslav Draganović. He helped Croatian fascists, as well as many well-known Nazi war criminals, to escape. The report of an American agent in Rome reads:

> Many of the more prominent Ustaša war criminals and Quislings are living in Rome illegally, many of them under false names. Their cells are still maintained, their papers still published, and their intelligence agencies still in operation. All this activity seems to stem from the Vatican, through the Monastery of San Geronimo to Fermo, the Chief Croat Camp in Italy. Chief among the intelligence operatives in the Monastery of San Geronimo appear to be Dr. Draganović and Monsignor Madjarac [Magjerec].[139]

Monsignor Draganović was an imposing presence: tall and dark; always dressed in a long cassock, a flowing cloak, and a wide-brimmed priest's hat, he looked grim and sinister. Draganović had studied theology and philosophy in Sarajevo, where he received very strong support from the Archbishop Ivan Sarić. Sarić sent his protégé first to Budapest and then, in 1932, to Rome, where Draganović graduated from the Pontifical Gregorian University in 1935.[140] In 1941 the Fascist Ustaša party had set up a vassal state in Croatia under German control which was headed by the fascist leader Ante Pavelić. Soon afterwards, Draganović was promoted to a leading role in the Colonization Office in

Zagreb. The militant Catholic nationalism of the Croatian fascists made church people natural allies of the Pavelić government.

For the theologian Draganović, the Pavelić state was 'a wonderful decision of divine providence', 'which allowed a free and independent Croatia to return to existence after eight centuries'. Ustaša priest Draganović also found that one other area of the Yugoslavian landscape was deeply Catholic and needed to be evangelized accordingly: Bosnia, in the south of the country.[141] Within a year the Ustaša government had half a million Orthodox Serbs from Bosnia-Herzegovina murdered. Draganović admired the dictator Pavelić as a 'torchbearer of freedom', but he was troubled by the horrors in Croatia—or so he said later.[142] In 1943 he joined the Ustaša delegation in the Vatican as an intermediary and moved to the Collegio di San Girolamo degli Illirici, the Croatian National College of San Girolamo on Via Tomacelli. This institution was founded in 1901; it served as a home for pilgrims and students, represented the Croatian church to the Pope, and had a leading role in the Catholic mission of Croatia and Bosnia-Herzegovina.[143]

After the defeat of Yugoslavia and the foundation of the fascist state of Croatia in 1941, the leadership of the College adopted the new line of the Ustaša government, and the policy of the Yugoslavian mission was provided by Father Draganović. Matters concerning refugee assistance for Croatians were coordinated by a special 'confraternity' at the national College. The Confraternity of San Girolamo was founded in July 1945 within the context of the Vatican, but was probably never officially recognized. The confraternity derived its recognition from its association with an established college. In this way, the Croatian priests were able to work with the authority and under the protection of the Vatican. The Institute's official task was only to supply refugee relief for Croatians in the immediate post-war years. This included legal support for residents' permits, accommodations, issues relating to study, and letters of recommendation; the Confraternity was particularly keen to maintain contact with the PCA, and finally became associated with it, enabling it to assist fleeing Croatians, some of whom were war criminals.

At the end of the Second World War, Croatian refugees fled the revenge of Tito's partisans and sought refuge and aid in Austria and Italy. The US military listed a total of 475 leading Croatian Ustaša men who were living in Italy in 1946 and were wanted for war crimes in Yugoslavia. Rome soon became a safe haven for particularly tainted fascists from the Pavelić state. According to US sources, more than thirty leading Ustaša officials had sought refuge in the Monastery of San Girolamo alone, while other wanted war criminals were in hiding in Catholic monasteries or church institutions in the wider Italian metropolis. Archbishop Sarić, an ardent admirer of the Pavelić state, found refuge in the Oriental Institute in the Vatican. The reaction to the Ustaša state's war crimes was restricted to a protest at a diplomatic level. Senior circles in the Vatican all the way up to the Pope had contact with Ustaša leaders, many of them representatives of the Catholic Church in Croatia. So it is hard to imagine that the top levels of the Vatican knew nothing of the presence and outward transfer of Croatian war criminals and Ustaša officers. For the US authorities in Italy, the motivation for church support and the—at least passive—attitude of the Vatican lay without a doubt in the 'anti-Communist attitude of these men':

> Draganović's sponsorship of these Croat Quislings definitely links him up with the plan of the Vatican to shield these ex-Ustaša nationalists until such time as they are able to procure for them the proper documents to enable them to go to South America. The Vatican, undoubtedly banking on the strong anti-communist feelings of these men, is endeavouring to infiltrate them into South America in any way possible to counteract the spread of Red doctrine.[144]

Even during the war, Pope Pius XII and his closest colleagues—Under-Secretaries of State Montini and Tardini—had met with representatives of the Ustaša government, including the fascist leader Pavelić himself. In 1941 Pavelić set about winning recognition for his 'independent Croatian state' from the Vatican. During the genocide of Serbs and Jews in the Balkans, the Vatican had drawn up lists of Catholic priests who had been involved and wanted them to face up to their responsibility. But the assumption of power by Tito's communist troops changed these plans. For Pius XII, this was no longer the time to deal with fascism, but to take energetic action against communism.

The US government had other ideas at first. It hoped to be able to arrest escaping prisoners of war and hand them over to Yugoslavia. The Cold War had not yet begun, and the war coalitions and the accords reached at war conferences still held, even though the first cracks were showing. Above all, the Americans wanted to get their hands on the leader of the Croatian fascists, Ante Pavelić, who had been in hiding in Austria and Italy since the end of the war. Had he been handed over to the Yugoslavian government, the Americans would have found it easier to push through their own demands. Allied intelligence services were aware that many Ustaša refugees were staying in the large complex of the San Girolamo Monastery in Rome. But the game of hide-and-seek with fake papers and the special status of church institutions remained in operation until the start of the Cold War brought Allied efforts to arrest the Croatian war criminals to an end. Pavelić and other leading fascists were finally able to leave for Argentina.[145]

With the end of the Ustaša regime and the arrival of thousands of Croatian refugees in Italy, Draganović saw that his hour had come: the Croatian College of San Girolamo in Rome became the hub of his activities against the communist regime in Belgrade. One US intelligence report from 1947 describes Draganović's activity very precisely. Draganović's National College 'is guarded by armed Ustashi youths in civilian clothes and the Ustashi salute is exchanged continually'. Several ministers and senior officers of the Ustaša government hid at least temporarily in the Monastery of San Girolamo at 132 via Tomacelli in Rome: Deputy Foreign Minister Vjekoslav Vrancić, Finance Minister Dragutin Toth, Education Minister Mile Starcević, General Dragutin Rupćić, Propaganda Minister Djordge Perić, General Vilko Pečnikar of the Ustaša gendarmerie, Air Force Commander Vladimir Kren, and Head of State Ante Pavelić.[146] It had not escaped the notice of US intelligence services that Ustaša war criminals had been allowed to travel abroad with fake papers and with the help of Vatican offices. 'Because of the Vatican's involvement in the hiding of war criminals', the information was to be secured in the safe of the US military intelligence service in Rome. Not even the British authorities were to be informed of the Vatican's involvement.[147]

Early in 1947 the US authorities still wanted to arrest Pavelić 'as soon as he leaves Vatican soil'.[148] But, in the end, they decided not to intervene because the political conditions had changed.[149] In March 1947 President Truman pledged the United States to the worldwide resistance of communism in a pioneering speech that entered history as the

Truman Doctrine. The CIA was founded in July 1947. The US information services now urgently needed experts in Eastern Europe and engaged fascists, including Draganović, to provide that expertise. The US historian Michael Phayer has examined these relationships in depth and reaches the conclusion: 'Not by accident did Ante Pavelić gain "hands off" status in July 1947, the date marks the year and the month of U.S. and papal convergence regarding war criminals.'[150] The Cold War had reached Italy. The year 1947 marks a turning point in the American attitude towards fleeing fascists. The tracing of Nazi perpetrators and collaborators by the US intelligence services, at first performed consistently and with great success, was abandoned in 1947/8.[151] In Phayer's words: 'The Holy See and the United States began the post-War era in totally divergent positions regarding fugitive refugees, but by the summer of 1947 they had converged onto the same course.'[152]

In December 1948 the CIC reported the arrival of Pavelić in Buenos Aires. According to the CIC, he had entered the country under a false name with an ICRC travel document. His first contacts, his discussions in Argentina with former Ustaša officers, were reported in detail to Washington by the US intelligence services.[153]

The activity of the Croatian Confraternity began very promisingly in 1945, its purposes largely charitable, although in conflict with those of the Allies. At first Draganović protested to the Tito government against the extradition of Croatians. He wrote a large number of memoranda and interceded with Allied offices in Italy, President Harry Truman, and US Foreign Minister Dean Acheson. His primary commitment was to the Ustaša, including a considerable number of war criminals. The Allies differentiated between two kinds of crime: crimes against humanity and political crimes such as collaboration with the Germans and treason. Italy's peace treaty with the Allies committed the Italians to taking the steps required to catch war criminals and hand them over to the relevant courts. In the case of crimes against humanity, Draganović also committed himself to the pursuit of perpetrators because they needed to be punished. As regards political crimes, he saw things quite differently: 'What is a traitor?' Draganović placed this question firmly at the centre of his argument.[154]

Whatever his motivations, Draganović saved those he helped from a grim fate, and the behaviour of the Yugoslavian government eventually convinced the Allies not to extradite Yugoslav refugees. The Yugoslavian government repeatedly demanded the extradition of Croatians, whether supposed or actual war criminals. It saw the refugees and their families solely as 'traitors' who were to be condemned quickly and across the board. At first the Allies' desires matched those of the Tito government, and they handed over Yugoslavs who had fought in German units. In May 1945 the British repatriated Yugoslavians who had been on the German side: Serbian Chetniks, Slovenian Domobranci—and Croatian Ustaša. In the town of Bleiburg/Pliberk and other places in southern Carinthia, Tito's communists accepted tens of thousands of collaborators, but also civilians, women, and children who had fled with them. On their return, during the marches to the prisoner-of-war camps, thousands of prisoners were massacred.[155] Tito's government also took action against senior Catholic dignitaries. The most famous example is Alojzije Stepinać, the archbishop and primate of Croatia. He was a convinced Croatian nationalist, so at first he also greeted the 'Independent Croatia' under its leader Pavelić. In 1946 Stepinać was sentenced to sixteen years' imprisonment in a trial that was severely criticized, above all by the Vatican. The Stepinać trial suddenly drew the world's attention to anti-church measures in Yugoslavia. In 1946/7 the Vatican informed the US government several times about arrests, camp detentions, and murders of priests. Draganović was considered to be a confidant of Stepinać and shared his hatred of the communists and Yugoslavian nationalism. The United States soon came to see Cardinal Stepinać as a martyr of freedom. His past as an advocate of the Pavelić regime was not an obstacle.

Thus Draganović, the former Croatian Ustaša priest in exile, was able to rely on the sympathy of the US authorities in Italy.[156] Immediately after the end of the war, the Croatian Confraternity could only take action against the extraditions within severe limits. Above all they requested information, documented the fate of those extradited, and demanded a fair judicial process for the accused. In the first months after the war, the bulk of Yugoslavian collaborators were taken to Yugoslavia, but a considerable number of Croatians managed to stay in Austria and Italy. Most of the refugees were in Italian camps and tried to stay there for as long as possible. On an exploratory tour of the camps in June 1945, Draganović estimated that there were some 15,000 Croatian refugees. In many ways, this fact brought the special situation of the Croats to the attention of the US ambassador in Rome. The president of the Croatian Confraternity informed the Vatican of Draganović's reports and received authorization for financial help. The money was to be distributed in the ratio of 60 per cent for the Croatians, 30 per cent for the Slovenians, and 10 per cent for the Serbs. The Croatians in exile in the United States were also asked for donations.[157]

The Croatian Confraternity also directly organized the emigration of the Croats. Argentina soon became their destination of choice because it already had a large Croatian community numbering around 130,000 people. But potential emigrants still faced considerable obstacles. The Argentinians preferred Spanish and Italian immigrants, mostly young workers and unmarried women under the age of 28, as well as skilled German workers, army officers, and engineers. Visa applications had to be made in person to the Argentinian Embassy in Rome. This was hardly possible for people in refugee camps. Draganović desperately wanted to assist the Croatian refugees in Austria through his efforts, but the length of the journey from Austria to Rome and the border controls did not make this any easier. In spite of all the difficulties, in 1947 the 'Emigration Office' set up work in the monastery. Draganović's many contacts with the Argentinian consulate, US officials, and the Italian authorities meant that his work was very successful. He sent lists of names to the Argentinians, and this meant that his protégés no longer had to appear at the embassy in person. By 1951 the monks had helped some 30,000 Croatians to emigrate, 20,000 of them overseas.

Draganović sometimes procured travel documents via the IRO, which had been set up by the United Nations in 1948 for the resettlement of Displaced Persons and was, therefore, responsible for victims of Hitler's war, not for Nazi war criminals and fascists. But Draganović had 'his man' in the IRO office, an American who transferred identity documents to him over a period of several years.[158] It was only when this man lost his nerve that Draganović had to turn to the International Red Cross, though not to its central office in Rome, where people were rather suspicious of him, but to the branch of the Red Cross in the port city of Genoa.[159] Here, at the suggestion of the 40-year-old new archbishop of Genoa, Giuseppe Siri, a special division of the papal relief mission had been formed; it bore the significant name 'Auxilium' on its letterhead and ran its own Centro Nazionale Emigrazione Argentina. Archbishop Siri stayed in close contact with Draganović and Karl

Petranović in Genoa. Siri's appointment was welcomed by antifascists because he negotiated the capitulation of German units in Genoa at the end of the war. He also campaigned during Mussolini's rule for Jewish citizens in his diocese and condemned the racial teaching of National Socialism.[160] Draganović went in and out of Siri's 'Auxilium' relief organization; in delicate cases, he also procured Bishop Hudal's 'recommendation'. In the Red Cross office and the Latin American consulates, all that was needed was Draganović's signature, even when it was confirming false names.[161] The head of the Croatian Red Cross in Italy also referred to the good services of university professor Draganović in Rome. As early as March 1946 US intelligence services reported on the Croatians:

> When Tito formed the Yugoslav Federation, the heads of the so called independent Croatian state fled and the majority of them are in Italy. Many of these people are considered as criminals of war. The 'Confraternita Croata' issues identity cards with false names even to these war criminals who with these false papers manage to evade arresting authorities. There are seven members of the board of directors of this organization. They are Don Krunoslav Draganović—secretary—actually the most important person in the fraternity...[162]

Draganović and his Croatians worked tirelessly, visiting refugee camps, intervening on behalf of Croatian refugees and prisoners of war, and procuring travel documents.[163] Draganović had close contacts with the Italian authorities, especially senior officials in the Italian domestic intelligence service and the branch of the police dealing with foreigners. They were not to get in the way of the emigration of refugees. The secret emigration channels began in Austria, where Father Vilim Cecelja acted as intermediary with Rome. Until 1944 Cecelja worked as military chaplain to the Ustaša militias and was a close confidant of Pavelić.[164] Then he returned to Salzburg, in and around which many war criminals and SS men were in hiding at the end of the war. Upon their arrival in Salzburg, the refugees received new documents, including Red Cross travel papers, accommodations, and financial support. After making previous arrangements, Cecelja sent precisely predetermined contingents of people to Draganović, arranging for them to stay at various monasteries on the way. The crucial destination for their outbound journey was Genoa, where they were looked after by another

Croatian cleric, Monsignor Karlo Petranović. Draganović regularly phoned Petranović to tell him how many seats he needed for passengers on the transatlantic steamers. But Petranović had only to organize the necessary number of seats and welcome the outbound passengers in Genoa.[165]

On denazification documents and applications of the best-known war criminals and the 'most sensitive cases', Draganović's signature repeatedly appears. There is a great deal of evidence to suggest that Draganović knew very well who he was helping to escape. Imam Omrcanin, a close confidant of Hudal and Draganović in Genoa, was, like Draganović, an activist in the Croatian nationalist cause. Asked about his contacts with Hudal and Draganović, he said in an interview: 'Whenever I saw Draganović or Hudal, it was mostly to discuss things. I was helping them, or they were giving me advice. I fought for Europe, and didn't want Europe to have to suffer so much.'[166] Omrcanin gives a detailed account of the escape routes and Draganović's good contacts with the Americans, who were interested in gathering information from refugees from the Soviet empire.[167] Among the prominent perpetrators that Draganović helped to escape was the Nazi criminal Gerhard Bohne, who had provided the organizational and formal legal framework for the euthanasia programme. After the war he escaped to Italy and applied for a Red Cross travel document in Rome in August 1948. Here he used the name Hans Bohne, describing himself as 'stateless'. As his profession, Bohne gave 'lawyer', and he described himself as Catholic. While he was waiting in Rome, Bohne hid in the bolt-hole used by Draganović's refugees at 27 Via dei Glicini. As his destination Bohne gave 'Argentina'; his details were confirmed by the Croatian Confraternity, and Draganović personally signed and stamped Bohne's application to the Red Cross. Bohne was successful: as early as 27 August 1948, he was given an ICRC travel document in Genoa.[168] Frau Gisela Bohne also applied, along with her husband, for an ICRC travel document in Rome in August 1948.[169]

After the death of Rector Magjerec, the Confraternity abandoned refugee aid, although without officially dissolving, and Draganović had to adapt to the changing times. When Pope John XXIII was striving for a better relationship with Yugoslavia in the early 1960s, Draganović had to clear his home in the Croatian College and rent rooms in the city like a private individual.[170] He had probably become too exposed and threatened to become a burden to the church leadership. Paul VI continued his policy of détente, and Draganović left for Austria, having assumed that country's nationality in Salzburg in 1956. In June 1966 the Vatican signed a treaty with Tito's Yugoslavia, committing the Holy See to take canon law proceedings against any clerics who abused their church position with political intent to the detriment of Socialist Yugoslavia. After this ceasefire between the Catholics and the Yugoslavian communists, men such as Draganović had no option but to wage a private war. In this, he could rely on the help of the United States.

The US intelligence community saw Draganović as a useful contact. In 1947 the CIC had already wooed Draganović and utilized him as one of the main people behind the US intelligence service's 'ratline' in Italy. This collaboration between US federal agents and a former fascist was not exceptional in the post-war years, but rather a symptom of the moral equivocation of the US intelligence services during the Cold War. In the early Cold War, the Monsignor was happy to make his services available to the Americans because this collaboration gave him invaluable support for his relief work for his Croatian compatriots. Draganović also received a generous emolument for his CIC services so that he was, in turn, able to help other refugees, mostly of Croatian nationality. After he was thrown out of the monastery of San Girolamo in 1959, the Americans came to his aid once more. He was again approached by the American intelligence service in Italy, this time by a new generation of agents, but his duties were generally the same as before: procuring military information about Yugoslavia. By this point, Draganović was no longer an excellent source because he had not seen his homeland since 1943 and certainly did not have the requisite contacts with the country's new elite. Nevertheless, he managed to persuade his American partners of his indispensability and the size of his supposedly large Croatian spy network in Italy. The CIC agents in Italy thus knew from the start with whom they were dealing. This seems not to have troubled them in the slightest. Thus Draganović financed his own private crusade with CIC funds and got hold of money and arms for guerrilla raids.[171]

But suddenly Draganović vanished from sight for a number of weeks. On 10 November 1967 the Yugoslavian state attorney declared that Draganović was in Sarajevo—as a free man.[172] On 15 November

1967 he even gave a press interview. Escorted by five policemen, the priest-politician said: 'I have voluntarily returned to my old homeland, to submit my case to the relevant court.' Draganović seems to have been cooperative, lest he lose his life. The Yugoslavians accepted his attitude—they were hoping for information. Moreover, they wanted to escape the stain of being kidnappers. But the cleric, experienced as he was in guerrilla fighting, made sure to leave two envelopes, one with a priest and another with a lawyer. In his statements he wrote that he was aware of being 'constantly exposed to the danger of murder or abduction by Titoist agents and spies'; Krunoslav Draganović assured his readers that 'whatever I should declare or write or sign, if I should fall into the hands of the Communist Yugoslavian police, it must all be considered as being against my free will and against my innermost conviction'.[173]

International diplomats correctly assessed the situation and predicted its likely conclusion. The Austrian government took a particular interest in the Draganović case because he had for some years been an Austrian citizen. The well-informed Austrian ambassador in Yugoslavia was happy to advise the US Embassy in Belgrade about this delicate matter. At last the Austrian diplomats reached this conclusion: 'Draganovic apparently learned in Rome that the Church no longer approves what he had been doing among the emigres, but could not face returning to Austria to live among them while refusing to lead them. Therefore, he sought to make a deal with the Yugoslav authorities that would permit his return here.'[174] Draganović was supposed to 'tell all' in Communist Yugoslavia, name his colleagues and like-minded people, hand his archive over to Tito's agents, and make some positive remarks about Communist Yugoslavia. In return, Belgrade would waive judicial condemnation and imprisonment. The priest-politician was to disappear quietly into a monastery. The Austrian diplomats were quite correct with this assessment. The priest's half-voluntary return made big waves internationally. Soon afterwards, however, things quietened down around Draganović. Shortly before going to ground in Yugoslavia, Draganović gave his assessment of his nation and himself:

> The Croatian nation is a people of pariahs in this world, through no fault of our own. And for many I am one of the worst representatives of this pariah nation, although I had neither the position nor the time, was

unimportant and bear no guilt. I have not deserved this contempt either.
In all my unhappiness, this is the one thing that makes me happy.[175]

He died in Yugoslavia in 1983, without experiencing the end of Tito's regime.[176]

5. The Role of the Church in South Tyrol

When La Vista's report reached Washington, the monasteries of the Italian peninsula were all crammed with emigrants. From 1945 well into the 1950s, a stream of Central and Eastern European nationals wishing to emigrate illegally reached the Italian ports via church organizations, giving many the impression that the Pope himself had issued the relevant protection order. Church organizations shielded escapees and hid some of them for years.[177] The Catholic Church helped—not officially, but very effectively. South Tyrol was the first stop from Germany and Austria on the escape route to Rome or Genoa. The Diocese of Brixen provides a good picture of the existing escape networks and of the motives that incited some members of the Catholic clergy to help Nazis to escape. The chief motivations of these clerics were probably the same as those that animated Hudal and Draganović: a fervent anticommunism and a desire for religious renewal. The national question and a strong feeling of solidarity with Germans in South Tyrol also played a central role. The Bishop of Brixen, Johannes Geisler, his Vicar General Alois Pompanin, and some of his clergy were to take an active part in escape assistance. Some prominent figures of the Church in South Tyrol were very heavily involved in making this borderland a place of refuge for Nazis. These connections, however, were officially hushed up. Today, one even discerns a trend to heroize the players in this recent history of the diocese.

The Nazi era is indeed known by local church historians as a dark period, and Bishop Geisler's attitude is recognized as an error, but the generous level of damage control is extremely interesting.[178] The emphasis is clearly on anti-Nazi resistance by individual members of the Church in South Tyrol; thus the clergy's degree of complicity is significantly minimized.[179] Bishop Geisler's biographer Josef Gelmi writes: 'Immediately after the war, Prince-Bishop Geisler was fully committed to the population under pressure by the Italians. His commitment extended to the emigrants in South Tyrol and to all those affected by the war.'[180] On the Church's escape assistance, the historian limits himself to a few remarks: 'After the war various senior Nazis stayed in South Tyrol and found support, not least in church circles.'[181] Gelmi also mentions the rebaptism of SS Hauptsturmführer Erich Priebke in 1948, on the instructions of the Bishop of Brixen, and concludes his brief digression with this rather cryptic sentence: '[After 1945] Geisler also repeatedly wrote petitions for persecuted individuals.'[182] Who these 'persecuted individuals' might have been after the end of the Nazi regime remains an open question. Were these people persecuted by the Allies and the democratic Italian government? The extent of the involvement of some senior church officials, not least in the Diocese of Brixen, possibly falls under this unconvincing blanket clause. At the same time, the Diocese refuses to allow access to its archives for the period after 1939. More research needs to be done and sinister aspects of the situation and the excessively forgiving attitude of the Church in Brixen after 1945 should not be ignored. The German Anima church in Rome opened Bishop Hudal's archives; the Diocese of Brixen should follow this example.

The Diocese of Brixen was on the escape route through the Brenner Pass, and although in Italy, it was run spiritually and administratively by a German-speaking clergy. Vicar General Pompanin in particular had a great influence on Bishop Geisler. Pompanin was born in 1889 in Cortina d'Ampezzo. He finished his secondary school studies at the Vinzentinum in Brixen and with the Franciscans in Bolzano, then studied in Rome and Innsbruck. During the First World War, he became a priest. It was then that he developed his 'antipathy to all things Italian and love of everything to do with Germany'.[183] In 1933 Pompanin was appointed Vicar General to Prince-Bishop Geisler and gained firm control of the diocese. Pompanin was able to make the most important decisions in the diocese by himself and to persuade Bishop Geisler to go along with him. In fact, important letters were often written by Pompanin and then signed by Geisler.[184]

A man of great intellectual abilities, Pompanin embodied the type of enthusiastic German nationalist who made little distinction between National Socialism and Catholicism. He was anti-Italian and pro-Nazi. While studying in Rome at the German-Austrian Anima church, he was strongly influenced by the ideas of the rector, Alois Hudal.[185]

Pompanin and Hudal were not personally close, although 'they may have had closer contact in political matters'.[186]

Pompanin was not a 'Hitler-worshipper', as was often claimed, but he did fight resolutely for all things German and opposed the forces trying to undermine the German language and culture in South Tyrol. He deeply resented Italy's annexation of South Tyrol in 1920 and experienced it as a moment of profound impotence. His anti-Italian attitude later extended to Bishop Geisler, who had tried to find a modus vivendi with the Italian fascists before Pompanin came on the scene. In 1939 Hitler and Mussolini decided to solve the 'South Tyrol Problem' by resettling the population in the 'Third Reich'. According to the 'Option' proposed to them, the South Tyroleans had to choose between either accepting German nationality or keeping their Italian citizenship.[187] After opting for German citizenship, they were to emigrate to Germany. On the other hand, choosing Italian nationality involved the risk of forced Italianization. Pompanin argued for a strong German nationalist line among the clergy and encouraged allegiance to Hitler's Germany.

While the clergy generally sympathized with the authoritarian Catholic corporate state of Austria, a gulf began to form when the 'Option' was proposed in 1939, and clergy and church leadership in Brixen slowly drifted apart. Pope Pius XI's 1937 encyclical 'Mit brennender Sorge' against violations of the Concordat by the Third Reich could not be read out in the Diocese of Brixen, unlike in the neighbouring diocese of Trento. Geisler and Pompanin did not welcome open criticism of the Nazi regime by the Vatican.[188] The Bishop of Trento, for his part, shared the Pope's scepticism about the National Socialists. In his encyclical, Pius XI clearly criticized National Socialism, also its racial doctrine: the Nazi leaders were 'like enemies of humanity', and there was even talk of a battle to the death by the National Socialists against the Church. But in South Tyrol, the wheel of history was turning in a different direction.

The special situation in South Tyrol incited Nazi leaders to avoid openly confronting the Church, which was seen as an ally in the struggle for German identity in the region. Even leading representatives of the Nazi movement in South Tyrol still described themselves as 'Catholic' in 1943. For this reason, one South Tyrolean SS Obersturmführer justified himself to the SS superiors in Berlin: 'Because of the difficult

political-religious conditions in South Tyrol, at the request of the Volksgruppenführer and with the knowledge of the Reich Commissariat for
the Consolidation of German Ethnicity, I have long refrained from
publicly leaving the Church [...].'[189]

The question of nationality made the church leadership in the Diocese of Brixen an ally of 'a strong Germany' and, thus, of the Hitler
regime. Most of the clergy in South Tyrol, on the other hand, initially
saw Nazi ideology as their chief enemy. For example, one South
Tyrolean Franciscan priest publicly declared that there were no compromises to be made between National Socialism and Catholicism:
'They are deadly enemies. National Socialism is the work of the
devil.'[190] But after the battle of Stalingrad in 1943, a certain change of
attitude occurred within the Church: recalling the Spanish Civil War
when the clergy had sided solidly with Franco against the 'atheist-
Bolshevik' republicans, some priests now thought it appropriate to
consider a partial and temporary collaboration with the Nazi regime—
nolens volens—in order to 'resist the Bolshevik threat and save the
Christian West.'[191] In May 1945 they found themselves facing a completely new situation: the collapse of the Nazi regime left a vacuum in
South Tyrol as well. In spite of its partial compromise with German
National Socialism and Italian fascism, the Church won new legitimi-
zation from the failure of Nazi policy towards South Tyrol. By falling
back on traditional values and old structures, the Church's influence
was strengthened in every area.[192]

Contacts between Hudal, Pompanin, and Geisler also provide clues
to the attitude of the church leadership in Brixen. Hudal maintained
close contacts with South Tyrol, always presenting himself as an advocate of German culture.[193] The 'German bishop in Rome' supposedly
even wanted to become Bishop of Brixen after Geisler's retirement in
1951—a hopeless undertaking for the Austrian, though he considered
himself a 'great friend of South Tyrol' and had the support of Vicar
Pompanin.[194] One great concern of Hudal's was the release of prisoners
of war and amnesty for war criminals. He suggested to Monsignor
Montini that the Vatican should endorse a general amnesty for German soldiers.[195] Montini replied that the Holy Father would welcome
an 'extensive amnesty', but that the German clergy had a different attitude.[196] Hudal also championed an amnesty with his colleague in
Brixen. In spite of the public influence of Pompanin, however, Bishop

Geisler was not ready to assume an unambiguous position. In October 1949 Alfons Ludwig of the Institut Johanneum near Merano, on the explicit instructions of Hudal, inquired into the attitude of the Bishop of Brixen. Geisler was supposed to support Hudal's call for a general amnesty for Nazis, but Hudal's constant interventions and requests to Geisler were obviously not always heard. On 15 October Joseph Prader, secretary to the Bishop of Brixen, replied tersely to Father Ludwig: 'The Very Reverend Prince-Bishop [Geisler] does not consider it opportune to comply with the suggestion made by His Excellency Bishop Hudal concerning an amnesty for ex-Nazis.'[197]

Thus in 1949 Hudal experienced a distinct lack of success in his attempts to connect with Bishop Geisler. Monsignor Prader was Hudal's confidant from 1945 to 1947; he witnessed Hudal's activities and his support for war criminals at close quarters. In 1948, Prader moved to the Diocese of Brixen, where he worked initially as Bishop Geisler's private secretary.[198] Prader's unique position as confidant of the two 'German' bishops in Italy makes him a very special eyewitness. Hudal's repeated demands and suggestions concerning amnesty for war criminals were politely but coolly dismissed, in large part thanks to Prader's influence on Bishop Geisler while in Brixen. Sixty years later, Prader still 'recollected' his correspondence with Hudal: 'I personally advised [Bishop Geisler] against it because I knew who the people in hiding in Hudal's Anima church were, and I knew about their [Nazi] record.'[199]

A number of monasteries in South Tyrol became major stops for refugees on the way to Rome and Genoa. In those days, people talked about the 'monastery tour' of the war criminals. Eichmann remembered this journey years later: 'It was curious that Catholic priests kept helping me on my journey. They helped without asking any questions. In their eyes, I was just one person among many who needed their help.'[200] Hudal's colleagues near Rome sheltered Eichmann.[201] He was also helped by the German Pallottine priest Anton Weber. During the war, Weber ran an aid office for 'Catholic-baptised non-Aryans'.[202] Father Weber later recalled: 'Yes, someone called Richard Klement came to me. He said he came from East Germany and didn't want to go back there to live under the Bolsheviks, so I helped him.'[203] In the years after the end of the war, Italian monasteries were swarming with SS men and war criminals from all over Europe who were in hiding.

The well-known fighter pilot Hans-Ulrich Rudel gratefully recalled the help he had received from monasteries in Italy:

> There were some who had hiked through the Alps from monastery to monastery in monks' habits. One can take whatever position one likes about Catholicism, but the significant number of our people that were saved, often from certain death, by the Church during those years, above all by individuals of towering humanity, should certainly never be forgotten![204]

On 1 December 1945 Italian carabinieri searched the monastery of the German Order of Knights in Lana near Merano. The authorities suspected that the 'right to asylum' was being abused by German military officers hiding in the monastery. The operation was a great success: a total of fifteen soldiers and collaborators from France, Croatia, Czechoslovakia, and Germany were arrested. In the monastery, the carabinieri also found a large amount of weapons and military equipment, three confiscated cars, and a considerable sum of money. Several art pieces that had been stolen by the staff of Tyrolean Gauleiter Franz Hofer were also among the war booty. Their value came to over 15 million lire—a huge sum at the time. On 12 December 1945, carabinieri commander General Bruno Brunetti sent his report on the operation to the Ministry of the Interior in Rome and to the Allied military government.[205]

The event at the German Order of Knights monastery was unusual in every respect; according to the Lateran Treaties, monasteries were, in a sense, protected areas to which the Italian authorities normally had no access. As a result, monasteries were hardly ever searched, and escaping soldiers, even war criminals, could feel safe there. The raid at Lana was only possible because permission had been granted by the Allied authorities. Earlier, in August 1945, Italian partisans had wanted to search the Catholic boys' school (Knabenseminar) in Salern near Brixen, where they suspected SS men were in hiding. Father Albert Steiner demanded written permission from the Allied military government, whereupon the partisans referred to a verbal order. The priest was unyielding and threatened to inform the carabinieri, since without written permission the partisans had no right to enter the monastery. A partisan presented his Communist Party membership card as justification, and Steiner was even threatened with a pistol, but to no effect. The priest refused to budge, and the partisans had to withdraw.[206] This example demonstrates the traditional safety of monasteries as refuges for people on the run.

After the end of the war when Hudal tried to prevent Germans and Austrians from being arrested and interned in prisoner-of-war camps or extradited from Italy, part of his strategy was to shelter refugees in monasteries. That was one of the reasons why Hudal's contacts with South Tyrolean clergy were so important. Hudal's archives also contain the Red Cross travel document of a man giving his name as Rudolf von Luden, son of Rudolf von Luden. He had given his profession as 'student', the date as Epiphany 1950, and the document mentioned that 'Rudolf von Luden, staying with the venerable Capuchins of Brixen monastery, has reached his destination'.[207] 'The venerable fathers, he writes, have welcomed him lovingly, above all Magister Leopold', meaning the former parachutist Father Leopold von Gumppenberg, who worked closely with Hudal.[208]

The priest came from the old aristocratic Bavarian family of the barons of Gumppenberg. He was born in Ebersberg in 1901, joined the Bavarian Capuchins at the age of 20 after graduating from secondary school, and completed his philosophical and theological studies at the Pontifical Gregorian University in Rome. In 1938 he was appointed Superior of the Bavarian Capuchins of Latvia, who performed their pastoral work in parishes, schools, and universities. As a fanatical anti-communist, he frequently and readily acted before 1945 as intermediary between National Socialism and the Catholic Church.[209] Driven out of Latvia by the Soviets in 1941, Gumppenberg came to Rome, and from 1943 served as a soldier with a parachute regiment in northern Italy. As early as December 1944, Gumppenberg was a secret guest of the Capuchins in Brixen: he 'came to us in the night as a Wehrmacht soldier', as the diary of the Brixen Capuchins observed.[210] A few days after the end of the war, on 13 May 1945, Gumppenberg again sneaked into the monastery of the Capuchins in Brixen, got rid of his Wehrmacht uniform, and changed into a monk's habit. The former 'Superior of the Capuchins in Latvia' remained as a guest of the Capuchins in Brixen, as there was 'currently no possibility of getting over the Brenner', as the monastery diary records.[211] Soon a new task was found for Gumppenberg: the 'training of the Capuchin priests in South Tyrol'.[212] Gumppenberg stayed in the monastery in Brixen for two years, taught there, and in May 1947 transferred to a Capuchin Institute in Rome.[213] But two years later, the busy priest returned to Brixen, where he worked as a so-called 'organizer of socio-political activities' and delivered political lectures, gradually making things uncomfortable for his superiors.[214] Senior SS officers repeatedly went into hiding at Gumppenberg's monastery while on their way to Rome or Genoa.

Thus, for example, the Kreisleiter of Braunschweig, Berthold Heilig, was taken in by the venerable Capuchins in Bressanone monastery and dressed in a monastic habit. Heilig later praised the 'warm and paternal care of Father Leopold'. In August 1949 Gumppenberg wrote to Hudal in Rome that he should take care of 'the man who has escaped the sphere of communist domination', who 'has experienced much that was grave and unjust, but is deeply rooted in our faith'. The answer was positive, and by October 1949 Heilig was staying in Rome at 20 Via della Pace, Bishop Alois Hudal's residence.[215] Like his contact Hudal, Gumppenberg was not overly concerned with discretion. His 'disciplinary transfer' to Bolzano in 1951 could not trouble his church superior in the long term, either.[216] After his removal from Italy by the Capuchin order, Gumppenberg briefly looked after the protégés of the Church in Spain.[217] From 1958 he was a pilgrimage pastor in the Capuchin monastery of St Magdalena-Altötting, and he died in 1982 in a retirement home in Munich.[218]

The Franciscan monastery in Bolzano was also a well-known asylum address for 'senior Nazis'. Adolf Eichmann enjoyed its hospitality for a few weeks. In the 1960s the philosopher Hannah Arendt, in her report on the Eichmann trial, mentioned the new South Tyrolean identity of the Nazi perpetrator and the help of the Franciscan priest.[219] The Franciscan monastery in Bolzano constantly sheltered guests in the first years after the war, often church members in transit.[220] As a result, guests such as Eichmann did not stand out particularly. The most important supporter was the legendary Father Franz. Oswald Pobitzer (Father Franz Borgias), born in Bolzano in 1908 and brought up there,[221] was seen as a 'pioneering fascist'.[222] After his ordination as a priest, Pobitzer became a teacher at the Franziskanergymnasium in Bolzano, where he taught principally Italian, history, and geography, and for two years also 'military principles'. For a short time he was an army chaplain with the mountain troop Divisione Brennero.[223] Nazi spy Reinhard Kops, a confidant of Hudal's, repeatedly approached Pobitzer for advice and financial assistance for his escape.[224] In May 1948 Kops reported to Hudal from Genoa about the escape assistance he received from Gumppenberg and Pobitzer on the Brenner Line to Rome:

> During those days four people arrived, who were sent by Father Leopold and were supposedly to get away for 20,000 lire. No one got away. The address named by F.[ather] L.[eopold von Gumppenberg] failed. Personally I cannot say who the person is who was supposed to help these four here in Genoa on their way. A certain Herr Fuchs helped financially and with accommodation. [...] In Bolzano I introduced myself to Father Franz Pobitzer. He made me acquainted with various refugees waiting in his care. I was able to give some advice about how to procure a Red Cross passport, Certificato Penale, Medico etc.[225]

In the monasteries were many willing helpers, such as Pobitzer's fellow priest in the Franciscan monastery in Bolzano, Patrick Rudolfi, who was officially in charge of war grave care, prisoners of war, and internees.[226] In the months after the war, the priest was also vice-president of the Italian Red Cross in South Tyrol, and in this capacity he had close contact with the Allied authorities.[227] Father Patrick also, like Pobitzer, looked after emigrants in transit for South America at the monastery in Bolzano.[228] The priest at the Merano hospital is also mentioned in complimentary terms in the memoirs of fleeing Nazis: Father Koger, who 'found room for indigent strangers in the hospital, where they were able to gather their strength'. Plainly this business was not without its dangers because Father Koger always kept a loaded pistol under his mattress. According to Kops, the priest was 'working in a dangerous place' and needed such safety measures.[229] The life of the Protestant pastor Julius Giese in Merano was not without its dangers, either. The German was working as an informant for Reich German authorities in South Tyrol. In his annual report for 1932, Pastor Giese mentions for the first time that he holds the post of representative of the German Consulate General, which already made considerable demands on him in 1933, and from 1934 onwards demanded a really large amount of work from him, which he tried to justify, when other pastoral duties were forced into the background, as 'the service of charity, which may build bridges over the borders of denomination and also often of the nation'.[230] The Italian police had been suspicious of him for a long time because of his activities, but there was little they could do about the churchman. After the end of the war, Giese was a contact point in Nazi escape assistance, and Protestant Reich Germans in transit knew his address. On a raid in October 1945, officials found various kinds of loot at his residence and confiscated all of it.[231] The issue of what motivated these churchmen is a striking one. Simon Wiesenthal devoted almost his whole life to exploring it and reached this carefully assessed conclusion:

> It is difficult to guess the motives of these priests. Many no doubt acted from a misunderstood Christian love of one's neighbour—some of them, indeed may have done the same for Jews under Nazi rule. The fact that of Rome's 8000 Jews 4000 survived the Third Reich is certainly due, above all, to the Church. [...] It seems to me probable that the Church was divided: into priests and members of the religious orders who had recognised Hitler as the Antichrist and therefore practised Christian charity, and those who viewed the Nazis as a power of order in the struggle against the decline of morality and Bolshevism.[232]

6. Denazification through Baptism

In some cases, the ticket for a safe passage through Italy was the 'return' of former Catholics or the 'conversion' of Protestants to the Catholic Church. Sometimes non-Catholics even converted through new Christian baptism. Former fanatical SS men and Party leaders with tainted pasts probably had to undergo baptism as a proof of repentance, but then enjoyed the advantage of mercy as a result. For the clergy, the significance of the sacraments was the most important thing. Through baptism, the SS men were effectively turned into new people and freed from the 'heresy of National Socialism'. Through 're-baptism', the Church took repentant sinners back into the community. Baptismal registers demonstrate the accumulation of these Catholic 'adult baptisms' in the post-war years. In particular, former Protestant SS men were re-baptized as Catholic in Italy. These re-baptisms often occurred on the clergy's instructions; this is all the more surprising in that the re-baptisms were barely permitted by canon law. Among those re-baptized by the Brixen bishop was SS Hauptsturmführer Erich Priebke. On 13 September 1948 Priebke—a Protestant until then—was baptized as a Catholic by the town priest of Sterzing, Johann Corradini, on the instructions of Brixen's Prince-Bishop Geisler. In the baptismal register, the priest explicitly observed that he had received instructions to re-baptize Priebke from the bishop:

> According to the letter from the Ordinariate No. 1259 of 9 July 1948, concerning acceptance into the Cathol.[ic] Church of Herr Priebke Erich, he has been re-baptised by [...] Town Priest Johann Corradini *sub conditione*, in the presence of his wife Alice Priebke Roman Catholic, as witness and as second witness Thaler Karolina [and] accepted into the Catholic Church. [...] Erich Priebke was of Protestant denomination like his parents [...][233]

Priebke's wife Alice and their children Jörg and Ingo had already been re-baptized in Sterzing by Corradini on 22 April 1946.[234] The driving force behind Priebke's baptism and the assignment of Corradini was probably Vicar General Alois Pompanin. Corradini was, like Pompanin, to a certain extent well-disposed towards National Socialism. The two men had known each other since their youth and supported one another.[235] The personal correspondence between Pompanin and Corradini shows the friendly relationship the two churchmen enjoyed. Corradini continued to serve as Sterzing's town priest for over twenty years until 1958.[236] Priebke's 'conversion' was by no means an exception. In his memoirs, Eichmann refers several times to the help he received from Father Corradini when he was escaping to Italy via the Brenner.[237] Catholic baptism was maybe also required of Eichmann, as it was of many others. Eichmann's notes also hint in that direction. Eichmann, baptized as a Protestant after his birth, saw his new Catholic identity only as an 'honorary membership', and no inner avowal of Christianity was involved with it: 'Without hesitation I described myself as Catholic. In fact I did not belong to any church, but the help I received from the Catholic priests had remained deep within my memory, so I decided to honour the Catholic Church by becoming its honorary member.'[238]

Father Anton Weber in Rome checked that only those who had been (re)baptized or converted in one way or another were helped to leave the country: baptized Jews, for example, had to 'recite the Lord's Prayer and the Ave Maria; then it was revealed quickly enough who was real and who was not.'[239] When Eichmann, plainly an Austrian from his dialect, told Father Weber he was an East German and did not want to be sent to the Bolsheviks, he did not have to say an Ave Maria or undergo any test of his Catholic faith.[240] At any rate, Eichmann's application for an ICRC travel document included one important entry: 'Religion: Catholic'.

Several adult Protestant Reich Germans were re-baptized as Roman Catholic in Sterzing between 1946 and 1950. For example, Ludwig Schäfer, who was born in Halberstadt in 1927, Corradini baptized *sub conditione* on 6 August 1947 on the orders of Bishop Geisler of Brixen. Reinhold Ziegler from Berlin, born in 1917, was baptized in Sterzing on 17 July 1948 on the orders of the Episcopal Ordinariate. Father Corradini observed of Ziegler in the baptismal register: 'conditionate, without ceremony, after prior acceptance into the Catholic Church and *absolutis ex haeresis excommunicate* (Protestant denomination)'. So the Protestant had been freed from the 'heresy of delusion' by re-baptism. In this case, too, the instruction came from the Bishop, as revealed in a note: 'Letter of Ordination, 9 July 1948'.[241] In 1947 the Retzlaff family from Bromberg converted from the 'Protestant denomination' to Catholicism. The Protestant Politzschke family from Silesia also became Catholic in Sterzing. Frau Gerda Thiel, born in East Prussia in 1923, was re-baptized at the request of the Bishop in April 1946, and confirmed in Sterzing by Geisler in person in July 1946. Some Hungarians were also among the baptized in Sterzing, such as Tibor Kiss from Budapest.[242] Corradini remarked, not without pride, that these converts were freed from the 'heresy' of Protestantism and 'excommunication' by Catholic baptism.[243]

Several SS men and Nazi functionaries also stayed in the hospital in Brixen at the end of the war; former SS men converted to the Catholic faith there and had themselves baptized.[244] Father Pobitzer himself seems to have baptized some of Nazi refugees in the sanatorium of the Sisters of the Cross in Brixen, or at least helped their baptism to occur.[245] According to eyewitnesses, after the end of the war dozens of 'German soldiers' were baptized in the Episcopal Hofburg.[246] In 1994 the journalist Hartmuth Staffler was the first to look into these cases of 'converts', 're-baptists' or 're-acceptances into the Catholic Church'. For this he consulted the chronicles of the Sisters of the Cross in Brixen sanatorium and copied out certain interesting entries.[247]

When Staffler uncovered the adult baptism of Erich Priebke in Sterzing, the people of Brixen were surprised by the 'excitement' that it caused. It soon turned out that it had been quite normal in the former episcopal town after the Second World War for former senior Nazis to be welcomed into the bosom of the Church. In the Sacred Heart Chapel of Brixen hospital, in 1946 alone four major National Socialists joined the Catholic Church and 'renounced the heresy of National Socialism', as the internal chronicle of the Sisters of the Cross at the sanatorium records:

22 March 1946: Johann Weinstetter, Ex-Deputy of Gauleiter Hofer, as a patient at the hospital, rejoins the Church and renounces the heresy [...]

29 March 1946: Guido A. and station chairman Luigi R. return to the Church. In the case of A. this is a real surprise, during the Nazi period he was one of the worst and urged that the church be turned into a cinema. [...]

30 March 1946: Friedrich T., Communist from Berlin, recently interpreter with the Allies, joins the Church. He utters the *Domine non sumus dignus* [Lord we are not worthy] so convincingly loudly that he drowns out the priest.

21 April 1946: Many patients who had stayed away from the sacraments during the Nazi period, fulfilled their Easter duties once more.

24 June 1946: Prince-bishop Geisler confirms two converts from Berlin, Kurt F. and Frau W. (two senior Nazis who had previously been baptized in Sterzing).

14 December 1946: Herr Fritz Jüptner is accepted back into the Church.[248]

The Capuchins in Brixen also did their part in 'welcoming people into the Church' or helping them to 'convert' from Protestantism. On 23 May 1947, for example, Father Viktor accepted the Berliner Heinrich Bode, born in 1905, *sub conditione* into the Catholic Church in the Capuchin Church in Brixen.[249] In July 1949 'Father Leopold von Gumppenberg de Ebersberg', who had himself once taken refuge with the Capuchins, personally acted as baptismal sponsor for 35-year-old Hildegard Dalmer. Originally from Düsseldorf, she was of the 'Protestant denomination'; present as witness was Andreas Geisler, a brother of the Prince-Bishop.[250]

Only a few refused the sacraments and 'persisted in unbelief'; some of those returning to the Church were National Socialists who were tainted by their Nazi past, but hardly had to fear prosecution. This was true, for example, of Jakob Strickner, who was re-baptized on 22 March 1946 and later made Mayor of Gries am Brenner. SS Sturmbannführer Strickner had been a member of the illegal NSDAP in Austria, involved in the July Putsch in 1934, and in the 1930s a co-founder of the Tyrolean NSDAP. In the course of Reichskristallnacht, he took over a shop in Innsbruck that belonged to some Jews; 'Aryanization', as it was called at the time. Strickner repeatedly described himself to the SS as *'gottgläubig'*, meaning not registered as a member of a church or religious community, which was expected of SS members. Thus when he married Hildegard in 1939, having a church wedding didn't occur to him. In a letter to the SS Race and Settlement Office, he stressed that his wife, too, had left the Catholic Church: 'I wish to inform you at the same time that my fiancée also left the Roman Catholic Church on 15 August 1939, and is now only *gottgläubig*. I ask that my application be treated most urgently for economic reasons, and sign off with the German salute: Heil Hitler!'[251] After 1945, however, Stickner sided 'fully with the Church' again. But that did not keep him from earning his livelihood by assisting with the escape of Nazis.

Others among the re-baptized had even more cause to hide, such as Fritz Jüptner, who was admitted as a Catholic by the house chaplain of the Sisters of the Cross in Brixen, Father Viktor, on 14 December 1946. Jüptner came from Hall in Tyrol and seemed to have had good reasons to go into hiding. After escaping to South Tyrol at the war's end, he was hidden by the Sisters of the Cross in a shepherd's hut above Brixen, and in 1948 was smuggled to Argentina. From there he remained in correspondence with the Sisters of the Cross in Brixen, who had been very helpful to him. When Jüptner was about to cross a railway line near Buenos Aires on his bicycle, he was run down by a train. It was the pious sisters who spread the sad news of his death in his homeland.[252] The chronicle of the Sisters of the Cross refers several times to the change of heart on the part of a number of petitioners in Brixen: 'Only some within the people have not remained loyal to the Federal Lord [Jesus] and were beguiled by the Nazi spirit.'[253]

The South Tyrolean escape agent and Waffen-SS member Karl Nicolussi-Leck also found his way back to the bosom of the Church after 1945. After the Wehrmacht invaded Italy in autumn 1943, less attention had to be paid to the Church in South Tyrol; Nicolussi-Leck therefore decided to leave the Church 'after the last change to internal conditions in South Tyrol'.[254] After the Second World War he acted quite differently. In his Red Cross emigration papers in 1948, he describes himself without hesitation as 'Roman Catholic'.

Despite these examples of recorded re-baptisms, this practice is not in alignment with Church practice. A second baptism by Catholic priests after the first baptism is an infringement of canon law; this is true of both Catholic and Protestant denominations. Even bearing in mind the post-war chaos, a second baptism is completely forbidden by the Catholic Church. But in the Catholic Church in Italy, a way out was found which might have been questionable, but at least had some kind of legal safe-guard: baptism *sub conditione*. Until the Second Vatican Council, the relationship between the Catholic and Protestant churches was very tense. The baptisms were fundamentally acknowledged in principle, but could be repeated in dubious cases if (*sub conditione*) the first baptism was incomplete or was invalid. That is normally extremely rare. By canon law, baptism *sub conditione* could only occur in four cases:

1. if it is questionable whether the baptized is alive;
2. if there is a suspected lack of intention on the part of the baptismal sponsor or the baptized;
3. if the baptismal formula was badly corrupted at the 'first baptism';
4. if the baptismal water did not touch the body.[255]

If someone has been properly baptized either Catholic or Protestant, normally a re-baptism is an offence against canon law. For some bishops and parish priests, it seems to have been quite clear: anyone who was a Nazi cannot have been properly baptized.

Belief in the effectiveness of the sacraments is one of the foundations of the Catholic Church. Pope Pius XII also emphasized the significance of this principle. In 1944, when he returned to his palace from a meeting with previously Protestant American soldiers, he said: 'At the big audience in the morning there was a group of twenty-one, all of whom have now found their way back to the holy Church and received their First Communion. This harvest of souls is worth any sacrifice!'[256] For the Italian clergy, too, the 'harvest of souls' among former members of the SS was quite central. The baptizing priests in South Tyrol kept to the regulations of canon law, but interpreted them quite liberally:

The following general stipulations apply to all sacraments: because the sacraments were deployed by Christ the Lord as a chief means of sanctification and salvation, the greatest care and respect should be shown to ensure that they are administered correctly and in a timely fashion, and received correctly and in a timely fashion. Heretics and schismatics, even if they are mistaken in good faith and ask for the sacraments to be administered, may only have the sacraments administered to them if they set aside their error and reconcile themselves with the Church. The sacraments of Baptism, Confirmation and Ordination, which are indissoluble in nature, cannot be administered; if, however, there is justified doubt about whether they have in fact been administered, they should be administered again conditionally [*sub conditione*].'[257]

In the view of some priests, the (former) Nazis were the new heretics. If the former Hitler devotees showed repentance, the baptism could be repeated because the outsiders could hardly be expected to provide evidence that the first baptism had been administered correctly.

Against this background, in some cases baptism (but also conversion without re-baptism) became an element of church denazification. Oswald Pohl, as head of the SS Head Administrative Office, was considerably involved in the exploitation of concentration camp inmates. After the end of the war, Pohl was condemned to death and was awaiting his execution in the fortress of Landsberg am Lech. There the mass murderer found his way back to Christ; he was re-baptized on instructions from above and confirmed a year later.[258] Pohl was now able to rely on the intercession of Catholic dignitaries, who asked the Allies to spare his life. Encouraged by prison priest Karl Morgenschweis and with the imprimatur of the church, the 'former General of the Waffen-SS' had been able to give an account of his conversion to the Catholic Church in the summer of 1950 in a brochure in an edition of 9,000 copies.[259] Morgenschweis wanted to incorporate the SS man's conversion story into the Catholic tradition and place Oswald Pohl beside St Augustine. In the blurb, Pohl's transformation was thus honoured accordingly:

In the description of his journey through life, the shattering events and serious political events [*sic*] are touched upon more at the edges, while in the foreground are those motives that led the officer, who had a strict religious upbringing, to leave the Protestant church, to see himself as '*gottgläubig*', and finally to convert to the Catholic Church. Pohl shows that salvation from the current moral degradation of the whole of humanity can *only* come through unconditional commitment to the holy Trinity as the absolute standard of all moral values.[260]

Examples of war criminals who found Christ after the war abound. One was Hans Frank, governor general of the occupied Polish territories. He grew up as a Protestant, later became a convinced National Socialist *Gottgläubiger*, and finally found his way to the Catholic faith and converted. The SS Obergruppenführer and radical anti-Semite was responsible for the deportation of millions of Polish Jews to the extermination camps. At the war's end, he effectively cosied up to the Church. But his 'conversion' could not save him from the gallows in Nuremberg.[261] Unsurprisingly, Rudolf Höss, commandant of Auschwitz, also found his way back to faith before his execution.[262] Reinhard Spitzy, a counter-intelligence agent in Madrid, also found moral support in the Church and refuge in a Spanish monastery. Speaking for hundreds of Nazis, Spitzy described this inner transformation in his memoirs:

If they [priests and monasteries] were far from harmful to our future, the deeper reason for that lay in the fact that one thought once more about the old ideals, as the 'modern' ones had collapsed so miserably. Yes, we loved the warm cloak of the Church when we stood by the ruins and knew that bad things awaited us.[263]

National Socialism had turned out to be a heresy, and the Church celebrated its moral victory. It had come to a kind of moral crusade for souls. In the planned re-Christianization of Europe, Protestant and Catholic churches were in competition.

The Pope and his Brixen bishop also granted denazification through baptism to the family of Reichsleiter Martin Bormann, who had fled to South Tyrol at the end of the war. Parish priest Theodor Schmitz looked after Bormann's seriously ill wife Gerda. Mrs Bormann said of the South Tyrolean priests: 'They're concerned about German people. The decent German people that we have here help each other quite naturally. Regardless of whether they're from East Prussia, Bohemia, Vienna or the Rhine. They can't take that feeling of solidarity away from us, even if they tear Germany up into tiny little pieces.'[264]

Soon after this, Gerda Bormann's state of health deteriorated rapidly. Already fatally ill, she was further troubled by the uncertain future of her children. On 5 February 1946, the 'solemnly undersigned wife' Gerda Bormann, being of the firm conviction that Martin Bormann could no longer be alive, made her brother Hans Walter Buch—*pro forma*—guardian of her underage children. To everyone's surprise, she called for the loyal helper of her final days and friend to her children, the Catholic cleric Theodor Schmitz. She asked him to ensure the personal and financial wellbeing of the Bormann children. In the last weeks before her death, Gerda Bormann became increasingly preoccupied with religious questions. In the hospital in Merano, she probably converted to the Catholic faith, as the American authorities maintained: 'Frau Bormann found her way back to the Christian religion, having been an agnostic for the last few years.'[265] Gerda Bormann died on the evening of 23 March 1946 at the age of 36 in Merano. Her death left eight children needing care. The Bishop of Brixen initially gave permission for the orphans to be looked after by the Catholic priest Schmitz, and helped with a large sum from his private assets.

On the instructions of the Bishop, Father Josef Obergasser from St Lorenzen in the Pustertal sought foster families for the children, and they were later adopted by them. Seven of the eight Bormann children in South Tyrol converted to the Catholic faith in 1946. The eldest son, Martin Bormann, Jun., had been baptized as a Protestant in 1930, and the Catholic Adolf Hitler had been present at the ceremony as godfather. In 1947 Martin Bormann Junior was re-baptized as a Catholic, again *sub conditione*. This renewed baptism was officially explained with reference to the possibly invalid (Protestant) first baptism of 1930. Martin Bormann, who later became a Catholic cleric and missionary, wrote: 'On 4 May 1947 I was accepted into the Catholic Church. My godfather for the conditional baptism (because no certainty could be had about my baptism as an infant) was my Querleitner.'[266] The older children attended Catholic monastery boarding schools so that they could get used to their new surroundings. The Italian government's plans to put the Bormann children in a southern Italian children's home were thus thwarted.[267]

Father Karl Bayer, head of Caritas in Rome, was very involved in the Bormann story:

Because of the children. You see, Bormann's wife and children were living in the South Tyrol, where, as of course you know, Frau Bormann died in 1945 [*sic*]. Theo Schmitz, the POW chaplain in Merano, was with her much of the time; he helped her die. But during all that time we were working on finding solutions for the children; they were very young and homes had to be found for them.[268]

Father Bayer went in search of Reichsleiter Martin Bormann, 'just because of the children' and 'huge amounts of financial problems'. But Bormann remained missing, and Bishop Alois Hudal, the keen escape agent, remained silent about the case. In 1950 Father Anton Weber, who was in contact with Bishop Hudal, arranged for the Bormann children to have a special audience with Pope Pius XII in Rome.[269] The Italian Ministry of the Interior and the Foreign Ministry looked into Martin Bormann's whereabouts and the fate of his children several times. The Ministry of the Interior saw the issue as a possible threat to public security. The Foreign Ministry feared foreign policy problems and accusations from the Allies. Both ministries wanted to hand the children of the 'German war criminal Martin Bormann' to the care of the state. Bormann's children were to be 'removed from South Tyrol' and brought to a home in southern Italy. In May 1947 the Foreign Ministry gave the Ministry of the Interior a detailed report about the case of Martin Bormann, 'one of the chief defendants in the Nuremberg war crimes trial'. The Italian officials thought it was likely that Bormann had died in May 1945, although 'Bormann's survival could never be absolutely ruled out';[270] ascertaining with certainty the facts of his death still held great importance for the Italian authorities and Bormann's orphaned children:

> In this situation a message from the Ministry that Bormann might be in Italy could have serious consequences, so the investigations of the Ministry of the Interior require absolute exactitude. Bormann's presence in Italy could have serious political effects on the Allies, the goodwill of the Italian authorities must be quite clear here. The efforts to identify and arrest the named war criminal must be beyond question. [Hence, also according to the Foreign Ministry] the children of the aforementioned are to be removed from the Alto Adige [South Tyrol] and interned in southern Italy. Because of their age, they could perhaps be accommodated in a children's home or a church institution under the supervision of the security authorities.[271]

In November 1948 the Italian authorities took concrete steps to find accommodation for the Bormann children in Naples. The Prefect of Naples was prepared to place the children in a home, and even the daily rate, of '120 lire at the most' was already established.[272] But in the end it was not to happen: while Schmitz, the children's *de facto* guardian, managed to have his charges placed with foster parents in the South Tyrol in the long term, the worldwide search for their father continued.

4

The Intelligence Service Ratline

What is almost entirely missing from the La Vista report is any reference to America's own activity in the area of Nazi border-crossing, even
though that, too, existed. In the initial phase of the Cold War, US intelligence services began employing former SS officers with spy experience. This also made border-crossing more professional. Organized
escape routes and networks of people who would assist the fleeing Nazis
in various ways began to take shape in the summer of 1946. At that
time, a mass escape of SS members from the large prisoner-of-war
camp in Rimini began, and the fugitives seemingly vanished without a
trace. The US authorities were concerned and began in-depth investigations. US State Department official Vincent La Vista eventually discovered that the SS members were being sheltered in monasteries and
supplied with Red Cross travel papers. Vatican authorities also confirmed invented identities for people with particularly tainted pasts.
Individual SS officers in Italy who had built up contacts with the clergy
even before the end of the war now worked as escape agents within the
context of the Vatican.

   The underground escape routes used by National Socialists were not
only discovered by the Americans, but soon came to be used by them
also. Shortly after the end of the war, the Americans had a great interest in SS intelligence agents with anticommunist expertise. These secret
service specialists were soon to be 'recycled' and deployed against the
'common enemy'. Hence, from 1947 onwards, the Americans supported
the escape of SS members from Europe. Almost anyone who had intelligence and/or anticommunist experience was eligible for a job. Starting in 1947 the US CIC used the overseas escape route for National
Socialists via Italy for its own agents. In spy jargon, 'ratlines' refers to
prepared routes along which refugees or agents can be smuggled in or
out of enemy territories. They are a standard part of the secret operations

of any major country. When the Iron Curtain came down over Europe, the ratlines were originally used to get endangered agents out of the Soviet-occupied part of Austria and out of Eastern Europe. On this underground line, SS men from all over Europe were also smuggled via Italy to South America. The precondition for this was their usefulness to the US intelligence services in the struggle against communism. The Italian ratline was a well-organized escape route that made legendary and well-known National Socialist organizations such as ODESSA look amateurish.

The general conditions in Italy were particularly favourable for the recruitment of former SS officers for the anticommunist 'shadow war'. At the end of the war in 1945, SS commanders and the Wehrmacht in Italy sought contact with the Americans. In secret, German officers and Allied officials negotiated the surrender of German forces in Italy; the secret negotiations code-named 'Operation Sunrise' led to the strategic surrender in Italy. These SS members wanted to emerge from the war with as little punishment as possible, while the Americans hoped for a victory with very minor losses on their side. For the Soviets, the German–American secret negotiations were the first shot in the Cold War between the blocs. After reaching an agreement, the Americans' German negotiating partners could rely on pledges of protection, and a few years later, some of them were even working for the American intelligence services.

Any involvement between the US intelligence services and war criminals would have done terrible damage to the United States in the public eye. The true extent of this involvement became apparent only in 1998 when parts of the related files of the CIA (and the organizations that preceded it) were released in the National Archives in Washington, DC. The combination of protection for certain war criminals and, at the same time, the active prosecution of others responsible for genocide by the same American authorities still has after-effects today. The positive contributions of US intelligence at the Nuremberg Trials, for example, should not be ignored here, but the contradictions are plain. The American historian Richard Breitman sums it up: 'The post-war fate of the perpetrators of wartime atrocities remains controversial and [...] during the 1980s the international hunt for Josef Mengele and the trial of Klaus Barbie raised questions about how some Nazi war criminals managed to escape post-war justice, or at least postpone it for decades.'[1]

The case of the head of the Gestapo in Lyons, Klaus Barbie, clearly demonstrated to the world that repeated interventions by US intelligence services showed their complicity with Nazi escapes. Worse than that, people such as Barbie, 'the butcher of Lyons', were soon back as agents on the payroll of US intelligence agencies.

1. Operation Bernhard

One passage in the La Vista report has kept researchers busy for over twenty years. It is quoted in various works, although without being examined more precisely:

> On the Brenner Pass route from Austria the first stop on the underground railroad in Italy is at a castle in Merano where German is the language of the directors. This castle is believed to be 'Schloss Rametz' belonging to Crastan, Albert, a Jew, who poses as a Swiss Consul and as a member of the International Red Cross. During the war he was agent of the SS task force 'Schloss Labers' sometimes called 'Group Wendig' under the command of Schwendt, Col. Frederick [Friedrich Sschwend], who was responsible only to Kaltenbrunner and Himmler. Four other Jewish agents of this group are known to be at large. One, van Harten, Jaac, is at present at 184 Hayarkonstr., Tel Aviv, Palestine, from where he claimed 5.000.000 Dollars from the U.S. Government for property confiscated at Merano after the war's end. All this property was the loot of the SS group which had been stored in Schloss Rametz, Schloss Labers, Schwendt's HQ, and other buildings in Merano. Included in this loot were large quantities of counterfeit British Pound notes. One of the plants producing these bills is reported still in operation in the Milan area [...].[2]

La Vista had happened upon a Nazi underground network. 'Operation Bernhard' was an SS initiative devoted to the forgery of British pound notes. On the orders of the SS leaders Heinrich Himmler and Ernst Kaltenbrunner, the project was designed to sabotage the British economy. SS-Sturmbannführer Bernhard Krüger was in charge of the preparation and execution of the counterfeiting operation.[3] A total of 142 prisoners were busy on it. The Jewish workers in Sachsenhausen concentration camp were forced to work under threat of death. One of them, Adolf Burger, wrote that by the end of the war the entire sum of forged pound notes came to around 134 million British pounds, about

8 per cent of which were successfully put into circulation.[4] The operation's goal was chaos and the destabilization of the British currency and economy. But this plan was never realized. Instead, the forged money was used to purchase raw materials for the armaments industry, the financing of major foreign arms deals, and to pay agents.[5]

From the summer of 1943 the production of fake pound notes was operating at full speed after a successful test of the counterfeit notes at Swiss and Italian banks.[6] Leading members of the SS wanted to believe in Operation Bernhard and its pound notes as a miracle weapon. These were probably the most perfect forgeries that had been produced by this time. The man responsible for the global distribution of the forged money was Friedrich Schwend, a shrewd Swabian businessman, who used the rank of SS-Sturmbannführer as a cover.

Schwend's spying career began gradually. He was born on 6 November 1906 in Heilbronn-Böckingen, where he trained as a mechanic in his father's workshop. After completing his training, in 1925 he became a driving instructor. Then he moved to Nuremberg and, to the surprise of his family, married Baroness Agnes von Gemmingen. At the time he was chiefly working at selling car engines. His foreign travels related to this activity and led him to, amongst other places, the Soviet Union, Persia, South America, and the United States.[7] In 1940 the Schwend family settled in a villa in Abbazzia, at the time a popular Italian spa town near Fiume (Rijeka). During the war his first marriage collapsed. Friedrich Schwend then married his secretary Hedda Neuhold in Trieste.[8] Schwend had been a member of the NSDAP since 1932, and his wife was a member of the National Socialist Women's League. The Kreisleiter of Rosenheim was wild about Schwend: 'He is an entirely irreproachable, politically reliable man, who offers the guarantee that he will always whole-heartedly support the Führer and the National Socialist movement.'[9] In 1940 the Nazi Kreisleitung of Rosenheim gave Schwend a very positive political appraisal: his behaviour was 'impeccable, and even today he supports the concerns of the Reich and the movement at home and abroad'.[10] Probably his work as an agent was also beginning at that time. At first it involved simple and limited spying on his trips abroad for the SS Security Service and the Wehrmacht. During the war Schwend was then taken on by the German counterintelligence service (Abwehr) to locate hidden deposits of foreign currency. The SS had plenty of uses for the shrewd man, who worked as an agent for the Security Service (SD) from 1943 onwards. Schwend's experience in the foreign currency trade, his contacts, and his successes as a confidence trickster were the most excellent references for the SS officers in Berlin. SS officer Wilhelm Höttl met Schwend in Italy in 1943 and suggested him to Kaltenbrunner as leading agent in the counterfeiting operation code-named 'Bernhard'.[11]

The Bernhard agents, under Schwend, set up numerous safe houses in Italy even during the war. After the collapse of the 'Third Reich', what was left of Operation Bernhard became, presumably, a useful component of the Nazi war criminals' escape route through Italy.[12] Wilhelm Höttl, Kaltenbrunner's special courier, described Schwend as a 'big businessman living in Italy' whose extensive business contacts 'could supply valuable services' to the SS and the Security Service in the distribution of counterfeit money.[13] According to the information of the US military intelligence service, Schwend's tasks were to 'acquire various goods such as gold, diamonds, securities, raw materials, manufactured products, silk goods and expensive perfume etc.'.[14] Schwend allegedly reported directly to Himmler about his activities. Höttl raved about his friend Schwend, as the 'model of a type that has become very rare, the daring pioneering businessman who also adheres to a very strict professional code of honour.'[15] Schwend put his international financial experience at the disposal of Operation Bernhard and took over the distribution of the forged pound notes. Kaltenbrunner was apparently enthusiastic about his well-thought-out suggestions and the extensive distribution organization that his new agent was able to supply. Schwend's central offices, disguised as 'Staff of the 4th Germanic Tank Corps', were first located in Abbazzia and Trieste.[16] In late summer 1944, headquarters transferred to Meran.[17] Höttl describes the appropriate accommodations that the SS made available to the self-styled 'financial genius' to facilitate his work:

> As the director of such complex marketing machinery, who had to be contactable at all times or at least as a rule, Schwend could not, as before, live as a travelling businessman in a dozen or more flophouses. He needed a fixed base, which had if possible to be remote and easy to guard, and a reliable security force, that could also be used as couriers for dealings with Berlin. Within two weeks Schwend had found the requisite location: it was Schloss Labers, which lies about half an hour away from Merano amidst extensive vineyards and orchards. Schwend bought

it [the castle had only been requisitioned by the SS] and had it equipped
for his purposes, while I supplied him with a guard unit consisting of 24
Waffen-SS men.[18]

Schwend, a notorious braggart, repeatedly stressed the clandestine
nature if his work: 'The field of activity of my office was a complete
secret. [...] The only people who really knew about current or planned
operations were General Kaltenbrunner and me. To have broken my
duty of silence would have meant the rope or the bullet.'[19] Schwend was
supposed to be the buyer of the aforementioned Germanic Tank Corps.
Of course, in order to obstruct the investigations of foreign agents and
German offices as well, he had to use a false name; he was now called
Dr Fritz Wendig. It was in this name that he received pay as a Major of
the Waffen-SS, a legitimation as Gestapo Kriminalrat, a German min-
isterial passport, and a normal German passport.[20]
Schwend was presumably given a relatively free hand in his business dealings. After the war he gave a clearly exaggerated account of
his own position of power: 'I was given a completely free hand in the
way I threw the pounds into the market; I could have given millions
of them away, if doing so had encouraged the war effort.'[21] Schwend's
share of each pound note brought into circulation was 33⅓ per cent—a
vast sum, although from it he had to finance the entire operation and
also pay his middlemen, his so-called 'chief salesmen'. Schwend
bought houses, ships, cars, shares of companies, and raw materials
and paid out huge sums of money in bribes. In this way, within a comparatively short time he had created a relatively dense network of
bases and courier connections. The global network of distributors
consisted of a fairly large group of agents. They included Alberto
Crastan, a Swiss consular official and owner of Schloss Rametz near
Merano, and the former German consul Georg Gyssling. What is
amazing is the relatively large number of Jews who worked for
Schwend. The most important agent among them was Jaac van
Harten, who presented himself as a delegate of the International
Committee of the Red Cross, and in this way provided the necessary
disguise for the operations in Merano. Also living at Schloss Labers,
aside from Schwend's main agents, were his extended family, including
his brother-in-law and companion Hans (Giovanni) Neuhold.[22] According to Schwend, the organization in Merano was getting bigger and

FIG. 5. The 'minister of propaganda' of the French Vichy government in exile, Jean Luchaire, at the moment of his arrest in Meran; next to him stands his daughter Corinne, a well-known actress at the time.

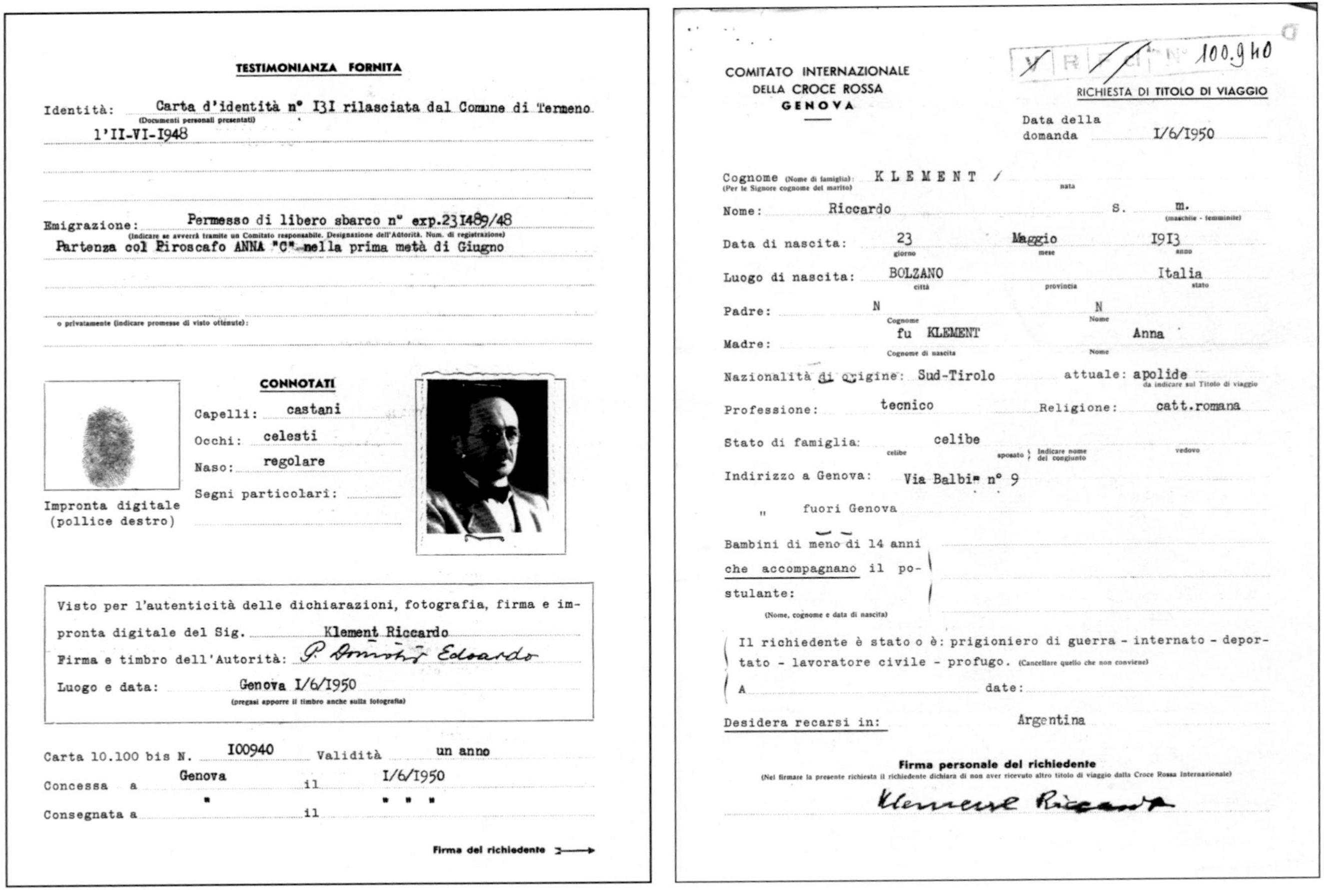

FIG. 6. In 1950 Adolf Eichmann, the 'bureaucrat of the Holocaust', fled from justice with a new identity. He travelled under the name of Richard Klement, a resident of Tramin, the South Tyrolean village world famous for its Gewürztraminer variety of grapes.

COMITATO INTERNAZIONALE
DELLA CROCE ROSSA
GENOVA

RICHIESTA DI TITOLO DI VIAGGIO

N° 100.940

Data della domanda 1/6/1950

Cognome (Nome di famiglia) (Per le Signore cognome del marito): **KLEMENT /** nato S. m.

Nome: **Riccardo**

Data di nascita: **23** giorno **Maggio** mese **1913** anno

Luogo di nascita: **BOLZANO** città **Italia** stato

Padre: N Nome

Madre: N fu **KLEMENT** Nome Cognome **Anna** Nome

Nazionalità di Origine: **Sud-Tirolo** attuale: **apolide**

Professione: **tecnico** Religione: **catt.romana**

Stato di famiglia: celibe **celibe**

Indirizzo a Genova: **Via Balbi n° 9** " **fuori Genova**

Bambini di meno di 14 anni che accompagnano il postulante:

Il richiedente è stato o è: prigioniero di guerra - internato - deportato - lavoratore civile - profugo. date:

Desidera recarsi in: **Argentina**

Firma personale del richiedente

Ricardo Klement

TESTIMONIANZA FORNITA

Identità: **Carta d'identità n° 131 rilasciata dal Comune di Termeno.**
1'II-VI-1948

Emigrazione: **Permesso di libero sbarco n° exp.23145/48**
Partenza col Piroscafo ANNA "C" nella prima metà di Giugno

CONNOTATI

Capelli: **castani**
Occhi: **celesti**
Naso: **regolare**
Segni particolari:

Impronta digitale (pollice destro)

Visto per l'autenticità delle dichiarazioni, fotografia, firma e impronta digitale del Sig. **Klement Riccardo**

Firma e timbro dell'Autorità: *P.Brivio Edoardo*

Luogo e data: **Genova 1/6/1950**

Carta 10.100 bis N. **100940** Validità **un anno**

Concessa a **Genova** il **1/6/1950**

Consegnata a " " "

Firma del richiedente ➔

COMITATO INTERNAZIONALE
DELLA CROCE ROSSA
GENOVA

RICHIESTA DI TITOLO DI VIAGGIO

Data della
domanda .... 16 maggio 1949

Cognome (Nome di famiglia): .... G R E G O R /
(Per i Sposo il Sepione cognome del marito)

Nome: HELMUT .... nata .... S. ..... M. ..... (marchio - femminile)

Data di nascita: .... 6 agosto 1911
                        giorno   anno

Luogo di nascita: ..... Termeno (Alto Adige)
                        città   provincia   stato

Padre: ..... N N

Madre: ..... fu Berta Gregor
              Cognome di nascita   Nome

Nazionalità di origine: italiana ..... attuale: ..... germanica p.ognisa.
                                                      da indicare sul Titolo di viaggio

Professione: ..... tecnico- meccanico ..... Religione: ..... cattolica

Stato di famiglia: ..... celibe ..... vedovo
                        celibe
                        sposa } Indicare nome
                               del congiunto

Indirizzo a Genova: ..... Via Vincenzo Ricci,3 ..... Termeno
   "   fuori Genova ..... Via Montello,22

Bambini di meno di 14 anni
che accompagnano il po-
stulante: .....
              (Nome, cognome e data di nascita)

Il richiedente è stato o è: ~~prigioniero di guerra~~ - internato - depor-
~~tato~~ ~~internato civile rifugiato~~. (Cancellare quello che non conviene)
A .... date: .....

Desidera recarsi in: ..... Argentina

Firma personale del richiedente
Gregor Helmut

(Nel firmare la presente richiesta il richiedente dichiara di non aver ricevuto altro titolo di viaggio dalla Croce Rossa internazionale)

TESTIMONIANZA FORNITA

Identità: ..... carta d'identità ..... rilasciata dal Comune di Termeno N°114-
                                       del 11/4/1948
                          (Documenti asserzioni presenti)

- Certificato di residenza rilasciato dal Comune di Termini risaliente
  la residenza in Italia dal 1944

-Libero sbarco Buor. 2177-1948 permesso P.1588 rilasciato dalla Repub
 Argentina in data 7/9/1948

Emigrazione: ..... per Argentina (Genova Rossa) in proprio Passaggio prenotato
nella m/n "NORTH KING " della Compagnia Transatlantica" partenza 25/5/49

° privatamente (indicare) presenze di visto ottenuto)

CONNOTATI

Capelli: ..... castani
Occhi: ..... castani
Naso: ..... regolare
Segni particolari: ..... nessuno

Impronta digitale
(pollice destro)

Visto per l'autenticità delle dichiarazioni, fotografia, firma e im-

pronta digitale del Sig. ..... GREGOR HELMUT

Firma e timbro dell'Autorità: .....

Luogo e data: .....
                (pregasi apporre il timbro anche sulla fotografia)

Carta 10.100 bis N. ..... 100501 ..... Validità ..... un anno

Concessa ..... a ..... Genova ..... il 12/6/1949
         .   .   .   .

Consegnata a .... il ....

Firma del richiedente :—————►

Fig. 7. Josef Mengele became a South Tyrolean, and his travel document from the International Committee of the Red Cross gave his new identity as Helmut Gregor from Tramin. His stated profession was 'technician—mechanic'.

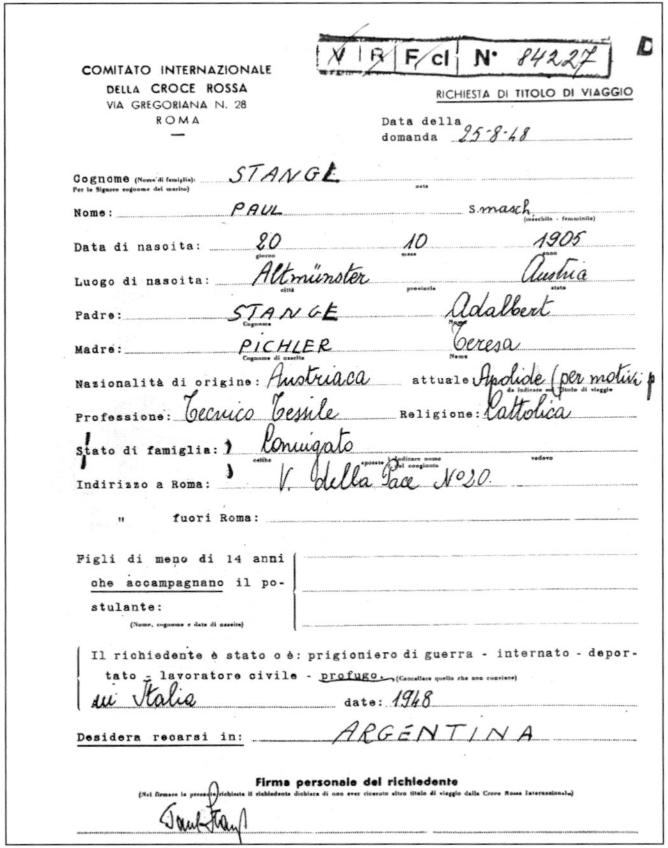

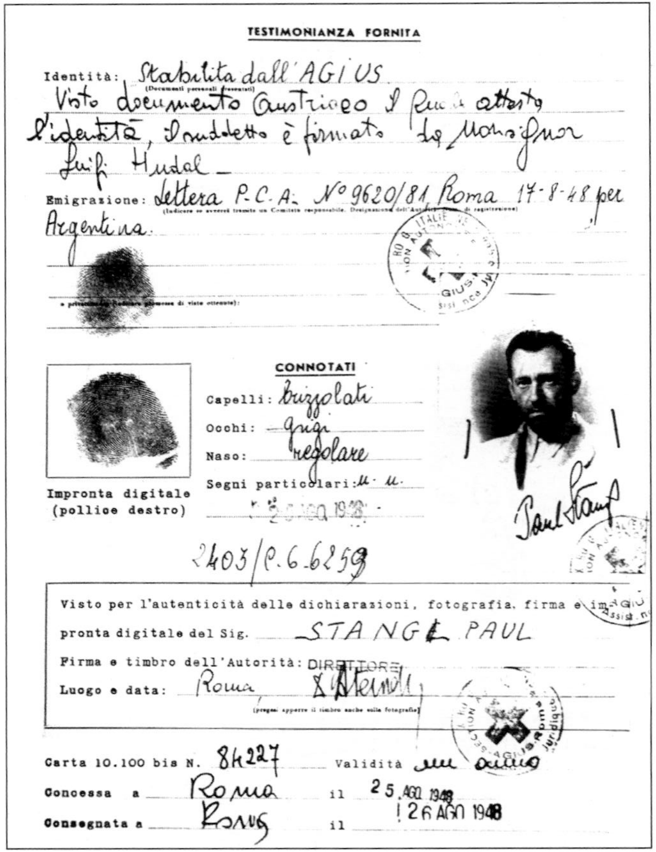

TESTIMONIANZA FORNITA

Identità: Stabilita dall'AGIUS
Visto documento Austriaco I Paul è attesta l'identità, Suddetto è firmato Lg Monaghan
Luf. Hudal
Emigrazione: lettera P.C.A. No 9620/81 Roma 17-8-48 per Argentina.

CONNOTATI
Capelli: bruzolati grigi
Occhi: grigi
Naso: regolare
Segni particolari: u. u.

Impronta digitale (pollice destro)

2403/P.C.6259

Visto per l'autenticità delle dichiarazioni, fotografia, firma e impronta digitale del Sig. STANGE PAUL
Pronta digitale del Sig. STANGE PAUL
Firma e timbro dell'Autorità: DIRETTORE
Luogo e data: Roma

Carta 10.100 bis N. 84227   Validità ___
Concessa a Roma il 25 AGO 1948
Consegnata a ROMA il 26 AGO 1948

FIG. 8B

COMITATO INTERNAZIONALE
DELLA CROCE ROSSA
VIA GREGORIANA N. 28
ROMA

N | R | F | cl | N° 84227

RICHIESTA DI TITOLO DI VIAGGIO

Data della domanda 25-8-48

Cognome: STANGE
Nome: PAUL   S.mach
Data di nascita: 20 giorno 10 mese 1905 anno
Luogo di nascita: Altmünster   Austria
Padre: STANGE   Adalbert
Madre: PICHLER   Teresa
Nazionalità di origine: Austriaca   attuale Apolide (per motivi)
Professione: Lavoratore Genile   Religione: Cattolica
Stato di famiglia: coniugato
Indirizzo a Roma: V. della via No 20
          fuori Roma:
Figli di meno di 14 anni che accompagnano il postulante:
Il richiedente è stato o è: prigioniero di guerra - internato - deportato - lavoratore civile - PROFUGO - in Italia   date: 1948
Desidera recarsi in: ARGENTINA

Firma personale del richiedente

FIG. 8A

Fig. 8a–c. Franz Stangl, the commandant of Treblinka extermination camp, fled from Italy overseas with the help of Bishop Alois Hudal. Stangl's address was given as Via della Pace 20, the bishop's residence in Rome. The papal aid commission supplied a letter supporting Stangl's request for travel documents from the ICRC.

PONTIFICIA COMMISSIONE ASSISTENZA
SEZIONE STRANIERI
Piazza Cairoli, 117

Roma, *17-8* 1948

Prot. N. *962₃/81*
OGGETTO: *Richiesta passaporto.*

On. Comitato Inter. Croce Rossa
ROMA. - Via Gregoriana, 28

Si prega codesto On. Comitato di voler

cortesemente disporre per il \ rilascio del passa-

porto della Croce Rossa Internazionale al

Sig. *Stangl Paul*

di nazionalità *apolide aust.*

per recarsi *Argentina*

Con vivi ringraziamenti.

Haruga Mathias
SEGRETARIO

Fig. 9. Bishop Hudal dedicated his book The Foundations of National Socialism to Hitler. Hudal wanted to build bridges between the Nazis and the Catholic Church. After the war he helped many Nazis and SS officers, including criminals, to escape from justice.

+ Hudal

Die Grundlagen
des Nationalfozialismus

Eine ideengeſchichtliche Unterſuchung

von

Biſchof Dr. Alois Hudal
Rom

Johannes Günther Verlag

Leipzig und Wien

November 6, 1944

My dear Walter:

      While Archbishop Spellman was in Rome he had forwarded to the Bishops' War Emergency and Relief Committee a request for a monthly allotment of twenty thousand lire for the work of relieving Austrian residents in Rome. The request was evidently brought to the attention of the Archbishop by Barone Berger de Waldenegg.

      The inclosed check in the amount of Four Hundred Dollars ($400.00) represents an allotment by the Bishops' Committee for this work. The question of continuing the allotment will be discussed at the coming meetings. May I ask your kindness in seeing that the money reaches the proper authorities?

      We here are hoping for another glimpse of you before you leave for foreign soil.

      With every good wish, I remain

Very sincerely yours,

[signature]

General Secretary

The Right Rev.Msgr.Walter S. Carroll,
8521 Frankstown Road,
Pittsburgh, Pennsylvania.

FIG. 10. In 1944 Archbishop Spellman from New York agreed to support financially the Austrian Refugee Committee in Rome.

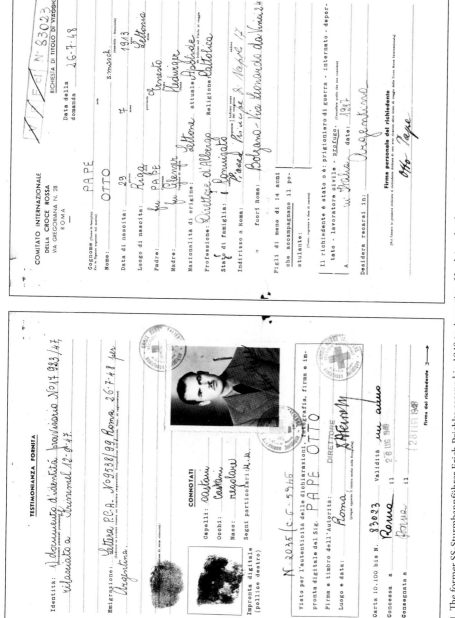

Fig. 11. The former SS-Sturmbannführer Erich Priebke escaped in 1948 to Argentina. He claimed to be a stateless Volksdeutscher from the Baltic and managed to get travel papers from the ICRC. At the end of the war he went into hiding in South Tyrol and was helped by Catholic priests.

FIG. 12. Ante Pavelić, the leader of fascist Croatia, and his war minister in the German propaganda journal *Signal*, 1941. Pavelić is one of the most prominent war criminals who emigrated to South America.

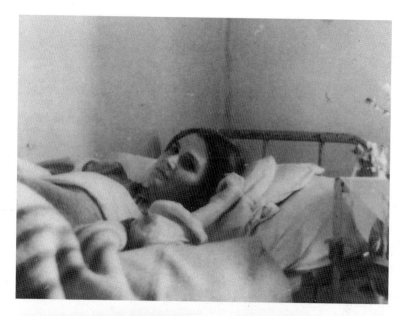

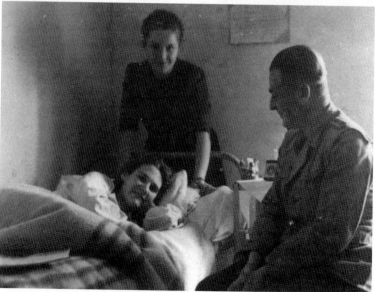

Fɪɢ. 13. The seriously ill Gerda Bormann in the hospital in Meran. The wife of Reichsleiter Martin Bormann managed to escape with her numerous children to South Tyrol where she changed her name, went into hiding, and converted to Catholicism. Gerda Bormann died in 1946 and is buried in the military cemetery in Meran. The local bishop took care of the orphans, who were baptized and later adopted by Catholic South Tyrolean families.

FIG. 14. Allied officers in front of a hotel in the Bolzano town centre a few days after the capitulation of the Germans in Italy in May 1945. In the background are German officers enjoying the spring sunshine. Such scenes were quite common, and the situation in Bolzano seemed rather Kafkaesque to US soldiers.

FIG. 15. German Special Police, South Tyrol, May 1945. The Special Police consisted of German and US soldiers; the Allies hoped that by working together the victorious and defeated soldiers would be able to guarantee security and maintain calm in the first days after the end of the war. The US public and many GIs were displeased by so much liberty being given to the former enemy in northern Italy.

Fıg. 16. Karl Wolff, the Höchste SS- and Polizeiführer for Italy, in a POW camp in Bolzano in May 1945. Thanks to his secret negotiations with Allen Dulles from the US wartime intelligence service, the former deputy of Heinrich Himmler was spared the gallows.

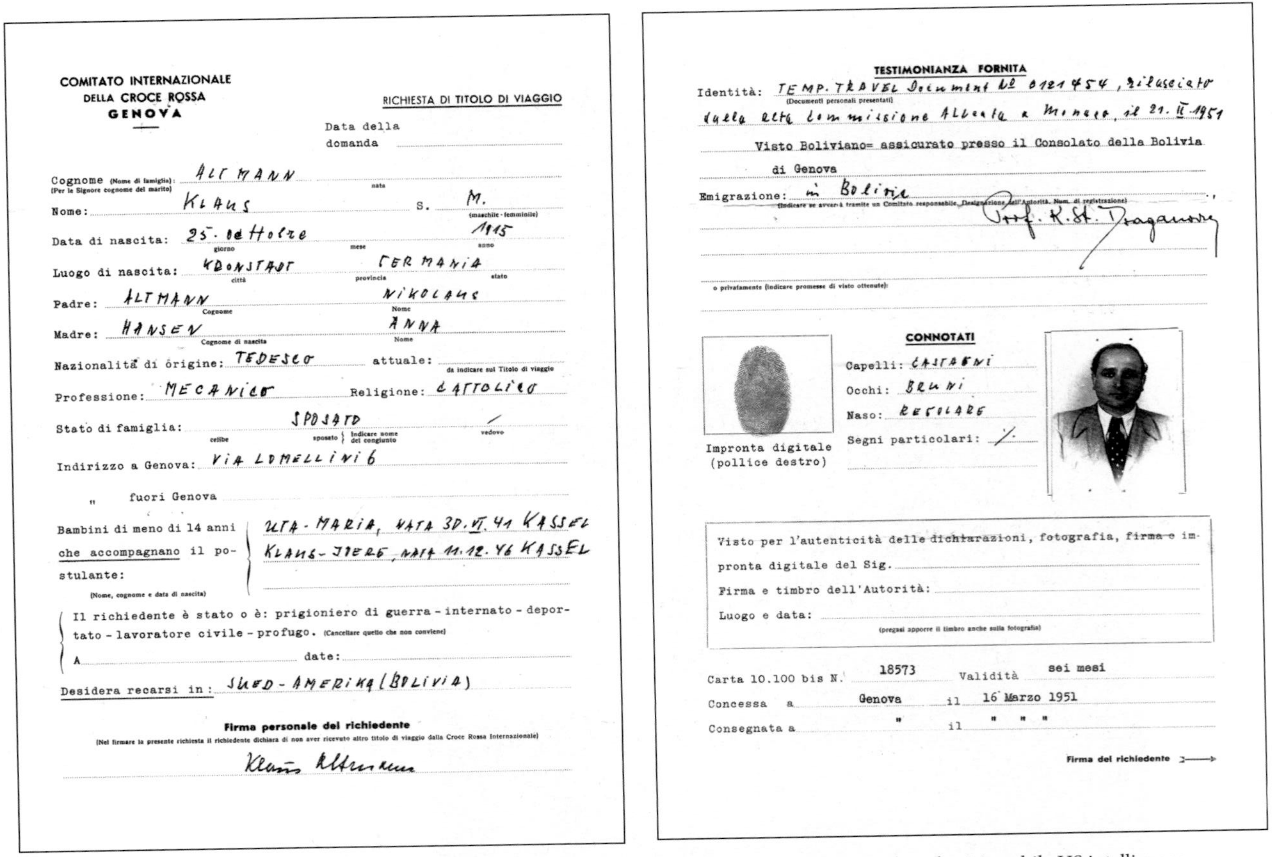

COMITATO INTERNAZIONALE
DELLA CROCE ROSSA
GENOVA

RICHIESTA DI TITOLO DI VIAGGIO

Data della domanda

Cognome (Nome di famiglia): (Per le Signore cognome del marito) ALTMANN nata

Nome: KLAUS s. M. (maschile - femminile)

Data di nascita: 25. Oktober 1915 (giorno, mese, anno)

Luogo di nascita: KRONSTADT GERMANIA (città, provincia, stato)

Padre: ALTMANN NIKOLAUS (Cognome, Nome)

Madre: HANSEN ANNA (Cognome di nascita, Nome)

Nazionalità di origine: TEDESCO attuale: (da indicare sul Titolo di viaggio)

Professione: MECANICO Religione: CATTOLICO

Stato di famiglia: SPOSATO / (celibe, sposato } Indicare nome del congiunto, vedovo)

Indirizzo a Genova: VIA LOMELLINI 6

" fuori Genova

Bambini di meno di 14 anni che accompagnano il postulante: UTA-MARIA, NATA 30.VI.41 KASSEL
KLAUS-JIERG, NATO 11.12.46 KASSEL
(Nome, cognome e data di nascita)

Il richiedente è stato o è: prigioniero di guerra - internato - deportato - lavoratore civile - profugo. (Cancellare quello che non conviene)
A date:

Desidera recarsi in: SUED-AMERIKA (BOLIVIA)

Firma personale del richiedente
(Nel firmare la presente richiesta il richiedente dichiara di non aver ricevuto altro titolo di viaggio dalla Croce Rossa Internazionale)

Klaus Altmann

TESTIMONIANZA FORNITA

Identità: TEMP. TRAVEL Document No 0121454, rilasciato (Documenti personali presentati)
dalla alta Commissione Alleata a Monaco, il 21. II. 1951

Visto Boliviano= assicurato presso il Consolato della Bolivia di Genova

Emigrazione: in Bolivia
(Indicare se avverà tramite un Comitato responsabile. Designazione dell'Autorità. Num. di registrazione)
Prof. K. St. Draganović

o privatamente (indicare promesse di visto ottenute):

Impronta digitale (pollice destro)

CONNOTATI

Capelli: CASTAGNI

Occhi: BRUNI

Naso: REGOLARE

Segni particolari: ./.

Visto per l'autenticità delle dichiarazioni, fotografia, firma e impronta digitale del Sig.

Firma e timbro dell'Autorità:

Luogo e data:
(pregasi apporre il timbro anche sulla fotografia)

Carta 10.100 bis N. 18573 Validità sei mesi

Concessa a Genova il 16 Marzo 1951

Consegnata a " il " " "

Firma del richiedente →

Fig. 17. Klaus Barbie, the former chief of the Gestapo in Lyons, was wanted for war crimes by the French authorities while US intelligence services were smuggling him to South America. They organized travel papers from the ICRC for him in the name of Klaus Altmann, and Croatian Monsignor Krunoslav Draganovič took care of the rest.

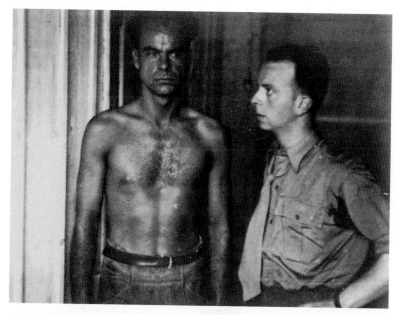

Fig. 18. In 1938 Gerhard Lausegger was leading the SS squad which murdered the head of the Jewish community in Innsbruck, Richard Berger. Berger's son, Frederik R. Benson, who had changed his last name and was by 1945 a soldier in the British army, traced down his father's killer after the war. This photo shows Benson, right, next to the just captured Lausegger. In 1947 Lausegger escaped and managed to reach Argentina.

Fig. 19. The family of the Austrian engineer Walter Haasler in front of the Pyramids, posing for a photo for their loved ones back home in Europe. In 1951 the Haaslers moved from Egypt to South America where well-educated military and technical experts from the ruins of the Third Reich were in demand.

FIG. 20. The Eichmann trial in Jerusalem in 1961 attracted worldwide attention. Oddly enough, prosecutors raised hardly any questions as to how he and other Nazis escaped to Argentina. The involvement of Christian churches, the Red Cross, Western intelligence services, and governments was not to be made public.

bigger. Three large warehouses were available near the Merano race-track. From there the goods were transported by train every three to four weeks. Forged pound notes were smuggled in an apposite manner to Denmark, Holland, and France: the fake notes were hidden in racehorse boxes. Along with weapons, Schwend's people got hold of everything that was in short supply in wartime.[23]

In the autumn of 1942 managers for American Express found over 10,000 forged pound notes, probably test notes for the Swiss market. They included notes so perfect that they looked like part of a government operation. This suspicion was absolutely correct. The distributor of the forged notes in Switzerland was Rudolf Blaschke, an Austrian by birth, who worked from Abbazzia. When Blaschke was arrested by the Swiss authorities, he named Friedrich Schwend as the source of the notes. American diplomats in Switzerland followed the case very closely and drew the accurate conclusion that Schwend and Blaschke must be German agents. So authorities knew very early on about the German forgery operation, but the whole thing was handled in great confidence. Wherever counterfeit notes appeared in future, they were discreetly withdrawn by British officials. No one wanted to broadcast the fact that fake notes were in circulation.

Over time, the US military had developed detailed information about Schwend's activities. In March 1945 they had an accurate map of Labers showing its secret passages, guard units, barracks, and so forth. The OSS in Switzerland identified Schloss Labers as a 'bombing target', and passed on the information, along with the location map, to the various headquarters of the US intelligence services in Caserta and Washington.[24] At this point, Schwend was not exactly displeased that the Americans knew about him and his operations.

It is reasonable to assume that men such as Schwend and Höttl began to play a double game quite early on and to shift the focus of their activities. The secret operation provided the perfect disguise for the preparation of escape routes along which war criminals and SS members could get out of Europe. Towards the end of the war, members of the Schwend group initially tried to save their own skins. Their official task faded into the background, and the quite selfish interests of the operation's members came to the fore. By the close of 1944 Schwend was already preparing for the war's conclusion. The last days of the Thousand-Year Reich could not be far off, and he began to buy property for himself, a hotel or two here, buildings and shares there.

He bought majority shares in a Spanish bank and opened bank accounts in Switzerland, Liechtenstein, and other countries to ensure that his future was as secure as possible after the war.[25] Particularly in Trieste and Merano, members of the Bernhard group were responsible for large numbers of property purchases. There were also some buildings that were used as hiding-places by the Merano profiteers, or as accommodation for their contacts. These included the marble quarries of Laas, some tunnels in the Upper Vinschgau, Hotel Paradise in the Martell Valley, Castle Dornsberg in Naturns, and the castle of Hochnaturns as well as Villa Rheingold on the Reschen.[26]

For his business deals, Schwend usually drew his relations into his confidence; in his personal dealings, he relied on family and friends. Schwend hid gold in the Kaunertal valley in Austria and with a friend in Bavaria. His brother had bricked up about 26 kg of gold coins, jewellery, and 15,000 US dollars in the cellar of their parents' house.[27] Towards the end of the war, Schwend's agents also took money, gold, and items of jewellery into Switzerland. After investigations, American agents reached the conclusion: 'There is good reason to suspect that the purpose of Van Harten's frequent journeys was to carry off valuables, whether this was to ensure a later livelihood for Van Harten and Schwendt [*sic*] alone, or whether the shipment of valuables to Switzerland occurred in the interest of higher-ranking personalities is also worthy of examination.'[28] For the transport of their loot, Schwend's colleagues repeatedly used the International Red Cross as a disguise. As the Red Cross's supposed couriers, they had a car with diplomatic plates and were able to drive to Switzerland without hindrance.[29] But Schwend and his colleagues also tried to hedge their futures in other ways.

The American intelligence officer Vincent La Vista had researched not only the network of escape routes for wanted Nazis through Italy, but even more the routes used by Jewish emigrants who wanted to emigrate illegally to Palestine. The Holocaust survivors were brought to Palestine illegally by Jewish underground organizations and against the will of the British. These emigrants would construct the new Jewish state of Israel. Their goal was to reach the Italian international ports—generally Trieste and Genoa—from Germany, Poland, and Austria. Nazis on the run took the same route to reach the same ports. In the case of Schloss Labers, these two very contrasting underground lines had probably entered an unusual alliance, for some of Friedrich

Schwend's most important 'chief salesmen' had been Jewish business-men, bank directors, and hoteliers. Vincent La Vista stated in his report: 'The exact connection between the remains of "Schloss Labers" and the Jewish underground is unknown at the present time, but the link seems to exist.'[30] The La Vista report provides some hints that the infra-structure of Operation Bernhard was used after the war by National Socialists, but also by Holocaust survivors. The hospital city of Merano was particularly suited to this. Apart from the sanatorium, a number of private houses, chiefly Schloss Rametz and Schloss Labers, were used as accommodations. Merano, not far from the Swiss and Austrian bor-der, was strategically very well located on the way to Genoa.

The most important figure in this network was probably the Jewish agent for Operation Bernhard, Julius Levy, known by his assumed name, Jaac van Harten. As early as April 1945, van Harten established contact with members of Jewish emigration organizations who were on the way to Austria and Hungary and repeatedly passed on to them large numbers of forged pound notes. These pound notes and valuables from the Bernhard booty were intended to help finance the illegal Jew-ish escape routes to Palestine. The Israeli journalist Shraga Elam did intensive research on the van Harten case.[31] But the connections between Jewish underground and Nazi escape routes in Italy still require closer examination, and further archive material on the subject may exist in US and Israeli archives.

In the first months after the war, the SS agents risked walking a dif-ficult tightrope between the camps in order to save their own lives. But van Harten's and Schwend's pasts could not be hushed up for long. The CIC soon discovered that van Harten was an SS agent who was wanted for questioning. On 17 May 1945 he was arrested by the CIC in Mer-ano after the Americans had discovered the many SS depots protected by fake ICRC signs reading 'property of the Red Cross' and filled with plunder that was both costly and rare. When he was arrested by the Allies, van Harten was found to be in possession of pound notes which US authorities at the time consfiscated, estimating their worth at 5,000 dollars.[32] After a brief spell in prison, van Harten, like his boss Schwend, managed to reach an agreement with the US intelligence service to collaborate with its agents. For van Harten, the generous support of the Jewish refugee groups had paid for itself. In 1946 he moved to Tel Aviv, opened a jeweller's shop, and, in spite of his past as an SS collaborator, remained undisturbed. Even Golda Meir, the future Israeli Prime Minister, argued that he could remain in the country 'for his merits'.[33]

By placing their expertise at the disposal of the Allies, some of the distributors of the forged British pound notes found a way into the world of the Cold War intelligence services. After the end of the war, van Harten and fellow agent Crastan presented themselves as Red Cross delegates and issued many tainted SS members—including their boss Schwend—with Red Cross documents.[34] On 28 April 1945 van Harten gave Schwend a forged Red Cross letter confirming 'that he [Schwend] has helped the Committee of the Red Cross [...] J. L. van Harten of the ICRC in Merano will provide all desired information about the forenamed Herr Schwend'.[35] This letter of acknowledgement shielded Schwend for the first few days after the war. Then Schwend—like many of his old comrades—saved his own skin by switching sides and working for the CIC.

On 12 May 1945 Schwend handed himself in to a US unit in Tyrol and began his metamorphosis from Nazi agent to Cold War operative. At first he hushed up his own activity, hoping in this way to save his nest egg beyond the end of the Third Reich. Schwend ended up on remand in Stadelheim prison in Munich and was—by his own account—blackmailed by CIC agents and one of his former chief buyers to tell them where his money was hidden.[36] Under interrogation by the CIC in Munich, Schwend would eventually talk and cooperate and, thus, remain unpunished. After he had finally yielded to pressure and given his consent, the Americans took Schwend under their wing. He led the Americans to various hiding-places in Austria and South Tyrol where he had buried and stashed gold and jewels.[37] The gold alone was worth 200,000 dollars. When he had handed himself over in Augsburg, 2,000 dollars, Swiss francs, and gold coins had been confiscated from him.[38] Finally Schwend was taken on by the Americans as a CIC informant under the code name 'Major Klemp' for 'certain counter-intelligence work'. In May 1945 his American interlocutors held on to Schwend: 'Schwend hopes that his efforts for the Allied cause will be recognized by the US government.'[39] This cooperation won him some concessions from the US officers. Until 1946 Schwend worked for the US agents as a lure to flush out other wanted men in Italy, hence his code-name, 'Flush'.[40] Schwend was only one of many former SS agents who made themselves useful after a short period of imprisonment. A CIC report from the time puts it succinctly: 'The groups consist of Nazis who have been discharged from internment camps. These people use the tensions between the East and the West to work themselves into leading positions where they will become more or less indispensable personnel, thus creating a basis of power and influence for Pro-Nazi activities.'[41]

The positive attitude towards Schwend and his unusually prompt adoption by the US intelligence services had a lot to do with the special situation in Italy; senior SS and Wehrmacht officers had tried to end the pointless struggle a few months before the end of the war, and with this aim they made contact with Allen Dulles, the head of the US wartime intelligence service, the Office of Strategic Services (OSS), in Berne, Switzerland. Shortly before the end of the war, the SS spies around Schwend also became involved in the negotiations with the Americans because these contacts seemed to them to be promising from the point of view of 'building a bridge for the future'.[42] Schwend finally met the SS leaders in Italy and offered to help in the negotiations.[43] Their efforts were finally successful, and the surrender of the SS and the Wehrmacht in Italy, called Operation Sunrise, occurred in a largely orderly fashion. Schwend played a very marginal and minor part in this, but his involvement in the German surrender in Italy was to benefit himself and his agents.

2. The Special Case of Italy

The surrender negotiations with the Americans created a particularly favourable climate for former SS men in Italy such that the whole of the SS and Wehrmacht leadership in Italy could expect accommodating treatment. In many ways, Italy was unique. It was not only the chief negotiators on the German side who profited from the secret negotiations with the SS in Italy code-named Operation Sunrise; the Allied Sunrise negotiators largely had a positive attitude towards the German Wehrmacht and SS officers in Italy. The anticommunism of some American negotiating partners played a crucial role in this; Dulles had certain interests in common with the German generals and, therefore, repeatedly intervened on behalf of his German partners in Sunrise. All SS officers who took part in the operation managed to escape serious punishment after the war. Some were later hired by US intelligence services; others were able to flee to South America or start new careers as private businessmen.[44] The negotiations and contacts within the framework of Operation Sunrise are thus worth examining more closely. Even before the end of the war, they created the context for the Allied treatment of SS officers in Italy.

When the defeat of the Third Reich gradually became foreseeable, some leading German commanders in Italy made contact with Allied offices in 1944. At an appropriate moment, the German forces in Italy were to surrender independently, thus crucially shortening the war. The German officers wanted to achieve favourable conditions for themselves in the event of a surrender, but until the end they all maintained the hope of being able to continue the war against the Soviet Union side by side with the Western Allies.[45] Northern Italian industrialists and Swiss military officers also recognized the advantages in this arrangement. The German commanders in Italy had to proceed with great caution and discretion. If Hitler had learned of their surrender negotiations, the 'conspirators' would certainly have been executed; until Hitler's suicide, no one was safe from denunciation and kangaroo courts, right up to the very last.

From 1944 Karl Wolff, the 'Supreme Commander of the SS and the police in Italy', acted as spokesman for the German conspirators. The best chance of keeping the negotiations quiet was to make contact with the Americans via neutral Switzerland where the OSS had one of its offices. Most of the secret operations in northern Italy, Germany, and Austria were organized via the OSS outpost in Berne, led by the future director of the CIA, Allen Dulles.

No senior OSS agent developed such a keen interest in the political face of post-war Germany as Dulles did. From mid-1943 the head of the OSS in Berne had used his secret contacts to sound out the political landscape within the SS. The Washington headquarters of the OSS felt obliged to point out to Dulles that 'the interest of the OSS is entirely unpolitical', and that his duties lay in 'supporting the army, not in encouraging political doctrines'. Dulles was to stop playing politics off his own bat, came the word from Washington.[46] Still, early in 1944 Dulles struck a tone that—very directly—reveals the urgency of a post-war commitment on the part of the US intelligence service: in order to avert political chaos in Germany, which could produce a communist state, the Americans were prepared to support particular individuals and groups. These people were later to assume key roles in German politics and finance.[47]

Dulles's pro-German attitude came as no surprise. Allen Dulles and his brother, John Foster Dulles, had both worked in the diplomatic service. Even during the First World War, Allen Dulles had worked as a young diplomat in the US embassy in Berne, collecting information about Austria-Hungary and Germany. At the 1919 Paris Conference, he had worked as a Central European adviser within the US delegation. The severe peace conditions for Germany and the break-up of the Austro-Hungarian monarchy had come as a terrible disappointment to him. Even at this time he must have believed in the necessity of incorporating Germany into the West as a stabilizing element within Europe. In 1941 he began to work for the OSS, and in 1942 he took over the running of its important outpost in Berne. Neutral Switzerland had been encircled by the Axis Powers and in many respects represented the ideal platform for intelligence activities, for it offered a window into fascist Europe. In his work, Dulles concentrated particularly on Italy, Germany, and Austria. Two months after Dulles's arrival in Berne, US President Franklin Delano Roosevelt and British Prime Minister Winston Churchill identified the doctrine of the 'unconditional surrender' of Germany as their non-negotiable war objective. Dulles spoke out against this and rejected any objective that would lead to the fragmentation, starvation, or humiliation of Germany. Dulles feared that this position on the part of the West would only lead to a Soviet-dominated Germany. Quite early on, Dulles saw the war as a dispute between East and West. He repeatedly called for the West to fight for the hearts and minds of the Germans and to incorporate Germany into the West after the war. Mistakes like those made after the First World War could not be repeated; the head of the OSS in Berne always remained loyal to that position.[48]

Dulles was convinced that the Germans would continue to play an important part in the future of Europe. He wanted to know that they were on the American side in the struggle against communism. Dulles's SS negotiating partners were aware of this attitude on his part; therefore, they took the same line. From the outset, the SS men stressed to the British and American officials their 'shared view of the Communist danger'. The Sunrise conspirators wanted to offer the Western Allies the 'German Reich as a stronghold in the struggle against Communism', as one colleague of General Wolff's noted in his diary. In northern Italy they wanted to demonstrate how the German Wehrmacht could function as a power for order in the service of the Allies. This 'model' would then apply to Germany.[49] Kept only half-informed by the Americans, the Soviet Union was very suspicious about this planned special surrender. With his attitude, Dulles was ahead of his time—his positions were the opposite of US policy under Roosevelt at the time.[50]

Seen from a purely military point of view, the Operation Sunrise negotiations were practically insignificant because the treaty was signed only a few days before the general end of the war in Europe in 1945. But the negotiations were *politically* significant; in some aspects, they marked the first signs of the Cold War. The surrender of the Wehrmacht in Italy on 2 May 1945 was the climax of a lengthy process of discussion in which political considerations on the part of the major players were at the forefront. Wolff and Dulles were certainly not in political agreement about many things, but they did share some common viewpoints, particularly the fear of a communist-dominated Europe. These discussions, and the secrecy with which they were conducted, made the Soviets doubt the principled nature of the Western Allies and their shared war objective of 'unconditional surrender'.[51]

In his autobiographical accounts of the Sunrise negotiations in 1945, Dulles does not mention promises of protection. But the files of the US State Department contain clues that shed a new light on its attitude towards war criminals who took part in the Sunrise negotiations. In a memo of 17 September 1947, the political adviser to the United States working in Germany asked headquarters in Washington for instructions on dealing with war criminals who maintained that they had taken part in Sunrise. The text of the request is missing from the archives, but the answer to the question has been preserved: 'Officials concerned with Operation Sunrise report no, repeat, no promises furnished,' the head of security in the State Department, Jack Neal, wired back. 'However these officials are of the opinion [...] that allies owe some moral obligation in return for aid given and risks taken; therefore definite consideration should be given to those positive aspects, when assessing war crimes with which they are charged.'[52]

Always officially denied by Dulles, the German Sunrise conspirators were able to rely on his promises of protection, 'even without any kind of written contract',[53] and a few years later some of them were working for the US intelligence services. What promises Dulles made to Wolff will probably never be known in detail. Even colleagues of Wolff were not let in on what was happening. 'What Wolff tried to negotiate, or negotiated, for himself and the forces supporting him, in the discussions he constantly held without my presence in Switzerland and later in Bolzano, I don't know.'[54] But Allen Dulles wanted to ensure that Wolff's side of the story never fully came to light. As Kerstin von Lingen has made clear in her research over the past few years, the anticommunist, anti-Soviet line of the Sunrise negotiations could not be made public. That was one reason why Dulles and other chief Allied negotiators repeatedly intervened vigorously on behalf of SS officers.[55] It was a deal: the Americans would protect the former Nazi leaders whose services were valuable, but in exchange, they would not reveal too much about Sunrise.

At the end of the war in May 1945, the situation in Bolzano was very unusual, even Kafkaesque. SS members and Wehrmacht officers could move relatively freely after the arrival of the American troops. There were even mixed German–American military police patrols in South Tyrol that were guarding buildings and controlling traffic together. Allied officials had to ask the German commanders for accommodations. For weeks, Swastika stamps still decorated German passes, documents, and reports to the Allies. Some of the South Tyrolean mayors and parts of the administration remained in office for another two months. Even bloody clashes between partisans and Wehrmacht at the end of the war were examined by a mixed German–American commission. As a member of the German commission in Bolzano, the war criminal SS-Obersturmbannführer Herbert Kappler took part in local inspections. His incident reports to the Allies reveal as much.[56] The almost absurd situation in Bolzano was also made clear by an article in the American soldiers' magazine *Stars and Stripes*, under the headline 'Did we beat the Nazis or not? You couldn't tell at Bolzano':

> Bolzano, Italy, May 17. This is the city where SS General Karl Wolff made his headquarters, and the city where American GIs spent VE-Day wondering who won the war. Days after the unconditional surrender of the German armies in Italy, armed and arrogant Germans wearing the SS death's head still roamed the streets of Bolzano, in freedom. It was an almost unbelievable situation. When the 88th Division moved into town, it was forced to ask General Wolff for permission to set up a CP. All

billeting was done through the SS—to the infantrymen's profound disgust. When rooms were asked for five American Red Cross girls, the Germans showed their defiance by billeting them next to the local Wehrmacht pro station. Men of the 88th, from rifleman to staff colonels, were disappointed. 'What is this?' they asked. 'What did our guys get killed for? These aren't just German soldiers—they're the men who were Himmler's representatives in Italy.' [...] On VE-Day, two correspondents—Sid Feder of the Associated Press and this Stars and Stripes reporter [Stan Swinton]—wrote what was happening in Bolzano. Both stories were stopped.[57]

But the honeymoon period between the Germans and the Americans only lasted until the middle of May 1945. Washington was disturbed by the reports from Bolzano—what would the international public think, what would the suspicious Soviets assume? On 13 May 1945 Wolff celebrated his forty-fifth birthday in grand style at the villa of the Dukes of Pistoia in Bolzano. The most senior SS and police commander in Italy did not expect to be pursued and was banking on his crucial role in Operation Sunrise to guarantee his safety. He was all the more surprised to be arrested during his birthday party in Bolzano, just as he was opening the last bottle of champagne. Wolff responded with a violent letter of protest, pointing out that Dulles had 'promised him honourable treatment'.[58] Dulles wrote of the ungrateful SS man: 'Between you and me KW [Karl Wolff] doesn't realize what a lucky man he is not to be spending the rest of his days in jail, and his wisest policy would be to keep fairly quiet [...].'[59]

SS General Wolff would have had every reason to keep quiet because he, too, was charged with war crimes. Wolff had joined the SS in 1931 and was soon promoted to the Chief of Staff of the Reichsführer SS thanks to his friendship with Himmler. Himmler, the powerful head of the SS, often authorized Wolff to make decisions about important matters on his behalf. He had been repeatedly involved in the genocide of the Jews. In 1943 Wolff was sent to Italy as head of the SS and the police and, thus, was freed from his close connection to Himmler. That was probably what saved his skin. After his arrest in May 1945, Wolff was interned in Italy to speak as a witness rather than to sit as a defendant at the Nuremberg war crimes trial from autumn 1945 onwards, a shocking turn of events. The Allies made no accusations against him. In 1949 Himmler's former personal adjutant was placed in custody in Nuremberg as part of a denazification process and then immediately released. The former deputy to the mass murderer Himmler went on living undisturbed in Germany until January 1962, and 'Herr General' spent his holidays in South Tyrol. It was only when what had long been known and documented came back into the public eye during the Eichmann trial that Wolff had to swap his comfortable villa on Lake Starnberg for a Munich prison cell. In 1964 a German court sentenced him to fifteen years' imprisonment. His closeness to Himmler and his involvement in deportations of the Jews to Poland until 1943 were considered far weightier than his merits in speeding up the end of the war.[60]

In the early Cold War, the US intelligence services had no qualms about employing Nazi war criminals. If a former SS man who had been involved with the intelligence services could contribute important information about the struggle against the Soviet bloc, in many cases the criminal past of the informant was overlooked. What mattered was the Nazi agent's appropriately anticommunist attitude and the key information he could provide. In some cases, the US authorities were even prepared to protect these agents from prosecution.[61] Particularly intriguing was the gall with which members of the SS secret service took jobs directly from the staffs of the occupying armies. The CIA employed many former Nazis as agents after the war. Of them, a significant number were specialists in the armaments industry. The victorious powers had a great interest in their knowledge and the advances in German technology. The US government exploited their agents' expertise in what was probably one of the biggest 'transfers of specialists and knowledge from one country to the other' that the world has ever seen.[62] The Allied intelligence services had the major task of finding these specialists, questioning them, and perhaps taking them to their new home; the top scientists were absorbed by the US, the Soviet Union, and Great Britain. Small allies got only the crumbs from the table of the German and Austrian specialists—and they included people with tainted pasts; for example, Wernher von Braun ran a missile factory that used thousands of forced labourers and concentration camp inmates, many of whom died. The slave labourers were forced to work themselves to death, or were starved.

American decision-makers justified the employment of former Nazis and collaborators after 1945 with reference to the immediate threat from the Soviet Union. Another war was expected within a short time, and the United States seemed to be ill-prepared for it. It was particularly short of reliable information about its new enemy. Because of this situation, President Truman ordered the establishment of a programme of psychological warfare, covert operations, and espionage. The first deliberations on the subject were made in 1945. Three years later Truman authorized a secret multimillion-dollar programme by the National Security Council to assist 'underground movements, guerrillas and refugee liberation groups [...] against hostile states', meaning the USSR and its satellites. Many of these 'refugee liberation groups' were fascist organizations that had collaborated with the Third Reich during the war. Some of their leaders were perpetrators directly involved in the deportation and murder of Jews in Eastern Europe. In spite of this history, senior officials in the National Security Council were convinced of the necessity to support precisely these groups and reactivate German spy networks.

The US reliance on intelligence from these turncoats yielded optimism about the West's anticommunist campaign, but few positive results, an outcome hardly worth the backlash that would occur once the facts about the recycled spies became public knowledge. Ukrainian and Russian exile groups told the Americans they still had big underground armies in the Soviet Union. This optimistic view was shared by German secret service experts such as Reinhard Gehlen, who ran spy networks of this kind in Eastern Europe during the war. According to Gehlen, most of the spy networks that could easily be reactivated with American money and his spy staff were still in operation. There was no shortage of grand promises and visions of a guerrilla army against the Soviets in Eastern Europe. Compared to all these assurances, the results were rather feeble. In fact, the majority of the programmes to recycle Nazi secret service staff were complete failures. Most of the networks in Eastern Europe did not exist at all, or else had been infiltrated by the Soviets. The secret underground conflict waged during the early years of the Cold War was amateurish in every respect, and that sloppiness cost the lives of thousands of anticommunists in Eastern Europe. In the eyes of the American public, too, this recycling of Nazi war criminals would turn out to be a severe setback for the intelligence services and politics generally. Allen Dulles played a considerable part in that.[63]

3. 'Recycled' War Criminals

One of the most prominent cases of a post-war SS career within the context of the Cold War is that of Wilhelm Höttl. Kaltenbrunner's right-hand man was arrested by US troops in mid-May 1945, in the Ausseer Land in the heart of the 'Alpine fortress'. But the busy Höttl still wouldn't admit defeat even though he faced an inevitable trial because of his involvement in the murder of the Hungarian Jews. He suddenly mutated into an Austrian patriot and stressed to the Americans his anticommunist convictions from the very first. Even while he was being questioned for the first time while in US custody in May 1945, he confidently went on record as telling the US official that the future of Austria could only lie in a strong alliance with the West against communism. As well as words, Höttl offered the US something that was of concrete value: his network of agents in Hungary, Yugoslavia, and Romania. He had preserved these SS contacts throughout the end of the war in order to put them at the service of the United States. But at first, in July 1945, Höttl's information was used only to eliminate existing networks as potential Werewolf cells, the code name for Nazis who stayed behind and formed guerrilla units against the Allied forces.[64] At the same time, Höttl tried to activate his 'American spy connections', and made contact with Dulles.[65]

Any SS criminals who could demonstrate their services in the context of Sunrise, however small they might have been, could count on Dulles's protection after 1945. Höttl had jumped on the Sunrise bandwagon at the last minute, via his comrade Friedrich Schwend. Höttl later stressed these few contacts that he had with the Sunrise officers in completely exaggerated terms. But this method paid off for him.[66] In the main Nuremberg war crimes trial, Höttl was an important witness for the prosecution. His statement that Eichmann had told him about six million murdered Jews was to assume worldwide historical importance. For Höttl, his role as witness rather than defendant at Nuremberg was proof that the Allies planned to spare his life; in the end, his willingness to collaborate with the Americans had, indeed, probably saved him from the gallows.

Höttl was thus able to return to Upper Austria in October where he began by working for the CIC. From 1948, Höttl ran several secret service operations for the agency in Soviet-occupied eastern Austria, as well as in Hungary and Romania. His old contacts and SS networks were now to be reactivated for the anticommunist struggle. Höttl's colleagues were all old SS comrades who became turncoats. The Cold War made Höttl, with his supposed and real contacts, into a valuable ally of the West. In summer 1948 he carried out an espionage project for Thomas A. Lucid who, as the director of the CIC 430th Detachment, was the head of the CIC in Upper Austria.[67] But the CIC commander in Austria, Major James (Jim) Milano, observed Höttl's work with increasing scepticism. Höttl seemed to be driven by greed and a lust for power, sometimes lied immoderately, and often exaggerated his opportunities and contacts. At the same time, he offered his services to anyone interested as long as that person paid him. Sometimes he even earned his livelihood from several intelligence services at once. When the CIC dropped him for the first time in 1950, the French immediately took him on, and it even seems likely that the Soviet Komitet gosudarstvennoy bezopasnosti (KGB, Committee for State Security) was interested in him, too. Höttl repeatedly had contact with the former SS officer Karl Hass, who was also in the service of the CIC. Hass also played a prominent key role in the world of Italian espionage. In addition to that, Hass and Höttl tried to sign up for a new West German secret service. It was only in the early 1960s that Höttl became persona non grata to the CIA and the Western services because of his supposed KGB contacts. Höttl's involvement in war crimes never particularly disturbed the Americans: rumours that he was close to the communists, on the other hand, immediately led to his downfall.[68]

One close colleague of Höttl's was the Austrian Dr Helmut Triska, an SS-Sturmbannführer in the Foreign Office from 1940 onwards, who worked with Höttl in Budapest. After the 'successful operation against the Jews' in Hungary, Triska was with Ambassador Rahn in Fasano on Lake Garda from the end of 1944 until May 1945. At the end of the war, he was arrested by American troops in Merano. Triska was soon making a career for himself again in private business, and from 1954 he was the director of a trading company. Between 1953 and 1954 the CIC and the CIA drew up a detailed report on Triska. The reasons are not entirely clear from the file. But there are clear indications that Triska had worked as a spy in the 1950s. The Americans knew him as a fanatical Nazi with a gold Party medal. Triska may have used his contact with Höttl to work as an informant for the US intelligence services. A note in his CIA file reads: 'Helmut Triska has been assigned the number V-9134.2 and the cover name Triebe'.[69]

Yet another former Nazi who found a career as a Cold War operative was Guido Zimmer. The Sunrise conspirator SS-Obersturmführer Zimmer completely escaped prosecution and went to Argentina as a businessman. His case illustrates very clearly the treatment of German Sunrise conspirators after 1945. Guido Zimmer was born in 1911 in Buer, Westphalia. In 1932 he joined the NSDAP, the SS as early as 1936, and the Security Service (SD) of the SS. In 1940 he was sent to Rome as a member of the foreign espionage service of the SD. Zimmer worked as a specialist with the German embassy in Rome under Herbert Kappler.[70] After Mussolini's fall from power and the German invasion of Italy in 1943, Zimmer was sent to Genoa where he was involved in the arrest of Jews. Then he was called to Milan, where his superior, Walter Rauff, was living. Rauff had already made a name for himself within the SS as the inventor of the gas truck before he was appointed head of the SS in northwest Italy. When the defeat of the Third Reich was becoming increasingly obvious, Zimmer suggested making contact with the Allies via neutral Switzerland. According to Zimmer, the Italian baron and businessman Luigi Parrilli was to act as intermediary. Parrilli had already spent some time working as an informant for Zimmer; he also had contacts with the partisan commanders in northern Italy. Zimmer was thus seen as one of the early initiators of the Sunrise operation.

At the end of the war, the SS-Obersturmführer was neither arrested nor interrogated in any depth by the Allies. On the contrary, the OSS hired him to uncover Nazi underground organizations. In the summer of 1945, Zimmer worked repeatedly for the OSS in Milan and even wore an American uniform.[71] In December 1945 CIC headquarters for Europe confirmed that Zimmer and his colleagues had been 'of material assistance to the Allied cause during the recent war. At great risk to their own lives, they helped in the defeat of the enemy and saved the lives of numerous Allied military personnel.' Consequently, 'the Chief, Counter Intelligence Branch, G-2 Division, Headquarters United States Forces, European Theater has directed that the above individuals will not be arrested for their actions, or otherwise molested because of their membership in the SS. This information will not be disseminated unnecessarily, but will be used for reference and to prevent arrest or molestation of the subjects.'[72]

This letter of acknowledgement was issued not only for Zimmer, but also for the officer Baron Günther von Haniel from Munich. With this writ of protection from the head of the CIC in Europe, Zimmer and his SS comrades were practically inviolable. Zimmer was able to move freely around Italy; if he was checked, he presented his CIC letter of acknowledgement. As early as November 1945, one of Dulles's senior colleagues wrote to the head of the OSS in Washington, DC about Zimmer's contributions to Sunrise:

> Guido Zimmer, a member of the SS, played an outstanding part in the secret operations, which resulted in the unconditional surrender of the German Armies in Northern Italy. It was he who, early in 1945, set the ball rolling by entering into secret discussions with the Italian Baron Parrilli, for the purpose of establishing the first contact with Allied representatives in Switzerland. [...] There can be no doubt that Guido Zimmer was of outstanding help in bringing about the surrender of the German Armies in Northern Italy. In so doing he contributed materially to hastening the end of the war and saving the lives of many Allied soldiers.[73]

At this time OSS chief General William Donovan was working closely with the American chief prosecutors in the Nuremberg war crimes trial. Dulles wrote this letter for Zimmer as a kind of security. With this CIC pass, no limits were put on his freedom of movement in Italy, and his letter of acknowledgement to Donovan helped to protect him in the future. As a result, Zimmer escaped potential prosecution as an SS war criminal.

In 1946 Zimmer settled for a time in Erlangen. In 1948 he received a visit there from his friend Baron Luigi Parrilli, who was on one of his first business trips in post-war Germany. Zimmer's business was doing badly, and the country was in ruins. Baron Parrilli offered his former superior a job as a private secretary in Italy and a very high salary— on the condition that he would now work for him. Zimmer did not hesitate and accepted the offer. He wanted to make a new start in Italy and even tried to acquire Italian citizenship.[74] But apparently South America and offers from former comrades in Argentina were more tempting. Zimmer may also have been worried about being prosecuted after his former comrade Herbert Kappler was sentenced in Italy. His fear was not unfounded. In the 1950s Zimmer was actually wanted by the state prosecutor of Dortmund for his involvement in the deportation of Jews in Genoa. But Zimmer had moved to Argentina long before then. He arrived in Argentina from Genoa on 22 October 1949, describing himself as a 'farming expert' and risking a new start with Parrilli's help.[75] Once again the US intelligence service had gotten rid of an agent long past his usefulness by sending him abroad.

The best-known and best-established example of uninterrupted recycling is the career of Hitler's head of espionage in the East, Reinhard Gehlen. Gehlen, who had been in the Reichswehr since 1920, joined the General Staff in 1935, and from 1942 was responsible for counter-intelligence against the Soviet army as head of the Foreign Armies East department. He worked particularly closely with the SS. After the announcement of the Soviet attack on Berlin in spring 1945, he was dismissed. He presented himself to the Americans in person. When he was questioned in June 1945, he provided more than just useful information; the protocol of the Interrogation Centre of the 7th US Army reads like an employment application for the US secret service. Gehlen had to change neither conviction nor jargon. By the very fact that he didn't change his position, he told the Americans what they wanted to hear. The recording officer remarked: Gehlen 'is an anti-Communist and expects a conflict between Russia and the Allies'.[76] From March 1945 Gehlen had been preparing for the defeat by putting his officers and archives out of reach of the Red Army. The 'Gehlen Organization' came into being in July 1946: Gehlen and some of his comrades were working in the United States for the country's intelligence services, gathering information on Eastern Europe and helping to shape the UD government's image of the Russian enemy there. From 1949 the Gehlen Organization was entrusted to the CIA and maintained close contact with the West German government under Konrad Adenauer. In the selection of agents and informers, their usefulness was crucial, but not their past. Gehlen stated: 'A German intelligence organization is being created using the available potential, to do intelligence on Eastern Europe, i.e. to continue the old work in the same direction. The foundation is a shared interest in the defence against Communism.'[77] In 1956 the Gehlen Organization became the Federal Information Service of Western Germany (Bundesnachrichtendienst, BND), and Gehlen remained its head until 1968. The Gehlen Organization enjoyed certain advantages in that the CIA was able to approach Gehlen for delicate operations.[78] In such cases his contacts could be very useful to former SS and Gestapo members. Although it relied on this organization outside its agency, the CIA also directly recruited amongst former SS officers.

The US had recruited an SS veteran from Adolf Eichmann's Jewish Affairs department. A close colleague of Eichmann, Otto Albrecht von Bolschwing had been involved in the persecutions of the Jews in Hungary, amongst other things. After the end of the war he worked initially for the CIA and emigrated to the United States where his life was quiet and orderly until 1960, when he learned of Eichmann's abduction. Von Bolschwing became nervous and immediately contacted his former CIA superior. Although he was a respected US citizen and had a good job in a pharmaceuticals company, von Bolschwing was frightened. He told his superior that he was always worried about being deported to Israel. The retired CIA man, who knew von Bolschwing's biography only superficially, could not at first understand his former agent's anxieties, so he asked the CIA about von Bolschwing. As he learned more and more about him, he was shocked. He immediately declared that he knew nothing about his agent's past. What the officer was supposedly unable to remember had been known to the CIA since von Bolschwing's engagement: his brutal SS past.

Von Bolschwing's biography, specifically his role in Nazi war crimes and his government-aided avoidance of justice, would be enough to disturb anyone. He was born in 1909 into an old aristocratic Junker family, and his education had included the study of languages and learning good manners. Anti-Semitism was not typical of Junkers, but was expected by the NSDAP, which von Bolschwing joined in 1929. In 1936 he was employed as an adviser in Himmler's SS. After only a few weeks in his new job, he presented a highly regarded study of the 'solution of the Jewish problem'. In 1937 von Bolschwing developed, with Eichmann, the first programme for the systematic expropriation of the European Jews. The German Jews were to be forced through terror to emigrate to Palestine. After the annexation of Austria—in Nazi terms the so-called Anschluss—in 1938 he was able to turn his theories into practice. Von Bolschwing helped Eichmann in the dispossession and forced migration of the Jews of Vienna. During the war he took part in special operations in Romania and Hungary.

In the eyes of the CIA, von Bolschwing was an opportunist who first enriched himself from Jewish property in Hungary, then from the German defeat. As the end of the Hitler regime approached, he sought a way to secure his future. His second marriage to an Austrian gave him the chance to reinvent his biography. His brother-in-law was a member of the Austrian O5 resistance movement, which had been organized from 1943 onwards with American help. In late 1944 von Bolschwing brought his family to safety in Salzburg. In the spring of 1945 he had already begun to cooperate actively—one might even say enthusiastically—with the Allies when US troops rolled through western Austria. Von Bolschwing's talent was such that he was able to metamorphose from Prussian Junker to Tyrolean peasant in the Alps. Von Bolschwing's contacts with the CIC proved reliable. He used his position and the active support of the US intelligence services to apply for Austrian citizenship in 1948 and have himself whitewashed by an Austrian denazification commission.[79] Von Bolschwing, too, was finally recruited for the newly founded CIA in 1949. One of his duties was to find informants, and he specialized in border-crossing operations in which spies were smuggled into Hungary and Romania. For reasons that are so far unclear, in January 1954 the CIA brought von Bolschwing to the United States. The former SS officer, Nazi, and SD agent was authorized to enter the United States illegally and, thus, start a new life. The CIA worked out a complicated plan and produced a whole range of fake documents for their top man.[80] The American historian Christopher Simpson thus reaches this conclusion: 'Considering that Otto von Bolschwing had spent most of his adult life working full-time as a salaried executive of the Nazi party security service and SS police apparatus, the CIA's refusal even to *suspect* that he might have committed crimes against humanity appears to give him a presumption of innocence of truly munificent proportions.'[81]

4. The Origins of the Italian Ratline

The CIC spies had already constructed an overseas escape route for their agents in 1947: the Italian 'ratline'. When the Iron Curtain came down across Europe, the ratline originally served to bring endangered agents out of the Soviet-occupied parts of Austria and Eastern Europe. Along that underground line, SS people from all over Europe were smuggled via Italy to South America or the Middle East. It was set up to be used by the US intelligence services in the struggle against communism after 1945. The start of the Italian 'ratline' can be precisely dated. On 22 July 1946 forty prisoners of war escaped from the Rimini prisoner-of-war camp. They included twenty dangerous German secret service officers and SS members. Holding 150,000 prisoners, Rimini was the largest camp for members of the German Wehrmacht and SS in Italy. Previously, hundreds of Wehrmacht soldiers and SS men had disappeared from Rimini, apparently into thin air. Finally, from 1946, a mass break-out from Rimini began, and hundreds of SS men made off and disappeared completely. The Allies were increasingly concerned. Fugitives included prominent perpetrators such as the SS officers Erich Priebke, Walter Rauff, and Willem (Wilhelm) Maria Sassen, as well as the commandant of the Riga Ghetto, Eduard Roschmann.[82] The former head of the Security Service in Rome, Karl Hass, was only a 'guest' in Rimini for a month before escaping from Allied imprisonment on 20 July 1946.[83] 'There were break-outs from the camp almost every night, we were 220,000 German soldiers,' Priebke said in an interview in 1996.[84]

The Americans were alarmed and went off in search of the escapees. Where had the absconders from Rimini gone? A large-scale inquiry began. When the Americans learned of illegal, possibly well-organized Nazi escape routes, they launched 'Operation Circle' to get to the bottom of the matter. Vincent La Vista, a senior officer in the Rome office of Foreign Activity Correlation, was put in charge of the investigation. Born in 1907 in Dobbs Ferry, New York, La Vista had taken part in various inquiries into fascist spy cells in the United States and South America. He came to Italy in July 1945 to work on Mussolini's archive. La Vista was then involved in 'Operation Safe Haven'. The purpose of this large-scale operation was to uncover hidden Nazi assets. Various US authorities, including the OSS and the State Department, went in search of Nazi money and property after 1943. Within this framework, La Vista was to investigate the whereabouts of escaped SS officers in Italy. He was successful. His report on 'illegal emigration to and through Italy', dated 15 May 1947, was classified as 'top secret' and was—as mentioned above—kept under wraps for a long time.[85] La Vista wrote at the start of his report: 'An examination of this list of organizations and the individuals involved will readily disclose the reason for the necessity of treating this matter with the utmost discretion.'[86]

The most important escape routes that have so far come to light, including the ones that smuggled National Socialists, were led by church groups. Understanding why and how some proponents of the Catholic Church were involved in Nazi smuggling facilitates a better understanding of the post-war alliances between former Nazis and Western intelligence services. One of the church organizations in particular is worth closer examination: the Catholic group Intermarium. Monsignor Krunoslav Draganović, who took care of the escape routes of Croatian fascists amongst other things, was the most senior Croatian representative in the self-appointed management committee of Intermarium. The organization was, according to American historian Christopher Simpson, hugely involved in Nazi border-crossing. Later Intermarium became an important source for the recruitment of exiled Eastern Europeans for the anti-communist propaganda machine or exile organizations sponsored by the CIA. Leading members of Intermarium ended up in CIA-sponsored media such as Radio Free Europe, Radio Liberty, or the Assembly of Captive European Nations (ACEN).[87]

The leadership of the Catholic Church saw the Second World War as an intermezzo in a bigger struggle against 'atheist Communism'. In this dispute, the Vatican allied itself with a series of Christian conservative and clerical-fascist political movements in Europe. The Vatican saw the National Socialists as the lesser evil. Even before the Second World War, the German counter-intelligence departments used members of Intermarium, who were seen as very effective and valuable because of their contacts. By the time the Wehrmacht overran half of Europe, Intermarium was already an 'instrument of the German intelligence', as one US Army report noted.[88] With the collapse of the Third Reich in 1944/5, senior Catholic clerics organized humanitarian relief programmes for refugees from Eastern Europe. The members of these organizations barely differentiated between Catholics who were persecuted by the Soviets, deportees, and Nazis. The mass of refugees certainly had nothing to do with Nazi crimes; they were simply in the wrong place at the wrong time when the Wehrmacht or the Red Army laid waste their villages. At the same time, however, these channels became the most important escape route for SS members, collaborators, and war criminals. Within the Catholic Church were factions that had long sympathized with the Nazis and their fanatical opposition to communism and that wanted to forge an alliance with them. These groups organized programmes to bring tens of thousands of SS men and collaborators from Germany, Austria, Hungary, Croatia, Slovakia,

Ukraine, and other Eastern European states to safety.[89] One striking example may serve to illustrate the work of Intermarium in Italy.

The rescue of an entire division of the Ukrainian Waffen-SS—some 11,000 men and women—was perhaps the most dramatic action of Intermarium. In the Rimini internment camp, these Ukranians faced an uncertain future. Most were members of the Galicia grenadier division, which had been formed in 1943. Some members of this division were veterans of Ukrainian police and militia units who had collaborated with the Germans and taken part in anti-Semitic and anticommunist pogroms in their homeland. Some of these men may have even served as guards in concentration camps. Most of these men (with their families) were, however, private soldiers who had committed no war crimes and only found themselves in this compromising situation as a result of circumstances. These Catholic Ukrainians hoped for an independent, anticommunist Ukrainian state after the final victory of the Third Reich.[90] The Ukrainian Waffen-SS soldiers finally surrendered to the Western Allies in May 1945.[91]

During the soldiers' interment in Rimini, Ukrainian Archbishop Ivan Buchko now came to their aid. Along with other Ukrainian clerics—and with the blessing of the Pope—Buchko took a leading role in Intermarium. He petitioned the Pope in person for the 'blossom of the Ukrainian nation'—meaning the Waffen-SS men in Rimini. The result was that the collaborators were ultimately not handed over to Stalin, but allowed to emigrate as 'free colonists' to Great Britain, Canada, Australia, and other Commonwealth states.[92] Thus, thanks to the papal initiative, they escaped safely abroad.[93] Securing International Red Cross travel documents for the Ukrainians was a crucial step in their emigration, so on 4 December 1946 Archbishop Buchko approached the ICRC in Rome and asked for 9,000 travel documents to be issued for the interned Ukrainians in Rimini.[94] After several interventions from church and other relief organizations, the Red Cross decided to issue travel documents for this group—their tickets to freedom.[95] The former SS men soon attracted the attention of the Western intelligence services. With these men's support, the West hoped that it would be possible to unleash an intensified guerrilla war within the Soviet Union. A good number of the former Ukrainian members of the Galicia SS Division thus ended up on the payroll and in the training camps of the British US intelligence services and military.[96]

Intensive attempts by Intermarium to help with border crossings began as early as the summer of 1945. The President of Intermarium was the Slovene Miha Krek, but the driving force behind the whole organization was the Hungarian Ferenc Vajta, who was promoted to speaker of Intermarium.[97] CIC agents soon developed close contacts with representatives of Intermarium. One of the first common projects concerned the situation in Hungary. In 1947 the pro-Western head of the Hungarian government was toppled by the Soviets. US intelligence services such as the CIC and Intermarium now tried to join forces to prevent the Sovietization of Hungary.[98] The speaker of Intermarium, Vajta, was exactly the right contact for this enterprise and was soon recruited as a CIC agent in Rome. But Vajta had a dark history: the Allies officially wanted him for the murder of Hungarian Jews. In the Second World War, he had had a career among the Hungarian Arrow-Cross fascists and, along with other Hungarian fascists, had to flee to Italy to escape the Soviets. At first he worked within the framework of the PCA in Rome. His employers were the escape agents Bishop Hudal and Father Gallov. In 1947 Vajta was briefly arrested as a wanted war criminal in Italy, but soon escaped from a Roman police cell and hid in the Pope's summer residence, Castel Gandolfo, where he was granted asylum. There, under the aegis of the French, he began to set up spy-rings in Innsbruck, Bolzano, Rome, Freiburg, and Paris. This network probably involved members of the Jesuit order, who operated as agents of the Vatican, especially in the Soviet-occupied countries of Europe. This network was later co-sponsored by the CIA. Once his work was finished, Vajta reached the United States in the 1950s and later Colombia, where he worked for the CIA and as a correspondent for foreign newspapers.[99]

For the organizers of the ratline, contacts with church escape agents in Italy were central because, strictly speaking, the US intelligence services did not actually create the ratline but took over existing escape routes. These church connections were already being created at the end of the war in 1945, and by the time of the La Vista report in 1947, they were in full operation. Former SS men in Italy established contacts between the CIC and the Church. Most of them were SS men who had won the trust of the Allies.

One escape agent associated with the Catholic Church was SS-Standartenführer Walter Rauff. Rauff, a former SS commander in

Milan, was able to escape Allied imprisonment in Rimini with church help in 1946. His superior recalled: 'Walter Rauff—he was from Brandenburg, by his accent, whether he's still alive or where he is I don't know; I last saw him in 1945 in the POW camp in Rimini/Ital[y].'[100] Rauff's first stop after escaping was Rome, where he was given a friendly welcome by Bishop Hudal and put up in a monastery. Hudal allegedly found the SS man a job as a teacher of French and math at the Catholic school on Via Pia. With the help of the Church, Rauff's family reached Rome from the Soviet-occupied zone of Austria.[101] According to Simon Wiesenthal, Rauff and Hudal organized what was known as the 'route via Rome' for escaping senior Nazis. Even in the prisoner-of-war camps, the comrades were told who they could approach in Rome and elsewhere. The political background that made it easier to disguise this enterprise was the seizure of power by communist regimes in Eastern Europe. In all the former Nazi satellite states—Slovakia, Hungary, and Croatia—mass arrests were carried out by the new rulers, with former fascists their first targets. As these were all 'good Catholics', the Vatican set up relief agencies for this category of refugees. Rauff made contact with these institutions via Bishop Hudal to ensure that his colleagues were not forgotten. Rauff's comrades included Eugen Dollmann, Hitler's interpreter in Italy and a confidant of Himmler.

SS Standartenführer Dollmann is a good example of the way the US secret services got rid of an SS officer who was no longer very useful as a source. Dollmann played a supporting role in Operation Sunrise. After the war he was employed as an American agent against Italian communists. Eugen Dollmann was born on 8 August 1900 in Regensburg. In the summer of 1918 he served briefly in a Bavarian field artillery regiment. After the end of the First World War, he studied history and literature at the Ludwig Maximilian University in Munich and graduated magna cum laude in 1926. As a Protestant, he dedicated his doctoral thesis to the Counter-Reformation; that in itself was good preparation for his later contacts with the Vatican. From 1927 until 1930, he studied at various Italian universities on a research grant. In 1934 he joined the NSDAP, and from 1935 he ran the press department at the Nazi Auslandsstelle in Rome, where he also frequently worked as a translator. In 1937 he joined the SS and was promoted to Obersturmführer. Then he worked very closely with SS General Karl Wolff on Heinrich Himmler's staff. As an intermediary with Mussolini's government and the Vatican, Dollmann became the important bearer of a great deal of secret knowledge.[102] This quiet work in the shadows paid off—he was soon appointed SS-Standartenführer. He was educated and worldly, speaking perfect Italian and English, and also some French. He was somehow 'everybody's man', as OSS chief Allen Dulles observed.

It is hardly surprising that, given his history, skills, and contacts, Dollmann was one of the first SS men to knock on Dulles's door. Dollmann doubtless wanted to save his own skin, but his love of Italian art and history may also have been a motivation. He wanted to prevent the destruction of northern Italy, his cultural homeland, with all means at his disposal. After Claus Schenk Graf von Stauffenberg's assassination attempt on Hitler in July 1944, Dollmann sought a way out of the war. He worked as Mussolini's interpreter in the Wolf's Lair in Rastenburg immediately after the assassination attempt on 20 July 1944.[103] This made him an eyewitness to Hitler's pathological rages and ravings. 'I thought to myself, the man must be mad. I don't know why I didn't go over to the Allies there and then,' Dollmann said when being questioned by the Americans.[104] After his return to Italy, Dollmann immediately began to establish contact with those who might help him; after all, Dollmann had valuable, diverse contacts: he had discussions with Mussolini, with churchmen, with Italian industrialists, and finally with SS General Karl Wolff.

Wolff gave his agreement to Dollmann's ideas for ending the fight, but imposed certain conditions: an honourable surrender for the Wehrmacht in Italy and an amnesty for himself and his SS men. Cardinal Ildefonso Schuster of Milan offered his services as intermediary. Dollmann wrote: 'During this period my intensive contacts with the Cardinal of Milan and Bologna began. The Catholic Church intended to bring about a ceasefire of German troops in Italy under the protectorate of the Church. These contacts produced the connections with the American secret service in Switzerland, which finally led to the surrender of Caserta on 2 May 1945.'[105]

Dollmann played a role in the negotiated German surrender in Italy. For varying reasons, the Germans, Americans, and the Vatican were pursuing a common goal: the prevention of a communist assumption of power. According to US historian Robert Wolfe: 'Operation Sunrise closely resembled a performance of the Commedia dell'Arte, replete with mistaken identities, missed connections, surprise entrances and exits, with everything falling into place just in time for the final curtain.'[106] Much information about Sunrise is based on records of interrogations and memories, in which numerous German, Italian, American, and Swiss agents each stressed his 'crucial' role in the successful outcome of the negotiations. The secret surrender in Italy was finally successful—although it was a last-minute success. For Allen Dulles, Operation Sunrise marked the crucial step in his appointment as director of the CIA. Dulles always remained obliged to his German partners in Sunrise and where possible tried to protect them from prosecution as war criminals.[107] For the Americans, it seemed clear 'that Dollmann did actively participate in the surrender negotiations at no small risk to himself'.[108] Although Dulles made no binding promises to Dollmann, 'it seems that we owe some consideration to those men', the American intelligence service concluded.[109] Dulles made it clear once more that they should at least help him.

The US agents took Dollmann under their wing and brought him to Rome, urging him to remain calm because a publication by Dulles about Operation Sunrise would purge him and the other German SS and Wehrmacht members of all charges.[110] Despite these reassurances, in December 1945 Dollmann fled from an Italian prisoner-of-war camp and was hidden by the Bishop of Milan. He stayed under the protection of Cardinal Schuster in a monastery in the city, where he observed in his memoirs:

> Summer 1946. After successfully escaping from an Allied prisoner-of-war camp, I had battled adventurously all the way to Milan. Shortly afterwards, scruffy and wrapped in an old English officer's coat, I stood facing Cardinal Schuster. The cardinal smiled gently: 'You don't need to say anything, Dr Dollmann. Over the past few years you have done a great deal for the Church. Now the Church will do something for you.' [...] The Church did something for me. It sheltered me [...].'[111]

In 1947 the Italians demanded that Dollmann be handed over as a Nazi criminal.[112] According to the indictment, he had been involved in the deportation of Italian Jews. Counterintelligence chief James Angleton successfully intervened on Dollmann's behalf; as a result, he was moved to the American zone of Germany, where he underwent a fast-track denazification process.[113] The Central Intelligence Group (a predecessor of the CIA) expressly warned him against returning to Italy, for he would be arrested there and possibly prosecuted as a war criminal. Dollmann and his colleague Eugen Wenner were thus to remain in the US-occupied zone and 'stay calm'. They were given a large sum in Swiss francs to make a new start.[114] But Dollmann had no accommodations or work opportunities in Bavaria and, consequently, stayed in Innsbruck. In 1948 American agents smuggled him over the Brenner and back to Milan, where he worked as a CIC agent.

Dollmann was a talented liaison officer and diplomat, but he had little knowledge about or experience with intelligence services. Because he urgently needed money, he initially offered the CIC, and later the CIA, dubious information. Occasionally he promised the CIC that he would recover the Bormann archive in Bolzano and find the 'Hitler treasure' in the South Tyrolean mountains. In 1950, with members of the Brandenburg Division, he tried to recover the Hitler 'treasure'. The motivation for his cooperation with the Americans becomes clear from his letter: 'And in the spirit of our fighting comradeship, low-key but often tried and tested, I have been honestly delighted that you now have a good chance of returning from passive nothingness back into the active reality of global political events.'[115] There is a grain of truth to the Dollmann 'treasure' story. At the end of the war, Frau Bormann and the children fled from Berchtesgaden to South Tyrol. In Gerda's luggage in Wolkenstein there were also parts of the archive of the Bormann family, including private correspondence and records of Hitler's dinner conversation.

At first the Americans believed and supported Dollmann, who often wildly exaggerated. He was probably trying to capitalize on his knowledge as much as he could. On 12 July 1950 he crossed the border again and travelled to Innsbruck. There he met former members of the Brandenburg Division and discussed a possible search operation in South Tyrol. At that time, Dollmann's spymasters were keen on him and called him a 'first-class man'. Dollmann repeatedly demanded money, which they happily handed over. He travelled several times to South Tyrol; in the end, nothing came of the search.[116] In 1951 Dollmann also offered what he claimed was the Bormann Archive to the Italian military secret service. The handover was to take place in Bolzano.[117] Exactly what Dollmann wanted to give the Italians is unclear.

At any rate, the Italian agent Rodolfo Siviero had been commissioned by Rome in 1945 to secure stolen art treasures in South Tyrol. Interestingly, in 1984 some drawings by Hitler that had been in Bormann's possession were shown in public by Siviero's heirs, for he had died the previous year. Whether they could have been part of the Bormann Archive that Dollmann offered to the Italians is an uncertain but tantalizing possibility. Officially, Siviero had bought the pictures legally in Bolzano.[118] In his memoirs, Siviero records that the Italian state had 'forgotten' to pay him an income at the time—even so, he didn't seem to manage too badly if he was able to purchase art with no income.[119]

As a result of his dealings with the intelligence services, Dollmann got himself a fake South Tyrolean identity paper made out in the name of 'Eugen Amonn' from Bolzano. This made him a stateless ethnic German, who was to emigrate to Argentina with a Red Cross travel document. In 1952 he was smuggled along the CIC ratline via Genoa to Spain, where he spent some years in the circle around Otto Skorzeny. At the end of the 1950s, he was still trying to capitalize on his American contacts, although generally in vain.

Dollmann's fellow-SS man Walter Rauff became an important member of the Nazi escape organization after 1945. In the summer of 1941, Rauff was running a 'technical affairs' group in the Reich Security headquarters in Berlin, which developed the 'gas trucks' used by the directors of the 'Einsatzgruppen', mobile murder units. With these an estimated 200,000 Jews in the East, mostly children, women, and old people, were murdered. In 1943 he was sent to Italy. Rauff's chief duty as head of the SD and the Gestapo in Milan was to fight the Italian partisans.[120] The well-known Milan journalist Indro Montanelli was one of those who fell into his clutches. Rauff wanted to force Montanelli to work as a spy for the SS, but Montanelli escaped to Switzerland.[121]

Rauff had a whole staff of Italian spies and fascists; after 1945 he was able to fall back on these contacts. He was thus very well suited to act as an escape agent in Italy after the end of the war. In the first few postwar weeks, Rauff and Dollmann were able to feel safe among Catholic clerics in Rome, particularly since they were under the protection of the OSS chief in Berne, Dulles. It is quite likely, though, that Dulles never intervened directly on behalf of Rauff. After his arrest in April 1945, Rauff became very uncooperative.[122] In his very first interrogation on 1 May 1945, he was stubborn: 'Rauff stated categorically that he would never give any information dealing with the operation or personnel of SD or SS in this or any other region,'[123] Stephen Spingarn, the head of the CIC in Italy, noted with frustration. Rauff constantly railed against the Allies, suggesting that he would run amok if he was ever freed. 'Source is considered a menace if ever set free, and failing actual elimination, is recommended for life-long internment,' said Spingarn.[124] But things were to turn out quite differently. As in the case of other SS officers, Rauff's 'merits' were probably acknowledged within the context of the secret Sunrise negotiations. In his first interrogations by Spingarn, Rauff referred explicitly to the fact that Dulles, 'Allied agent in Switzerland', was able to confirm his details with regard to negotiations with the Allies.[125]

Rauff found a post-war career that was almost as adventurous and criminal as his SS activities. Essential to Rauff's flight were his good contacts with the Catholic Church, not least with the Archbishop of Milan, Ildefonso Schuster. An in-depth study by the Simon Wiesenthal Center suggests that Schuster's secretary, Monsignor Giuseppe Bicchierai, helped Rauff and others to escape a war crimes trial by enabling them to flee from Europe.[126] In 1984 the Simon Wiesenthal Center in New York produced a detailed study of 'Rauff and the Church'. After listing a long chain of evidence, the Wiesenthal Center challenged Pope John Paul II to set up 'an immediate and complete investigation of the Rauff case'. The Church could, it was argued, contribute a great deal to the clarification of Rauff's claims that he was able to escape from Europe with help from the Vatican.[127] Rauff did receive help from the Church while in San Vittorio prison in Milan. First a Catholic priest arranged for his transfer to a US military hospital in Milan. Rauff Planned a possible later escape, which was finally successful. Rauff went into hiding in Italy, working undercover as an escape agent. In the 1948 election campaign, Bicchierai and the CIA probably worked collaboratively to prevent a Communist assumption of power. Rauff made himself useful with his espionage services and his network of agents. The CIA strategy in Italy was a complete success, although other factors had also certainly played a part. The Italian Communists lost the election by a considerable margin, and the US intelligence services had found a powerful ally in the Catholic Church.[128] There are later suggestions that Rauff also worked for the Italians: 'Rauff too was persona grata after the war in Italy, without anything happening to him. Herr Katz assumes that Rauff performed services for the Italians in return.'[129]

As the former SS chief in Milan, Rauff was very well acquainted with Italy because even before the end of the war he had taken numerous precautions and established connections with the Church. Networks like the ones Rauff set up with the assistance of the Church helped serious criminals such as Franz Stangl, the ex-commandant of Treblinka; Josef Schwammberger, who was responsible for thousands of murders in the Przemysl Ghetto; and Adolf Eichmann, who escaped from US imprisonment under the identity SS-Untersturmführer Otto Eckmann in 1945 and arrived in Argentina in 1950 as the South Tyrolean 'Richard Klement'.[130] Fascist solidarity helped people like them to acquire new identities. The last official acts by Gestapo agencies were sometimes to declare the death of colleagues in order to assist their escape. In this way, for example, Gestapo inspector Gustav Jürges became the victim of a bombing raid and fled via Italy to South America as 'Federico Pahl'. From there he maintained close contact with his wife. Rauff looked after the Nazi community for a long time. At any rate, Jürges obediently wrote home from South America to the SS-Standartenführer and signed off: 'Heil Hitler! Gustav'.[131]

As the former head of the SS in Milan responsible for northwestern Italy, Rauff had a network of acquaintances and comrades in Italy, but apart from Italian fascists, he relied particularly on South Tyrolean SS men. Bolzano SS-Untersturmführer Dr Walter Segna played his part in Rauff's network.[132] In 1946 Segna was arrested in his hiding place on the Ritten above Bolzano. He had been a prominent South Tyrolean Nazi official in the 1930s and was later a member of the Gestapo. During the war, as a colleague of the Gestapo and SD chief in Holland, Wilhelm Harster, he helped with the deportation of Dutch Jews. In 1943 he followed Harster to Verona, where he took a key role in the German espionage network in Italy.[133] As an intermediary between Rauff and Cardinal Schuster as well as Don Bicchierai, the South Tyrolean played a not inconsiderable part in the successful Sunrise negotiations. Along with Rauff, Segna was arrested by the Americans on 30 April 1945 in the Regina Hotel in Milan, and was automatically interned because of his SS membership. After an adventurous escape from the Torretta camp—he and his comrades dug an escape tunnel—he went into hiding in a monastery near Ancona. Then, early in

1946, he battled on to South Tyrol and hid on a farm. Maybe he was supposed to be working as a South Tyrolean intermediary in Rauff's border-crossing operation. According to information from the local residents, he was literally surprised in his sleep and arrested. At first he denied his true identity, although that did not protect him from being handed over to the Allies again.[134] Otherwise, he proved to be very open at his first interrogation by the CIC in Verona: 'Segna indicated that he would be willing to collaborate fully with Allied intelligence.'[135] After a brief imprisonment, he appears to have been released.

5. The Ratline Players

From 1947 until 1950 Jim Milano served as director of the CIC in Austria and was one of the founders of the ratline. The political parameters had changed, and only a few years after the war, the antagonism between East and West occupied the centre ground. Even fifty years later, Milano justified his ratline with particular reference to political targets: 'In their favor, it can be argued that, at least after 1949, the Western Allies, as a matter of policy, suspended all war crime prosecutions and consciously allowed former Nazi officials, SS officers, judges, and others to assume senior posts in West German government and industry.'[136] Milano, who had spent the war in Italy as an agent, officially wanted to save agents who had worked for the West and who were now in the Soviet sphere of influence. As early as 1945, the Lieutenant Colonel established a Nazi escape route in Austria. At first this operation assumed a very simple form: the CIC simply procured forged travel documents, which it either produced itself or bought on the black market. Most of the forgery was performed in the CIC's offices in Salzburg. But it was only during a later phase that Nazis managed to profit from these services. At first the clientele consisted of agents and specialists from the Soviet-occupied part of Austria. After the Russians had started intensifying their checks, at the end of 1947 a better ratline had to be constructed. It was the creation of Milano and his colleague Paul Lyon. People who had previously worked in church border-crossing operations were now recruited by the CIC in Austria, Germany, and Italy.

The SS officer Karl Hass was a particularly important intermediary between the Americans and church circles in the context of the ratline. Karl Hass, born on 5 October 1912 in Elmchenhagen near Kiel, had an unusual career. Even while studying political science at Berlin University, he joined the SS, which would soon have a positive professional effect. A friend in the SS found him a job with the SS intelligence service (SD) in Berlin. Hass worked in the press department there, mostly assessing newspapers from Italy. After Mussolini's fall in July 1943, Hass became director of the SD in Rome and built up his own spy network. After the liberation of Rome in June 1944, the staff of which Hass was a part moved back to Parma. In April 1945 Hass went first to stay with Erich Priebke in Bolzano and finally settled in the mountains of South Tyrol, where he must have felt very safe. On 15 July 1945 the wanted man even got married to Anna Maria Giustini in Bolzano. He was arrested six times, but was always able to escape. Finally he was transferred to the prisoner-of-war camp in Rimini, from which he escaped on 20 July 1946, fleeing to Rome. At the time, Hass was chiefly assisting Nazis who were escaping via Rome and Genoa to South America. US agent Vincent La Vista reported about it in detail and also quoted Hass's code name, 'Franco'. After their successful escape from Rimini prisoner-of-war camp, SS men were to report to Karl Hass, alias 'Franco', in Rome. There he would help them escape to South America, on the instructions of Bishop Hudal. Meanwhile the PCA procured Red Cross travel documents for their travel overseas. This was of great benefit to Hass's comrades, too. They included his colleague Karl-Theodor Schütz, who worked with the Gestapo in Rome. In the last days of April 1945, Schütz fled from Merano to Germany with fake papers. Because of his experience in the intelligence service, he worked first for the Gehlen Organization, then the German Federal Intelligence Service, and finally with his boss Hass again.[137]

Hass must have helped dozens of former comrades to escape to South America.[138] The SS escape agent was finally arrested and interrogated by the Americans, but was freed only to work again as an escape agent for SS members—this time on behalf of the US military. Hass was only one of many SS secret service men with anticommunist expertise whom the CIC had recycled. He was later taken on by the Italian military intelligence service, for which Hass performed important work as a liaison with the Federal Intelligence Service. 'I presume I was valuable to them,' Hass observed decades later.[139]

In November 1947 Karl Hass was brought to Austria by the CIC to participate in its burgeoning Cold War activities. The Americans invited him to work for them. 'Dear Major Hass, we have a common enemy; won't you work for us?' Hass recalled, fifty years later, of his fateful new start. Hass was transferred to Linz in Upper Austria where he wore a US uniform.[140] In the years that followed, CIC chief Milano was now able to fall back on the services of his agent in Italy. Hass initially received 150 dollars a month from Lucid, Milano's superior, and was soon running the 'Los Angeles' spy ring in Italy.[141] In the 1950s Hass was part of the CIC information network in Salzburg, but worked with the Italian Ministry of the Interior. Hass maintained contact with Rome via officials of the intelligence services in Bolzano. He was now a Cold War spy.[142] He therefore acquired new identities as 'Carlo Steiner' or 'Rodolfo Giustini'.[143] His supposed origin in South Tyrol made it easy for him to acquire Italian, Austrian, or German papers. From 1947 Hass settled in Bolzano for some period of time, and in 1952 he founded the Mercital Company in Bozen with its office at 1 Musterplatz.[144] As a businessman and spy, he worked closely with the American agent Joseph Luongo, whose name is repeatedly mentioned in connection with terrorism in Italy. Major Joseph Luongo was born on 3 May 1916 in New Haven and came to Italy in 1943. After the war he had the task of feeding and lodging Nazis on the run—evidence of the recycling of Nazis for Western intelligence services. Luongo repeatedly met Hass and gave him money and instructions.[145] In Rome the fascists Giorgio Almirante and Pino Romualdi, both founders of the Movimento Sociale Italiano (MSI) Party, helped Hass by supplying him with new papers. Hass's example corresponded precisely to the most prevalent Italian pattern: new and old fascists working for the Italian and US secret services in defence against communism. It was the invisible front of the Cold War, drawn up immediately after the end of the war to protect the Western European states against Soviet influence. Thus in most Western European states with US support, 'stay-behind' networks were set up for guerrilla warfare in the event of a Soviet invasion.[146]

In 1954 the CIC lost interest in Hass. At their Linz headquarters, they were planning the future of the informants mentioned above, and Argentina was suggested as a new home for 'Carlo Steiner'. But Hass stayed in Italy. In spite of an Italian arrest warrant, Hass hadn't left the country. He probably felt very safe there.[147] Officially, Hass had been 'deceased' since 1947. The Americans had created the necessary preconditions, which consisted of the appropriate protection and a new identity for him. His knowledge as a secret agent was now used by the CIA in the Cold War. One curious concluding detail: in the well-known 1969 film *The Damned* (*La caduta degli dei*) by Luchino Visconti, the supposedly dead Hass had a part as an extra, playing himself—a Nazi officer. While the war criminal was on the Italian authorities' wanted list, he was flickering on cinema screens across the length and breadth of Italy. This almost unbelievable detail also reflects the atmosphere in Italy during the Cold War. In 1953, when the CIC shelved its collaboration with Hass, the trained spy had to find another employer because he had also been stonewalled by the Gehlen Organization; most Wehrmacht spies were unwilling to work with former SS men. Hass was then taken on by Italian information services.

As an SS officer, Hass pursued independent secret operations alongside his official activities. First he extended his contacts into church circles, but maintained contacts with Bishop Hudal in Rome—even after the Allied occupation of Rome—and finally he was able to win over clerics in northern Italy to help him set up his escape routes. Aside from church support, of course, an organization of this kind needed financial means. Getting hold of money was one of Hass's most significant achievements. Amongst other methods of obtaining funds, he relied upon a man who had also ended up in Italy after the war, Friedrich Schwend. The head of Operation Bernhard lived in Schloss Labers near Merano and had access to considerable funds. Schloss Labers and the other safe houses of Operation Bernhard thus played a part in the escape of war criminals. Rauff was allegedly also soon working with Schwend.[148] Thus the SS profiteer was also brought back into service. In the course of a raid at the end of 1946, the Italian authorities found proof that some remaining networks and personnel of Operation Bernhard were still active.[149]

Then, when Schwend was put under pressure by the American authorities, he did the only sensible thing he could in that situation: he offered the still existing remnants of Operation Bernhard in Italy to the Americans of the CIC. Apart from Schwend, some of his closest colleagues at first worked for the CIC. These included the Viennese Jewish banker of Operation Bernhard, Georg Spitz. Spitz was arrested by the CIC in May 1945 and served at first as an informant, investigating his boss Schwend.[150] According to the CIC, Spitz was eager to bring about Schwend's arrest. He had previously supported the arrest of Heinrich

Hoffmann, Hitler's photographer and publisher. The CIC in Munich found Spitz very useful, 'although strictly speaking he was not an agent', as his superiors stressed.[151] He worked as a mole and an informant for the Americans until May 1948. Obviously, Spitz knew all about Schwend's dealings and thus represented a very important source of information for the Americans. Schwend was now to help in 'Operation Ratline'. He himself used this route to emigrate via Genoa to Argentina at the end of 1946 and was one of the first SS refugees to do so. Schwend procured Red Cross travel documents with invented personal details. In South America, above all in the first few years after the war, he became a contact for some fleeing Nazis and war criminals. Schwend's brother-in-law and right-hand man in his profiteering operations, Giovanni Neuhold, left Merano in September 1947. He duly reported to the town hall, stating that he wanted to emigrate 'to Argentina'. But Neuhold only got as far as Genoa, apparently becoming stranded in the port city.[152]

6. Escape along the Ratline

Vincent La Vista's report provided the United States with facts that would have been enough to identify and dismantle the escape apparatus in Italy. But, in the end, nothing happened: no storm of outrage in the US media and no political pressure on the ICRC or the Vatican. Why it didn't happen is explained by the altered situation of the postwar era.

The expansive efforts of the Soviet Union not only created an external threat, but the communist worldview increasingly created a spirit of discord within the US-oriented states of Western Europe. The Americans had soon come to see Italy as the key country in Europe, not only because of its strategic proximity to the oil fields in the Middle East, but also because the communists were becoming increasingly influential there. President Truman had made the containment of communism a principle of US foreign policy. For the Italian Prime Minister De Gasperi, the integration of Italy into the West and the country's economic revival were also priorities.[153] He worked very closely with the Americans.[154] In the years immediately after the war, Italy seemed to be on the brink of turning communist, the first to do so democratically. This nightmarish prospect and the fear of a domino effect led the United

States to give the peninsula around 350 million US dollars in civilian and military aid during the 1948 Italian election.[155] The country's Catholic Church had fully supported the initiative: both partners in the Cold War worked together against the common threat of communism. The illegal escape routes via Austria and Italy described by La Vista, which had just been discovered by the US authorities, were now no longer suppressed, but used. In this way the Cold War, the struggle against the Soviet Union and communism, soon covered over the 'inherited waste' of the Second World War. For many war criminals, the general political climate of the Cold War had soon provided a context that was generally favourable.

The US was drawn into using the underground escape routes for war criminals on a large scale when the CIC recruited the Croatian head of Intermarium, Krunoslav Draganović, to do the Americans' dirty work. At first, the Americans did not want to assume responsibility for operating this ratline to smuggle senior Nazis through the country. Instead, the CIC assumed responsibility for the financing and protection of Draganović's activities. War criminals were also brought into the US along 'illegal routes'. According to Ivo Omracanin, a former official in the Croatian Foreign Office and an assistant to Draganović who now lives in Washington, DC, his mentor used human and institutional church resources and finances to ensure the passage of several thousand Ustaša fascists. Among the Croatian 'refugees' were head of state Ante Pavelić and his police minister Andrija Artuković, who were responsible for the murders of at least 400,000 Serbs and Jews. The CIC did not arrest a single Ustaša in Draganović's charge, or report the hiding places of the war criminals to the relevant United Nations commission or the Yugoslavian government. The investigations by the US Department of Justice in the Klaus Barbie case made public dozens of government files containing evidence of Draganović's activities for US intelligence services. The Department confirmed that Draganović was working for the Americans and smuggling refugees into the United States.[156]

Draganović became a leading figure of the CIC ratline in Italy: 'Draganović was listed as CIC ratline chief in Italy', as an American secret service report unambiguously records.[157] A CIC report on this network is very informative:

Thanks to the Vatican contacts of Father Draganović, Croatian, head of the Vatican resettlement projects for refugees, a provisional agreement was reached to support this organization. The agreement consists of simple mutual support, that is, these CIC agents help individuals who are of interest to Father Draganović to leave Germany; to this end Father Draganović will procure the necessary Argentinian and South American visas for individuals who are of interest to this [CIC] headquarters. It can be observed that some of these individuals who interest Father Draganović could be of interest to the Allies' denazification policy [that is, these individuals might be war criminals]. But these individuals are also of interest to our Russian allies. For that reason this operation cannot be officially authorized, but must be put into effect without delay and with minimal publicity.[158]

Allied High Command in Italy knew all about Draganović's activities. He was issuing fake identification papers, he had good contacts with the Red Cross, and travel documents could be acquired from the Red Cross 'with the agreement of the Papal Refugee Relief Mission at 41 Via Piave in Rome'.[159] Although the CIC had exposed Father Krunoslav Draganović as a fascist, it still agreed to do business with him. The CIC wanted to smuggle agents out of Europe, and to do so it needed travel documents. Draganović was able and willing to help. The cleric they called 'The Golden Priest' was perfect for the needs of the CIC because he could easily get hold of the coveted Red Cross travel documents.[160] Whenever the Croatian smuggled his Ustaša people out of the country, the CIC kept its eyes tightly shut. At the CIC in Salzburg, they were accommodated in a safe or 'rat' house, if possible equipped with forged papers, and then brought across the border to the Italian ports of Genoa or Naples.

The unmasking of agents by the opposing side is hardly uncommon in espionage, and governments must make the appropriate preparations should that occur. In the years after the war, it often happened that accusations were levelled at German CIC agents about their pasts, and sometimes international warrants were even issued. In such situations, the intelligence service found itself forced to bring the now useless spy to safety, supplying him with a new identity as a reward for his services and getting him out of Europe. After all, he had served in the agency's own ranks, and the embarrassing situation of making a statement in court on the subject had to be avoided. The seedy transport route was worked out and tested very precisely, so that it would not fail and reflect badly on the US government. The man in question received a US uniform, and a three-man CIC team brought him to Bad Gastein. From there his route took him across the Italian border to South Tyrol, then on to Genoa or Naples, wherever an Atlantic steamer docked first. In Genoa, the ratline organizers had been able to find contacts in the form of a Croatian priest and fellow-travellers of Draganović's. The CIC paid very generously for its own people to be smuggled out, between 1,000 and 1,400 US dollars per person, a great deal of money at the time. In return, Draganović had to ensure that the operation was kept quiet and that the individuals in question were supplied, if necessary, with papers—usually a Red Cross travel document—as well as an entry visa for a South American country.

Early in 1946 agent Schwend decided to leave Europe. But he had planned to escape to South America for a long time. Even before the end of the war, he and his brother Albert Schwend formed serious escape plans: 'When we were collecting the dollars he said he wanted to take us all to South America, we wouldn't have to work any more. There was enough there to live on.'[161] Albert Schwend also emigrated to Peru in 1949 and founded a business there with his brother, but returned to Germany in 1958.[162] On his escape Schwend used the CIC ratline which he himself had helped to install. Schwend probably had contacts with the church escape agent Draganović in Rome, who was, quite certainly, very involved in Schwend's escape, having procured Red Cross travel documents for him.

Schwend was one of the first Nazi fugitives who used Red Cross travel documents bearing a false name. He and his wife Hedda travelled to Rome where they received Croatian papers with which they were able to acquire ICRC travel documents. Schwend now called himself 'Venceslav Turi', born on 1 November 1904 in Zara, and presented himself as an agronomist. Schwend alias Turi gave his destination as 'Spain and Venezuela'.[163] The PCA was very involved in the acquisition of the papers. The Commission wrote on 30 September 1946 to the International Red Cross, also in Rome: 'The honoured committee is requested to issue a Red Cross travel document for Herr Turi Venceslav [*sic*] and his wife Hedda, of Yugoslavian nationality (Zara).'[164] Schwend was also able to show the ICRC a letter of recommendation from the Italian Red Cross in Rome. In it his identity was confirmed and two witnesses were named: Gottfried Melcher and Georg Carli, who, perhaps, were two of Schwend's escape agents. They both confirmed the details of the 'Yugoslav Venceslav Turi'. During his time in Rome, Schwend stayed with the nuns at 77 Via Mura Giani-colensi.[165] His wife Hedda Schwend, née Moretti, applied for an ICRC travel document in the name of Hedda Turi at the same time. Her details were also confirmed by the Italian Red Cross in Rome and again by the two 'witnesses', Melcher and Carli.[166]

In Germany too, the army and the intelligence services had abandoned old standards. Given the acutely threatening situation that they faced, Allied intelligence officers were falling back on trusted anticommunist fighters, such as the former head of the Gestapo in Lyons, Klaus Barbie, who occupied a prominent position on France's lists of criminals. He was taken on by the CIC in 1947 and supplied the intelligence service with information, falling back on the still operational networks of the SD and Gestapo coteries.[167] In December 1950 the German CIC decided to provide Barbie with a new identity and bring him via Italy to South America. The Barbie family arrived in Genoa on 12 March 1951. They were put up in a hotel and taken under the wing of Father Draganović.[168] In March 1951 Barbie received a visa for Bolivia and the familiar travel documents of the International Committee of the Red Cross made out in the name of 'Klaus Altmann'. Altmann claimed to be an ethnic German from Romania, and was thus officially deemed to be stateless. This, too, was typical of the usual processes discussed in previous chapters. Draganović had personally authorized the issuing of a Red Cross travel document for the former SS-Hauptsturmführer Klaus Barbie. On 23 March 1951, Barbie boarded the *Corrientes* and left Italy for Bolivia.[169] The US intelligence services concisely summed up Barbie's outward transfer: 'In 1951 because of the French and German efforts to apprehend subject, the 66th Detachment resettled him in South America. Subject was documented in the name of Klaus Altmann and routed through Austria and Italy to Bolivia. Since that time, Army has had no contact with Subject.'[170]

Barbie was only outwardly a businessman in Bolivia, but his various sidelines show that he went on working at his trade for the CIA and, of course, for his fascist friends in Bolivia. The powerful German community in Bolivia had its own candidate for head of state: Colonel Hugo Banzer, a US-trained army officer of German descent. When Banzer lacked weapons, Barbie, head of the Transmaritima Boliviana trading company,[171] saw an interesting task for himself in the struggle against communism. His son Klaus represented the shipping company in Hamburg, while Barbie senior travelled the whole of the Western world with his diplomatic pass and supplied his generals with arms.[172] Barbie's important business partner in Latin America was Schwend in Lima. The various dubious arms deals that 'Fritz Wendig' undertook, not least with other National Socialists, but mainly with Barbie, passed through Lima. When Barbie had to leave the Bolivian capital temporarily in 1970 because of a fraudulent collapse of his company, his friend Schwend in Peru was his guardian angel. He acquired a residence permit for the former Gestapo chief of Lyons and organized the necessary contacts with Peruvian businessmen. Klaus Barbie wrote to a comrade in 1966:

> We, Herr Schwend, you and I now have every reason to team up together, as we have become the victim[s] of a particular race whose hatred for us will probably never end. I regret to an extraordinary degree what happened [...]. You can depend all the more on my and Herr Schwend's help and comradeship. I too have lately, after a long-prepared action by the German embassy, been removed from the German Club here, on the basis of a committee decision, for supposed 'anti-Semitic statements'.[173]

Apart from some business problems, Barbie found life very pleasant at the time. His daughter Ute had lived in Kufstein in Tyrol since 1969, where Barbie had found her a teaching post with the help of Hans-Ulrich Rudel (he was also living in Kufstein at the time)—the idea of his daughter marrying a Bolivian man had considerably troubled him. Ute later married a Tyrolean teacher.[174] For a time, Schwend and Barbie became a team in more or less dubious financial transactions. But in the familiar circle of his 'master race' beyond the Atlantic Ocean, Altmann/Barbie became too confident of his safety.

Apart from arms deals, Schwend and Barbie were still practising espionage.[175] The Americans repeatedly showed an interest in them as a result. In 1964 they remembered the former agents Barbie and Schwend. Like other members of the German community in South America, they were now to work as spies for the Americans, after being recruited by the CIA in La Paz, and to help the struggle against communism in South America.[176] The US agents were 'interested in re-establishing contact with subject for purposes of an assessment of his present capabilities', as a CIA report explains. In short, they wanted to know if Barbie was still valuable as an agent.[177] But at the same time they were cautious because Barbie was still wanted in France for his war crimes. The US authorities thus feared negative effects if the US involvement in the Barbie case became public. On 5 April 1967 the CIA therefore stated in a secret memorandum: 'The war criminal charges against Altmann require serious consideration, since exposure of CIC's role in evacuating him from Germany to avoid prosecution would have serious consequences for the U.S. Government; these would be still graver if a current operational relationship could be claimed (or demonstrated).'[178]

When Barbie was prosecuted, Schwend approached the Bolivian President Hugo Banzer to demand protection for his friend: 'I met Altmann [Barbie's alias] in the first years of the war as a young soldier who fulfilled his duty,'[179] Schwend stressed. An FBI report records the supportive side of Schwend:

> Altmann-Barbie deportation—Lima, 8 September: an examining magistrate in Lima has begun the extradition process against Klaus Altmann—it is assumed that he is identical with the Nazi war criminal Klaus Barbie, who is currently living in Bolivia. Altmann-Barbie is accused of smuggling foreign currency. The chief accused in this case is another former Nazi by the name of Friedrich Schwend.[180]

Unlike Barbie, Schwend had never made a secret of his presence in Peru. In 1964 Schwend wrote a letter of recommendation for a 'serious international press man' to the President of Paraguay, General Alfredo Stroessner. Schwend proudly signed the letter to the Germanophile dictator 'Federico Schwend, Ex-Commander of the Sonderstab Generalkommando III germanisches SS-Panzerkorps'.[181]

Schwend's confidant Barbie enjoyed a run of good luck after his arrest; however, justice finally caught up to him. In June 1972, in spite of incriminating documents about war crimes in France, his file was closed by the German examining magistrate for lack of evidence. The journalist Beate Klarsfeld took note of this outrage and put all the machinery in motion to have the Gestapo Chief of Lyons arrested. In 1983 Barbie was tracked down in Bolivia and extradited to France.[182] In the course of the trial, facts surfaced that Klaus Barbie had been on the payroll of the CIC and had reached Bolivia in 1951 via the ratline. Barbie's CIC past was a source of shame and embarrassment to the US government in 1983. Proof of this may be found in the large CIA file on Barbie in the US National Archives.[183] The Department of Justice described the role of the US Army as a 'hindrance to justice and illegal action'.[184] In 1986 the Barbie affair developed into a national scandal officially compounded at the highest level by the fact that the US government publicly apologized to the French government.[185] The trial against Barbie in Lyons degenerated into a sad piece of theatre. Several times the trial was postponed and the charge changed. A trial of the century along the lines of the Eichmann trial in Jerusalem did not take place. A detailed examination of France's past, particularly of collaboration in the Vichy state, was probably not thought desirable.[186] The name of the 'Butcher of Lyons' took its place in the story of inhumanity alongside Himmler, Mengele, Kaltenbrunner, and Eichmann. Barbie was the most prominent example of a war criminal turned spy, but was by no means a singular case.[187]

Jim Milano later justified Barbie's appointment with reference to the general political situation in the early Cold War:

> Why, then, should not the CIC in Augsburg avail itself of the services of a junior Gestapo official whose contacts throughout Germany were so good? Indeed, as former SS men were allowed to resume senior positions in German society, the network of comrades became a very valuable source of intelligence—and Barbie's chief use to the Americans was that he was a trusted member of the SS old-boys' network. Furthermore, he was an expert in anti-French intelligence gathering at a time when the Americans greatly feared the dangers of the French Communist Party, one of the organizations Barbie had fought during the war. Last, although Barbie was the 'Butcher of Lyons', he was a minor war criminal. There were thousands of more dangerous men on the loose. He was no Eichmann or Mengele. General Heinz Lammerding, who had commanded the Nazi division that wiped out a French village, Oradour-sur-Glane, in 1944, was living openly in Germany despite every effort by France to have him extradited. Why bother with an SS captain who was actually useful to the CIC?[188]

Milano's justification for shielding Barbie from justice in order to use him as a Cold War spy is a rationalization that seems to explain the general attitude of the US intelligence community regarding its programme of recruiting war criminals as agents.

The case of Klaus Barbie is full of parallels with another case of espionage in the early Cold War, that of Robert Jan Verbelen who worked for the CIC in Austria from 1946 until 1955. The Belgian SS-Sturmbannführer had supported the Flemish independence movement since the 1930s. During the war, he fought against the resistance in Belgium and recruited Flemish volunteers for the Waffen-SS. Since July 1945, Verbelen had appeared on the American Central Register of war criminals and suspicious enemy officers, not as a war criminal, but as a potential security risk. In Belgium in 1947, Verbelen was condemned to death in his absence for collaboration and war crimes, but went on living unmolested in Vienna. He was finally arrested in Austria in 1962 as a potential war criminal. The Verbelen trial attracted a great deal of media attention, and details of his story gradually came out. After 1955, Verbelen seems also to have worked for the Austrian state police as a spy in the right-wing camp; according to the Office of Special Investigation he was 'one of the best informants of the Austrian [State] Police on the activities of rightist extremist groups in Austria'. In his 1965 trial, he was acquitted after three years on remand. There was an appropriately furious response in Belgium. But it was not until 1984 that justice officials in Washington, DC, began a deeper investigation of the Verbelen case and the related involvement of US authorities. These investigations were prompted by the Klaus Barbie case and the role of the CIC in it. Closer investigations into the CIC's working methods in Austria in the early Cold War followed.[189]

The investigators revealed a pattern for the ramshackle spying methods of the CIC at the start of the Cold War. The 430th Counter Intelligence Corps Detachment was deployed in Austria from May 1945 until August 1955. This CIC detachment had its headquarters in Vienna, with subdetachments in Salzburg and Linz. The CIC was originally set up to combat saboteurs and spies and track down SS officers and war criminals. But towards the end of 1946 the focus began gradually to change, and activities against the Soviets increasingly came to the fore because the Soviet troops were numerically far superior to the US forces. Thus the Soviet Union was also showing its influence more and more clearly in Austria. Due to this situation, the 430th Detachment of the CIC was deployed in espionage against the Soviet military presence in Austria and Central and Eastern Europe and the Austrian Communist Party.[190] Finally, in May 1947, the CIC largely suspended its active search for war criminals in Austria. With its new duties, the mission and procedures of the CIC changed. As well as counter-espionage, it now engaged in active espionage. Years later, the CIC's active espionage work struck the investigators of the US Justice Department as thoroughly amateurish. In their report, the investigators were not reticent about expressing their opinion, stating, 'The American personnel who worked for CIC during the immediate postwar years had one significant common characteristic: inexperience.'[191]

In the summer of 1945, most CIC officers who had been able to gain spying experience during the war returned to their civilian life in the United States. Their successors came from other Army units, or were young recruits. The staff shortage led to the employment of many inexperienced officers and agents unsuited to the duties of the CIC.[192] Above all, the CIC lacked experts in active espionage who were needed in the early Cold War. Thus the CIC had to fall back on other sources. The intelligence services with the best and most up-to-date knowledge of the East and the Soviet Union were those of the defeated enemy, Nazi Germany. Experts with experience in anti-Soviet espionage who might still have contacts in the Soviet Union received a warm welcome from the CIC. Hence agents from German military counter-intelligence, the Security Service (SD), or the Gestapo were in great demand.

It was thus that Verbelen was employed by the CIC in Vienna in 1946. At the end of the war, he first acquired fake papers for himself and presented himself as a displaced person from the Sudetenland, the stateless ethnic German 'Peter Mayer'. By his own account, he met a former SS comrade in 1946 who asked him if he would help the Americans in their fight against the communists. That was his first contact with the CIC. Verbelen first worked for the CIC as 'Peter Mayer', then from 1951 as 'Alfred Heinrich Gustav Schwab'. By 1955, however, his CIC superiors knew his true identity and his history as an officer in the Waffen-SS. Verbelen ran a spy ring in eastern Austria, but also helped former SS comrades to flee Austria.[193] He concealed his own activities as an SS-Sturmbannführer. In 1955 the CIC withdrew from Austria and ended its collaboration with Verbelen. The CIC invited Verbelen to emigrate to the United States or South America, but he wanted to remain in Austria. After 1955 he worked therefore for the Austrian state police, delivering reports on Soviet and Eastern European agents in Vienna; in return for his services, he was given Austrian citizenship.

Walter Rauff, who, according to Wiesenthal, had himself been involved in running the ratline, emigrated to Syria, and finally moved to Ecuador. According to US sources, his crossing was paid for by Monsignor Bicchierai, Secretary to the Archbishop of Milan. The former SS-Standartenführer was worth a 40,000 lire ticket as far as the Church was concerned.[194] In Ecaudor he worked until 1958 as a salesman. The CIA suspected that Rauff was also involved in secret service activities in the capital, Quito, but could never prove it. The CIA possibly never subjected Rauff's activities in Quito to closer examination. From Ecuador he moved to Chile in 1958. In April 1960 Rauff was already such a confident traveller that he was able to visit acquaintances in the Federal Republic of Germany with his wife, travelling on a Chilean passport in his real name.[195]

In the context of the Eichmann trial in 1961, Walter Rauff's name cropped up repeatedly, and the West German authorities swung into action. In 1962 Germany demanded that Chile extradite the fugitive. In December 1962 the Chilean authorities arrested the former SS man in Punta Arenas. The representative of the Federal Republic of Germany in the extradition process accused Rauff of crimes against humanity:

> Walter Rauff was directly and immediately involved in the invention, conversion, perfection and delivery of the special trucks that were deployed in the mass killings of thousands of people. He was aware that he was thus providing the means for the execution of the massacres, and he was willing to cooperate on this in the context of the duties assigned to him. With this attitude he accepted the demands of those who had set this criminal enterprise in motion.[196]

Five months later, the Supreme Court in Chile established that the period of limitations for murder (fifteen years) had already passed—and as Rauff had broken no Chilean law, he was not extradited. Rauff was a free man once again. All subsequent Chilean governments adhered to the Supreme Court's 1963 ruling. Neither the Christian Democrat Eduardo Frei, the Socialist Salvador Allende, nor the dictator Augusto Pinochet changed the Chilean government's position on the issue. Even a personal intervention by Simon Wiesenthal with President Allende in August 1972 did not bring about a change in Chile's attitude.[197] The Socialist Allende wrote to Wiesenthal in Vienna:

As you know, the Supreme Court of Chile decided against the application by the Justice Authorities of the Federal Republic of Germany to
extradite Rauff on the grounds that the crime has lapsed [...]. Meanwhile Article 38 of this judgment contains the sharpest condemnation of
the treacherous crimes of National Socialism and its enforcers. [...]
I deeply regret, esteemed Herr Wiesenthal, that I must give a negative
reply to your request. Time and again I have admired the tireless per-
sistence with which you have pursued the perpetrators of the greatest
crimes in human history. But I also know that you respect applicable law
within political governments; hence I am sure that you will understand
my attitude as President of the Republic.[198]

Rauff went on living unmolested as a businessman in Chile, first in
Punta Arenas in the southernmost province of Chile and later in Santiago itself. He remained in permanent secret contact with associations
of former SS men, including Colonel Rudel's 'Kameradenwerk'.[199] At
his funeral in Santiago in May 1984, friends from all over South America gave him a final escort with their arms raised in the Hitler salute.
Although many were present, some were missing, having preceded him
in death: the commandant of the Riga Ghetto, Eduard Roschmann;
the supervisor of the Sobibór gas chambers, Gustav Wagner; and the
Commandant of Treblinka extermination camp, Franz Stangl. Adolf
Eichmann was, of course, also unable to take part in the funeral, having been executed in Israel in 1962 after his trial there for war crimes.
Rauff had helped men like these to escape via Italy, but in the end they
made crucial errors, Wiesenthal remarks.[200] The story of the US ratline
and the turncoat agents it ferried to freedom is one of expediency and
hypocrisy justified by the advent of the Cold War. For some Nazis, SS
men, and collaborators, it proved to be a salvation, for others, merely a
temporary respite from eventual justice.

5

Destination Argentina

After 1945, Argentina became the most popular refuge for Nazi criminals. Like other countries, Argentina was interested in German scientists and specialists after the collapse of the Third Reich. President Perón wanted to modernize Argentina, particularly its army, but Argentina faced recruitment problems. Unlike the occupying powers, the Argentinians were unable to engage overtly specialists from Germany and Austria, so a plan to exploit the chaotic refugee situation in Europe suggested itself. Because many emigrants wanted to leave Europe via Italian ports, the Argentinians concentrated their efforts on Italy. The Argentinian consular representatives in Genoa and Rome were given the task of recruitment, and special cosmmissions were sent to Italy. Recruiters spoke to the refugees in Italy or smuggled them over the border into the country. Between 1946 and 1955 Argentina and other nations were very busy in northern Italy in what became in some ways 'Germany's backyard'.

The Argentinians concentrated on recruiting mostly the middle level of scientists and military officers, leaving the top people to the Soviets, the British, and the Americans. For practical work related to recruitment, Perón's diplomats liked to use Argentinians of German origin. Working together with SS men and Italian people-smugglers, they organized an effective system of official, and also illegal, recruitment in Italy. The SS men had the appropriate contacts and often pursued agendas of their own; they were less concerned with recruiting specialists for Perón and more with helping old comrades over the border— including war criminals and SS officers with seriously tainted pasts. For Perón, importing war criminals was not an official policy, but a tolerated fact.

The particular attractiveness of Argentina for German specialists and emigrants did not emerge overnight. Even during the war Argentina was known for its Germanophile attitude, and it was only after massive pressure from the United States that Argentina declared war on the German Reich in March 1945, making Argentina the last country to enter the war against Nazi Germany. The existence of large German and Italian communities in Argentina meant that there were many links between Argentina and the Axis powers. Simon Wiesenthal consistently saw Argentina as the most important country of refuge for the 'pro-Nazi world community', and the Argentinian journalist Uki Goñi has described the role that Argentina (and above all its president, Juan Domingo Perón) played in escape assistance as 'the real ODESSA'. Most Nazis, however, did not flee overseas, but stayed in Germany and Austria. The often one-sided focus on Argentina as a Nazi refuge has been predominant for decades and has meant that the immigration of German-speakers and the recruitment of specialists by other states after 1945 have been largely overlooked. As discussed previously, apart from Syria, Egypt, Canada, and Spain, the United States itself was also a popular destination for Nazi perpetrators and tainted scientists. But the sheer amount of research that has been done on Argentina makes it a very good case study for the way the system of recycling SS men and war criminals worked.[1]

1. Argentinian Immigration Policy

For economic reasons, Argentina had from the 1880s onwards become a very popular destination for emigrants from Europe, particularly southern Europe. They had settled predominantly in Buenos Aires and shaped the atmosphere and culture of the port city. Between the end of the First World War and the end of the 1920s, many economic migrants arrived in search of a new start. The proportion of Italians in Argentina was particularly high. By the late 1930s two million Italian nationals were living there, forming about one-sixth of the entire Argentinian population. Including those of Italian descent, around 40 per cent of Argentinians had Italian roots.[2] But Argentina was also a very popular destination for German and Austrian emigration between the wars, and around 240,000 people of German descent lived in the country. About 45,000 German speakers settled in the capital, Buenos Aires. Around three-quarters of the immigrants were so-called 'ethnic Germans', German-speakers from the former Austro-Hungarian and

Russian empires. They included many Volga Germans who settled in the interior.[3]

After Hitler's assumption of power in 1933, a new group of German-speaking immigrants—around 30,000 to 40,000 German refugees fleeing for political or 'racial' reasons, most of them Jews—arrived in Argentina.[4] In the years after the Anschluss in 1938, an estimated 2,000 Austrian Jews found refuge from Nazi persecution—more than in any other Latin American country.[5] This resulted in the first major split in Argentina's German-speaking community. The official 'German colony' adopted the political line of the new rulers in the German Reich.[6] The anti-Nazi newcomers remained distant from the German community that aligned itself politically with Hitler's Reich. But Argentina, or more specifically Greater Buenos Aires, was big enough, with its 13 million inhabitants, for them to stay out of each other's way. Cultural associations developed that were divided into the 'Jewish, emigrant' and the former 'Reich-German, pro-Nazi' camps, and no exchanges or common points of contact existed between the two groups.[7] From 1933 at least two German-speaking communities in Argentina, the pro- and anti-Hitler groups, existed, in addition to the Jewish community which had its own specific agenda. Thus the country can be understood to have had 'two or more German-speaking communities'.[8]

Given its sizeable European population, Argentina was an attractive destination for Nazis after the Axis powers' defeat. In Europe during the first months after the end of the war in 1945, Germans and Austrians found it nearly impossible to emigrate overseas. Only from 1946 onwards did a large wave of emigration begin again. According to official sources, between 1946 and 1955 66,327 people born in Germany migrated into Argentina. Of these, 51,398 Germans left the Perón republic after a few years. There were 14,929 settlers from Germany who spent a longer time in Argentina.[9] For the number of Austrian immigrants, the figures are apparently equally precise. Between 1947 and 1955 the Argentinian immigration authorities recorded 13,895 immigrants born in Austria; 9,710 of them later left Argentina again, which leaves 4,185 people who stayed in the country.[10] But the statistics don't tell the whole story. Ethnic Germans, from Eastern Europe for example, were registered according to their country of birth. Complete statistical data for German-speaking immigration to Argentina is, thus, difficult to determine precisely.[11]

Contemporary attempts to estimate more accurately the number of immigrants to Argentina still fall short for a few reasons. According to Holger Meding, some 300 to 800 senior Nazi officials had immigrated to Argentina, including fifty war criminals and mass murderers among them,[12] while historian Volker Koop estimated in 2009 that 600 Nazis and military experts from Germany and Austria immigrated to Argentina alone.[13] The Argentinian commission of historians, Comisión para el Esclarecimiento de las Actividades del Nacionalsocialismo en la Argentina (CEANA), has listed 180 biographies of prominent National Socialists, Nazi perpetrators, fascists, and war criminals from Austria, Germany, Belgium, France, and Yugoslavia who fled to Argentina, sixty-five of them described in brief biographies.[14] But this list is only provisional and incomplete. CEANA recorded only the best-known cases, yet thousands of less-prominent Fascists, SS men, and Nazi collaborators from all over Europe resettled in Argentina, too. It is, therefore, also a matter of definition that affects which group to include in the statistics and which not. One major reason why arriving at precise figures is difficult stems from the fact that the fugitives often entered the country with false identities or nationalities. Their given names, places of origin, and nationalities were, in many cases, false. Politics provided another reason why numbers of immigrants with tainted pasts tended to be underestimated after 1945. Established conservative representatives of the German-Argentinian community played down the extent of Nazi immigration. The German Club in Buenos Aires, for example, claims in its *History of the Germans in Argentina*, that from the end of the war until 1950 there was hardly any immigration from Germany, an attempt to deflect unwanted attention, perhaps.[15] No matter what the true count of immigrants after the war may be, Argentina was clearly a much sought-after destination, and the Perón government's policies ensured that this was the case.

Understanding Argentinian immigration policy after 1945 requires understanding the nature of the Perón regime. General Perón's steep political ascent began in 1943 with his appointment as the military junta's labour minister, after which he quickly conquered the hearts of the poor with worker-friendly decrees. His wife 'Evita' acted as spokeswoman for the *descamisados*, the 'shirtless ones'. She was revered by the people and despised by the oligarchy for her humble origins and her provocative speeches. When her husband was temporarily unseated as minister in 1945, Evita called for resistance. Protest demonstrations paralysed Buenos Aires. The protests died down only when Perón, supported by the German community in particular, returned to his post. In 1946 he was elected president with a large majority.

Because Perón had always been an admirer of Hitler's Germany and Mussolini's Italy, German-speaking immigrants profited from his attitude in many ways after the war. For instance, when presenting his first five-year plan (1947–51), Perón deliberately catered to the German and Italian immigrants, introducing forty guidelines for immigration into Argentina. Immigration was to be specific and selective. Certain groups of people, particular specialists, and those from a list of preferred countries of origin were given preferential treatment. In addition, immigrants were targeted who came from a particular cultural and linguistic background which would make them easily integrated into society. Perón's directives were not solely based on his political leanings, however; with the help of European immigrants, Perón hoped to advance the modernization of the army and the industrialization of the country.

On the basis of these vague precepts, the director of the immigration authority, Santiago Peralta, drew up some rather more concrete stipulations. In 1945 Peralta had been appointed head of the Dirección General de Migraciones (DGM), which was, at first, directly answerable to Perón's presidential chancellery. Peralta sympathized with both Perón and National Socialism. He had studied literature and philosophy in Buenos Aires, worked at the Anthropological Institute in Berlin in the 1930s, and maintained close connections with the Latin American institutes of the Third Reich. For the 'braune Flüchtlinge'—the pro-Nazi refugees—his appointment as director of the immigration authority was a victory because Peralta established the guidelines for immigration in their favour. Although many of his instructions and pronouncements were distinctly obscure, he was nevertheless very clear on certain points: where possible, immigrants were to belong to the 'white race', come from Europe, have a good education, be Catholic, and ideally speak a romance language as their mother tongue. Asians and black Africans were excluded by Peralta's racial guidelines because they would not meet the criterion of being 'easily able to assimilate'. Since the population in Argentina was mostly of Spanish, Italian, and German origin, the new arrivals would preferably belong to one of these groups.[16] But there was often a gulf between the theory and practice of the official immigration laws in Argentina. The practice was considerably more liberal, and officials often turned a blind eye towards the emigrants in terms of how well they fit the immigration guidelines.

Wilfred von Oven, formerly Goebbels' personal press adviser, was one of those who profited from Peralta's precepts. At the end of the war, von Oven presented himself as an exiled ethnic German and assumed the false name 'Willy Oehm'.[17] Wilfred von Oven was born on 4 May 1912 in La Paz (Bolivia), the son of German immigrants. He had gone to Germany with his father as a 2-year-old and later attended school there. In the early 1930s he made a career for himself as a Nazi journalist. But his rapid rise came to an end in 1937. He was turned down for membership in the SS when the medical examination board assessed him as 'unsuitable'.[18] In 1951 von Oven travelled with a fake identity via Hamburg to Argentina, where he died in 2008. When the Nazi archives in Argentina were opened in 1992, von Oven's past was revealed. No arrest warrant was ever issued for Goebbels' man, by now almost forgotten. In his new life, von Oven worked as a journalist, with stints as a foreign correspondent. The former Nazi journalist spotted a great chance for a new start that was offered by Perón's immigration policy:

> Now Perón was in charge (since 1946). He wanted to have as many hard-working immigrants as possible, and thus became involved in the clearance sale of the German intelligentsia, whose beneficiaries all the Allies were, and he himself was one, after all, even if he had entered the war only at the very last minute [...]. He—like the United States—was chiefly concerned with the abilities and skills of those wishing to enter the country, less than with their Party membership. An important German immigrant could by all means be a so-called 'Nazi' or even a 'war criminal'. It made no difference.[19]

Von Oven was hardly a special case in which an immigrant's past was overlooked; in fact, for some countries, not only was a Nazi past not an impediment for immigration, it was a positive attribute. In 1947 the American delegation in Vienna confirmed the interest of South American countries in taking in emigrants from Europe; Nazi sympathies could even prove to be an advantage:

> An interview with the Minister from Panama disclosed the fact that they are willing to allow a certain number of Europeans to enter Panama

early in 1947. There is some investigation made when possible by the Consulates, however this stress is being placed upon whether the person is Communist or has any previous connections with the Communistic elements. It was stated that there is a definite fear of increasing Communistic activities in South America and for this reason persons possessing a Fascist background are favourably considered rather than permitting a person with tainted Communistic ideas.[20]

News of work opportunities in Argentina spread like wildfire, particularly in Italy.[21] The Italian press wrote at length about the open doors of the Perón state. As one article had it: 'News of the possibility of emigration to Argentina has provoked an absolute stampede to the labour exchange of people wanting to emigrate to the country.'[22] Italian labour exchanges tried to channel this flood by publicizing bilateral bureaucratic hurdles that still had to be overcome. Interested parties could apply to the labour exchanges and their various branches for emigration. On the Italian side, the unemployed would receive preferential treatment: 'Recruitment is based in every case on professional and medical suitability, and the status of unemployment', the Italian authorities stated.[23] Millions of Europeans had knocked on the doors of Argentina's consulates and embassies in the hope of acquiring a passport and a visa for the 'promised land', 'as if the soil of their homelands was burning their feet'.[24] In August 1947, for example, an article appeared in the *Wiener Zeitung*, praising Argentina as an ideal country of emigration. Unlike other countries, the article read, Argentina had an interest in taking in 'millions of emigrants' and even in paying for their crossing. The economic conditions for this were ideal, and the country promised affluence for all.[25] Probably in order to halt the stampede of would-be emigrants, German-language newspapers also warned against reckless emigration. Germans should be wary of tempting offers of cheap land in Argentina, they wrote, because many Europeans had already fallen victim to criminals.[26]

After a war that had destroyed so much and with no hope of speedy reconstruction, many people impatiently sought a new future in a new country, but they were often faced with bureaucratic hurdles and delays. All professionals were represented among the emigrants, from engineers to bricklayers. Many of them claimed to have been in the navy or the Luftwaffe during the war, for 'the Argentinian government had declared that members of the navy or the Luftwaffe were to receive preferential treatment'.[27] But before the would-be emigrants set off on their journey, mostly by ship, they needed a visa and a ticket. Anyone wishing to emigrate first had to find a job or at least a pledge of assistance from acquaintances in Argentina. Only then could he or she hand in an application for immigration to an Argentinian consulate. The consulates then sent the documents to the national immigration authority for visas. Because of the large numbers of people involved, the whole procedure could take several months.[28] Those wishing to emigrate simply had to wait their turn. They often had to wait for months in Italy, their transit country, and make do with temporary jobs. The escape agents in Italy generally based their advice on their own experiences: 'I regret to inform you that because of major staff reshuffles at the emigration authority nothing can currently be undertaken. I therefore advise your protégé go to South Tyrol or other places in Italy and get on with some work until this matter can be dealt with here.'[29]

The Argentinians at first had no diplomatic representation in Germany and Austria, so emigrants had to apply for Argentinian visas in Italy. Argentina's embassies and consulates in Italy thus became major points of contact for European emigrants. Italy quickly developed into a springboard for those travelling overseas. Thus the Argentinians deliberately concentrated their recruitment activities on Italy. Constant abuse in the issuing of visas and rampant corruption led to frequent reshuffles and dismissals amongst the Argentinian immigration authorities there. This was a serious setback to the pro-Nazi network, as a former Nazi reported from Buenos Aires to Bishop Hudal in 1949:

> There is currently complete chaos amongst the immigration authorities here. Is it not possible that information could emerge via the Vatican (Croats?) concerning the indefensible situation at present? Half the immigration authority is behind bars for profiteering, and the respectable ones no longer have the opportunity to present their cases. But by now the profiteers have found new 'channels' long since. The respectable ones, though, will have to wait until applications are being officially accepted again.[30]

2. The Recruitment of Specialists

After the defeat of the Axis powers, the Argentinians proved to be particularly interested in taking on specialist workers from Germany. It was a sound financial investment: Argentina had only to pay their travel costs, while Germany had invested millions in the training of these scientists and technicians. Years later, when Spanish journalists questioned the former Argentinian president about the recruitment of German specialists after 1945, Perón very clearly remembered this transfer, which was intended to modernize his country:

> Long before the war ended, we had already prepared for the post-war period. Germany was defeated; we knew that, and the victors wanted to take advantage of the massive technological achievements that the country had accomplished over the previous ten years. The engineering complexes could no longer be exploited, as they had been destroyed. The only thing that could be used was the people, and they were what we were interested in.[31]

The fighter pilot and friend of Perón, Adolf Galland, succinctly summarized the viewpoint of the German specialists in Argentina when he wrote:

> In this situation, the idleness of many German scientists, technicians, and other specialists after 1945 suited Argentina very well. It also secured its stake in them. But the German specialists who went to Argentina did so entirely voluntarily and had the feeling not only of being treated fairly, but also of serving a nation that approached them sympathetically and without prejudice, and serving their own fatherland at the same time.[32]

In Argentina, emigration was a win-win proposition for both the recruiting country and the emigrants.

Perón's positive experiences with German senior executives and his government's recruitment of former Nazis and fellow travellers brought him into conflict with the victorious powers.[33] Argentina's global obligations forbade the intake of people from the former Axis powers without the permission of the Allies. Scientists from the war industry were ostracized, and war criminals had to be extradited. Under pressure from the United States, the countries of the South American continent, including Argentina, were obliged by the 1945 Act of Chapultepec to take common action against the Axis powers. This included freezing their bank accounts and hunting out members of enemy states who had gone into hiding in South America.[34] Immigration from the defeated Third Reich was to be closely monitored, but neither Argentina nor the

United States adhered to these policies. Nevertheless, the United States strongly criticized Argentina's lax attitude.[35]

In the summer of 1945, the United States had discussed the supposedly 'critical situation' in Argentina with other North and South American countries and published its severe accusations against Argentina in a 'Blue Book'. The main working points in it were German military aid to Argentina, German espionage activities, and Nazi companies and business interests in Argentina.[36] Furthermore, the Argentinians had supposedly delayed the extradition of Nazi agents and German embassy staff. The Blue Book concluded that:

> In October 1945, when consultation concerning the Argentina situation was requested by the United States, it had substantial reason to believe from the evidence then at its disposal that the present Argentine government and many of its high officials were so seriously compromised in their relations with the enemy that trust and confidence could not be reposed in that government. Now the Government of the United States possesses a wealth of incontrovertible evidence. This document, based on that evidence, speaks for itself.[37]

The declared purpose of the Blue Book was to prevent the election of Perón; if necessary, this was to be achieved through direct massive intervention by the United States. Perón's government replied clearly and immediately with an Argentinian 'White Book' designed to refute the allegations.

The debate was not merely a diplomatic one. Elements of the American press painted a picture of Argentina as a Nazi refuge.[38] As early as 1946 there was talk of '90,000 Nazis carrying on in Argentina, and tinkering away on a "Fourth Reich"'.[39] While such reports often contained a grain of truth, their broader conclusions were generally not warranted. The assumption that all Germans were working as part of a major conspiracy for the rise of a new Nazi movement was exaggerated beyond measure. But Perón's pro-German attitude and the existence of an active German-speaking community provided a great deal of ammunition for such conspiracy theories. The US government's repeated attacks on the overly ambitious Argentinian president also had their effect in the US media. An article in the magazine *Prevent World War III*, for example, reads thus:

Well entrenched in their local communities, these Germans have been able to return to their power and influence within the last ten months. Their fortunes, temporarily embargoed, have been returned and their business is booming again since the abolishing of the Black Lists. Thus, much sooner than expected by the Germans themselves, the next steps for the future aggression against the United States can be undertaken. Again, as before the war, Americans are forgetting the dangers which are being conjured in the south and which shortly before Pearl Harbor were close to bringing destruction to the Panama Canal. Argentina's propensities to fight 'Yankee imperialism' are well-known. That Perón will not hesitate to use any German help he can get is also well-known.[40]

Despite the criticism, Argentina continued its recruitment of former SS men, former Wehrmacht officers, and Nazis in order to pursue its own agenda. A 1953 CIA report on Argentina describes the wide range of German 'experts' and groups coming to Argentina:

Evidence of intention to carry on Nazi activities, and of belief in Nazi resurgence in Germany and other parts of the world, has been apparent among Germans in Argentina since 1946. A substantial stream of German immigration, including Wehrmacht and SS veterans, Nazi economists, propagandists, intelligence agents, scientists, and military specialists, has flowed into Argentina since 1945.[41]

The myths surrounding the 'Fourth Reich' in Argentina also served US interests after 1945. In particular, the emigration of German armaments experts for the modernization of Latin American militaries disturbed some circles in Washington. The blame for Argentina's pro-German policy was soon laid at the door first of the minister, then of President Perón himself.[42] Perón, like the Americans, British, Soviets, and French, placed himself beyond such matters; the legal principle of contract was always subordinate to *raison d'état*. But the chances of recruitment were divided extremely unequally.

The Soviets cared little about the pasts of 'their' specialists; they recruited considerably more German armaments experts than all the other victorious powers together.[43] The figure of 5,000 German scientists working for the USSR is well documented.[44] But in many cases the Soviet authorities forced the scientists to emigrate and collaborate.[45] Most migrants to Argentina, on the other hand, emigrated voluntarily.

Their chief motivation was the possibility of continuing their own work because there would not have been enough opportunities in post-war Germany to do so. This applied particularly to those emigrants whose previous work had been prohibited by Allied Control Council Law No. 25: scientists in the fields of applied nuclear research, aviation, and missile technology.

Like Argentina, the United States was also involved in recruiting top German experts. The Americans had a whole arsenal of recruitment possibilities at their disposal. They made scientifically and financially attractive offers or threatened employment bans and worse. Under the code name 'Operation Paperclip', the US Army set about reeling in German specialists on a grand scale. The recruitment of a team of German rocket technologists around the designer of the V2, Wernher von Braun, was probably the most striking US achievement in the competition for top German personnel.[46] Rather than ending up in the dock, hundreds of Nazi scientists launched new careers in the United States in this way. The facts that von Braun, the head of the Peenemünde rocket research institute, was an SS officer and that thousands of forced labourers and concentration camp inmates had died miserable deaths working in the underground armaments centre of Mittelbau-Dora were simply ignored by the US military.[47]

Eventually in the early 1950s the US authorities did not obstruct Argentina in any way because it, too, was now officially permitted to recruit German scientists. The US authorities had an interest in an economically successful West German state and encouraged cooperation between Germany and Argentina. The US High Commissioner for Germany, John McCloy, repeatedly authorized the export to Argentina of machine tools manufactured in Germany. In 1952 the Argentinian Foreign Minister Jeronimo Remorino cautiously sounded out McCloy and asked for permission to import machines manufactured by the Meissner Company near Cologne. Remorino made no secret of their intended purpose. The machines were purchased by the Argentinian Directorate General for the production of armaments and served to rearm and modernize the Argentinian military.[48]

The emigration of specialists after the war resulted in what has come to be called the German 'brain drain'. The victorious United States and USSR recruited the top German scientists and technicians and benefited financially from doing so. The La Plata Republic contented itself with mid-level specialists. News of Argentina's interest in such specialists quickly spread, resulting in a flood of detailed applications swiftly reaching the delegations in Europe and even arriving directly in Buenos Aires. The focus of Argentinian interest was quite clearly on scientists and armaments experts as historian Holger Meding stresses.[49] But the projects of the German researchers in Argentina were by no means always successful.

Argentina's attempt to join the circle of nuclear powers with the help of German scientist Ronald Richter, for example, was a total fiasco. Although Perón had invested huge sums in the program, he had been pursuing an unrealistic goal. Argentina had technically overreached itself. But the transfer of experts was also, in some cases, very useful for introducing the latest technology.

A prominent example illustrates the positive effects of the transfer of German specialists to Argentina. One of the most famous airplane designers in the world, Kurt Tank, the director of the Focke-Wulf aeronautic works in Bremen, had arrived in Buenos Aires in 1947. Having with him the very latest jet plane designs, Tank persuaded Perón that Argentina needed to build jet planes and was capable of doing so with the help of German experts.[50] Political momentum was required, he said, as well as the requisite finances and experienced aeronautical engineers from Germany. Perón accepted Tank's proposal, and the airplane designer immediately drew up a list of necessary specialists. The Argentinian government used its connections with Monsignor Krunoslav Draganović of the papal relief agency for Croatians to bring them into the country. With his connections and experience in the smuggling of fugitives, Draganović was able to demand the intake of a certain number of Croatians without paperwork and arrange for payment of their travel to Argentina. In June 1948 a group of engineers was finally brought to Salzburg because the Argentinian consulate there played an important part in the recruitment of specialists. The emigrants' paperwork was ready: Red Cross travel documents for displaced persons, personally signed by Father Draganović, together with residence permits issued by the Italian embassy in Vienna. After several stopovers in Italian monasteries, the engineers finally reached Argentina via Rome.

Within three years, Kurt Tank and his highly specialized team of experts built several of the first fully operational jet fighters of any South

American country: the Pulqui II, which reached speeds of around 1,000 km/h.[51] In February 1951, the Argentinian government presented Tank's jet plane to the international public at a large air show in front of cameras, radio reporters, and the press, thereby demonstrating that Argentina was a country capable of fast technological progress. Perón had much to be pleased about.[52] In 1952, the fighter pilot and 'inveterate far-right-winger'[53] Hans-Ulrich Rudel, noted admiringly in his diary:

> The Pulqui II jet fighter designed by Tank and his team remains the dominant topic of many technical discussions. I was amazed at the way the Argentinian workers, who were quite unfamiliar with this kind of metal-working, adapted to it in a very short time and achieved really fabulous results. They rightly deserve the greatest praise. The Argentinians in general have great technical ability and learn very quickly.[54]

After 1945 the German specialists were able to continue almost a century's tradition of German–Argentinian relations in the fields of military technology and training. Most prominently, Germans had helped to build the aeronautics industry in Argentina, and the Argentinian air force was considered especially pro-German. The two countries' long history of cooperation played a part, no doubt, in Rudel feeling that he was in good hands when he immigrated to Argentina. Having been the most decorated soldier in the whole of the German forces in the Second World War, Rudel would have had no future in post-war Germany, so in 1948 he travelled via Austria and Italy to Argentina. Once he arrived, Perón appointed him to serve as his air force adviser. Rudel also became the director of a German group of airplane designers—including Focke-Wulf, Messerschmidt, Dornier, Daimler-Benz, and Siemens—that was working for the German air force. Equipped with this kind of financial support and professional success, Rudel soon became politically active again. Rudel's 'Kameradenwerk' acted as a social club of sorts for former National Socialists in Argentina and South America as a whole.[55] After the fall of his patron Perón in 1955, Rudel switched his allegiance to the Paraguayan dictator Alfredo Stroessner. Reaching across borders and continents, Rudel's activities rapidly extended back to Europe. After 1950, he appeared repeatedly and illegally at the events of various neo-Nazi organizations. He never made a secret of his continued Nazi beliefs and remained active in various far-right organizations in Germany and Austria until his death in 1982.[56]

For German emigrants, Rudel among them, Argentina proved to be a comfortable, profitable, and professionally fulfilling new home. One of Rudel's long-time business partners was the former Dutch war reporter Willem (Wilhelmus Antonius) Maria Sassen, who had been given a long prison sentence in the Netherlands.[57] As advisers and arms dealers, they both maintained excellent contacts with Latin American dictators such as Stroessner in Paraguay and Augusto Pinochet in Chile. During the Second World War, Sassen was the director of a Nazi magazine in Holland and worked for Goebbels' propaganda ministry. By all accounts, the Nazis in Argentina remained loyal to their politics, meeting for coffee in the mornings and clinking glasses in the evening to toast the 'good old days.' Sassen and Eichmann had known each other since 1954 when the SS officer Otto Skorzeny introduced them to each other.[58] Adolf Galland also came to Argentina in Rudel's wake. The major general was one of the best-known fighter pilots in the Third Reich. In 1948 he, like Rudel, had escaped to Argentina via South Tyrol and Genoa. In South America, Galland was promoted to Perón's military adviser.[59] In his memoirs, Galland explains the temptation for pilots such as himself to go to Argentina:

> The offer of a job as air force adviser in Argentina led me to cross the Atlantic. Two days after my arrival in Buenos Aires, I was received by the then-aviation minister, Brigadier Major César Ojeda. He extended the President's greetings and welcomed me with a respect and friendliness that made a considerable impression on me after the bitter years of imprisonment and the time that followed, for throughout the whole world, hatred was directed at all things German. Here in the circles of the Argentinian army, we encountered no prejudices. In their eyes, we might have lost the war, but not our honour.[60]

However, the most that can be said about the lasting effect of the German emigrants on Argentina, according to historian Gabriele Ley, is that it:

> [...] in most cases remained limited, for they did not stay long enough in the host country to be able to achieve any continuity in their work. Even the Perón government's ambitious project of giving a powerful boost to the development of Argentinian universities by recruiting

European scientists can only be considered successful within certain bounds. A lack of medium- and long-term research that could have put the work of the European scientists on a more solid footing prevented both technological breakthroughs and the training of future specialists. The effects of the experts generally remained small; the German scientists had a crucial effect only on Argentina's economy.[61]

Many roads led to the Río de la Plata. What they all shared was the fact that they had to be travelled illegally—past the Allied checkpoints. Most emigrants to Argentina—above all the fleeing National Socialists—chose the path via Italy into safety abroad.

3. Argentinian Diplomats and Agents in Italy

Argentina was only indirectly active in the recruitment of German specialists, being at a disadvantage because it had no official presence in Germany. Before the opening of the General Consulate in Frankfurt am Main in 1949, diplomats in the neighbouring countries had been brought in to coordinate recruitment, examine requests, and organize transfers.[62] Soon the hubs of Argentinian recruitment in Europe included the embassy and the general consulate in Rome, the consulate in Genoa, and later the consulates in Vienna and Salzburg.

In Italy, the Argentinians were able to build on many personal, family, and political contacts. A third of them came from Italy, and Argentinian politicians and military officers were closely connected with their Italian colleagues. The most prominent example is President Perón himself. In 1939/40 Perón took part in a training course for Argentinian officers in the Italian army, a program designed to reinforce the close connections between Argentina and fascist Italy.[63] For Perón, an admirer of Mussolini, this was a unique opportunity and an experience to which he would later refer repeatedly. After a brief stay in Rome, the young officer spent several months in the northern Italian spa town of Merano. At the end of 1939, Perón left for Rome where he worked until December 1940 as a military attaché at the Argentinian embassy. On the eve of the Second World War, Perón probably also supplied Argentinian military intelligence with frequent reports on the mood among the population and the Italian officers. At any rate, Perón built connections with Italian military officers that he was able to reactivate after the war.[64] Thus, for Italian fascists, Argentina became an obvious country of refuge. Carlo Scorza, the last Party secretary; Piero Parini, the head of the province of Milan in the last years of the war; and Vittorio Mussolini, one of Il Duce's sons, all emigrated to Buenos Aires.[65] Perón always remained closely linked to Italy. Thus Eva Perón's much-vaunted European trip in 1947 was supposed to win sympathy for the Perón regime: in Spain she met Francisco Franco, in France she was the fashionable darling of the press, and in Italy she was received by the Pope. Perón also wanted to demonstrate his empathy with war-torn Italy and was careful not to send Doña Maria Eva on her travels empty-handed. In the name of Juan and Eva Perón, food parcels were distributed in Rome and other Italian cities. Ships arrived in the port of Genoa with relief deliveries for the starving Italian population, 'for the Italian people in the name of the Argentinian President,' as the newspapers reported.[66]

When Perón briefly experienced Germany during his military training tour of Europe in 1939/40, the country was at the peak of its successes in the Second World War. Perón was deeply impressed by the German military machinery and the efficiency of the Blitzkrieg. As captain of the General Staff and teacher at the military academy, Perón himself published works about operations by German commanders in the First World War. His admiration for the German military machine survived its defeat in 1945. Perón's training by Germans at the start of his career as an officer had long-term consequences, according to Rudel:

> It's amazing what a deep impression was made by the German officers who worked in several South American countries as teachers in higher military training and how tenacious is the friendship with Germany that General Perón was the first statesman in the world after the war, in public and before the complete assembly of military attachés, to give the highest praise to German soldiers. [...] For this, we soldiers owe, Germany owes thanks to General Perón, as we do for many of the official acts with which he has expressed his enduring sympathy for Germany.[67]

Perón had given instructions to his consulates and embassies in Europe, in the context of his immigration policy after 1945, to endeavour to smooth the way for interested German parties. Incomplete and even missing documents were deliberately overlooked, and the administrative process was kept to a minimum. The Argentinian immigration commission reached its first agreement with the Italian government in February 1947, by which time 100,000 Italians had already applied to emigrate to Argentina.[68] Immediately after the war's end, Rome became the project's central hub. Beginning in 1946, the Salesian priest José Clement Silva was head of the Argentinian immigration office there. He had express orders to organize the movement of four million Europeans to Argentina in order to realize Perón's dream of an economic and social revolution. Even after an Argentinian immigration delegation was dispatched to Italy, Rome remained the departure point from which specialists found their way to Buenos Aires, while mass relocation was channelled via Genoa. In December 1946 the Italian ambassador in the Vatican reported to the Foreign Ministry that Silva saw the task of the Argentinians as enabling between 400,000 and 500,000 people to emigrate to their country. The Vatican authorities wished to make the organization and funds of the pontifical refugee commission (PCA) available for this purpose. This document shows that the promotion of immigration both conformed to the purposes of the Perón government and corresponded entirely with the interests of the Vatican. The Italian government, in turn, hoped to be able to rid itself of the burden of the refugee problem and, therefore, supported the Argentinians in their organization of immigration and recruitment offices in Italy.[69]

A diplomat with the rank of minister, Adolfo Scilingo (Schilling), who was of German descent, coordinated the recruitment of emigrants in Italy as a special envoy from Argentina.[70] Each month, the Argentinian consulate in Rome issued at least 400 visas; in April 1948 it was more than 1,000 per month. Particularly common were visas for refugees from the Ukraine, Poland, Croatia, and Russia.[71] Of central importance was the Argentinian general consulate in Genoa, where the Argentinian immigration authority, the Delegación Argentina de Inmigración en Europa (DAIE), was located. Argentinian authorities, Catholic clerics, and the Red Cross worked there hand in hand.

In Perón's recruitment office, German-Argentinians and former Wehrmacht officers and SS men very often pursued their own interests. They were less concerned with the recruitment of specialist workers, and more with helping their comrades to escape. As a result, they helped to shape the work of Perón's immigration policy at a practical level. The head of Perón's secret service who had an information office in the presidential palace in Buenos Aires, Rodolfo Freude, was a young, fair-haired Argentinian of German origin. He played a key role in crafting immigration policy. During the war, his father, the German businessman Ludwig Freude, seemed to have maintained close contacts with the National Socialists and particularly with the German foreign intelligence service. He worked for the German embassy and was a representative of several German companies in Buenos Aires. According to FBI reports, before the end of the war Freude repeatedly received money from General Friedrich Wolf of the German embassy in Buenos Aires to keep the local German spy networks active.[72]

The successful entrepreneur Ludwig Freude lived in the German-speaking heartland of Bariloche and had been an Argentinian citizen since 1935.[73] As a good friend of Perón's and until 1945 the president of the influential German Club in Argentina, Freude was selected very early on as a key figure in the pro-Nazi network. The Americans accused him of working as a spy and repeatedly urged for his extradition. Freude also assumed a prominent role in the US government's Blue Book on 'Argentina as a Nazi Haven'. In March 1946 the US authorities triumphed, and the *Washington Post* wrote, under the headline 'Argentina's No. 1 Nazi to Lose Citizenship,' about Freude's imminent extradition.[74] But a few months later, Perón won the presidential election and had no interest in sacrificing his friend and financier. The US's accusations were examined by an Argentinian court in October 1946 and declared baseless; thus Freude was not extradited or stripped of his Argentinian citizenship.[75] In 1955, under Perón's protection, he founded the Federation of German–Argentinian Associations; as its chair, he became highly involved in the cultural life of the German community.[76] The CIA was particularly concerned about Freude's influence:

> Since consolidation of President Juan Domingo Perón's political power in the 1946 election, German interests have had abundant opportunity for growth and profit. Principal personages in the German colony, especially Ludwig Freude, have been in close touch with many officials at high levels in the Argentine Government and armed forces and also directly with President Peron. He employed Freude's son Rodolfo from the early post-war period to 1951, as one of his private secretaries, with the title of Chief of Investigations, Division of the Presidency. As such, Rodolfo directed Perón's domestic intelligence service.[77]

Fritz Mandl, owner of an Austrian arms factory, was almost as influential as Freude. Mandl had contacts with Austro-fascists and was, thus, able to extend his influence and his monopolist position. Mandl had close contacts with Argentina even before 1939 and had founded companies there. During the war, Mandl lived in Argentina and, beginning in 1946, became one of Perón's advisers. The CIA even identified him as an *éminence grise* behind Perón's economic plans. Freude, they claimed, had been nothing but Mandl's front man.[78]

One important mastermind behind Nazi escape assistance in Italy was the former SS-Hauptsturmführer and German Argentinian Horst Carlos Fuldner who acted as a liaison with the Argentine immigration authority and successfully procured visas and employment for the escapees in South America. He was born in Buenos Aires in 1910 and attended school there. In 1926 his family moved to Germany, where he was graduated from the Realgymnasium in Kassel. In 1931 he joined the SA and, shortly afterwards, the SS. He quickly rose through the ranks. 'Herr SS-Hauptsturmführer' worked on the staff of the Reichsführer SS Himmler and as an adjutant with the SS head of administration in Munich. But suddenly his career changed course due to circumstances in his private life. Fuldner's marriage was in ruins, and he was living the high life, buying himself an expensive BMW on credit, for instance. He was constantly thinking about his escape option: 'Argentina was always an alternative for me,' Fuldner wrote later.[79] In 1936, Fuldner actually tried to flee the SS, making an adventurous bid to escape to South America; only on the high seas was Fuldner apprehended and 'persuaded' to return. A civilian court acquitted Fuldner of fraudulent borrowing. The Munich district court articulated its finding that the reasons for his attempted escape were 'marital disputes' and civic duties: 'he wanted to do his military service in Argentina as he is also an Argentine citizen,' and the 'accused was to be acquitted'.[80] Fuldner gradually restored his reputation; towards the end of the war, his contacts with Argentina became more and more important. In March 1945 he travelled to Madrid to set up escape routes for the SS.[81] When the Allies demanded his extradition, he fled to Argentina in 1947. As a German Argentinian and former SS officer, he brought valuable expertise with him and was immediately hired by Rodolfo Freude. He became an agent in Freude's information office as a specialist in the field of German immigration. But with a series of arrivals of war criminals from Europe, Fuldner was charged with one preeminent task: saving National Socialists, including SS men.

Fuldner was sent to Italy as an official representative of Argentina to organize improved recruitment. Perón saw him as his personal delegate and granted him special powers: the Argentinian delegations in Italy and Austria had to collaborate with him.[82] In December 1947, Fuldner arrived back in Europe and made himself useful in the Argentinian immigration commission, DAIE, in Genoa. The venue was well chosen; Genoa was one of the most important ports for ships to Argentina at that time.[83] The Argentinian officials at DAIE in Genoa changed often, while the group of former of SS and Wehrmacht officers now working for the Argentinians was something of a stable element.

Mario Franz Ruffinengo (Rufinatscha), a former Wehrmacht officer, was secretary of the DAIE, which was well known to fleeing National Socialists. Ruffinengo was born an illegitimate son of Leopoldine Wizenetz on 22 February 1919 in Waidhofen an der Ybbs (Austria). His mother came from Moravia and was a teacher in Waidhofen at the time. His Italian father, Dominico Ruffinengo, did not legally declare his paternity until early October 1924. Soon afterwards, his parents were officially married in the small town of Canelli, sixty miles north of Genoa.[84] Young Mario grew up in Italy. In 1940, the Italian army drafted him. In autumn 1943, he was briefly imprisoned by the Germans in the Balkans and then served in the Wehrmacht. At the end of the war, he was imprisoned by the Americans and worked for them as an interpreter until 1946. As an Italian citizen, he received an identity card in 1946 without any difficulty. A year later in July 1947, he applied for an Italian passport to emigrate to Argentina and first reached Buenos Aires via Genoa on 3 May 1948. However, his first stay there was very short because Fuldner soon recruited him for his 'Argentinian immigration commission' and in 1949 gave him a key position in Genoa. Soon Rufinatscha became a central figure; his Italian citizenship together with his knowledge of German and Italian were invaluable for his new task.[85] Rufinatscha stayed in Genoa until 1952, then had his family join him in Argentina. His last address in Genoa was 3 Via Gobetti where his Austrian mother also lived for a long time.

Franz Rufinatscha found a ready and enterprising aide for his work at the DAIE in the form of the National Socialist Reinhard Kops. Kops was a Wehrmacht spy in Hungary and had served in the Balkans.

After escaping to Italy in 1947, he contacted Rufinatscha in Genoa, and they were soon working together. Kops, who now called himself Hans (Juan) Maler, was quickly involved in smuggling SS men to Argentina. In his memoirs, Kops gave an account of his first contact with Rufinatscha:

> In this connection it was fortunate that in the context of an extensive immigration agreement made with Italy the Argentinian government of General Perón sent as a secretary to Genoa a gentleman who was of South Tyrolean origin and who had been a German officer in the Second World War, Franz R[ufinatscha]. The hand that Franz extended from Genoa I took in Rome.[86]

In tricky cases, Kops and Rufinatscha had to improvise and were seen as very stubborn and imaginative. Thus Rufinatscha in Genoa soon became the 'Robin Hood' of the 'disenfranchised'.[87]

4. Perón's Escape Agents in Italy

The Argentinians sought partners for their immigration activities and worked very closely with church organizations, particularly in Genoa. Escape agent Fuldner became an important contact for Italian churchmen. In several letters to the Austrian Bishop Hudal in Rome, Carlos Fuldner was repeatedly described as the driving force of the Argentinians:

> The number of Germans waiting in Rome, Genoa, and Bolzano is vanishingly small compared to the Croatians who have been taken away. At any rate, it proves once again that the presence of a German priest here would be desirable. This emerges above all from the statements of one 'Don Carlos' [...]. Don Carlos seems to have been a leading member of the SS, but even before the collapse he seems to have deviated. For our concerns he is now at the crucial point.[88]

Hudal's informant knew what he was talking about; the Catholic Monsignors enjoyed almost unlimited trust from the Red Cross, the Argentinians, and the Italian authorities, for who would openly question the word of a priest? Consequently, the help of churchmen was often vitally important in procuring papers: 'However as a non-Italian you can only enter this post [...] if you have a cleric at hand. Monsignor Draganović is going in and out. So is Father Dömöter. So it is to be recommended that a priest should be working here at least from time to time, when a steamer is leaving.'[89]

The assistance of the Church, clergy, and charities was integral to the success of any immigration programme. Father Draganović remained especially effective in obtaining visas for emigrants. In October 1947, he set up his own Croatian emigration committee in Genoa and Rome.[90] The Archbishop of Genoa, Giuseppe Siri, worked closely with Fuldner. Siri had also founded a committee of his own to facilitate emigration to Argentina.[91] In Genoa all the threads came together, and influential local contacts were of huge importance. Siri was particularly interested in bringing as many anticommunists from Eastern Europe to South America as possible, in order to remove them from the clutches of the Soviets. The term "anticommunist" was applied very broadly in describing individuals who had compromised themselves in the eyes of the communists, and hence included fascists, National Socialists, Ustaša members, and similar groups. The Croatian charity Hrvatski Karitas in Buenos Aires was one source of help with border crossing for the refugees. In March 1949, for example, a secret gathering of Croatians in exile met to solve problems regarding the financing of Croatian emigration to South America. Draganović proposed a secret fund to bring German and Croatian fascists to Latin America and spoke of 25,000 Croatian refugees in Italy, Germany, and Austria, as well as around 3,600 Germans who had earned the help of Croatia. As the IRO considered many Croatians to be politically tainted and undesirable, it often refused aid for them, according to Draganović. Finance for emigration thus had to come from other sources. Father Draganović suggested that every Croatian in Argentina should pay at least 10 pesos a month to the secret fund. Although the Argentinian government officially wanted to end the immigration of Slavs, there were ways and means of moving Croatians to Argentina; falsifying the origin of refugees, for example, was not a big problem for Draganović.[92]

Thus a working system came into being: the Catholic Church provided accommodation and shelter, the Red Cross supplied the documentation, and the Argentinian general consulate in Genoa distributed the visas in agreement with the immigration authorities in Buenos Aires and in many cases sorted out the sea crossing. If passengers—mostly Italians—had not appeared before a ship was due to leave, Rufinatscha filled the passenger lists with German fugitives and emigrants. Officially, the new passengers were identified as Italians from South Tyrol, which was supposed to explain the fact that they spoke German. By taking on passengers as specified by Rufinatscha, the Argentinian Dodero shipping company did not comply with the wishes of the general consulate. This system, described in quantitative terms as the most significant opportunity for emigration from Italy, worked very smoothly until it was halted around the beginning of 1948 due to a scandal. Shortly after the ship sailed, a hundred Germans who had embarked with Italian papers had started singing the 'Engeland song' to the alarm of the carabinieri on the shore. 'Engeland' was a popular battle song among the German Luftwaffe in the first years of the war. After the illegal people-smuggling had been exposed in such a provocative way, the complicity of the Italian authorities came to an end. The fake South Tyroleans now came under the closer scrutiny of the carabinieri, in whom their poor command of Italian immediately aroused suspicion. This practice almost led to disaster for Mengele alias Helmut Gregor from the South Tyrolean village of Tramin; he was even imprisoned in Genoa for several days in June 1949.[93] Reinhard Kops alias Hans Maler travelled several times—like Mengele—from his hiding place in Merano to Genoa. There he had to acquire a crossing and an Argentinian visa. To do so, he relied on the help of South Tyrolean contacts of the Argentinians and their partners in Genoa. In his memoirs, Kops mentions in passing that he was under the protection of South Tyrolean people-smugglers: 'The next day we consulted Genoese friends of my South Tyrolean protectors about how one could board a ship "illegally" (without papers), what was called a "blind" passenger. It soon turned out that this was not nearly so easy for these Genoese to arrange as it appeared from a distance.'[94]

Rufinatscha and Fuldner had contacts all over Italy, and the route over the Brenner Pass to Genoa was of particular importance to their work. At the Italian–Austrian border, the escape agents in Perón's network were reliably present. The Bolzano SS officer and holder of the Knight's Cross, Karl Nicolussi-Leck, played an important part in this. Nicolussi-Leck and Fuldner may already have known each other from their time in the SS; in any case, they became friends after the war. Even late in life, Nicolussi-Leck spoke with respect of his friend 'Don Carlos'.[95] The two men were ideal complements for one another. Nicolussi-Leck knew the Tyrolean and South Tyrolean SS men, the South

Tyrolean borderland, the smugglers, and the safe routes over the border. His network brought fugitives over the border to Genoa, where Fuldner sorted out the next stage of the journey. Nicolussi-Leck's work in cross-border people smuggling was almost a seamless continuation of his work in the Nazi movement before 1945. The South Tyrolean was born on 14 March 1917 in Pfatten near Bozen and reared in a family with many other children. As a young man, he became involved with the Völkischer Kampfring Südtirol (VKS), in opposition to the de-nationalization policy of Italian fascism. From 1933 the VKS increasingly came under Nazi influence. Nicolussi-Leck soon became one of the leading and most active participants in the ranks of the VKS. In SS documents, he confidently gave his profession as 'political leader and organizational director of the Nazi movement in South Tyrol'.[96]

After accepting German citizenship, in 1940 Nicolussi-Leck voluntarily joined the Waffen-SS (no. 423,876[97]) 'because it claimed to be an elite unit'.[98] From 1942 until 1945 he served in the ranks of the Wiking 5th SS Tank Division, which initially consisted of volunteers and was chiefly deployed on the Eastern Front. As a result of his service, in 1944 Nicolussi-Leck received the Knight's Cross of the Iron Cross—one of the Third Reich's highest decorations. After the defeat at Stalingrad and Reich propaganda minister Goebbels' announcement of 'total war,' all available Heimatfront forces were mobilized, even in South Tyrol. In a personal telegram to Himmler on 3 February 1943, Volksgruppenführer Peter Hofer declared his willingness to 'completely mobilize the forces of the Volksgruppe'. SS-Obersturmführer Nicolussi-Leck was one of the chief supporters of this propagandistic order, praising it. Nicolussi-Leck had already complained of the unwillingness of South Tyroleans to mobilize for the Third Reich, accusing them of Verschweizerung (Swissification), and in all his speeches, he expressed his sympathy for the SS as the 'elite troop of the Reich'.[99]

Even today Nicolussi-Leck bears the reputation in initiated circles of being a 'reckless daredevil'; stories of his 'Hussar rides' can even be read on the Internet.[100] The French journalist Jean Mabire wrote of him, 'He comes from Bozen in South Tyrol—which the Italians renamed Bolzano in 1918—and thus belongs to the southernmost German minority abroad. He is a young, slim and dashing daredevil, who wages war in the Hussar style, and attracted attention even in the battles in the Caucasus.'[101]

Nicolussi-Leck's wartime service showed his daring and fearlessness, qualities that would serve him well in his new post-war career. In the last year of the war, Nicolussi-Leck served with distinction: he had led a Wiking tank company, was promoted to SS-Hauptsturmführer in January 1945, and was awarded the German Cross in gold in March 1945, having been wounded several times on the Eastern Front.[102] In early April 1945, Nicolussi-Leck was transferred with a unit of 150 men from Hungary to northwest Germany. After adventurous battles while retreating, Nicolussi-Leck finally gave the order in mid-April 1945 to dissolve the unit, and each soldier had to make his own way home. Nicolussi-Leck and most of his men underwent US imprisonment in Austria and Germany.[103] In 1947, Nicolussi-Leck was released from the US prisoner-of-war camp at Glasenbach and returned to South Tyrol[104] where he initially worked as an escape agent. Nicolussi-Leck's protégés also included the well-known fighter pilots Hans-Ulrich Rudel and Adolf Galland. In 1948, he smuggled them both, though not in the same month, across the Brenner Pass to Italy. For several weeks, the flying aces were guests of Nicolussi-Leck in Bolzano where they received their Red Cross travel documents with false identities or citizenship.

Nicolussi-Leck was a popular contact for Austrian SS men escaping through Italy because they all had something in common: they had been interned for two years in the Glasenbach camp in Austria where former SS men and active National Socialists were imprisoned by the Allies. 'The American internment camp for the bad Nazis is well known all over Austria', as one former SS man caustically put it.[105] Glasenbach is a classic example of how friendships forged in prison cells turned into the basis of escape networks. At the end of the war, the Counter Intelligence Corps issued automatic arrest warrants; individuals who might, because of their rank or knowledge, try to preserve or revive Nazi organizations were arrested. Some detention camps had to be set up. The largest one in Austria was Glasenbach near Salzburg, where up to 12,000 people were interned. Groups of prisoners in the camps soon turned into networks of friends. The head of one such group of prisoners, according to US reports, was Franz Haja.[106] Haja, from Vienna, had been a member of the NSDAP since 1933 and worked as a mechanic. After the Anschluss of Austria, he joined the SS in 1938, and then served in a Waffen-SS unit at the end of the war. As an SS-Untersturm-führer, Haja soon became very active again in various internment camps. In June 1948 he was released from Glasenbach camp and then lived in Upper Austria. Old comrades also met up at Haja's wedding in 1948. Apart from a number of Austrian SS men from Upper Austria, Styria, and Vienna, there was 'in addition, one Nicolussi Karl, also a former fellow-prisoner. Nicolussi is about 30 years old, and resides in Bozen, Italy.'[107] Under questioning, he stressed to the Americans that there was nothing political behind gatherings of former comrades. The Americans launched detailed investigations and kept the correspondence of the group from Glasenbach camp under surveillance, particularly that between the Austrians and Nicolussi-Leck in Bolzano. After six months of investigations, the CIC in Austria reached the conclusion, 'Investigation revealed no information which would indicate that the meetings held by the group mentioned in basic papers are of any political significance. All members, when questioned individually and separately, gave the same reasons for the meetings: social gatherings of former POW camp inmates.'[108]

The men were less concerned with politics than with friendship and mutual assistance. For many people, a new start after 1945 was harder to achieve without such support. According to one letter from the Glasenbach group, 'of course we are closely connected and help each other as much as we can'.[109] Better than many secret service reports, this statement sums up the nature of most networks after 1945: there was no secret, all-powerful organization of 'former SS-men' at work. Rather, groups of SS comrades helped one another, mostly to start again at home, but also to escape overseas. In the Allied prisoner-of-war camps, social networks began to develop, and new friendships were made. The rumour that SS members were beginning to escape overseas started to spread in the camps. The Glasenbach group had one very important contact on the route to Italy in Karl Nicolussi-Leck, but contact with Bishop Hudal and church escape agents in Italy came through Franz Hieronymus Riedl.

Riedl, a journalist, was born in Vienna in 1906, came from a Catholic nationalist background, and attended the Gymnasium in the Benedictine abbey of Seitenstetten near Vienna. He then studied at the universities of Vienna and Marburg an der Lahn, among others. In Marburg he lived at the Deutsche Burse, a student organization for ethnic and foreign Germans from all over the world. This was the basis of a lifelong network of acquaintances in influential positions. After completing his studies, Riedl embraced politics that tended more and more to National Socialism, a stance his journalism increasingly reflected. Through his many contacts with the Reich Press Chamber, Riedl came to Budapest as a correspondent of the German embassy, writing for several newspapers and also working as a war reporter. In 1945 he fled from Hungary to escape the Red Army. When the war ended, he hid in the Ötztal valley in the Austrian Tyrol before crossing the mountains to South Tyrol, where he had many friends dating back to his student days in Marburg.[110] At the same time, Riedl established contact with Hudal and with various church agencies in Italy and Austria. For a long time, Riedl, like Hudal, believed in the possibility of building bridges between the Catholic Church and National Socialism. In the 1930s this placed him very much in accord with Bishop Hudal, whom he knew well. After 1945 Riedl began to reactivate these old contacts, particularly stressing his anticommunism. For the Italian authorities, for example, he asked the Benedictines in Bolzano to confirm that he was 'of Catholic conviction and a resolute opponent of communism'.[111] Riedl had powerful advocates: on 10 December 1948 Hudal wrote to him: 'Today I sent a recommendation, hopefully successful. Unfortunately intrigues and gossip always belong to times of decay. Bravely fulfil duty, show strong character and contribute firmly to Italy's rise, that is very important today, not least for us guests and foreigners. God bless you. Bishop Alois Hudal.'[112]

Due to their shared sympathies before and after the war, Riedl and Hudal soon worked closely and well together. As early as April 1948, Hudal had written a first long letter to Riedl: 'Dear Doctor, I am very glad to hear from you after such a long and sadly rather too eventful time, and congratulate you on escaping the first flood. May we be spared another. I received the visit I had been told about yesterday. You can rely on me in all things.'[113] By 'the first flood' Hudal means the measures to arrest SS members and leading National Socialists. Riedl had escaped them by fleeing to South Tyrol. Hudal was convinced that he could depend on Riedl's agreement in his hatred of Jews, communists, and socialists. Hudal now once again asked his protégé for favours. Hence Riedl began working, alongside his own personal interests, for 'would-be emigrants'. The emigration plans were not a secret. One comrade wrote to Riedl in 1948: 'Otherwise I am busy preparing for my crossing to Argentina, and that is giving me enough to do. I would like to start around the end of July. Here we are stagnating.'[114] At the same time he informed Riedl that he would soon be arriving in Bolzano, strategically the most favourable stopping place on the route to Genoa.

Austrian and Reich German acquaintances could depend on safe lodgings in South Tyrol. During stopovers in Bolzano, the former comrades were recommended to Hudal, who found accommodation for them in Rome or Genoa. Soon camp commandant Franz Stangl would knock on the doors of the escape agents. Like other members of the SS, he had heard of Hudal and the Italian escape route while in the Glasenbach camp. One of the fugitives in Riedl's circle was SS-Sturmbannführer Gustav Otto Wächter. Wächter had been heavily involved in war crimes in occupied Poland, and in 1946 he escaped via Bolzano to Rome where he sought refuge with Bishop Hudal. Escape assistance was flourishing. Riedl was suitably optimistic in letters to Bishop Hudal in Rome: 'Many thanks for your kind letter, for sending the monthly journal *Mann in der Zeit*, and for taking in my friend Raschhofer. His appearance finally brought me back in contact with part of my scattered circle of friends and reminded me that we can now to some extent return to work'.[115] Riedl knew Hudal's guest Hermann Raschhofer from Upper Austria, probably since they had studied together at the Burse in Marburg.

Raschofer's case is typical of the assistance Riedl and Hudal provided for former Nazis. Raschhofer was a member of the illegal NSDAP in Austria and, as a teacher of international law in the 1930s, played a significant part in the National Socialist conception of ethnicity. On the personal wishes of Secretary of State for Bohemia and Moravia Karl Hermann Frank, he was given an appointment at the German University in Prague. Raschhofer became Frank's legal adviser. The German rulers wanted to make Bohemia and Moravia 'German within a few years'. The (pseudo-)scientific framework for this came from 'experts' such as Raschhofer.[116] He was also a close personal friend of Frank's. In the autumn of 1944 Raschhofer was also involved, on the instructions of SS-Gruppenführer Frank and as 'political adviser' to the Waffen-SS Obergruppenführer Hermann Höfle, in the suppression of the armed nationalist uprising in the Nazi puppet state of Slovakia.[117] It is worth noting, however, that Raschhofer remained loyal to the Nazi regime to the very last: he planned a special issue about Bohemia in honour of

Hitler's birthday for April 1945. In that month Frank finally sent Rasch-hofer as a negotiator to General George S. Patton, but after a number of detours, he stayed instead in South Tyrol.[118] After spending some time in the border region, in April 1948 on Riedl's recommendation he finally went into hiding in church institutions in Rome, courtesy of Bishop Hudal.[119]

Over the course of time, escape aid and escape agents changed. The network was becoming increasingly tight, and its members were also acting with ever greater openness and confidence. Denazification cooled as the Cold War between East and West grew increasingly heated. Riedl had good contacts and safe houses in South America; he also wrote for German magazines in Chile, Brazil, and Argentina. At first, Riedl himself wanted to emigrate to Argentina, but because of his 'ignorance of Western languages' the Eastern European expert saw no future for himself there.[120] After the adventurous years of 'emigration assistance', in the 1950s Riedl continued his career as a journalist and author in Bolzano.[121]

Nicolussi-Leck saw things differently than Riedl. He saw no profes-sional future for himself in Europe. As an escape agent, he used the tried and tested routes and headed for South America. Shortly after his return from US imprisonment, Nicolussi-Leck learned that the Perón government was welcoming Germans with open arms. The country needed specialists, particularly technicians, in every profession. His goal was the construction of a new life—and at first Nicolussi-Leck sim-ply wanted to get 'away from ruined Europe'.[122] On 31 August 1948 Nicolussi-Leck applied for a Red Cross travel document in Rome. The South Tyrolean SS man could truthfully fill out the forms, with one crucial detail included: 'citizenship—stateless'. There was no doubt as to his destination: for the South Tyrolean, as for many others, Argen-tina meant a major opportunity for a new start. Nicolussi-Leck could not prove his identity with any kind of card or document, but there was a safe way out because the escape agent Nicolussi-Leck had close con-tacts with the Croatian priest Draganović in Rome. According to Nico-lussi-Leck, 'the good Father Draganović was the most important con-tact and colleague of Fuldner's in Italy'.[123] He knew what he was talking about. On the morning of 31 August 1948 the former SS man approached Draganović in Rome. The papal relief mission had no trouble issuing him with a letter of recommendation, but didn't stop

there: Draganović signed in person Nicolussi-Leck's application for a
Red Cross travel document, which the stamp of Draganović's College
of St Jerome of the Illyrians (Collegio di San Girolamo degli Illirici) in
Rome somehow made more official.[124] Along with his wife Maria and
daughter Reinhild, Nicolussi-Leck emigrated to Argentina.[125] He and
his wife were placed on list 169 of Draganović's Croatians and duly
received visas for Argentina as 'Croatians'. Nicolussi-Leck deliberately
left his nationality of origin open, saying only that he was stateless and
giving his place of birth as 'W[V]adena' (Pfatten, near Bolzano) without a country of birth. Nicolussi-Leck's lack of data made it possible for
Draganović to present him as an ethnic German from Croatia.[126]
Finally Nicolussi-Leck himself set out on an established route and emigrated to Argentina 'to earn some money'.

5. Austrian Pioneers in the Escape Network

Particularly striking is the escape of one circle of people who had known
each other well since the days of National Socialism's illegality in Austria and had contacts in South Tyrol. This was a group of senior SS
members from the Austrian region of Tyrol who all belonged to the
hard core of the Austrian National Socialist movement. They maintained their solidarity after 1945: 'These individuals were all members
of the SS, officials of the former NSDAP or participants in pogroms
against the Jews,'[127] as the police department in Innsbruck wrote in
1948 about 'fugitive National socialists in South Tyrol'.[128] For the
Tyrolean National Socialists, escape to Italy was very easy. They had
only to travel a few miles over the mountains to join their comrades in
South Tyrol. Personal friendships and comradeships quickly turned
into contacts and safe houses. Tyrolean and South Tyrolean National
Socialists prepared the way for former SS men from the German Reich
to Italy and, finally, Argentina.

   According to the available data from the Argentinian immigration
authority, Franz Rubatscher was the first of the Tyrolean group to reach
Argentina. In October 1947 he travelled by land via Uruguay to Argentina. SS-Hauptsturmführer Rubatscher could have served as a contact
for the others, and upon his immigration in October 1948, SS-Hauptsturmführer Fridolin Guth explicitly gave 'Franz Rubatsher [*sic*], Hotel
San Carlos de Bariloche' as a reference.[129] Rubatscher was part of the

committed core of the Tyrolean NSDAP. Among his intimates, aside from Gauleiter Franz Hofer and Kreisleiter Klaus Mahnert, was Fritz Lantschner, Gauamtsleiter of Tyrol.[130] Rubatscher was thus a key figure in escape assistance, and his activity behind the scenes warrants closer examination. Rubatscher entered the service of the state police in Innsbruck in 1930 and shortly afterwards continued his professional activity as a policeman in the service of the NSDAP.[131] He was significantly involved in the attempted Nazi putsch in Tyrol in 1934. He had been a member of the SS and the NSDAP since June 1932, and the Nazi authorities later recognized him as an 'old combatant' from the NSDAP.[132]

Given his Nazi record, Rubatscher would need to flee or else be prosecuted, perhaps, by the Allies. During the war Rubatscher served in a police squad in Cracow; in 1944 he was promoted to commander of the Trentino Security Unit, fighting Italian partisans.[133] In May 1945 he was arrested by the Americans in Innsbruck, but by November 1946 had been released from Darmstadt camp. He then moved to South Tyrol, where he had many acquaintances from his time in the war. The police in Innsbruck were well informed about his location. In a 1947 report they wrote:

> On 18 May 1945 Rubatscher was handed over to the CIC in the police prison house [Innsbruck], from which he was transferred by the CIC to a camp in Germany. As has now been shown, Rubatscher was released from Darmstadt Camp on 29 November 1946. He came to Innsbruck around 1 or 2 December, spent a night with his family at 4 Gaswerkstrasse, and the following day crossed the border to South Tyrol. There he is to stay chiefly with his relatives.[134]

But Italy was only a stopping-point of his for a few months. From here SS-Hauptsturmführer Rubatscher organized his journey overseas. The main precondition for this was valid identification papers—and the Red Cross travel documents were particularly coveted. In June 1947 he applied for them as a stateless technician and builder. As his address in Italy he gave 'Bozen, 12 Via Molini, at the home of Dr Pircher'. His identity was confirmed by the Red Cross in Rome and by the PCA. Rubatscher travelled with his wife Heilwig and their two children. The ICRC in Rome sent the travel documents for Rubatscher to the delegation in Verona. Rubatscher was to collect them from there, as he 'is resident in Bolzano', and 'cannot come to Rome', as it said in a letter from the Italian Red Cross.[135] From that moment everything went smoothly and relatively swiftly for him.

Rubatscher finally arrived in Argentina in October 1947,[136] and he then moved to the winter sports resort in the Andes, San Carlos de Bariloche, which is 1,200 miles from Buenos Aires, helping to found a community of SS men. This refuge soon became the second home of many National Socialist fugitives. The concentration of Nazis among the former comrades in this place, which is very like skiing resorts in the Alps, was relatively high. Living there, besides Erich Priebke, whose butcher's shop, Wiener Delikatessen, became a popular meeting-point, were a number of senior SS officers from Austria and Germany. They included Gauamtsleiter Friedrich (Fritz) Lantschner, who escaped in 1948 via South Tyrol to Argentina, where he set up a construction company.[137]

Lantschner made a wise decision in fleeing to Argentina; his Nazi record certainly made him a target of the Allied authorities. Originally from Innsbruck, Lantschner was a major mastermind of the July Putsch in 1934 against the Austrian government led by Engelbert Dollfuss; then he fled to Nazi Germany, where he was soon working in the Reich office for agricultural policy. Meanwhile, Lantschner was wanted in Austria for murder.[138] After the Anschluss of Austria in March 1938, he returned to Tyrol in the wake of the German Wehrmacht and assumed provisional direction of the Tyrolean Farmers' Association. Until the end of the war, he was government director of the 'Agriculture, Economy, Labour' department in the Gau administration of Tyrol-Vorarlberg, and for a long time he was even the right-hand man of the Gauleiter of the Tyrol.[139] During and after 'Reichskristallnacht', Fritz Lantschner played an inglorious role in the confiscation of Jewish property.

Lantschner travelled along with Gustav 'Guzzi' Lantschner, a very well-known skiing ace and film-maker, who in the 1930s had been one of the stars of Alpine skiing and was world champion of downhill skiing in 1932. Guzzi won a total of three Olympic medals and three world championship medals, and his success enabled him to become a well-known star of various adventure and mountain films. Guzzi was already making films with Leni Riefenstahl in the 1930s, and he also knew Luis Trenker. Lantschner delighted the cinema audience with his skiing skills in the hit 1931 film *Der Weisse Rausch*, which he shot with

Riefenstahl. Guzzi left Austria years before the Anschluss and became a German citizen to serve the Third Reich as a sportsman and to make a career for himself. He seemed to have admired Hitler, but he was foremost an opportunist. He was also a cameraman in Leni Riefenstahl's propaganda film *Olympia* about the Olympic games of 1936 in Berlin. This was one reason why he probably 'became persona non grata in Austria and Germany' after Hitler's downfall.[140] In any case, like Fritz, Guzzi Lantschner decided to emigrate overseas after the war. So it was that on 25 May 1948, Guzzi applied for an ICRC travel document with the correct details, 'Gustav Lantschner', born on 12 August 1910 in Innsbruck, Tyrol. He gave his original citizenship as 'Austro-Hungarian', and his current nationality as 'stateless'. Of course Lantschner gave his religion on the application form as Catholic and his profession as film-maker. Lantschner probably had money, because during his journey he stayed in expensive hotels rather than monastery cells. In South Tyrol he stayed in the well-known Hotel Figl on Kornplatz in Bolzano, and in Rome he stayed in the Universo. In Italy Lantschner received support from Hudal, as his letter of thanks to the bishop reveals.[141] Lantschner had already acquired his entry permit for Argentina in December 1947 via Hudal's contacts,[142] and on arrival lived in the Andean resort of San Carlos de Bariloche, where he reunited with his fellow countrymen, including Fritz. Guzzi had spent time there between the wars and lived there after the Axis powers' defeat: 'He drew more friends here after the Second World War,' as the Austrian folklorist and writer Karl Ilg enigmatically observed in 1976.[143]

After moving to Argentina, Guzzi Lantschner continued to make films, shot mainly around Bariloche; he, like most of the German and Austrian community there, relied upon his talents to make a living. The films, which featured mainly blond, Nordic people, were in the genre of the skiing films of Trenker and Riefenstahl. Fritz Lantschner supported Guzzi financially for his film work in Argentina. Lantschner's close friend Rubatscher was a trained and experienced skier,[144] a skill that the escapees in the ski resort of Bariloche were able to exploit by working as guides and instructors. Fritz Lantschner was, alongside Rubatscher, probably the leading mind among the Tyrolean fugitives. In Bariloche the South Tyrolean Cornelius Dellai, from a family of South Tyrolean hoteliers, was also an acquaintance of Guzzi's. So it can hardly be a surprise that the Argentinian government commissioned Dellai to run a hotel complex in Bariloche. During the pre-war period, Cornelius Dellai was landlord and owner of the Dellai guest-house. From 1943 he ran a local police unit, which was entrusted amongst other things with the search for Allied pilots and deserters. Immediately after the end of the war, the persistent attention paid to Dellai by the Italian police at the Berghotel Dellai apparently became too much for his family, and in 1948 he sold his little mountain hotel to Hans Steger and set off for San Carlos.[145] Dellai managed hotels for Perón, while his son-in-law leased the Hotel Cardena in Bariloche. The choice of name for the hotel was supposed to keep alive the memory of the Val Gardena (Grödner valley in South Tyrol). After his 'emigration', Dellai kept in contact with his old home in South Tyrol; for example, he and his family corresponded for a long time with Paula Wiesinger. In the inter-war years, Wiesinger was a well-known skier who also knew Luis Trenker and Riefenstahl. Along with her husband, Hans Steger, she ran the Hotel Steger-Dellai in Seis near Bolzano until her old age.

In 1961 the state court of Innsbruck once again issued an arrest warrant for Friedrich (Fritz) Lantschner. Lantschner's residence in South America, 'San Carlos de Bariloche, Rio Negro/Argentina', was now known to the court. As he was already an Argentinian citizen according to the state court, an extradition application for him seemed pointless, since Argentina refused to extradite its own citizens.[146] Lantschner's friend Hans Aichinger was also involved in the skiing business in San Carlos. He arrived in Argentina via Italy in 1948.[147] The son of innkeepers from Innsbruck, Aichinger had been a member of the NSDAP and the SS since 1932. Along with Lantschner, he had formed the hard core of the SS in Tyrol. At the end of the war, he chose flight over a trial. He was able to escape shortly before his impending arrest in 1945, moving to Argentina and working in San Carlos as a skiing instructor. In 1959 he gave himself up to the Austrian authorities, but proceedings against him were suspended in 1961.

In Lantschner's wake, Franz Sterzinger also came to Argentina. He was born on 5 December 1903 in Vienna, but grew up in Innsbruck.[148] As SS-Führer and deputy Gauleiter throughout the whole of the Nazi period, Sterzinger was an important personality in the region of Tyrol-Vorarlberg. Within the Speer empire, he played a particular role in the exploitation of water power and the war efforts in northern Italy. After the First World War, Sterzinger joined the right-wing Freikorps 'Bund

Oberland'. From November 1931 he was a member of the NSDAP.[149] In 1933 he joined the SS with the relatively low SS number of 167,540. After the failed Nazi putsch in Austria in 1934, Sterzinger spent several months in prison for 'high treason'.[150] From 1935 until 1937 he was deputy Gauleiter in Tyrol and at the same time ran NSDAP Landkreis Innsbruck. Sterzinger refers clearly to this in his curriculum vitae: 'As SS-Führer and deputy Gauleiter, I was at the front line throughout the whole illegal time [of the Nazis in Austria before the Anschluss].'[151] After the Wehrmacht invaded Austria in March 1938, Sterzinger quickly made a career for himself. He was promoted to Hauptsturmführer in the SS, and the former underdog of his employer Tiroler Wasserwerke (TIWAG) was now catapulted up to the status of director and works manager. In May 1942 Armaments Minister Albert Speer gave him the task of coordinating the 'new order of the German energy economy', particularly the development of hydroelectric power stations in the Alpine region: 'In March 1943 Reichsminister Speer appointed me director of the work group "hydraulic power stations", thus making me head of this branch of the economy for the whole of Germany.'[152] After the occupation of Italy by the Wehrmacht in September 1943, Speer made the Innsbruck engineer his representative for the electricity economy in Italy. In 1943 he also founded the 'Energy Company based in Bolzano' (Energie-Gesellschaft mbH in Bozen), whose boss was Sterzinger. Sterzinger placed trusted South Tyrolean SS comrades in key positions in this company and its electrical sub-companies, creating contacts that were extremely useful during his escape after the end of the war.[153] As an expert in hydroelectric power stations, Sterzinger also became a coveted specialist among the Argentinians. In order to emigrate, though, Sterzinger would have to make use of the Italian escape route to South America.

Sterzinger's situation and path to freedom followed that of many fugitives after the war. Sterzinger was wanted by the Allies as the former Kreisleiter of Innsbruck, deputy Gauleiter of the Tyrol, and SS-Sturmbannführer, and the US military police finally arrested him on 12 May 1945 and took him to a prisoner-of-war camp in Germany. After his escape from Glasenbach camp in 1947, Sterzinger hid with his comrades in South Tyrol and travelled to Argentina via Genoa. He found help and support among Catholic clerics in Italy. SS-Sturmbannführer Sterzinger had left the Catholic Church during the Third Reich and described himself, like many SS men, as '*gottgläubig*'.[154] While escaping through Italy, he reversed that step and almost penitently re-entered the bosom of the Catholic Church. In the documents used in his escape in 1947, he once again described himself as 'Roman Catholic'. In June 1947 Sterzinger applied for a Red Cross travel document in Rome. His details on the form corresponded to the facts, and he probably felt very confident. He gave his profession as engineer, his destination as Vene-zuela. His details were confirmed by the Italian Red Cross and the PCA in Rome.[155] In April 1948 his wife and their four children followed him via Genoa to Buenos Aires. In 1953 the Sterzinger family finally moved to São Paulo, Brazil.[156]

Sterzinger's colleague Gerhard Lausegger, responsible as leader of an SS commando unit for the brutal murder of the head of the Jewish community in Innsbruck,[157] was arrested in Carinthia at the end of the war, but escaped from Allied imprisonment and probably moved to South Tyrol.[158] For his escape he acquired an ICRC identification paper and emigrated to Argentina.[159] His superior officer in the killing opera-tions of Kristallnacht, SS-Oberführer Johann Feil, was also able to escape. The actual commander of the night of pogroms in Innsbruck was born in Upper Austria, a member of the NSDAP from 1932 and, at the end of the war, a senior SS officer. With the help of Bishop Hudal, he was able to flee via South Tyrol to Argentina; he returned to Europe after a few years and died in 1956 in Mittenwald in Bavaria. The Aus-trian authorities often knew of the escape and whereabouts of war crim-inals and Nazi perpetrators: 'It has been known to the court for a long time that those chiefly responsible for the serious outrages of 9 Novem-ber 1938, above all the former SS General [Johann] Feil, escaped responsibility by fleeing to South America.'[160] Nevertheless, the efforts of the legal system were often rather modest. The escape of Nazi war criminals was a way for the legal system to avoid the responsibility of prosecution. In order to evade justice, the war criminals didn't need to escape to South America, just jump across the Brenner.

Fridolin Guth also followed the simple procedure of crossing the Brenner when he fled with Tyrolean comrades seeking emigration to South America. Guth was born in Schönberg in Tyrol in 1908, and took part along with Lantschner and Rubatscher in the failed Nazi putsch attempt in Tyrol in 1934. Like his comrades, he escaped to Munich afterwards and only returned to Austria after the Anschluss in

1938. As an SS-Hauptsturmführer, he is supposed to have been involved in the killing of partisans, from 1944 onwards, as company head of a police regiment in France, although these accusations have never been definitively proven.[161] After the end of the war, Guth hid with comrades, although at the time he was never sought either by German or Austrian authorities. In April 1948, SS-Hauptsturmführer Guth applied for an ICRC travel document in Genoa. Guth presented himself as a stateless German, a technician by profession. He claimed to have been in an Allied prisoner-of-war camp in North Africa from August 1944 until December 1947. In Genoa Guth went into hiding in a convent and waited to leave the country. Guth already had an Argentinian entry permit, and he was booked to travel from Genoa.[162] Guth lived in Argentina from 1948 and maintained close contacts with Colonel Rudel. The Tyrolean was supposedly one of the founders of the Kameradenwerk, the relief organization for Nazi prisoners and their families run by Rudel. Until his death in 1989, 'Don Guth' lived in Agua de Oro, a town near Cordoba in the north of Argentina. He was a valued businessman in the town, and his cake-shop, 'Confiserie Tirol', was well-known for its outstanding Black Forest gateaux.[163] Between 1960 and 1981 Guth repeatedly travelled to Austria and Germany, presenting himself either as an Austrian or German.[164]

In many respects, the fleeing Tyrolean National Socialists were pioneers in escaping to Italy. They smoothed the way for comrades from other Austrian and German regions.

6. The Escape of the Concentration Camp Commandants

Franz Stangl was one of the most prominent camp commandants who fled to South America to find a new home. The first time Simon Wiesenthal came across his name was on a list of awards to senior SS officers. Added to it in pencil were the words 'secret Reich matter—for psychological stress'. Translated from Nazi terminology that means the commandant of Treblinka extermination camp received an award for special merits in the execution of mass murder. Wiesenthal doubts whether this caused Stangl particular mental stress. When Stangl was finally brought in front of a court, he explained to the judge what it was that had really caused him headaches, which Wiesenthal repeats: 'Some days he had been sent as many as 18,000 people at a time for extermination, yet it had been his duty to return all the railway wagons empty. He simply had no choice but to kill the people, there just wasn't the room to accommodate them.'[165] Stangl was later sentenced to life imprisonment for the murder of 900,000 people. How many people really died under his control as extermination camp commandant—first in Sobibór and later in Treblinka—will probably never be known.[166] As German historian Wolfgang Benz explains, Treblinka extermination camp, 'given its short existence and its staff—about twenty-five to thirty-five people [...was] the most efficient murder apparatus that has ever existed'.[167]

Stangl's career began early and culminated in his tenure as an extermination camp commandant. Stangl was born on 26 March 1908 in Altmünster in Austria. From 1931 he worked in the police service and in 1935 moved with his wife to Wels in Upper Austria. Wels was then at the heart of illegal Nazi activities, and as early as 1936 he joined the NSDAP, which was forbidden in Austria at the time. It was after the annexation of Austria in 1938 that his 'career' really got under way.[168] In January 1939 Stangl's department was transferred from Wels to Linz and incorporated within the Gestapo. Stangl was very ambitious and saw his work in the Gestapo as apolitical.[169] At that time he was increasingly involved with the persecution of Jews, particularly after the annexation of the Czechoslovakia. In 1941 Stangl was given a new duty: to work on the 'euthanasia' programme in the Hartheim mental institution near Linz. What happened there was state-decreed murder, first for economic, then for political, reasons and had nothing to do with 'helping people to die'. When the Third Reich deployed all its forces to organize the murder of the Jews, the SS leadership understood that it had ideal experimental laboratories in the euthanasia sanatoriums. In Hartheim and other institutions, methods could be tried out that would later be used on an industrial scale in Treblinka and Auschwitz: the killing of people with poison gas.[170] Then Stangl was transferred to Sobibór and Treblinka. His inner transformation began in the extermination camps. He became slowly deadened and saw the imprisoned humans only as commodities: 'I think it started the day I first saw the Totenlager in Treblinka. I remember [Christian] Wirth standing there, next to the pits full of blue-black corpses. It had nothing to do with humanity, it couldn't have; it was a mass—a mass of rotting flesh. Wirth said, "What shall we do with this garbage?" I think unconsciously that started me thinking of them as cargo.'[171]

In his function as camp commandant Franz Stangl allegedly asked several times to be removed and dismissed from his post:

> I saw no possibility of getting out of the whole thing after my work in Hartheim and Sobibór had made me a bearer of secrets. Now my efforts were devoted to not dealing directly with the killing of people. At the time I made no attempt to get out of that 'machinery', but hoped I had the chance to free myself from it in some other way.[172]

In the end Stangl was dispatched to north-eastern Italy in 1943. There he persecuted Jews and fought partisans, a dangerous task, since his predecessor in Treblinka had been killed by a partisan commando. But Stangl survived. At the end of the war, he was able to fight his way through to Wels in Upper Austria to join his wife. He made no attempt to hide because that would have made him appear suspicious. Instead, as an SS-Hauptsturmführer he came under the 'immediate arrest' directive of the Americans and was sent to the internment camp in Glasenbach near Salzburg. He kept quiet about the fact that he had been commandant of Treblinka, and it never came out during the two years that he spent in Glasenbach. But things suddenly became critical for Stangl in 1947: he was arrested by the Austrian judiciary for his involvement in the murder of disabled people in Hartheim. In May 1948 he was able to escape from remand in Linz. He didn't have much money—just a small amount of his wife's savings. Stangl joined forces with his comrade Hans Steiner. The two men first escaped to Graz on foot. There Stangl found his former subordinate Gustav Wagner.[173] In the notorious Glasenbach prisoner-of-war camp, Stangl had learned that the most important thing was somehow to get to Rome because there was a church agency there that could help him on his way. Catholics would find refuge with Bishop Hudal. 'I escaped from the Linz prison on May 30, 1948. Originally we had intended to ask my wife's former employer, the Duca di Corsini, to help us. But then I heard of a Bishop Hulda [*sic*] at the Vatican in Rome who was helping Catholic SS officers, so that's where we went.'[174] With the help of former comrades, he would cross the border to South Tyrol and ask Catholic agencies there to make contact with Rome. The information he had been given proved to be true.

Like many before and after him, Stangl would follow the route across the mountains to Rome and beyond. At night, Stangl and three comrades crossed the 'green border' over the Brenner to Sterzing in South Tyrol. Then Stangl first went to Merano, where his wife's cousin lived. He tried to find him, but without success. He finally met up again with his comrades in the mountains above Merano, then travelled to stay with acquaintances in Florence. Next his journey took him to Bishop Hudal in Rome who welcomed the concentration camp commandant with open arms. At first Stangl lived in the Anima with Hudal at 20 Via della Pace. The bishop allegedly also found Stangl a job in a library, where Stangl was able to work until he travelled abroad.[175] The question of how Stangl acquired his Red Cross travel document has been resolved. He himself claimed that Hudal had called him in and handed him the document.[176] Hudal procured Stangl a travel document in the name 'Paul Stangl'. They had turned his name around, and Stangl immediately pointed out the 'mistake': 'They made a mistake, this is incorrect. My name is Franz Paul Stangl'; Hudal only patted the SS-man reassuringly on the shoulder and said, 'Let sleeping dogs lie.'[177]

Obviously Hudal kept Stangl safe from every danger. On 25 August 1948 'Paul' Stangl calmly applied for his ICRC travel document in Rome. Many of the details that he gave were truthful. He was born in Altmünster in Austria and had lost his Austrian citizenship 'for political reasons'. He was Catholic and a tailor by trade. Since 1948 he had been in Italy as a refugee, and lived in Rome with Hudal at 20 Via della Pace. As in the case of Wagner, Stangl's details were then confirmed by Hudal. The application explicitly stated that Stangl had identified him-self 'with an Austrian identity document signed by Monsignor Luigi [Alois] Hudal'. Of course in the case of Paul Stangl, the PCA also asked for an ICRC travel document for his passage to Argentina.[178] After a few weeks Stangl had an ICRC travel document and initially used it to set off for Syria.[179] But Syria was only a stopping-off point for Stangl. In the end, he emigrated to Brazil where he found work as a mechanic in the Volkswagen factory in São Paulo.

Settling in Brazil proved to be a terrible blunder. Austria, the Federal Republic of Germany, Poland, and the United States all called for Stangl to be extradited. Brazil had never extradited a Nazi criminal before. But this time the international pressure was enormous, and in 1967 the Brazilian government finally gave in to Germany's calls for extradition. May 1970 saw the start of the long-prepared trial in which Stangl answered as he saw fit: 'I was just doing my duty'. On 22

December 1970 the court delivered its sentence: life imprisonment for the mass murder of at least 400,000 people. Stangl didn't have much of his sentence to serve. He died in June 1971 of a heart attack in Düsseldorf prison.[180] Shortly before his death, Stangl said, 'My conscience is clear about what I did, myself [...] But I was there.'[181]

Stangl's subordinate, Gustav Franz Wagner, on the other hand, was never put on trial. Wagner, the deputy camp commandant of Sobibór, died in 1980 at the age of 69 on his ranch in Itatiaia, about forty miles from São Paulo. Wagner allegedly committed suicide. Wagner, born on 18 July 1911 in Vienna, joined the Austrian NSDAP in 1931. After his arrest for prohibited Nazi agitation, he escaped to Germany. After the Anschluss of Austria, he came back to Linz in 1938, hoping to rise through the ranks of the SS. From May 1940 Wagner 'worked' in the killing institution of Hartheim near Linz in the context of the Nazi 'euthanasia' programme. Because of his experiences there, in March 1942 he was transferred to the construction of Sobibór extermination camp. After the facility was complete, Wagner was appointed deputy commandant of the camp and was responsible for the 'selection' of the prisoners. After an uprising by the inmates in October 1943, Wagner was instructed to close the camp and was finally transferred to Italy.

Wagner and Stangl stuck together as they sought to leave Europe and, perhaps, evade Allied justice. On the same day as Stangl, the afternoon of 25 August 1948, Wagner applied for an ICRC travel document to emigrate to Argentina. Wagner filled in the form truthfully and did not use any fake names for his escape. Wagner gave his original nationality as Austrian, saying that he had lost it 'for political reasons'. As a result, Wagner was now stateless and had a right to an ICRC travel document. Probably out of gratitude to Hudal, Wagner claimed to be Catholic. As his address in Rome, Wagner gave Hudal's address, 20 Via della Pace. Wagner's details were also confirmed by Hudal. The application explicitly noted that Wagner identified himself 'with an Austrian identity document, signed by Monsignor Luigi [Alois] Hudal'. On 17 August 1948, the PCA asked the ICRC to issue a travel document for the stateless Wagner Gustavo.[182] He had often been lucky before: in 1945, after his last deployment in Yugoslavia, he had escaped from US custody. In Austria he had met his old friend and superior in Sobibór, Franz Stangl, and disappeared with him via South Tyrol and Rome to Syria. Two years later, the two men turned up together in

Brazil, where Stangl soon found a job in a Volkswagen factory, while Wagner hired himself out as an assistant to affluent locals. But this quiet life would not last.

Stangl's arrest and extradition had consequences for Wagner, too. As described earlier, in 1967 Franz Stangl was discovered following an investigation by Simon Wiesenthal and extradited by Brazil's most senior judges to the German criminal prosecutors. After Stangl's discovery, life became dangerous for Wagner.[183] But his luck held out. By the 1966 Sobibór trial, even the searchers in West Germany knew who Wagner was—the 'hangman of Sobibór'—and where he was staying, which was near his boss and friend Stangl. But Stangl did not betray him during interrogation. When Stangl died after being sentenced to prison in 1971, Wagner suggested marriage to Stangl's widow, a proposal that she turned down with the remark that Wagner was too vulgar for her, a sadist. The Brazilian supreme court stated in June 1979 that Wagner would not be extradited. The court took the view that the statute of limitations for the offences with which he was charged had expired.[184]

Concentration camp commandants seemed to escape in each other's company. The 'travel group' around Stangl and Wagner, not only escaped to Italy together, but also applied for their ICRC travel documents together. Stangl and Wagner were obviously joined by August Steininger. In 1940/1 the Austrian Steininger was commandant of the 'Weyer workers' education camp and 'gypsy' camp near Linz. As such he repeatedly mistreated prisoners, some of whom died. Early in 1948 he was put on trial in Austria, and in June 1948 the former SA man escaped from custody. Along with concentration camp commandants Stangl and Wagner, Steininger set off for Italy in the summer of 1948,[185] and he applied for an ICRC travel document for his escape to Argentina on the same day as they did. He presented himself as a Sudeten German born in 1913 and, thus, 'stateless'. Steininger stayed with Hudal at 20 Via della Pace at the same time as Stangl. Unsurprisingly, the applications of Stangl, Wagner, and Steininger also show the sequence of numbers 84,227, 84,228, and 84,229. Steininger's details were confirmed by AGIUS and the PCA.[186] Steininger seemingly first fled to Syria and went into hiding. After a few years in Syria and South America, Steininger finally came back to Europe. From January 1952 he lived in West Germany and, through a lawyer, offered to return to

Austria under certain conditions. In April 1952 the main part of his trial took place, and he escaped with only two and a half years' imprisonment.[187]

Also among the Holocaust perpetrators escaping via Italy with a new identity and Red Cross travel papers was Horst Wagner. He was born on 17 May 1906 in Posen, served several months in the Reichswehr in 1933, and in January 1935 married Irmgard Spiess. Joining the SS in 1935 and the NSDAP in 1937, he began his rapid rise through the SS. He was promoted twice in a row in 1939, achieved the rank of Sturmbannführer in 1942, was made Obersturmbannführer in August 1943, and in 1944 finally became SS-Standartenführer.[188] His career as an official in the Foreign Office also reached its zenith in 1943 when he was promoted to 'Vortragender Legationsrat Inland II (Juden)' and was, therefore, in charge of 'Jewish questions' in the Foreign Office. Wagner owed his career to Foreign Minister Joachim von Ribbentrop but was also on good terms with SS chief Heinrich Himmler.[189] His daily work included organizing the deportation of Jews from many European countries, which meant that he worked closely with Adolf Eichmann.[190] Along with the 'Ambassador and Plenipotentiary of the Greater German Reich' in Budapest, SS-Brigadeführer Edmund Veesemayer, in 1944 Wagner was considerably involved in the 'diplomatic' preparation and safeguarding of deportations of Hungarian Jews to Auschwitz.[191]

After the war Wagner remained in Europe for a while before travelling abroad and eventually returning to face prosecution. He appeared as a witness during the Nuremberg Trials, but was released from custody in 1948. A Bavarian court immediately issued an arrest warrant for him, but he settled in the South Tyrolean town of Merano. After a few months in South Tyrol, he went to Rome and acquired new travel papers.[192] In November 1948 Wagner applied for a Red Cross travel document, calling himself 'Peter Ludwig'. 'Ludwig' was born in Königsberg in June 1908, a Protestant of German nationality. His name, place, and date of birth were completely invented. Wagner alias Ludwig presented himself as an agricultural specialist and gave his destination as Argentina. But Wagner seems to have changed his destination, for in November 1949 he received authorization for a visa from Peru, which was noted on his application form. Wagner's false data were confirmed by Monsignor Heinemann of the ecumenical mission for refugees in

Rome. Wagner was able to identify himself with a provisional identity card signed by Heinemann. The mission sisters in the Roman convent at Via Trionfale, where Wagner had found refuge for a long time, and the Italian Red Cross also confirmed his details. What else could the ICRC do but accept the facts as accurate and issue Ludwig/Wagner with an ICRC travel document on 11 November 1948 in Rome? In fact, on the basis of his own details he should not have received the travel document. He gave his current citizenship as 'German', but only stateless people had a right to an ICRC document. It seems that no one asked any further questions and took his supposed origin in Königsberg as evidence that he must be a displaced East German.[193] In 1950 Ludwig/Wagner fled first to Argentina, then lived in Peru, Italy, and Spain.

Wagner was eventually arrested, but like so many Nazis and war criminals, was never held accountable in a court of law for his actions. In 1956 he returned voluntarily to West Germany. In 1958 preliminary investigations of him began, but Wagner's lawyers protracted these. When the main trial finally began in May 1972, it was postponed because of Wagner's inability to follow the hearing, and 'temporarily suspended' in 1974 because of the defendant's poor state of health. In spite of the charge of 'contributing to the murder of 350,000 European Jews', he was never sentenced after his return to and arrest in Germany. He died in March 1977.[194] His colleague and Judenreferent in the Foreign Office, Franz Rademacher, fled to Syria.[195] Karl Klingenfuss, Secretary of the German Embassy in Buenos Aires in 1939/40 and later a colleague of Rademacher in the Judenreferat of the Foreign Office, escaped to Argentina in 1948.[196]

Tried and tested networks also enabled the Holocaust perpetrator Eduard Roschmann to escape to Argentina. Roschmann was born on 25 November 1908 in Graz-Eggenberg, was a liquor salesman before the war, and later worked for a Styrian brewery. Roschmann had joined the NSDAP and the SS while the Nazis were still outlawed in Austria. After the Anschluss of Austria to the Third Reich in 1938, he quickly advanced through the ranks. As a volunteer in the Waffen-SS, he took part in the French campaign. Early in 1941 he was taken on by the Security Police, and in June 1941 he was assigned to Einsatzkommando 2 of Einsatzgruppe A, which chiefly killed people in Latvia. There he worked in the Judenreferat of the commander of Security Police in

Latvia. From March 1943, he was commandant of the Riga Ghetto. In that position he was responsible, amongst other things, for the murder of at least between 2,000 and 2,500 Jews.[197] His 'work' won him the nickname the 'Butcher of Riga'.

At the end of the war, the SS-Untersturmführer was first arrested by the Americans and interned in the Rimini prisoner-of-war camp,[198] but, like many of his comrades, Roschmann was able to escape the camp and Europe. In 1947 after fleeing Rimini, he went into hiding with his family in Graz. His freedom lasted only a short time before he was arrested again, not because of his crimes in Riga, however, but because of his membership in a neo-Nazi organization. Roschmann became aware of the danger of his situation.[199] On the transport to Dachau, Roschmann was able to jump from the train and go into hiding. He hid in a brickworks until he was able to travel to Italy with help from comrades. Here he acquired a new identity as 'Federico Wegner', born in Eger, a displaced ethnic German from Czechoslovakia and, thus, stateless, making him eligible for ICRC travel documents. The profession he gave, 'mechanic', was one that was highly desirable to the Argentinians, and his Catholic denomination helped him a great deal with Hudal and his associates.[200] Tellingly, he gave his address in Rome as the 'Salvatorian Monastery'. Bishop Hudal had already acquired an Argentinian visa for Wegner on 4 August 1948. On the questionnaire of Hudal's Austrian relief organization, Wegner said he wanted to move to stay with his cousin in Buenos Aires. Roschmann applied to the International Red Cross in Rome on 4 August 1948, and that morning he visited Bishop Hudal, who personally gave him the church letter of recommendation to the Red Cross with the stamp of the Austrian sub-committee of the PCA.[201]

With his Red Cross travel document, Roschmann finally emigrated from Genoa to Argentina, where he stayed at the town of Villa de Mayo in the province of Buenos Aires.[202] Roschmann worked in Argentina in a travel agency and later ran a joinery business. In 1955—despite a wife and children in Graz—he married his secretary Irmtraud Schubert. His wife in Austria found out and informed the authorities. So it was that a warrant was issued for the arrest of Roschmann, alias Fritz Weg(e)ner, for bigamy. The German judicial authorities were aware that Roschmann was a resident in Argentina: 'Since October 1948 resident in Buenos Aires Argentina, Address 2717

Echevarria, Buenos Aires'.[203] Then his trail was lost again. A file memo in the Central Office of Justice Administrations in Ludwigsburg in 1972 states: 'Roschmann is reported to be living under the assumed name of Fritz Bernd Wegener, b. 21. 6. 1914 in Eger, in Buenos Aires (Argentina). Investigations into his whereabouts in Argentina have so far remained unsuccessful.'[204]

When the author Frederick Forsyth wrote his semi-fictional novel *The Odessa File*, he took advice from the Nazi-hunter Simon Wiesenthal. Wiesenthal had very personal reasons for wanting to catch Roschmann: he himself had been a concentration camp inmate, and most of his family were murdered. In 1945, after his liberation from the concentration camp, Wiesenthal began to work for the US Army in the search for war criminals in Austria and was at first employed by US intelligence services, then by the US Army's Counter Intelligence Corps. In 1947 he began to establish his Documentation Centre in Linz and later in Vienna.

Roschmann's biography was tailor-made for the main character in *The Odessa File*. Wiesenthal had asked Forsyth to use Roschmann as a character in his book in order to publicize the Roschmann case.[205] The film of the novel had its premiere in 1974 and was shown all around the world. Both the book and film were a great success and still shape popular ideas about the escape of the Nazis. In South America, at any rate, the film created considerable unease amongst Roschmann's former comrades, and Wiesenthal received countless clues about the former Ghetto commandant's whereabouts. Roschmann was probably given an increasingly wide berth by his comrades because, at Wiesenthal's suggestion, in the movie Roschmann was responsible for the cowardly murder of a Wehrmacht officer; his comrades could not know if this depiction was fictional or factual. As a result, they could no longer see Roschmann as an 'honourable' comrade, but only as a 'swinish' one. At any rate, from the moment 'his' film played in South America and 'his' book entered the bookshops, he constantly changed his place of residence and never stayed anywhere for longer than a few weeks. The newspaper reports about the film were also about him. Roschmann became the quarry, just as he had been the quarry in the film. In October 1976 the German embassy presented the Argentinian Foreign Ministry with the extradition request in the Roschmann case. Roschmann was warned and immediately fled to Paraguay.[206] In August 1977 he died of heart failure in Asunción. Because of the amputation of several toes, mentioned in the SS files, he was unambiguously identified after his death.[207] The dead man's fingerprints were also identical to the ones taken from Roschmann in 1947 the first time he was arrested in Graz, thus ensuring that the deceased was, in fact, the Butcher of Riga.[208]

7. A New Start in Argentina

The majority of Europeans who arrived at the port of Buenos Aires did not have an easy start in the 'New World'. The support of the Argentinian government was concentrated on experts from well-defined areas of the economy. Most immigrants began their new life with debts and repaid their passage in instalments. They also had to overcome language problems and cultural differences. Forty years after his arrival in the port, Reinhard Kops remembered the beginning of his new life in Argentina:

> Relief agencies alone get the least done. Anyone who goes out with foreign aid won't get far. Anyone who's unwilling to battle through with his own small means should stay at home. If I look around at the achievements of Germans (and other Europeans) abroad over the past forty years, what they have in common is that none of them begged.[209]

The majority of immigrants after 1945 could build on years of funded training in Europe. The experience of war and dictatorship had also hardened them and distinctly lowered their expectations. New arrivals often climbed the career ladder faster than their long-established colleagues. The words of former sales director of the Operation Bernhard, Friedrich Schwend, who emigrated to South America as early as 1946 and became a fairly successful businessman, speak for the experience of many; in 1959 he wrote to his brother-in-law in Genoa:

> Life here is much easier. A shame you didn't make tracks over here immediately after the end of the war. All the doctors that came from Europe have done very well for themselves after struggling for about two years. I'm thinking amongst other people about our doctor, a German. He hadn't a scrap to eat. Today he's building a luxury villa, his children are studying, and so forth.[210]

Hard work and tenacity allowed some emigrants to achieve moderate success in their careers.

Many people were also able to use in the skills they had acquired in Germany in Argentina. Small enterprises were founded with little capital, scraped together in the first years of working in Argentina. Sometimes a garage had to make do as a first office or production site. The number of successful people who had been able to accumulate a modest level of prosperity, however, was far larger than the number of those who failed. The major German companies, such as Siemens, which had established a significant presence in Argentina before the war, re-established its branches there after 1945.[211] West German companies and their branch offices in South America generally preferred the attitude of the new German and Austrian immigrants over that of locals, and some of the immigrants reached important positions. Practically the whole top level of Mercedes Benz in Argentina consisted of immigrants from Germany and Austria.

After a brief transition phase, immigrated businessmen were able to connect with German companies who had developed a strong presence in South America during the pre-war years. Simon Wiesenthal observed bitterly that Siemens, Krupp, and Volkswagen in Argentina had been 'a hotbed of Nazis'.[212] The boards of companies such as Bayer, Höchst, and Badische Anilin- und Soda-Fabrik (BASF) sometimes worked with old comrades in Europe and overseas. But one should not assume that these were always ideological networks—although these did exist. Practical reasons were more crucial: the new immigrants spoke perfect German and, after a few years, good Spanish; they were technically up to date; they often had good training; and they were industrious, flexible, and highly motivated, as Holger Meding stresses.[213] For some German and Italian escape agents, once their smuggling careers ended, emigration to the Río de la Plata was a natural choice, for they had the knowledge and the contacts needed to do so. The comrades who were now safely located in Argentina could show their gratitude for the escape assistance and hospitality they had received in Italy.

Scientists with SS connections had numerous networks and circles of friends, which made it easier for them to make a fresh start. Over time a reliable network of companies and professional opportunities developed, particularly in Argentina. Because President Perón was very interested in specialists from the former Third Reich, between 1945 and 1950 alone, sixty German scientists emigrated to Argentina where they worked in their professions. This exchange continued the tradition of German researchers coming to work in Argentina. 'Nevertheless, the post-war migration was not an exchange of scientists in the usual sense, as with guest professorships, because a large number of scientists planned to stay in Argentina on a more than temporary basis', probably a longer period, or possibly forever, as Gabriele Ley stresses.[214]

In order to create the sense of community that makes life in a new place easier, the immigrants founded various business and social organizations. The company for German-speaking immigrants to Argentina, CAPRI,[215] is a particularly prominent example of a hidden organization for Nazi fugitives in South America. CAPRI was set up by the businessman Horst Carlos Fuldner, and was nominally part of the large state water and energy company Agua y Energia Electrica, which was founded in 1947 and soon grew very large. The German Club in Buenos Aires, whose members had a great interest in the CAPRI businesses, later wrote cryptically: 'The achievements of CAPRI, even if they only remained starting points, are symptomatic of many more or less anonymous important German contributions to development.'[216]

South American organizations to which the former Reich Germans and others belonged soon became an area of interest for the United States. Its intelligence network was informed about Fuldner and his background as well as CAPRI. A 1953 CIA report reads:

> An Argentine-born SS leader named Fultner (aka Fuldner or Fuster), was reported to be Col. Gonzalez' liaison with the Argentine Office of Immigration. In 1948, Fultner was made a member of the Argentine Immigration Delegation for Europe, and was stationed in Genoa. From this key position he was able to help many Wehrmacht, Gestapo, and Waffen-SS veterans to enter Argentina. With funds allegedly provided by Ludwig Freude, as well as the Argentine Government, he made a trip to Spain for the same purpose. He now is business manager for a group of industrial designers composed largely of former Wehrmacht and Nazi technicians, who have organized in Argentina the Compañía Argentina para Proyectos y Realizaciones Industriales (CAPRI) […].[217]

Not only was the United States interested in Fuldner and CAPRI, but in all areas of commercial, political, and social organizations that might serve as contact points for Nazis and war criminals. As a result, the CIA was well aware of the German business networks in Argentina:

The German commercial and political penetration in Argentina went so deep that it was disturbed only slightly by Germany's military defeat. Neither domestic nor foreign anti-Axis forces were able to induce the Argentine Government to take effective action against the principal German business houses which had provided funds and cover for Nazi operations. The men who headed these firms continued to exert great influence on high-ranking officials in the Argentine Government and armed forces. The main German businesses suffered no major interference and the repatriation or extradition of a large number of the Nazi leaders on Allied 'wanted' lists was prevented.[218]

These German–Argentinian connections did, in fact, become increasingly close. Over the years, with the help of his friend August Siebrecht—another friend of Perón's who rose to become 'coordinator of hidden immigration'—Fuldner found positions for senior and junior National Socialist fugitives through CAPRI. There were around three hundred people on the CAPRI payroll. These included the internationally famous hydrologist Armin Schoklitsch, director of the Polytechnikum and rector of the University in Graz. In CAPRI the former SS officer was Eichmann's immediate superior. Schoklitsch finally found a new home at the University of Tucumán, where he enjoyed a fine reputation until his death, at which time he was an emeritus professor.

Schoklitsch applied for an ICRC travel document in Innsbruck on 8 January 1949, using his real name. But the Austrian gave a Hungarian place of birth and described himself as an 'ethnic German'. He didn't want to tell lies about his profession, which he gave as university professor and engineer. He named his destination as Argentina. As confirmation of his identity, the former SS-Untersturmführer presented an identity card from the city of Graz. In mid-January, the ICRC travel document was posted to Schoklitsch at Beethovenstrasse in Graz.[219] The police in Graz confirmed both Armin Schoklitsch's Hungarian origin and his birthplace of Farkasfalva and 'that the present details are correct and that from the police point of view there are no concerns about the issuing of a special exit permit to Argentina and re-entry to Austria'.[220] The town of Farkasfalva is now called Wolfau, in the southern Burgenland in Austria, but before 1921—at the time of Schoklitsch's birth—it still belonged to Hungary. So Schoklitsch skilfully used his origins in the formerly Hungarian border town of Farkasfalva to present himself as a stateless ethnic German. In 1948 the Argentinian immigration authorities in Buenos Aires finally sent 'Armin Schoklitsch, austriaco, catolico, de 50 años de edad' an immigration permit for Argentina.[221]

A similar case was that of the engineer Walter Haasler from Vienna. In the wake of Schoklitsch, the professor travelled to Innsbruck in 1949 and approached the ICRC for a travel document. In his application, Haasler said that he was from Lithuania and that he had been driven out as a German in 1944. He claimed to have come to Austria in May 1945. Haasler described himself as stateless and asked for the chance to emigrate to Egypt or Venezuela. Haasler's details were, of course, not always truthful.[222] He had, for example, simply invented an origin in Lithuania for himself. Originally from Vienna, he was a documented expert in hydraulic engineering and repeatedly planned large damming projects for power and irrigation. Before the Second World War he had been in Shanghai as a professor at the German Technical University there; in 1939 he moved to the protectorate of Bohemia and Moravia where he worked as dean at the Technical University in Brünn.

At the end of the war, Haasler went first to Salzburg and there organized, via contacts with colleagues in the field, the necessary documents for emigration. But he did not mention any of these facts to the Red Cross. Under the heading 'personal description', Haasler made an embarrassing blunder. In the field 'particular characteristics', he at first wrote 'none'. But the official at the ICRC in Innsbruck corrected this entry and noted: 'duelling scar on the left cheek'. Haasler's political and educational background was written on his face. The engineer had been in a right-wing duelling fraternity as a student, but was not a convinced National Socialist. According to his son, Haasler was never a member of the NSDAP and kept his head down during the Nazi period. One reason for Haasler's pursuit of invisibility was probably his membership in the Freemasons whose members were persecuted during the Third Reich. Nevertheless he kept his reservations private and allowed himself to be recruited for total war deployment.[223] This was all deliberately ignored by the Austrian authorities when the police in Vienna issued him with a 'Führungszeichnis' (Certificate of Good Conduct) in May 1949 which read: 'This Führungszeichnis provides no information about membership of the NSDAP or any of its branches. The information is, as the police record has been destroyed, based on incomplete information.' In other words: the police confirmed that nothing 'unfavourable is recorded against him [Haasler]' because the relevant documents no longer existed.[224] Thus Haasler's path to South America was clear and without obstacles.

Given his 'clean' record and impressive resume, Haasler lined up a teaching position for himself after the war and continued his engineering career abroad. The dean of the Faculty of Mathematics and Physics in Mérida, Venezuela, offered Haasler a job as lecturer in June 1949. The job was well paid and a second-class passage was financed by the University. The visa had been authorized by the Venezuelan consulate. Venezuela probably had a great deal of interest in Haasler's research.[225] In July 1949 the Egyptian General Consulate in Vienna confirmed that it was issuing an entry visa for Herr Universitätsprofessor Haasler 'as soon as a passport is presented'.[226] Thus in August 1949 Haasler was able to emigrate from Genoa to Egypt first, where he worked as one of the leaders on a major damming project. His wife and two small children followed him to Alexandria. In Egypt, eighty German and Czech experts were working for the Egyptian Ministry of War. The country wanted to arm itself against Israel with the help of German experts. The leader of these experts was Wilhelm von Voss, a former adjutant of Hitler's.[227] In 1951 the Haasler family moved to Paraguay, where the coveted expert again worked on large hydraulic engineering projects. Haasler returned to Europe in 1965, where he continued his career. He died in Vienna in 1976 at the age of 90.[228]

The route from Genoa to Argentina was also taken by Nazi Minister and General Commissar for Finance and Economy in the occupied Netherlands, Hans Fischböck.[229] Fischböck was born in Geras in Styria on 24 January 1895. He perhaps relied on the circle of Styrian comrades based around Dadieu and Schoklitsch to help him emigrate. Hudal had a soft spot for his Styrian compatriots, after all. Entering Argentina, Fischböck identified himself with a Red Cross travel document, number 100,980, issued on 9 January 1951 in Genoa, and a visa of the Argentinian Consulate in Genoa dated 2 February 1951. The documents were issued in the false name of 'Jakob Schramm', born on 24 May 1903 in Hof in Bavaria. On the application he gave his original nationality as German, and his current one as 'stateless'. During his residence in Italy, he lived in Genoa and was a technician by profession. Fischböck gave evidence of his identity in the form of an identity card from the city of Salzburg issued in May 1947. The details in the application were confirmed by the signature of Monsignor Krunoslav Draganović.[230] Years later Schramm himself informed the Austrian embassy that Fischböck and Schramm were one and the same person. As evidence for these statements, a confidant of the man in question presented a birth certificate and a solemn declaration. Thus Jakob Schramm once more became 'Hans Christian Fischböck, born on 24 January 1895 in Geras, Austria'.[231] In the 1960s Fischböck returned to Europe as an Argentinian citizen and lived in Germany. That no country undertook proceedings against Fischböck is interesting given his wartime service.

Upon emigrating to Argentina, Fischböck relied upon the social and business network of former Nazis to help to build his new life. One of Fischböck's employers in Argentina was SS officer Nicolussi-Leck, a close business partner of Fuldner's with whom he shared an office on the sixth floor of 375 Avenue Cordoba in Buenos Aires. Nicolussi-Leck and Fuldner's firms in Buenos Aires became employers of some Nazis with tainted pasts, including Hans Fischböck. Nicolussi-Leck also lectured on thermodynamics at Buenos Aires University and applied his knowledge practically. He founded the company Aspersión, Nicolussi & Cia, a very successful firm at the time;[232] when it was sold to Mannesmann a few years later, he was able to buy property near Bolzano with the profits.[233] Through his acquaintance with Ferdinand Porsche, Nicolussi-Leck was also given a job as salesman of agricultural machinery.[234]

Not only did the former SS in Argentina help one another professionally, but in South Tyrol, other groups of former Nazis set up thriving businesses, sometimes working in conjunction with their friends in South America. Once again, Perón's escape assistants in Italy played a key role in this. Connections from Germany, Italy, Spain, and Argentina often came together in companies and SS circles in South Tyrol. Thus the borderland developed from an escape hub into a business hub. In South Tyrol, for example, large quantities of agricultural machinery were imported from Germany and sold on the Italian market. Aedes-Landmaschinen in Bolzano and the firm Mengele & Steiner, operating a branch office in Auer and Merano, were involved in such transactions. There were also ideological networks within the South Tyrolean farming community, which was in large part organized into the Chief Agricultural

Association (Landwirtschaflicher Hauptverband).[235] Some networks of old comrades and their new careers in the agriculture industry were an open secret. Based on information of prominent local anti-Nazis, the British consulate in Bolzano reported to the embassy in Rome in May 1949: 'The headquarters of the Nazi movement in S. Tyrol is the ex-hotel Sti[e]gl at Bolzano, now occupied by the "Hauptverband Landwirtschaftlicher Genossenschaften" (Consorzio delle Co-operative Agricole), a very powerful body, the prominent Nazis inside this body are [...] Nicolussi, [...]'[236]

Former comrades in South Tyrol found more than a new professional home in the 'Agria' company, which serves as an example of the regional and international trade that provided a livelihood and professional community for the former SS men.[237] Agria Mediterranea, based in Bolzano, was founded in 1957 and, like the company Mengele & Steiner in Auer, distributed agricultural machinery as a subsidiary of the Agria Werke engineering works in Möckmühl in Germany.[238] After the war the legal representative and business manager of Agria was Michael Tutzer, from 1935 one of the most important organizers of the Nazi movement and a close comrade of Nicolussi-Leck.[239] SS-Sturmmann Tutzer frequented, amongst other things, courses on Nazi ideology at the NS-Ordensburg in Sonthofen, was decorated with the Alte-Kämpferwinkel, and in 1943 wrote proudly of his career: 'I am an SS-Führerbewerber'.[240] When Nicolussi-Leck and other comrades in Argentina were able to win numerous contracts from Perón, new companies were quickly established. Thanks to his good contacts with Mannesmann in Germany, Nicolussi-Leck was able to start some subsidiary companies in Italy. In 1950, in addition to Agria, Nicolussi-Leck and Tutzer founded the successful Generalpioggia sprinkler company and also the Agrotecnica Bolzano GmbH in Bolzano. The purpose of the Agrotecnica Bolzano GmbH was the 'manufacture, assembly and sale of agricultural and animal husbandry machines, and so forth'. The sole administrator was Bernd Ausserer; Nicolussi-Leck and Tutzer were special agents for the company. The networks based around shared worldviews, friendships, and business interests went on functioning until the 1980s.[241]

SS-Untersturmführer Paul Hafner could also rely on his comrade Nicolussi-Leck's business contacts. Hafner was born in 1923 in Mals in South Tyrol, joined the SS in 1941, and served from 1942 in the

Waffen-SS Division 'Nord' on the Finnish–Soviet border. Wounded several times there and highly decorated, he became in June 1944 a trainer at the SS-Junker School in Bad Tölz, where he also helped to set up the SS Grenadier Division 'Nibelungen', the last SS squad.[242] After some months as a prisoner of war in Bavaria, he escaped to Innsbruck, where he graduated in business studies in 1949. Nicolussi-Leck then found him a job with Generalpioggia in Bolzano. In 1954 he went to Spain, where he worked for Mannesmann and later set up a pig-breeding firm (Hafner wrote, 'For Spain a great success. Today there are at least 2 million Spanish pigs with German blood in their veins!'[243]). His job with Mannesmann was also owed to Nicolussi-Leck and Tutzer. After the Second World War the Spanish dictator Francisco Franco provided refuge for many former Nazis, and large numbers of National Socialists also fled overseas via Spain. To ease the pain of nostalgia among his SS comrades in Spain, Hafner opened the Cortijo Tiroles inn —('Tiroler Hof', or 'Tyrolean Courtyard')—which seated 500. It was not until 2007 that Pablo Hafner became widely known when the documentary film *Hafner's Paradise* by the Austrian director Günther Schwaiger caused a furore.[244] The former 'SS-Führer' Hafner, who lived unmolested in Madrid until his death in 2010, denied the Holocaust: 'Hitler was not the gasser of the Jews, but the promoter of efforts to establish the Jewish national state (Zionism!). [...] Not a single Jew was killed because he was a Jew! For me Hitler is the saviour of Europe and Christianity!'[245]

While Hafner stayed abroad for the long term, many refugees soon returned to their old homeland. In the late 1950s Nicolussi-Leck came back to Europe, as did 'Guzzi' Lantschner and Franz Rubatscher. Rubatscher died in Tyrol in old age, and Nicolussi-Leck died in the summer of 2008 as a respected art collector in Bolzano. In an obituary in the well-known South Tyrolean cultural magazine *Der Schlern*, not a word was devoted to his role in National Socialism, the SS, and escape assistance.[246] His Tyrolean countryman Lantschner still lives the life of an active pensioner in Germany. He does not like talking about Argentina, 'things were hard here so we went over there', is his brief commentary.[247] But many fleeing former SS men and Nazis remained in South America forever.

One immigrant who stayed in Argentina for the rest of his life was the South Tyrolean Karl Tribus. Years ago he died in Buenos Aires.

Tribus was born on 7 April 1914 in Lana an der Etsch near Merano and was a German citizen. In September 1943 he was involved in the arrest of the Jews of Merano.[248] From autumn 1943 Tribus tortured partisans and deserters at SS headquarters in Belluno. He is still remembered in Belluno as a 'cruel Nazi' who particularly distinguished himself in combat against the partisans. After the end of the war, the former SS-Oberscharführer escaped with the help of a Bolzano Franciscan priest on the tried and tested route to Argentina. At first, however, Tribus went into hiding in the South Tyrolean mountains, grew a long beard, and assumed a new identity. Before 1945 the mountains offered South Tyrolean deserters protection from the Nazis; after the war many wanted SS officers, Nazi collaborators, and war criminals from all over Europe used them as an ideal hiding place. In 1947 Tribus fled with his new identity via Genoa to Argentina, where he worked in a paper factory.

Although Tribus was safe in Argentina, he was not happy there. According to his letters to his sister in South Tyrol, he was anything but contented in South America. He was eaten up with homesickness, and meetings with South Tyrolean comrades did little to ease that.[249] But coming back was out of the question—he had too much blood on his hands from his career as an SS man in Belluno. In Buenos Aires he married Anita Wagner from Graz, who shared his life on the run. In 1957 she even sent a telegram to the village of Lana—his place of birth—announcing the supposed death of her husband Karl.[250] After the end of the Cold War, however, the judiciary reopened his case. In 1996 the Italian military public prosecutor's office in Verona began preliminary inquiries into Tribus for suspicion of war crimes in the area of Belluno in northern Italy. It asked the German judiciary for legal help regarding the precise personal details and current whereabouts of Tribus.[251] The Tribus case thus remained pending at the public prosecutor's office in Ludwigsburg until 2004.

One other prominent Nazi fugitive was SS-Obersturmbannführer Dr Kurt Christmann, but unlike Hafner, he returned to Europe after emigrating to Argentina. Even as a young man, he had been involved in the failed Hitler Putsch in Munich in 1923. As a Gestapo official, he was deployed after the Anschluss of Austria in Vienna, Innsbruck, Salzburg, and Klagenfurt. From the summer of 1942 until the summer of 1943, Christmann was head of Einsatzkommando 10a.[252] The official task of the unit, based in Krasnodar in southern Russia, was to 'combat partisans'. The SS took this as licence to murder everyone who, in their eyes, represented a threat, all those who were considered 'Slavic Unter-menschen' or Jews. Christmann himself murdered at least 105 people, each 'as an accessory'.[253] While serving in Krasnodar, he once had between forty and sixty predominantly Jewish men, women, and children killed in a gas truck. The victims were horribly suffocated by the exhaust fumes of the truck within ten to fifteen minutes. Christmann claimed only to have been present at the gassings by chance. He added: 'I think that if several people die together, it's still more pleasant than each one individually'. For Christmann, at any rate, it was 'not such a world-shattering event that I could remember it all that precisely'.[254]

After the end of the war, Christmann went on living in Stuttgart-Feuerbach, supposedly under a false name. In 1946 he was arrested by the Americans as a wanted Nazi perpetrator and interned in Dachau. He managed to escape from there after a short time and worked for the British occupation forces in Germany under his alias 'Dr Ronda'. In Rome he acquired new papers and travelled, probably on a Red Cross document, to Argentina. Under questioning, Christmann gave only a brief account of his escape: 'Via Munich I went to Italy, where thanks to the Vatican I got papers and an entry permit for Argentina for my wife and myself.'[255] From the autumn of 1948 until February 1956 he lived in South America.[256] Christmann was also political in his new homeland. He maintained close contact with the fighter pilot Hans-Ulrich Rudel, and the CIA identified him as one of the masterminds behind the Kameradenwerk neo-Nazi movement.[257] After his return to Germany in 1956, he lived as an estate agent in Munich. His denazification trial was suspended as only insufficient charges could be brought against him. An initial indictment in 1971 was immediately abandoned for lack of evidence.[258] Christmann was put on trial again only in 1980 and sentenced to ten years' imprisonment.[259]

On the whole, the SS perpetrators' collaboration worked in assisting one another to emigrate and to start new lives in Argentina. On 23 October 1948 the steamer *San Giorgio* left the port of Genoa with Erich Priebke and his family on board. On 18 July 1948 Josef Mengele travelled to Argentina. On 14 July 1950 Adolf Eichmann alias 'Richard Klement' from Tramin landed in Buenos Aires, the portal to a new life. Hans-Ulrich Rudel travelled with his closest comrades in the Luftwaffe to the New World. It would be entirely false to say that these men formed a branch of the fantasy 'ODESSA' on the Río de la Plata. But contact between the 'old comrades' was maintained even in South America, which continued to feed rumours of a 'secret organization'.

In May 1948 Franz Rufinatscha also arrived in Argentina and embarked upon a comfortable post-war existence. He decided to take advantage of his contacts and opened a travel agency in Buenos Aires that was soon very popular in German–Argentinian circles. Business was good, and Rufinatscha found his friends jobs: the Tyrolean SS-Standartenfürher Erwin Fleiss, for example, found a lucrative post as director of a travel agency in Rio Negro.[260] In Argentina Rufinatscha married Elina Margarita Albertina Hahn, a woman of German descent. They were wed in church on 29 September 1950 in Buenos Aires, the bride's home town.[261]

Even if the SS community demonstrably maintained their connections and shielded and protected one another, there was never a rigidly organized conspiratorial network. As long as Perón held his protecting hand over the Nazi criminals, such a thing wasn't necessary. In July 1949 the President even passed a general amnesty for foreigners who had entered Argentina illegally. Questions about the past were hardly asked. A certain 'Otto Pape' went to the immigration office and claimed to have found refuge in the German Embassy in Rome until the end of the war. In this way, Otto Pape once more became Erich Priebke—quite legally. He settled in one of the many German emigrant communities that had mutated into a stronghold of fleeing National Socialists; like many of his former comrades, Priebke, too, chose San Carlos de Bariloche, an idyllic ski resort in the Andes, where the former Nazi Reinhard Kops had already settled.

San Carlos de Bariloche proved to be a comfortable town with its familiar architecture, activities, and cultural ties. In Bariloche there were houses in the Tyrolean style; in the 1930s Austrian ski instructors had developed the area for winter sports, the Residencial Tirol and Edelweiss hotels and the pension Kaltschmidt were inviting places to stay, and the ski lifts were built by the Austrian Doppelmayr firm. The number of German-speaking settlers was large even before 1945, and connections with the old homeland abounded.[262] Thus the Innsbruck expert in Tyrolean folklore, Karl Ilg, was not surprised to note in 1976: 'The German-speaking inhabitants, whose immigration has still not come to an end—around and after the Second World War it was, as I have said, particularly strong!—[are members of associations].'[263] Here Priebke led a peaceful existence, opened his delicatessen, and even became the chairman of the German–Argentinian cultural association.[264] He travelled often around the world and regularly renewed his passport at the German Embassy in Buenos Aires.

Priebke's life continued uneventfully in Bariloche until 1994 when he spoke to an American television crew, which was actually searching for Reinhard Kops, and openly described his participation in a massacre near Rome and his own shooting of two Italians. The former SS-Sturmbannführer Priebke had been involved in a spectacular act of violence—the shooting of 335 hostages in the Ardeatine Caves near Rome on 24 March 1944. Officially this was an act of retaliation for a bombing attack by Italian partisans which cost thirty-three South Tyrolean police soldiers their lives.[265] This act of revenge in the Ardeatine Caves is seen to this day by most Italians as the worst symbol of Nazi barbarism in their country. The interview with Priebke caused a national outrage. An Italian call for extradition followed shortly after, and this was granted in November 1995. On 1 August 1996 a Roman military court declared in its verdict that Priebke could no longer be prosecuted for his crimes as they lay outside the statute of limitations. At the higher court, Priebke was sentenced to a limited period of imprisonment. But this sentence, too, came to nothing. In 1998 Erich Priebke and his fellow defendant Karl Hass were each sentenced to 'lifelong imprisonment'. As of this writing, Priebke lives under house arrest in Rome.[266]

In a part of the world in which prominent Nazis and some of the worst murderers of Jews from the Third Reich found a new home, many Germans thought the murder of millions was a malicious Allied—or Jewish—invention. This explains why so many escaped Nazi criminals found support among their compatriots. Simon Wiesenthal called Argentina the 'Cape of Last Hope', and in a way, it was: many Nazis saw it as their last refuge, and many long-established German settlers preserved their flattering image of the Third Reich.[267]

Conclusion

Simon Wiesenthal's demand of justice for the victims and judgment for the perpetrators faded away for the most part during the Cold War. It was no coincidence that Wiesenthal had the persona of the lone voice in the wilderness, the outsider, the moral authority that often became a source of discomfort to society and the leading elites, not only in his homeland of Austria, but in many countries around the world. His attitude didn't fit the zeitgeist of the Cold War. Today his position is enjoying a renaissance, even if—with the war generation fading away—it leads to the discovery and sentencing of wanted Nazi perpetrators less often than it once did. The 'Vienna Wiesenthal Institute of Holocaust Studies' has been in development for some years. Even twenty years ago this appreciation of the man who tirelessly reminded his country of the criminal role of certain Austrians during the war would have been difficult to imagine from a political point of view. In Austria the debate around President Kurt Waldheim's war record in 1986 finally shattered the myth of victimhood once and for all. Over the past few years, the Nazi past has provided fewer headlines than Austria's consistent record in its treatment of the Holocaust—as, for example, when the controversial British historian David Irving was sentenced to three years' imprisonment by an Austrian court in 2006 for trivializing the Holocaust, a violation of the law prohibiting National Socialist activities (Verbotsgesetz).

This example shows very clearly the transformation that has occurred in Western democracies' recent past, starting from the unprecedented prosecutions of the Nuremberg Trials, to silence about the Shoah, to today's naming of historical injustices and the 'mastering of an unmasterable past'.[1] As the Anglo-American historian Tony Judt has shown, members of Western democracies now approach the World War and the Shoah through examination and research.[2] But in the years of reconstruction immediately after the war, things were quite different. The years of the post-war economic miracle (*Wirtschaftswunder*) were a time both of double standards and of silence. The examination of the most recent past—and the Holocaust in particular—was still largely ignored. Thus the subject of Nazi flight reveals the difficulty of responding to the past. While this book has described the chief players and the mechanisms and conditions that enabled the flight in detail, the treatment of the subject since 1945 is of central importance and raises several questions: Why did it take so long for Nazi flight to come under scrutiny? What is the significance of this problematic area today? How different is the situation in individual countries that were particularly involved in the flight of Nazis? What is the reaction of the institutions involved in it, particularly the Red Cross and the Vatican? Finally, how are countries and individuals to respond to historical injustice?

Auschwitz casts a long shadow, and the ghosts of the past catch up with us time and again. Thus Aribert Heim's photo was seen everywhere in the media in the summer of 2008 when the media reported that Efraim Zuroff of the Simon Wiesenthal Centre would search for him in Chile. Heim, a concentration camp doctor in Mauthausen, had been tirelessly sought by Wiesenthal, unsuccessfully in the end. The Austrian Nazi perpetrator Heim had gone into hiding in 1962 and a warrant was still out for his arrest; for years he was suspected of being in South America. According to the latest newspaper reports, however, 'Dr Death' was supposed to have died in his hideaway in Egypt, yet in 2009 documentarians visiting Egypt could find no trace of his body or grave. Similarly, the case of the alleged Sobibór guard Ivan 'John' Demjanjuk is also keeping the courts and the international media busy. Demjanjuk emigrated to the US in 1951 and lived there undisturbed until the 1980s when first Israel, then Germany, prosecuted him. These more recent stories illustrate again the fact that Nazi perpetrators as well as tens of thousands of collaborators managed to flee when Europe lay in ruins.

The days and weeks immediately after the end of the war were of crucial importance for the Nazi leaders and perpetrators. Shortly before or after the arrival of the Allies, some of them committed suicide. These included not only the internationally notorious representatives of the Nazi dictatorship, such as Adolf Hitler, Joseph Goebbels, and Heinrich Himmler, but also many senior and middle-ranking executives of the Nazi regime, as well as some Gauleiters. In the period immediately after the war, especially high-ranking and prominent Nazi perpetrators were subject to penalties. The first trial against the main war criminals in Nuremberg in 1945–6 was sympathetically received by wide circles of the German and Austrian public, but that soon changed. Another group of SS perpetrators and National Socialists, not the largest by a long way, but a considerable contingent, fled in the years immediately after the war and emigrated overseas as a way of escaping justice.

For many, the escape routes through Italy were the path to the future, despite the hardships involved and the risk of Allied capture; over time, the Allies' use of these routes for their own purposes and their shifting focus to the Cold War lessened the risks, however. Around 1947, US officials such as Vincent La Vista described the escape agents and the institutions involved in great detail. But the relevant 'top secret' report ended up in the classified sections of the archives, and the underground channels were not suppressed, allowing Nazis, fellow perpetrators, and Jews illegally travelling to Palestine to use the 'ratlines' in their bid for a new life. Michael Phayer sums up the findings and effects of the report succinctly:

> 'Not until July 1947 did the U.S. State Department's Vincent La Vista produce his very important investigation of illegal emigration from Rome, by which time the United States had already made an executive decision to allow anticommunist black fascists to walk away from their World War II crimes. La Vista's report, a boon for historians, had no effect on history.[3]

There were good reasons for that. In the US State Department, La Vista's employer, the actual enemy was increasingly being identified as the Soviet Union. In 1947 the influential American diplomat George Kennan created the motto of 'containment'. He demanded harsher policies against the Soviet Union, which was to be put under constant pressure so as to hasten its inevitable collapse. Against this background, denazification went into abeyance a few years after the end of the war and so did the search for Nazi perpetrators. Shutting down the ratlines, which were also used by the Americans in their drafting of technical experts and Cold War operatives, would have seemed counterproductive to US intelligence services.

As the years passed, conditions made it possible for fugitives to escape Europe—and sometimes to return. As a result of the Allies turning a blind eye to the escape routes, perpetrators such as Adolf Eichmann and Josef Mengele, as well as the great majority of fugitives, were able to get away without great difficulty between 1947 and 1950. Not only did the Allies no longer have any great interest in prosecuting the perpetrators or destroying the escape routes precisely mapped out by La Vista, but the countries of continental Europe quickly realized that establishing an administration and a new start for the state could not be accomplished entirely without the old elites. Soon generous amnesty laws were passed—in Italy as early as 1946 and in Austria in 1948. The West German Amnesty Law of 1949 for fellow-travellers and minor criminals and the social reintegration of 30,000 officials and former professional soldiers in 1951 exonerated the majority of Germans. From the mid-1950s hardly anyone had to fear prosecution by the state and the judiciary over his past. What followed was a quickly spreading amnesia. In the 1950s denazification and judicial reappraisal of the events of the war had been not only suspended, but largely forgotten or repressed.[4]

The Cold War made it particularly difficult to reappraise the very recent past. The chapter on the Nazi past had supposedly been concluded in the mid-1950s. Even when trials against Nazi perpetrators were held, the sentences were very lenient.[5] In particular, the outbreak of the Korean War in 1950 marks a caesura, as the Cold War immediately escalated into an open conflict there. From 1950 onwards very few war criminals fled Europe; on the contrary, many returned from abroad. For those responsible for the genocide of the Jews, however, a return to Europe was too risky, even after amnesty laws were enacted. The connection between the escape movement and the outbreak of the Cold War is obvious. As the Allied prosecutions abated and the conflict between West and East heated up in 1947–8, emigration reached its peak. But even a few years later, when the conflict in Korea broke out openly and the Cold War turned hot, the movements of emigration and escape came to a standstill in 1950–1.

The Nazi past and the Shoah were repeatedly addressed from the 1960s onwards, but the Cold War also covered over many old crimes from the Second World War. This no longer holds true for Europe after 1989, in part because of a new generation born after the war that began to question its secrets. Tellingly, the first National Holocaust Memorial Museum outside Israel was not set up until 1992, and it was outside

Europe in Washington, DC. Similar memorials have been set up in Europe only over the last few years. Since 2005 there has also been a Holocaust Memorial (Memorial to the Murdered Jews of Europe) in the heart of Berlin. Yet these memorials point more to a tentative step at honouring, rather than re-examining, the past.

The acknowledgement of the Holocaust of the Jews was not only repressed in places where there were good reasons for feeling responsible (as in Austria or Germany), but also in Poland, France, and Italy. Even in Great Britain, the genocide of the Jews was barely mentioned, though that nation has always been proud of its uncompromising role in the struggle against the Third Reich. Tony Judt stresses this global phenomenon: 'In retrospect it is the universal character of the neglect that is most striking.'[6] The Holocaust was only one event among many that people simply wanted to forget but could, in the end, only repress. In the words of Hans-Magnus Enzensberger: 'In the affluent years after the War [...] the Europeans sought refuge in a collective amnesia'.[7] Everyone wanted to be a victim, even the Germans. They felt like the victims of a small clique of criminals around Hitler. They also felt like victims of the Allied 'bombing terror', the expulsions, the mass rapes by Soviet soldiers, and finally 'Hitler's war'. The Federal Republic under Konrad Adenauer acknowledged publicly that terrible crimes had been committed against Jews 'in the name of the German people', but for the most part the criminals were not given faces; they remained anonymous and abstract. The most recent past served in East and West as a quarry, so to speak, for selective historical images. In the German Democratic Republic, much more attention was devoted to the anti-fascist resistance fighters than to the perpetrators, who were in any case located for the most part in 'capitalist' West Germany.[8]

But Nazis on the run were a fact that could not be entirely ignored. Thus spectacular individual cases such as that of Eichmann became an outlet for suppressed feelings. The question of how Nazi criminals could escape prosecution after the war, and in which political context that was to occur, who covered up their escape, and what individual interests lay behind it, faded into the background. Sensational individual cases were a distraction, but at the same time they helped to keep the subject of Nazi flight and Nazi crimes alive. Simon Wiesenthal, the 'Nazi-hunter', knew that very clearly. For him, the ODESSA myth was maybe only a vehicle by which he could bring his concerns to a wider public. But myths alone can't explain the Nazi flight. Only since the 1990s have misrepresentations surrounding secret escape organizations such as ODESSA begun to unravel. From the fog of myths, the outlines of Nazi flight are beginning to emerge.

Over the last twenty years, historians and journalists have tried to identify the true impulses and determining factors of Nazi flight. Just as Heinz Schneppen convincingly demolished the ODESSA myth,[9] Uki Goñi has emphasized how Argentina under Perón's presidency was a major driving force behind the movement (the title of his book, *The Real Odessa*, is telling in this regard). Over the past few years, Richard Breitman and other American historians have clearly exposed the involvement of US intelligence services in the context of the 'ratline' in books such as *US Intelligence and the Nazis*. But the wider political context is only slowly coming into view, particularly when examining the relationship between the Cold War against the Soviet Union, on the one hand, and the repression of the genocide of the Jews, the Shoah, on the other. Both factors, the political parameters and the silence and repression of a whole generation, were what made the flight of Nazis possible.

Governments' silence, but also that of nongovernmental agencies, contributed to the flight of Nazis and the secreting of the past. In the 1961 Eichmann trial, little importance was given either to illegal emigration or the background to it. A great deal of attention was probably devoted to editing out the involvement of major institutions such as the Catholic Church or the ICRC, and this was done almost completely. As an observer of the trial in Jerusalem, the philosopher Hannah Arendt was able to tease out only a few references to the role of such institutions in Eichmann's flight. The notes that Eichmann took during his time in prison, 'My Escape: Report from the Cell in Jerusalem', could not be kept entirely hidden from the international press. But, in the end, such reports disappeared for decades into the CIA archives and were only released a few years ago.[10] So it can hardly come as a surprise that efforts were made to sweep this information under the carpet. What was largely edited out during the Jerusalem trial continued by means of deliberate concealment to obscure the truth about Nazi flight. The political implications in particular were ignored. But it is precisely in these connections between realpolitik and morality, legal reappraisal and the interests of the Cold War, that we may find the key to an understanding of why a considerable number of Nazi perpetrators were able to escape justice and responsibility.

Contradictions between public and private actions have further clouded the history of the post-war treatment of Nazis and other perpetrators. It was the United States that opened up a completely new chapter with regard to guilt and war crimes at the Nuremberg Trial. Traditional victors' justice was to be replaced by the rule of law and new international legal and moral norms and standards. For the first time, heads of state and military commanders had to take responsibility for 'crimes against humanity'. The massive, systematic, state-sponsored crimes led to the decision to set up an International Military Tribunal in Nuremberg against some (surviving) major war criminals such as Hermann Göring and Ernst Kaltenbrunner. But even in the 'selection' of the defendants, strategic and practical considerations sometimes found themselves in competition with moral and legal claims.[11] While SS General Karl Wolff, Himmler's deputy until 1943, was not prosecuted, but protected by US agencies against any kind of Allied prosecution, other perpetrators faced serious penalties. Rudolf Hess was sentenced to life imprisonment in Spandau Prison, which he ended in 1987 by taking his own life at the age of 93. In spite of repeated approaches by the Americans, the Soviets refused to put mercy before justice where the old man was concerned.[12] Nuremberg thus also represents the selective treatment of guilt, responsibility, and justice. The 1961 American film *Judgment at Nuremberg* brilliantly captures the question of morality, justice, and the interests of the early Cold War. Its cast, which includes such excellent actors as Spencer Tracy, Marlene Dietrich, and Maximilian Schell, doubtless contributes to this. The film is set in 1948 and examines the trial of four Nazi judges who were complicit in euthanasia and the persecution of political opponents: not only the Germans, but also the Allies wanted to draw a line under the past, and many people saw the trial and the 'rummaging around in the past' as unnecessary. The accused lawyer and Nazi Minister Dr Ernst Janning (played by Burt Lancaster) breaks through this silence and freely admits his moral guilt. But at a time of conflict between the Western and Eastern power-blocks, such positions were the exception.

Beyond Nuremberg, many examples reveal the uneven 'justice' that prevailed in the early Cold War years. After the suicide of his boss, Himmler, Karl Wolff could have been condemned at Nuremberg as a proxy for the SS, but nothing came of it. Because of his contacts with US intelligence services and his usefulness in the 'fight against Communism', the Allies decided not to prosecute him. In this respect Italy was an early 'testing ground' for future German–American cooperation. As historian Kerstin von Lingen has clearly shown, Wolff's US counterpart and protector, Allen Dulles, knew of Wolff's past as a perpetrator, but Dulles thought Wolff useful.[13] The Americans' treatment of Wolff was by no means an exception. Nazi criminals, scientists, officers, and collaborators were brought back into service—recycled for the new struggle against the Soviet power if they could be useful. Many such cases occurred in the intelligence services and the military. This coordinated recruitment of Nazi scientists has been the subject of heated debates in the United States over the past twenty years. One such example is that of Wernher von Braun. As SS-Sturmbannführer and technical director of the Peenemünde Military Research Establishment, he was responsible for the development and production of large rockets during the Second World War. His V-2 missiles terrorized people in British and Dutch cities. After the end of the war, the technician was immediately taken back into service by the Americans and became director of the NASA Marshall Space Flight Center. Braun's past was no great secret, even in the United States. But little was made of the fact that concentration camp inmates in camps such as Mittelbau Dora produced the V-2 rockets in appalling conditions, and thousands died of their slave labour. Braun helped the Americans to be the first on the moon, and that was all that counted. Usefulness rather than morality was at the top of the US agenda.

Similarly, General Reinhard Gehlen, former head of the counter-intelligence division 'Foreign Armies East' made a remarkable second career for himself after 1945. Even before the end of the war, Gehlen was aware that the Western powers would probably turn against their former ally, the Soviet Union, sooner or later. When they did so, they would need his knowledge and his colleagues in the fight against communist expansion because the Americans themselves had no agents in Germany and the Soviet states. Gehlen's calculations were correct. In 1946 the US military appointed him as head of the 'Gehlen Organization' spy network, which later became the West German intelligence service. Gehlen remained its head until 1968. He was the beneficiary of Allen Dulles' position of 'usefulness before prosecution'; Dulles had consistently fought for this policy and, in the end, became head of the CIA. Dulles and his intelligence agents were soon way ahead of the dilettantes of the Counter Intelligence Corps (CIC) where active espionage was concerned, particularly in terms of experience. SS officers such as Wilhelm Höttl repeatedly offered the Americans at the CIC sound spy networks behind the Iron Curtain, even entire underground armies consisting of former collaborators of the Germans and nationalists who could supposedly be easily reactivated against the Soviets. But in many cases, these 'underground armies' operated somewhere between boundless exaggeration and pure wishful thinking, making the CIC less effective than its counterpart, the CIA.

The story of Klaus Barbie, once a powerful and brutal Gestapo chief in Lyons in occupied France, explains better than any theoretical considerations the logic of the early Cold War. Barbie was one of those responsible for the torture and murder of members of the resistance—Jean Moulin among them—in the South of France. In 1947 he started working for the CIC and was smuggled to South America by US agencies. The Franco-German 'Nazi hunters' Beate and Serge Klarsfeld began to track Barbie down in Bolivia in the early 1970s. He was extradited to France and brought before the court there. The trial sparked intense controversies in France concerning the relationship between the occupying Germans and the Vichy regime. The first cracks appeared in France's attempts to suppress the past. Barbie was by no means the most significant war criminal in France, but Moulin became a martyr of the resistance, and his tormentor thus became a symbol of the Nazi terror in France. This case was significant in that it raised the question of the US's role in shielding Nazis from prosecution and the reasons behind that policy.

Since the Barbie case, the problematic role of the United States in Nazi smuggling has become an internationally debated topic. In 1983 the US government even had to give a formal apology for its involvement in helping Barbie to escape—an early example of an apology for historical injustice. US authorities in the early Cold War put the usefulness of former SS men before the prosecution of the perpetrators. Consistent reappraisal and the prosecution of Nazi crimes that went hand in hand with it soon fell victim to reasons of state.

One example will have to suffice here. In 1950 the Displaced Persons Commission of the US Congress stated: 'The Baltic Waffen-SS units are to be considered as separate and distinct in purpose, ideology, activities and qualifications from the German SS. Therefore the Commission holds them not to be a movement hostile to the government of the United States.' The historian Tony Judt concisely sums up these distortions on the part of the US authorities: 'The Baltic Waffen-SS had been among the most brutal and enthusiastic when it came to torturing and killing Jews on the Eastern Front; but in the novel circumstances of the Cold War they were of course "our Nazis".'[14] As this example clearly shows, decisions in the context of refugee policy were extremely political, and by no means purely humanitarian.

It becomes evident through this study that, in the larger context, fighting communism became more important to the West than punishing Nazis and justified a certain collaboration by US intelligence services and their high-tech community with former Nazis. Moral standards were subordinated to pragmatism. Some war criminals and Holocaust perpetrators were thus protected against prosecution by the US information services. The role of the US government and its intelligence services in the flight of the Nazis has been under examination by the Nazi War Crimes Interagency Working Group (IWG) since 1999. This commission of historians is concentrating its investigations on the role of the US intelligence services in the recruitment of anticommunist specialists from the periphery of Himmler's SS. Over the past ten years, the IWG has released some eight million pages of secret service reports, including 1.2 million pages on the SS, 74,000 pages of CIA personal and case files, and over 350,000 pages of FBI documents. Archive sources are the precondition for a solid reappraisal of this subject. The IWG's results are shocking, but also show that a democratic society is entirely capable of 'coming to terms with the past'.

The United States was not the only country that aided Nazis when it was in its interests to do so; Italy did the same thing and, like the United States, tried to keep it quiet. One telling—if rather drastic—Italian example of secreting the past was the 'cupboard of shame'. This was an old filing cabinet in the Palazzo Cesi, the headquarters of the Procura Generale Militare in Rome. Here, from the 1950s until the early 1960s, files in part deposited by the Allies concerning Nazi war crimes in Italy (committed by the SS, the Wehrmacht, and Italian fascists) were kept, even though they should have been sent to the responsible military state prosecutors. As Italy wanted to take its NATO partner Germany into account for reasons of state, the documents lay undisturbed, gathering dust. It was not until 1994 that a judicial officer in search of documents for the trial against former SS officer Erich Priebke opened the cupboard. Almost 700 files were revealed, and they were finally sent to the relevant military state prosecutors' offices. A series of trials and sentences followed, albeit in many cases far too late.[15]

The story of Karl Hass, Priebke's closest colleague in Rome, also draws a very clear picture of Italy's attempts to deal with the past. Hass, who took part in the massacre in the Ardeatine Caves near Rome in 1944 and was a war criminal wanted in Italy, stayed in the sunny south after the war and worked for the Italian and US intelligence services. In the 1950s he was seemingly declared dead, but in 1969 he took a minor role in Visconti's film *The Damned*, in which he played a Nazi officer. No one was troubled by that fact, and having been declared dead, he remained officially so. The 'Priebke case' unleashed a controversy about the recent past that was to last for decades. Now the 'long shadows of the Holocaust'[16] had caught up with Italy as well.

After the Priebke affair, a belated judicial reappraisal of the recent past occurred in Italy. At the same time, in the 1990s, critical voices about the country's own fascist past were also growing louder, in competition with the revisionist statements of leading politicians.[17] The special role of Italy as a 'highway (Reichsautobahn) for war criminals' has hitherto never been examined in its own right. The question of Italy's role was mostly only touched upon—as it was in the international media in 2007. In this case it concerned the archives of the Red Cross Tracing Service in Arolsen in Germany. There was repeated resistance to this from the Italian government, and journalists were not the only ones who surmised that the attitude of resistance might have something to do with Italy's involvement in 'Nazi-smuggling'. The Italian government delayed the process, supposedly 'because they fear the records will reveal just how many Nazis escaped through Italy after the war',[18] the *Washington Post* wrote in March 2007. For Italy, the process of coming to terms with the past seems to be a slow one.

Despite the stalling of the Italian government, historians' reappraisal of Nazi war crimes and the fascist past has without a doubt made great progress in Italy since the 1990s. This reappraisal by current historians also applies to the northern Italian border province of South Tyrol. Nevertheless, the image of South Tyrol as a 'victim' still prevails there among the wider public. After the First World War, the southern part of the Tyrol was assigned to Italy as spoils of war, even though German was, and remains, the majority language; this fact contributes to a victim mentality. In addition, for seventy years the German-speaking population has referred to the years of cultural oppression by Mussolini's fascism, which also furthers the victim mentality. The role of many South Tyroleans as perpetrators under National Socialism, however, tends to be overlooked. That has much to do with the 'ethnic pillarization' of South Tyrolean society—a division in many areas between Italian- and German-speaking populations.[19] The Italians in the region refer to their role as victims during the Nazi occupation of 1943–5, and the German-speakers to their role as victims during the twenty-year rule of Italian fascism. Each group has always seen itself as the victim, the other as the perpetrator. After 1945, 'fronts of unity' formed on both sides according to language groups, quite openly serving to achieve political goals. In South Tyrol this stance of national hostility produced a situation not unlike that seen elsewhere in the Cold War, and the reappraisal of the most recent past was made much more difficult.[20] Eichmann's and Mengele's new identities as South Tyroleans were in no way a coincidence and shed some light on the Nazi past of this border region. But as in Germany and elsewhere, in South Tyrol there were victims and perpetrators as well as victims who were also perpetrators.

Argentina, like Italy, was forced to confront its past with Priebke's extradition from Argentina to Italy in 1995. For the first time Argentina, too, officially requested clarification concerning his Nazi past. In 1997 the Argentinian government set up a special Commission (Comisión para el Esclarecimiento de las Actividades Nacionalsocialistas en la Argentina, CEANA). CEANA—whose panel included famous personalities from public life (Edgar Bronfman, President of the Jewish World Congress; Sir Ralph Dahrendorf, former Rector of the London School of Economics; and Richard Joseph Goldstone, former Chief Prosecutor at the Yugoslavian Criminals Tribunal in The Hague) and whose staff included renowned historians—was set up to cast a penetrating light on Argentina's relationship with National Socialism. But CEANA's work was repeatedly accompanied by controversies. Ignacio Klich, the head of CEANA, criticized the book by Argentine journalist Uki Goñi about Nazi flight to Argentina. *The Real Odessa*, he claimed, was 'unfair' for not showing that Argentina had taken in thousands of Jewish refugees between 1933 and 1945. But that was only half the truth—because Argentina had repeatedly prevented Jewish immigration.

The debate touched off by Goñi's reexamination of Argentina's past policy regarding Jewish immigration yielded startling results. From 1938 Argentina officially closed its borders to Jewish emigrants from Europe who were fleeing from National Socialism. In his book, Goñi had brought the relevant anti-Jewish decrees to international attention. After lengthy discussions, a remarkable moment in the recent history of Argentina took place: on 8 June 2005, in the presence of State President Néstor Kirchner, the secret decree of 1938, designed to prevent the immigration of Jewish refugees, was declared invalid. The revocation of this order represented a high point in the discussion of Argentina's past in which the country's relations with the Third Reich were re-examined. Argentina's immigration policy is often given as a prime example of the reception of Nazi refugees and collaborators, but a similar practice could also be seen in other countries in the Middle East and South America. Even America and Canada allowed Lithuanian and Ukrainian collaborators into their countries from 1946 onwards. The one-sided image of Argentina as the only Nazi refuge came into being in the years around 1945. Argentina's pro-German sympathies and her late declaration of war on Nazi Germany provoked US diplomats. The result was a demonization of the South American state by the media, an unfair portrayal that is now beginning to be revised.

The US, Italian, and Argentinian governments are not the only institutions that must answer for their role in the protection of Nazis; the Vatican, too, still faces questions about its activities. In the 1948 Italian election, the United States went to great expense to prevent a possible communist election victory. Anticommunist forces and parties were supported, and the intelligence services were also well prepared. In addition, fresh collaboration between US agencies and the Catholic Church arose. The idea of a communist Italy was a bugbear for the Vatican and the United States; thus Italy was one of the first battlegrounds of the Cold War. In the battle against communism, the Catholic Church immediately found strong allies, not least among them the United States. The priest Krunoslav Stjepan Draganović is an example that demonstrates collaboration between US intelligence services and the Catholic Church in Italy. Draganović was not a lone exception, and neither was he just anybody: as a representative of the Croatian refugee aid mission, he was involved with the agencies of the Vatican. The question of the Vatican's role in the escape of Nazis and other collaborators is thus posed with particular urgency.

Additionally, the attitude of the Pope and the Catholic Church towards National Socialism has been controversial for decades. Since Rolf Hochhuth's play *The Deputy* (1963), Pope Pius XII has been the focus of criticism for his silence about the Holocaust. The Vatican responded to Hochhuth's accusations by setting up an internal commission of historians consisting of four Jesuit priests. Commissioned by Paul VI, the churchmen produced between 1965 and 1981 several volumes about the Vatican and its policy in the Second World War; the priests alone had exclusive access to the Vatican archives during this period.[21] The commission exonerated the Pope and the Vatican of all moral guilt. Nevertheless, the topic of Pius XII and National Socialism has repeatedly stirred great interest among the public. In November 2008 an exhibition on 'Pius XII—The Man and His Pontificate' opened in Rome. It stressed his criticism of the Nazis and the Church's aid for the Jews. Pope Benedict XVI has also refused to criticize Pius XII, but has at the same time delayed the planned canonization of his controversial predecessor.

Church agencies did play a central part in helping National Socialists escape—particularly the PCA in Rome. This mission soon became a popular stopping-off point for serious war criminals from Central and Eastern Europe. Contemporary history still only touches on the subject of escape assistance by the Church, which is hardly surprising because access to the Vatican archive for the years after 1939 is still strictly limited. The Vatican's assistance to escaping Nazis also did not play a major role in discussions about the canonization of Pius XII.[22] Yet the history of the Vatican mission for refugees is key to understanding the Vatican's attitude towards National Socialism, denazification, and the early Cold War. Following the publication of the La Vista report, in February 1992 the Vatican spokesman Joaquín Navarro-Valls made a statement about the accusations that the refugee mission of the Holy See had acquired passports for Nazi war criminals that allowed them to escape. 'On the contrary, Pius XII and the Vatican helped to save the lives of thousands of Jews,' said Navarro-Valls, here coming to the defence of the PCA: 'In those days it was so easy to assume a fake identity and disappear among the refugees, but to represent the work of the Papal Aid Mission as supporting the escape of war criminals is historically false.' The Pope also gave a statement on the subject. In an interview, he followed up on the comments of his press spokesman Navarro-Valls and said that similar accusations had already been examined and rebutted in the past by the relevant agencies.[23]

Despite the words of such prominent defenders, the papal aid mission was, in fact, massively involved in helping war criminals and Nazis to escape. A difficult question that remains to be answered is why Catholic dignitaries helped Nazis in their escape. My research shows that their motives were both political and religious. On one hand, high-up members of the Catholic Church aimed to weaken communism as much as possible, and on the other, they hoped to revive religion in Europe at any cost. Radical nationalism and anti-Judaism also played a role, especially in the cases like those of Bishop Hudal and Monsignor Draganović. But 'the Vatican' was not a 'monolithic bloc', and different positions, 'different voices' inside the Catholic Church, could be heard.[24] Decisions at the highest level were made on the basis of sober strategic considerations. During the Second World War Pius XII worked to preserve the interests of the Church. It was a balancing act between the dictatorships of Stalin and that of Hitler, and the Pope was prepared for compromises. Although Pius XII's portrayal as 'Hitler's Pope' is unfair, Pius did see 'godless' communism as the main enemy of the Church.[25]

At the end of World War II, matters became simpler. With the end of Hitler's Nazi Germany, only one major enemy of the Catholic Church remained: the communist Soviet Union. Thus the Vatican waged its 'lonely Cold War'[26] against communism years before the United States did. Pope Pius XII was one of the first Cold War warriors.[27] The PCA was part of this fight. By helping National Socialists, collaborators, and fascists from all over Europe, church agencies were accomplishing two goals: rescuing Central and Eastern European Catholic refugees and anticommunists from Stalin and expanding the pro-Catholic political electorate in the new home countries of the refugees. Former SS men were clearly anticommunist, and these 'anticommunist fighters for Europe' (as Hudal called them) had to be helped by the Church. The fact that some war criminals and perpetrators could escape thanks to the PCA and the Red Cross was seemingly considered bearable in the interest of a greater good.

Religious renewal was also a clearly formulated and important aim in this context. Catholic priests' understanding of guilt and responsibility was dominated by forgiveness. 'We do not believe in the eye for an eye of the Jews,' as Hudal put it. This attitude of Hudal's was shared by other important people inside the Church. Pius XII and the Catholic Bishops repeatedly asked for mercy and even amnesty for war criminals and Holocaust perpetrators. They believed that the responsibility for the crimes lay only with a handful of leaders, foremost among them were Hitler, Himmler, and Goebbels. All others, including SS men, were not responsible, and were, perhaps, victims too. Priests and bishops helping war criminals and Nazis helped foremost Catholics. The lost sheep had to be brought back to the fold, they thought. The Catholic Church celebrated its moral victory over National Socialism. Former Nazi officials but also millions of simple Nazi party members were being freed from the 'false teachings of Nazism' and were welcomed back into the church. Better yet, non-Catholic Nazi criminals converted to Catholicism. In some cases, 're-baptism' was the pre-condition for Catholic aid. For instance, former Protestant and war criminal Erich Priebke underwent 'denazification through re-baptism', as I call it, before he was 'shipped' through Italy to Argentina. Holocaust perpetrator Oswald Pohl's conversion from Protestant Christian before the war to Nazi *Gottgläubiger* during the Hitler years, to Catholic was compared to St Augustine's conversion.

The involvement of the International Committee of the Red Cross in Nazi escape assistance is a similarly complex story. Individual ICRC delegations more or less actively helped war criminals to escape by issuing them with ICRC travel documents, whether out of sympathy for individuals, because of their political attitude, or simply because they were overburdened. The ICRC has a certain moral responsibility and bears a share of the blame for aiding the perpetrators of the war. But the ICRC is belatedly beginning to re-examine its role in the escape assistance for Nazis and fellow travellers. It was only a few years ago that the ICRC in Geneva made its archive generally accessible to research. Since then efforts have been made to find clarification in Geneva as well. Cornelio Sommaruga, the president of the ICRC until 1999, spoke of the 'failure' of the Red Cross in the context of escape assistance. ICRC spokespeople accused local ICRC delegates in Italy of joint responsibility and even of 'complicity with fleeing war criminals'.[28] Reference was also made to the extraordinary situation in the post-war years: 'At the time there were thousands of refugees from completely unchecked backgrounds. If really reliable checks had been introduced, help would inevitably not have been given to many genuine refugees.'[29] Was one to refuse help to the many genuine refugees because there might have been some criminals hiding among them? This is a tough question. On the other hand, the checks could easily have been improved, particularly towards the end of the 1940s, when the ICRC had already accumulated some experience. But Headquarters in Geneva delayed implementing these. Refugees from all over Europe were not creatures without biographies or histories; they all had a past. In a fair number of cases, this meant a past as a perpetrator or collaborator in Nazi crimes. But as long as people were able to demonstrate an anticommunist background, the ICRC plainly turned a blind eye. Still the ICRC's role in assisting Nazis, whether willingly or unknowingly, is not the only question about its World War II past that the agency must answer.

Was realpolitik placed above moral standards in the case of the ICRC's silence about the Holocaust? For a moral superpower like the ICRC, its behaviour as regards the Shoah represents a serious problem. The ICRC was three times awarded the Nobel Peace Prize for its charity work. Such high regard can be easily damaged. The Swiss historian Jean-Claude Favez, in his pioneering work on the ICRC and its attitude towards the Holocaust, has made it clear why the chief response in Geneva was one of silence.[30] In the ICRC, leaders prioritized Swiss national interests and subordinated all other concerns to it. Swiss security and economic interests were not to be jeopardized. References were also made in Geneva to the unconditional neutrality of the ICRC and its lack of legal authority. The clear anticommunist attitude within the ICRC probably played a major role in its policies after 1945. For all the justified criticism, however, the help that the ICRC gave to millions of POWs, casualties, and refugees from the Second World War remains undisputed and unforgotten. In the last years, the ICRC also has dealt more openly with its past and has supported academic research on these topics. It is about time, because the ICRC's involvement in Nazi escape is striking. Given its silence about the Holocaust and its

hesitation in rescuing Jews, the ICRC's involvement in helping Holocaust perpetrators to escape justice is a serious issue of moral guilt and
responsibility.

As the research presented in this book clearly shows, the escape of
Nazis and war criminals aided by the Red Cross and the PCA was an
open secret at the time. The US intelligence services knew, the US State
Department knew, the International Committee of the Red Cross knew,
its presidents Max Huber and Paul Ruegger knew, the Swiss government knew, the Italian government knew, Monsignors Carroll and
Montini from the Vatican knew. They all knew as early as 1946/47
about the misuse of the Red Cross travel documents and PCA papers.
Internal memos of the Red Cross in Geneva clearly show the agency's
awareness that war criminals escaped thanks to its papers. But the
agency decided to continue its practices with few changes. The consequences of turning a blind eye—illustrated so shockingly by the case of
Adolf Eichmann, who fled Europe with the help of the PCA and the
Red Cross in 1950, four years after the massive abuse had become
known inside the respective institutions—is still stunning to contem-
plate.

After the fall of the Berlin Wall in 1989, shifting historical perspec-
tives have once again been set in motion. States, nations, and groups
have discovered their history or completely reinterpreted it. In the process, historical guilt has assumed a new status. In his book *Guilt of Nations*,
the historian Elazar Barkan speaks of a new globalized morality—the
discovery of historical injustice.[31] According to Barkan, moral responsibility is becoming increasingly important in a post-Cold War world.
Today the acknowledgement of moral standards has also become a
political device. Apologies for historical injustice 'are simply proper' if
one wishes to survive as a politician in a democratic state. History has
once again become a major field of political and social debate. Today,
as in the past, competing images of history form the identity of both
perpetrators and victims, as each side arms itself with a particular
interpretation of the past. When studying the involvement of certain
institutions and states with Nazi flight, most striking are the great differences in the treatment of responsibility. The debates about guilt and
reconciliation range from total denial to confession of involvement and
responsibility and include cases where 'too little too late' is seen as a
great barrier to reconciliation.[32] In institutions such as the International

Committee of the Red Cross and the Catholic Church, the question of moral responsibility assumes a very central role because both institutions derive their authority from their own moral example. The discrepancy between realpolitik and moral standards is quite plain in the question of Nazi flight. These moral questions polarize, hurt, and provoke.

In the days of the Cold War, the trend was to throw 'mud' over the past,[33] while today things look very different: moral responsibility for historical crimes has an important status. A society that can face the dark episodes in its own history is capable of drawing lessons from the past in order to shape a better future, a goal which serves as the motivation for writing this book, for the years spent painstakingly documenting the stories of perpetrators and the prevailing political conditions, and for explaining the historical complicity of institutions and states in helping Nazis to escape. The Austrian writer Martin Pollack explains concisely the value of revisiting an accurately reconstructed past: 'We can only meet the ghosts of the past with openness. Any attempt to drive them out, to make them disappear by remaining silent, by closing our eyes or blocking our ears, is doomed inevitably to failure.'[34] It is no coincidence that the quotation from the Austrian author Ingeborg Bachmann is a leitmotif for this book: 'People can face the truth' (*'Die Wahrheit ist dem Menschen zumutbar'*). Although the truth about the escape of Nazi war criminals has not changed since 1947, what we make of it certainly has. The zeitgeist of the immediate post-war years was characterized by very different moral values and a very different concept of moral guilt and responsibility. Human rights and historical injustice were new concepts at the time. This change in worldview (Weltanschauung) in just two generations is, perhaps, the most striking revelation of this book.

Notes

Introduction

1 Simon Wiesenthal, *The Murderers among Us: The Simon Wiesenthal Memoirs* (New York: McGraw-Hill, 1967), 78.
2 Jonathan Littell, *The Kindly Ones*, tr. Charlotte Mandell (London: Chatto & Windus, 2008).
3 See the survey of the most recent literature on the subject in Matteo Sanfilippo, 'Ratlines and Unholy Trinities': A Review Essay on (Recent) Literature Concerning Nazi and Collaborators Smuggling Operations Out of Italy, *Unitas DSpace*, 2003, <http://hdl.handle.net/2067/24>, accessed 14 Mar. 2010.
4 Cf. Heinz Schneppen, *Odessa und das Vierte Reich: Mythen der Zeitgeschichte* (Berlin: Metropol, 2007). Cf. Carlos Widmann, 'Der Mythos Odessa: Die vermeintliche "Rattenlinie" der Nazis nach Argentinien', *Süddeutsche Zeitung* (7 May 2007) <http://www.sueddeutsche.de/panorama/legendenbildung-der-mythos-odessa-1.852906>, accessed 14 Jan. 2011.
5 Holger Meding, *Flucht vor Nürnberg? Deutsche und österreichische Einwanderung in Argentinien 1945–1955* (Cologne: Böhlau, 1992).

Chapter 1

1 'Subject: Recrudescence of Secret Activities of German Rightist Groups; Underground Route established by them via Tirol and Italy to Argentine, Encouragement given them by Perón Government', Maurice Altaffer, American Consulate, Bremen, 13 January 1949, to Secretary of State, Washington DC, NARA, RG 59, box 6744, Central Decimal File 862.20235/1-1349.
2 Cf. Luc van Dongen, *Un purgatoire très discret. La transition 'Helvétique' d'anciens nazis, fascistes et collaborateurs après 1945* (Paris: Société d'histoire de la Suisse romande, 2008).
3 Cf. Michael Phayer, *Pius XII, the Holocaust, and the Cold War* (Bloomington: Indiana University Press, 2008), 177 ff. Cf. Uki Goñi, *The Real Odessa: How Perón brought the Nazi War Criminals to Argentina* (London: Granta, 2003).
4 Gabriele Stieber, 'Die Lösung des Flüchtlingsproblems 1945–1960', in Thomas Albrich *et al.* (eds.), *Österreich in den Fünfzigern*, Innsbrucker Forschungen zur Zeitgeschichte 11 (Innsbruck: Österreichischer Studien Verlag, 1995), 67–93 at 68.
5 Cf. Klaus Eisterer, *Französische Besatzungspolitik: Tirol und Vorarlberg 1945/46*, Innsbrucker Forschungen zur Zeitgeschichte 9 (Innsbruck: Haymon, 1990), 77 ff.
6 SHAEF, Conference on Repatriation/Disposal of Prisoners of War, Surrendered Personnel, Displaced Persons, etc. held at Bozen 1945, first session, 14 June 1945, p. 10, National Archives of England, Wales, and the United Kingdom, WO 219/3556, 234, 237.
7 Michael R. Marrus, *The Unwanted: European Refugees in the Twentieth Century* (Oxford: Oxford University Press, 1985), 317 ff.
8 Stieber, 'Die Lösung des Flüchtlingsproblems', 68 f.

9 Cf. Federica Bertagna and Matteo Sanfilippo, 'Per una prospettiva comparata dell'emigrazione nazifascista dopo la seconda guerra mondiale', *Studi Emigrazione*, 441/155 (2004), 527–53.

10 Louise W. Holborn, *The International Refugee Organization, A Specialized Agency of the United Nations: Its History and Work, 1946–1952* (London: Oxford University Press, 1956), 9.

11 Stieber, 'Die Lösung des Flüchtlingsproblems', 69. But there were many exceptions: in 1947, 200,000 ethnic Germans in Austria were de facto given Austria as their country of origin and accepted into the IRO's emigration programme. Cf. Holborn, *International Refugee Organization*, 211.

12 Arthur Rucker, 'The Work of the International Refugee Organization', *International Affairs* (Royal Institute of International Affairs), 25/1 (Jan. 1949), 66–73.

13 DP Situation in Austria, Summary by UNRRA, 31 July 1946, National Archives of England, Wales, and the United Kingdom, FO 1020/2491.

14 See Bertagna and Sanfilippo, 'Per una prospettiva comparata dell'emigrazione nazifascista', 527–53.

15 Archivio Centrale di Stato, Roma (ACS), PCM, 1948–50, file 4028, Profughi stranieri in Italia, Migrazione dall'Europa. Pubblicazione compilata dall'I.R.O.

16 'Extension of activities of the Intergovernmental Committee on Refugees', 30 July 1946, signed Herbert Emerson, USHMM, RG 43.048 M, IRO, carton 62, reel 5.

17 Marrus, *The Unwanted*, 340 ff.

18 Ibid.

19 Letter from IRO office in Rio de Janeiro to IRO headquarters in Geneva, 17 June 1947, USHMM, RG 43.048 M, IRO, carton 566, reel 3.

20 Brochure 'IRO Refugee Problem in Italy' *c.*1947, ICRC Geneva, Archive, Archives Générales, G. 68, Titres de voyage, box 954, Italie 1944–8, folder 'Mission de M. Gallopin en Italie'.

21 Alessandro Agnoletti, *Enklave Rimini-Bellaria: Storia e storie di 150.000 prigionieri nei campi di concentramento alleati sulla costa romagnola (1945–1947)* (Rimini: Guaraldi, 1999), 55 ff. Deutsches Hauptquartier (ed.), *Die deutsche SEP-Enklave Rimini 1945/46. Ein Überblick* (Rimini-Miramare: Dt. Hauptquartier, 1946), 3.

22 Giovanna Padovani, 'Epilogo di guerra per la Wehrmacht in Italia: dalla resa nella montagna veneta all "Enklave" di Rimini-Bellaria', in Ferruccio Vendramini (ed.), *Montagne e veneti nel secondo dopoguerra* (Verona: Bertani, 1988), 217–37 at 233.

23 Agnoletti, *Enklave Rimini-Bellaria*, 64 ff.

24 Memo from the Italian Ministry of the Interior, Direzione Generale P.S. to the Prefects *et al.* [1947], ACS, Int. P.S. Aff. Gen. A5GP, 'Prigionieri di Guerra 1943–1949', file 1, folder 'Riconsegna Autorità Alleate'.

25 ACS, Ministero Interno, DG di PS, Div. AGR, A5G, 1944–8, Italia liberata, file 7, folder 21.

26 Report from the Prefect of Forli to the Ministry of the Interior, 14 July 1947, ACS, Int. P.S. Aff. Gen. A5GP, 'Prigionieri di Guerra 1943–1949', file 1, folder 'Riconsegna Autorità Alleate'.

27 US Ambassador Dunn in Rome to the Italian Foreign Minister Carlo Sforza, 25 July 1947, NARA, RG 319, entry 134 B, box 173, G-2 intelligence, personnel name files, folder 'Ante, Pavelić'.

28 Mediterranean Theater of Operations, US Army to the Italian Ministry of the Interior, signed U. G. Fetterman, Major, Asst. Adjutant General, 10 October 1947, ACS, Int. P.S. Aff. Gen. A5GP, 'Prigionieri di Guerra 1943–1949', file 1, folder 'Riconsegna Autorità Alleate'.

29 Holborn, *International Refugee Organization*, see 'Constitution of the International Refugee Organization', 575–89, esp. 586 f., 'persons who will not be the concern of the organization'.

30 Cf. Arieh J. Kochavi, *Prelude to Nuremberg: Allied War Crimes Policy and the Question of Punishment* (Chapel Hill: U of North Carolina P, 1998), 57. Cf. Phayer, *Pius XII*, 151, 267–8. Cf. Claudia Kuretsidis-Haider, 'Die von der Moskauer Konferenz der Alliierten vom 1. November 1943 verabschiedete Erklärung über die Verantwortlichkeit der Hitleranhänger für begangene Gräueltaten', *Alfred Klahr, Gesellschaft: Verein zur Erforschung der Geschichte der Arbeiterbewegung* (25 Oct. 2003) <http://www.klahrgesellschaft.at/Referate/Kuretsidis_2003.html>, accessed 28 Jan. 2009.

31 US embassy in Moscow to the State Department Washington, DC and the embassies in Vienna, Berlin, and Rome, signed Durbrow, 12 June 1947 (SECRET), NARA, RG 84, Rome embassy, box 20, folder 848, 'Displaced Persons'.

32 Memo Supreme Allied Commander, Mediterranean Theater, signed A. L. Hamblen, Colonel, Asst. Chief of Staff, G-5 to the Italian Ministry of the Interior in Rome, 3 May 1947, ACS, Int. P.S. Aff. Gen. A5GP, 'Prigionieri di Guerra 1943–1949', file 1, folder 'Riconsegna Autorità Alleate'.

33 Kosakische Völkische Bewegung in Deutschland to the Director of the IRO in the US Zone of Germany, 27 August 1948, USHMM, RG 43.048 M, IRO, carton 824, microfilm reel 5.

34 Franco Cantoni, 'Fattaccio a Fossoli provocato e voluto ma non accaduto', *L'Unità* (4 February 1947). Cf. also ACS, Istruzioni, subfile 77, folder 69, subfolder 41, insert 3, 'Visite al campo e relazioni'.

35 ACS, Istruzioni, file 78, folder 69, n. 70, Stranieri Internati, subfolder 41, M. Centro raccolta Fossoli di Carpi, insert 16, 'Assistenza religiosa'.

36 IRO Headquarters, Preparatory Commission, in Geneva to the US ambassador in Rome, James C. Dunn, 10 September 1947 (STRICTLY CONFIDENTIAL), NARA, RG 84, Italy, US Embassy Rome, Classified General Records, 1947, box 20.

37 Holborn, *International Refugee Organization*, 324.

38 ACS, Ministero dell'Interno, Direzione Generale Pubblica Sicurezza, Divisione Affari Generali e Riservati, Cat. A 16, Stranieri e Ebrei stranieri, Affari Generali (1930–56), file 39: 'IRO: tessera di riconoscimento per profughi'.

39 Holborn, *International Refugee Organization*, 208.

40 Ibid.

41 'Ultimas noticias', 13 June 1947, USHMM, RG 43.048 M, IRO, carton 566 IRO, reel 3.

42 Special Commissioner for IGCR, Vincent Meyer, Brig. Gen. US Army (retired). 15 June 1947, USHMM, RG 43.048 M, IRO, carton 566 IRO, reel 3.

43 Vincent La Vista to Herbert J. Cummings, 15 May 1947 (TOP SECRET), NARA, RG 84, Austria, Political Adviser, Gen. Records 1945–55, entry 2057, box 2, app. D, p. 2.

44 'Italia–Austria senza passaporto. Traffico clandestino di corrispondenza e di valuta estera scoperto dall'arma di carabinieri', *Alto Adige* (23 Sept. 1945), 2.

45 Research by Claus Larass for *Bunte* magazine 1985, MS, notes (copy in the possession of the author).

46 Vincent La Vista to Herbert J. Cummings, 15 May 1947 (TOP SECRET), NARA, RG 84, Austria, Political Adviser, Gen. Records 1945–55, entry 2057, box 2, p. 8.

47 Ufficio di P.S. di confine Brennero, Oggetto: Fermo Stranieri, Brennero, 3 February 1946, Staatsarchiv Bozen, Fondo Questura, file 'Soggiorno stranieri' 1946.

48 Monthly Security Report of Bozen State Police Department August 1947, 1 September 1947, Archiv des Regierungskommissariats für die Provinz Bozen, Monatsberichte der Quästur Bozen 1947.

49 Summary of the Monthly Security Reports of Bozen State Police Department 1947, 1948, and 1949, Archiv des Regierungskommissariats für die Provinz Bozen, Kabinett.

50 Cf. TLA, Repertorium Bezirkshauptmannschaft Innsbruck-Land, Abt. II. 1947, RZ 23.

51 Cf. Stefan Lechner, 'Rückoption und Rücksiedlung nach Südtirol', in Klaus Eisterer and Rolf Steininger (eds.), *Die Option: Südtirol zwischen Faschismus und Nationalsozialismus*, Innsbrucker Forschungen zur Zeitgeschichte 5 (Innsbruck: Haymon, 1989), 369 ff.

52 'Subject: Indiscriminate Issuing and Use of Identity Documents of the International Red Cross', US Consul General Laurence G. Frank in Vienna to the US Foreign Minister, 20 January 1947 (TOP SECRET), and accompanying 'Summary of Information', 16 December 1946, NARA, RG 84, Austria, Political Adviser, General Records 1945–55, entry 2057, box 2.

53 Simon Wiesenthal, *Doch die Mörder leben* (Munich: Droemer, 1967), 109. Idem, *The Murderers Among Us* (London: Heinemann, 1967), 85.

54 Cf. Eva Pfanzelter, 'Zwischen Brenner und Bari: Jüdische Flüchtlinge in Italien 1945 bis 1948', in Thomas Albrich (ed.), *Flucht nach Eretz Israel: Die Bricha und der jüdische Exodus durch Österreich nach 1945* (Innsbruck: Studien Verlag, 1998), 225–52.

55 Albrich, *Flucht*, 7.

56 Ibid.

57 Cf. Eva Pfanzelter, *Südtirol unterm Sternenbanner: Die amerikanische Besatzung Mai–Juni 1945* (Bozen: Edition. Rætia, 2005), 234 f.

58 Report, 'Responsibility for Frontier Control', 1 September 1945, NARA, RG 331, ACC Italy, 11202/Bozen/128/84, box 8920.

59 Cf. Thomas Albrich, *Exodus durch: Österreich: Die jüdischen Flüchtlinge 1945–1948*, Innsbrucker Forschungen zur Zeitgeschichte 1 (Innsbruck: Haymon, 1987), 46.

60 Anton Weissteiner, *Auf verlorenem Posten: Südtiroler an fernen Fronten: Erinnerungen an den Zweiten Weltkrieg* (Bozen: Athesia, 2004), 151 ff.

61 Cf. Rudi Wagner, 'Wir Schmuggler vom Brennerpass', *Rudolph Nautilus Wagner* [website] <http://rudolf-nautilus-wagner.info/7.htm>, accessed 10 May 2007. Cf. idem, *Übergänge: Aus dem Tiroler Tagebuch eines Bergvagabunden, Schmugglers und Suppenfechters* (Bozen: Frasnelli-Keitsch, 1996), 85 ff.

62 Karl Schedereit, *SS-Mann Karrasch: Unvollständige Wahrnehmungen* (Bozen: Edition Rætia, 2006).

63 One exception to this is the denunciation of the South Tyrolean Gunther Langes, who hid away in a mountain village. In summer 1945 the US authorities received an anonymous letter: 'Dr. Gunther Langes, SS-Untersturmführer, is in Seis, where he has not left his flat for some weeks; he has 2 cars that he organised during the war.' Letter to the Allied Governor William McBratney, 1945, NARA, RG 331, ACC Italy 11202/Bolzano/143/19, box 8922.

64 Schedereit, *SS-Mann Karrasch*, 215 f.

65 NSDAP file, Reinhard Kops, born 29 September 1914, membership no. 7524143, NARA, RG 242, formerly BDC, NSDAP-Ortsgruppenkartei, reel L054.

66 Juan Maler [Reinhard Kops], *Frieden, Krieg und 'Frieden'* (San Carlos de Bariloche: Maler, 1987), 287 ff.

67 Ibid. 314.

68 Maler to Hudal, 21 December 1948, Anima, Nachlass Hudal, box 39.

69 Schedereit, *SS-Mann Karrasch*, 219.
70 Personnel file action request, 17 February 1964, Dr Karl Babor (SECRET), NARA, RG 263, CIA name files, box 5. SS-file Karl Babor, born 23 August 1918, SS no. 296.670, NARA, RG 242, formerly BDC.
71 Rena Giefer and Thomas Giefer, *Die Rattenlinie: Fluchtwege der Nazis, Eine Dokumentation* (Frankfurt am Main: Haine, 1991), 64 f.
72 Adolf Eichmann, 'Meine Flucht. Bericht aus der Zelle in Jerusalem', NARA, RG 263 (CIA), War Crimes, CIA name files, IWG, box 14, Eichmann, Adolf, vol. 1.
73 Jochen von Lang, *Das Eichmann-Protokoll: Tonbandaufzeichnungen der israelischen Verhöre* (Berlin: Severin and Siedler, 1982), 254 f.
74 Adolf Eichmann, 'Meine Flucht. Bericht aus der Zelle in Jerusalem', NARA, RG 263 (CIA), War Crimes, CIA name files, IWG, box 14, Eichmann, Adolf, vol. 1.
75 Ibid.
76 Ibid.
77 Ibid.
78 Ibid.
79 Ibid.
80 Hannah Arendt, *Eichmann in Jerusalem: Ein Bericht von der Banalität des Bösen* (Munich: Piper, 1986), 282.
81 Holger Meding, *Flucht vor Nürnberg? Deutsche und österreichische Einwanderung in Argentinien 1945–1955* (Cologne: Böhlau, 1992), 73.
82 Teja Fiedler, 'Nazis auf der Flucht. Teil 5: Das Verschwinden der Nazis', *Stern*, 13 (2005).
83 State Department report on Luis Trenker, 13 January 1949, 862.20235/1-1349, NARA, RG 59, name card index 1945–9, entry 200, box 464, 'Trenker Luis'.
84 Luis Trenker, *Alles gut gegangen: Geschichten aus meinem Leben* (3rd edn, Munich: Bertelsman, 1979), 456 ff.
85 Quoted in Gitta Sereny, *Into That Darkness: From Mercy Killing to Mass Murder, a Study of Franz Stangl, the Commandant of Treblinka* (London: Deutsch, 1974), 315.
86 Ulrich Völklein, *Josef Mengele: Der Arzt von Auschwitz* (Göttingen: Steidl, 1999), 187 f.
87 Gerald Posner and John Ware, *Mengele: Die Jagd auf den Todesengel* (Berlin: Aufbau-Verlag, 1993), 95.
88 Ibid. 117.
89 Sven Keller, *Günzburg und der Fall Josef Mengele: Die Heimatstadt und die Jagd nach dem NS-Verbrecher*, Schriftenreihe der Vierteljahrshefte für Zeitgeschichte 87 (Munich: Oldenbourg, 2003), 49–50.
90 Conversation with Werner Wechselberger, 22 March 2004.
91 'Mengele-Trauma in Gries', *Neue Tiroler Zeitung* (8 July 1985), 5. Cf. File on Jakob Strickner, Simon Wiesenthal Documentation Centre, Vienna.
92 Conversation with Hartmut Staffler, 17 April 2004.
93 'Keiner fragte nach seinen Taten', *Bunte*, 28 (1985), 26–34, 108.
94 Conversation with Richard Penz, 11 May 2004.
95 'Mengele-Trauma in Gries', *Neue Tiroler Zeitung* (8 July 1985), 5.
96 'Mengeles Flucht: Kein Vergleich zwischen Strickner und Hörtnagl', *Tiroler Tageszeitung* (5 Sept. 1985), 4.
97 'Mengele-Trauma in Gries', *Neue Tiroler Zeitung* (8 July 1985), 5.
98 Conversation with Andreas Hörtnagl, 15 March 2005.
99 'Mengele-Trauma in Gries', *Neue Tiroler Zeitung* (8 July 1985), 5.
100 Handwritten curriculum vitae of Jakob Strickner, NARA, RG 242, formerly BDC, Rasse- und Siedlungshauptamt, SS-file Jakob Strickner, born 19 November 1915.

101 Ibid.
102 Memo from Jakob Strickner to the Rasse- und Siedlungshauptamt, 12 August 1939, ibid.
103 Rasse- und Siedlungshauptamt form of Jakob Strickner, 14 February 1939, SS-Hauptscharführer, SS-no. 295065, NARA, ibid.
104 Research by Claus Larass for *Bunte* magazine 1985, MS, notes (copy in the possession of the author).
105 Erinnerungen von Franz Sparer aus Eppan, handschriftliche Notizen über die Zeit der Option bis 1946, written 1946. Private collection.
106 Ibid.
107 Stefan Karner, *Die Steiermark im Dritten Reich 1938–1945: Aspekte ihrer politischen wirtschaftlich-sozialen und kulturellen Entwicklung* (Graz: Leykam, 1986), 469.
108 Edith Blaschitz, 'NS-Flüchtlinge österreichischer Herkunft: Der Weg nach Argentinien', in Christine Schindler and Dokumentationsarchiv des österreichischen Widerstandes (eds.), *Jahrbuch 2003* (Vienna: Taschenbuch, 2003) 103–36 at 108.
109 Ibid. at 114.
110 Interrogation of Josef Schwammberger, 10 May 1990, Zentrale Stelle der Landesjustizverwaltungen Ludwigsburg, Akt Josef Schwammberger (copy in the possession of the author).
111 Erhebungsabteilung Landesgendarmeriekommando für Tirol an die Staatsanwaltschaft in Innsbruck, Innsbruck, 28 April 1949, on the investigations into the case of Walter Spitaler and Karl Folie, TLA, Bestand Landesgericht, Akt 10 Vr 873/49, p. 5.
112 Niederschrift aufgenommen mit Maria Folie, 6 May 1949, TLA, Bestand Landesgericht, ibid. 17.
113 Bundesministerium für Inneres an die Sicherheitsdirektion für Tirol, z.Hd. Herrn Sicherheitsdirektor, 2 April 1949 'Betr.: Menschenschmuggel von Österreich und Deutschland nach Argentinien' (STRICTLY CONFIDENTIAL!), TLA, Bestand Landesgericht, ibid. 15.
114 Landesgendarmeriekommando, Niederschrift, Verhör mit Karl Folie, Innsbruck am 25. 4. 1949, TLA, Bestand Landesgericht, ibid. 19.
115 Meding, *Flucht vor Nürnberg?*, 91 f.
116 Hans-Ulrich Rudel, *Zwischen Deutschland und Argentinien: Fünf Jahre in Übersee* (Göttingen: Plesse, 1954), 44.
117 Ibid. 43 ff.
118 Adolf Galland, *Die Ersten und die Letzten: Die Jagdflieger im Zweiten Weltkrieg* (Munich: Schneekluth, 1953).
119 Military Intelligence Service in Austria, 5 August 1946, Subject: Gestapo Linz (Confidential), NARA, RG 319, Records of the Army Staff, box 3, IRR impersonal files, folder 'Linz Dienststelle Gestapo', XE 020505.
120 Conversation with Martin Pollack, 23 March 2005.
121 Ibid.
122 Martin Pollack, *Der Tote im Bunker: Bericht über meinen Vater* (Vienna: Zsolnay, 2004), 244–53.
123 'Il morto nel fortino—I particolari dell'assassinio del clandestino al passo del Brennero', *Alto Adige*, 12 April 1947, 2.
124 Pollack, *Der Tote im Bunker*, 244–53.
125 Ibid. 251 f.
126 Wagner, *Übergänge*, 107.
127 Quoted from Edith Blaschitz, 'NS-Flüchtlinge österreichischer Herkunft, 110.

128 Cf. Stefan Lechner, '*Die Eroberung der Fremdstämmigen*', *Provinzfaschismus in Südtirol 1921–1926*, Veröffentlichungen des Südtiroler Landesarchivs 20, (Innsbruck: Wagner, 2005). Cf. Leopold Steurer, *Südtirol zwischen Rom und Berlin 1919–1939* (Vienna: Europaverlag, 1980), 256–71. Cf. Martha Verdorfer, *Zweierlei Faschismus: Alltagserfahrungen in Südtirol 1918–1945* (Vienna:Verlag für Gesellschaftskritik, 1990).

129 Cf. Rolf Steininger, *Südtirol im 20. Jahrhundert: Vom Leben und Überleben einer Minderheit* (Innsbruck: Studien, 1997); idem, *South Tyrol: A Minority Conflict of the Twentieth Century* (New Brunswick: Transaction, 2003); idem, *Alto Adige/Sudtirolo 1918–1999* (Innsbruck: Studien, 1999).

130 Claus Gatterer, 'Südtirol 1930-45. Eine politische Landschaftsskizze', in *Aufsätze und Reden* (Bozen: Edition Rætia, 1991), 171–84 at 177. This essay by Gatterer first appeared in Reinhold Iblacker (ed.), *Keinen Eid auf diesen Führer* (Innsbruck: Tyrolia, 1979), 34–46.

131 Steurer, *Südtirol zwischen Rom und Berlin*, 256–71. Cf. Helmut Alexander *et al.*, *Heimatlos: Die Umsiedlung der Südtiroler 1939–1945* (Vienna: Deuticke, 1993). Cf. Steininger, *South Tyrol: A Minority Conflict*.

132 Jochen von Lang, *Der Sekretär: Martin Bormann: Der Mann, der Hitler beherrschte* (Munich: Herbig, 1987), 332.

133 Report by William E. McBratney to CIC Bolzano, 13 May 1945, NARA, RG 331, ACC Italy 11202/Bolzano/128/ Provincial Commissioner /16, box 8916.

134 Rudolf Rahn, *Ruheloses Leben: Aufzeichnungen und Erinnerungen* (Düsseldorf: Diederichs, 1949), 295.

135 Gerald Steinacher and Philipp Trafoier, '"Ich mache Sie zum Erzbischof von Paris, wenn Sie uns helfen!" Die Flucht der Vichy-Regierung nach Südtirol 1945', *Der Schlern*, 1 (2007), 24–35.

136 Report of the Commander of the Carabinieri for the Province of Bozen, Amedeo Girone, on Maximilian Bernhuber, 28 September 1945, Staatsarchiv Bozen, Fondo Questura, file Q 542 'Soggiorno stranieri' 1945, 'Bernhuber Massimiliano'. Cf. Götz Aly and Jefferson Chase, *Hitler's Beneficiaries: Plunder, Racial War, and the Nazi Welfare State* (New York: Metropolitan, 2007), 187.

137 Cf. Pfanzelter, *Südtirol unterm Sternenbanner*, 120 ff.

138 'Il capo delle SS-italiane ucciso con la sua amante', *Alto Adige* (24 May 1945), 2. Cf. Pfanzelter, *Südtirol unterm Sternenbanner*, 87.

139 Cf. Akte I 110 AR 259/76, Beschuldigter Alois Schintlholzer u.a., Bundesarchiv/ Außenstelle Ludwigsburg (Barch LB), Bestand Zentrale Stelle der Landesjustizverwaltungen zur Aufklärung von NS-Verbrechen (B 162).

140 'Roster of Italian SS, Province of Bolzano', CIC lists, 22 May 1945, signed Stephen J. Spingarn, Chief CIC, 5th Army, NARA, RG 226 (OSS), entry 174, box 55, folder 449 (X-2 Rome, situation reports Bolzano area).

141 Bericht der Sicherheitsdirektion für Tirol, 7 September 1946 über Erwin Fleiss u.a., TLA, Bestand Landesgericht, Akte 10 Vr 104/46, 'Erwin Fleiss u.a.'.

142 'Altra belva nazista al laccio. Arrestato il maggiore Schintlholzer detto il massacratore degli ebrei', *Alto Adige*, 27 June 1947, 2. Cf. Federico Steinhaus, *Ebrei/Juden: Gli ebrei dell'Alto Adige negli anni trenta e quaranta* (Florence: Giuntina, 1994), 95.

143 TLA, Bestand Landesgericht, Akte 20 Vr 876/61, 'Alois Schintlholzer'.

144 Günter Gyseke, *Der Fall Priebke: Richtigstellung und Dokumentation* (Berg am Starnberger See: Druffel, 1997), 79–83.

145 Quoted from Joachim Staron, *Fosse Ardeatine und Marzabotto: Deutsche Kriegsverbrechen und Resistenza, Geschichte und nationale Mythenbildung in Deutschland und Italien (1944–1999)* (Paderborn: Schöningh, 2002), 330–1.

146 Letter from Erich Priebke to Axel-Elmar Schütz, 17 July 2003 (copy in possession of the author).

147 'Witness protocol, Rudolf Stötter, Escape of the SS-Sturmbannführer Rudolf Thyrolf and other SS-Führers', 4 June 1945, NARA, RG 226 (OSS), entry 174, box 127, folder 959.

148 'German Reprisal at Adreatinische Caves', September 1947, National Archives of England, Wales, and the United Kingdom, WO 310/137.

149 Statement by Erich Priebke quoted from Agnoletti, *Enklave Rimini-Bellaria*, 90.

150 The involvement of the Vatican or Catholic clerics in Priebke's flight has been disputed by church historians including Robert A. Graham. Cf. e.g. 'Arrestato in Argentina il boia delle Ardeatine', *L'Opinione* (11 May 1994), 11. On the accusations of escape aid in the Priebke case, cf. Peter van Meijl, *Pater Pancratius Pfeiffer und sein Einsatz für die Juden während der Besatzung in Rom (1943–1944)*, ed. von der Österreichischen Provinz der Salvatorianer (Vienna: Vallendar, 2007).

151 Uki Goñi, *Operazione Odessa: La fuga dei gerarchi nazisti verso l'Argentina di Perón* (Milan: Garzanto, 2003), 340 ff., 315–16.

152 Vorermittlungen wegen der Ermordung einer unbestimmten Anzahl von Juden im September 1943 in Maina und anderen Orten am Lago Maggiore (Italien) durch deutsche SS-Angehörige, Auswertung der Vernehmung von Dr. Martin Sandberger, 10 May 1960. Zentrale Stelle der Landesjustizverwaltungen Ludwigsburg, Beschuldigter Bosshammer Fritz, Akte 518 ARZ 4/63, Bl. 400, Bundesarchiv/Außenstelle Ludwigsburg (Barch LB), B 162.

153 'Witness protocol, Rudolf Stötter, Escape of the SS-Sturmbannführer Rudolf Thyrolf and other SS-Führers', 4 June 1945, NARA, RG 226 (OSS), entry 174, box 127, folder 959 pp. 3–4.

154 'First detailed interrogation report on SS Sturmbannführer Schiffer, August', October 1945, NARA, RG 226 (OSS), entry 194, box 65, folder 286, London X-2, p. 41.

155 NSDAP-file, Epp, Waldemar, born 12 April 1912, membership no. 3,720,692, NARA, RG 242, formerly BDC, NSDAP-Ortsgruppenkartei, reel E012.

156 Cf. Maria Keipert *et al.* (eds.), *Biographisches Handbuch des deutschen Auswärtigen Dienstes, 1871–1945*, vol. 1, A–F (Paderborn: Schöningh, 2000), 511 f.

157 Cf. Staatsarchiv Bozen, Fondo Questura, file Q. 632 'Soggiorno stranieri' 1946, 'Epp, Waldemar'.

158 NSDAP-file, von Jagow, Dietrich, membership no. 110,538, NARA, RG 242, formerly BDC, NSDAP-Zentralkartei, reel K0042.

159 Entry for Gábor and Elisabeth Kemény, 3 May 1945, Stadtarchiv Meran, Melderegister 1945 (Registro Statistica delle Migrazioni).

160 Cf. Rahn, *Ruheloses Leben*, 294 f.

161 Information from David Fliri, 31 March 2009.

162 Letter from the camp administration of Fossoli di Carpi to Bozen State Police Department, 18 November 1946, Staatsarchiv Bozen, Fondo Questura, file Q. 632 'Soggiorno stranieri 1946, 'Epp, Waldemar'.

163 Letter from Waldemar Epp to Bozen State Police Department, 2 December 1946, ibid.

164 Letter from Berta Baumgartner to Bozen State Police Department, 29 November 1946, ibid.

165 Petra Young-zie Barthelmess Röthlisberger, 'Tarnoperationen und Geheimgeschäfte auf dem Schweizer Finanzplatz: Verdeckte deutsch-schweizerische Umgehungsgeschäfte und die Frage der nationalsozialistischen Täterkonten im Zweiten Weltkrieg', D. Phil. dissertation, University of Zurich, Switzerland, 2006, 183.

166 Vernehmung des Beschuldigten Anton Malloth, 16 January 1948, Landesgericht Innsbruck, Archiv, Strafakte 34 Vr 1775/00 (Anton Malloth). Cf. Peter Finkelgruen, *Haus Deutschland oder die Geschichte eines ungesühnten Mordes* (Berlin: Rowohlt, 1994). Cf. 'Der schöne Toni', in *Der Spiegel*, 23 (1998), 50–3.

167 Völklein, *Mengele*, 225 ff.

168 Stadtgemeinde Meran, Meldeamt, index card Martha Mengele.

169 Gründungsurkunde der Gesellschaft Mengele und Steiner Gesmbh mit Sitz in Meran, Meran, 30 April 1969, Firmenunterlagen, Gesellschaft Mengele und Steiner Gesmbh, Archiv der Handelskammer Bozen.

170 Amtliche Deutsche Ein- und Rückwandererstelle, Zweigstelle Meran, Zweigstellenleiter Otto Vonier an den Sonderbeauftragten des Reichsführers SS und Chef der Deutschen Polizei, Bozen u.a., 30 July 1941, Bundesarchiv Berlin, former BDC, Einwandererzentralstelle EWZ, Südtiroler, file on Steiner Franz.

171 Bundesarchiv Berlin, former BDC, Einwandererzentralstelle EWZ, Südtiroler, file on Steiner Adolf.

172 Gründungsurkunde der Gesellschaft Mengele und Steiner Gesmbh mit Sitz in Meran, Meran, 30 April 1969, Firmenunterlagen, Gesellschaft Mengele und Steiner Gmbh, Archiv der Handelskammer Bozen.

173 Cf. Sitzungsprotokoll der Generalversammlung der Gesellschaft Mengele und Steiner, 10 February 1975, ibid.

174 Auszug aus dem Handelskammerregister, 'Mengele und Steiner Land- und Industriemaschinen', Handelskammer Bozen, 19 March 2004.

175 Cf. Ludwig Walter Regele, *Meran und das Dritte Reich: Ein Lesebuch* (Innsbruck: Studien, 2008).

176 'L'Eldorado dei collaborazionisti', *Alto Adige* (22 May 1947), 3.

177 'Falso nome e falsi documenti di un "nazi" collaborazionista', *Alto Adige* (30 May 1947), 2.

178 Headquarters 2677th Regiment, OSS, APO 777, US Army, Subject: Report of German-Austrian Desk for period ending 14 July (SECRET), 15 July 1944, signed John McCulloch, NARA, RG 226 (OSS), entry 210, box 74, folder 1.

179 Ernst Klee, *Persilscheine und falsche Pässe: Wie die Kirchen den Nazis halfen* (Frankfurt am Main: Fischer, 1991), 32 f.

180 Henry Kamm, 'German in Rome denies he sought to help Nazis', *New York Times* (23 February 1984), A 8.

181 Klee, *Persilscheine und falsche Pässe*, 33.

182 Michael Phayer, *The Catholic Church and the Holocaust, 1930–1965* (Bloomington: Indiana University Press, 2000), 168.

183 Quoted in Markus Langer, 'Alois Hudal, Bischof zwischen Kreuz und Hakenkreuz: Versuch einer Biografie', D. Phil. dissertation, University of Vienna, Austria, 1995, 191. Cf. dazu Collegio Santa Maria dell'Anima, Rom, Nachlass Hudal, box 48 (Österreich Komitee).

184 Alois Hudal, *Römische Tagebücher: Lebensbeichte eines alten Bischofs* (Graz: Stocker, 1976), 229.

185 Gerald Steinacher, *Südtirol und die Geheimdienste 1943–1945*, Innsbrucker Forschungen zur Zeitgeschichte 15 (Innsbruck: Studien, 2000), 108 ff.

186 'Notes on Fritz Rienzner, Provisional Consul of Austria in Bolzano Province', signed Major Harrison, AMG Bolzano, 26 January 1946, NARA, RG 331 ACC Italy/Bolzano, 10,000/109/158, 'Relations between Italy and Austria October 1945 to March 1946'.

187 Letter from Fritz Rienzner to Bozen State Police Department, 7 April 1946, Staatsarchiv Bozen, Fondo Questura, file Q 649 'Soggiorno stranieri' 1946, 'Rienzner Fritz'.

188 Michael Fahlbusch, 'Im Dienste des Deutschtums in Südosteuropa: Ethnopolitische Berater als Tathelfer für Verbrechen gegen die Menschlichkeit', in Mathias Beer and Gerhard Seewann (eds.), *Südostforschung im Schatten des Dritten Reiches. Institutionen—Inhalte—Personen*, Südosteuropäische Arbeiten 119 (Munich: Oldenbourg, 2004), 203 ff.

189 Valjavec to Riedl, 14 January 1948, Südtiroler Landesarchiv, Nachlass Franz Hieronymus Riedl, box 9.2, folder 'Post 1947/48'.

190 Hudal to Riedl, 24 April 1948, ibid.

191 Holger Meding, 'Nationalsozialismus im Exil: Die deutschsprachige Rechtspresse in Buenos Aires, 1945–1977', in idem (ed.), *Nationalsozialismus und Argentinien: Beziehungen, Einflüsse und Nachwirkungen* (Frankfurt am Main: Lang, 1995), 192.

192 On the history of 'Der Standpunkt' see Philipp Trafojer, 'La Voce del Padrone, Der Standpunkt: Ein italienisches Propagandamedium in Südtirol 1947–1957', in Gerald Steinacher (ed.), *Im Schatten der Geheimdienste: Südtirol 1918 bis zur Gegenwart* (Innsbruck: Studien, 2003), 161–86.

193 RG 331, ACC Italy, Subject File 1943–7, Genova Province, 11002/143 Public Safety, boxes 7867–76, cf. Monthly Security Report of Bozen State Police Department for August 1946, Archiv des Regierungskommissariats für die Provinz Bozen, Monatsberichte der Quästur Bozen 1946, report dated 31 August 1946.

194 'Conclusa la prima parte delle indagini per gli scellini falsificati', *Alto Adige* (18 May 1947), 2.

195 Cf. Eva Braun, *Il mio diario*, introd. D. W. Hewlett (Rome: Editrice 'Farro', 1948). Paul Tabori (ed.), *The Private Life of Adolf Hitler: The Intimate Notes and Diary of Eva Braun* (London: Aldor, 1949). 'Il diario di Eva Braun è nelle mani dell'attore Luigi Trenker', *Alto Adige* (15 February 1948), 1. The historian Roman Urbaner has carried out a detailed investigation into the background of the forgery, cf. *Quart Heft für Kultur Tirol*, 13 (2009).

196 Pubblica sicurezza, case di tolleranza, Stadtarchiv Meran, Bestand Gemeinde Meran, ZA 15 K, no. 2412.

197 'Come vivono gli stranieri irregolari? Un'organizzazione segreta provvede alla loro sistemazione', *Alto Adige* (22 April 1947), 2.

198 'Una banda di falsari presente all'appuntamento. Il sequestro di valuta italiana e straniera per un ingente valore nonché della attrezzatura per la compilazione di carte d'identità', *Alto Adige* (1 May 1947), 2.

199 'Come vivono gli stranieri irregolari? Un'organizzazione segreta provvede alla loro sistemazione', *Alto Adige* (22 April 1947), 2.

200 'Falso nome e falsi documenti di un "nazi" collaborazionista', *Alto Adige* (30 May 1947), 2.

201 Bundespolizeidirektion Innsbruck, Dringende Fahndung nach Kriegsverbrechern, 3 January 1948, Dokumentationsarchiv des Österreichischen Widerstandes Wien (DÖW), file Josef Schwammberger, signature 14848.

202 Aaron Freiwald, Martin Mendelsohn, *The Last Nazi: Josef Schwammberger and the Nazi Past* (New York: Norton, 1994), 163.

203 Carlota Jackisch, Cuantificación de Criminales de Guerra Según Fuentes Argentinas, informe final, *CEANA*, (1998) <http://www.ceana.org.ar/final/final.htm>, accessed 1 April 2007.

204 Application for a Red Cross travel document for Riccardo Klement, Italian Red Cross in Genoa, 1 June 1950. ICRC Geneva, Archive, 'Titres de Voyage CICR 1945–1993', application 100,940. Cf. Goñi, *Operazione Odessa*, 340 ff. Cf. 'Eichmanns gefälschter Pass entdeckt', *Der Spiegel* (30 May 2007).

205 David Cesarani, *Adolf Eichmann: Bürokrat und Massenmörder: Biografie* (Berlin: Propyläen, 2004), 296.

206 Application for a Red Cross travel document for Helmut Gregor, Italian Red Cross in Genoa, 16 May 1949. ICRC, Geneva, Archive, 'Titres de Voyage CICR 1945–1993', application 100, 501.

207 Pierangelo Giovanetti, 'La salvezza arrivò da Termeno', *l'Adige*, 30 July 2003, 15.

208 Application for a Red Cross travel document for Helmut Gregor, Italian Red Cross in Genoa, 16 May 1949, ICRC Geneva, Archive, 'Titres de Voyage CICR 1945–1993', application 100, 501.

209 Ibid.

210 Baptismal register of the parish of Tramin, 1911, microfilm, Südtiroler Landesarchiv Bozen.

211 Application for a Red Cross travel document for Francesco Noelke, Italian Red Cross in Genoa, 1 November 1950. ICRC Geneva, Archive, 'Titres de Voyage CICR 1945–1993', application 100, 958.

212 In the Bozen baptismal register, no birth is recorded in the name of Franz Noelke for 7 December 1906. Cf. Taufmatriken der Pfarre Maria Himmelfahrt Bozen, 1906, microfilm, Südtiroler Landesarchiv Bozen.

213 Report from Security Official Arno Pettinari to Bozen State Police Department, 28 December 1946, Staatsarchiv Bozen, Fondo Questura, file Q. 641 'Soggiorno stranieri' 1946, 'Kremhart Lona'.

214 Report from Security Official Lona Kremhart to the police (record section) in Bozen, 30 November 1946, Staatsarchiv Bozen, Fondo Questura, ibid.

215 Application for a Red Cross travel document for Kremhart Teodoro, ICRC Genoa, 31 October 1949, ICRC Geneva, Archive, 'Titres de Voyage CICR 1945–1993', application 100, 569.

216 Information from Deutsche Dienststelle (WASt) Berlin to the author concerning the case of Theodor Kremhart, b. 18 September 1905 in Posen, letters dated 8 March 2006 and 1 March 2007.

217 Cf. e.g. 'Una banda di falsari presente all'appuntamento: Il sequestro di valuta italiana e straniera per un ingente valore nonché della attrezzatura per la compilazione di carte d'identità', *Alto Adige*, 1 May 1947, 2.

218 Cf. e.g. Pierangelo Giovanetti, 'La salvezza arrivò da Termeno', 15.

219 Letter from the Marktgemeinde of Tramin to the author, 12 February 2004.

220 Cf. Hannah Arendt, *Eichmann in Jerusalem: A Report on the Banality of Evil* (New York: Viking, 1963), 240.

221 Adolf Eichmann, 'Meine Flucht: Bericht aus der Zelle in Jerusalem', NARA, RG 263 (CIA), War Crimes, CIA name files, IWG, box 14, Eichmann, Adolf, vol. 1.

222 Memorandum from the Director of Central Intelligence to the Asst. Chief of Staff, G-2, Department of the Army, 'Subject: Eugene Dollmann', 9 November 1951, NARA, RG 263 (CIA), War Crimes, IWG, box 11, Dollmann, Eugen.

223 Meding, *Flucht vor Nürnberg?*, 91 f.

224 Rudel, *Zwischen Deutschland und Argentinien*, 44 f.

225 Cf. Ronald C. Newton, *The 'Nazi Menace' in Argentina, 1931–1947* (Stanford: Stanford University Press, 1992), 376.

226 Application for a Red Cross travel document for Hermann Rudolf, ICRC Verona, 20 December 1946, ICRC Geneva, Archive, 'Titres de Voyage CICR 1945–1993', application 36, 079.

227 Application for a Red Cross travel document for Hufnagl Hermann, ICRC Verona, 20 December 1946, ICRC Geneva, ibid. application 36, 081.

228 Carabinieri report, Bozen, 4 June 1945, signed Renato Galgano, NARA, RG 331, ACC Italy, 11202/Bolzano 143/19/ box 8922.
229 'Un ufficiale delle SS. Fuori dal campo di Rimini dentro le carceri cittadine', *Alto Adige*, 1 June 1947, 3.

Chapter 2

1 'Subject: Indiscriminate Issuing and Use of Identity Documents of the International Red Cross', US Consul General Laurence G. Frank in Vienna to the US Secretary of State, 20 January 1947 (TOP SECRET), and accompanying 'Summary of Information', 16 December 1946, NARA, RG 84, Austria, Political Adviser, General Records 1945–55, entry 2057, box 2.
2 Robert Dempfer, *Das Rote Kreuz: Von Helden im Rampenlicht und diskreten Helfern* (Vienna: Deuticke, 2009), 63 ff.
3 The Geneva Conventions are a matter for individual states. Only those states who had ratified it could sign new conventions such as those concerning the protection of civilians. The role of the ICRC is limited; it is effectively mandated by the states bound by the convention to check their compliance and bring help and protection to the victims of war.
4 ICRC, ed., *The International Committee of the Red Cross in Geneva 1863–1943* (Zurich: Corzett & Huber, 1943).
5 Jean-Claude Favez, *The Red Cross and the Holocaust* (Cambridge: Cambridge University Press, 1999), 43.
6 Heiner Lichtenstein, *Angepasst und treu ergeben: Das Rote Kreuz im Dritten Reich* (Cologne: Bund, 1988), 93.
7 Ibid. 36.
8 Ibid.
9 Ibid. 63.
10 Ibid. 96.
11 Favez, *Red Cross and the Holocaust*, 224 ff., 270.
12 Margarethe Reimann, Meran, to the Secretariat of the Red Cross, Displaced Persons Section, Geneva, 11 October 1948, ICRC Geneva, Archives Générales, G. 68, Titres de voyage, box 954, Italie 1944–8, folder 'Titres de voyage: Italie'.
13 *Report of the International Committee of the Red Cross on its Activities during the Second World War (1939–1947)*, I. *General Activities*, Geneva 1948, 669 ff.
14 O. Lampanen, ICRC delegation in Rome, to ICRC Headquarters in Geneva, 29 September 1945, ICRC, Geneva, Archive/Agence, Titres de voyage, 1945–93, TVCR 1994.060, folder 00639.
15 Quoted in Langer, 'Alois Hudal, Bischof zwischen Kreuz und Hakenkreuz', 215.
16 Letter from Madame E. de Ribaupierre, ICRC Geneva, Division for Prisoners of War and Civilian Internees, 1949, ICRC Geneva, Archives Générales, G. 68, Titres de voyage, Italie 1949–50, box 955, folder 'Circulaire Fr. 30 c'.
17 Ibid.
18 H. W. de Salis, ICRC Rome to the Director of ICRC Milan, Samuel Girod, 29 January 1947, ICRC Geneva, Archive/Agence, Titres de voyage, 1945–93, TVCR 1994.060, folder 00642.
19 E. de Ribaupierre to the liaison office in Rome, 13 October 1949, ICRC Geneva, Archive/Agence, Titres de voyage, 1945–93, TVCR 1994.060, folder 00639.
20 List of the travel papers for the delegation in Rome, assembled by ICRC Headquarters in Geneva, December 1948, ICRC Geneva, Archive/Agence, Titres de voyage, 1945–93, TVCR 1994.060, folder 00639.

21 Letter from H. W. de Salis in Rome to Paul Kuhne in Geneva, 24 May 1947, ICRC Geneva, Archive/Agence, Titres de voyage, 1945–93, TVCR 1994.060, folder 00639.

22 List of the camp administration of Capua, signed Camp Director W. J. C. Davidge, 28 July 1949, ICRC, Geneva, Archive/Agence, Titres de voyage CICR (TV CICR) 1945–93.

23 Elías Juan Agusti, Consulate General of the Republic of Argentina in Genoa to the ICRC Delegate in Genoa, Leo Biaggi de Blasys, 24 August 1948, ICRC Geneva, Archive, Archives Générales, G. 68, Titres de voyage, box 954, Italie 1944–8, folder 'Titres de voyage: Italie'.

24 Letter from the ICRC delegate in Genoa, Leo Biaggi de Blasys, to the ICRC in Geneva, 3 September 1948, ICRC Geneva, Archive, Archives Générales, G. 68, Titres de voyage, box 954, Italie 1944–8, folder 'Titres de voyage: Italie'.

25 E. de Ribaupierre in Rome to the ICRC delegation for Italy in Rome, 27 October 1948, letter from the ICRC in Buenos Aires, 12 October 1948, to Geneva Headquarters, ICRC Geneva, Archive/Agence, Titres de voyage, 1945–93, TVCR 1994.060, folder 00639.

26 P. Kuhne of the ICRC in Geneva to the delegations in Rome, Genoa, Paris, and Vienna, 5 August 1948, ibid.

27 Dr. H. Zimmermann, Chief, IRO-Department of Repatriation and Resettlement in Rome, to ICRC Rome, 29 September 1948, ibid.

28 Letter from the IRO Mission in Rome to the ICRC in Rome, 14 December 1951, ICRC, Geneva, Archive, Titres de voyage, CICR 1945–93, application 65, 694.

29 Christiane Uhlig *et al.*, *Tarnung, Transfer, Transit: Die Schweiz als Drehscheibe verdeckter deutscher Operationen (1938–1952)*, ed. Unabhängige Expertenkommission Schweiz—Zweiter Weltkrieg (Zurich: Chronos, 2001), 190 f.

30 Memo Ministero dell'Interno, Direzione Generale della Pubblica Sicurezza, Rome, 1 March 1946 (URGENT), 'Oggetto: Apolidi—Documento speciale rilasciato dalla Croce Rossa Internazionale', ICRC Geneva, Archive, Archives Générales, G. 3/ 24 b /Titres de voyage, box 91 (1).

31 Quoted in Sereny, *Into that Darkness*, 312.

32 Hansjakob Stehle, 'Pässe vom Papst? Aus neuentdeckten Dokumenten: Warum alle Wege der Ex-Nazis nach Südamerika über Rom führten', *Die Zeit* (4 May 1984), 9–12 ('Dossier') at 10.

33 Horst Schreiber, *Die Machtübernahme: Die Nationalsozialisten in Tirol 1938/39*, Innsbrucker Forschungen zur Zeitgeschichte 10 (Innsbruck: Haymon, 1993), 65.

34 Wolfgang Meixner, ' "Arisierung"—die "Entjudung" der Wirtschaft im Gau Tirol-Vorarlberg', in Rolf Steininger and Sabine Pitscheider (eds.), *Tirol und Vorarlberg in der NS-Zeit*, Innsbrucker Forschungen zur Zeitgeschichte 19 (Innsbruck: Studien, 2003), 319–40.

35 Thomas Albrich, ' "Die Juden hinaus" aus Tirol und Vorarlberg: Entrechtung und Vertreibung 1938 bis 1940', in Steininger and Pitscheider (eds.), *Tirol und Vorarlberg in der NS-Zeit*, 299–317 at 305.

36 The political representative of the Austrian government in Rome, Dr Buresch, to Vice Prefect Giuseppe Migliore in the Ministry of the Interior and with an accompanying letter to Conte Vittorio Zoppi, Direttore Generale degli Affari Politici, Ministero Affari Esteri, Rome, 21 December 1946, ACS, Int. D. G., P. S., Div. AA. Massime 14, 'Istruzione di Polizia Militare', file 83, folder 69.

37 The political representative of the Austrian government in Rome, Dr. Buresch, collective passport, 10 June 1947, ibid.

38 Letter from the Fossoli di Carpi camp administration to the Ministry of the Interior in Rome about Hermann Duxneuner, 23 June 1947, ACS, Int. D.G., P.S., Div. AA. Massime 14, 'Istruzione di Polizia Militare', file 83, folder 69.

39 Application for a Red Cross travel document for Duxneuner Hermann, ICRC Rome, December 1946, letter from the PCA to ICRC Rome, 19 January 1948, ICRC Geneva, Archive, Titres de voyage CICR 1945–93, application 36, 075.

40 Report by the police chief of Bozen on Kurt Baum, 8 October 1946, Staatsarchiv Bozen, Fondo Questura, file Q. 628 'Soggiorno stranieri' 1946, 'Baum Kurt'.

41 Fossoli di Carpi camp administration to Bozen Questura, 4 September 1946, ibid.

42 Report from Carabinieri Commander of Bruneck, Aldo Pistono, on Kurt Baum, 20 July 1946, ibid.

43 SS file, Kurt Baum, born 3 November 1918, NARA, RG 242, formerly BDC, SS enlisted men.

44 Application for a Red Cross travel document for Baum Kurt, ICRC in S. Giovanni Lupatoto-Verona, 20 December 1946. ICRC Geneva, Archive, Titres de voyage CICR 1945–93, application 36, 074.

45 Maler [Kops], *Frieden, Krieg und 'Frieden'*, 325.

46 Vincent La Vista to Herbert J. Cummings, 15 May 1947 (TOP SECRET), NARA, RG 84, Austria, Political Adviser, Gen. Records 1945–55, entry 2057, box 2, p. 4.

47 Vincent La Vista to Herbert J. Cummings, 15 May 1947 (TOP SECRET), ibid. 2.

48 Ibid. appendix B, 10.

49 Department of State in Washington to the US Ambassador in Berne, Leland Harrison, 11 July 1947, letter accompanying the report by Vincent La Vista to Herbert J. Cummings, 15 May 1947 (TOP SECRET), NARA, RG 59, D-File 1945–49, box 4082, 800.142/5-1547.

50 Graham Parsons to the Division of Southern European Affairs, Department of State, Washington DC, 29 August 1947 (TOP SECRET), copy, Simon Wiesenthal Dokumentationszentrum Wien, Akte Walter Rauff.

51 Stehle, 'Pässe vom Papst?', 10.

52 *L'Unità* reported on this on 29 and 31 January, *Il quotidiano* on 1, 2, and 4 February, and *L'Osservatore Romano* on 2 February 1947.

53 ICRC Geneva to the Italian Ambassador in Berne, Egidio Reale, 21 March 1947, signed by the Vice-Presidents of the ICRC, Martin Bodmer und Ernest Gloor, ICRC Geneva, Archive, Agence, Titres de voyage, 1945–93, TVCR 1994.060, folder 00637.

54 Sereny, *Into that Darkness*, 315.

55 Ibid. 316.

56 Quoted in ibid. 317.

57 Uhlig *et al.*, *Tarnung, Transfer, Transit*, 193.

58 Red Cross travel documents; visit from Herr Kühne, Schürch to Rothemund, 17 February 1948, Schweizerisches Bundesarchiv BAR, E 4260 (C) 1974/34, vol. 194.

59 Margarethe Reimann, Meran, to the Secretariat of the Red Cross, Displaced Persons Section, Geneva, 11 October 1948, ICRC Geneva, Archive, Archives Générales, G. 68, Titres de voyage, box 954, Italie 1944–8, folder 'Titres de voyage: Italie'.

60 ICRC Geneva, Prisoners of War Section, to ICRC Rome, 7 May 1948, signed E. de Ribaupierre, ICRC Geneva, Archive, Archives Générales, G. 3/ 24 b /Titres de voyage, box 91 (1).

61 Hans Wolf de Salis, ICRC Director in Rome, to M. P. Kuhne, 5 March 1948, ICRC Geneva, Archive/Agence, Titres de voyage, 1945–93, TVCR 1994.060, folder 00639.

62 ICRC Geneva to the ICRC delegation in Rome, 18 January 1949, ibid.

63 Letter from Denise Werner, ICRC Rome, to Geneva Headquarters, 15 December 1948, ibid.

64 Application for a Red Cross travel document for Marko Ćalušić, ICRC Rome, 19 November 1947; letter from the PCA to ICRC Rome, 18 November 1947. ICRC Geneva, Archive, 'Titres de voyage CICR 1945–1993', application 68,676. ICRC Rome, June 1946, application 26, 420.

65 Letter from Denise Werner, ICRC Rome, to Geneva headquarters, 21 December 1948, ICRC Geneva, Archive/Agence, Titres de voyage, 1945–93, TVCR 1994.060, folder 00639.

66 Quoted in Sereny, *Into that Darkness*, 317.

67 Application for a Red Cross travel document for Bottcher Enrico, ICRC Rome, 25 September 1947, ICRC Geneva, Archive, 'Titres de Voyage CICR 1945–1993', application 65, 609.

68 ICRC Rome to E. de Ribaupierre, Legal Department, ICRC Geneva, 28 September 1949, ICRC Geneva, Archive/Agence, Titres de voyage, 1945–93, TVCR 1994.060, folder 00639.

69 ICRC Geneva, Archive, Archives Générales, G. 68, Titres de voyage, Italie 1949–50, box 955, folder 'passeports Croix-Rouge falsifiés'.

70 ICRC delegation in Rome to the Legal Department of the ICRC Geneva, 4 February 1949 (CONFIDENTIAL), signed Denise Werner, ICRC Geneva, ibid.

71 His time in office coincided with the commencement in 1949 of the version of the Geneva Convention still valid today and a revision of the statutes of the International Red Cross. Numerous trips in 1948 brought him, among other places, to the United States in 1948, the Soviet Union in 1950, and China in 1951. In September 1955 he was replaced by Léopold Boissier as President of the ICRC. Even after stepping down from this post, he remained a member of the ICRC until his death in 1988.

72 Cf. Stefan Glur, *Vom besten Pferd im Stall zur persona non grata: Paul Ruegger als Schweizer Gesandter in Rom 1936–1942* (Bern: Lang, 2005).

73 After several years as an ICRC special delegate, Burckhardt had been unanimously elected president of the ICRC on 4 December 1944, effective 1 January 1945. Burckhardt initially admired some facets of Nazi ideology. Apart from a fundamental love of German history and culture, he also displayed a perceptible trace of anti-Semitism. Cf. Paul Stauffer, 'Grandseigneuraler "Anti-Intellektueller": Carl J. Burckhardt in den Fährnissen des totalitären Zeitalters', in Aram Mattioli (ed.), *Intellektuelle von rechts: Ideologie und Politik in der Schweiz 1918–1939* (Zurich: Orel Füssli, 1995), 113–34. Cf. Paul Stauffer, *'Sechs furchtbare Jahre...': Auf den Spuren Carl J. Burckhardts durch den Zweiten Weltkrieg* (Zurich: Verlag Neue Zürcher Zeitung, 1998).

74 'Procès-verbal d'une séance', 24 May 1949, ICRC, Geneva, Archive, Archives Générales, G. 68, Titres de voyage, Italie 1949–50, box 955, folder 'passeports Croix-Rouge falsifiés'.

75 Dr Ercole Costa, ICRC liaison office, Rome, to Paul Ruegger, ICRC President, Geneva, 5 July 1950. Archiv für Zeitgeschichte Zürich, NL Paul Ruegger 28.2.9.1, correspondence spring 1948 to mid-August 1955.

76 Paul Ruegger to Ercole Costa, 14 July 1950, ibid.

77 Memo Ministero dell'Interno, Direzione Generale della Pubblica Sicurezza, Rome, 2 April 1948, 'Oggetto: Documento di viaggio per profughi stranieri', ICRC Geneva, Archive, Archives Générales, G. 3/ 24 b /Titres de voyage, box 91 (1).

78 PCA Rome, foreign office, President Ferdinando Baldelli to ICRC President Paul Ruegger, Geneva, 6 September 1947, ICRC Geneva, Archive, Archives Générales, G. 68, Titres de voyage, Italie 1944–7, box 954.

79 IRO, Department of Repatriation and Resettlement, Rome, to ICRC Geneva, 5 September 1947, signed C. B. Findlay, Chief of the Department of Repatriation and Resettlement, ICRC Geneva, Archive, Archives Générales, G. 68, Titres de voyage, Italie 1944–7, box 954.

80 Cf. e.g. a letter from the ICRC delegate in Genoa, Leo Biaggi de Blasys, to ICRC Geneva, 19 June 1950, ICRC Geneva, Archive, Archives Générales, G. 68, Titres de voyage, Italie 1949–50, box 955, folder 'Titres de voyage: Italie'.

81 Slovenian Welfare Society for Emigration in Rome to the President of the ICRC Paul Ruegger, Geneva, 9 June 1950, ibid.

82 La Confraternità dei Croati di San Girolamo, Roma, 132 Via Tomacelli, to the President of ICRC Geneva, Paul Ruegger, 7 June 1950, signed Krunoslav Draganović and Juraj Magjerec, ibid.

83 Ibid.

84 Ibid.

85 ACS, Stranieri ed Ebrei Stranieri (1930–56), file 32, folder 15, IRO—Emigrazione: Imbarco per Bolivia 1951.

86 Letter from E. de Ribaupierre of ICRC in Geneva to Draganović in Rome, 4 September 1950, ICRC Geneva, Archive, Archives Générales, G. 68, Titres de voyage, Italie 1949–50, box 955, folder 'Circulaire Fr. 30 c'.

87 Krunoslav Draganović to E. de Ribaupierre in Geneva, 22 September 1950, ICRC Geneva, Archive/Agence, Titres de voyage, 1945–93, TVCR 1994.060, folder 00639.

88 E. de Ribaupierre in Geneva to Krunoslav Draganović in Rome, 28 May 1951, ibid.

89 Letter from Prof. Krunoslav Draganović to Mme de Ribaupierre of ICRC Geneva, 2 August 1950, ibid.

90 Ibid.

91 E. de Ribaupierre in Geneva to Krunoslav Draganović in Rome, 4 September 1950, ibid.

92 Letter from the ICRC delegate in Genoa, Leo Biaggi de Blasys, to Madame E. de Ribaupierre of ICRC Geneva, 6 July 1950, ICRC Geneva, Archive, Archives Générales, G. 68, Titres de voyage, Italie 1949–50, box 955, folder 'Circulaire Fr. 30 c'.

93 Letter from E. de Ribaupierre to ICRC President Paul Ruegger, 28 August 1950, ICRC Geneva, Archive, Archives Générales, G. 68, Titres de voyage, Italie 1949–50, box 955, folder 'Titres de voyage: Italie'.

94 E. de Ribaupierre to Umberto Vaccari, AGIUS in Rome, 15 March 1951, ICRC Geneva, Archive/Agence, Titres de voyage, 1945–93, TVCR 1994.060, folder 00639.

95 'Konzept für einen Tätigkeitsbericht der Freiw. Rett. Ges. Ibk.', Bericht über die erste Jahreshauptversammlung der Freiwilligen Rettungsgesellschaft Innsbruck nach dem Krieg, 25 January 1947, Freiwillige Rettung Innsbruck, Archiv.

96 Ibid.

97 Cf. Titres de voyage Innsbruck 1950, ICRC, Archives Générales G. 68, 'Titres de Voyage', 6/1/28, Autriche 1944–50.

98 Application for a Red Cross travel document for Mohr Josef, ICRC Innsbruck, 26 January 1949. Letter from the IRO delegate in Graz to ICRC Innsbruck, 21 January 1949, ICRC Geneva, Archive, 'Titres de voyage CICR 1945–93', application 86, 739.

99 Application for a Red Cross travel document for Peter Grün, ICRC Innsbruck, 5 July 1949, ICRC Geneva, Archive, 'Titres de Voyage CICR 1945–93', application 100, 669.

100 See ICRC Geneva, Archive, G. 68, Titres de voyage, Autriche, folder 'Innsbruck 1950'.

101 Cf. Peter Gosztonyi, *A Kormányzó Horthy Miklós és az Emigráció* (Budapest: Százszorszép Kiadó, 1992).

102 Conversation with Ferencz Stolicz, 27 December 2005.

103 Application for a Red Cross travel document for Dr Wilhelm Bako, ICRC Rome, September 1945, ICRC Geneva, Archive, 'Titres de Voyage CICR 1945–1993', application 7, 106.

104 Application for a Red Cross travel document for Dr Detre Barczy, ICRC Rome, September 1945, ibid. 7, 107.

105 Conversation with Piroska Sapinsky, 7 January 2006.

106 Norman J. W. Goda, 'Nazi Collaborators in the United States: What the FBI Knew', in Richard Breitman *et al.* (eds.), *U.S. Intelligence and the Nazis* (Washington, DC: National Archives and Records Administration, 2004), 227–64 at 231.

107 Mark Aarons and John Loftus, *Unholy Trinity: How the Vatican's Nazi Networks Betrayed Western Intelligence to the Soviets* (New York: St Martin's, 1992), 59–69.

108 Vincent La Vista to Herbert J. Cummings, 15 May 1947 (TOP SECRET) NARA, RG 84, Austria, Political Adviser, Gen. Records 1945–55, entry 2057, box 2, app. D, 2.

109 OSS Report 'Hungarian Red Cross in Rome', June 1945 (SECRET), NARA, RG 226 OSS, entry 211, box 49, folder 'Hungarian Red Cross'.

110 CIC Report 'Additional information on agents and suspects recently arrived in Rome', 8 February 1946 (SECRET), NARA, RG 263 (CIA), box 51, folder 'Tarno de Tharno Ladislao'.

111 William E. McBratney to ICRC Geneva, 21 May 1945, NARA, RG 331, ACC Italy, 11202/Bolzano/128/Prov. Commissioner/6, box 8916.

112 AMG II. Corps Josephine McNamara to McBratney, 25 May 1945, ibid.

113 Application for a Red Cross travel document for Klaus Altmann, ICRC Genoa, 16 March 1951, ICRC Geneva, Archive, Titres de Voyage CICR 1945–1993, application 18, 573.

114 Application for a Red Cross travel document for Altmann Regina, ICRC Genoa, 15 March 1951, ibid. 18, 574.

115 Letter of recommendation for Franz Geyer, PCA, Foreign Section, Rome, 3 March 1947, signed F. Echarri, ibid. 47, 801.

116 PCA, Foreign Section, 23 Via Piave, Rome, letter of recommendation to ICRC Rome for Franz Geyer, 3 March 1947, ibid.

117 Application for a Red Cross travel document for Franz Geyer, ICRC Rome, 5 March 1947, ibid.

118 Letter from the Styrian State Archive to the author, 4 January 2005.

119 Application for a Red Cross travel document for Otto Pape, ICRC Rome, 26 July 1948, ICRC Geneva, Archive, 'Titres de Voyage CICR 1945–1993', application 83, 023.

120 Christoph Franceschini, 'Der Feinschmecker aus Bariloche', in *Südtirol profil*, 20/16 (May 1994), 12–16 at 15.

121 Erich Priebke and Paolo Giachini, *Autobiographie 'Vae victis' (Wehe den Besiegten)* (Rome: n.pub., 2003), 200.

122 Ibid. 201.

123 Application for a Red Cross travel document for Otto Pape, ICRC Rome, 26 July 1948, ICRC Geneva, Archive, 'Titres de Voyage CICR 1945–1993', application 83, 023.

124 Application for a Red Cross travel document for Richwitz Hans, ICRC Rome, 10 November 1949, ibid. 97, 583.

125 Eckhard Schimpf, *Heilig: Die Flucht des Braunschweiger Nazifführers auf der Vatikan-Route nach Südamerika* (Braunschweig: Appelhans, 2005), 106.

126 Application for a Red Cross travel document for Freisleben Hubert Karl, ICRC Rome, 28 August 1947, ICRC Geneva, Archive, 'Titres de Voyage CICR 1945–1993', application 62, 175.

127 SS-file, Dr Hubert von Freisleben, born 20 September 1913, SS no. 304,163, NARA, RG 242, formerly BDC.

128 Application for Red Cross travel documents for Filippo, Theresia, und Susanne Heimberger, ICRC Rome, 17 November 1948, ICRC Geneva, Archive, 'Titres de Voyage CICR 1945–1993', applications 90,167; 90,168; 90,169.

129 Application for a Red Cross travel document for Ernst Wilhelm, ICRC Rome, 31 March 1948, letter of recommendation from the PCA in Rome for Ernst Wilhelm, 7 April 1948, ibid. 74, 974.

130 Letter from Evangelische Kirchengemeinde Hermannstadt (Sibiu) to the author, 31 May 2006.

131 Application for a Red Cross travel document for Gualtiero Schindler, ICRC Rome, 20 November 1947, letter of recommendation from the PCA in Rome for Schindler Gualtiero, 14 January 1948, ICRC Geneva, Archive, 'Titres de Voyage CICR 1945–1993', application 65, 607.

132 Application for a Red Cross travel document for Josef Schwammberger, ICRC Rome, 13 November 1948, letter from the PCA for Josef Schwammberger, 3 November 1948, ibid. application 90, 143.

133 'Una banda di falsari presente all'appuntamento. Il sequestro di valuta italiana e straniera per un ingente valore nonché della attrezzatura per la compilazione di carte d'identità', *Alto Adige* (1 May 1947), 2.

134 Application for a Red Cross travel document for Riccardo Klement, ICRC Genoa, 1 June 1950, ICRC Geneva, Archive, 'Titres de Voyage CICR 1945–1993', application 100, 940.

135 Ibid.

136 David Cesarani, *Eichmann, His Life and Crimes* (London: Heinemann, 2004), 209. Cf. Andrea Casazza, *La fuga dei nazisti: Mengele, Eichmann, Priebke, Pavelić da Genova all'impunità* (Genoa: Il melangolo, 2007). On pp. 43–8 Casazza pays particular attention to the background of the Hungarian Franciscan priest Eduard (Lajos) Dömöter.

137 Goñi, *Operazione Odessa*, 356.

138 Cesarani, *Eichmann*, 209 ff.

139 Simon Wiesenthal to Nahum Goldmann, 30 March 1954, NARA, RG 263 (CIA), War Crimes, CIA name files, IWG, box 14, Eichmann, Adolf, vol. 1.

140 Application for a Red Cross travel document for Helmut Gregor, ICRC Genoa, 16 May 1949, ICRC Geneva, Archive, 'Titres de Voyage CICR 1945–1993', application 100, 501.

141 Application for a Red Cross travel document for Francesco Noelke, ICRC Genoa, 1 November 1950, ibid. 100, 958.

142 Application for a Red Cross travel document for Niermann Ernst August, ICR Genoa, 7 June 1948, ibid. 13, 131.
143 Application for a Red Cross travel document for Werner Baumbach, ICRC Genoa, 7 June 1948, ibid. 13, 132.
144 Georg Brütting, *Das waren die deutschen Kampfflieger-Asse 1939–1945* (Stuttgart: Motorbuch, 1991), 34 ff.
145 Application for a Red Cross travel document for Bauer Herbert, ICRC Rome, 5 April 1948, letter of recommendation from the PCA in Rome, signed Francesco Echarri, 6 April 1948, ICRC Geneva, Archive, Titres de Voyage CICR 1945–1993, application 74, 969.
146 Uhlig *et al.*, *Tarnung, Transfer, Transit*, 195 f.
147 Lichtenstein, *Angepasst und treu ergeben*, 148.

Chapter 3

1 Vincent La Vista to Herbert J. Cummings, 15 May 1947 (TOP SECRET), NARA, RG 84, Austria, Political Adviser, Gen. Records 1945–55, entry 2057, box 2, 2.
2 Cf. amongst others: 'Two Church Historians Deny that Vatican Helped Nazis Escape', *New York Times* (30 January 1984), A 1, A 7.
3 Pierre Blet *et al.* (eds.), *Actes et Documents du Saint Siège relatifs à la Seconde Guerre mondiale*, 11 vols. (Vatican City: Libreria Editrice Vaticana, 1965–81).
4 'Tod in Rom', *Der Spiegel*, 6 (1984), 122–5 at 125.
5 Monsignor Montini served as Under-Secretary of State when Pius II appointed him to that post in 1939. He served in that capacity until 12 January 1953 when Pius II appointed Montini Pro-Secretary of State for Ordinary Affairs and Monsignor Tardini Pro-Secretary of State for Extraordinary Affairs. J. L. Gonzalez and T. Perez, *Paul VI*, tr. Edward L. Heston (Boston: Daughters of St Paul, 1964), 20, 171.
6 Pontificia Commissione Assistenza Profughi, *Organizzazione* (Rome: n.pub., 1944). Comune di Roma, Archivio storico capitolino, library. Cf. *Caritas. Bollettino della Pontificia Commissione Assistenza* 1 (May 1947). Cf. 'Charitas' nella Diocesi dell'Aquila. 'L'opera della Pontificia Commissione Assistenza, dal febbraio 1945 al febbraio 1950', extract from *Bollettino Diocesano dell'Aquila*, 29/3–4 (March–April 1950).
7 'I Nazisti a Genova', *Il secolo XIX* <http://www.ilsecoloxix.it/Oggetti/3431.pdf >, accessed 15 May 2007.
8 Andrea Lazzarini, *Papst Paul VI: Sein Leben und seine Gestalt* (Freiburg: Herder, 1964), 156.
9 Pascalina Lehnert, *Ich durfte ihm dienen: Erinnerungen an Papst Pius XII* (Würzburg: Naumann, 1982), 103.
10 Lazzarini, *Papst Paul VI*, 59.
11 Bishop Jakob Weinbacher in Sereny, *Into That Darkness*, 306.
12 Lehnert, *Ich durfte ihm dienen*, 101.
13 John Cornwell, *Hitler's Pope: The Secret History of Pius XII* (New York: Viking, 1999).
14 Peter C. Kent, *The Lonely Cold War of Pope Pius XII: The Roman Catholic Church and the Division of Europe 1943–1950* (Montreal: McGill-Queen's University Press, 2002), 26 ff.
15 Cf. Gerhard Besier, 'Eugenio Pacelli, die Römisch-Katholische Kirche und das Christentum (1933–1945) in historisch-religiöser Kritik', in Rainer Bendel (ed.), *Die katholische Schuld? Katholizismus im Dritten Reich zwischen Arrangement und Widerstand* (Munich: Lit, 2002), 200–20 at 200 f.

16 Cf. Pietro Scoppola, 'Gli orientamenti di Pio XI e Pio XII sui problemi della società contemporanea', in Elio Guerriero (ed.), *La chiesa in Italia: Dall'unità ai nostri giorni* (Milan: San Paolo, 1996), 359–90.

17 Cf. Lucia Scherzberg, 'Theologie und Vergangenheitsbewältigung im interdisziplinären Vergleich, Tagungsbericht von der Tagung des Instituts für Katholische Theologie der Universität des Saarlandes und der Katholischen Akademie Trier, Abteilung Saarbrücken, im Robert-Schuman-Haus, Trier, 14–16 January 2005', *Theologie Geschichte* [website], (2006), http://aps.sulb.uni-saarland.de/theologie.geschichte/inhalt/2006/04.html>, accessed 3 October 2008.

18 Cf. Kevin P. Spicer, *Hitler's Priests: Catholic Clergy and National Socialism* (DeKalb: Northern Illinois University Press, 2008), 168.

19 Cf. Cornwell, *Hitler's Pope*; cf. Phayer, *The Catholic Church and the Holocaust* and idem, *Pius XII*. Cf. Susan Zuccotti, *Under His Very Windows: The Vatican and the Holocaust in Italy* (New Haven: Yale University Press, 2000). Daniel J. Goldhagen, *A Moral Reckoning: The Role of the Catholic Church in the Holocaust and its Unfulfilled Duty of Repair* (New York: Knopf, 2002). Cf. Giovanni Miccoli, *I dilemmi e i silenzi di Pio XII* (Milan: Rizzoli, 2000).

20 Matteo Napolitano and Andrea Tornielli have repeatedly defended Pope Pius XII. Recently, Tornielli's book *Pius XII: A Man on St Peter's Throne*, caused a furore when it was published in Italy in 2007; in it the author claims that the Pope was engaged in large-scale rescue operations for the Jews of Rome. Cf. Andrea Tornielli, *Pio XII: Eugenio Pacelli, un' uomo sul trono di Pietro* (Milan: Mondadori, 2007). Cf. 'Bertone; il nazismo e Pio XII. Leggenda nera la sua indulgenza', *Corriere della Sera* (6 June 2007), 17. Cf. also 'Le accuse a Pio XII: quando nasce Israele', *La Repubblica* (6 June 2007), 50. Matteo Luigi Napolitano and Andrea Tornielli, *Pio XII: Il papa degli ebrei* (Casale Monferrato: Piemme, 2002). Andrea Tornielli and Matteo Luigi Napolitano, *Pacelli, Roncalli e i battesimi della shoah* (Casale Monferrato: Piemme, 2005).

21 The Vatican reacted to the altered situation and made available archives on the Papal Nuncio in Germany until 1939, Eugenio Pacelli, the future Pope Pius XII. The archives on the pontificate of Pius XII (from 1939) remain inaccessible. Individual dioceses, religious orders, and institutes in Italy are granting researchers more access to archives. Cf. Suzanne Brown-Fleming is working on the book *The Vatican–German Relationship Re-Examined, 1922–1939* (research in progress). A study of the recently released (2003) records of the Vatican nunciature in Munich and Berlin during the Weimar Republic and the period of Eugenio Pacelli's tenure as Secretary of State (1930–9) have been available (since 2005) in the archives of the USHMM in Washington, DC.

22 Peter Hebblethwaite, *Paul VI: The First Modern Pope* (New York: Paulist, 1993), 214.

23 Cf. Lazzarini, *Papst Paul VI*.

24 Phayer, *Catholic Church*, 211.

25 Hebblethwaite, *Paul VI*, 166.

26 Central amongst the predecessors of the Papal refugee agency was Relief for Converted Jews and Persecuted Catholics from Germany and Austria. The Vatican helped several hundred people to travel overseas, mostly to South America. This relief largely came to an end when Italy entered the war in 1940. The organization of emigration via Spain to South America was transferred to a representative of the St Raphael Association in the Pallotine Convent in Rome. Cf. Klaus Voigt, *Zuflucht auf Widerruf: Exil in Italien 1933–1945*, 2 vols. (Stuttgart: Klett-Cotta, 1989), i, 374 ff.

27 As a research term, 'anticommunism' (not in the sense in which it has been developed individually in the extensive Eastern European and sparse transatlantic anticommunism research and literature, but in a general sense) characterizes an attitude which fundamentally rejects all social models that it deems to be communist. It includes within its critique all the considerations, conceptions, and ideas that are

supposedly aimed at the same communist model of society that it sees as being realized in the states it deems to be communist. These communist states, in turn, are
reduced only to their negative historical manifestations.

28 Sereny, *Into That Darkness*, 301.

29 Gertrude Dupuis in Sereny, *Into That Darkness*, 315.

30 Vincent La Vista to Herbert J. Cummings, 15 May 1947 (TOP SECRET), NARA, RG
84, Austria, Political Adviser, Gen. Records 1945–55, entry 2057, box 2, app. B,
p. 5.

31 Ferdinando Baldelli, 'Activity of P.C.A. in Italy from 1944–1947', 1947, Catholic
University of America, Washington, DC, University Archives, File NCWC, box 22,
folder 'Church Holy Father 1944–1949', 10/22/7.

32 Cf. Lisa C. Moreno, 'The National Catholic Welfare Conference and Catholic
Americanism, 1919–1966', Ph.D. dissertation, University of Maryland, College
Park, 1999.

33 John Cooney, *The American Pope: The Life and Times of Francis Cardinal Spellman* (New
York: Times Books, 1984).

34 Years later, for example, Spellman saw the deployment of American troops in the
Vietnam War as an 'anticommunist crusade'.

35 Kent, *The Lonely Cold War*, 63 ff.

36 Paul I. Murphy and René Arlington, *La Popessa* (New York: Warner, 1983), 184.

37 Stehle, 'Pässe vom Papst?', 12.

38 Cf. 'Monsignor Andrew P. Landi (1906–1999)', in the Catholic Church, Diocese of
Brooklyn (ed.), *Diocese of Immigrants: The Brooklyn Catholic Experience 1853–2003* (Strasbourg: Éditions du Signe, 2004), 103.

39 Stehle, 'Pässe vom Papst?', 16.

40 Paul Ginsborg, *A History of Contemporary Italy: Society and Politics 1943–1988* (London:
Penguin, 1990), 79.

41 Charles R. Morris, *American Catholic: The Saints and Sinners Who Built America's Most
Powerful Church* (New York: Times Books, 1997), 246 f.

42 Memorandum from the Papal Delegate to the USA, Amleto Giovanni Kardinal
Cicognani to Monsignor Howard J. Carroll von der Katholischen Bischofskonferenz
NCWC, 7 February 1948, Catholic University of America, Washington, DC, Uni-
versity Archives, Bestand NCWC, box 25, folder 'Communism Italy 1944–1954'.

43 IRO-Hauptquartier, Preparatory Commission, in Geneva to the US Ambassador in
Rome, James C. Dunn, 10 September 1947 (STRICTLY CONFIDENTIAL), NARA, RG
84, Italy, US embassy Rome, Classified General Records, 1947, box 20.

44 Cf. Suzanne Brown-Fleming, *The Holocaust and Catholic Conscience: Cardinal Aloisius
Muench and the Guilt Question in Germany, 1946–1959* (Notre Dame: U of Notre Dame
P, 2005).

45 Letter from Bishop Aloisius Muench, Apostolic Nuncio in Germany, to John J. Mc-
Cloy, US High Commissioner for Germany, 19 December 1949, NARA, RG 466
HICOG, McCloy papers, entry 1, 1950, box 6, folder D (50) 57.

46 'Report. War Relief Services—National Catholic Welfare Conference. Mission
to South America in interest resettlement of Displaced Persons. Rev. Msgr. John
O'Grady, Carl C. Taylor, J. Henry Amiel', 1 July 1947, Catholic University of
America, Washington, DC, University Archives, file NCWC, box 36, folder 'Displaced Persons 1947' 10/36/35.

47 Edward J. Killion of the Vatican Migration Bureau in Geneva to Bruce M. Mohler
of the NCWC Immigration Bureau, Washington, DC, 21 November 1949, Catholic University of America, Washington, DC, University Archives, file NCWC, box
36, folder 'Displaced Persons 1948–49' 11/21/49.

48 Edward J. Killion of the Vatican Migration Bureau in Geneva to Howard J. Carroll of the NCWC in Washington, DC, 6 November 1948, Catholic University of America, Washington, DC, University Archives, ibid. 11/12/48.

49 Klee, *Persilscheine und falsche Pässe*, 33.

50 Pontificia Commissione Assistenza Profughi, *Organizzazione*.

51 Christopher Simpson, *Blowback: America's Recruitment of Nazis and Its Effects on the Cold War* (New York: Weidenfeld & Nicolson, 1988), 217.

52 Cf. Manfred Gailus, *Protestantismus und Nationalsozialismus: Studien zur nationalsozialistischen Durchdringung des protestantistischen Sozialmilieus in Berlin* (Cologne: Böhlau, 2001).

53 Cf. Alois Hudal, *Die deutsche Kulturarbeit in Italien* (Munich: Aschendorff, 1934), 166 ff. One example of Catholic relief for Protestants is Ernst Fritz Böhme from Dresden. Böhme presented himself as stateless, saying that he was an engineer by profession and Protestant by denomination. The Croatian subcommittee confirmed the Protestant's data, and the Papal relief agency confirmed Böhme's data and the Böhme family's wishes to travel to Argentina. Application for Red Cross travel document for Böhme Fritz Ernst, ICRC Rome, 27 August 1948, letter from the PCA to ICRC Rome, 31 August 1948, ICRC Geneva, Archive, 'Titres de Voyage CICR 1945–1993', application 83, 501.

54 Cf. Reports of the Camp Directors Centro Raccolta Profughi Stranieri Farfa Sabina, ACS, Int. D.G., P.S., Div. AA. Massime 14, 'Istruzione di Polizia Militare', file 82.

55 The Prefect of Modena to the Ministry of the Interior, 'Agitazione da parte di internati', 3 January 1947. ACS, Istruzioni, file 77, folder 69, N. 30 Stranieri internati, subfolder 41, 'Centro raccolta profughi a Fossoli di Carpi'.

56 Letter from Alois Hudal to the Italian Minister of the Interior, Mario Scelba, 31 August 1947, ACS, Int. D.G., P.S., Div. AA. Massime 14, 'Istruzione di Polizia Militare', file 89.

57 Uhlig *et al.*, *Tarnung, Transfer, Transit*, 190 f.

58 Langer, *Hudal*, 213.

59 Letter of recommendation by the PCA, Foreign Section, Francesco Echarri, for Josef Schwammberger, 3 November 1948, ICRC Geneva, Archive, 'Titres de Voyage CICR 1945–1993', application 90, 143.

60 'Tod in Rom', *Der Spiegel*, 6 (1984), 122–5 at 125.

61 Hudal, *Römische Tagebücher*, 21.

62 Sereny, *Into That Darkness*, 289.

63 Goñi, *Operazione Odessa*, 305.

64 Klee, *Persilscheine und falsche Pässe*, 39.

65 Application for a Red Cross travel document for Bla(a)s Maximilian, ICRC Rome, 9 April 1948. ICRC travel document for Maximilian Blaas; letter of recommendation from the Italian Red Cross Hilfsstelle AGIUS Rome, 16 April 1948. ICRC Geneva, Archive, 'Titres de Voyage CICR 1945–1993', application 75, 040.

66 ICRC Rome application form for Blaas Maximilian, undated; letter of recommendation from the PCA Rome, 19 July 1947, ibid. 75, 040.

67 The baptismal register for Partschin confirms Blaas's date of birth and parents. Entry for Maximilian Blaas, 13 March 1921, in Partschin baptismal register, microfilm, Südtiroler Landesarchiv Bozen.

68 Michael Krek in Cleveland to Secretary General Revd Paul Tanner of the NCWC in Washington, DC, 24 October 1947, Catholic University of America, Washington, DC, University Archives, file NCWC, box 36, folder 'Displaced Persons 1948–49' 10/36/36.

69 Application for a Red Cross travel document for Drago Sedmak, ICRC Rome, 3 April 1947, ICRC Geneva, Archive, 'Titres de Voyage CICR 1945–1993', application 48, 741.

70 Application for a Red Cross travel document for Jan Baduniec, ICRC Rome, 2 September 1947, letter from the PCA Polish Section to ICRC Rome, 1 September 1947, ibid. 62, 198.

71 OSS-Report 'Stay-Behind Italy', undated, *c.* December 1944, NARA, RG 226 (OSS), entry 210, box 9, folder 1. Cf. also Phayer, *Catholic Church*, 168 f.

72 Letter from Rechtsanwalt Karl Mayer an Erzbischof Aloisius Muench, 11 September 1951 sowie Amtsgericht Mühldorf, Streitgericht, Urteil gegen Zoltàn Kòtai, 31. Mai 1950, Catholic University of America, Washington, DC, University Archives, file Aloisius Muench, box 37, folder 6 'Hungarian Priests'.

73 Cf. e.g. letter from Giovanni B. Montini to Bishop Aloisius Muench, 9 June 1951, Catholic University of America, Washington, DC, University Archives, file Aloisius Muench, box 37, folder 6 'Hungarian Priests'.

74 Phayer, *Catholic Church*, 168 f.

75 Stehle, 'Pässe vom Papst?', 12.

76 Hebblethwaite, *Paul VI*, 206.

77 'Pending release of ambassador Eizenstadts vol. II, Report on WW II. victim gold' (SECRET), 29 April 1998, Botschafter Stuart Eizenstadt Report RG 263 (CIA), name files, box 12, Draganovic, Krunoslav.

78 Simon Wiesenthal, *Justice Not Vengeance: Memoirs*, tr. Ewald Osers (London: Weidenfeld & Nicolson, 1989), 35.

79 Peter Godman, *Hitler and the Vatican: Inside the Secret Archives that Reveal the New Story of the Nazis and the Church* (New York: Free, 2004), 5.

80 Philippe Chenaux, 'Pacelli, Hudal et la question du nazisme (1933–1938)', *Rivista di storia della Chiesa in Italia*, 57/1 (2003), 133–54.

81 The hospital for German pilgrims was probably founded in 1350, but the actual boom of the German National Church began in the fifteenth century. Even today Santa Maria dell'Anima bears the title 'German National Church'. It is at the religious centre of the college of priests that was associated with the hospital in 1859, where young priests from German-speaking dioceses stay when doing their specialist studies.

82 *Personalstand der Säkular- und Regular-Geistlichkeit der Diözese Seckau in der Steiermark im Jahre 1946* (Graz: Ordinariats-Kanzlei, 1946), 312.

83 Godman, *Hitler and the Vatican*, 45.

84 'Will the modern cult of state and nation, which is leading the world into a cultural change with its claims to totality and a myth of blood and race, accept another leadership side by side with it, one that is not of this world?' Hudal brooded in 1935. Quoted in Alois Hudal, *Der Vatikan und die modernen Staaten* (Innsbruck: Tyrolia Verlag, 1935), 7.

85 Cf. Alois Hudal, *Deutsches Volk und christliches Abendland* (Innsbruck: Tyrolia, 1935).

86 Godman, *Hitler and the Vatican*, 54.

87 Guido Zagheni, *La croce e il fascio: I cattolici italiani e la dittatura* (Milan: San Paolo, 2006), 211 ff.

88 Alois Hudal, *Die Grundlagen des Nationalsozialismus: Eine ideengeschichtliche Untersuchung* (Leipzig: Günther, 1937).

89 Maximilian Liebmann, *Kirche in Gesellschaft und Politik: Von der Reformation bis zur Gegenwart* (Graz: Austria Medien Service, 1999), 271. Cf. the chapter 'Bischof Hudal und der Nationalsozialismus—Rom und die Steiermark', 260–72.

90 Hudal, *Grundlagen*, 13.

91 Hudal, *Römische Tagebücher*, 116.

92 Interview with Joseph Prader, 3 May 2005.

93 Michael Buchberger (ed.), *Kirchliches Handlexikon: Ein Nachschlagebuch über das Gesamtge-biet der Theologie und ihrer Hilfswissenschaften*, 2 vols. (Freiburg: Herder, 1907), i. 257 f.

94 Hudal, *Grundlagen*, 86 f.

95 Ibid. 88. For Hudal's Rassismus cf. Dominik Burkard, 'Alois Hudal—ein Anti-Pacelli? Zur Diskussion um die Haltung des Vatikans gegenüber dem Nationalsoz-ialimus', *Zeitschrift für Religions- und Geistesgeschichte*, 59/1 (2007), 61–89 at 66.

96 Cf. Voigt, *Zuflucht auf Widerruf*, i. 370–6.

97 Interview with Joseph Prader, 3 May 2005.

98 Langer, *Hudal*, 197.

99 Letter from Michael J. Ready, Secretary General of the NCWC, to Monsignor Walter Carroll, 6 November 1944, Catholic University of America, Washington, DC, University Archives, File NCWC, box 49, folder 'Relief Italy'.

100 Letter from Archbishop Samuel A. Cardinal Stritch to Monsignor Michael J. Ready, NCWC, 25 September 1944, ibid.

101 Headquarters 2677th Regiment, OSS, APO 777, US Army, Subject: Report of German-Austrian Desk for period ending 14 July (SECRET), 15 July 1944, signed John McCulloch, NARA, RG 226 (OSS), entry 210, box 74, folder 1.

102 German and Austrian Personality Section, Research Department of the Foreign Office, London, 'Austrian Personalities, Dr. Alois Hudal', 9 February 1948, NARA, RG 319, CIC collection, G-3 intelligence IRR name files, box 424, Hudal, Alois, AC 854314.

103 Interview with Joseph Prader, 3 May 2005.

104 Klee, *Persilscheine und falsche Pässe*, 39.

105 Schilling to Hudal, 29 January 1949, quoted in Langer, *Hudal*, 226.

106 In Shraga Elam, *Hitlers Fälscher: Wie jüdische, amerikanische und Schweizer Agenten der SS beim Falschgeldwaschen halfen* (Vienna: Ueberreuter, 2000), 171.

107 'Subject: Indiscriminate Issuing and Use of Identity Documents of the Interna-tional Red Cross', US Consul General Laurence G. Frank in Vienna to the US Foreign Minister, 20 January 1947 (TOP SECRET), and the accompanying 'Summary of Information', 16 December 1946, NARA, RG 84, Austria, Political Adviser, General Records 1945–55, entry 2057, box 2.

108 Hudal to Perón, 31 August 1948, Collegio Santa Maria dell'Anima, Nachlass Hudal, box 27 (Aug. 1948).

109 Cf. Matteo Sanfilippo, 'Los papeles de Hudal como fuente para la historia de la migración de alemanes y nazis después de la segunda guerra mundial', 12, *Comisión para el esclarecimiento de las actividades del nazismo en la República Argentina*, <http://www.ceana.org.ar/final/sanfilippo.zip>, accessed 1 May 2005. Cf. idem, 'Los pa-peles de Hudal como fuente para la historia de la migración de Alemanes y Nazis después de la Segunda Guerra Mundial', *Estudios Migratorios Latinoamericanos*, 43 (1999), 185–209.

110 Hans-Ulrich Rudel, *Aus Krieg und Frieden: Aus den Jahren 1945 und 1952* (Göttingen: Plesse, 1954), 200.

111 CIA report, 'German Nationalist and Neo-Nazi Activities in Argentina', 8 July 1953, 11f. (SECRET. SECURITY INFORMATION), NARA, RG 263, General CIA Records, 62-00865R, box 0003, folder 0003. This report was approved for release in April 2000.

112 Interview with Joseph Prader, 3 May 2005.

113 Confirmation of Hudal, 10 September 1946, Collegio Santa Maria dell'Anima, Nachlass Hudal, box 37.

114　Hudal to Truman, 8 March 1951, ibid. box 45.

115　Hudal to the Commandant of Terni prisoner-of-war camp, 8 September 1946, ibid. box 37.

116　Filippo Focardi, *Criminali di guerra in libertà. Un accordo segreto tra Italia e Germania federale, 1949–1955* (Rome: Carocci, 2008), 161 f.

117　Ibid. 54.

118　In Klee, *Persilscheine und falsche Pässe*, 45 f.

119　Ibid. 46.

120　Application for a Red Cross travel document for Walther Ottowitz, ICRC Rome, 26 March 1948. Affidavit from Walther Ottowitz, 22 March 1948; confirmation for Walther Ottowitz from Bishop Alois Hudal, 24 March 1948; letter of recommendation from the PCA Rome for Walther Ottowitz, 23 March 1948. ICRC Geneva, Archive, 'Titres de Voyage CICR 1945–1993', application 74, 988.

121　Interview with Kurt Schrimm, 26 August 2004.

122　Giovanni Maria Pace, *La via dei demoni: La fuga in Sudamerica dei criminali nazisti: Secreti, complicità, silenzi* (Milan: Sperling & Kupfer, 2000), 44.

123　In Langer, *Hudal*, 241.

124　Alois Hudal, 'Die katholische Caritas in einer Zeitenwende: Predigt gehalten am 11. 9. 1949 in der Deutschen Nationalkirche der Anima in Rom', *Anima-Stimmen: Lose Blätter zur Förderung des kollegialen Geistes der ehemaligen Anima-Priester*, 3/4 (1951), 26–30.

125　'Non è opportuno, non si difende un vescovo nazista', Hudal, *Römische Tagebücher*, 299.

126　Hudal, *Römische Tagebücher*, 299.

127　In Stehle, 'Pässe vom Papst?', 12.

128　In Giefer and Giefer, *Rattenlinie*, 98.

129　Sereny, *Into That Darkness*, 305–6.

130　Ibid. 306.

131　Lehnert, *Ich durfte ihm dienen*, 1027.

132　Liebmann, *Kirche in Gesellschaft und Politik*, 271, esp. 'Bischof Hudal und der Nationalsozialismus—Rom und die Steiermark', 260–72.

133　Cf. Stefan Moritz, *Grüß Gott und Heil Hitler: Katholische Kirche und Nationalsozialismus in Österreich* (Vienna: Picus, 2002).

134　Cf. 'A te, mio Fuehrer', *Avanti!* (6 and 8 April 1961).

135　Letter from the Austrian Bishops, 19 April 1951, to Bishop Alois Hudal, in Langer, *Hudal*, 15.

136　Hudal, *Römische Tagebücher*, 317.

137　Cf. ibid.

138　In Hansjakob Stehle, 'Bischof Hudal und SS-Führer Meyer: Ein kirchenpolitischer Friedensversuch 1942/43', *Vierteljahreshefte für Zeitgeschichte*, 39 (1989), 299–322 at 316.

139　Headquarters Counter Intelligence Corps, Allied Forces Headquarters APO 512, Background Report on Krunoslav Draganović, 12 February 1947, Robert Clayton Mudd, Special Agent CIC, NARA, RG 263 (CIA), War Crimes, CIA name files, IWG, box 12, Krunoslav Draganović, vol. 1 of 4.

140　Cf. Marko Babić, 'Prof. Dr. Krunoslav Stjepan Draganović, u prigodi 10. obljetnice smrti i 90. onljetnice rodenja (1903–1983)', *Hrvatska revija, Kroatische Rundschau*, 44 (1994), 1(173), 184–6.

141　Cf. Krunoslav Draganović, *Katolička crkva u Bosni i Hercegovini nekad i danas. Prilog zu istoimenu historijsko-statističku kartu* (Zagreb: n.pub., 1934).

142　'Draganović. Wolga in Rom', *Der Spiegel* (27 November 1967), 138–43.

143 On the 100th anniversary of the Croatian College, Pope John Paul II delivered a lengthy speech, acknowledging the institution's merits. Cf. 'Discorso di Giovanni Paolo II. alla comunità del Pontificio Collegio Croato di San Girolamo in Roma', *Vatican: The Holy See*, 16 November 2001, <http://www.vatican.va/holy_father/john_paul_ii/speeches>, accessed 12 July 2005.

144 Headquarters Counter Intelligence Corps, Allied Forces Headquarters APO 512, Background Report on Krunoslav Draganović, 12 February 1947, Robert Clayton Mudd, Special Agent CIC, NARA, RG 263 (CIA), War Crimes, CIA name files, IWG, box 12, Krunoslav Draganović, vol. 1 of 4.

145 Phayer, *Catholic Church*, 169f.

146 Headquarters Counter Intelligence Corps, Allied Forces Headquarters APO 512, Background Report on Krunoslav Draganović, 12 February 1947, Robert Clayton Mudd, Special Agent CIC, NARA, RG 263 (CIA), War Crimes, CIA name files, IWG, box 12, Krunoslav Draganović, vol. 1 of 4. Vgl. CIC report, 'Whereabouts of ex-Croat Leaders', 11 October 1946, NARA, RG 263 (CIA), War Crimes, CIA name files, IWG, box 12, Krunoslav Draganović, vol. 1 of 4.

147 Mediterranean Theater of Operations, Office of the Assistant Chief of Staff, G-2, APO 512, US Army, G. F. Blunda, Lt. Col., Assistant Chief of Staff G-2 to Colonel Carl F. Fritzsche, Assistant Deputy Director of Intelligence, Headquarters, US Army, Subject: Ante Pavelić (TOP SECRET), 8 November 1947, NARA, RG 319, entry 134 B, box 173, G-2 intelligence personnel name files, folder Ante Pavelić.

148 Ibid.

149 Headquarters Counter Intelligence Corps, Allied Forces Headquarters APO 512, Background Report on Krunoslav Draganović, 12 February 1947, Robert Clayton Mudd, Special Agent CIC, NARA, RG 263 (CIA), War Crimes, CIA name files, IWG, box 12, Krunoslav Draganović, vol. 1 of 4.

150 Phayer, *Pius XII, the Holocaust, and the Cold War*, 250.

151 For a detailed account of the flight of Ante Pavelić, see ibid. 220–30.

152 Ibid. 248.

153 CIC report, 'Reported Arrival of Ante Pavelić in Argentina', 2 December 1948, NARA, RG 263 (CIA), War Crimes, CIA name files, IWG, box 12, Krunoslav Draganović, vol. 1 of 4.

154 Cf. 'La confraternità di San Girolamo per l'aiuto ai profughi croati (1945–1957)', *Studia Croatica* <http://www.studiacroatica.org/jero/luki4.htm>, accessed 12 July 2005.

155 Cf. Stefan Dietrich, 'Der Bleiburger Opfermythos', *Zeitgeschichte*, 35/5 (2008), 298–317.

156 Subject: Persecution of the Catholic Church in Yugoslavia, According to the Holy See, US ambassador to the Vatican, Myron C. Taylor, to the US Foreign Minister and US ambassador in Rome, 26 January 1947, NARA, RG 84, Rome embassy, box 20, folder 840.4 'Yugoslavia'.

157 Cf. the critical study by Marco Aurelio Rivelli, *L'arcivescovo del genocidio: Monsignor Stepinac, il Vaticano e la dittatura ustascia in Croazia, 1941–1945* (Milan: Kaos, 1999).

158 Report on Draganović, 31 March 1950, NARA, RG 263 (CIA), name files, box 12, Draganović, Krunoslav.

159 Stehle, 'Pässe vom Papst?', 12.

160 Cf. Nicola Buonasorte, *Siri: Tradizione e Novecento* (Bologna: Il mulino, 2007).

161 Stehle, 'Pässe vom Papst?', 12.

162 CIC report, 7 March 1946, NARA, RG 263 (CIA), War Crimes, CIA name files, IWG, box 12, Krunoslav Draganović, vol. 1 of 4.

163 Cf. 'La confraternità di San Girolamo per l'aiuto ai profughi croati (1945–1957)', *Studia Croatica* <http://www.studiacroatica.org/jero/luki4.htm>, accessed 12 July 2005.

164 Aarons and Loftus, *Unholy Trinity*, 91–6.

165 Ibid. 104–9.

166 In Giefer and Giefer, *Rattenlinie*, 108.

167 Ibid. and Simpson, *Blowback*, 185.

168 Application for a Red Cross travel document for Bohne Hans, ICRC Rome, 22 August 1948, letter from the PCA to ICRC Rome, 22 August 1948, ICRC, Geneva, Archive, 'Titres de Voyage CICR 1945–1993', application 83, 465.

169 Application for a Red Cross travel document for Bohne Gisela, ICRC Rome, 22 August 1948, letter from the PCA to ICRC Rome, 22 August 1948, ICRC Geneva, Archive, 'Titres de Voyage CICR 1945–1993', application 83, 470.

170 Norman J. W. Goda, 'The Ustaša: Murder and Espionage', in Breitman *et al.* (eds.), *U.S. Intelligence and the Nazis*, 203–26 at 216 ff.

171 Cali Ruchala, 'The Return of the Golden Priest: The Verona Reports and the Second Recruitment of Krunoslav Draganović, 1959', *The Pavelić Papers, An Independent Project Researching the History of the Ustase Movement 1929–2003* [website], n.d., <http://www.Pavelicpapers.com/features/essays/verona.html>, accessed 12 October 2005.

172 'Draganović: Wolga in Rom', *Der Spiegel* (27 November 1967), 138–43 at 140.

173 Ibid. at 143.

174 US embassy in Belgrade to the Department of State and its delegations in Vienna, Trieste, Rome, and Zagreb, 25 December 1967 (CONFIDENTIAL), signed Elbrick, NARA, RG 263 (CIA), War Crimes, CIA name files, IWG, box 12, Krunoslav Draganović, vol. 3 of 4.

175 In Babić, 'Prof. Dr. Krunoslav Stjepan Draganović', 184–6. Cf. also Ivan Tomas, *Krunoslav Stj. Draganović, Prilikom 60. godišnjice njegova života* (Buenos Aires: Hrvatska Revija,1964).

176 Cf. F. Nevistić, 'La muerte del Prof. Draganović', *Studia Croatica*, 90/1 (Dec. 1983), 153–5.

177 Meding, *Flucht vor Nürnberg?*, 81.

178 Cf. the works of the two Brixner church historians Josef Gelmi and Josef Inner-hofer, e.g. Josef Gelmi, *Fürstbischof Johannes Geisler (1882–1952): Eines der drama-tischsten Kapitel der Südtiroler Geschichte* (Brixen: Weger, 2003). Cf. idem, *Geschichte der Kirche in Tirol: Nord-, Ost- und Südtirol* (Innsbruck: Tyrolia, 2001). Cf. Josef Innerhofer, *Die Kirche in Südtirol, Gestern und Heute* (Bozen: Athesia, 1982), 168 ff. The opening of the relevant archive sources will bring greater clarity about the relationship between the leadership of the church in Brixen and Hudal's escape assistance. But the Brixen Diocesan Archive has been closed for seventy years, making contempo-rary historical research very difficult.

179 Josef Innerhofer, *Er blieb sich selber treu: Josef Mayr-Nusser 1910–1945* (Bozen: Ath-esia, 2005). Cf. idem, *Die Kirche in Südtirol.*

180 Gelmi, *Fürstbischof*, 10.

181 Ibid. 114.

182 Ibid. 115.

183 Ibid. 25.

184 Ibid. Cf. also 'Unser Gedenken an Dompropst Dr. Alois Pompanin von Brixen', *Südtirol in Wort und Bild*, 10/3 (1966), 14.

185 Interview with Joseph Prader, 3 May 2005.

186 Ibid.

187 Cf. Klaus Eisterer and Rolf Steininger (eds.), *Die Option: Südtirol zwischen Faschismus und Nationalsozialismus*, Innsbrucker Forschungen zur Zeitgeschichte 5 (Innsbruck: Haymon, 1989). Cf. Steurer, *Südtirol zwischen Rom und Berlin*.

188 Cf. Gelmi, *Fürstbischof*. Cf. idem, *Die Brixner Bischöfe in der Geschichte Tirols* (Bozen: Athesia, 1984), 269 ff.

189 Handwritten curriculum vitae of Karl Nicolussi-Leck to the Rasse- und Siedlungshauptamt (RuSHA), October 1943, SS personnel files, Nicolussi-Leck, Karl, born 14 March 1917, SS. no. 341.499, NARA, RG 242, formerly BDC.

190 Leopold Steurer, 'Meldungen aus dem Land: Aus den Berichten des Eil-Nachrichtendienstes der ADO (Jänner–Juli 1943)', *Sturzflüge: Eine Kulturzeitschrift*, 29/30 (Dec. 1989), 31–125 at 40.

191 Ibid. at 35.

192 Joachim Goller, 'Die Brixner Nebenregierung: Der politische Einfluss des Bistums Brixen auf die SVP 1945–1964', D.Phil. dissertation, University of Innsbruck, Austria, 2004, 49.

193 Cf. Hudal, *Grundlagen*, 21.

194 Interview with Joseph Prader, 22 November 2005.

195 Hudal to Giovanni Montini, 5 April 1949, Collegio Santa Maria dell'Anima, Rome, Nachlass Hudal, box 40.

196 Montini to Hudal, 12 May 1949, ibid. box 39.

197 Joseph Prader to Alfons Ludwig, 15 October 1949, ibid. box 41.

198 'Josef Prader ist verstorben', *Dolomiten* (21 January 2006), 12.

199 Interview with Joseph Prader, 3 May 2005.

200 Adolf Eichmann, 'Meine Flucht: Bericht aus der Zelle in Jerusalem', NARA, RG 263 (CIA), War Crimes, CIA name files, IWG, box 14, Eichmann, Adolf, vol. 1.

201 Hudal, *Römische Tagebücher*, 229.

202 Klee, *Persilscheine und falsche Pässe*, 25 ff.

203 Sereny, *Into That Darkness*, 320.

204 Rudel, *Zwischen Deutschland und Argentinien*, 46.

205 Report from Bruno Brunetti, Carabinieri Commander in Rome, 12 December 1945, ACS, Ministero dell'Interno, Direzione Generale. Pubblica Sicurezza, Divisione Affari Generali e Riservati, A16—Stranieri ed Ebrei Stranieri, AA.GG. (1930–56), file 48, 'Fascicolo Bolzano Convento Teutonico. Abusivo ricovero militari tedeschi e ricettazione materiali trafugati'.

206 Report to the Allied Military Government Bozen, 18 August 1945, signed Alberto Steiner, NARA, RG 331, ACC Italy, 11202/Bolzano/143/37, box 8924.

207 Klee, *Persilscheine und falsche Pässe*, 45.

208 Interview with Joseph Prader, 3 May 2005.

209 Cf. Maler, *Frieden, Krieg und 'Frieden'*, 322.

210 Chronik des Kapuzinerklosters Brixen am Eisack, Jahr 1944, Kapuzinerkloster Brixen, Archiv.

211 Ibid.

212 Cf. 'In memoriam Fr. Leopoldus von Gumppenberg de Ebersberg (1901–1982)', in Istituto Storico Cappuccini (ed.), *Collectanea Franciscana* 53 (1983), folders 1–2, 51–60. Cf. also the obituary: 'Pater Leopold von Gumppenberg ist heimgegangen', *Altöttinger Liebfrauenboten* (25 July 1982).

213 Letter from the Provincial Benedikt Frei, 8 May 1947, Klosterarchiv der Kapuziner Bozen, folder III, no. 105.

214 Chronik des Kapuzinerklosters Brixen am Eisack, Jahr 1947, Kapuzinerkloster Brixen, Archiv.

215 Schimpf, *Heilig*, 92 ff.

216 Letter from Provinzial Josef Oberhollenzer of 6 July 1951, Südtiroler Kapuziner-provinz, Provinzial-Archiv 1c22.

217 Klee, *Persilscheine und falsche Pässe*, 45.

218 See note 213.

219 Cf. Arendt, *Eichmann in Jerusalem: A Report*, 236 f.

220 Chronik des Bozner Franziskanerklosters V. Teil, Beginn: Juli 1938, 296, Franciscan Monastery Library, Bozen.

221 Cf. obituary for Prof. Dr Franz Borgias Pobitzer in the annual report 1974/5 of the Franziskanergymnasium in Bozen, Bozen 1975.

222 Interview with Leopold Steurer, 16 April 2004.

223 Bruno Klammer *et al.* (eds.), *200 Jahre Franziskanergymnasium Bozen 1781–1981: Festschrift zum 200 jährigen Bestehen des Franziskanergymnasiums in Bozen* (Bozen: Athesia, 1981), 250.

224 Maler, *Frieden, Krieg und 'Frieden'*, 332.

225 Hans Maler to Alois Hudal, 14 May 1948, Anima, Nachlass Hudal, box 27.

226 Federico Zweifel, ICRC delegate in Verona, to Captain Dawson, Commander of AMG Evacuation Camp 23, Bolzano, 24 July 1946, ICRC Geneva, Archives Générales G. 3/24 b/cV box 84 (1).

227 Father Patrick, Vice-President of the Italian Red Cross, Bozen, to William E. McBratney, 9 July 1945, NARA, RG 331, ACC Italy, 11202/Bolzano/128/9, box 8916, 'Italienische Rote Kreuz'.

228 Interview with N. N., 20 June 2005.

229 Maler, *Frieden, Krieg und 'Frieden'*, 321.

230 Cf. Hans H. Reimer, *Lutherisch in Südtirol: Die Geschichte der Evangelischen Gemeinde Meran* (Bozen: Edition Rætia, 2009), 345.

231 Report by the Carabinieri Commander of Merano, Salvatore Palermo, 4 October 1945, NARA, RG 331, ACC Italy, box 8921, 11202/143/11, Folder 'Arresti civili'.

232 Wiesenthal, *Justice Not Vengeance*, 55.

233 Entry for 13 September 1948 in the baptismal register of Sterzing, Pfarre Unsere Liebe Frau im Moos 1943–1951, Pfarramt Sterzing; cf. also Gelmi, *Geschichte der Kirche in Tirol*, 427.

234 Entry for 22 April 1946 in the baptismal register for Sterzing, Pfarre Unsere Liebe Frau im Moos 1943–51, Pfarramt Sterzing.

235 Interview with Josef Gelmi, 30 June 2004.

236 Interview with Alexander Mesner, 1 July 2004.

237 Adolf Eichmann, 'Meine Flucht: Bericht aus der Zelle in Jerusalem', NARA, RG 263 (CIA), War Crimes, CIA name files, IWG, box 14, Eichmann, Adolf, vol. 1.

238 Ibid.

239 Sereny, *Into That Darkness*, 322.

240 Ibid. 320.

241 Entry for 17 July 1948 in the baptismal register of Sterzing, Pfarre Unsere Liebe Frau im Moos 1943–1951, Pfarramt Sterzing.

242 Ibid., entry for 26 May 1946.

243 Entry in the baptismal register of Sterzing, Pfarre Unsere Liebe Frau im Moos 1943–1951, Pfarramt Sterzing.

244 Letter from the Order of the Sisters of the Cross (in Varese) to the author, 22 November 2004. Cf. also Chronik der Brixner Kreuzschwestern im Haus St Agnes von 1945 bis 1950 (copy). The original is in the mother house in Besozzo Varese.

245 Interview with Hartmut Staffler, 22 June 2004.

246 Statement by N. N., 30 June 2004.

247 Letter from Hartmuth Staffler to the author, 16 July 2004. According to the Sisters of the Cross, the Chronicle is no longer in their possession, but in the archive of the mother house. It was not possible to access it again.

248 Copies by Hartmuth Staffler from the Chronicle of the Sisters of the Cross at the Sanatorium in Brixen 1943–46. Copy in possession of the author. Some surnames in this quotation are given only with initials by the author.

249 Baptismal entry Heinrich Bode 23 May 1947, Pfarrarchiv Brixen, Taufbuch Brixen, XIV, 1943–50, 196.

250 Baptismal entry Hildegard Dalmer 24 July 1949, ibid. 358.

251 SS-Hauptscharführer Jakob Strickner to the SS-Rasse- und Siedlungshauptamt in Berlin, concerning engagement and marriage permissions, 25 August 1939, SS-Personalakte Jakob Strickner, Bundesarchiv Berlin, formerly BDC.

252 Hartmuth Staffler, 'Heimkehrer der katholischen Kirche. Brixen vor 48 Jahren: Viele Absagen an die Irrlehre des Nationalsozialismus', *Dolomiten* (14 May 1994), 33.

253 Chronik der Brixner Kreuzschwestern im Haus St. Agnes von 1945 bis 1950 (copy), entry for June 1946.

254 Handwritten curriculum vitae for Karl Nicolussi-Leck to the Rasse- und Siedlungshauptamt (RuSHA), October 1943, SS personnel files, Nicolussi-Leck, Karl, born 14 March 1917, SS no. 341.499, NARA, RG 242, formerly BDC.

255 Cf. Carl Holboeck, *Handbuch des Kirchenrechtes*, 2 vols. (Innsbruck: Tyrolia, 1951), ii, 521–30.

256 Lehnert, *Ich durfte ihm dienen*, 111.

257 Anton Perathoner, *Das kirchliche Gesetzbuch (Codex juris canonici). Sinngemäß wiedergegeben und mit Anmerkungen versehen*, i. *Von den Sakramenten (can. 731–1153)* (3rd edn, Brixen: Druck and Weger, 1923), 225 f.

258 Anton Posset, 'Der Priester und der SS-General. Die Bekehrungsgeschichte des Oswald Pohl', in *Themenhefte Landsberger Zeitgeschichte*, 1 (1993), 20–4. Cf. extract from the register (Matrikelbuch) of the Seelsorgestelle des Kriegsgefangenen- und Strafgefängnisses Landsberg, 8 June 2006, entry for Oswald Poh, born 30 June 1892.

259 Norbert Frei, *Vergangenheitspolitik: Die Anfänge der Bundesrepublik und die NS-Vergangenheit* (Munich: Beck, 1996), 65.

260 Oswald Pohl, *Credo: Mein Weg zu Gott* (Landshut: Girnth, 1950).

261 Cf. Niklas Frank, *Der Vater: Eine Abrechnung* (Munich: Bertelsmann, 1987).

262 Manfred Deselaers, *'Und Sie hatten nie Gewissensbisse?' Die Biografie von Rudolf Höß, Kommandant von Auschwitz, und die Frage seiner Verantwortung vor Gott und den Menschen* (Leipzig: Benno, 1997).

263 Reinhard Spitzy, *So entkamen wir den Alliierten: Bekenntnisse eines 'Ehemaligen'* (Munich: Müller, 1989), 17.

264 Anna Maria Sigmund, *Die Frauen der Nazis II* (Vienna: Ueberreuter, 2000), 41.

265 CIC report on Frau Martin Bormann, 17 April 1947, NARA, RG 319, IRR name files, box 270, Bormann Martin, XE187975. *Der Spiegel* wrote on 24 July 1948, 15: 'Martin Bormann, the son of the still missing Reichsleiter, is training for the profession of priest in Ingolstadt. His mother, who died of cancer in Merano in October 1946, had also become Catholic shortly before.'

266 Martin Bormann, *Leben gegen Schatten: Gelebte Zeit, geschenkte Zeit, Begegnungen, Erfahrungen, Folgerungen* (Paderborn: Blindenscher, 1998), 83.

267 Headquarters 970 Counter Intelligence Corps, Sub-Region Regensburg Region V, Subject: Buch Hermann, 3 August 1947, NARA, RG 319, IRR, name files, box 270, Bormann Martin, XE187975.

268 Quoted in Sereny, *Into That Darkness*, 311.
269 Ibid. 321.
270 'Oggetto: Martin Bormann', 12 May 1947, Archivio storico del Ministero degli Affari Esteri Roma (AAER), Affari Politici 1946–50, file 175, 'Criminali di guerra'.
271 Ibid.
272 'Oggetto: Ricovero dei minori Bormann', Ministry of the Interior in Rome to the Foreign Ministry, 24 November 1948, ibid.

Chapter 4

1 In Michael Salter, *Nazi War Crimes, US Intelligence and Selective Prosecution at Nuremberg: Controversies Regarding the Role of the Office of Strategic Services* (Abingdon: Routledge-Cavendish, 2007), 5. See also idem, 'The Prosecution of Nazi War Criminals and the OSS: The Need for a New Research Agenda', *Journal of Intelligence History*, 2/1 (Summer 2002), 77–119.
2 Vincent La Vista to Herbert J. Cummings, 15 May 1947 (TOP SECRET), NARA, RG 84, Austria, Political Adviser, Gen. Records 1945–55, box 2, app. C, 4.
3 Letter from Bernhard Krüger in the case of Friedrich Schwend, 2 June 1960, Beschuldigter Friedrich Schwend, Akt 518 AR 339/69, Bl. 68, Bundesarchiv Ludwigsburg (Barch LB), B 162.
4 Adolf Burger, *Unternehmen Bernhard: Die Fälscherwerkstatt im KZ Sachsenhausen* (Berlin: Hentrich, 1992), 112.
5 Walter Schellenberg, *Memoiren* (Cologne: Verlag für Politik und Wirtschaft, 1959), 322.
6 Giefer and Giefer, *Rattenlinie*, 78–86.
7 Landgericht München I., Anklageschrift in der Strafsache gegen Schwend Friedrich Paul, 14 September 1978, Beschuldigter Friedrich Schwend, Akte 518 AR 339/69, Bl. 241, Barch LB, B 162.
8 Interrogation of Albert Gottfried Schwend, 1 August 1960, ibid. Bl. 81, Barch LB, B 162.
9 NSDAP-Kreisleitung Rosenheim an die Außenhandelsstelle für Südbayern München, Munich, 25 January 1940, NARA, RG 263 (CIA), War Crimes, IWG, CIA name files, box 47, Fritz Venceslav Schwend.
10 NSDAP-Kreisleitung Rosenheim, Politische Beurteilung für Friedrich Schwend, 18 January 1940, ibid.
11 Interrogation of Wilhelm Höttl, 28 December 1961, Beschuldigter Friedrich Schwend, Akte 518 AR 339/69, Bl. 160, Barch LB, B 162.
12 Ibid.
13 Walter Hagen [Wilhelm Höttl], *Unternehmen Bernhard: Ein historischer Tatsachenbericht über die größte Geldfälschungsaktion aller Zeiten* (Wels: Welsermühl, 1955), 101.
14 Report from the OSS in Berne, 12 April 1945, 'Subject: Sonder-Kommando Schwendt', NARA, RG 263 (CIA), War Crimes, IWG, CIA name files, entry ZZ-16, box 47, Fritz Venceslav Schwend.
15 Hagen, *Unternehmen Bernhard*, 102.
16 Interrogation of Martin Mader, 16 January 1962, Beschuldigter Friedrich Schwend, Akte 518 AR 339/69, Bl. 147, Barch LB, B 162.
17 Interrogation of Gertrud Tacke, 14 March 1961, ibid. Bl. 104, Barch LB, B 162.
18 Hagen, *Unternehmen Bernhard*, 8 f.
19 Friedrich Schwend to Klaus Dieter Langenstein, 15 June 1961, Fritz-Bauer-Institut, Frankfurt am Main, copy of Schwend-Archives, folder II./3.

20 Hagen, *Unternehmen Bernhard*, 8 f.
21 Letter from Friedrich Schwend to the Staatsanwaltschaft bei dem Landgericht München I, 26 June 1960, Beschuldigter Friedrich Schwend, Akte 518 AR 339/69, Bl. 86, Barch LB, B 162.
22 Gerichtsurteil des Landgerichts München I. in der Strafsache gegen Friedrich-Paul Schwend, 8 June 1979, Akte 518 AR 339/69, Bl. 282, ibid.
23 FBI Director John Edgar Hoover to the CIA Director, Deputy Director, Plans, 21 December 1966 (CONFIDENTIAL), attached letter from Friedrich Schwend to Julius Mader, 18 August 1966 in the original and in English translation, NARA, RG 263 (CIA), War Crimes, IWG, CIA name files, entry ZZ-16, box 47, Schwend, Fritz Venceslav, folder 2.
24 Report by the OSS in Berne on Bela Tar, 16 March 1945, NARA, RG 263 (CIA), War Crimes, IWG, CIA name files, box 47, Fritz Venceslav Schwend. Schloss Labers was soon given a literary monument: *Where Eagles Dare* by Alistair MacLean is based around a castle on the southern slopes of the Alps where the German secret service has its southern headquarters. In this 1967 novel, certain details such as locations, including the Weissspitze, indicate Schloss Labers. In the film version, the OSS and British agents launch a death-defying raid on the castle. Is this a deliberate reference to operations planned in reality? Schloss Labers had, in fact, entered the sights of the US secret service from 1944, and had been identified as a 'bombing target'. At any rate, the film of the novel starring Clint Eastwood was a worldwide hit.
25 Anthony Pirie, *Operation Bernhard* (New York: Grove, 1963), 119.
26 Report by Artur Schoster, 'Gruppe Wendig in Meran. Mündliche Unterrednung am 31. 7. 1945 bei der CIC und beim Intelligence Service in Meran', 1 August 1945, NARA, RG 226 (OSS), entry 194, box 65, folder 286.
27 Letter from Friedrich Schwend to the Bundeskriminalamt in Wiesbaden, 12 March 1959, Beschuldigter Friedrich Schwend, Akte 518 AR 339/69, Bl. 28, Barch LB, B 162.
28 Report by Artur Schoster, 'Gruppe Wendig in Meran. Mündliche Unterredung am 31. 7. 1945 bei der CIC und beim Intelligence Service in Meran', 1 August 1945, NARA, RG 226 (OSS), entry 194, box 65, folder 286.
29 Ibid.
30 Vincent La Vista to Herbert J. Cummings, 15 May 1947 (TOP SECRET), NARA, RG 84, Austria, Political Adviser, Gen. Records 1945–55, box 2, app. C, 4.
31 Elam, *Hitlers Fälscher*.
32 CIC Report, Situation Summary, Merano Area, 4 June 1945, NARA, RG 226 (OSS), E 174, B 59, F 109. Cf. Report SCI 12. Army Group, Munich, 28 July 1945, NARA, RG 263 CIA, Entry ZZ-16, box 50, latest release, Georg Spitz file.
33 Cf. Elam, *Hitlers Fälscher*, 133–55.
34 Vincent La Vista to Herbert J. Cummings, 15 May 1947 (TOP SECRET), NARA, RG 84, Austria, Political Adviser, Gen. Records 1945–55, box 2, app. C, 4.
35 ICRC Meran, 28 April 1945 (copy in the possession of the author).
36 Richard Breitman, 'Follow the Money', in Richard Breitman *et al.* (eds.), *U.S. Intelligence and the Nazis* (Washington, DC: National Archives and Records Administration, 2004), 121–36 at 121–7.
37 Lawrence Malkin, *Krueger's Men: The Secret Nazi Counterfeit Plot and the Prisoners of Block 19* (Boston: Little, 2008), xx.
38 Letter from Friedrich Schwend to the Bundeskriminalamt in Wiesbaden, 16 June 1959, Beschuldigter Friedrich Schwend, Akte 518 AR 339/69, Bl. 42, Barch LB, B 162.

39 'Interrogation Summary, Friedrich Schwend, Sturmbannführer Wendig, Doctor Sauter, Major Klemp', 21 May 1945 (SECRET), (copy in the possession of the author).

40 Report by US Army Intelligence Germany on Friedrich Schwend, 5 February 1948 (SECRET), NARA, RG 263 (CIA), War Crimes, IWG, CIA name files, entry ZZ-16, box 47, Fritz Venceslav Schwend.

41 Headquarters Sub Region Baden, 970th CIC Detachment, Region I, European Command, 'Subject Underground in Austria and American Zone of Germany', 2 June 1948 (Confidential), 41, records concerning Austrian Intelligence Services ZF400006WJ, Department of the Army, US Army Intelligence and Security Command, Fort George G. Meade, Maryland (copies in the possession of the author).

42 Report by Artur Schoster, 'Gruppe Wendig in Meran. Mündliche Unterredung am 31. 7. 1945 bei der CIC und beim Intelligence Service in Meran', 1 August 1945, NARA, RG 226 (OSS), entry 194, box 65, folder 286.

43 Max Waibel, *1945 Kapitulation in Norditalien: Originalbericht des Vermittlers* (Basle: Helbing & Lichtenhahn, 1981), 103.

44 Cf. Peter Grose, *Gentleman Spy: The Life of Allen Dulles* (Boston: Houghton Mifflin, 1994), 253.

45 Allen Dulles, *The Secret Surrender* (New York: Harper & Row, 1966), 67 ff.

46 Christof Mauch, *Schattenkrieg gegen Hitler: Das Dritte Reich im Visier der amerikanischen Geheimdienste 1941 bis 1945* (Stuttgart: Deutsche, 1999), 282–3.

47 Ibid. 283.

48 Ibid. 152 ff.

49 Extracts from the diary of Guido Zimmer, copy commissioned by the CIA, NARA, RG 263 (CIA), War Crimes, IWG, CIA name files, entry ZZ-16, box 59, Zimmer, Guido.

50 After Dulles had been working as a lawyer again after 1945, in the 1950s the Cold Warrior was brought back to head the CIA. Now Dulles could put his policy into action unhindered. In the hot phase of the Cold War he, as head of the CIA, and his brother, as US Secretary of State, held leading roles in the US power structure. Neal H. Petersen, 'From Hitler's Doorstep: Allen Dulles and the Penetration of Nazi Germany', in George C. Chalou (ed.), *The Secret War: The Office of Strategic Services in World War II* (Washington, DC: National Archives and Records Administration, 2002), 273–94.

51 Bradley F. Smith and Elena Agarossi, *Operation Sunrise: The Secret Surrender* (New York: Basic, 1979), 3.

52 Christopher Simpson, *Blowback*, 93.

53 Elam, *Hitlers Fälscher*, 114.

54 Interrogation of Wilhelm Harster, 22 August 1962, Bl. 700 f., Ermittlungssache gegen Karl Wolff, Akte 208 ARZ 203/59, Barch LB, B 162.

55 Kerstin von Lingen, *SS und Secret Service: 'Verschwörung des Schweigens': die Akte Karl Wolff* (Paderborn: Schöningh, 2010). Cf. idem, 'Conspiracy of Silence: How the "Old Boys" of American Intelligence Shielded SS General Karl Wolff from Prosecution', *Holocaust and Genocide Studies*, 22 (2008), 74–109 at 80. Idem, 'Der lange Weg zum Verhandlungsfrieden: Hintergründe und Interessen an "Operation Sunrise"', in Gerald Steinacher and Hans-Günter Richardi, *Für Freiheit und Recht in Europa: Der 20. Juli 1944 und der Widerstand gegen das NS-Regime in Deutschland, Österreich und Südtirol* (Innsbruck: Studien, 2009), 174–206 at 192. Idem, 'La lunga via verso la pace. Retrosceni e interessi all'"Operation Sunrise"', *Geschichte und Region/Storia e regione*, 17/1, *Faschismus und Architektur/Architettura e fascismo* (2008), 159–78 at 173.

56 'Headquarters 2677th Reg. OSS (Prov.), Trip to General Wolff's HQ 9–12 May 1945 by T. S. Ryan', 1 June 1945, Seeley G. Mudd Library, Princeton, Allen Dulles Papers, box 106. Cf. also Herbert Kappler, 'Bericht über Zusammenstoß zwischen Kräften des CNL und deutschen Einheiten im Raum Predazzo im Val di Cembra', 6 May 1945, Bundesarchiv Berlin, R 70, Italien, 7, Bl. 15–22. Cf. also Giuseppe Pantozzi, *Il Minotauro Argentato: Contributi alla conoscenza del movimento di resistenza di val di Fiemme* (Trento: Museo Storico, 2000).

57 *Stars and Stripes*, 17 May 1945, NARA, RG 338 (Fifth US-Army Records/Liasion Section Italy), box 3, format X.

58 Letter from Karl Wolff to US-General Kendall in Bozen, 13 May 1945 (SECRET), ibid.

59 Allen Dulles to Max Waibel, 12 June 1950, Seeley G. Mudd Library, Princeton, Allen Dulles Papers, box 57.

60 Dulles, *Secret Surrender*, 252 f.

61 Timothy Naftali, 'The CIA and Eichmann's Associates', in Breitman *et al.*, *U.S. Intelligence and the Nazis*, 337–74.

62 Richard J. Aldrich, *The Hidden Hand: Britain, America, and Cold War Secret Intelligence* (Woodstock: Overlook, 2002), 187.

63 Simpson, *Blowback*, 3 ff.

64 OSS Mission for Germany, X-2 Branch APO 655, 18 July 1945 (SECRET), concluding report on 'Mount Operation', NARA, RG 226 (OSS), entry 210, box 305, folder 'Mount Case'.

65 'Nachrichtendienstliche Planungen des Herrn Dr. Wilhelm Höttl', Stapo-Bericht, 23 September 1948, NARA, RG 263 (CIA), CIA name files, entry ZZ-16, box 24, Höttl, Wilhelm, vol. 2.

66 Norman J. W. Goda, 'The Nazi Peddler: Wilhelm Höttl and Allied Intelligence', in Breitman *et al.*, *U.S. Intelligence and the Nazis*, 265–92.

67 'Proposed Russian Zone Austria Network' and 'Network Montgomery', memoranda from Thomas A. Lucid, Counter Intelligence Corps, 40th CIC Detachment Land Upper Austria, APO 174, US Army, 3 September 1948, NARA, RG 263 (CIA), name files, entry ZZ-16, box 24, Höttl, Wilhelm, vol. 1.

68 Goda, 'The Nazi Peddler', 265–92.

69 Reports on Triska 1953, NARA, RG 263 CIA name files, box 52, folder Triska, Helmut.

70 Chief, Foreign Division M, Chief of Station, Karlsruhe, Operational, Guido Zimmer, 28 March 1951, NARA, RG 263 (CIA), War Crimes, IWG, CIA name files, entry ZZ-16, box 59, Zimmer, Guido.

71 Ibid.

72 CIC Headquarters, CIC, US Forces, European Theater, 'Subject: German Nationals who aided the Allies, to all CIC Regional Chiefs', 13 December 1945, signed Dale M. Garvey, Lt. Col. Infantry, S-3, for the Chief, CIC (SECRET), NARA, RG 319, IRR personal name files, box 546, folder 'Guido Zimmer'.

73 'Memorandum to General Donovan, from: G. Gaevernitz', 20 November 1945, NARA, RG 319, IRR personal name files, box 546, folder 'Guido Zimmer'. Handwritten note in file: 'for Zimmer'.

74 Chief, Foreign Division M, Chief of Station, Karlsruhe, Operational, Guido Zimmer, 28 March 1951, NARA, RG 263 (CIA), War Crimes, IWG, CIA name files, box 59, Zimmer, Guido.

75 Pace, *La via dei demoni*, 146. Cf. Grose, *Gentleman Spy*, 253.

76 Jens Scholten, 'Offiziere: Im Geiste unbesiegt', in Norbert Frei (ed.), *Karrieren im Zwielicht: Hitlers Eliten nach 1945* (Frankfurt: Campus, 2001), 135.

77 Ibid.

78 Cf. Reinhard Gehlen, *The Service: The Memoirs of General Reinhard Gehlen*, ed. David Irving (New York: World, 1972). Cf. Dieter Schenk, *Die braunen Wurzeln des BK* (Frankfurt am Main: Fischer, 2001).

79 Naftali, 'The CIA and Eichmann's Associates', 343–54.

80 Simpson, *Blowback*, 301 ff. Cf. also Salter, 'The Prosecution of Nazi War Criminals and the OSS', 77–119.

81 Simpson, *Blowback*, 259.

82 On the biography of Roschmann cf. Heinz Schneppen, *Odessa und das Vierte Reich: Mythen der Zeitgeschichte* (Berlin: Metropol, 2007), 138 ff. Agnoletti, *Enklave Rimini-Bellaria*, 88 ff.

83 CIC personnel file for Karl Hass, 1 January 1950, NARA, RG 263 (CIA), War Crimes, CIA name files, IWG, entry ZZ-16, box 19, Haas, Karl Theodor.

84 Goñi, *Real Odessa*, 260.

85 Vincent La Vista to Herbert J. Cummings, 15 May 1947 (TOP SECRET), NARA, RG 84, Austria, Political Adviser, Gen. Records 1945–55, entry 2057, box 2, app. B, 1.

86 Vincent La Vista to Herbert J. Cummings, 15 May 1947 (TOP SECRET), ibid. box 2, 1.

87 Simpson, *Blowback*, 184.

88 Ibid. 181.

89 Ibid. 177 ff.

90 Ibid. 180.

91 On the Ukrainians in the Rimini camp, see the memoirs of Jaroslaw Pankiw, *Rimins'kyi ansambl 'Burlaka' v moij pam'jati: Belljarija-Rimini Italija 1945–1947* (Kiev: Vyd-vo im. Oleny Telihy, 1999).

92 Agnoletti, *Enklave Rimini-Bellaria*, 102 ff.

93 Klee, *Persilscheine und falsche Pässe*, 29.

94 For the applications and distribution, Buchko had already assembled a five-man committee which immediately passed on detailed lists of names to the ICRC. The whole correspondence in the case of the Ukrainians in Rimini was classed as 'confidential!' by the Red Cross. Letter from Bishop Giovanni Buchko to the Italian Section of the ICRC in Rome, 4 December 1946, ICRC Geneva, Archives Générales, G. 68, Titres de voyage, box 954, Italie 1944–8, folder 'Titres de voyage: Italie 1944–Décembre 1947'.

95 Cf. ICRC Geneva, Archiv, Archives Générales, G. 68, Titres de voyage, box 954, Italie 1948–50, folder 'Ukrainiens Rimini'.

96 Aldrich, *Hidden Hand*, 142 ff.

97 Aarons and Loftus, *Unholy Trinity*, 126.

98 Simpson, *Blowback*, 182.

99 Ibid. 183.

100 Preliminary investigations into the murder of an uncertain number of Jews in September 1943 in Maina and other places on Lake Maggiore (Italy) by German members of the SS, statement from Dr Wilhelm Harster, 9 June 1960, Bl. 96, Akte 8 ARZ 16/1959, Barch LB, B 162.

101 Ralph Blumenthal, 'Vatican Is Reported to Have Furnished Aid to Fleeing Nazis', *New York Times* (26 January 1984), A 14.

102 Memorandum from the Director of Central Intelligence to the Assistant Chief of Staff, G-2, Department of the Army, 'Subject: Eugene Dollmann', 9 November

1951, NARA, RG 263 (CIA), War Crimes, IWG, entry ZZ-16, box 11, Dollmann, Eugen.

103 Cf. Jerzy Szynkowski *et al.*, *Das Führerhauptquartier Wolfschanze* (Kętrzyn: Kengraf, 2004).

104 Robert Wolfe, 'Coddling a Nazi Turncoat', in Breitman *et al.* (eds.), *U.S. Intelligence and the Nazis*, 317–31 at 322.

105 Interrogation of Eugen Dollmann, 23 February 1965, Beschuldigter Bosshammer Fritz, Akte 518 ARZ 4/63, Bl. 3189, Barch LB, B 162.

106 Wolfe, 'Coddling a Nazi Turncoat', 317–31 at 325.

107 Ibid. 317–31.

108 'Eugenio Dollmann und Eugene Wenner', document accompanying report from the Central Intelligence Group to Washington Headquarters, 20 November 1946 (SECRET), NARA, RG 263 (CIA), War Crimes, IWG, entry ZZ-16, box 11, Dollmann, Eugen.

109 Ibid.

110 Report from the Central Intelligence Group to Washington Headquarters, 20 November 1946 (SECRET), NARA, RG 263 (CIA), War Crimes, IWG, box 11, Dollmann, Eugen.

111 Eugen Dollmann, *Dolmetscher der Diktatoren* (Bayreuth: Hestia, 1963), 89.

112 Memorandum, Department of State, Leghorn, to Secretary of State, 13 April 1947 and 15 May 1947 (SECRET), NARA, RG 263 (CIA), War Crimes, IWG, Box 11, Dollmann, Eugen.

113 Memorandum Department of State, Leghorn, to Secretary of State, 8 May 1947 (SECRET), ibid.

114 Telegram from Central Intelligence Group, Special Operations in Washington, DC to the Heidelberg base, 22 October 1947 (SECRET), ibid.

115 Letter from Eugen Dollmann to a former SS comrade, 29 September 1950, (SE-CRET), NARA, RG 263 (CIA), War Crimes, CIA name files, IWG, box 7, Bormann, Martin, vols. 1, 2 of 3.

116 Report on Dollmann's activities in July 1950, NARA, RG 263 (CIA), War Crimes, IWG, box 11, Dollmann, Eugen.

117 Command from the SIM in Milan, signed Guido Bruno to headquarters in Rome, 27 August 1951, ibid.

118 'Martin Bormann im west-östlichen Zwielicht', *Die Zeit* (6 June 1997), 72.

119 Rodolfo Siviero and Mario Ursino Bertoldi (eds.), *L'arte e il nazismo: Esodo e ritorno delle opere d'arte italiane, 1938–1963* (Florence: Cantini édition d'arte, 1984). Cf. Tilmann Lahme and Holger Stunz, 'Wo sind Wagner-Partituren?', *FAZ* (28 July 2007), Z 1.

120 'Interrogation Report of SS-Standartenführer Rauff, Walther', 29 May 1945, NARA, RG 263 (CIA), War Crimes, IWG, CIA name files, box 42, Rauff, Walter, folder 1. Cf. interrogation of Dr Wilhelm Harster, 9 June 1960, Bl. 10, Zentrale Stelle der Landesjustizverwaltungen Ludwigsburg, Akt 8 ARZ 16/1959, Bundesarchiv/Außenstelle Ludwigsburg (Barch LB), B 162. Cf. Aarons and Loftus, *Unholy Trinity*, 37–40.

121 'Interrogation Report of SS-Standartenführer Rauff, Walther', 29 May 1945, NARA, RG 263 (CIA), War Crimes, IWG, CIA name files, box 42, Rauff, Walter, folder 1. Cf. Paolo Granzotto, *Montanelli* (Bologna: Mulino, 2004), 83 f. Cf. Serena Gana Cavallo and Granzotto e Montanelli, 'Due giornalisti', *Deportati* [website] <http://www.deportati.it/recensioni/montanelli.html>, accessed 21 October 2008.

122 Memorandum from Stephen J. Spingarn, CIC Director, 5th US Army, 3 May 1945 (SECRET), NARA, RG 263 (CIA), War Crimes, IWG, CIA name files, box 42, Rauff, Walter, folder 1.

123 Report from Stephen J. Spingarn, 1 May 1945 (SECRET), NARA, RG 263 (CIA), War Crimes, IWG, CIA name files, box 42, Rauff, Walter, folder 1.

124 'Interrogation Report of SS-Standartenführer Rauff, Walther', 29 May 1945, NARA, RG 263 (CIA), War Crimes, IWG, CIA name files, entry ZZ-16, box 42, Rauff, Walter, folder 1.

125 'Subject: Interrogation of SD Officers', report by Stephen J. Spingarn, 1 May 1945 (SECRET), NARA, RG 263 (CIA), War Crimes, IWG, CIA name files, box 42, Rauff, Walter, folder 1.

126 Simon Wiesenthal Center, New York, 'Declassified Documents Reveal Close Relationship Between Nazi War Criminal Walter Rauff and High Church Officials' and 'Summary of Facts and Documents Simon Wiesenthal Center Investigation on Rauff and the Church', 1984, copy, Simon Wiesenthal Dokumentationszentrum Vienna, Walter Rauff files.

127 Ibid.

128 Simpson, *Blowback*, 92–5.

129 'File memo' about an interview by the Higher State Prosecution Service with Robert Katz on the Rauff case, 16 January 1963, Akte 8 AR Z 16/1959, Barch LB, B 162.

130 Christian Habbe, 'Im Visier der Nazi-Jäger', *Der Spiegel*, 36 (2001), 164–72 at 168.

131 Ibid. at 172.

132 Cf. 'Interrogation Report on Dr. Segna Walter', 13 May 1945 (SECRET), NARA, RG 263 (CIA), War Crimes, IWG, CIA name files, box 47, Segna, Walter.

133 Preliminary investigations into the murder of an uncertain number of Jews in September 1943 in Maina and other places on Lake Maggiore (Italy) by German members of the SS, statement from Dr Wilhelm Harster Bl. 4, Zentrale Stelle der Landesjustizverwaltungen Ludwigsburg, 13 June 1960, Akte 8 ARZ 16/1959, Barch LB, B 162.

134 'I particolari dell'arresto di uno spione della Gestapo', *Alto Adige* (1 September 1946), 2.

135 'Subject: Interrogation of SD Officers', report by Stephen J. Spingarn, 1 May 1945 (SECRET), NARA, RG 263 (CIA), War Crimes, IWG, CIA name files, Rauff, Walter, folder 1.

136 James V. Milano and Patrick Rogan, *Soldiers, Spies and the Rat Line: America's Undeclared War Against the Soviets* (Washington: Brassey's, 2000), 203.

137 Curriculum vitae of Karl-Theodor Schütz, born 11 April 1907 in Mayen/Rheinland, assembled by Axel-Elmar Schütz for the author, 13 February 2002 (original in the possession of the author).

138 Vincent La Vista to Herbert J. Cummings, 15 May 1947 (TOP SECRET), NARA, RG 84, Austria, Political Adviser, Gen. Records 1945–55, entry 2057, box 2, app. B, 1.

139 'Ich war wertvoll für die', *Der Spiegel*, 4 (1997), 71 f.

140 Robert Katz, *Dossier Priebke* (Milan: Rizzoli, 1996), 130.

141 CIC briefing on Karl Hass, 1948 (SECRET), NARA, RG 263 (CIA), War Crimes, CIA name files, IWG, box 19, Haas [*sic*], Karl Theodor.

142 Katz, *Dossier Priebke*, 130.

143 'Subject: Karl Hass', Overview of the activities of Hass for the CIC, August 1954, NARA, RG 263 (CIA), War Crimes, CIA name files, IWG, box 19, Haas [*sic*], Karl Theodor.

144 CIC report on Karl Hass, 16 April 1951 (SECRET), ibid.

145 Notes on the meeting of Joseph Luongo with Karl Hass in 3. 1951 (SECRET), ibid.

146 Cf. Erwin A. Schmidl (ed.), *Spione, Partisanen, Kriegspläne. Österreich im frühen Kalten Krieg 1945–1958* (Vienna: Böhlau, 2000).

147 Katz, *Dossier Priebke*, 64 ff.

148 Aarons and Loftus, *Unholy Trinity*, 43.

149 Breitman, 'Follow the Money', 121–7.

150 CIA note, 'George Spitz (Tarbaby)' undated, NARA, RG 263 (CIA), War Crimes, CIA name files, IWG, entry ZZ-18, box 50, second release, Georg Spitz.

151 Mitteilung über Tarnaby [Tarbaby?], 24 February 1948, ibid.

152 Register of population movements [Bevölkerungsbewegungen], September 1947, entry for 'Giovanni Neuhold', Stadtarchiv Meran, Bestand Gemeinde Meran, ZA 15 K, no. 2599.

153 Michele Battini, *Peccati di memoria: La mancata Norimberga italiana* (Rome: GLF editori Laterza, 2003).

154 Ginsborg, *History of Contemporary Italy*, 79.

155 Simpson, *Blowback*, 118 f.

156 Ibid. 185.

157 Subject: OSI [Office of Special Investigations] investigation of Klaus Barbie (SECRET), 15 April 1983, NARA, RG 263 (CIA), War Crimes, CIA name files, IWG, entry ZZ-16, box 12, folder 1 of 4, second release, Draganović, Krunoslav.

158 Quoted in Elam, *Hitlers Fälscher*, 180 f.

159 Report AFHQ Liaison Office (Secret), 26 November 1947, Subject: Draganovic Krunoslav, NARA, RG 263, CIA, War Crimes, CIA name files, IWG, entry ZZ-16, box 12, folder 1 of 4, Draganović, Krunoslav.

160 Milano and Rogan, *Soldiers, Spies and the Rat Line*, 203, 204–7.

161 Interrogation of Albert Gottfried Schwend, 1 August 1960, Beschuldigter Friedrich Schwend, Akte 518 AR 339/69, Bl. 83, Barch LB, B 162.

162 Ibid.

163 Application for a Red Cross travel document for Venceslav Turi, ICRC Rome, 30 September 1946, ICRC Geneva, Archive, 'Titres de Voyage CICR 1945–1993', application 28, 192.

164 Letter from the PCA to the ICRC Rome, 30 September 1946, ibid. 28, 192.

165 Letter from the Italian Red Kross in Rome (AGIUS) to the ICRC Rome concerning Turi Venceslav, 30 September 1946, ibid. 28, 192.

166 Letter presumably from AGIUS to the ICRC in Rome concerning Turi Hedda, 2 October 1946, ibid. 28, 191. Application for a Red Cross travel document for Hedda Turi, ICRC Rome, 2 October 1946, ibid. 28, 191.

167 Cf. Erhard Dabringhaus, *Klaus Barbie, the Shocking Story of How the U.S. Used This Nazi War Criminal as an Intelligence Agent* (Washington, DC: Acropolis, 1984), 69 ff.

168 'The Rat Line. Barbie's Exit was U.S.-Made', *Washington Post*, 5 July 1983, NARA, RG 263 (CIA), War Crimes, CIA name files, entry ZZ-16, box 4, Klaus Barbie, vol. 2.

169 Klee, *Persilscheine und falsche Pässe*, 29.

170 Report from the Department of the Army, Office of the Assistant Chief of Staff for Intelligence, Memorandum for Central Intelligence Deputy Director in the Barbie Case, 18 February 1967, RG 263 (CIA), War Crimes, CIA name files, entry ZZ-16, box 4, Barbie, Klaus.

171 Cf. Ermittlungsverfahren gegen Klaus Barbie, Zentrale Stelle der Landesjustizverwaltungen Ludwigsburg, Akte II 107 ARZ 164/75, Bl. 82, Barch LB, B 162.

172 Alice Kaufmann, *Klaus Barbie: Dem Schlächter von Lyon entkommen* (Vienna: Edition S Verlag der Österreichischen Staatsdruckerei, 1987), 179 ff.

173 Klaus Barbie to Consul J. Hieber, copied to Friedrich Schwend, 25 February 1966, Fritz-Bauer-Institut, Frankfurt am Main, Kopie des Schwend-Archivs, folder IV./3.

174 Tom Bower, *Klaus Barbie: Lyon, Augsburg, La Paz—Karriere eines Gestapo-Chefs* (Berlin: Rotbuch, 1984), 229.

175 CIA investigation into the connections between Schwend und Klaus Barbie, 23 February 1983, NARA, RG 263 (CIA), War Crimes, IWG, CIA name files, entry Z-16, box 47, Schwend, Fritz Venceslav, folder 2.

176 CIA memorandum for the record, subject meeting with ASCI re Klaus Altmann aka Barbie 5 April 1967 (SECRET), RG 263 (CIA), War Crimes, IWG, CIA name files, entry Z-16, box 4, Barbie, Klaus.

177 Barbie Klaus, RG 263, CIA, box 4, report by the Department of the Army, Office of the Assistant Chief of Staff for Intelligence, Memorandum for Central Intelligence Deputy Director 18 February 1967, RG 263 (CIA), War Crimes, IWG, CIA name files, entry Z-16, box 4, Barbie, Klaus.

178 CIA memorandum for the record, subject meeting with ASCI re Klaus Altmann aka Barbie 5 April 1967 (SECRET), RG 263 (CIA). War Crimes, IWG, CIA name files, entry Z-16, box 4, Barbie, Klaus.

179 In Elam, *Hitlers Fälscher*, 167.

180 FBI, report 11 September 1972 (copy in the possession of the author).

181 Letter of recommendation for Herbert John, issued by Friedrich Schwend to the President of Paraguay Alfredo Strössner, 25 July 1964, Fritz-Bauer-Institut, Frankfurt am Main, Kopie des Schwend-Archivs, folder I./82/3.

182 Kaufmann, *Klaus Barbie*, 11.

183 Cf. NARA, RG 263 (CIA), War Crimes, IWG, CIA name files, box 4, Klaus Barbie. Cf. also Salter, 'The Prosecution of Nazi War Criminals and the OSS', 77–119.

184 Thomas O'Toole, 'U.S. Admits Sheltering Barbie', *Washington Post*, 17 August 1983, A 1.

185 Meding, *Flucht vor Nürnberg?*, 84.

186 Heinz Höhne, 'Der Schlächter von Lyon', *Der Spiegel*, 19 (1987), 192–207.

187 Milano and Rogan, *Soldiers, Spies and the Rat Line*, 205 f.

188 Ibid. 203.

189 Report from the Office of Special Investigation (OSI): Robert Jan Verbelen and the United States Government. A Report to the Assistant Attorney General, Criminal Division, US Department of Justice, June 1988, NARA, RG 263 (CIA), name files, entry ZZ-16, box 53, folder 'Verbelen, Robert Jan'.

190 'Historical Report for the Year 1949, Vienna Sub-Detachment', NARA, RG 407 World War II. Operation Reports 1940–8, entry 427, Central Intelligence, box 18337, folder History 430 CIC Detachment, 1949.

191 OSI report, June 1988, 14.

192 Ibid. 15.

193 Ibid. 22.

194 CIA report on Walter Rauff alias Abdullah Rauf, 24 February 1950, NARA, RG 263 (CIA), War Crimes, IWG, CIA name files, Rauff, Walter, folder 1.

195 Richard Breitman, Norman J. W. Goda, and Paul Brown, 'The Gestapo', in Breitman *et al.*, *U.S. Intelligence and the Nazis*, 137–64 at 153–9.

196 In Victor Farías, *Die Nazis in Chile* (Berlin: Philo, 2002), 311.

197 Tom Segev, *Simon Wiesenthal: The Life and Legends* (New York: Random House, 2010), 330 f.

198 Salvador Allende to Simon Wiesenthal in Vienna, 1972, 'Doy respuesta a su carta de 21 agosto último, relativa al caso Rauff', Simon-Wiesenthal-Dokumentation-szentrum Vienna, folder Walter Rauff.

199 Michael Wildt, *Generation des Unbedingten: Das Führungskorps des Reichssicherheitshauptamtes* (Hamburg: Hamburger Edition, 2002), 739 f.

200 Wiesenthal, *Justice Not Vengeance*, 91.

Chapter 5

1 Cf. Argentinian Commission of Historians, 'Comisión para el Esclarecimiento de las Actividades del Nacionalsocialismo en la Argentina', *CEANA*, Final Report, Buenos Aires, (1999) <http://www.ceana.org.ar/final/final.htm>, accessed 1 Apr. 2007.

2 Ronald C. Newton, 'Italienischer Faschismus und deutscher Nationalsozialismus in Argentinien. Eine vergleichende Analyse', in Meding, *Nationalsozialismus und Argentinien*, 117–38 at 120.

3 Ibid. at 121.

4 Blaschitz, 'NS-Flüchtlinge österreichischer Herkunft', 103–36 at 104.

5 Regula Nigg and Philipp Mettauer, '"Wir sind für euch immer noch die Emigranten". Eine österreichisch-argentinische Lebensgeschichte', in Dokumentationsarchiv des österreichischen Widerstandes, *Jahrbuch 2003*, 12–41.

6 Cf. Carlota Jackisch, *El nazismo y los refugiados alemanes en la Argentina, 1933–1945* (Buenos Aires: Editorial de Belgrano, 1989).

7 Cf. Regula Nigg, Philipp Mettauer, and Oliver Kühschelm (eds.), *ÖsterreicherInnen im Exil: Die La Plata-Staaten Argentinien, Uruguay, Paraguay 1934–1945* (Vienna: Documentation Centre of Austrian Resistance, 2004), 66. Cf. also the history of the German-speaking colony in Cobán in Guatemala.

8 Cf. Anne Saint Sauveur-Henn, 'Deutsche Einwanderung an den Río de la Plata während des Dritten Reiches und die Polarisierung der deutschen Gemeinschaft in Argentinien', in Holger M. Meding (ed.), *Argentinien und das Dritte Reich* (Berlin: Wissenschaftlicher, 2008), 57–72.

9 Holger M. Meding and Lucia de Stoia, *La ruta de los nazis en tiempos de Perón* (Buenos Aires: Emecé, 2000), 195.

10 Blaschitz, 'Austrian National Socialists in Argentina after 1945', 226–7.

11 Meding and Stoia, *La ruta de los nazis*, 194.

12 Cf. Bertagna and Sanfilippo, 'Per una prospettiva comparata dell'emigrazione nazifascista dopo la seconda guerra mondiale', 532.

13 Volker Koop, *Hitlers fünfte Kolonne: Die Auslands-Organisation der NSDAP* (Berlin: Be.bra, 2009), 260.

14 Cf. Carlota Jackisch, 'Cuantificación de Criminales de Guerra Según Fuentes Argentinas, informe final', *CEANA* (1998) <http://www.ceana.org.ar/final/jackicsh.zip>, accessed 22 March 2004.

15 Wilhelm Lütge et al., *Deutsche in Argentinien 1520–1980* (2nd edn, Buenos Aires: Alemann, 1981), 306.

16 Cf. Fernando Devoto, 'Las politicas migratorias Argentinas (1930–1955). Continuidades, tensiones y rupturas', *CEANA*, Final Report, Buenos Aires (1999) <http://www.ceana.org.ar/final/final.htm>, accessed 1 Apr. 2007. Cf. Federica Bertagna, *La Patria di riserva: L'emigrazione fascista in Argentina* (Rome: Donzelli, 2006), 159 ff.

17 Wilfred von Oven, *Ein 'Nazi' in Argentinien* (Duisburg: VAWS, 1999), 33.

18 NARA, RG 242, BDC, SS-Enlisted Men, von Oven, Wilfred, born 4 May 1912, reel N060, 2826–32.

19 Oven, *Ein 'Nazi' in Argentinien*, 53.

20 'Subject: Indiscriminate Issuing and Use of Identity Documents of the International- al Red Cross', US Consul General in Vienna, Laurence G. Frank, to the US Foreign Minister, 20 January 1947 (TOP SECRET), and enclosed 'Summary of Information', 16 December 1946, NARA, RG 84, Austria, Political Adviser, General Records 1945–1955, entry 2057, box 2.

21 Fernando J. Devoto, 'Italia como país de transito a la Argentina para Nazis y otros crimi- nales de guerra', Argentinian Historians' Commission, *CEANA*, Final Report, Buenos Aires (1999) <http://www.ceana.org.ar/final/devoto.zip>, accessed 22 March 2004.

22 'L'emigrazione in Argentina', *Alto Adige* (1 March 1947), 2.

23 Ibid.

24 'Gli emigranti bussano alla porta. 1200 alto atesini attendono di partire per l'Argentina', *Alto Adige* (3 August 1947), 2.

25 Blaschitz, *Austrian National Socialists*, 226 f.

26 'Argentinien spekuliert mit Grund und Boden', *Dolomiten* (22 June 1949), 4.

27 'Gli emigranti bussano alla porta. 1200 alto atesini attendono di partire per l'Argentina', *Alto Adige* (3 August 1947), 2.

28 Meding, *Flucht vor Nürnberg?*, 71.

29 Hans Maler to Alois Hudal, 8 April 1949, Nachlass Hudal, Anima, box 41.

30 Hans Maler to Alois Hudal, 22 April 1949, ibid.

31 In Meding, *Flucht vor Nürnberg?*, 87.

32 Galland, *Die Ersten und die Letzten*, 9.

33 Matthias Schönwald, *Deutschland und Argentinien nach dem Zweiten Weltkrieg: Politische und wirtschaftliche Beziehungen und deutsche Auswanderung 1945–1955*, (Paderborn: Schön- ingh, 1998).

34 Cf. Marc Jean Masurovsky, 'The Safehaven Program: The Allied Response to Nazi Post-defeat Planning 1944–1948', M.A. thesis, American University, Washington DC, 1990.

35 Cf. Bertagna, *La Patria di riserva*, 209 ff.

36 'Consultation among the American Republics with Respect to the Argentine Situation', Memorandum of the US Government, February 1946, NARA, RG 59, Argentine Bluebook, E 1083/1084, box 1.

37 Memorandum of the US Government, February 1946, 131, ibid. Cf. the Argentin- ian response to the US's Blue Book: República Argentina, Ministério de Relaciones Exteriores y Culto (ed.), *La República Argentina frente al Libro Azul* (Buenos Aires: Direc- ción de información al exterior, 1946).

38 Cf. Victoria Caudery Allison, 'The Bitch Goddess and the Nazi Elvis: Peronist Argentina in the U.S. Popular Imagination', Ph.D. dissertation, State University of New York, Stony Brook, 2001.

39 Virginia Prewett, '90,000 Nazis Carry On in Argentina', *Prevent World War III*, 17 (Oct./Nov. 1946), 13–15.

40 Eric Rath, 'The Mission of Argentina's Senor Bracamonte', ibid. 35–6.

41 CIA report, 'German Nationalist and Neo-Nazi Activities in Argentina', 8 July 1953 (SECRET), P. 5, NARA, General CIA Records, 62-00865R, box 0003, folder 0003.

42 Report from the State Department, 'Nelson Rockefeller statement, January 11', State Department, 2 February 1946, NARA, RG 59, Decimal Files 862.20235, Ar- gentina, box 6738.

43 Ulrich Albrecht, 'Deutscher Wissenschaftlerexodus in der Nachkriegszeit', in Med- ing, *Nationalsozialismus und Argentinien*, 139–48 at 140.

44 Ulrich Albrecht *et al.*, *Die Spezialisten: Deutsche Naturwissenschaftler und Techniker in der Sowjetunion nach 1945* (Berlin: Dietz, 1992).

45 Albrecht, 'Deutscher Wissenschaftlerexodus', 144.

46 Tom Bower, *The Paperclip Conspiracy: The Hunt for the Nazi Scientists* (Boston: Little, 1987).

47 Cf. the CIA file on Wernher von Braun, NARA, RG 263 (CIA), War Crimes, IWG, CIA name files, box 8.

48 Undated letter from the Argentinian Foreign Minister Dr Jeronimo Remorino to US High Commissioner, letter from John McCloy to Foreign Minister Jeronimo Remorino, 5 May 1952, NARA, RG 466, HICOG, McCloy Papers, Classified General Records 1949–52, entry 1, box 41, folder D (52), 1089–1120.

49 Meding, *Flucht vor Nürnberg?*, 87–9.

50 Cf. Newton, *The 'Nazi Menace' in Argentina*, 376 ff.

51 The first prototypes of the Pulqui were designed by Émile Dewoitine. The designer had to flee from France, for he was wanted by the French authorities as a Nazi collaborator. In Argentina he found new work opportunities and later, in Tank, a powerful competitor. Cf. Linda Hunt, *Secret Agenda: The United States Government, Nazi Scientists and Project Paperclip* (New York: St Martin's, 1991), 150.

52 Ruth Stanley, 'Der Beitrag deutscher Luftfahrtingenieure zur argentinischen Luftfahrtforschung und -entwicklung nach 1945: das Wirken der Gruppe Tank in Argentinien, 1947–1955', in Meding, *Nationalsozialismus und Argentinien*, 161–83.

53 In Ernst Klee, *Was sie taten—was sie wurden: Ärzte, Juristen und andere Beteiligte am Kranken- und Judenmord* (Frankfurt am Main: Fischer, 1986), 40.

54 Rudel, *Aus Krieg und Frieden*, 194.

55 CIA report, 'German Nationalist and Neo-Nazi Activities in Argentina' (SECRET), 8 July 1953, NARA, General CIA Records, 62-00865R, box 0003, folder 0003.

56 Cf. Frei, *Vergangenheitspolitik*, 326 ff.

57 Cf. Gerard Gröneveld, *Kriegsberichter, Nederlandse SS-oorlogsverslaggevers 1941–1945* (Nijmegen: Vantilt, 2004), 356–402.

58 CIA report on Otto Skorzeny to the Department of State, Deputy Assistant Secretary for Security, 20 February 1967, NARA, RG 263 (CIA), War Crimes, IWG, CIA name files, box 49, Skorzeny, Otto, vol. 2, 4 of 4.

59 Klee, *Persilscheine und falsche Pässe*, 25.

60 Galland, *Die Ersten und die Letzten*, 17.

61 Gabriele Ley, 'Deutsche Naturwissenschaftler an argentinischen Universitäten nach 1945', in Meding, *Nationalsozialismus und Argentinien*, 149–60 at 160.

62 NARA, RG 466 Office of the US High Commissioner for Germany, Bonn, Security-Segregated General Records 1949–1952, entry 10, box 1, Decimal Files 301–301G, folder 301 'Diplomatic and Consular Relations 1949–1952 by country'.

63 On Italian–Argentinean relations cf. the book by Fernando J. Devoto, *Historia de los italianos en la Argentina* (Buenos Aires: Biblos, 2006).

64 Paolo Valente, *Porto di Mare, frammenti dell'anima multiculturale di una piccola città europea: Italiani (e molti altri) a Merano tra esodi, deportazioni e guerre (1934–1953)* (Trento: Temi, 2003–5), 69 ff. Cf. Paolo Valente, 'Juan Domingo Perón a Merano', *Paolo 'Bill' Valente* [website] <http://www.webalice.it/valente.paolo/peron.htm>, accessed 2 Jan. 2005; also in *Alto Adige* (7 October 2004), 48.

65 Cf. Bertagna, *La Patria di riserva*, and Pace, *La via dei demoni*, 6.

66 Peron Gift Packages in Italy, US Embassy in Rome to the State Department Washington DC, 5 June 1947 (CONFIDENTIAL), NARA, RG 84, Embassy Rome, box 20, file 848, 'Argentine Gift Packages'.

67 Rudel, *Aus Krieg und Frieden*, 309 f.

68 Newton, '*Nazi Menace*', 375.

69 Devoto, 'Italia como país de transito a la Argentina'.

70 ACS Roma, Presidenza del Consiglio dei Ministri, 1944–47, file 3402, Emigrazione per la Repubblica Argentina, subfolder II, Accordo italo-argentino di Emigrazione (Missione Jacini).

71 Matteo Sanfilippo, 'Archival Evidence on Postwar Italy as a Transit Point for Central and Eastern European Migrants', in Oliver Rathkolb (ed.), *Revisiting the National Socialist Legacy: Coming to Terms with Forced Labor, Expropriation, Compensation, and Restitution* (Innsbruck: Studien, 2002), 241–58 at 244.

72 FBI report, John Edgar Hoover and Department of State, 8 March 1946, 'Subject: Ludwig Freude—Argentina', NARA, RG 59, Decimal Files, 862.20235 Argentina, box 6739.

73 US Embassy Buenos Aires to the Department of State, 19 February 1946, NARA, RG 59, E 1084, box 3, folder Ludwig Freude.

74 'Argentina's No. 1 Nazi to Lose Citizenship', *Washington Post* (14 March 1946), 19; ibid.

75 FBI Report, John Edgar Hoover to Department of State, 8 March 1946, 'Subject: Ludwig Freude—Argentina', NARA, RG 59, Decimal Files, 862.20235 Argentina, box 6739.

76 Lütge *et al.*, *Deutsche in Argentinien*, 308.

77 CIA report, 'German Nationalist and Neo-Nazi Activities in Argentina', 8 July 1953 (SECRET), p. 8, NARA, General CIA Records, 62-00865R, box 0003, folder 0003.

78 Cf. US War Department files on Fritz Mandl, NARA, RG 153, Judge Advocate General, entry 144, dossier file, box 58, folder 100-608 'Fritz Mandl', CIA Report, 'German Nationalist and Neo-Nazi Activities in Argentina' (SECRET), 8 July 1953, NARA, General CIA Records, 62-00865R, box 0003, folder 0003. On Mandl, see Newton, '*Nazi Menace*', 315 ff.

79 SS personnel files, Fuldner, Horst, born 16 December 1910, SS-Officer, SS no. 31,710, NARA, RG 242, formerly BDC.

80 Munich Court, judgment against Horst Fuldner, 5 May 1937, NARA, RG 242, formerly BDC, SS-Personalunterlagen, Horst Fuldner, born 16 December 1910, SS-Officer, SS no. 31,710.

81 Cesarani, *Eichmann, His Life*, 206 f.

82 Beatriz Gurevich, 'Agencias estatales y actors que interviniero en la inmigracion de criminales de Guerra y colaboracionistas en la pos segunda guerra mundial. El caso Argentina', in Comisión para el Esclarecimiento de las Actividades del Nazismo en la Argentina (CEANA) (ed.), *Tercer Informe de Avance*, 2 vols. (Buenos Aires: CEANA, 1998).

83 Goñi, *Operazione Odessa*, 150–3.

84 Cf. baptismal register of the parish of Waidhofen an der Ybbs, entry for Mario Franz Ruffinengo, 27 February 1919.

85 Jackisch, 'Cuantificación de Criminales de Guerra'.

86 Maler, *Frieden, Krieg und 'Frieden'*, 323.

87 Ibid.

88 Hans Maler to Alois Hudal, 14 May 1948, Nachlass Hudal, Anima, box 27.

89 Ibid.

90 Letter from the President of the Croatian Committee in Rome, Antonio Budimirovic, to the Italian Ministry of the Interior, 29 October 1947, ACS, Int. D.G., P.S., Div. AA. Massime 14, 'Istruzione di Polizia Militare', file 89, folder 'Croati'.

91 Meding, *Flucht vor Nürnberg?*, 86.

92 CIA report, 'Subject: Slav Immigration to Argentina', 1 March 1949 (CON-FIDENTIAL), NARA, RG 263, CIA Databank Document no. CIA-RDP82-00457R0024001600048.

93 Posner and Ware, *Mengele*, 119.

94 Maler, *Krieg und 'Frieden'*, 318.

95 Interview with Karl Nicolussi-Leck, 10 May 2004.

96 File Karl Nicolussi-Leck, born 14 March 1917, Rasse- und Siedlungshauptamt (RuSHA), SS no. 341.499, NARA, RG 242, formerly BDC.

97 SS personnel files, SS Officers, Nicolussi-Leck, Karl, born 14 March 1917, SS no. 423,876, NARA, RG 242, formerly BDC.

98 Ulrich Saft, *Der Krieg in der Heimat: Das bittere Ende zwischen Weser und Elbe* (Langen-hagen: U. Saft, 1990), 54.

99 Steurer, 'Meldungen aus dem Land', 41.

100 Maik Fuchs, 'Ein Husarenritt', *MF-Panzermodellbau* (July 2001) <http://www.mf-panzermodellbau.de/Artikel der Husarenritt.htm>, accessed 3 Sept. 2004. On the British homepage *Sig-Rune*, Nicolussi-Leck applied, with a personal letter with dedi-cation, for Nazi souvenirs, <http://www.sigruneuk.com>, accessed 16 Nov. 2004.

101 Jean Mabire, *Die SS-Panzer-Division 'Wiking'* (Eggolsheim: Dörfler, 2002), 282–97. Cf. also Erich Kern, *Kampf in der Ukraine 1941–1944* (Göttingen: Plesse, 1964), 134 ff.

102 Wilhelm Eppacher and Karl Ruef, *Hohe Tapferkeitsauszeichnungen an Tiroler im Zweiten Weltkrieg*, Veröffentlichungen des Innsbrucker Stadtarchivs 6 (Innsbruck: Stadtmag-istrat, 1975), 41. For a heroic version of Leck's 'achievements' as an SS soldier, see Franz Kurowski, *Panzer Aces II: Battle Stories of German Tank Commanders in World War II* (Mechanicsburg: Stackpole Books, 2004), 273 ff.

103 Saft, *Der Krieg in der Heimat*, 53–66.

104 Eppacher and Ruef, *Hohe Tapferkeitsauszeichnungen an Tiroler*, 41.

105 Counter Intelligence Corps, 430th CIC Detachment, City of Vienna, 'Subject: Possible Nazi Group', June 1948 (CONFIDENTIAL), Records Concerning Austrian In-telligence Services ZF400006WJ, Department of the Army, US Army Intelligence and Security Command, Fort George G. Meade, Maryland, 107 ff. (copies of the files in the possession of the author).

106 Ibid.

107 Ibid. 118.

108 'Conclusion and Recommendations', ibid.

109 Letter from Ambros Murbitzer, Vienna, Civil Censorship Group Austria, APO 777 US Army, Vienna Station, 20 March 1948 (CONFIDENTIAL), ibid.

110 Conversation with Franz Berger, 24 April 2007.

111 Confirmation from Josef Hoby OSB, Gries Benedictine Monastery, Bozen, for Franz Riedl, 9 December 1948, Südtiroler Landesarchiv, Nachlass Franz Hierony-mus Riedl, box 9.2, folder 'Post 1947/48'.

112 Hudal to Riedl, 10 December 1948, ibid.

113 Hudal to Riedl, 24 April 1948, ibid.

114 Letter to Riedl, no sender, 19 May 1948, ibid.

115 Riedl to Hudal, 2 May 1948, ibid.

116 Cf. also Isabel Heinemann, 'Die Rassenexperten der SS und die bevölkerungspoli-tische Neuordnung Südosteuropas', in Beer and Seewann (eds.), *Südostforschung im Schatten des Dritten Reiches*, 135–57.

117 Samuel Salzborn, 'Zwischen Volksgruppentheorie, Völkerrechtslehre und Volks-tumskampf. Hermann Raschhofer als Vordenker eines völkischen Minderheiten-rechts', *Sozial. Geschichte*, 21/3 (2006), 29–52 at 43.

118 Ibid. 47.
119 Raschhofer to Riedl, 2 April 1948, Südtiroler Landesarchiv, Nachlass Riedl, box 9.2, folder 'Post 1947/48'.
120 Letter from Riedl to Hudal, 2 May 1948, ibid.
121 Franz Riedl and Theodor Veiter (eds.), *Volkstum zwischen Moldau, Etsch und Donau: Festschrift für Franz Hieronymus Riedl dargeboten zum 65. Lebensjahr* (Vienna: Braumüller, 1971). Cf. curriculum vitae of Prof. Dr Franz Hieronymus Riedl, ibid. 1–22.
122 Interview with Karl Nicolussi-Leck, 10 May 2004.
123 Ibid.
124 Application for a Red Cross travel document for Karl Nicolussi-Leck, Italian Red Cross in Rome, 31 August 1948, ICRC Geneva, Archive, 'Titres de Voyage CICR 1945–1993', application 83, 519.
125 Application for a Red Cross travel document for Maria Nicolussi-Leck, ICRC Rome, 31 August 1948, ibid., application 83, 526.
126 Application for a Red Cross travel document for Karl Nicolussi-Leck, ICRC Rome, 31 August 1948, ibid., application 83, 519.
127 Report of the Federal Police, Innsbruck, to the State Prosecution Office, Innsbruck, 19 January 1948, Tiroler Landesarchiv (TLA), Bestand Landesgericht, file 10 Vr 2138/47 'Franz Rubatscher'.
128 Ibid.
129 Jackisch, 'Cuantificación de Criminales de Guerra'.
130 NARA, RG 263 (CIA), War Crimes, CIA name files, IWG second release, box 109, Franz Rubatscher.
131 Report of the Federal Police, Innsbruck, to the State Prosecution Office, Innsbruck, 15 April 1947, TLA, Bestand Landesgericht, file 10 Vr 2138/47 'Franz Rubatscher', 2.
132 Ibid., file 'Franz Rubatscher'.
133 NARA, RG 263 (CIA), War Crimes, CIA name files, IWG second release, box 109, Franz Rubatscher. Cf. also Gerald Steinacher, 'Das Trentino in der Operationszone Alpenvorland 1943–1945', D.Phil. Arb., Innsbruck University, Austria, 1995, 66 ff.
134 Report of the Federal Police, Innsbruck, to the State Prosecution Office, Innsbruck, 15 April 1947, TLA, Bestand Landesgericht, file 10 Vr 2138/47 'Franz Rubatscher', 5.
135 Application for a Red Cross travel document for Francesco Rubatscher, ICRC Rome, 6 June 1947, letter from PCA to ICRC Rome, 10 March 1947; letter from AGIUS in Rome to ICRC Rome in the case of Franz Rubatscher, 15 March 1947, ICRC Geneva, Archive, 'Titres de Voyage CICR 1945–1993', application 48, 735.
136 Jackisch, 'Cuantificación de Criminales de Guerra'.
137 Jorge Camarasa, *Organizzazione Odessa: dossier sui nazisti rifugiati in Argentina* (Milan: Murcia, 1998), 2.
138 Richard Schober, 'Auf dem Weg zum Anschluss: Tirols Nationalsozialisten 1927–1938', *Tiroler Heimat*, 59 (1995), 132–61, at 149.
139 Schreiber, *Die Machtübernahme*, 137.
140 Jürgen Leyerer, *Argentinien, die Flieger und wir: Eine Erzählung aus den Nachkriegsjahren* (Vienna: Liber Libri, 2010), 262.
141 Letter from Guzzi Lantschner (Innsbruck) to Hudal, Anima, Nachlass Hudal, box 27 (Apr. 1948).
142 Application for a Red Cross travel document for Lantschner Gustav, ICRC Rome, 25 May 1948, ICRC Geneva, Archive, 'Titres de Voyage CICR 1945–1993', application 13, 489.

143 Karl Ilg, *Pioniere in Argentinien, Chile, Paraguay und Venezuela: Durch Begwelt, Urwald und Steppe erwanderte Volkskunde der deutschsprachigen Siedler* (Innsbruck: Tyrolia, 1976), 107.

144 Military Registration Record for Franz Rubatscher, TLA, Bestand Landesgericht, file 10 Vr 2138/47, 'Franz Rubatscher'.

145 Cf. Edgar Moroder, *Hans Steger, and Paula Wiesinger zum 100. Jahre-Jubiläum und das Hotel Steger-Dellai auf der Seiser Alm* (Seis: n.pub., 2007), 56.

146 Warrant, 2 November 1961, for the arrest of Fritz Lantschner, TLA, Bestand Landesgericht, file 10 Vr 924/47 'Fritz Lantschner'.

147 Jackisch, 'Cuantificación de Criminales de Guerra'.

148 Handwritten curriculum vitae of Franz Sterzinger, 28 October 1943, Bundesarchiv Berlin, SS-Führer-Personalunterlagen (formerly BDC) Sterzinger, Franz.

149 Bundesarchiv Berlin, NSDAP-Zentralkartei (formerly BDC) Sterzinger, Franz.

150 Franz Sterzinger, 28 October 1943, Bundesarchiv Berlin, SS-Führer-Personalunterlagen (formerly BDC) Sterzinger, Franz.

151 SS-Personalbogen, Bundesarchiv Berlin, SS-Führer-Personalunterlagen (formerly BDC) Sterzinger, Franz.

152 Handwritten c.v. of Franz Sterzinger. Cf. dazu Ernennungsurkunde für Franz Sterzinger zum Mitglied der Energieplanung und zum Leiter des Arbeitskreises Wasserkraftwerke im Reichsministerium für Bewaffnung und Munition, signed Speer, 12 March 1943, Bundesarchiv Berlin, SS-Führer-Personalunterlagen (formerly BDC) Sterzinger, Franz.

153 Handwritten c.v. of Franz Sterzinger.

154 Franz Sterzinger's application for promotion to SS-Sturmbannführer, 11 December 1943, Bundesarchiv Berlin, SS-Führer-Personalunterlagen (formerly BDC) Sterzinger, Franz.

155 Application for a Red Cross travel document for Francesco Sterzinger, ICRC Rome, 4 June 1947; letter of recommendation from the PCA, 10 May 1947, ICRC Geneva, Archive, 'Titres de Voyage CICR 1945–1993', application 54, 202.

156 Blaschitz, *NS-Flüchtlinge österreichischer Herkunft*, 103–36 at 134.

157 Cf. State Prosecution Office, Düsseldorf, Action 8 Js 195/69 against Franz Hofer.

158 Report of the Federal Police, Innsbruck, to the State Prosecution Office, Innsbruck, 19 January 1948, TLA, Bestand Landesgericht, file 10 Vr 2138/47 'Franz Rubatscher'.

159 'Dokumente betreffend Verfahren wegen Judenverfolgungen in Tirol', Dokumentationsarchiv des österreichischen Widerstandes Wien (DÖW), Signatur 19652/3. Cf. also Gretl Köfler, 'Wir wollen sehen, ob das Kreuz oder der siebenarmige Leuchter siegt! Antisemitismus in Nord- und Osttirol seit 1918', *Sturzflüge: Eine Kulturzeitschrift*, 5/15–16 (Dec. 1986), 89–95 at 93.

160 Gesuch um Einbeziehung in die Weihnachtsamnestie, Herr Hans Aichinger to the Austrian President, 12 November 1959, TLA, Bestand Landesgericht, file 10 Vr 104/46, 'Erwin Fleiss u.a.'.

161 Cf. Meding, *Flucht vor Nürnberg?*, 150.

162 Application for a Red Cross travel document for Guth Friedolin, ICRC Genoa, April 1948, ICRC Geneva, Archive, 'Titres de Voyage CICR 1945–1993', application 13, 092.

163 Michel Faure, 'Sur la piste des derniers nazis', *L'Express* (9 April 1998) <http://www.lexpress.fr/info/monde/dossier/argentine/dossier.asp?ida=418659>, accessed 9 Nov. 2007.

164 Blaschitz, *NS-Flüchtlinge österreichischer Herkunft*, 103–36 at 124.

165 Wiesenthal, *Justice Not Vengeance*, 80.

166 Cf. Yitzhak Arad, *Bełżec, Sobibor, Treblinka: The Operation Reinhard Death Camp* (Bloomington: Indiana University Press, 1987).

167 Wolfgang Benz, 'Treblinka', in Wolfgang Benz *et al.* (eds.), *Der Ort des Terrors: Geschichte der nationalsozialistischen Konzentrationslager* (Munich: Beck 2008), viii, 407–43 ff. at 407.

168 Sereny, *Into That Darkness*, 30.

169 Tom Segev, *Die Soldaten des Bösen: Zur Geschichte der KZ-Kommandanten* (Reinbek: Rowohlt,1992), 245–57.

170 Cf. Bogdan Musial (ed.), *'Aktion Reinhard': Der Völkermord an den Juden im Generalgouvernement 1941–1944* (Osnabrück: Fibre, 2004).

171 Sereny, *Into That Darkness*, 201.

172 Interrogation of Franz Stangl, 26 June 1968, defendants Franz Stangl *et al.*, file 208 ARZ 230/59, Bl. 3950, Barch LB, B 162.

173 Theresa Stangl in Sereny, *Into That Darkness*, 273.

174 Sereny, *Into That Darkness*, 275.

175 Goñi, *Operazione Odessa*, 305.

176 Sereny, *Into That Darkness*, 289.

177 Ibid.

178 Application for travel document for Stangl Paul, ICRC Rome, 25 August 1948, ICRC, Geneva, Archive, 'Titres de voyage CICR 1945–1993', application 84, 227.

179 Klee, *Persilscheine und falsche Pässe*, 39.

180 Ibid.

181 Sereny, *Into That Darkness*, 365.

182 Application for Red Cross travel document for Wagner Gustav, ICRC Rome, 25 August 1948, letter of recommendation from the PCA for Gustavo Wagner, 17 August 1948, ICRC Geneva, Archive, 'Titres de Voyage CICR 1945–1993', application 84, 228.

183 Julian Schelvis, *Vernichtungslager Sobibór* (Hamburg: Unrast, 2003), see Wagner's biography, 311–12.

184 Dietrich Strothmann, 'Der Wolf ist wieder frei: Brasilien lehnt die Auslieferung des Massenmörders Wagner ab', *Die Zeit* (28 September 1979), 11.

185 Siegwald Ganglmair, 'Das "Arbeitserziehungslager" Weyer im Bezirk Braunau am Inn 1940–1941: Ein Beitrag zur Zeitgeschichte Oberösterreichs', *Oberösterreichische Heimatblättter*, 37/1 (1983).

186 Application for a Red Cross travel document for August Steininger, ICRC, Rome, 25 August 1948, letter of recommendation from the PCA for August Steininger, 17 August 1948, ICRC Geneva, Archive, 'Titres de Voyage CICR 1945–1993', application 84, 229.

187 Information from Ludwig Laher, 13 July 2006. Cf. also Ludwig Laher, *Heart Flesh Degeneration* (Riverside: Ariadne, 2006).

188 SS file Wagner, Horst, born 17 May 1906, SS No. 276,847, NARA, RG 242, formerly BDC.

189 See Eckart Conze *et. al* (eds.), *Das Amt und die Vergangenheit: Deutsche Diplomaten im Dritten Reich und in der Bundesrepublik* (Munich: Blessing, 2010), 145–6. NARA, RG 238, Microfilm, Records of the United States Nuremberg war crimes trials WA series 1940–1945, pamphlet describing M946, p. 5, concerning the activities of Horst Wagner.

190 Hans-Jürgen Döscher, *Das Auswärtige Amt im Dritten Reich: Diplomatie im Schatten der 'Endlösung'* (Berlin: Siedler, 1987), 264–76.

191 Raul Hilberg, *Die Vernichtung der europäischen Juden: Die Gesamtgeschichte des Holocaust* (Berlin: Olle & Wolter, 1982), 541–84.

192 Information from Gisela Heidenreich, 11 January 2006.

193 Application for Red Cross travel document for Peter Ludwig, ICRC Rome, 10 November 1948, ICRC Geneva, Archive, 'Titres de Voyage CICR 1945–1993', application 90, 092.

194 Schneppen, *Odessa und das Vierte Reich*, 178–9. Files on the trial of Horst Wagner, Wiener Library London, War Crime Trials: Various Papers (1947–67), file 1185/3, Horst Wagner.

195 Cf. Christopher R. Browning, *Der Weg zur 'Endlösung': Entscheidungen und Täter* (Bonn: Dietz, 1998), 105–15.

196 Annette Weinke, *Die Verfolgung von NS-Tätern im geteilten Deutschland. Vergangenheitsbewältigungen 1949–1969, oder, eine deutsch-deutsche Beziehungsgeschichte im Kalten Krieg* (Paderborn: Schöningh, 2002), 260 ff.

197 Schneppen, *Odessa und das Vierte Reich*, 138 ff.

198 Camarasa, *Organizzazione Odessa*, 236 ff.

199 Cf. State Prosecution Office, Hamburg, against Eduard Roschmann, 141 Js 534/60 and 14 Js 210/49 (copy in the possession of the author).

200 Application for a Red Cross travel document for Federico Wegner, ICRC Rome, 5 August 1948, ICRC Geneva, Archive, 'Titres de Voyage CICR 1945–1993', application 83, 967.

201 Ibid. Letter of recommendation from the PCA Foreign Section (Austria), Rome, signed by Bishop Alois Hudal, 4 August 1948.

202 Wiesenthal, *Justice Not Vengeance*, 131.

203 Cf. Eduard Roschmann Trial, State Prosecution Office, Hamburg, 141 Js 534/60.

204 Zentrale Stelle der Landesjustizverwaltungen Ludwigsburg, memorandum of 30 May 1972, defendants Eduard Roschmann *et al.*, I-110 AR 796/72, Bl. 11, Barch LB, B 162.

205 Segev, *Wiesenthal*, 255 ff.

206 Schneppen, *Odessa und das Vierte Reich*, 141.

207 Trial by the State Prosecution Office, Hamburg, of Eduard Roschmann, 141 Js 534/60 and 14 Js 210/49 (copy in possession of the author).

208 Cf. Barch LB, B 162, file II 207 ARZ 7/59.

209 Juan (Hans) Maler [Pseudonym of Reinhard Kops], *Rette sich wer kann!* (Buenos Aires: Maler, 1989), 224.

210 Letter from Friedrich Schwend to Johann Neuhold, 2 October 1959, Fritz-Bauer-Institut, Frankfurt am Main, copy of the Schwend Archives, folder II./3.

211 Cf. Stefan Rennicke, *Siemens in Argentinien: Die Unternehmensentwicklung vom Markteintritt bis zur Enteignung 1945* (Berlin: Wissenschaftlicher, 2004).

212 In Meding, *Flucht vor Nürnberg?*, 226.

213 Ibid. 226.

214 Cf. Ley, 'Deutsche Naturwissenschaftler an argentinischen Universitäten nach 1945', in Meding, *Nationalsozialismus und Argentinien*, 149–60 at 149.

215 Compañía Argentina para Proyectos y Realizaciones Industriales—Fuldner y Cía.

216 Lütge *et al.*, *Deutsche in Argentinien*, 334.

217 CIA report, 'German Nationalist and Neo-Nazi Activities in Argentina', 8 July 1953 (SECRET), p. 22, NARA, General CIA Records, 62-00865R, box 0003, folder 0003.

218 Ibid. 17.

219 Application for a Red Cross travel document for Armin Schoklitsch, ICRC Innsbruck Delegation, 8 January 1949, ICRC Geneva, Archive, 'Titres de Voyage CICR 1945–1993', application 86, 724.

220 Certificate, Police Headquarters Graz, for Armin Schoklitsch, 4 January 1949; ICRC, Geneva, Archive 'Titres de Voyage CICR 1945–1993', application 86, 724.

221 Confirmation from Dirección General de Migraciones in Buenos Aires for Armin Schoklitsch of unrestricted entry to Argentina, November 1948, ICRC, Geneva, Archive, 'Titres de Voyage CICR 1945–1993', application 86, 724.

222 Criminal record from Vienna Police for Walter Haasler, 24 May 1949; application for a Red Cross travel document for Walter Haasler, ICRC Innsbruck Delegation, 6 August 1949, ICRC Geneva, Archive, 'Titres de Voyage CICR 1945–1993', application 100, 680.

223 Interview with Walter Haasler, 30 November 2005.

224 Criminal record from Vienna Police for Walter Haasler, 24 May 1949; application for Red Cross travel document for Walter Haasler 100, 680.

225 Letter from Dean Marcelo Gonzalez in Mérida to Walter Haasler in Vienna, 3 June 1949; application for Red Cross travel document for Walter Haasler 100, 680.

226 Application for Red Cross travel document for Walter Haasler 100, 680.

227 NARA, RG 263 (CIA), War crimes, IWG, name files, box 51, folder Tiefenbacher Joseph.

228 Interview with Walter Haasler, 30 November 2005.

229 Blaschitz, 'Austrian National Socialists in Argentina after 1945', 226–40 at 228.

230 Application for a Red Cross travel document for Jakob Schramm, ICRC Genoa, 9 January 1951, ICRC, 'Titres de Voyage CICR 1945–1993', application 100, 980.

231 Cf. Jackisch, 'Cuantificación de Criminales de Guerra'.

232 Information from Uki Goñi, 29 July 2010.

233 Interview with Karl Nicolussi-Leck, 10 May 2004. Information from Uki Goñi, 29 July 2010. Lütge *et al.*, *Deutsche in Argentinien*, 334.

234 Eppacher and Ruef, *Hohe Tapferkeitsauszeichnungen an Tiroler im Zweiten Weltkrieg*, 41.

235 Information from Leopold Steurer, 14 January 2007.

236 British consulate, Bolzano, to British embassy, Rome, Savingram, 27 May 1949 (CONFIDENTIAL), copy in the possession of the author.

237 Cf. Leopold Steurer, 'Südtirol zwischen schwarz und braun', in Godele von der Decken (ed.), *Teilung Tirols: Gefahr für die Demokratie?* (Bozen: Redaktion Sturzflüge, 1988), 25–40 at 36. Cf. Veronika Mittermair, 'Bruchlose Karrieren? Zum Werdegang der Südtiroler Politikerschicht bis zur "Stunde Null"', in Hans Heiss and Gustav Pfeifer (eds.), *Südtirol—Stunde Null? Kriegsende 1945–1946*, Veröffentlichungen des Südtiroler Landesarchivs 10 (Innsbruck: Studien, 2000), 169–202.

238 Extract from Bozen Chamber of Commerce register for 'AGRIA Mediterranea Spa', 9 March 2005, Handelskammer Bozen.

239 Steurer, *Südtirol zwischen Rom und Berlin*, 269–70.

240 Handwritten c.v. for Michael Tutzer, 11 April 1943; personal record, Ordensburg Sonthofen, for Michael Tutzer, 4 September 1940; assessment sheet, Reichsschulungsburg [state training castle] Erwitte, for Michael Tutzer, 15 March 1941. The author is grateful to Leopold Steurer for lending copies of the documents concerning the Nazi career of Michael Tutzer. Cf. Company charter for 'AGRIA Mediterranea', 13 December 1957, articles of incorporation, 'AGRIA Mediterranea', Archive, Chamber of Commerce, Bozen.

241 Bozen Chamber of Commerce, statement from the company register concerning Agrotecnica Bolzano GmbH, 9 March 2005.

242 NARA, RG 242, formerly BDC, SS-Personalakt Hafner, Paul, born 24 February 1923, SS no. 490, 167.

243 The c.v. of Pablo Hafner for Innsbruck University, 7 March 1999. Copy in the possession of the author.

244 Cf. Katja Stumpp, 'Er bereut nichts—und macht noch immer den Hitler-Gruß: SS-Offizier zockt Rente in 3 Ländern ab', *Bild.de Online* (10 Dec. 2007) <http://www.bild.de/>, accessed 11 Dec. 2007.

245 The c.v. of Pablo Hafner for Innsbruck University.

246 Christoph Pan, 'In memoriam Karl Nicolussi-Leck', *Der Schlern*, 8 (2008), 48 f.

247 Conversation with Guzzi Lantschner, 21 May 2007.

248 Karl Prossliner, *Sprechen über Südtirol, Zeugen eines Jahrhunderts* (Vienna: Folio, 1996), 61–3.

249 Interview with Karl von Marsoner, 14 September 2004.

250 Baptismal register of the parish of Lana an der Etsch 1914, entry for Karl Tribus, born 7 April 1914.

251 Cf. file 518 ARZ 25/96, Carl Tribus, Barch LB, B 162.

252 French L. MacLean, *The Field Men: The SS Officers Who Led the Einsatzkommandos, the Nazi Mobile Killing Units* (Atglen: Schiffer, 1999), 28, 49; Andrej Angrick and Ulrick Prehn, *Besatzungspolitik und Massenmord: Die Einsatzgruppe D in der südlichen Sowjetunion 1941–1943* (Hamburg: Hamburger Edition, 2003), 677 ff., 706 f.

253 Helmut Krausnick, *Hitlers Einsatzgruppen: Die Truppe des Weltanschauungskrieges 1938–1942* (Frankfurt am Main: Fischer, 1985), 364.

254 Erwin Tochtermann, 'Ohne Emotionen saubere Arbeit geleistet', *Süddeutsche Zeitung* (27 September 1980).

255 Interrogation of Kurt Christmann, 3 March 1956, LHAK, 584/1/1419; databank of the IfZ: list of the case records of the prosecution of Nazi crime by West German authorities since 1945.

256 MacLean, *Field Men*, 49 n. 44.

257 CIA Report, German Nationalist and Neo-Nazi Activities in Argentina, 8 July 1953, NARA, General CIA Records, 62-00865R, box 0003, folder 0003.

258 IfZ, ED 342/22–31.

259 Johann Freudenreich, 'Wegen schwerer Kriegsverbrechen in Rußland: Vor 5 Jahren angeklagt—erst gestern festgenommen', *Süddeutsche Zeitung* (14 November 1979).

260 Blaschitz, *Austrian National Socialists*, 226–40 at 236.

261 Cf. baptismal register for the parish of Waidhofen an der Ybbs, entry for Mario Franz Ruffinengo, 27 February 1919.

262 Ilg, *Pioniere in Argentinien*, 106 ff.

263 Ibid. 108.

264 Elena Llorente and Martino Rigacci, *El último nazi: Priebke, de la Argentina a Italia, juicio a medio siglo de historia* (Buenos Aires: Editorial Sudamericana, 1998), 62.

265 Steffen Prauser, 'Mord in Rom? Der Anschlag in der Via Rasella und die deutsche Vergeltung in den Fosse Ardeatine', in Gerald Steinacher (ed.), *Südtirol im Dritten Reich/L'Alto Adige nel Terzo Reich 1943–1945: NS-Herrschaft im Norden Italiens/L'occupazione nazista nell'Italia settentrionale*, Veröffentlichungen des Südtiroler Landesarchivs 18 (Innsbruck: Studien, 2003), 295–307. Cf. Friedrich Andrae, *Auch gegen Frauen und Kinder: Der Krieg der deutschen Wehrmacht gegen die Zivilbevölkerung in Italien 1943–1945* (Munich: Piper, 1995), 115–23. Cf. Staron, *Fosse Ardeatine und Marzabotto*.

266 Cf. Schneppen, *Odessa und das Vierte Reich*, 143–5.

267 Wiesenthal, *Justice Not Vengeance*, 135.

Conclusion

1 Charles S. Maier, *The Unmasterable Past: History, Holocaust, and German National Identity* (Cambridge: Harvard University Press, 1997).

2 Tony Judt, *Postwar: A History of Europe since 1945* (New York: Penguin, 2005).

3 Phayer, *Pius XII, the Holocaust, and the Cold War*, 232.

4 Cf. Christoph Cornelissen *et al.* (eds.), *Erinnerungskulturen. Deutschland, Italien und Japan seit 1945* (Frankfurt am Main: Fischer, 2003).

5 Frei, *Vergangenheitspolitik*, 13 f.

6 Judt, *Postwar*, 808.

7 Ibid.

8 Robert G. Moeller, 'Germans as Victims? Thoughts on a Post-Cold War History of World War II Legacies', in *History and Memory*, 17/1–2 (2005), 147–94. Jeffrey Herf, *Divided Memory: The Nazi Past in the Two Germanys* (Cambridge: Harvard University Press, 1997).

9 Schneppen, *Odessa und das Vierte Reich*.

10 Adolf Eichmann, 'Meine Flucht. Bericht aus der Zelle in Jerusalem', NARA, RG 263 (CIA), War Crimes, CIA name files, IWG, box 14, Eichmann, Adolf, vol. 1.

11 Donald Bloxham, *Genocide on Trial: War Crimes and the Formation of Holocaust, History and Memory* (Oxford: Oxford University Press, 2001).

12 Cf. Norman J. Goda, *Tales from Spandau: Nazi Criminals and the Cold War* (New York: Cambridge Univeristy Press, 2007).

13 Cf. Lingen, 'Conspiracy of Silence', 74–109.

14 Judt, *Postwar*, 808.

15 Cf. Mimmo Franzinelli, *Le stragi nascoste: L'armadio della vergogna: impunitá e rimozione dei crimini di guerra nazifascisti 1943–2001* (Milan: Mondadori, 2002).

16 Judt, *Postwar*, 813.

17 Cf. Michele Battini, *The Missing Italian Nuremberg: Cultural Amnesia and Postwar Politics* (New York: Palgrave Macmillan, 2007). Cf. Aram Mattioli, ' "Die Resistenza ist tot, es lebe Onkel Mussolini!" Vom Umdeuten der Geschichte im Italien Berlusconis', *Mittelweg*, 36/17 (2008), 75–93, <http://www.eurozine.com/journals/mittelweg36/issue/2008-10-29.html>, accessed 1 March 2009. Cf. idem., *Viva Mussolini! Die Aufwertung des Faschismus im Italien Berlusconis* (Paderborn: Schöningh, 2010). Cf. Carlo Moos, 'Die "guten" Italiener und die Zeitgeschichte: Zum Problem der Vergangenheitsbewältigung in Italien', *Historische Zeitschrift*, 259 (1994), 671–94.

18 Anne Applebaum, 'An Archive With Tales To Tell', *Washington Post* (6 March 2007), A 19.

19 Günther Pallaver, 'Abhängigkeit, Verspätung, ethnische Versäulung: Folgen einer verfehlten Epurazione und Entnazifizierung in Südtirol', in Steinacher (ed.), *Südtirol im Dritten Reich*, 361–74.

20 Ibid.

21 Blet *et al.* (eds.), *Actes et Documents*. Cf. Hubert Wolf, *Papst und Teufel: Die Archive des Vatikan und das Dritte* (Munich: Beck, 2008).

22 Michael Phayer, 'Canonizing Pius XII: Why Did the Pope Help Nazis Escape?', *Commonweal* (9 May 2003), 22–3.

23 US Embassy in Rometi Secretary of State, 20 February 1992, NARA, RG 263 (CIA), box 5, folder 'Nazis in South America', 2 of 7.

24 Thomas Brechenmacher, 'Die Enzyklika "Mit brennender Sorge" als Höhe- und Wendepunkt der päpstlichen Politik gegenüber dem nationalsozialistischen Deutschland', in Wolfram Pyta *et al.* (eds.), *Die Herausforderungen der Diktaturen: Katholizismus in Deutschland und Italien 1918–1943/45* (Tübingen: Niemeyer, 2009), 271–300 at 274.

25 Cornwell, *Hitler's Pope*. Cf. also Daniel J. Goldhagen, *A Moral Reckoning*.

26 Kent, *Lonely Cold War*.

27 Phayer, *Pius XII, the Holocaust, and the Cold War*.

28 Riccardo Orizio, 'Cosi' la Croce Rossa salvo' i nazisti', *Corriere della Sera*, 19 June 1998, 11, <http://archiviostorico.corriere.it/1998/giugno/19/Cosi_Croce_ Rossa_salvo_nazisti_co_0_98061914498.shtml>, accessed 8 May 2009.

29 'Neue Forschungsresultate zeigen das Mass der Fluchthilfe auf', *Neue Zürcher Zeitung am Sonntag* (7 September 2008) <http://www.nzz.ch/nachrichten/schweiz/ das_rote_kreuz_verhalf_tausenden_nazis_zur_flucht_1.825790.html>, accessed 12 Feb. 2009.

30 Cf. Favez, *Red Cross and the Holocaust.*

31 Elazar Barkan, *The Guilt of Nations: Restitution and Negotiating Historical Injustices* (New York: Norton, 2000).

32 Cf. Giorgio Agamben, *Remnants of Auschwitz: The Witness and the Archive* (New York: Zone, 2002).

33 Pallaver, 'Abhängigkeit, Verspätung, ethnische Versäulung.'

34 Martin Pollack, 'Mutmassungen über ein Verbrechen: Was ist es, das den Menschen den Mund verschliesst? Das Massaker im österreichischen Rechnitz im März 1945', *Neue Zürcher Zeitung* (20 June 2009), 'Literatur und Kunst', B 1.

Bibliography

Archival Sources

Archive of the International Committee of the Red Cross, Geneva
Archiv der Südtiroler Kapuzinerprovinz, Brixen
Archiv des Instituts für Zeitgeschichte, ETH Zurich
Archivio Centrale dello Stato, Rome
Archivio storico del Ministero degli Affari Esteri, Rome
Bundesarchiv-Militärarchiv Freiburg
Bundesarchiv Berlin, formerly Berlin Document Center
Bundesarchiv/Außenstelle Ludwigsburg
(Bestand 162 = Ehemalige Zentrale Stelle der Landesjustizverwaltungen zur Aufklärung von NS-Verbrechen)
Catholic University of America, Washington, DC, Archive, National Catholic Welfare Conference
Dokumentationsarchiv des Österreichischen Widerstandes, Vienna
Dokumentationszentrum des Bundes jüdischer Verfolgter des Naziregimes (Simon Wiesenthal Dokumentationszentrum), Vienna
Franziskanerkloster Bozen, Bibliothek
Fritz-Bauer-Institut, Frankfurt am Main
Handelskammer Bozen, Archiv
Handelskammer Triest, Archiv
Harvard University, Widener Library
Hessisches Hauptstaatsarchiv, Wiesbaden
Institut für Zeitgeschichte, Munich
Institut für Zeitgeschichte, Universität Innsbruck
Istituto Santa Maria dell'Anima, Rome
Landesgericht Innsbruck, Archiv
Library of Congress, Washington, DC
Museo Storico Italiano della Guerra, Rovereto
National Archives and Records Administration, College Park, Maryland
Pfarramt Brixen, Archiv
Pfarramt Sterzing, Archiv
The National Archives of England, Wales and the United Kingdom
(Public Record Office), London-Kew
Rotes Kreuz Stadt Innsbruck, Archiv
Schweizerisches Bundesarchiv, Berne
Seeley G. Mudd Library, Princeton
Siemens-Archiv, Munich
Staatsarchiv Bozen
Staatsarchiv Marburg
Stadtarchiv Brixen
Stadtarchiv Meran
Steiermärkisches Landesarchiv, Graz

Südtiroler Landesarchiv, Bozen
Tiroler Landesarchiv, Innsbruck
Tiroler Landesmuseum Ferdinandeum, Innsbruck
United States Holocaust Memorial Museum, Library and Archives, Washington, DC

Secondary Sources

AARONS, MARK, and LOFTUS, JOHN, *Unholy Trinity: How the Vaticans Nazi Networks Betrayed Western Intelligence to the Soviets* (New York: St Martin's, 1992).

AGAMBEN, GIORGIO, *Remnants of Auschwitz: The Witness and the Archive* (New York: Zone, 2002).

AGNOLETTI, ALESSANDRO, *Enklave Rimini-Bellaria: Storia e storie di 150.000 prigionieri nei campi di concentramento alleati sulla costa romagnola (1945–1947)* (Rimini: Guaraldi, 1999).

AHARONI, ZVI, and DIETL, WILHELM, *Der Jäger: Operation Eichmann: Was wirklich geschah* (Stuttgart: Deutsche, 1996).

ALBRECHT, ULRICH, 'Deutscher Wissenschaftlerexodus in der Nachkriegszeit', in Holger Meding (ed.), *Nationalsozialismus und Argentinien*, 139–48.

—— et al., *Die Spezialisten: Deutsche Naturwissenschaftler und Techniker in der Sowjetunion nach 1945* (Berlin: Dietz, 1992).

ALBRICH, THOMAS, *Exodus durch Österreich: Die jüdischen Flüchtlinge 1945–1948*, Innsbrucker Forschungen zur Zeitgeschichte 1 (Innsbruck: Haymon, 1987).

—— and MEIXNER, WOLFGANG, 'Zwischen Legalität und Illegalität: Zur Mitgliederentwicklung, Alters- und Sozialstruktur der NSDAP in Tirol und Vorarlberg vor 1938', *Zeitgeschichte* 22/5–6 (1995), 149–87.

—— (ed.), *Flucht nach Eretz Israel: Die Bricha und der jüdische Exodus durch Österreich nach 1945* (Innsbruck: Studien, 1998).

—— '"Die Juden hinaus" aus Tirol und Vorarlberg: Entrechtung und Vertreibung 1938 bis 1940', in Rolf Steininger and Sabine Pitscheider (eds.), *Tirol und Vorarlberg in der NS-Zeit*, Innsbrucker Forschungen zur Zeitgeschichte 19 (Innsbruck: Studien, 2003), 299–317.

—— et al. (eds.), *Holocaust und Kriegsverbrechen vor Gericht: Der Fall Österreich* (Innsbruck: Studien, 2006).

ALCOCK, ANTHONY E., *The History of the South Tyrol Question* (London: Joseph, 1970).

ALDRICH, RICHARD, *The Hidden Hand: Britain, America, and Cold War Secret Intelligence* (Woodstock: Overlook, 2002).

ALEXANDER, HELMUT, et al., *Heimatlos: Die Umsiedlung der Südtiroler 1939–45* (Vienna: Deuticke, 1993).

ALLISON, VICTORIA CAUDERY, 'The Bitch Goddess and the Nazi Elvis: Peronist Argentina in the United States Popular Imagination', Ph.D. dissertation, State University of New York, Stony Brook, 2001.

ALVAREZ, DAVID, and GRAHAM, ROBERT A., *Nothing Sacred: Nazi Espionage against the Vatican 1939–1945* (London: Cass, 1997).

ALY, GÖTZ, and CHASE, JEFFERSON, *Hitler's Beneficiaries: Plunder, Racial War, and the Nazi Welfare State* (New York: Metropolitan, 2007).

ANDRAE, FRIEDRICH, *Auch gegen Frauen und Kinder: Der Krieg der deutschen Wehrmacht gegen die Zivilbevölkerung in Italien 1943–1945* (Munich: Piper, 1995).

ANGRICK, ANDREJ, and PREHN, ULRICK, *Besatzungspolitik und Massenmord: Die Einsatzgruppe D in der südlichen Sowjetunion 1941–1943* (Hamburg: Hamburger Edition, 2003).

APPLEBAUM, ANNE, 'An Archive With Tales To Tell', *Washington Post* (6 March 2007), A 19.

Bibliography

ARAD, YITZHAK, Bełżec, Sobibór, Treblinka: The Operation Reinhard Death Camps (Bloomington: Indiana University Press, 1987).
ARENDT, HANNAH, Eichmann in Jerusalem: A Report on the Banality of Evil (New York: Viking, 1963).
—— Eichmann in Jerusalem: Ein Bericht von der Banalität des Bösen (Munich: Piper, 1986).
ASTOR, GERALD, The Last Nazi: The Life and Times of Dr. Joseph Mengele (New York: Fine, 1985).
AZÉMA, JEAN-PIERRE, and WIEVIORKA, OLIVIER, Vichy 1940–1944 (Paris: Perrin, 2004).
BABIĆ, MARKO, 'Prof. Dr. Krunoslav Stjepan Draganović, u prigodi 10. obljetnice smrti i 90. onljetnice rodenja (1903–1983)', Hrvatska revija, Kroatische Rundschau, 44 (1994), 1(173), 184–6.
BARKAN, ELAZAR, Völker klagen an: Eine neue internationale Moral (Düsseldorf: Patmos, 2000).
—— The Guilt of Nations: Restitution and Negotiating Historical Injustices (New York: Norton, 2000).
BARUCH, MARC OLIVIER, Vichy-Regime: Frankreich 1940–1944 (Stuttgart: Reclam, 1999).
BATTINI, MICHELE, Peccati di memoria: La mancata Norimberga italiana (Rome: GLF editori Laterza, 2003).
—— The Missing Italian Nuremberg: Cultural Amnesia and Postwar Politics (New York: Palgrave Macmillan, 2007).
BECKER, OTTO H., '"Ici la France": Die Vichy-Regierung in Sigmaringen 1944/45', in Fritz Kallenberg (ed.), Hohenzollern, Schriften zur politischen Landeskunde Baden-Württembergs 23 (Stuttgart: Kohlhammer, 1996), 428–46.
BEER, MATHIAS, and SEEWANN, GERHARD (eds.), Südostforschung im Schatten des Dritten Reiches. Institutionen—Inhalte—Personen, Südosteuropäische Arbeiten 119 (Munich: Oldenbourg, 2004).
BENDEL, RAINER (ed.), Die katholische Schuld? Katholizismus im Dritten Reich zwischen Arrangement und Widerstand (Munich: Lit, 2002).
BENEŠOVÁ, MIROSLAVA, Malá pevnost Terezín 1940–1945 (Terezín: Vráji, 1996).
BENOIN, DANIEL, and HORN, MATTHIAS, Als Paris an der Donau lag: Sigmaringer Erinnerungen an eine große Zeit, Tübinger Programme 2 (Tübingen: Landestheater Württemberg-Hohenzollern, 1991).
BEN-TOV, ARIEH, Das Rote Kreuz kam zu spät: Die Auseinandersetzung zwischen dem jüdischen Volk und dem Internationalen Komitee vom Roten Kreuz im Zweiten Weltkrieg, die Ereignisse un Ungarn (Zurich: Ammann, 1990).
BENZ, WOLFGANG, 'Treblinka', in Wolfgang Benz et al. (eds.), Der Ort des Terrors: Geschichte der nationalsozialistischen Konzentrationslager (Munich: Beck 2008), viii, 407–43.
BERGMANN, GUENTHER, Auslandsdeutsche in Paraguay, Brasilien, Argentinien (Bad Münstereifel: Westkreuz, 1994).
BERTAGNA, FEDERICA, La Patria di Riserva: L'emigrazione fascista in Argentina (Rome: Donzelli, 2006).
—— and SANFILIPPO, MATTEO, 'Per una prospettiva comparata dell'emigrazione nazi-fascista dopo la seconda guerra mondiale', Studi Emigrazione/Migration Studies, 41/155 (2004), 527–53.
BESIER, GERHARD, 'Eugenio Pacelli, die Römisch-Katholische Kirche und das Christentum (1933–1945) in historisch-religiöser Kritik', in Rainer Bendel (ed.), Die katholische Schuld? Katholizismus im Dritten Reich zwischen Arrangement und Widerstand (Munich: Lit, 2002), 200–20.
BLACK, PETER, Ernst Kaltenbrunner: Vasall Hitlers, Eine SS-Karriere (Paderborn: Schöningh, 1991).

BLASCHITZ, EDITH, 'Austrian National Socialists in Argentina after 1945', in Oliver Rathkolb (ed.), *Revisiting the National Socialist Legacy: Coming to Terms with Forced Labor, Expropriation, Compensation, and Restitution* (Innsbruck: Studien, 2002), 226–40.

——'NS-Flüchtlinge österreichischer Herkunft: Der Weg nach Argentinien', in Christine Schindler and Dokumentationsarchiv des österreichischen Widerstandes (eds.), *Jahrbuch 2003* (Vienna: Taschenbuch, 2003), 103–36.

BLET, PIERRE, *et al.* (eds.), *Actes et Documents du Saint Siège relatifs à la Seconde Guerre mondiale*, 11 vols. (Vatican City: Libreria Editrice Vaticana, 1965–81).

BLOXHAM, DONALD, *Genocide on Trial: War Crimes and the Formation of Holocaust, History and Memory* (Oxford: Oxford University Press, 2001).

BLUMENTHAL, RALPH, 'Vatican Is Reported to Have Furnished Aid to Fleeing Nazis', *New York Times* (26 January 1984), A 14.

BORMANN, MARTIN JUN., *Leben gegen Schatten: Gelebte Zeit, geschenkte Zeit, Begegnungen, Erfahrungen, Folgerungen* (Paderborn: Blindenscher, 1998).

BORMANN, MARTIN SEN., *The Bormann Letters: The Private Correspondence between Martin Bormann and his Wife from January 1943 to April 1945*, ed. Hugh R. Trevor-Roper (London: Weidenfeld & Nicolson, 1954).

BORNSCHEIN, JOACHIM, *Gestapochef Heinrich Müller: Technokrat des Terrors* (Leipzig: Militzke, 2004).

BOWER, TOM, *Klaus Barbie, Lyon, Augsburg, La Paz: Karriere eines Gestapo-Chefs* (Berlin: Rotbuch, 1984).

——*The Paperclip Conspiracy: The Hunt for the Nazi Scientists* (Boston: Little, Brown, 1987).

BRAHAM, RANDOLPH L. (ed.), *The Holocaust in Hungary: A Selected and Annotated Bibliography 1984–2000* (New York: Rosenthal Institute for Holocaust Studies, 2006).

BRAUN, EVA, *Il mio diario*, introd. D. W. Hewlett (Rome: Editrice 'Farro', 1948).

BRECHENMACHER, THOMAS, 'Die Enzyklika "Mit brennender Sorge" als Höhe- und Wendepunkt der päpstlichen Politik gegenüber dem nationalsozialistischen Deutschland', in Wolfram Pyta *et al.* (eds.), *Die Herausforderungen der Diktaturen*, 271–300.

BREITMAN, RICHARD, 'Follow the Money', in Breitman *et al.* (eds.), *U.S. Intelligence and the Nazis*, 121–36.

——*et al.*, 'The Gestapo', in Breitman *et al.* (eds.), *U.S. Intelligence and the Nazis*, 137–64 at 153–9.

——*et al.* (eds.), *U.S. Intelligence and the Nazis* (Washington, DC: National Archives and Records Administration, 2004).

BRENDER, REINHOLD, *Kollaboration in Frankreich im Zweiten Weltkrieg: Marcel Déat und das Rassemblement national populaire* (Munich: Oldenbourg, 1992).

BROSZAT, MARTIN, and HÖSS, RUDOLPH, *Kommandant in Auschwitz: Autobiografische Aufzeichnungen* (Munich: Deutscher Taschenbuch, 1963).

BROWN-FLEMING, SUZANNE, *The Holocaust and Catholic Conscience: Cardinal Aloisius Muench and the Guilt Question in Germany, 1946–1959* (Notre Dame: University of Notre Dame Press, 2005).

BROWNING, CHRISTOPHER R., *Der Weg zur 'Endlösung': Entscheidungen und Täter* (Bonn: Dietz, 1998).

BRÜTTING, GEORG, *Das waren die deutschen Kampfflieger-Asse 1939–1945* (Stuttgart: Motorbuch, 1991).

BUCHBERGER, MICHAEL (ed.), *Kirchliches Handlexikon: Ein Nachschlagebuch über das Gesamtgebiet der Theologie und ihrer Hilfswissenschaften*, 2 vols. (Freiburg: Herder, 1907).

BUONASORTE, NICLA, *Siri: Tradizione e Novecento* (Bologna: Il mulino, 2007).

BURGER, ADOLF, *Unternehmen Bernhard: Die Fälscherwerkstatt im KZ Sachsenhausen* (Berlin: Hentrich, 1992).

BURKARD, DOMINIK, 'Alois Hudal—ein Anti-Pacelli? Zur Diskussion um die Haltung des Vatikans gegenüber dem Nationalsozialimus', in *Zeitschrift für Religions- und Geistesgeschichte*, 59/1 (2007), 61–89.

BURRIN, PHILIPPE, *La Dérive fasciste: Doriot, Déat, Bergery* (Paris: Seuil, 1986).

CAIMARI, LILA M., *Perón y la Iglesia Católica: religión, Estado y sociedad en la Argentina 1943–1955* (Buenos Aires: Ariel Historia, 1995).

CAMARASA, JORGE, *Organizzazione Odessa: Dossier sui nazisti rifugiati in Argentina* (Milan: Murcia, 1998).

CAPORALE, RICCARDO, *La 'Banda' Carità: Storia del Reparto Servizi Speciali (1943–1945)* (Lucca: S. Marco liotipo, 2005).

CASAZZA, ANDREA, *La fuga dei nazisti: Mengele, Eichmann, Priebke, Pavelić da Genova all'impunità* (Genoa: Il melangolo, 2007).

CAVALLO, SERENA GANA, and MONTANELLI, GRANZOTTO, 'Due giornalisti', *Deportati* [website] <http://www.deportati.it/recensioni/montanelli.html>, accessed 21 October 2008.

CESARANI, DAVID, *Adolf Eichmann: Bürokrat und Massenmörder: Biografie* (Berlin: Propyläen, 2004).

——*Eichmann: His Life and Crimes* (London: Heinemann, 2004).

CHALOU, GEORGE C. (ed.), *The Secret War: The Office of Strategic Services in World War II* (Washington, DC: National Archives and Records Administration, 2002).

CHENAUX, PHILIPPE, 'Pacelli, Hudal et la question du nazisme (1933–1938)', *Rivista di storia della Chiesa in Italia*, 57/1 (2003), 133–54.

COMISIÓN PARA EL ESCLARECIMIENTO DE LAS ACTIVIDADES DEL NACIONALSOCIALISMO EN LA ARGENTINA, CEANA, Final Report, MRE, Buenos Aires 1999, <http://www.ceana.org.ar/final/final.htm>, accessed 1 April 2007.

CONZE, ECKART, *et. al* (eds.), *Das Amt und die Vergangenheit: Deutsche Diplomaten im Dritten Reich und in der Bundesrepublik* (Munich: Blessing, 2010).

COONEY, JOHN, *The American Pope: The Life and Times of Francis Cardinal Spellman* (New York: Times Books, 1984).

CORNELISSEN, CHRISTOPH, *et al.* (eds.), *Erinnerungskulturen. Deutschland, Italien und Japan seit 1945* (Frankfurt am Main: Fischer, 2003).

CORNI, GUSTAVO, *Il sogno del 'grande spazio': Le politiche d'occupazione nell'Europa nazista* (Rome: Laterzza, 2005).

CORNWELL, JOHN, *Hitler's Pope: The Secret History of Pius XII* (New York: Viking, 1999).

——*Der Papst, der geschwiegen hat* (Munich: Beck, 1999).

COSTA, STEFAN, 'Auswirkungen der "Sunrise"—Waffenstillstandsverhandlungen: Aspekte des Übergangs vom Zweiten Weltkrieg in den Kalten Krieg?', Master's thesis, University of Berne, Germany, 1998.

CRIVELLI, LUIGI, *Montini arcivescovo a Milano: Un singolare apprendistato* (Cinisello Balsamo: San Paolo, 2002).

CZECH, DANUTA, *Kalendarium der Ereignisse im Konzentrationslager Auschwitz-Birkenau 1939–1945* (Hamburg: Rowohlt, 1989).

DABRINGHAUS, ERHARD, *Klaus Barbie: The Shocking Story of How the U.S. Used This Nazi War Criminal as an Intelligence Agent* (Washington, DC: Acropolis, 1984).

DEL BOCA, ANGELO, *Italiani, brava gente? Un mito duro a morire* (Vicenza: Pozza, 2005).

DELLE DONNE, GIORGIO (ed.), *Alto Adige 1945–1947: Ricominciare* (Bozen: Provincia Autonoma di Bolzano, 2000).

DEMPFER, ROBERT, *Das Rote Kreuz: Von Helden im Rampenlicht und diskreten Helfern* (Vienna: Deuticke, 2009).

DESELAERS, MANFRED, *'Und Sie hatten nie Gewissensbisse?' Die Biografie von Rudolf Höß, Kommandant von Auschwitz, und die Frage seiner Verantwortung vor Gott und den Menschen* (Leipzig: Benno, 1997).

DEUTSCHES HAUPTQUARTIER (ed.), *Die deutsche SEP-Enklave Rimini 1945/46: Ein Überblick* (Rimini-Miramare: Dt. Hauptquartier, 1946).

DEVOTO, FERNANDO J., 'Las politicas migratorias Argentinas (1930–1955). Continuidades, tensiones y rupturas', *CEANA*, Final Report, Buenos Aires (1999) <http://www.ceana.org.ar/final/final.htm>, accessed 1 Apr. 2007.

——*Historia de los italianos en la Argentina* (Buenos Aires: Biblos, 2006).

DICKMANN, ENRIQUE, *La infiltración nazi-fascista en la Argentina* (Buenos Aires: Ediciones socials argentinas, 1939).

DIETRICH, STEFAN, 'Der Bleiburger Opfermythos', *Zeitgeschichte*, 35/5 (2008), 298–317.

DIOCESE OF BROOKLYN (ed.), *Diocese of Immigrants: The Brooklyn Catholic Experience 1853–2003* (Strasbourg: Éditions du Signe, 2004),

DI MICHELE, ANDREA, *Storia dell'Italia repubblicana 1948–2008* (Milan: Garzanti, 2008).

DJUROVIĆ, GRADIMIR, *L'agence centrale de recherches du Comité International de la Croix-Rouge* (Geneva: Institut Henry Dunant, 1981).

DOERRIES, REINHARD R. (ed.), *Diplomaten und Agenten: Nachrichtendienste in der Geschichte der deutsch-amerikanischen Beziehungen* (Heidelberg: Winter, 2001).

——(ed.), *Hitler's Last Chief of Foreign Intelligence: Allied Interrogations of Walter Schellenberg* (London: Cass, 2003).

DOLIBOIS, JOHN E., *Pattern of Circles: An Ambassador's Story* (Kent: Kent State University Press, 1989).

DOLLMANN, EUGEN, *Dolmetscher der Diktatoren* (Bayreuth: Hestia, 1963).

DONGEN, LUC VAN, *Un purgatoire très discret: La transition 'Helvétique' d'anciens nazis, fascistes et collaborateurs après 1945* (Paris: Société d'histoire de la Suisse romande, 2008).

DÖSCHER, HANS-JÜRGEN, *Das Auswärtige Amt im Dritten Reich: Diplomatie im Schatten der 'Endlösung'* (Berlin: Siedler, 1987).

DRAGANOVIĆ, KRUNOSLAV, *Katolička crkva u Bosni i Hercegovini nekad i danas: Prilog zu istoimenu historijsko-statističku kartu* (Zagreb: n.pub., 1934).

DULLES, ALLEN, *The Secret Surrender* (New York: Harper & Row, 1966).

EISTERER, KLAUS, *Französische Besatzungspolitik, Tirol und Vorarlberg 1945/46*, Innsbrucker Forschungen zur Zeitgeschichte 9 (Innsbruck: Haymon, 1990).

——and STEININGER, ROLF (eds.), *Die Option: Südtirol zwischen Faschismus und Nationalsozialismus*, Innsbrucker Forschungen zur Zeitgeschichte 5 (Innsbruck: Haymon, 1989).

ELAM, SHRAGA, *Hitlers Fälscher: Wie jüdische, amerikanische und Schweizer Agenten der SS beim Falschgeldwaschen halfen* (Vienna: Ueberreuter, 2000).

EPPACHER, WILHELM, and RUEF, KARL, *Hohe Tapferkeitsauszeichnungen an Tiroler im Zweiten Weltkrieg*, Veröffentlichungen des Innsbrucker Stadtarchivs 6 (Innsbruck: Stadtmagistrat, 1975)

FAHLBUSCH, MICHAEL, 'Im Dienste des Deutschtums in Südosteuropa: Ethnopolitische Berater als Tathelfer für Verbrechen gegen die Menschlichkeit', in Beer and Seewann (eds.), *Südostforschung im Schatten des Dritten Reiches*, 175–214.

FARAGO, LADISLAS, *Scheintot: Martin Bormann und andere NS-Größen in Südamerika* (Hamburg: Hoffmann and Campe, 1975).

FARÍAS, VÍCTOR, *Die Nazis in Chile* (Berlin: Philo, 2002).

FARMER, PAUL, *Vichy: Political Dilemma* (New York: Columbia University Press, 1955).

FATTORINI, EMMA, *Pio XI, Hitler e Mussolini: La solitudine di un papa* (Turin: Einaudi, 2007).

FAURE, MICHEL, 'Sur la piste des derniers nazis', *L'Express* (9 April 1998) <http://www.lexpress.fr/info/monde/dossier/argentine/dossier.asp?ida=418659>, accessed 9 Nov. 2007.

FAVEZ, JEAN-CLAUDE, *The Red Cross and the Holocaust* (Cambridge: Cambridge University Press, 1999).

FELDKAMP, MICHAEL, *Pius XII und Deutschland* (Göttingen: Vandenhoeck & Ruprecht, 2000).

FEST, JOACHIM C., *Speer: Eine Biographie* (Berlin: Fest, 1999).

—— *Der Untergang: Hitler und das Ende des Dritten Reiches* (Berlin: Fest, 2002).

—— *Hitler: Eine Biographie* (Berlin: Ullstein, 2005).

FIEDLER, TEJA, 'Nazis auf der Flucht. Teil 5: Das Verschwinden der Nazis', *Stern*, 13 (2005).

FINKELGRUEN, PETER, *Haus Deutschland oder die Geschichte eines ungesühnten Mordes* (Berlin: Rowohlt, 1994).

FINKIELKRAUT, ALAIN, *Remembering in Vain: The Klaus Barbie Trial and Crimes against Humanity* (New York: Columbia University Press, 1992).

FLOTO, JOBST H., *Die Beziehungen Deutschlands zu Venezuela 1933 bis 1958* (Frankfurt am Main: Lang, 1991).

FOCARDI, FILIPPO, *Criminali di guerra in libertà: Un accordo segreto tra Italia e Germania federale, 1949–1955* (Rome: Carocci, 2008).

FORSYTH, FREDERICK, *The Odessa File* (London: Hutchinson, 1972).

FRANCESCHINI, CHRISTOPH, 'Der Feinschmecker aus Bariloche', in *Südtirol profil*, 20/16 (May 1994), 12–16.

FRANK, MICHAEL, *Die letzte Bastion, Nazis in Argentinien* (Hamburg: Rütten & Loening, 1962).

FRANK, NIKLAS, *Der Vater: Eine Abrechnung* (Munich: Bertelsmann, 1987).

FRANZ, CORINNA, *Fernand de Brinon und die deutsch-französischen Beziehungen 1918–1945* (Bonn: Bouvier, 2000).

FRANZINELLI, MIMMO, *Le stragi nascoste: L'armadio della vergogna: impunitá e rimozione dei crimini di guerra nazifascisti 1943–2001* (Milan: Mondadori, 2002).

FREI, NORBERT, *Vergangenheitspolitik: Die Anfänge der Bundesrepublik und die NS-Vergangenheit* (Munich: Beck, 1996).

—— (ed.), *Karrieren im Zwielicht: Hitlers Eliten nach 1945* (Frankfurt: Campus, 2001).

FREIWALD, AARON, and MENDELSOHN, MARTIN, *The Last Nazi: Josef Schwammberger and the Nazi Past* (New York: Norton, 1994).

FREUDENREICH, JOHANN, 'Wegen schwerer Kriegsverbrechen in Rußland: Vor 5 Jahren angeklagt—erst gestern festgenommen', *Süddeutsche Zeitung* (14 November 1979).

FRIEDMAN, MAX PAUL, *Nazis and Good Neighbors: The United States Campaign against the Germans of Latin America in World War II* (Cambridge: Cambridge University Press, 2003).

FUCHS, MAIK, 'Ein Husarenritt', *MF-Panzermodellbau* (July 2001) <http://www.mf-panzermodellbau.de/Artikel der Husarenritt.htm>, accessed 3 Sept. 2004.

GADDIS, JOHN LEWIS, *The Cold War* (London: Lane, 2006).

GAILUS, MANFRED, *Protestantismus und Nationalsozialismus: Studien zur nationalsozialistischen Durchdringung des protestantistischen Sozialmilieus in Berlin* (Cologne: Böhlau, 2001).

GALLAND, ADOLF, *Die Ersten und die Letzten: Die Jagdflieger im Zweiten Weltkrieg* (Munich: Schneekluth, 1953).

—— *The First and the Last: The German Fighter Force in World War II* (London: n.pub., 1955).

GANGLMAIR, SIEGWALD, 'Das "Arbeitserziehungslager" Weyer im Bezirk Braunau am Inn 1940–1941: Ein Beitrag zur Zeitgeschichte Oberösterreichs', *Oberösterreichische Heimatblättter*, 37/1 (1983).

GANN, CHRISTOPH, *Raoul Wallenberg: So viele Menschen retten wie möglich* (Munich: Beck, 1999).

GATTERER, CLAUS, *Schöne Welt, böse Leut: Kindheit in Südtirol* (Vienna: Europaverlag, 1982).

—— 'Südtirol 1930–45. Eine politische Landschaftsskizze', in *Aufsätze und Reden* (Bozen: Edition Rætia, 1991).

GAUDIG, OLAF, and VEIT, PETER, *Hakenkreuz über Südamerika: Ideologie, Politik, Militär* (Berlin: Wissenschaftlicher, 2004).

GEHLEN, REINHARD, *Der Dienst: Erinnerungen 1942–1971* (Mainz: Hase & Koehler, 1971).

——*The Service: The Memoirs of General Reinhard Gehlen*, ed. David von Irving (New York: World, 1972).

GELMI, JOSEF, *Die Brixner Bischöfe in der Geschichte Tirols* (Bozen: Athesia, 1984).

——*Geschichte der Kirche in Tirol: Nord-, Ost- und Südtirol* (Innsbruck: Tyrolia, 2001).

——*Fürstbischof Johannes Geisler (1882–1952): Eines der dramatischsten Kapitel der Südtiroler Geschichte* (Brixen: Weger, 2003).

GENTILE, CARLO, 'Politische Soldaten: Die 16. SS-Panzer-Grenadier-Division "Reichsführer-SS", in Italien 1944', *Quellen und Forschungen aus italienischen Archiven und Bibliotheken*, 81 (2001), 529–61.

——and KLINKHAMMER, LUTZ, 'Gegen den Verbündeten von einst: Die Gestapo in Italien', in Paul and Mallmann (eds.), *Die Gestapo im Zweiten Weltkrieg*, 521–40.

GERLACH, CHRISTIAN, *Das letzte Kapitel: Realpolitik, Ideologie und der Mord an den ungarischen Juden 1944/1945* (Stuttgart: Deutsche, 2002).

GIEFER, RENA, and GIEFER, THOMAS, *Die Rattenlinie: Fluchtwege der Nazis, Eine Dokumentation* (Frankfurt am Main: Haine, 1991).

GINSBORG, PAUL, *A History of Contemporary Italy: Society and Politics 1943–1988* (London: Penguin, 1990).

GIOVANETTI, PIERANGELO, 'La salvezza arrivò da Termeno', *l'Adige*, 30 July 2003, 15.

GLUR, STEFAN, *Vom besten Pferd im Stall zur persona non grata: Paul Ruegger als Schweizer Gesandter in Rom 1936–1942* (Bern: Lang, 2005).

GODA, NORMAN J. W., 'Nazi Collaborators in the United States: What the FBI Knew', in Breitman *et al.* (eds.), *U.S. Intelligence and the Nazis*, 227–64.

——'The Nazi Peddler: Wilhelm Höttl and Allied Intelligence', in Breitman *et al.* (eds.), *U.S. Intelligence and the Nazis*, 265–92.

——'The Ustaša: Murder and Espionage', in Richard Breitman *et al.* (eds.), *U.S. Intelligence and the Nazis*, 203–26.

——*Tales from Spandau: Nazi Criminals and the Cold War* (New York: Cambridge University Press, 2007).

GODMAN, PETER, *Hitler and the Vatican: Inside the Secret Archives that Reveal the New Story of the Nazis and the Church* (New York: Free, 2004).

GOLDHAGEN, DANIEL J., *A Moral Reckoning: The Role of the Catholic Church in the Holocaust and Its Unfulfilled Duty of Repair* (New York: Knopf, 2002).

——*Die katholische Kirche und der Holocaust: Eine Untersuchung über Schuld und Sühne* (Berlin: Siedler, 2002).

GOLLER, JOACHIM, 'Die Brixner Nebenregierung: Der politische Einfluss des Bistums Brixen auf die SVP 1945–1964', D.Phil. dissertation, University of Innsbruck, Austria, 2004.

GOÑI, UKI, *La autèntica Odessa: La fuga nazi a la Argentina de Perón* (Buenos Aires: Paidós, 2002).

——*Operazione Odessa: La fuga dei gerarchi nazisti verso l'Argentina di Perón* (Milan: Garzanto, 2003).

——*The Real Odessa: How Perón Brought the Nazi War Criminals to Argentina* (London: Granta, 2003).

——*Odessa: Die wahre Geschichte: Fluchthilfe für NS-Kriegsverbrecher* (Berlin: Assoziation A, 2006).

GONZALEZ, J. L., AND PEREZ, T., *Paul VI*, tr. Edward L. Heston (Boston: Daughters of St Paul, 1964).

GÖSCHEL, CHRISTIAN, 'Suicide at the End of the Third Reich', *Journal of Contemporary History*, 41/1 (2006), 153–73.

GOSZTONYI, PÉTER, *A Kormányzó Horthy Miklós és az Emigráció* (Budapest: Százszorszép Kiadó, 1992).

GRABHER, MICHAEL, *Irmfried Eberl: "Euthanasie"-Arzt und Kommandant von Treblinka* (Frankfurt am Main: Lang, 2006).

GRANZOTTO, PAOLO, *Montanelli* (Bologna: Mulino, 2004).

GRIECH-POLELLE, BETH A., *Bishop von Galen: German Catholicism and National Socialism* (New Haven: Yale University Press, 2002).

GRÖNEVELD, GERARD, *Kriegsberichter, Nederlandse SS-oorlogsverslaggevers 1941–1945* (Nijmegen: Vantilt, 2004).

GROSE, PETER, *Gentleman Spy: The Life of Allen Dulles* (Boston: Houghton Mifflin, 1994).

GUERRIERO, ELIO (ed.), *La chiesa in Italia: Dall'unità ai nostri giorni* (Milan: San Paolo, 1996).

GUREVICH, BEATRIZ, 'Agencias estatales y actors que interviniero en la inmigracion de criminales de Guerra y colaboracionistas en la pos segunda guerra mundial. El caso Argentina', in Comisión para el Esclarecimiento de las Actividades del Nazismo en la Argentina (CEANA) (ed.), *Tercer Informe de Avance*, 2 vols. (Buenos Aires: CEANA, 1998).

GYSEKE, HERMANN, *Der Fall Priebke* (Berg am Starnberger See: Druffel-Verlag, 1997).

HAAS, ALEXANDRA, *Ungarn in Tirol: Flüchtlingsschicksale 1945–1956*, Innsbrucker Forschungen zur Zeitgeschichte 25 (Innsbruck: Studien, 2008).

HABBE, CHRISTIAN, 'Im Visier der Nazi-Jäger', *Der Spiegel*, 36 (2001), 164–72.

HAFFNER, SEBASTIAN, *Anmerkungen zu Hitler* (Frankfurt am Main: Fischer, 2008).

HAGEN, WALTER [Pseud. Wilhelm Höttl], *Die geheime Front* (Linz: Nibelungen, 1950).

—— *Unternehmen Bernhard: Ein historischer Tatsachenbericht über die größte Geldfälschungsaktion aller Zeiten* (Wels: Welsermühl, 1955).

HAREL, ISSER, *The House on Garibaldi Street* (London: Cass, 1997).

HEBBLETHWAITE, PETER, *Paul VI: The First Modern Pope* (New York: Paulist, 1993).

HEIDEKING, JÜRGEN, *Geschichte der USA* (Tübingen: Francke, 2006).

HEINEMANN, ISABEL, 'Die Rassenexperten der SS und die bevölkerungspolitische Neuordnung Südosteuropas', in Beer and Seewann (eds.), *Südostforschung im Schatten des Dritten Reiches*, 135–57.

HEISS, HANS, and PFEIFER, GUSTAV (eds.), *Südtirol—Stunde Null? Kriegsende 1945–1946*, Veröffentlichungen des Südtiroler Landesarchivs 10 (Innsbruck: Studien, 2000).

HERBERT, ULRICH, 'NS-Eliten in der Bundesrepublik', in Wilfried Loth and Bernd-A. Rusinek (eds.), *Verwandlungspolitik: NS-Eliten in der westdeutschen Nachkriegsgesellschaft* (Frankfurt: Campus, 1998), 93–115.

HERF, JEFFREY, *Divided Memory: The Nazi Past in the Two Germanys* (Cambridge: Harvard University Press, 1997).

HILBERG, RAUL, *Die Vernichtung der europäischen Juden* (Frankfurt am Main: Olle & Wolter 1991).

—— *Täter, Opfer, Zuschauer: Die Vernichtung der Juden 1933–1945* (Frankfurt am Main: Fischer, 1992).

HILTON, STANLEY E., *Hitler's Secret War in South America 1939–1945: German Military Espionage and Allied Counterespionage in Brazil* (Baton Rouge: Louisiana State University Press, 1981).

HOCHHUTH, ROLF, *Der Stellvertreter: Schauspiel* (Hamburg: Reinbek, 1963).

HÖHNE, HEINZ, *Zolling Hermann, Pullach intern: General Gehlen und die Geschichte des Bundesnachrichtendienstes* (Hamburg: Hoffmann and Campe, 1971).

—— 'Der Schlächter von Lyon', *Der Spiegel* 19 (1987), 192–207; 22 (1987), 182–98.

—— *Der Orden unter dem Totenkopf: Die Geschichte der SS* (Augsberg: Weltilt, 1994).

HOLBOECK, CARL, *Handbuch des Kirchenrechtes*, 2 vols. (Innsbruck: Tyrolia, 1951).

HOLBORN, LOUISE W., *The International Refugee Organization: A Specialized Agency of the United Nations: Its History and Work 1946–1952* (London: Oxford University Press, 1956).

HUDAL, ALOIS, *Vom Deutschen Schaffen in Rom* (Innsbruck: Tyrolia, 1933).
—— *Die deutsche Kulturarbeit in Italien* (Munich: Aschendorff, 1934).
—— *Deutsches Volk und christliches Abendland* (Innsbruck: Tyrolia, 1935).
—— *Der Vatikan und die modernen Staaten* (Innsbruck: Tyrolia, 1935).
—— *Das Rassenproblem*, Schriftenreihe im Dienste der Katholischen Aktion 10/11 (Lobnig: Schlusche, 1936).
—— *Die Grundlagen des Nationalsozialismus: Eine ideengeschichtliche Untersuchung* (Leipzig: Günther, 1937).
—— 'Die katholische Caritas in einer Zeitenwende: Predigt gehalten am 11. 9. 1949 in der Deutschen Nationalkirche der Anima in Rom', *Anima-Stimmen: Lose Blätter zur Förderung des kollegialen Geistes der ehemaligen Anima-Priester*, 3/4 (1951), 26–30.
—— *Römische Tagebücher: Lebensbeichte eines alten Bischofs* (Graz: Stocker, 1976).
HUNT, LINDA, *Secret Agenda: The United States Government, Nazi Scientists and Project Paperclip* (London: St Martin's, 1991).
HYE, FRANZ-HEINZ, *Innsbruck im Spannungsfeld der Politik 1918–1938: Berichte—Bilder—Dokumente*, Veröffentlichungen des Innsbrucker Stadtarchivs NS 16/17 (Innsbruck: Stadtmagistrat Innsbruck, 1991).
ICRC (ed.), *The International Red Cross Committee in Geneva 1863–1943* (Zurich: Corzett & Huber, 1943).
ILG, KARL, *Pioniere in Argentinien, Chile, Paraguay und Venezuela: Durch Begwelt, Urwald und Steppe erwanderte Volkskunde der deutschsprachigen Siedler* (Innsbruck: Tyrolia, 1976).
—— *Das Deutschtum in Chile und Argentinien*, Eckartschriften 83 (Vienna: Österreichische Landsmannschaft, 1982).
INNERHOFER, JOSEF, *Die Kirche in Südtirol, Gestern und Heute* (Bozen: Athesia, 1982).
—— *Er blieb sich selber treu: Josef Mayr-Nusser 1910–1945* (Bozen: Athesia, 2005).
IRNBERGER, HARALD, *Nelkenstrauss ruft Praterstern: Am Beispiel Österreich: Funktion und Arbeitsweise geheimer Nachrichtendienste in einem neutralen Staat* (Vienna: Promedia, 1983).
JÄCKEL, EBERHARD, *Frankreich in Hitlers Europa* (Stuttgart: Deutsche, 1966).
JACKISCH, CARLOTA, *El nazismo y los refugiados alemanes en la Argentina, 1933–1945* (Buenos Aires: Editorial de Belgrano, 1989).
—— 'Cuantificación de Criminales de Guerra Según Fuentes Argentinas, informe final', *CEANA* (1998) <http://www.ceana.org.ar/final/jackicsh.zip>, accessed 22 March 2004.
JACKSON, JULIAN, *France: The Dark Years, 1940–1944* (Oxford: Oxford University Press, 2001).
JUDT, TONY, *Postwar: A History of Europe since 1945* (New York: Penguin, 2005).
KAMM, HENRY, 'German in Rome denies he sought to help Nazis', *New York Times* (23 February 1984), A 8.
KARNER, STEFAN, *Die Steiermark im Dritten Reich 1938–1945: Aspekte ihrer politischen wirtschaftlich-sozialen und kulturellen Entwicklung* (Graz: Leykam, 1986).
KATER, MICHAEL H., *Das 'Ahnenerbe' der SS 1935–1945: Ein Beitrag zur Kulturpolitik des Dritten Reiches* (Munich: Oldenbourg, 2006).
KATZ, ROBERT, *Dossier Priebke* (Milan: Rizzoli, 1996).
KAUFMANN, ALICE, *Klaus Barbie: Dem Schlächter von Lyon entkommen* (Vienna: Edition S Verlag der Österreichischen Staatsdruckerei, 1987).
KEIPERT, MARIA, *et al.* (eds.), *Biographisches Handbuch des deutschen Auswärtigen Dienstes*, 1871–1945, vol. 1, A–F (Paderborn: Schöningh, 2000).
KELLER, SVEN, *Günzburg und der Fall Josef Mengele: Die Heimatstadt und die Jagd nach dem NS-Verbrecher*, Schriftenreihe der Vierteljahrshefte für Zeitgeschichte 87 (Munich: Oldenbourg, 2003).
KEMPNER, ROBERT, *SS im Kreuzverhör: Die Elite, die Europa in Scherben schlug* (Nördlingen: Greno, 1987).

KENT, PETER C., *The Lonely Cold War of Pope Pius XII: The Roman Catholic Church and the Division of Europe 1943–1950* (Montreal: McGill-Queen's University Press, 2002).

KERN, ERICH, *Kampf in der Ukraine 1941–1944* (Göttingen: Plesse, 1964).

KERSHAW, IAN, *Hitler 1936–1945* (New York: Norton, 2000).

KLAMMER, BRUNO, et al. (eds.), *200 Jahre Franziskanergymnasium Bozen 1781–1981: Festschrift zum 200jährigen Bestehen des Franziskanergymnasiums in Bozen* (Bozen: Athesia, 1981).

KLEE, ERNST, *Was sie taten—was sie wurden: Ärzte, Juristen und andere Beteiligte am Kranken- und Judenmord* (Frankfurt am Main: Fischer, 1986).

——*Persilscheine und falsche Pässe: Wie die Kirchen den Nazis halfen* (Frankfurt am Main: Fischer, 1991).

——*Auschwitz, die NS-Medizin und ihre Opfer* (Frankfurt am Main: Fischer, 1997).

KLINKHAMMER, LUTZ, *Zwischen Bündnis und Besatzung: Das nationalsozialistische Deutschland und die Republik von Salò 1943–1945* (Tübingen: Niemeyer, 1993).

KNOPP, GUIDO, *Die SS: Eine Warnung der Geschichte* (Munich: Bertelsmann, 2003).

KOCHAVI, ARIEH J., *Prelude to Nuremberg: Allied War Crimes Policy and the Question of Punishment* (Chapel Hill: University of North Carolina Press, 1998).

KÖFLER, GRETL, 'Wir wollen sehen, ob das Kreuz oder der siebenarmige Leuchter siegt! Antisemitismus in Nord- und Osttirol seit 1918', *Sturzflüge: Eine Kulturzeitschrift*, 5/15–16 (Dec. 1986), 89–95.

KOGON, EUGEN, *Der SS-Staat: Das System der deutschen Konzentrationslager* (Munich: Kindler, 1979).

——(ed.), *Nationalsozialistische Massentötungen durch Giftgas* (Frankfurt am Main: Fischer, 1983).

KOOP, VOLKER, *Hitlers fünfte Kolonne: Die Auslands-Organisation der NSDAP* (Berlin: Be.bra, 2009).

KRAUSNICK, HELMUT, *Hitlers Einsatzgruppen: Die Truppe des Weltanschauungskrieges 1938–1942* (Frankfurt am Main: Fischer, 1985).

KROYER, SILVIA, *Deutsche Vermögen in Argentinien 1945–1965: Ein Beitrag über deutsche Direkt-investitionen im Ausland* (Frankfurt am Main: Vervuert, 2005).

KUBE, ALFRED, *Pour le mérite und Hakenkreuz: Hermann Göring im Dritten Reich*, Quellen und Darstellungen zur Zeitgeschichte 24 (Munich: Oldenbourg, 1986).

KULKA, OTTO DOV, and JÄCKEL, EBERHARD (eds.), *Die Juden in den geheimen NS-Stimmungs-berichten 1933–1945*, Schriften des Bundesarchivs 62 (Düsseldorf: Droste, 2004).

KURETSIDIS-HAIDER, CLAUDIA, 'Die von der Moskauer Konferenz der Alliierten vom 1. November 1943 verabschiedete Erklärung über die Verantwortlichkeit der Hitleranhänger für begangene Gräueltaten', *Alfred Klahr, Gesellschaft: Verein zur Erforsch-ung der Geschichte der Arbeiterbewegung* (25 Oct. 2003) <http://www.klahrgesellschaft.at/Referate/Kuretsidis_2003.html>, accessed 28 Jan. 2009.

——and GARSCHA, WINFRIED R., *Keine 'Abrechnung': NS-Verbrechen, Justiz und Gesellschaft in Europa nach 1945* (Leipzig: Akademische, 1998).

KUROWSKI, FRANZ, *Panzer Aces II: Battle Stories of German Tank Commanders in World War II* (Mechanicsburg: Stackpole Books, 2004).

LAHER, LUDWIG, *Heart Flesh Degeneration* (Riverside: Ariadne, 2006).

LAHME, TILMANN, and STUNZ, HOLGER, 'Wo sind Wagner-Partituren?', *FAZ* (28 July 2007), Z 1.

LANFRANCHI, FERRUCCIO, *La resa degli ottocentomila: Con le memorie autografe del barone Luigi Parrilli* (Milan: Rizzoli, 1948).

LANG, JOCHEN VON, *Das Eichmann-Protokoll: Tonbandaufzeichnungen der israelischen Verhöre* (Berlin: Severin and Siedler, 1982).

——*Der Adjutant: Karl Wolff: Der Mann zwischen Hitler und Himmler* (Munich: Herbig, 1985).

——— *Der Sekretär: Martin Bormann: Der Mann, der Hitler beherrschte* (Munich: Herbig, 1987).

LANGBEIN, HERMANN, *Menschen in Auschwitz* (Vienna: Europaverlag, 1995).

LANGER, MARKUS, 'Alois Hudal, Bischof zwischen Kreuz und Hakenkreuz: Versuch einer Biografie,' D.Phil. dissertation, University of Vienna, Austria, 1995.

LAZZARINI, ANDREA, *Papst Paul VI: Sein Leben und seine Gestalt* (Freiburg: Herder, 1964).

LEBERT, NORBERT, and LEBERT, STEPHEN, *Denn du trägst meinen Namen: Das schwere Erbe der prominenten Nazi-Kinder* (Munich: Blessing, 2000).

LECHNER, STEFAN, *'Die Eroberung der Fremdstämmigen': Provinzfaschismus in Südtirol 1921–1926*, Veröffentlichungen des Südtiroler Landesarchivs 20 (Innsbruck: Wagner, 2005).

——— 'Rückoption und Rücksiedlung nach Südtirol', in Klaus Eisterer and Rolf Steininger (eds.), *Die Option: Südtirol zwischen Faschismus und Nationalsozialismus*, Innsbrucker Forschungen zur Zeitgeschichte 5 (Innsbruck: Haymon, 1989).

LEHNERT, PASCALINA, *Ich durfte ihm dienen: Erinnerungen an Papst Pius XII* (Würzburg: Naumann, 1982).

LENZENWEGER, JOSEF, *Sancta Maria de Anima* (Vienna: Herder, 1959).

LEY, GABRIELE, 'Deutsche Naturwissenschaftler an argentinischen Universitäten nach 1945', in Meding (ed.), *Nationalsozialismus und Argentinien*, 149–60.

LEYERER, JÜRGEN, *Argentinien, die Flieger und wir: Eine Erzählung aus den Nachkriegsjahren* (Vienna: Liber Libri, 2010),

LICHTENSTEIN, HEINER, *Angepaßt und treu ergeben. Das Rote Kreuz im 'Dritten Reich'* (Cologne: Bund, 1988).

LIEBMANN, MAXIMILIAN, *Kirche in Gesellschaft und Politik: Von der Reformation bis zur Gegenwart* (Graz: Austria Medien Service, 1999).

LINGEN, KERSTIN VON, *Kesselrings letzte Schlacht: Kriegsverbrecherprozesse, Vergangenheitspolitik und Wiederbewaffnung: Der Fall Kesselring* (Paderborn: Schöningh, 2004).

——— 'Conspiracy of Silence: How the "Old Boys" of American Intelligence Shielded SS General Karl Wolff from Prosecution', *Holocaust and Genocide Studies*, 22/1 (2008), 74–109.

——— 'Der lange Weg zum Verhandlungsfrieden: Hintergründe und Interessen an Operation Sunrise', in Richardi and Steinacher (eds.), *Für Freiheit und Recht in Europa*, 174–206.

——— 'La lunga via verso la pace. Retrosceni e interessi all' "Operation Sunrise"', in Gerald Steinacher and Aram Mattioli (eds.), *Faschismus und Architektur / Architettura e fascismo, Geschichte und Region / Storia e regione*, 17/1 (2008), 159–78.

——— *SS und Secret Service: 'Verschwörung des Schweigens': Der Fall Karl Wolff* (Paderborn: Schöningh, 2010).

LITTELL, JONATHAN, *The Kindly Ones*, tr. Charlotte Mandell (London: Chatto & Windus, 2008).

LLORENTE, ELENA, and RIGACCI, MARTINO, *El último nazi: Priebke, de la Argentina a Italia, Juicio a medio siglo de historia* (Buenos Aires: Editorial Sudamericana, 1998).

LONGERICH, PETER, *Hitlers Stellvertreter: Führung der Partei und Kontrolle des Staatsapparates durch den Stab Heß und die Partei-Kanzlei Bormann* (Munich: Saur, 1992).

LOTH, WILFRIED, and RUSINEK, BERND-A. (eds.), *Verwandlungspolitik: NS-Eliten in der westdeutschen Nachkriegsgesellschaft* (Frankfurt: Campus, 1998).

LÜTGE, WILHELM *et al.*, *Deutsche in Argentinien 1520–1980*, ed. Deutschen Klub (2nd edn, Buenos Aires: Alemann, 1981).

MABIRE, JEAN, *Die SS-Panzer-Division 'Wiking'* (Eggolsheim: Dörfler, 2002).

MACLEAN, FRENCH L., *The Field Men: The SS Officers Who Led the Einsatzkommandos—the Nazi Mobile Killing Units* (Atglen: Schiffer, 1999).

——— *The Camp Men: The SS Officers Who Ran the Nazi Concentration Camp System* (Atglen: Schiffer, 1999).

MAIER, CHARLES S., *The Unmasterable Past: History, Holocaust, and German National Identity* (Cambridge: Harvard University Press, 1997).

MALER, JUAN [Reinhard Kops], *Das Jüngste Gericht* (Buenos Aires: Maler, 1982).

—— *Frieden, Krieg und 'Frieden'* (San Carlos de Bariloche: Maler, 1987).

—— *Rette sich wer kann!* (Buenos Aires: Maler, 1989).

MALKIN, LAWRENCE, *Hitlers Geldfälscher: Wie die Nazis planten, das internationale Währungssystem auszuhebeln* (Bergisch Gladbach: Lübbe, 2006).

—— *Krueger's Men: The Secret Nazi Counterfeit Plot and the Prisoners of Block 19* (Boston: Little, 2008).

MALLMANN, KLAUS-MICHAEL, and PAUL, GERHARD (eds.), *Karrieren der Gewalt: Nationalsozialistische Täterbiographien* (Darmstadt: Wissenschaftliche, 2004).

MARGOLIAN, HOWARD, *Unauthorized Entry: The Truth about Nazi War Criminals in Canada* (Toronto: University of Toronto Press, 2000).

MARRUS, MICHAEL R., *The Unwanted: European Refugees in the Twentieth Century* (Oxford: Oxford University Press, 1985).

MASUROVSKY, MARC JEAN, 'The Safehaven Program: The Allied Response to Nazi Post-defeat Planning 1944–1948', M.A. thesis, American University, Washington DC, 1990.

MATTIOLI, ARAM, ' "Die Resistenza ist tot, es lebe Onkel Mussolini!" Vom Umdeuten der Geschichte im Italien Berlusconis', *Mittelweg*, 36/17 (2008), 75–93.

—— *Viva Mussolini! Die Aufwertung des Faschismus im Italien Berlusconis* (Paderborn: Schöningh, 2010).

MAUCH, CHRISTOF, *Schattenkrieg gegen Hitler: Das Dritte Reich im Visier der amerikanischen Geheimdienste 1941–1945* (Stuttgart: Deutsche, 1999).

MEDING, HOLGER, *Flucht vor Nürnberg? Deutsche und österreichische Einwanderung in Argentinien 1945–1955* (Cologne: Böhlau, 1992).

—— (ed.), *Nationalsozialismus und Argentinien: Beziehungen, Einflüsse und Nachwirkungen* (Frankfurt am Main: Lang, 1995).

—— *'Der Weg': Eine deutsche Emigrantenzeitschrift in Buenos Aires 1947–1957* (Berlin: Wissenschaftlicher, 1997).

—— and STOIA, LUCIA DE, *La ruta de los nazis en tiempos de Perón* (Buenos Aires: Emecé, 2000).

—— 'La emigración a la República Argentina de los Nacional-socialistas buscados. Una aproximación cuantitativa', *Estudios Migratorios Latinoamericanos*, 43 (1999), 241–59.

—— and ISMAR, GEORG (eds.), *Argentinien und das Dritte Reich: Mediale und reale Präsenz, Ideologietransfer, Folgewirkungen* (Berlin: Wissenschaftlicher, 2008).

MEIJL, PETER VAN, *Pater Pancratius Pfeiffer und sein Einsatz für die Juden während der Besatzung in Rom (1943–1944)*, ed. Österreichischen Provinz der Salvatorianer (Vienna: Vallendar, 2007).

MEISSL, SEBASTIAN, et al. (eds.), *Verdrängte Schuld, verfehlte Sühne: Entnazifizierung in Österreich 1945–1955* (Munich: Oldenbourg, 1986).

MEIXNER, WOLFGANG, ' "Arisierung"—die "Entjudung" der Wirtschaft im Gau Tirol-Vorarlberg', in Steininger and Pitscheider (eds.), *Tirol und Vorarlberg in der NS-Zeit*, 319–40.

MEZZALIRA, GIORGIO, and ROMEO, CARLO (eds.), *'Mischa' l'aguzzino del Lager di Bolzano: Dalle carte del processo a Michael Seifert (Quaderni della memoria 2/02)* (Bozen: Circolo Culturale ANPI, 2002).

MICCOLI, GIOVANNI, *I dilemmi e i silenzi di Pio XII* (Milan: Rizzoli, 2000).

MILANO, JAMES V., and ROGAN, PATRICK, *Soldiers, Spies and the Rat Line: America's Undeclared War against the Soviets* (Washington: Brassey's, 2000).

MITTERMAIR, VERONIKA, 'Bruchlose Karrieren? Zum Werdegang der Südtiroler Politikerschicht bis zur "Stunde Null"', in Heiss and Pfeifer (eds.), *Südtirol—Stunde Null?*, 169–202.

MLAKAR, BORIS, *Slovensko Domobranstvo 1943–1945: Ustanovitev, organizacija, idejno ozadje* (Ljubljana: Slovenska matica, 2003).

MOELLER, ROBERT G., *War Stories: The Search for a Usable Past in the Federal Republic of Germany* (Berkeley: University of California Press, 2001).

—— 'Germans as Victims? Thoughts on a Post-Cold War History of World War II Legacies', *History and Memory*, 17/1–2 (2005), 147–94.

MOISEL, CLAUDIA, *Frankreich und die deutschen Kriegsverbrecher: Politik und Praxis der Strafverfolgung nach dem Zweiten Weltkrieg*, Beiträge zur Geschichte des 20. Jahrhunderts 2 (Göttingen: Wallstein, 2004).

MOOS, CARLO, 'Die "guten" Italiener und die Zeitgeschichte: Zum Problem der Vergangenheitsbewältigung in Italien', *Historische Zeitschrift*, 259 (1994), 671–94.

MORENO, LISA C., 'The National Catholic Welfare Conference and Catholic Americanism, 1919–1966', Ph.D. dissertation, University of Maryland, College Park, 1999.

MORITZ, STEFAN, *Grüß Gott und Heil Hitler: Katholische Kirche und Nationalsozialismus in Österreich* (Vienna: Picus, 2002).

MORODER, EDGAR, *Hans Steger, and Paula Wiesinger zum 100. Jahre-Jubiläum und das Hotel Steger-Dellai auf der Seiser Alm* (Seis: n.pub., 2007).

MORRIS, CHARLES R., *American Catholic: The Saints and Sinners Who Built America's Most Powerful Church* (New York: Times Books, 1997).

MOTL, STANISLAV, *Nacisté pod ochranou: aneb kdo vlastně prohral válku?* (Prague: Rybka, 2001).

MURPHY, PAUL I., and ARLINGTON, RENÉ, *La Popessa* (New York: Warner, 1983).

MUSIAL, BOGDAN (ed.), *'Aktion Reinhard': Der Völkermord an den Juden im Generalgouvernement 1941–1944* (Osnabrück: Fibre, 2004).

NAFTALI, TIMOTHY, 'Creating the Myth of the Alpenfestung: Allied Intelligence and the Collapse of the Nazi Police-State', in Günter Bischof and Anton Pelinka (eds.), *Austrian Historical Memory and National Identity*, Contemporary Austrian Studies 5, (New Brunswick: Transaction 1997), 203–46.

—— 'The CIA and Eichmann's Associates', in Breitman *et al.* (eds.), *U.S. Intelligence and the Nazis*, 337–74.

NAPOLITANO, MATTEO LUIGI, *Pio XII Tra Guerra e Pace: Profezia e diplomazia di un papa (1939–1945)* (Rome: Città nuova, 2002).

—— and TORNIELLI, ANDREA, *Pio XII: Il papa degli ebrei* (Casale Monferrato: Piemme, 2002).

—— *Pacelli, Roncalli e i battesimi della shoah* (Casale Monferrato: Piemme, 2005).

NEVISTIĆ, F., 'La muerte del Prof. Draganović', *Studia Croatica*, 90/1 (Dec. 1983), 153–5.

NEWTON, RONALD C., *The 'Nazi Menace' in Argentina, 1931–1947* (Stanford: Stanford University Press, 1992).

—— 'Italienischer Faschismus und deutscher Nationalsozialismus in Argentinien: Eine vergleichende Analyse', in Meding (ed.), *Nationalsozialismus und Argentinien*, 117–38.

NIETHAMMER, LUTZ, *Die Mitläuferfabrik: Die Entnazifizierung am Beispiel Bayerns* (Berlin: Dietz, 1982).

NIGG, REGULA, and METTAUER, PHILIPP, ' "Wir sind für euch immer noch die Emigranten": Eine österreichisch-argentinische Lebensgeschichte', in Christine Schindler and Dokumentationsarchiv des österreichischen Widerstandes (eds.), *Jahrbuch 2003* (Vienna: Taschenbuch, 2003), 12–41.

NIGG, REGULA, METTAUER, PHILIPP, and KÜHSCHELM, OLIVER (eds.), *ÖsterreicherInnen im Exil: Die La Plata-Staaten Argentinien, Uruguay, Paraguay 1934–1945* (Vienna: Documentation Centre of Austrian Resistance, 2004).

ORIZIO, RICCARDO, 'Cosi' la Croce Rossa salvo' i nazisti', *Corriere della Sera*, 19 June 1998, 11, <http://archiviostorico.corriere.it/1998/giugno/19/Cosi_Croce_Rossa_salvo_nazisti_co_0_98061914498.shtml>, accessed 8 May 2009.

OVEN, WILFRED VON, *Ein 'Nazi' in Argentinien* (Duisburg: VAWS, 1999).

PACE, GIOVANNI MARIA, *La via dei demoni: La fuga in Sudamerica dei criminali nazisti: Secreti, complicità, silenzi* (Milan: Sperling & Kupfer, 2000).

PADOVANI, GIOVANNA, 'Epilogo di guerra per la Wehrmacht in Italia: dalla resa nella montagna veneta all "Enklave" di Rimini-Bellaria', in Ferruccio Vendramini (ed.), *Montagne e veneti nel secondo dopoguerra* (Verona: Bertani, 1988).

PALLAVER, GÜNTHER, 'Abhängigkeit, Verspätung, ethnische Versäulung. Folgen einer verfehlten Epurazione und Entnazifizierung in Südtirol', in Steinacher (ed.), *Südtirol im Dritten Reich*, 361–74.

PANKIW, JAROSLAW, *Rimins'kyi ansambl 'Burlaka' v moïj pam'jati: Belljarija-Rimini Italija 1945–1947* (Kiev: Vyd-vo im. Oleny Telihy, 1999).

PANTOZZI, GIUSEPPE, *Il Minotauro Argentato: Contributi alla conoscenza del movimento di resistenza di val di Fiemme* (Trento: Museo Storico, 2000).

PAUL, GERHARD, and MALLMANN, KLAUS-MICHAEL (eds.), *Die Gestapo im Zweiten Weltkrieg: "Heimatfront" und besetztes Europa* (Darmstadt: Primus, 2000).

—— (eds.), *Die Gestapo: Mythos und Realität* (Darmstadt: Primus, 2003).

PAZ, CARLOS, and DEUTSCH, OSCAR, *Eva Perón: peronismo para el socialismo* (Buenos Aires: Ediciones del Mirador, 1974).

PERATHONER, ANTON, *Das kirchliche Gesetzbuch (Codex juris canonici): Sinngemäß wiedergegeben und mit Anmerkungen versehen*, i. *Von den Sakramenten (can. 731–1153)* (3rd edn, Brixen: Druck and Weger, 1923).

Personalstand der Säkular- und Regular-Geistlichkeit der Diözese Seckau in der Steiermark im Jahre 1946 (Graz: Ordinariats-Kanzlei, 1946).

PETERSEN, NEAL H., 'From Hitler's Doorstep: Allen Dulles and the Penetration of Nazi Germany', in Chalou (ed.), *The Secret War*, 273–94.

PFANZELTER, EVA, 'Zwischen Brenner und Bari: Jüdische Flüchtlinge in Italien 1945 bis 1948', in Albrich (ed.), *Flucht nach Eretz Israel*.

—— 'Prominente am Pragser Wildsee: Eine Episode zum Kriegsende in Südtirol', in Heiss and Pfeifer (eds.), *Südtirol—Stunde Null?*, 117–37.

—— 'Kriegsende und amerikanische Verwaltung', in Steinacher (ed.), *Südtirol im Dritten Reich*, 347–60.

—— *Südtirol unterm Sternenbanner: Die amerikanische Besatzung Mai–Juni 1945* (Bozen: Edition Rætia, 2005).

PFEIFER, BARBARA, 'Im Vorhof des Todes: Das Polizeiliche Durchgangslager Bozen 1944–1945: Ansätze einer Gesamtdarstellung', D.Phil. dissertation, University of Innsbruck, Austria, 2003.

PHAYER, MICHAEL, *The Catholic Church and the Holocaust, 1930–1965* (Bloomington: Indiana University Press, 2008).

—— *Pius XII, the Holocaust, and the Cold War* (Bloomington: Indiana University Press, 2008).

PIRIE, ANTHONY, *Operation Bernhard* (New York: Grove, 1963).

POHL, OSWALD, *Credo: Mein Weg zu Gott* (Landshut: Girnth, 1950).

POLLACK, MARTIN, *Der Tote im Bunker: Bericht über meinen Vater* (Vienna: Zsolnay, 2004).

—— 'Mutmassungen über ein Verbrechen: Was ist es, das den Menschen den Mund verschliesst? Das Massaker im österreichischen Rechnitz im März 1945', *Neue Zürcher Zeitung* (20 June 2009), 'Literatur und Kunst', B 1.

POSNER, GERALD, and WARE, JOHN, *Mengele: Die Jagd auf den Todesengel* (Berlin: Aufbau, 1993).

POSSET, ANTON, 'Der Priester und der SS-General. Die Bekehrungsgeschichte des Oswald Pohl', *Themenhefte Landsberger Zeitgeschichte*, 1 (1993), 20–4.

POTASH, ROBERT, *The Army and Politics in Argentina*, i. *1945–1962, Peron to Frondizi*, 2 vols. (Stanford: Stanford University Press, 1980).

PRAUSER, STEFFEN, 'Mord in Rom? Der Anschlag in der Via Rasella und die deutsche Vergeltung in den Fosse Ardeatine', in Steinacher (ed.), *Südtirol im Dritten Reich*, 295–307.

PRESIDENZA DEL CONSIGLIO DEI MINISTRI (ed.), *Rapporto Generale, Commissione per la ricostruzione delle vicende che hanno caratterizzato in Italia le attività di acquisizione dei beni dei cittadini ebrei da parte di organismi pubblici e privati* (Rome: Presidenza del Consiglio dei ministri, Dipartimento per l'informazione e l'editoria, 2001).

PREWETT, VIRGINIA, '90,000 Nazis Carry On in Argentina', *Prevent World War III*, 17 (Oct./Nov. 1946), 13–15.

PRIEBKE, ERICH, and GIACHINI, PAOLO, *Autobiographie: 'Vae Victis' (Wehe den Besiegten)*, (Rome: n.pub., 2003).

PROSSLINER, KARL, *Sprechen über Südtirol, Zeugen eines Jahrhunderts* (Vienna: Folio, 1996).

PYTA, WOLFRAM, *et al.* (eds.), *Die Herausforderung der Diktaturen: Katholizismus in Deutschland und Italien 1918–1943/45* (Tübingen: Niemeyer, 2008).

RAHN, RUDOLF, *Ruheloses Leben: Aufzeichnungen und Erinnerungen* (Düsseldorf: Diederichs, 1949).

RATH, ERIC, 'The Mission of Argentina's Senor Bracamonte', *Prevent World War III*, 17 (Oct./Nov. 1946), 35–6.

RAUCHENSTEINER, MANFRIED, and ETSCHMANN, WOLFGANG (eds.), *Österreich 1945, Ein Ende und viele Anfänge* (Graz: Styria, 1997).

REGELE, LUDWIG WALTER, *Meran und das Dritte Reich: Ein Lesebuch* (Innsbruck: Studien, 2008).

REIMER, HANS H., *Lutherisch in Südtirol: Die Geschichte der Evangelischen Gemeinde Meran* (Bozen: Edition Rætia, 2009).

REITLINGER, GERALD, *SS: Alibi of a Nation 1922–1945* (New York: Viking, 1957).

RENNICKE, STEFAN, *Siemens in Argentinien: Die Unternehmensentwicklung vom Markteintritt bis zur Enteignung 1945* (Berlin: Wissenschaftlicher, 2004).

REPÚBLICA ARGENTINA, MINISTÉRIO DE RELACIONES EXTERIORES Y CULTO (ed.), *La República Argentina frente al Libro Azul* (Buenos Aires: Dirección de información al exterior, 1946).

RICHARDI, HANS-GÜNTER, *SS-Geiseln in der Alpenfestung: Die Verschleppung prominenter KZ-Häftlinge aus Deutschland nach Südtirol* (Bozen: Rætia, 2005).

——and STEINACHER, GERALD (eds.), *'Für Freiheit und Recht in Europa': Der 20. Juli 1944 und der Widerstand gegen das NS-Regime in Deutschland, Österreich und Südtirol*, ZeitgeschichtsSchriften Pragser Wildsee 2 (Innsbruck: Studien, 2009).

RIEDL, FRANZ, and VEITER, THEODOR (eds.), *Volkstum zwischen Moldau, Etsch und Donau: Festschrift für Franz Hieronymus Riedl dargeboten zum 65. Lebensjahr* (Vienna: Braumüller, 1971).

RIESS, CURT, *The Nazis Go Underground* (London: Boardman, 1944).

RISTELHUEBER, RENÉ, *The International Refugee Organization* (New York: Carnegie Endowment for International Peace, 1951).

RIVELLI, MARCO AURELIO, *L'arcivescovo del genocidio: Monsignor Stepinac, il Vaticano e la dittatura ustascia in Croazia, 1941–1945* (Milan: Kaos, 1999).

RÖTHLISBERGER, PETRA YOUNG-ZIE BARTHELMESS, 'Tarnoperationen und Geheimgeschäfte auf dem Schweizer Finanzplatz. Verdeckte deutsch-schweizerische Umgehungsgeschäfte und die Frage der nationalsozialistischen Täterkonten im Zweiten Weltkrieg', D.Phil. dissertation, University of Zurich, Switzerland, 2006.

ROUSSO, HENRY, *Pétain et la fin de la collaboration: Sigmaringen 1944–1945* (Brussels: Editions Complexe, 1984).

RUCHALA, CALI, 'The Return of the Golden Priest: The Verona Reports and the Second Recruitment of Krunoslav Draganović, 1959', *The Pavelić Papers, An Independent Project Researching the History of the Ustase Movement 1929–2003*, [website], n.d., <http://www.Pavelicpapers.com/features/essays/verona.html>, accessed 12 October 2005.

RUCKER, ARTHUR, 'The Work of the International Refugee Organization', *International Affairs* (Royal Institute of International Affairs), 25/1 (Jan. 1949), 66–73.

RUDEL, HANS-ULRICH, *Aus Krieg und Frieden: Aus den Jahren 1945 und 1952* (Göttingen: Plesse, 1954).

——*Zwischen Deutschland und Argentinien: Fünf Jahre in Übersee* (Göttingen: Plesse, 1954).

RUHL, KLAUS-JÖRG, *Franco, Falange y III Reich: España durante la II Guerra Mundial* (Madrid: Akal, 1986).

RUSINEK, LOTH, *Verwandlungspolitik: NS-Eliten in der westdeutschen Nachkriegsgesellschaft* (Frankfurt: Campus, 1998).

SAFT, ULRICH, *Der Krieg in der Heimat: Das bittere Ende zwischen Weser und Elbe* (Langenhagen: U. Saft, 1990), 54.

SALE, GIOVANNI, *Hitler, la Santa Sede e gli Ebrei: Con i documenti dell'Archivio Segreto Vaticano* (Milan: Jaca, 2004).

SALIERNO, PAOLINO, *Giovanni Battista Montini: Dalla cattedra di Ambrogio alla cattedra di Pietro* (Milan: Greco, 1992).

SALTER, MICHAEL, 'The Prosecution of Nazi War Criminals and the OSS. The Need for a New Research Agenda', *Journal of Intelligence History*, 2/1 (Summer 2002), 77–119.

——*Nazi War Crimes, US Intelligence and Selective Prosecution at Nuremberg* (London: Routledge-Cavendish, 2007).

SALZBORN, SAMUEL, 'Zwischen Volksgruppentheorie, Völkerrechtslehre und Volkstumskampf. Hermann Raschhofer als Vordenker eines völkischen Minderheitenrechts', *Sozial. Geschichte*, 21/3 (2006), 29–52.

SÁNCHEZ, JOSÉ, *Pius XII and the Holocaust: Understanding the Controversy* (Washington, DC: Catholic University of America Press, 2001).

SANFILIPPO, MATTEO, 'Los papeles de Hudal como fuente para la historia de la migración de alemanes y nazis después de la segunda guerra mundial', *Estudios Migratorios Latinoamericanos*, 43 (1999), 185–209. See also <http://www.ceana.org.ar/final/sanfilippo.zip>.

——'Archival Evidence on Postwar Italy as a Transit Point for Central and Eastern European Migrants', in Oliver Rathkolb (ed.), *Revisiting the National Socialist Legacy: Coming to Terms with Forced Labor, Expropriation, Compensation, and Restitution* (Innsbruck: Studien, 2002), 241–58.

——'Ratlines and Unholy Trinities': A Review Essay on (Recent) Literature Concerning Nazi and Collaborators Smuggling Operations Out of Italy, *Unitas DSpace*, 2003, <http://hdl.handle.net/2067/24>, accessed 14 Mar. 2010.

SAUVEUR-HENN, ANNE SAINT, 'Deutsche Einwanderung an den Río de la Plata während des Dritten Reiches und die Polarisierung der deutschen Gemeinschaft in Argentinien', in Meding and Ismar (eds.), *Argentinien und das Dritte Reich*, 57–72.

SAVEGNAGO, PAOLO, and VALENTE, LUCA, *Il mistero della missione giapponese: Valli del Pasubio, giugno 1944: La soluzione di uno degli episodi più enigmatici della guerra nell'Italia occupata dai tedeschi* (Verona: Cierre, 2006).

SCHEDEREIT, KARL, *SS-Mann Karrasch: Unvollständige Wahrnehmungen* (Bozen: Rætia, 2006).

SCHELLENBERG, WALTER, *Memoiren* (Cologne: Verlag für Politik und Wirtschaft, 1956).

SCHELVIS, JULIAN, *Vernichtungslager Sobibór* (Hamburg: Unrast, 2003).

SCHENK, DIETER, *Die braunen Wurzeln des BKA* (Frankfurt am Main: Fischer, 2003).

SCHERZBERG, LUCIA, 'Theologie und Vergangenheitsbewältigung im interdisziplinären Vergleich, Tagungsbericht von der Tagung des Instituts für Katholische Theologie der Universität des Saarlandes und der Katholischen Akademie Trier, Abteilung Saarbrücken', im Robert-Schuman-Haus, Trier, 1416 January 2005', *Theologie Geschichte*, [website], (2006), <http://aps.sulb.uni-saarland.de/theologie.geschichte/inhalt/2006/04.html>.

SCHIMPF, ECKHARD, *Heilig: Die Flucht des Braunschweiger Naziführers auf der Vatikan-Route nach Südamerika* (Braunschweig: Appelhans, 2005).

SCHMIDL, ERWIN A. (ed.), *Spione, Partisanen, Kriegspläne: Österreich im frühen Kalten Krieg 1945–1958* (Vienna: Böhlau, 2000).

SCHNEPPEN, HEINZ, *Odessa und das Vierte Reich: Mythen der Zeitgeschichte* (Berlin: Metropol, 2007).

——*Ghettokommandant in Riga: Eduard Roschmann, Fakten und Fiktionen* (Berlin: Metropol, 2009).

SCHOBER, RICHARD, 'Auf dem Weg zum Anschluss: Tirols Nationalsozialisten 1927–1938', *Tiroler Heimat*, 59 (1995), 132–61.

SCHOEPP, SEBASTIAN, *Das 'Argentinische Tageblatt' 1933 bis 1945: Ein Forum der antinationalsozialistischen Emigration* (Berlin: Metropol, 1996).

SCHOLTEN, JENS, 'Offiziere: Im Geiste unbesiegt', in Norbert Frei (ed.), *Karrieren im Zwielicht: Hitlers Eliten nach 1945* (Frankfurt: Campus, 2001).

SCHÖNWALD, MATTHIAS, *Deutschland und Argentinien nach dem Zweiten Weltkrieg: Politische und wirtschaftliche Beziehungen und deutsche Auswanderung 1945–1955* (Paderborn: Schöningh, 1998).

SCHREIBER, HORST, *Die Machtübernahme: Die Nationalsozialisten in Tirol 1938/39*, Innsbrucker Forschungen zur Zeitgeschichte 10 (Innsbruck: Haymon, 1994).

SCHRÖM, OLIVER, and RÖPKE, ANDREA, *Stille Hilfe für braune Kameraden: Das geheime Netzwerk der Alt- und Neonazis* (Berlin: Links, 2001).

SCHUSTER, WALTER, and WEBER, WOLFGANG (eds.), *Entnazifizierung im regionalen Vergleich* (Linz: Archiv der Stadt Linz, 2004).

SCHWARCZ, ALFREDO JOSÉ, *Trotz allem... Die deutschsprachigen Juden in Argentinien* (Vienna: Böhlau, 1995).

SCHWARZ, SIMONE, *Chile im Schatten faschistischer Bewegungen: Der Einfluss europäischer und chilenischer Strömungen in den 30er und 70er Jahren* (Frankfurt am Main: VAS, 1997).

SCOPPOLA, PIETRO, 'Gli orientamenti di Pio XI e Pio XII sui problemi della società contemporanea', in Guerriero (ed.), *La chiesa in Italia*, 359–90.

SEBERECHTS, FRANK, and VERDOODT, FRANS-JOS, *Leven in twee werelden: Belgische collaborateurs en de diaspora na de Tweede Wereldoorlog* (Leuven: Davidsfonds, 2009).

SEEGER, ANDREAS, '*Gestapo-Müller*': *Die Karriere eines Schreibtischtäters* (Berlin: 1996).

SEGEV, TOM, *Die Soldaten des Bösen: Zur Geschichte der KZ-Kommandanten* (Reinbek: Rowohlt, 1992).

——*Simon Wiesenthal: The Life and Legends* (New York: Random House, 2010).

SERENY, GITTA, *Das Ringen mit der Wahrheit: Albert Speer und das deutsche Trauma* (Munich: Kindler, 1995).

——*Into That Darkness: From Mercy Killing to Mass Murder* (London: Pimlico, 1995).

SHIRER, WILLIAM L., *The Rise and Fall of the Third Reich: A History of Nazi Germany* (New York: Simon and Schuster, 1960).

SIGMUND, ANNA MARIA, *Die Frauen der Nazis II* (Vienna: Ueberreuter, 2000).

SIMPSON, CHRISTOPHER, *Blowback: America's Recruitment of Nazis and Its Effects on the Cold War* (New York: Weidenfeld & Nicolson, 1988).

SIVIERO, RODOLFO, and BERTOLDI, MARIO URSINO (eds.), *L'arte e il nazismo: Esodo e ritorno delle opere d'arte italiane, 1938–1963* (Florence: Cantini édition d'arte, 1984).

SKORZENY, OTTO, *Meine Kommandounternehmen: Krieg ohne Fronten* (Wiesbaden: Limes, 1976).

——*Missioni segrete* (Milan: Garzanti, 1951).

SMITH, BRADLEY F., and AGA-ROSSI, ELENA, *Operation Sunrise: The Secret Surrender* (New York: Smith, 1979).

SOFISTI, LEOPOLDO, *Male di frontiera: Difesa del Brennero* (Bozen: Cappelli, 1949).

SPICER, KEVIN P., *Hitler's Priests: Catholic Clergy and National Socialism* (DeKalb: Northern Illinois University Press, 2008).

SPITZY, REINHARD, *So entkamen wir den Alliierten:Bekenntnisse eines 'Ehemaligen'* (Munich: Müller, 1989).

STANLEY, RUTH, 'Der Beitrag deutscher Luftfahrtingenieure zur argentinischen Luftfahrtforschung und -entwicklung nach 1945: das Wirken der Gruppe Tank in Argentinien, 1947–1955', in Meding (ed.), *Nationalsozialismus und Argentinien*, 161–83.

——*Rüstungsmodernisierung durch Wissenschaftsmigration? Deutsche Rüstungsfachleute in Argentinien und Brasilien, 1947–1963* (Frankfurt am Main: Verveurt, 1999).

STARON, JOACHIM, *Fosse Ardeatine und Marzabotto: Deutsche Kriegsverbrechen und Resistenza, Geschichte und nationale Mythenbildung in Deutschland und Italien (1944–1999)* (Paderborn: Schöningh, 2002).

STAUFFER, PAUL, 'Grandseigneuraler "Anti-Intellektueller": Carl J. Burckhardt in den Fährnissen des totalitären Zeitalters', in Aram Mattioli (ed.), *Intellektuelle von rechts: Ideologie und Politik in der Schweiz 1918–1939* (Zurich: Orel Füssli, 1995), 113–34.

——'Sechs furchtbare Jahre…': Auf den Spuren Carl J. Burckhardts durch den Zweiten Weltkrieg* (Zurich: Neue Zürcher Zeitung, 1998).

STEHLE, HANSJAKOB 'Pässe vom Papst? Aus neuentdeckten Dokumenten: Warum alle Wege der Ex-Nazis nach Südamerika über Rom führten', *Die Zeit*, 4 (May 1984), 9–12 ('Dossier').

——'Bischof Hudal und SS-Führer Meyer: Ein kirchenpolitischer Friedensversuch 1942/43', *Vierteljahreshefte für Zeitgeschichte*, 39 (1989), 299–322.

STEINACHER, GERALD, 'Das Trentino in der Operationszone Alpenvorland 1943–1945', D.Phil. Arb., Innsbruck University, Austria, 1995.

——*Südtirol und die Geheimdienste 1943–1945*, Innsbrucker Forschungen zur Zeitgeschichte 15 (Innsbruck: Studien, 2000).

——'The Special Operations Executive (SOE) in Austria 1940–1945', *International Journal of Intelligence and Counterintelligence*, 15/2 (2002), 211–21.

——(ed.), *Südtirol im Dritten Reich/L'Alto Adige nel Terzo Reich 1943–1945: NS-Herrschaft im Norden Italiens/L'occupazione nazista nell'Italia settentrionale*, Veröffentlichungen des Südtiroler Landesarchivs 18 (Innsbruck: Studien, 2003).

——(ed.), *Im Schatten der Geheimdienste: Südtirol 1918 bis zur Gegenwart* (Innsbruck: Studien, 2003).

——'"The Cape of Last Hope": The Postwar Flight of Nazi War Criminals through Italy/South Tyrol to South America', in Klaus Eisterer and Günter Bischof (eds.), *Transatlantic Relations: Austria and Latin America in the 19th and 20th Century*, Transatlantica 1 (New Brunswick: Transaction, 2006), 203–24.

——'Alto Adige come regione di transito dei rifugiati 1945–1950', in Matteo Sanfilippo (ed.), *Italia come paese dei profughi dal 1945 ad oggi, Studi Emigrazione*, 164 (2006), 821–34.

——'Argentinien als NS-Fluchtland: Die Emigration von Kriegsverbrechern und Nationalsozialisten durch Italien an den Rio de la Plata: Mythos und Wirklichkeit', in Meding and Ismar (eds.), *Argentinien und das Dritte Reich*, 231–54.

——*Nazis auf der Flucht: Wie Kriegsverbrecher über Italien nach Übersee entkamen*, Innsbrucker Forschungen zur Zeitgeschichte 26 (Innsbruck: Studien, 2008).

——' "Berufsangabe: Mechaniker": Die Flucht von Gestapo-Beamten nach Übersee', in Klaus-Michael Mallmann and Andrej Angrick (eds.), *Die Gestapo nach 1945: Karrieren, Konflikte, Konstruktionen* (Darmstadt: Wissenschaftlicher, 2009), 56–70.

——and TRAFOIER PHILIPP, ' "Ich mache Sie zum Erzbischof von Paris, wenn Sie uns helfen!" Die Flucht der Vichy-Regierung nach Südtirol 1945', *Der Schlern*, 1 (2007), 24–35.

STEINHAUS, FEDERICO, *Ebrei/Juden: Gli ebrei dell'Alto Adige negli anni trenta e quaranta* (Florence: Giuntina, 1994).

——and PRUCCOLI, ROSANNA (eds.), *Storie di Ebrei/Jüdische Schicksale: Contributi sulla presenza ebraica in Alto Adige e nel Trentino/Beiträge zu einer Geschichtsforschung über die jüdische Ansässigkeit in Südtirol und im Trentino* (Meran: Comunità Ebraica, 2004).

STEININGER, ROLF, *Südtirol im 20. Jahrhundert: Vom Leben und Überleben einer Minderheit* (Innsbruck: Studien, 1997).

——*South Tyrol: A Minority Conflict of the Twentieth Century* (New Brunswick: Transaction, 2003).

——and PITSCHEIDER, SABINE (eds.), *Tirol und Vorarlberg in der NS-Zeit*, Innsbrucker Forschungen zur Zeitgeschichte 19 (Innsbruck: Studien, 2003).

STEURER, LEOPOLD, *Südtirol zwischen Rom und Berlin 1919–1939* (Vienna: Europaverlag, 1980).

——'Südtirol zwischen schwarz und braun', in Godele von der Decken (ed.), *Teilung Tirols: Gefahr für die Demokratie?* (Bozen: Redaktion Sturzflüge, 1988), 25–40.

——'Meldungen aus dem Land: Aus den Berichten des Eil-Nachrichtendienstes der ADO (Jänner–Juli 1943)', in *Sturzflüge: Eine Kulturzeitschrift*, 29/30 (Dec. 1989), 31–125.

STIEBER, GABRIELE, 'Die Lösung des Flüchtlingsproblems 1945–1960', in Thomas Albrich *et al.* (eds.), *Österreich in den Fünfzigern*, Innsbrucker Forschungen zur Zeitgeschichte 11 (Innsbruck: Studien, 1995), 67–93.

STIEFEL, DIETER, *Entnazifizierung in Österreich* (Vienna: Europaverlag, 1981).

STROTHMANN, DIETRICH, 'Der Wolf ist wieder frei: Brasilien lehnt die Auslieferung des Massenmörders Wagner ab', *Die Zeit* (28 September 1979), 11.

STUMPP, KATJA, 'Er bereut nichts—und macht noch immer den Hitler-Gruß: SS-Offizier zockt Rente in 3 Ländern ab', *Bild.de Online* (10 Dec. 2007) <http://www.bild.de/>, accessed 11 Dec. 2007.

SZÖLLÖSI-JANZE, MARGIT, *Die Pfeilkreuzlerbewegung in Ungarn: Historischer Kontext, Entwicklung und Herrschaft*, Studien zur Zeitgeschichte 35 (Munich: Oldenbourg, 1989).

SZYNKOWSKI, JERZY, *et al.*, *Das Führerhauptquartier Wolfschanze* (Rastenburg: Kengraf, 2004).

TABORI, PAUL (ed.), *The Private Life of Adolf Hitler: The Intimate Notes and Diary of Eva Braun* (London: Aldor, 1949).

TAYLOR, TELFORD, *The Anatomy of the Nuremberg Trials: A Personal Memoir* (New York: Knopf, 1992).

THEIL, EDMUND, *Kampf um Italien: Von Sizilien bis Tirol, 1943–1945* (Munich: Müller, 1983).

TOCHTERMANN, ERWIN, 'Ohne Emotionen saubere Arbeit geleistet', *Süddeutsche Zeitung* (27 September 1980).

TOMAS, IVAN, *Krunoslav Stj. Draganović, Prilikom 60. godišnjice njegova života* (Buenos Aires: Hrvatska Revija,1964).

TORNIELLI, ANDREA, *Pio XII: Eugenio Pacelli un'uomo sul trono di Pietro* (Milan: Mondadori, 2007).

——and NAPOLITANO, MATTEO LUIGI, *Pacelli, Roncalli e i battesimi della shoah* (Casale Monferrato: Piemme, 2005).

TRAFOJER, PHILIPP, 'Bei Kriegsende: Die Flucht der Kollaborateure, Vichy-Franzosen im Vinschgau', *Der Vinschger*, 16/17 (9 Aug. 1996), 6–7.

——' "Der Standpunkt": Politisch-historische Analyse über Funktion, Form und Wirkungsweise eines Propagandamediums', D.Phil. dissertation, University of Innsbruck, Austria, 1999.

——'Das Paradies der Schieber: Das Wirken der "Gruppe Wendig" im Vinschgau bei Kriegsende', *Der Vinschger*, 15 (1 Aug. 2002), 6–7.

——'La Voce del Padrone, Der Standpunkt: Ein italienisches Propagandamedium in Südtirol 1947–1957', in Steinacher (ed.), *Im Schatten der Geheimdienste*, 161–86.

TRENKER, LUIS, *Alles gut gegangen: Geschichten aus meinem Leben* (3rd edn, Munich: Bertelsman, 1979).

TUTOROW, NORMAN E. (ed.), *War Crimes, War Criminals, and War Crime Trials: An Annotated Bibliography and Source Book* (New York: Greenwood, 1986).

UHLIG, CHRISTIANE et al., *Tarnung, Transfer, Transit: Die Schweiz als Drehscheibe verdeckter deutscher Operationen (1938–1952)*, ed. von der Unabhängigen Expertenkommission Schweiz–Zweiter Weltkrieg (Zurich: Chronos, 2001).

VALENTE, PAOLO, 'Juan Domingo Perón a Merano', *Paolo 'Bill' Valente* [website] <http://www.webalice.it/valente.paolo/peron.htm>, accessed 2 Jan. 2005.

——*Porto di Mare, frammenti dell'anima multiculturale di una piccola città europea: Italiani (e molti altri) a Merano tra esodi, deportazioni e guerre (1934–1953)* (Trento: Temi, 2005).

VERDORFER, MARTHA, *Zweierlei Faschismus: Alltagserfahrungen in Südtirol 1918–1945* (Vienna: Verlag für Gesellschaftskritik, 1990).

VIETINGHOFF-SCHEEL, HEINRICH VON, *Appunti dell'ultimo comandante in capo tedesco in Italia (Recoaro, ottobre 1944–aprile 1945)*, ed. Peter Hattenkofer et al. (Valdagno: n.pub., 1997).

VIGANÒ, MARINO, and PEDRAZZINI, DOMINIC M. (eds.), *'Operation Sunrise': Atti del convegno internazionale (Locarno, 2 maggio 2005)* (Lugano: EUSI, 2006).

VILLANI, CINZIA, *Zwischen Rassengesetzen und Deportation: Juden in Südtirol, im Trentino und in der Provinz Belluno 1933–1945*, Veröffentlichungen des Südtiroler Landesarchivs 15 (Innsbruck: Wagner, 2003).

VILLEMAREST, PIERRE DE, *Untouchable: Who Protected Bormann and Gestapo Müller after 1945?* (Slough: Aquilion, 2005).

VOIGT, KLAUS, *Zuflucht auf Widerruf: Exil in Italien 1933–1945*, 3 vols. (Stuttgart: Klett-Cotta, 1989).

VOLBERG, HEINRICH, *Auslandsdeutschtum und Drittes Reich: Der Fall Argentinien* (Cologne: Böhlau, 1981).

VÖLKLEIN, ULRICH, *Josef Mengele: Der Arzt von Auschwitz* (Göttingen: Steidl, 1999).

WAGNER, RUDI, *Übergänge: Aus dem Tiroler Tagebuch eines Bergvagabunden, Schmugglers und Suppenfechters* (Bozen: Frasnelli-Keitsch, 1996).

——'Wir Schmuggler vom Brennerpass', *Rudolph Nautilus Wagner* [website] <http://rudolf-nautilus-wagner.info/7.htm>, accessed 10 May 2007.

WAIBEL, MAX, *1945 Kapitulation in Norditalien: Originalbericht des Vermittlers* (Basle: Helbing & Lichtenhahn, 1981).

WALSER, HARALD, *Die illegale NSDAP in Tirol und Vorarlberg 1933–1938*, Materialien zur Arbeiterbewegung 28 (Vienna: Europaverlag, 1983).

WEDEKIND, MICHAEL, *Nationalsozialistische Besatzungs- und Annexionspolitik in Norditalien 1943 bis 1945: Die Operationszonen 'Alpenvorland' und 'Adriatisches Küstenland'* (Munich: Oldenbourg, 2003).

WEGNER, BERND, *Hitlers politische Soldaten: Die Waffen-SS 1933–1945, Studien zu Leitbild, Struktur und Funktion einer nationalsozialistischen Elite* (Paderborn: Schöningh, 1999).

WEINKE, ANNETTE, *Die Verfolgung von NS-Tätern im geteilten Deutschland: Vergangenheitsbewältigungen 1949–1969, oder, eine deutsch-deutsche Beziehungsgeschichte im Kalten Krieg* (Paderborn: Schöningh, 2002).

WEISSTEINER, ANTON, *Auf verlorenem Posten: Südtiroler an fernen Fronten: Erinnerungen an den Zweiten Weltkrieg* (Bozen: Athesia, 2004).

WHITE, ELIZABETH B., *German Influence in the Argentine Army 1900–1945* (New York: Garland, 1991).

WIDMANN, CARLOS, 'Der Mythos Odessa: Die vermeintliche "Rattenlinie" der Nazis nach Argentinien', *Süddeutsche Zeitung* (7 May 2007).

WIESENTHAL, SIMON, *The Murderers among Us* (London: Heinemann, 1967).

——*Justice Not Vengeance: Memoirs*, tr. Ewald Osers (London: Weidenfeld & Nicolson, 1989).

WILDT, MICHAEL, *Generation des Unbedingten: Das Führungskorps des Reichssicherheitshauptamtes* (Hamburg: Hamburger Edition, 2002).

——(ed.), *Nachrichtendienst, politische Elite und Mordeinheit: Der Sicherheitsdienst des Reichsführers SS* (Hamburg: Hamburger Edition, 2003).

WILSON, ROBERT, *The Confessions of Klaus Barbie, the Butcher of Lyon* (Vancouver: Arsenal, 1984).

WOJAK, IRMTRUD, *Eichmanns Memoiren: Ein kritischer Essay* (Frankfurt am Main: Campus, 2001).

WOLF, HUBERT, *Papst und Teufel: Die Archive des Vatikan und das Dritten Reich* (Munich: Beck, 2008).

WOLFE, ROBERT, 'Coddling a Nazi Turncoat', in Breitman *et al.* (eds.), *U.S. Intelligence and the Nazis*, 317–31.

YOUNG-ZIE BARTHELMESS RÖTHLISBERGER, PETRA, 'Tarnoperationen und Geheimgeschäfte auf dem Schweizer Finanzplatz: Verdeckte deutsch-schweizerische Umgehungsgeschäfte und die Frage der nationalsozialistischen Täterkonten im Zweiten Weltkrieg', D.Phil. dissertation, Zurich, Switzerland, 2006.

ZAGHENI, GUIDO, *La croce e il fascio: I cattolici italiani e la dittatura* (Milan: San Paolo, 2006).

ZOFKA, ZDENEK, 'Der KZ-Arzt Josef Mengele. Zur Typologie eines NS-Verbrechers', *Vierteljahrshefte für Zeitgeschichte*, 2 (1986), 245–67.

ZUCCOTTI, SUSAN, *Under His Very Windows: The Vatican and the Holocaust in Italy* (New Haven: Yale University Press, 2000).

ZWEIG, RONALD W., *The Gold Train: The Destruction of the Jews and the Looting of Hungary* (London: Lane, 2002).

Interviews and conversations

Conversation with Guzzi Lantschner, 21 May 2007.
Conversation with Franz Berger, 24 April 2007.
Conversation with Richard Breitman, 14 May 2006.
Conversation with Piroska Sapinsky, 7 January 2006.
Conversation with Ferencz Stolicz, 27 December 2005.
Conversation with Walter Haasler jun., 30 November 2005.

Interview with Joseph Prader, 3 May 2005, 22 Nov. 2005.
Conversation with Josef Steinacher, 20 August 2005.
Conversation with Martin Pollack, 23 March 2005.
Conversation with Andreas Hörtnagl, 15 March 2005.
Conversation with Kurt Schrimm, 26 August 2004.
Conversation with Alexander Mesner, 1 July 2004.
Conversation with Josef Gelmi, 30 June 2004.
Conversation with Johann Hörist, 3 June 2004.
Conversation with Richard Penz, 11 May 2004.
Interview with Karl Nicolussi-Leck, 10 May 2004 (video recording).
Conversation with Hartmut Staffler, 17 April 2004.
Conversation with Leopold Steurer, 16 April 2004, 14 Jan. 2007.
Conversation with Werner Wechselberger, 22 March 2004.

Index of Names

Abkhasi, Giorgio 83
Acheson, Dean 132
Adenauer, Konrad 124, 181, 275
Agusti, Elías Juan 62
Aichinger, Hans 245
Allende, Salvador 209–10
Almirante, Giorgio 197
Altmann, Klaus (alias of Klaus Barbie) 91, 203–5
Altmann, Klaus Jörg (alias of Klaus Jörg Barbie) 91
Altmann, Regina (alias of Regina Barbie) 91
Altmann, Uta Maria (alias of Uta Maria Barbie) 91
Amonn, Eugen (alias of Eugen Dollmann) 53, 192
Anders, Wladyslaw 115
Angleton, James 190
Apor (Baron) 89
Arendt, Hannah 52, 146, 276, 294n80, 300n221, 318n218
Artuković, Andrija 200
Ausserer, Bernd 265

Babor, Karl 21
Bachmann, Ingeborg viii, 289
Baduniec, Jan 115–16
Baduniec, Rosaria 115–16
Bako, Wilhelm 86–7
Baldelli, Ferdinando 80, 102–3, 117, 126
Banzer, Hugo 203–4, 205
Barbie, Klaus 91, 94, 160–1, 200, 203–7, 279
Barbie, Klaus Jörg 91, 203, 204
Barbie, Regina 91, 203
Barbie, Uta Maria 91, 203, 204
Barcata, Louis 45
Barczy, Detre 87
Bardossy, Làszlò 87
Barkan, Elazar 288
Bast, Gerhard 31–2, 91–2, 94
Bauer, Herbert 30

Bauer, Wilhelm 37, 98–9
Baum, Kurt 68–9
Baum, Otto 9
Baumbach, Werner 98
Bayer, Fr Karl 24, 65, 156–7
Benson, Frederik R. *Fig18*
Benz, Wolfgang vi, 249
Berger, Franz 333n110
Berger, Fritz (son of Richard Berger) *Fig18*
Berger, Richard *Fig18*
Berger-Waldenegg, Egon 44, 120–1
Bernini, Gian Lorenzo 103
Bernhuber, Maximilian 36
Bertagnolli, Georg 47–8
Besson-Rapp, André 35
Beuer, Herbert 54
Bicchierai, Giuseppe 193–4, 209
Blaas, Maximilian 114–15
Blaschke, Rudolf 165
Blet, Pierre 101–2
Bode, Heinrich 151
Bohne, Gerhard 136
Bohne, Gisela 136
Bohne, Hans (code name of Gerhard Bohne) 136
Boissier, Léopold 304n71
Bolschwing, Otto Albrecht von 182–3
Bonnard, Abel 35
Bormann, Gerda 35, 155–7, 191
Bormann, Martin xvi, 35, 155–8, 191–2
Bormann, Martin, jun. 35, 156
Bottcher, Heinrich 76
Braun, Eva 47,
Braun, Wernher von 175, 222, 278
Breitman, Richard v, xxii, 160, 276, 306n106, 316n169, 321n36, 323n61, 325n104, 327n149, 328n195
Bronfman, Edgar 282
Brunetti, Bruno 144
Bucard, Marcel 35
Buch, Hans Walter 156
Buchko, Ivan 186
Burckhardt, Carl Jacob xix, 40, 77

Buresch (diplomat) 67
Burger, Adolf 161–2
Byrnes, James 110

Ćalušić, Marko 74–5
Carità, Mario 36,
Carli, Georg 203
Carroll, Walter 71, 90, 108, 109, 117,
   121, 288
Cecelja, Vilim 135
Christmann, Kurt 267–8
Churchill, Winston 34, 171
Cornwell, John xx, 105, 309n19, 340n25
Corradini, Johann 148–50
Costa, Ercole 79
Crastan, Albert 161, 164, 168

Dadieu, Armin 27, 263
Dahrendorf, Ralph 282
Dalmer, Hildegard 151
Darnand, Joseph 35
Déat, Marcel 35
De Blasys, Leo Biaggi 62–3, 83
De Gasperi, Alcide 13, 88, 199
de Ribaupierre, E. 60–1, 81–3
de Salis, Hans W. 61–2, 76–7, 79, 80
Dellai, Cornelius 244–5
Demjanjuk, Ivan 'John' 272
Didinger, Josef 54
Dietrich, Marlene 277
Dollfuss, Engelbert 243
Dollmann, Eugen 53, 188–92
Dömöter, Eduard (Lajos) 97, 111, 232
Donovan, William 180
Draganović, Krunoslav Stjepan 13, 65, 74,
   81–2, 91, 93, 98, 111, 114–15, 117,
   128–39, 185, 200–3, 223, 232–3, 240–1,
   264, 283–4, 285
Dressler, Willi 28
Dulles, Allen W. xxiii, 169–74, 176, 177,
   180, 189–90, 192–3, 278–9
Dulles, John Foster 171
Dupuis, Gertrude 65, 72, 75, 122
Duxneuner, Hermann 66–8

Echarri, Francesco 91, 95, 112–13
Eckmann, Otto (alias of Adolf
   Eichmann) 194
Eichmann, Adolf xv, xvi, xviii, 21–3, 25,
   41, 49, 50, 51–3, 94, 97, 143, 146,
   149–50, 175, 177, 182, 194, 206, 209,
   210, 225, 254, 261, 268, 274, 275, 276,
   282, 288
Eichmann, Dieter 97
Eichmann, Horst 97
Eichmann, Klaus 97
Eichmann, Veronika (née Liebl) 97
Eizenstadt, Stuart 312n76
Elam, Shraga vi, 167, 313n105, 321n31;33,
   322n53, 327n158, 328n179
Enzensberger, Hans-Magnus 275
Epp, Waldemar 39–41
Ernst, Wilhelm 94–5
Ernst, Wilhelm (son) 95

Faulhaber, Michael 127
Favez, Jean-Claude xviii, 287, 301n5;11,
   341n30
Feder, Sid 174
Feil, Hanns 66
Feil, Johann 247
Fiedler, Karl 19
Fischböck, Hans 263–4
Fleiss, Erwin 269
Florian, Radu 76
Flush (code name of Friedrich
   Schwend) 168
Folie, Karl 28–9
Forsyth, Frederick xiv, 257
Franco (code name of Karl Hass) 196
Franco, Francisco 142, 227, 266
Frank, Hans 155
Frank, Karl Hermann 239–40
Franke-Griegsch [Gricksch], Alfred 123
Frei, Eduardo 209
Freisleben, Gertrude 93
Freisleben, Hubert Karl 93–4
Freude, Ludwig 229–30, 260
Freude, Rodolfo (Rudolf) 229–30
Fuchs (escape aide) 147
Fuldner, Horst Carlos 230–5, 240,
   260–1, 264

Gabolde, Maurice 35
Galgano, Renato 54
Galland, Adolf 30, 219, 225, 236
Gallov, Josef 89, 111, 187
Gatterer, Claus 33
Gehlen, Reinhard 176, 181, 196, 198,
   278–9
Geisler, Andreas 151
Geisler, Johannes 139–43, 148, 150, 151

Gelmi, Josef 139–40
Gelny, Emil 21
Gemmingen, Agnes von 162
Geyer, Franz (alias of Gerhard Bast) 31, 32, 91–2
Giese, Julius 40, 147–8
Giustini, Anna Maria 196
Giustini, Rodolfo (code name of Karl Hass) 197
Goda, Norman J.W. xxii, 306n106, 316n169, 323n66;68, 329n195, 340n12
Goebbels, Joseph 45, 46, 50, 88, 97, 124, 216, 225, 235, 272, 286
Goldgasser (code name of Walter Spitaler) 29
Goldhagen, Daniel J. 105, 340n25
Goldstone, Richard Joseph 282
Goñi, Uki vi, xxiii, 106, 212, 276, 282–3
Gonzalez (Colonel) 260
Göring, Hermann 277
Graham, Robert A. 101, 102
Graubart, Richard 37
Gregor, Helmut (alias of Josef Mengele) 49–50, 234
Greil, Johannes P. 124–5
Greitemberg, Georg (alias of Georg Bertagnolli) 47
Grün, Elisabetha 85
Grün, Eva 85
Grün, Katharina 85
Grün, Peter 85
Gumppenberg, Leopold von 145–7, 151
Guth, Fridolin 241, 247–8
Gyssling, Georg 164

Haasler, Walter 262–3
Hackel, Josef (alias of Josef Schwammberger) 48
Hafner, Paul 265–6, 267
Hahn, Elina Margarita Albertina 269
Haja, Franz 236–7
Haniel, Günther von 180
Hampel, Desiderius 9
Hans (intelligence operative) xv
Harrison, Leland 70
Harster, Wilhelm 194
Hartungen, Christoph von 52
Hass, Karl 37, 178, 184, 195–8, 270, 281
Häuser, Philipp 105
Hebblethwaite, Peter 117, 309n22;24, 312n75

Heilig, Berthold 93, 146
Heim, Aribert 272
Heimberger, Philipp 94–5
Heimberger, Susanne 94
Heimberger, Theresia 94
Heinemann, Karl 43–4, 93, 111, 254–5
Hermann, Rudolf 53–4
Herr, Traugott 9
Hess, Rudolf 277
Himmler, Heinrich 35, 44, 53, 57, 161, 163, 174–5, 182, 188–9, 206, 230, 235, 254, 272, 277, 280, 286
Hitler, Adolf xx, 30, 33–4, 39, 52, 104–5, 118, 119, 124, 141, 148, 154, 156, 170, 182, 189, 191, 192, 213, 244, 266, 267, 272, 275, 285, 286
Hochhuth, Rolf 105, 106, 284
Hofer, Franz 66, 144, 151, 242
Hofer, Peter 235
Hoffmann, Heinrich 198–9
Höfle, Hermann
Hollmann, Fritz (alias of Josef Mengele) 24
Horthy, Miklós 87
Höss, Rudolf 155
Höttl, Wilhelm 163, 165, 177–8, 279
Huber, Max 56, 71, 288
Hudal, Alois xx, xxii, 27, 43–4, 46, 92, 97, 99, 105, 111–14, 117, 118–28, 135, 136, 139–43, 145–7, 157, 187–8, 196, 198, 218, 232, 237–40, 244, 247, 250–3, 256, 263, 285–6
Hufnagl, Hermann 54

Ilg, Karl 244, 269
Irving, David 271

Jackisch, Carlota xxiii, 299n204, 329n6;14, 332n85, 334n129;136, 335n147, 338n231
Jagow, Dietrich von 40
Jakobi, Ludwig 68
Janning, Ernst 277
John XXIII, Pope 136
John Paul II, Pope 193, 315n142
Judt, Tony 271–2, 275, 280
Jüptner, Fritz 151, 152
Jürges, Gustav 194

Kaltenbrunner, Ernst 161, 163–4, 177, 206, 277
Kappler, Herbert 38–9, 116, 173, 179, 180

Karrasch, Robert (alias of Karl Schedereit) 20
Katschner (officer) 30
Katz, Robert 194, 326*n*140;142, 327*n*147
Kelemen, Marten 89
Kemény, Elisabeth von 297*n*159
Kemény, Gábor von 40
Kennan, George 273
Kernmayer, Erich 45
Kiechl, M. 85
Killion, Edward J. 110
Kircher, Rudolf 45
Kirchner, Néstor 283
Kirdorf, Emil xv
Kiss, Tibor 150
Klarsfeld, Beate 102, 205, 279
Klarsfeld, Serge 102, 279
Kleine, Richard 104
Klement, Anna 49
Klement, Riccardo (alias of Adolf Eichmann) 49, 53, 97, 143, 194, 268
Klemp (code name of Friedrich Schwend) 168
Klich, Ignacio 282
Klingenfuss, Karl 255
Koger (priest) 147
Koop, Volker 214
Kops, Reinhard 20–1, 69, 146, 147, 231–2, 234, 258, 269, 270
Kótay, Zoltàn 116
Krek, Miha 187
Kremhart, Lona 50–1
Kremhart, Theodor 50–1, 54
Kren, Vladimir 131
Krüger, Bernhard 161
Krupp, Gustav xv, 259
Kühne, Paul (ICRC staff) 62, 73

La Vista, Vincent 15, 43, 44, 69–71, 89, 91, 101–2, 107, 139, 159, 161, 166–7, 184, 187, 196, 199, 200, 273–4, 284
Laher, Ludwig 336*n*187
Lammerding, Heinz 206
Lancaster, Burt 277
Landi, Andrew P. 108, 109
Langes, Gunther 45, 293*n*63
Lantschner, Friedrich (Fritz) 242, 243, 244, 245, 247
Lantschner, Gustav (Guzzi) 243–4, 245, 266
Lausegger, Gerhard 247

Laval, Pierre 35, 36
Lehnert, Pascalina 103, 308*n*9;12, 314*n*130, 319*n*255
Lemelsen, Joachim 9
Levy, Julius 167
Ley, Gabriele 225, 260
Lichtenstein, Heiner 57, 100
Lingen, Kerstin von xxii, 173, 278
Littell, Jonathan xiii
Luchaire, Corinne *Fig5*
Luchaire, Jean 35
Lucid, Thomas A. 178, 197
Luden, Rudolf von 145
Ludwig, Alfons 143
Ludwig, Peter (alias of Horst Wagner) 254–5
Luongo, Joseph 197
Luttor, Ferenc 89
Lyon, Paul 195

Mabire, Jean 235
Maclean, Fitzroy 14
MacLean, Alistair 321*n*24
Magjerec, Juraj 111, 128, 136
Maier, Charles S. 339*n*1
Maler, Hans (Juan) (code name of Reinhard Kops) 21, 232, 234
Malloth, Anton 41
Mältzer, Kurt 123
Mandl, Fritz 230
Mahnert, Klaus 242
Martini, Angelo 101
Mayer, Peter (alias of Robert Jan Verbelen) 208
McBratney, William 293*n*63, 296*n*133, 306*n*111;112, 318*n*226
McCloy, John 109, 222
Meding, Holger xv, xxiii, xxiv, 46, 214, 223, 259
Meier, Hans (Emilio) (alias of Hans-Ulrich Rudel) 53
Meir, Golda 168
Melcher, Gottfried 203
Mengele, Alois 41, 42
Mengele, Irene 25
Mengele, Josef 24–6, 41–2, 49–52, 97, 160, 206, 234, 264–5, 268, 274, 282
Mengele, Karl Heinz 41, 42
Mengele, Martha 41, 42
Mengele, Rolf 25
Miccoli, Giovanni 105

Michel, William H. 85
Milano, James 178, 195, 197, 206
Mohr, Josef 85
Montanelli, Indro 192
Montini, Giovanni Battista xix, 13, 102–6,
    109, 116–17, 121, 126, 127, 130, 142, 288
Morgenschweis, Karl 154
Mosley, Oswald 123
Moulin, Jean 279
Muench, Aloisius 109, 116
Müller, Erich 50, 52, 97–8
Müller, Josef Erich (alias of Josef
    Didinger) 54
Mussolini, Benito xvii, xx, 33–4, 52, 53,
    77, 135, 141, 179, 184, 189, 196, 215,
    226, 282
Mussolini, Vittorio 227

Naftali, Timothy xxii, 323n61, 324n79
Napolitano, Matteo 105, 309n20
Navarro-Valls, Joaquín 284–5
Neal, Jack 172
Neuhold, Hans (Giovanni) 164, 199
Neuhold, Hedda 162
Neurath, Konstantin von 124
Nicolodi, Giovanni 41–2
Nicolussi-Leck, Karl 28, 29–30, 152–3,
    234–7, 240–1, 264, 265–6
Nicolussi-Leck, Maria 241, 334n125
Nicolussi-Leck, Reinhild 241
Niermann, Ernst August 30, 98–9
Nix, Willi 43–5
Noelke, Francesco (alias of Erich
    Müller) 50, 97

Obergasser, Josef 156
Oehm, Willy (alias of Wilfred von
    Oven) 216
Ojeda, César 225
Omrcanin, Ivo 136, 200
Ottowitz, Walther 125
Oven, Wilfred von 216

Pacelli, Eugenio (later Pius XII) xx, 105,
    108, 118
Pagmotta, Leo 44
Pahl, Federico (alias of Gustav Jürges) 194
Pape, Otto (alias of Erich Priebke) 93, 269
Parini, Piero 227
Parrilli, Luigi 179–81
Parsons, Graham 71

Pasche, Alfred 16
Patton, George S. 240
Paul VI, Pope xx, 101, 106, 137, 284
Pavelić, Ante 128–33, 135, 200
Pečnikar, Vilko 131
Peralta, Santiago 215–16
Perić, Djordje 131
Perón, Eva (Evita) 227
Perón, Juan Domingo 122, 211, 212, 213,
    214–17, 219–21, 223–31, 232, 234, 240,
    245, 261, 264, 265, 269, 276
Perrier (Captain) 87
Petranović, Karl 135, 136
Phayer, Michael 105, 132, 273, 290n3,
    292n30, 298n182, 312n70;73,
    315n144;149, 340n3;22;27
Pinochet, Augusto 209, 225
Piola (Msgr) 90
Pircher, Johann 104, 242
Pius XI, Pope 105, 119, 141
Pius XII, Pope xix, xx, xxi, 13, 102–6,
    108, 118, 126, 127, 130, 153, 157, 284–6
Pobitzer, Oswald Franz 92, 146–7, 150
Pohl, Oswald 154–5, 286
Politzschke (family) 150
Pollack, Martin 31, 289
Pompanin, Alois 139, 140–2, 149
Porsche, Ferdinand 264
Prader, Joseph xxii, 121, 123, 143
Priebke, Alice 38, 149
Priebke, Erich 37–9, 92–3, 140, 148–9,
    150, 184, 196, 243, 268, 269–70, 281,
    282, 286
Priebke, Ingo 149
Priebke, Jörg 149

Rademacher, Franz 255
Rahn, Rudolf 40, 178
Raschhofer, Hermann 239–40
Rauff, Walter 54, 102, 179, 184, 187–8,
    192–5, 198, 209–10
Reale, Egidio 71
Remer, Otto Ernst 124
Remorino, Jeronimo 222
Retzlaff (family) 150
Ribbentrop, Joachim von 254
Richter, Ronald 223
Richwitz, Hans (alias of Berthold
    Heilig) 93
Riedl, Franz Hieronymus 45, 237–40
Riefenstahl, Leni 243–4, 245

Rienzner, Fritz 44–5
Romagnoli, Antonino 75
Romualdi, Pino 197
Ronda, Dr (alias of Kurt Christmann) 268
Roosevelt, Franklin Delano 108, 171, 172
Roschmann, Eduard 184, 210, 255–8
Rotberg, Eberhard 124
Rubatscher, Franz 241–4, 247, 266
Rubatscher, Heilwig 242
Rudel, Hans-Ulrich 30, 53, 98, 99, 123,
  144, 204, 210, 224–5, 227, 236, 248,
  268–9
Rudolfi, Patrick 147
Ruegger, Paul xviii, xix, 56, 77–81, 83,
  99, 288
Ruffinengo, Domenico 231
Ruffinengo (Rufinatscha),
  Mario Franz 231–4, 269
Rufinatscha, Franz, *see* Ruffinengo,
  Mario Franz
Rupčić, Dragutin 131

Sarić, Ivan 128, 130
Sassen, Wilhelm (Willem) Maria 184, 225
Scelba, Mario 112
Schachleiter, Alban 104
Schäfer, Ludwig 150
Schedereit, Karl 20
Schell, Maximilian 277
Schindler, Walter 95
Schintlholzer, Alois 36–7
Schmidt, Paul 1
Schmidtke (officer) 122
Schmitz, Theodor 155–6, 157, 158
Schneider, Burkhardt 101, 106
Schneppen, Heinz xvi, 276, 290n4, 324n82,
  337n194;197;206, 339n266, 340n9
Schoklitsch, Armin 261–2, 263
Schramm, Jakob (alias of Hans
  Fischböck) 263–4
Schrimm, Kurt vi, 125
Schröder, Hans 40
Schubert, Irmtraud 256
Schulze (secretary) 43–4
Schuster, Ildefonso 189, 190, 193, 194
Schütz, Karl-Theodor 196
Schwab, Alfred (alias of Robert Jan
  Verbelen) 208
Schwaiger, Günther 266
Schwammberger, Josef 27, 32, 48–9, 96,
  113, 125, 194

Schwend, Albert 202
Schwend, Friedrich (Fritz) 162–9, 177,
  202–3, 204, 205, 258
Schwend, Hedda 162, 203
Schwentner, Georg 29
Scilingo (Schilling), Adolfo 228
Scorza, Carlo 227
Sedmak, Drago 115
Segna, Walter 194–5
Siebrecht, August 261
Silva, José Clement 228
Simpson, Christopher 183, 185
Siri, Giuseppe 134–5, 233
Siviero, Rodolfo 192
Skorzeny, Otto 192, 225
Sommaruga, Cornelio 286–7
Speer, Albert 245, 246
Spellman, Francis 108, 109, 120–1
Spicer, Kevin 104
Spiess, Irmgard 254
Spingarn, Stephen 193
Spitaler, Walter (code name
  Goldgasser) 28–30
Spitz, Georg 198–9
Spitzy, Reinhard 155
Springenschmied, Karl 45
Staffler, Hartmuth 150, 294n92, 318n244,
  319n246;247;251
Stalin, Joseph 12, 104, 106, 186
Stangl, Franz xviii, 27, 113–14, 194, 210,
  239, 248–53
Stangl, Paul (alias of Franz Stangl) 251
Starcević, Mile 131
Stauffenberg, Claus Schenk von 124, 189
Steger, Hans 245
Steiner, Adolf 25, 42
Steiner, Albert 144–5
Steiner, Carlo (code name of Karl
  Hass) 197
Steiner, Franz 42, 264, 265
Steiner, Hans 250
Steininger, August 253–4
Steininger, Rolf vi
Stepinać, Alojzije 133
Sterzinger, Franz 245–7
Stöll, Alice 38
Stötter, Rudolf 39
Strassoldo, Cesare 68
Strickner, Hildegard 152
Strickner, Jakob 25–7, 152
Stritch, Samuel Alphonsus 121

Stroessner, Alfredo 205, 224, 225
Swinton, Stan 174

Tank, Kurt 223–4
Tardini, Domenico 109, 130
Thaler, Karolina 149
Thiel, Gerda 150
Thyrolf, Rudolf 39
Thyssen, Fritz xv
Tito (Josip Broz) 2, 9, 11, 13, 111, 115, 129, 130, 132–3, 135, 137, 138–9
Tornielli, Andrea 105
Toth, Dragutin 131
Tracy, Spencer 277
Trenker, Luis 24, 47, 243, 244, 245
Tribus, Karl 266, 267
Triska, Helmut 178–9
Troy, Karl 29
Truman, Harry S. 123, 131–2, 176, 199
Tuck, William Hallam 77, 78
Turi, Hedda (alias of Hedda Schwend) 202–3
Turi, Venceslav (alias of Friedrich Schwend) 202–3
Tutzer, Michael 265–6

Uhlig, Christiane 99, 302n29, 303n57, 308n146, 311n56

Vajta (Vajda), Ferenc 88
Valjavec, Fritz 45–6
van Harten, Jaac (alias of Julius Levy) 90, 161, 164, 167–8
Veesenmayer, Edmund 254
Verbelen, Robert Jan 207–8
Vietinghoff, Heinrich von 9

Visconti, Luchino 198, 281
Volk, Ludwig 128
Voss, Wilhelm von 263
Vrančić, Vjekoslav 131

Wächter, Gustav Otto 125–6, 127, 239
Wagner, Anita 267
Wagner, Gustav Franz 210, 250, 251, 252–3
Wagner, Horst 254–5
Wagner, Rudi 19
Wallenberg, Raoul 57, 80
Weber, Anton 113, 143, 149, 157
Wegner, Fritz Bernd (alias of Eduard Roschmann) 256–7
Weinbacher, Jakob 127
Weinstetter, Johann 151
Wendig, Fritz (code name of Friedrich Schwend) 161, 164, 204
Wenner, Eugen 191
Werner, Denise 74–6, 79
Wiesenthal, Simon xiii, xiv, xv, 18, 26, 29, 118, 148, 188, 193, 209–10, 212, 248, 253, 257, 259, 270, 271, 272, 275–6
Wiesinger, Paula 245
Wirth, Christian 249
Wizenetz, Leopoldine 231
Wolf, Friedrich 229
Wolfe, Robert xxii, 189
Wolff, Karl 38, 53, 170, 172–5, 188, 189, 277–8

Zako, Andras 87–8
Zeltmann (pilot) 30
Ziegler, Reinhold 150
Zimmer, Guido 179–81
Zuccotti, Susan 105

General Index

Afragola camp 38
aircraft engineering, Argentina and 223–4
Alatri camp 5, 61
Alberobello camp 6, 61
Allied Command Mediterranean 10
Allied Headquarters, Bozen conference 4
Allies, definition issues 10–11
Alto Adige (South Tyrol)
    escape route through xvi–xvii
    escape networks 19–23
    German-speaking refugees and 19–23,
        43, 157
    see also South Tyrol
America see United States
American Catholic Bishops' Conference,
        and Austrian PCA xix–xx, 121
American military governor Bozen 90
amnesty laws 274
anticommunism and Nazi perpetrators
        protection 280, 283–4, 285–6
    and Croatian war criminals 130–3, 135,
        136–8
    ICRC xix, 287
    NCWC 108–9, 110, 120
    Operation Sunrise and 171–2
    PCA and 103, 104, 105–9
    PCA and 103, 104, 105–9, 113
    US government & agencies 11–12,
        105–9, 131, 135, 137, 280
    and Italy 105–9, 199–200
    Vatican xix, xx, 102, 109, 130–3, 136–8
anti-Semitism
    Catholic clergy 109, 110, 119–20
    ICRC officials xix
archives
    access to xv–xvi, xxii, xxiv
    CIA 160, 276, 280
    ICRC Geneva, travel documents xxiv,
        xxv, 69–70, 73, 74–5, 286–8
    NCWC xxiv
    Red Cross Tracing Service,
        Germany 281
    US National Archives xxv, 160
    Vatican, access to xxii

Argentina
    as Nazi refuge xxiii–xxiv, 220–1, 229
        and extradition 220, 229, 245, 257–8,
            261, 270
        CEANA Commission 214, 282–3
        Nazi past 214–15, 220–1, 282–3
        US Blue Book 220, 229
        White Book 220
    escapes to 21, 28, 59
        immigrant ships, German fugitives
            and 233–4
        infrastructure Italy 232–41
    German postwar immigrants 213–15
        and Argentina work
            opportunities 217–18
        and South Tyrol businesses 264–6
        armaments industries 221–6
        CAPRI 260–1
        mutual assistance 260–4
        settlement 258–64, 266, 268–70
        West German machine tools
            import 222
    history
        Germanophile 211–12
        ties with Italy 226–7
        German population 212–13
        Italian population 212
        Jewish community 213
    immigration authority (DAIE),
        Genoa 228–9, 231–2
    immigration policy 212
        ethnic stipulations 215–16
        German Nazi officials
            influence 228–32
    recruitment
        Italy as recruitment centre 218, 226–32
        Nazi specialists 211, 218–26
    visas 62, 122–3, 134, 228
        forgery 76
        and ICRC travel documents 62
        and IRO identification papers 63
Arrow Cross members 86–8, 89, 187
Association of Hungarian Comrades-
        at-Arms 87–8

Australia, and refugees 8, 86, 186
Austria
   Catholic Church and Nazi regime xxi
   Holocaust, modern attitude 271
   Jews, Argentina 213
   escapes/refugees
      border crossings, unofficial 15–19
      detention camp escapees 236–9
      escape network 2–3, 241–8
      ICRC travel documents 84–5
         local letters of recommendation 85
      collective passports 67
   offices 44, 45
   NSDAP members 236, 239, 241–2,
      245–7, 249, 252, 254, 255
   see also specific organizations

Balkans, genocide 130
Baltic
   refugees 7
   Waffen-SS units 279
baptism, denazification through xxi–xxii,
      148–58, 286
Bavaria
   escapees in 1, 84, 125, 254, 266
   refugees, ICRC travel documents
      84–5
Blue Book (US), on Argentina as Nazi
      refuge 220, 229
Bolivia, and ICRC travel documents 59, 62,
      81, 82
Bozen (Bolzano)
   Argentine escape agents and 234–40
   camps 5, 40, 76
   escape networks 9, 16–19, 23, 26–30,
      33–40, 43, 89, 91–2, 95, 99,
      146–7, 194, 196, 267
   fake ICRC delegates 90
   former Nazis, businesses 246, 264–8
   German-American administrative
      collaboration 173–4
   returning Italians 84
   spy rings 187, 191, 197
   stateless persons 49–52, 53, 67, 192
Brazil
   and extradition 251, 253
   and Jewish refugees 8
   and ICRC travel documents 59, 67
Brenner border
   escape networks 19–23, 31–2, 49, 84,
      140, 161, 234, 236

smugglers, and refugees xvii, 15–19,
      23–32
Brenner Pass route 7
   Argentine escape agents and 234–40
   rail route, homecoming transports 84
Britain
   and Holocaust acknowledgement 275
   and Nazi fugitives xxiii, xxiv
   and specialist immigrants xxiii, 175
   and Ukranians xxiv, 186
   screening team 14
British currency forgery, Operation
      Bernhard 161–2, 165, 167
Brixen South Tyrol Diocese
   clergy and escape networks 28, 47,
      139–48
   denazification through baptism 148–56
businessmen, as immigrants 259

camps, Italy 4, 61
   poor conditions 111–12
   see also specific camps
Canada, emigrant destination 59, 61,
      186, 212
   Hungarian refugees 86
   IRO office 7
   Nazi refugees & collaborators xxiv,
      283
CAPRI (company for German-speaking
      immigrants to Argentina)
      260–1
Capuchins, Brixen monastery 145–6, 151
Caritas
   attitude to re-baptism 156–7
   Croatia Hrvatski Karitas 233
   Hungary, visas 115
   International, and authenticity
      checking 65
   Rome, and escapees 24, 118, 156–7
Catholic aid commission for Croatian
      refugees 64–5, 81–2
Catholic Church
   agencies, and Nazi aid
      reappraisal 284–6, 289
   and 'renegade' Catholics xxi
   and collaborators 12–13
   and converted Protestants xxi–xxii
   and ICRC xix, xxii
   and Nazi regimes xx–xxi, 276
   and Nazi smuggling xix–xxii
   Argentine escape agents and 232–41

Catholic Church (*cont.*)
  clergy
    and Nazi party 104–5, 119–20
    anti-Semitism 109, 110, 119–20
    Argentine escape agents and 232–41
  denazification through baptism
    xxi–xxii, 148–58, 286
  'discovers' democracy xxi
  South Tyrol role 139–48
Catholic Church of America xxii
CEANA Commission 282–3
Central Office for Germans in Italy
  (ZDI) 43–4
Chapultepec Act 1945 219–20
Chile
  and extradition 209–10
  and ICRC travel documents 62
CIA *see* US Central Intelligence Agency
  (CIA)
CIC *see* US Counter Intelligence Corps
  (CIC)
civilian prisoners, Red Cross and 56–7
Cold War
  and Croatian war criminals 131
  and denazification 240
  and escape movement 274
  and spy networks in Soviet Union 176
  and spy recycling 159–60, 167–9,
    175–6, 177–83
  attitudes to Nazis 272, 273–4, 275–8
  Operation Sunrise and 172
  Vatican's 285–6
  war criminal recycling 176, 177–83
collaborators *see* specific groups
Collegio Germanico Ungarico 42
Compalto camp 10
concentration camp commandants,
  escape 248–58
Cossacks 11, 12
Croatia, Catholic nationalism 128–30
Croatian Brotherhood in Rome, and
  ICRC travel documents 62, 82
Croatian Confraternity of San
  Girolamo 10, 13, 129–36
Croatians
  and Italian ratline 200–1
  collaborators, flee to South Tyrol 35
  emigration to Argentina 62, 232–3
  in Italian camps 133–4
  refugees 13
  repatriation 6

travel documents 134
Ustaša 11, 111, 117, 128–33, 135,
  200–1, 233
Vatican refugee committees for xx
Cuba, and ICRC travel documents 62

definitions, official
  displaced persons (DPs) 3
  Ex-Enemy Displaced Persons 4
  prisoners of war 10–11
  refugees 6, 10–11
  war criminals 10–11
denazification
  certificates 111, 114, 115, 117, 123, 127,
    136, 148–58
  Cold War and 240
  through baptism xxi–xxii, 148–58, 286
Der Standpunkt 45–6
Der Weg 46
Dodero shipping company 234

Eastern Europe
  Jewish refugees from 19
  anticommunist underground, NCWC
    financial support 109
Ecumenical Aid Organization, Rome 111
Egypt, emigrant destination 212, 263
  and ICRC travel documents 62
El Salvador, and ICRC travel
  documents 62
escape networks 123
  Alto Adige (South Tyrol) xvi–xvii,
    19–23, 96–8
  Austria 2–3, 241–8
  Bozen (Bolzano) 9, 16–19, 23, 26–30,
    33–40, 43, 89, 91–2, 95, 99,
    146–7, 194, 196, 267
  Brenner border 19–23, 31–2, 49, 84,
    140, 161, 234, 236
  Brixen clergy and 28, 47, 139–48
  Cold War and 274
  German-speaking refugees 19–23,
    25–32
  Holocaust survivors 2, 166–7
  Jewish refugees 19
  and Operation Bernhard 163, 165, 198
Ethiopia, escapes to 21
European countries, and ICRC travel
  documents 73
European nations, and Holocaust
  acknowledgement 274–5

Evangelical churches and Evangelical
refugees 7, 28, 40
extradition 11
Argentina 220, 229, 245, 257–8,
261, 270
Brazil 251, 253
Chile 209–10
Yugoslavia 130–4

false identities 9, 43–54
ethnic German 90–100
Gestapo/SS false papers from
RSHA xiii
see also forgery; ICRC, travel documents
Farfa Sabina camp 6, 9, 61, 112
FBI, and Association of Hungarian
Comrades-at-Arms 87
FBI documents, IWG and 280
Fermo camp 128
forgery
British currency 161–2, 165, 167
Gorizia 74
ICRC travel documents 70, 72, 74–7,
91–2
rings, South Tyrol 46–7
visas 76
see also false identities
Fossoli di Carpi camp 5, 6, 13, 15, 40, 41,
53, 54, 67, 68, 111–12
France
and Association of Hungarian
Comrades-at-Arms 87–8
and ICRC travel documents 62, 73
and Nazi fugitives xxiii, 203, 205, 206
collaborators 144, 214
Holocaust acknowledgement 275
Vichy regime and Nazis 35–6, 206, 279
Franciscan monastery, Bolzano 146–7
Franzensfeste fortress 36
Fraschette di Alatri camp 6, 61, 112
Freemasons 20, 88, 262

Geneva Conventions 56, 57
Geneva
Vatican emigration delegation 110
ICRC *see* ICRC
IRO 7, 13
see also IRO
Genoa
church organizations, Argentine escape
agents and 232–41

ratline and 166–7, 196, 201–2
local church offices, letters of
recommendation 85–6
departure point to Argentina xv, 1, 2, 7,
20, 22, 32–3, 91, 97–8, 228
ICRC and travel documents 56, 61, 62,
64–5, 82–3, 113, 134–5
Georgian seminary, Rome 116
German-American secret negotiations,
Operation Sunrise 160, 169–74
German Anti-Nazi Association (DAV)
43, 44
German Club, Buenos Aires 214
German Democratic Republic, and
Holocaust acknowledgement
275
German Federal Republic, and Holocaust
acknowledgement 275
German National Church of the Anima,
Rome xxii
German Order of Knights monastery,
Merano 144
German-speaking refugees
and Alto Adige 19–23
and ICRC travel documents 63–4
as Hungarian refugees 88
as South Tyrol Italians 233–4
escape networks 19–23, 25–32
South Tyrol 36–43
see also specific destinations; groups;
organizations
Glasenbach camp, escapees 28, 236–9
Gorizia forgers 74
Group of National Socialist Priests 104

Harvard University, Center for European
Studies vi
Holocaust
Cold War attitudes to 273–4, 275–8
European nations,
acknowledgement 274–5
ICRC silence xvii–xviii, 56, 287–8
trivialization, Austrian law and 271
Vatican silence xix, 105
Holocaust Memorials v, 274–5
Holy Year 1950 124
Höttinger camp 36
Hungarian Jews, Swedish passports
for 57–8
Hungarian Red Cross delegation,
Rome 89

Hungarian refugees
 Arrow Cross members 86–8, 89, 187
 German Nazis as 88
 collaborators 35
 Innsbruck 86–9
 report forged ICRC travel
        documents 77
 Vatican committees for xx

immigrant ships, German fugitives
        and 233–4
Innsbruck, refugee hub 17, 84–100
Intermarium 88, 185–7, 200
International Committee of the Red Cross
        (ICRC) xvii–xix, 7
 and anticommunism xix, 287
 and Catholic Church xix, xxii
 and civilian prisoners 56–7
 and German refugees [general] 15, 16,
        40, 45, 55–6
 and Nazi flight 57
   involvement suppressed 276
   reappraisal 286–9
 and Vatican relief agencies xix
 Argentine escape agents and 232, 233
 delegates, fake 89–90
   Operation Bernhard 161, 164, 166, 168
 silence on Holocaust xvii–xviii, 56, 287–8
 staff
   political attitudes 77
   anti-Semitic officials xix
 travel documents xvii–xix, 13–14, 49,
        50–1, 55–6, 58
   10.100 documents 59
   and Swedish passport rescue 57–8
   archives xxiv, xxv, 69–70, 73, 74–5,
        286–8
   Argentina escapees and 242, 244,
        247, 248, 251–3, 255, 256, 261,
        262
   authenticity checking 64–6, 66–7,
        68–9, 71–2
     delegated responsibility 64–5, 72–3
   new documents recognition 61–9
   provisional function stressed 60–1,
        71, 75–6, 77–8
   Red Cross Passports 60
   suspension recommended 69–71, 77–9
International Committee of the Red Cross
        (ICRC) local offices
 Bozen 90

Buenos Aires 62
Genoa, travel documents 56, 61, 62,
        64–5, 82–3, 113, 134–5
Innsbruck
 and ethnic German refugees 84–100
 identity checking lax 84–6, 99
Italy, paperless individuals 59, 60–1,
        61–9
Milan 61, 89
Naples 61
Rome
 financial abuse accusation 79
 planned closure reactions 80–2
 travel documents 61, 62, 74–6
   forgery 70, 72, 74–7, 91–2
   fraud 75–6, 100
   multiple issue 74–5
   theft/blanks sales 75, 76
   double numbering 74, 75
Verona 61
International Military Tribunal
        see Nuremberg Trials
International Refugee Organization
        (IRO) 4, 6–8, 11–15, 85
 travel documents 13–15, 60–1
   and Croatians 134
   recognition 78, 80, 82
   South American states and 63–4
 active screening process 99–100
 and war criminal escapes to South
        America 14–14
 Division for Prisoners of War and
        Civilian Internees 60–1
 Rome, inconsistencies investigated 76
Iron Curtain, ratlines through 160, 195
Italian Concordat (Lateran
        Treaty) xx–xxi, 144–5
Italian government 5, 9
 1947 Peace Treaty 5
 Allied Military Government 2
 and burden of refugees 6, 64, 78–9
 and travel documents issue 78, 79–80
 government camps 11
 police, and prisoner of war escapes 9–10
 race laws xx
Italian ratline, CIC 159–60
 escape agents 195–9, 200–1
 Operation Bernhard infrastructure 161,
        163, 164, 165, 166–7, 198–9
 origins 183–95
 Croatians and 200–1

Italian Red Cross
  and ICRC travel documents 61–2
  refugee aid service (AGIUS) travel
        documents issue 72, 78, 81–2, 83
Italians
  and Argentina work opportunities 217
  returning 19, 84
Italy
  and Argentina
      historical ties 226–7
      recruitment centre 218, 226–32
  anticommunism, US and 105–9,
        199–200
  border controls 16
  camps, Italy 4, 61, 111–12
      see also specific camps
  Catholic Church and Nazi
        regime xx–xxii
  escape route through xvi–xvii, xxiii, 1–54
  illegal immigrants 15–23
  importance to US 199–200
  Nazi past reappraisal 280–2
  paperless individuals, ICRC and 59,
        60–1, 61–9
  press, on Austrian PCA 127

Jewish agents, Operation Bernhard 161, 164
Jewish refugees 7, 8
  baptized, testing 149
  escape routes 2, 16, 18, 19, 166–7
  see also Holocaust

Kindly Ones, The (Littell) xiii
Korea conflict, escape movements
        cease 274

Lateran Treaties xx
  monastery protection 144–5
Latvian anticommunists 12
Leopold Franzens University, Innsbruck v
Lipari camp 6, 112
Lithuanian anticommunists 12
London Agreement, travel documents 13,
        79, 83
Los Angeles spy ring, Italy 197
Luftwaffe, Argentina migrants 217–18,
        224–5

Maison Rouge xiv
Meran
  Austrian office 44, 45

escape route to Bozen 17–21, 25
French collaborators at 35–6
hospital 147
Jewish refugees at 18–19
Nazi escapees at 37, 40–7, 52–4, 90, 94,
        95, 114, 143–4, 147, 156–7, 161,
        163–8, 178, 196, 198–9, 234, 251,
        254, 264
  Operation Bernhard 162–7
Mexico, and ICRC travel documents 62
Middle East nations, and Nazi refugees &
        collaborators 283
Milan
  ICRC 61, 89
  escape route 18, 190, 193, 209
  Operation Bernhard 161
monastery tours, war criminals 143–8
Moscow Declaration 11
Murderers among Us, The (Wiesenthal) xiii,
        xv

NASA Marshall Space Flight Center 278
National Catholic Welfare Conference
        (NCWC)
  and PCA 107
  and anticommunism 108–9, 110, 120
  archives xxiv
  local aid organizations 107, 108
Navy, Argentina preferential treatment
        for 217–18
Nazi party
  Catholic Church and xxi, 12–13,
        103–4, 109
  Catholic priest members 104–5, 119–20
Nazi perpetrators/collaborators
  Argentina, activity 220–1, 229–30
  as possible victims, Catholic Church
        and 286
  Cold War attitudes to 272, 273–4,
        275–8, 280
      preferential treatment 12–13
  extradition 11
      Argentina 220, 229, 245, 257–8,
            261, 270
      Brazil 251, 253
      Chile 209–10
      Yugoslavia 130–4
  false papers from RSHA xiii
  flight
      modern historical study 276–80
      NGOs involvement suppressed 276

flight (*cont.*)
  Soviet Union and xxiii
  modern attitudes to 271–2
  Nuremberg Trials 11, 155, 157, 160,
      174–5, 177, 180, 254, 271,
      273, 277–8
  PCA Relief Committees and
    Austrian 113–14, 118, 120–8
    Croatian 114–15, 128–39
    Hungarian 115
    Polish 115–16
  scientists, recruitment 259–60, 278
    Argentina 211, 218–26
    Soviet Union 221–3
    USA 222–3, 278
  suicides 272
  US Displaced Persons Commission
      and 279–80
Nazi propagandist newspapers 45–6
Nazi War Crimes Interagency Working
    Group (IWG) 280
NSDAP members 236, 239, 241–8, 249,
    252, 254, 255
nuclear industry, Argentina and 222, 223
Nuremberg trials

Odessa File, The (Forsyth) xiv, 257
Office of Strategic Services (OSS) xxii, 43,
    121, 179–80, 184
  and Operation Sunrise 170–4
  and SS xxiii
  Berne 165, 169, 170–1, 189, 192
  finance to Austrian PCA 121
Opera Nazionale Assistenza Religiosa
    Morale Operai 102–3
Operation Bernhard vi, xxiii, 90, 161–9,
    198, 258
  infrastructure 161, 163, 164, 165, 166–7,
    198–9
  Holocaust survivors and 166–7
Operation Sunrise 160, 169–74
  and Cold War/anticommunism 171–2
  pro-German US attitudes 170–4
Organisation of former SS members
    (ODESSA) xiv–xvi, 29, 160, 212,
    269, 275–6

Panama, immigration policy 216–17
Paraguay
  aircraft engineering 224
  and ICRC travel documents 62

  travel to 54, 59, 62, 91, 93, 257, 263
PCA *see* Pontificia Commissione Assistenza
Peenemünde Military Research
    Establishment 278
Peru, and travel documents 62, 86, 115
Polish refugees 7
  Argentinian visas 62
  Eastern, DPs 4
  repatriation 6
Pontificia Commissione Assistenza
    (PCA) xix–xx, 102–10
  and anticommunism 103, 104, 105–9,
    113
  and emigration to Argentina 228
  and South America 110
  and travel documents
    authenticity checking 65–6, 95, 97
    letters of recommendation 64, 72, 80,
      85–6, 112–14, 122–3
  Austrian Relief Committee 111
    and Nazis 113–14, 118, 120–8
    denazification certificates 114, 123, 127
    dissolution 126
  Croatian Relief Committee 111
    and Nazis 114–15, 128–39
    denazification certificates 114,
      123, 136
  Geneva delegation 110
  German Relief Committee 111
  Hungarian Relief Committee, and
      Nazis 115
  ICRC delegated responsibility 64–5
  Lithuanian Relief Committee 111
  national subcommittees 102, 106, 110–17
    abuse for personal gain 116–17
    denazification certificates 111, 114, 115
    letters of recommendation 112–14,
      122–3
  Nazi aid reappraisal 288
  Polish Relief Committee 111
    and Nazis 115–16
  Russian Relief Committee 111
  Slovenian Relief Committee xx, 111,
    115, 120, 134
  Ukrainian Relief Committee 111
  US financial support 105–9
Popes
  and Vatican Nazi aid reappraisal 284–6
  see also Vatican
post-war economic miracle 272
postal traffic, illegal 16

prisoners of war
  camps, Italy 5
  definition issues 10–11
  escapes 9–10
Procura Generale Militare, Rome 280–1
Protestants, Catholic conversion xxi–xxii
  re-baptism 148–56, 286

Red Army 2, 12, 24, 181, 185, 238
Red Cross *see* International Committee of
    the Red Cross (ICRC)
Red Cross Tracing Service, Germany,
    archives 281
refugees [general] 2
  camps, Italy 5
  definition issues 6, 10–11
Reich Concordat xx
Reich Main Security Office (RSHA) xiii
Reichenau camp 84, 86
Repubblica di Salò, army 36
Reschenpass 17, 18, 20, 27
Rimini camp 8–9, 10, 19, 37, 38–9, 44,
    54, 188, 196, 256
  SS mass escape 159, 184–6, 196
Roman Committee for migrants 102
Rome 2
  local church offices, letters of
    recommendation 85–6
  specialists departure point to
    Argentina 228
  see also Catholic Church; ICRC office,
    Rome; Vatican
Russian exiles 59, 228
  and spy networks in Soviet Union
    176

Sachsenhausen concentration camp xv,
    44, 161
  Operation Bernhard and 161
San Geronimo Monastery 128
Santa Maria dell'Anima, Rome xx, xxv,
    43, 118
Schloss Labers, Merano 161, 164, 165,
    166–7
Schloss Rametz, Merano 161, 164, 167
Schutzstaffel *see* Nazi perpetrators;
    Waffen-SS
scientists, recruitment 259–60, 278
  Argentina 211, 218–26
  Soviet Union 221–3
  USA 222–3, 278

scientists, recruitment 259–60, 278
  Argentina 211, 218–26
  Soviet Union 221–3
  USA 222–3, 278
sensationalism, individual cases 275–6
Serbs 59, 134
  genocide 129, 130, 200
  nationalists 4
  repatriation 6, 133
Shoah *see* Holocaust
Sisters of the Cross, Brixen
    sanatorium 150–1
Slovakian collaborators 35, 188
Slovenes
  Argentinia xxiv, 62
  repatriation 6
  stateless 59, 62, 81
  PCA subcommittee xx, 111, 115,
    120, 134
smugglers
  Brenner border, and refugees 15–19,
    23–32
  routes, Austria/Italy 15–19, 23–32
South American states
  and Hungarian refugees 86
  and ICRC refugee identification
    documents 58–9
  and IRO identification papers 63–4
  and Jewish refugees 8
  and Nazi refugees & collaborators 283
  concentration camp commandants
    escape to 248–58
  PCA and 110
  ratline to *see* CIC Italian ratline
  treaty obligations against war
    criminals 219–20
South Tyrol
  Catholic Church role 139–48
  escape networks 96–8
  former Nazis, businesses 264–8
  German/Italian, history 33–5
  Italian Red Cross 147
  Italians, German fugitives as 233–4
  Nazi past reappraisal 281–2
  Nazis/collaborators flee to 32–43
  see also Alto Adige
South Tyroleans, as stateless ethnic
    Germans 95–6
Soviet Union
  and definition issues 11–12
  and Nazi fugitives xxiii

Soviet Union (*cont.*)
  and refugee problem 6
  citizens
    repatriation 6
    UNRRA and 5
  Nazi scientist recruitment 221–3
  on Allies and Soviet Displaced
      Persons 11–12
  on collaborators preferential
      treatment 12
  POWs, outside ICRC scope 57
Soviet Zone Germany, and ICRC travel
      documents 73
Spain
  and ICRC travel documents 62, 63
  escape to xvii, xviii, xxiv, 1, 123, 146,
      212, 255, 266
Spanish Civil War, clergy and 142
specialist recruitment *see* scientists
    recruitment
SS *see* Waffen-SS; *see also* Nazi
    perpetrators
Stalingrad, battle of 142
statistics, and imprecise definitions
    xxiii–xxiv
Sterzing (Vipiteno)
  baptisms 148–51
  escape route 17, 23, 38–9, 251
Supreme Headquarters, Allied
    Expeditionary Force
    (SHAEF) 3
Swedish passports, for Hungarian
    Jews 57–8
Switzerland
  and ICRC travel documents 62, 72–3,
    74
  bank accounts 41
  Swiss hub escape route 1
Syria, emigrant destination 212

Terni camp 40, 124
Tokyo draft convention 56–7
travel documents 13–15
  see also International Committee of
    the Red Cross (ICRC);
    International Refugee
    Organization (IRO)
Trieste
  escape route 1
  Gorizia forgers 74
  refugees, travel documents 81, 83

Tyrol
  smuggling as occupation 23–4
  Tyrolean NSDAP 241–8
  see also South Tyrol

Ukrainians 4
  anticommunists 12
  collaborators, flee to South Tyrol 35
  exile groups, spy networks in Soviet
    Union 176
  refugees 7
  screening 14
  Vatican refugee committees for xx
United Nations
  High Commission for Refugees
    (UNHCR) 8
  Relief and Rehabilitation
    Administration (UNRRA)
    4–5, 7
United States
  and Nazi fugitives xxiii, 10, 130–4, 283
  Arrow Cross members and 87
  Croatian war criminals,
    anticommunism 131, 135, 137
  emigrant destination 212
  financial support
    anticommunist groups 105–9
    PCA 105–9
  Italy, importance of 199–200
  Nazi scientist recruitment 222–3, 278
  Nazi smuggling & protection 279–80
  public opinion, and war criminal
    recycling 176
  see also specific US organisations below
United States Catholic Church
  and Catholic refugees 7
  and PCA finance 107–9
United States Central Intelligence Agency
    (CIA) xxii, 132
  and Italian communists 109, 193
  and ratline 160
  archives 276, 280
  former Nazis, agents 175, 178–9, 181–3,
    185, 187, 191, 198, 279
  on Argentina as Nazi refuge 221, 229,
    260
  on escape networks 123
United States Congress, Displaced Persons
    Commission, and Baltic
    Waffen-SS units 279–80
United States Consulate, Bremen 1

United States Counter Intelligence Corps
(CIC) xiv, xxii
Austria
and Italian ratline 195–6, 201–7
Cold War activities
investigated 207–8
files release 160
fugitives from 24
Italian ratline xxii–xxiii, 159–60
escape agents 195–9, 200–1
Operation Bernhard
infrastructure 161, 163, 164,
165, 166–7, 198–9
origins 183–95
and Nazi agents xxii
recruits SS with spy
experience 159–61, 167–9,
175–83
unmasked agents, escape route 201–2,
203–7
United States Embassy Moscow, on
anticommunists 11–12
United States intelligence services
and anticommunist recruitment 280
and Nazi refugees xxii
and underground escape routes 159–61
at Nuremberg Trials 160
Blue Book, on Argentina as Nazi
refuge 220, 229
Cold War operatives recruitment
278–9
ratlines expedience 273
Nazi flight involvement suppressed 276
Operation Sunrise 160, 169–74
pro-German attitudes 170–4
recruit SS with spy experience 159–61,
167–9, 175–83
see also US Central Intelligence Agency
(CIA); US Counter Intelligence
Corps (CIC)
United States Jewish Joint Distribution
Committee 7, 62, 77
United States National Archives xxv,
160
United States State Department
and ICRC authenticity checking 70–1
on Croatian Ustasa 117
Report
on DAV and ZDI 43
on ICRC travel documents 69–71,
89, 91

on intelligence service ratline 159,
161, 166–7, 184, 196, 199–200,
273–4, 284
on people smuggling 15–16
on Vatican network 101–2, 107, 139
Uruguay, and ICRC travel documents 62
Ustica camp 6

Vatican
accused of sheltering Nazis 101–2
and Croatian Ustasa 130
and proposed general amnesty for
German soldiers 142–3
anticommunism 102
and Croatian war criminals 130–33,
136–8
finance to Austrian PCA 121–2
'impartial historical investigation' 101–2
Nazi aid reappraisal 283–6, 289
silence on Holocaust xix, 105
standing damaged by Austrian
PCA 125–8
see also Catholic Church
Vatican Archives, access to xxii
Vatican Bank 106–7
Vatican Relief Commission for refugees
see Pontificia Commissione
Assistenza (PCA)
Venezuela, war criminals smuggled to 14–15
Vichy regime and Nazis 279
Vienna
and ODESSA 29
Argentine consulate 226
CIC detachment 207–8
ICRC 64
Nazi refugees in 122
Wiesenthal Institute of Holocaust
Studies 271
US delegation 18, 55, 216

Waffen-SS
Baltic 279–80
Division 'Nord' 266
Division Galizien xxiv
false papers from RSHA xiii
mass escape, Rimini camp 159,
184–5, 196
members 20, 38, 48, 68, 152, 154, 164,
207–8, 235–6, 239, 260
organisation of former (ODESSA)
xiv–xvi, 29, 160, 212, 269, 275–6

Waffen-SS (*cont.*)
　prisoners of war 8
　OSS and xxiii
　Protestant, re-baptized as Catholic
　　148–56
　support networks xvi, 123–4
　Ukrainian 186
　US recruits SS with spy experience
　　159–61, 167–9, 175–83
　volunteers 207, 235, 255
war criminals
　Allied interest in 10
　definition issues 10–11
　recycling 176, 177–83
　see also Nazi perpetrators; Nuremberg
　　trials
West Germany
　Amnesty Law 274

'brain drain' 222–3
economic success encouragement 222
establishment, former Nazis in 195
Western Allies, and Nazi refugees xxii
Western democracies
　Cold War attitudes to Nazis 272, 273–4,
　　275–8
　modern attitudes to WWII 271–2
White Book (Argentina), on Argentina as
　Nazi refuge 220

Yugoslav refugees 7, 13–14
　forged travel documents 74
　see also Croatians; Serbs
Yugoslav Welfare Society in Rome
　114–15
Yugoslavia 2
　and war criminals extradition 130–4